POWER WITHOUT VICTORY

Anil —
From one
idealistic,
civic nationalist,
radical internationalist
to another!
Thanks for
your support
and friendship —
TPYG

POWER WITHOUT VICTORY

Woodrow Wilson and the American
Internationalist Experiment

TRYGVE THRONTVEIT

THE UNIVERSITY OF CHICAGO PRESS
CHICAGO AND LONDON

The University of Chicago Press, Chicago 60637
The University of Chicago Press, Ltd., London
© 2017 by Trygve Throntveit
Published 2017.
Printed in the United States of America

26 25 24 23 22 21 20 19 18 17   1 2 3 4 5

ISBN-13: 978-0-226-45987-5 (cloth)
ISBN-13: 978-0-226-45990-5 (paper)
ISBN-13: 978-0-226-46007-9 (e-book)
DOI: 10.7208/chicago/9780226460079.001.0001

Library of Congress Cataloging-in-Publication Data

Names: Throntveit, Trygve, author.
Title: Power without victory : Woodrow Wilson and the American internationalist experiment / Trygve Throntveit.
Description: Chicago ; London : The University of Chicago Press, 2017. | Includes bibliographical references and index.
Identifiers: LCCN 2016049354| ISBN 9780226459875 (cloth : alk. paper) |
    ISBN 9780226459905 (pbk. : alk. paper) | ISBN 9780226460079 (e-book)
Subjects: LCSH: Wilson, Woodrow, 1856–1924. | United States—Foreign relations—1913–1921. | League of Nations.
Classification: LCC E768 .T47 2017 | DDC 327.73009/04—dc23 LC record available at https://lccn.loc.gov/2016049354
♾ This paper meets the requirements of ANSI/NISO Z39.48–1992 (Permanence of Paper).

CONTENTS

In May 1919, W. E. B. Du Bois threw in his lot with Woodrow Wilson. It was not the first such gamble for the prominent African American reformer and social critic, but that made it all the more surprising. His previous bets on Wilson had been bad ones.

Du Bois and hundreds of thousands of other African Americans had helped put Wilson in the White House in 1912. In Du Bois's view, they took their decision as "a step toward political independence." Wilson's progressive leadership as governor of New Jersey and his campaign promises to do blacks "justice" suggested his potential to tame the economic predators corrupting the nation's politics, leash the southern racists infesting his own Democratic Party, and "become the greatest benefactor of his country since Abraham Lincoln."[1] Despite launching a historic program of reform, however, the new president reneged on his pledge to fight racial injustice. Indeed, he was complicit in it. Shortly after taking office, he permitted cabinet members to segregate their departments. Soon it became clear that his promised national race commission was chimerical. Finally, when the United States entered World War I in 1917—ostensibly to help redeem Europe from its homicidal chauvinism—black soldiers were assigned to segregated units abroad and attacked by white mobs at home. Du Bois himself chronicled the African American soldier's ordeal in Europe and joined hundreds who called on the president to suppress the white vigilantes targeting black troops stationed in American towns. By the spring of 1919 Wilson had met such appeals with little but stony silence.

Yet in May 1919, as the president negotiated peace at Paris, Du Bois urged African Americans to lend full support to Wilson's top domestic priority: US membership in the League of Nations, the peacekeeping body that Wilson had helped make the lynchpin of the settlement. The League's constitution, or "Covenant," was under attack from variously striped nationalists in the Republican Party, the traditional political home of black Americans since Lincoln's day. Prominent Republicans in Congress worried, with some Democrats, that the Covenant impinged on national sovereignty and bound the country to defend unjust regimes in the name of peace and stability. Du Bois saw things differently. A powerful League, he predicted, would preserve peace *and* advance justice. In fact, it was "absolutely necessary to the salvation of the negro race." The fates of nonwhite peoples everywhere were linked, and though the Covenant did not dismantle the colonial system that subjugated so many of them, its provisions bore the seeds of imperial demise—and even of redemption for its own greatest champion, the United States. US membership would bring the plight of African Americans to the attention of an officially interested and legally empowered world body, just as membership for Europe's powers would subject their colonial policies to scrutiny. Under the glare of global publicity, crimes long ignored by "the choked conscience of America" might finally be addressed, and redressed, by "the organized Public Opinion of the World."[2]

As the League fight unfolded in 1919–20, Wilson's campaign for membership gained other surprising endorsements. The very month that Du Bois urged African Americans to support the League, Jane Addams, advocate for women, workers, and immigrants and among the nation's best-known pacifists, helped draft a systematic critique of the settlement to which the Covenant was tied. Like Du Bois, Addams had a list of grievances against Wilson, including his halting support for women's suffrage; his decision to join Britain, France, and their Allies in a horrific war against Germany and the Central Powers; and his failure to halt the anti-immigrant and antiradical excesses of wartime hyperpatriots. When the Treaty of Versailles ending hostilities with Germany was leaked to the public in the spring of 1919, Addams and several European colleagues convened in Zurich to compile an exhaustive catalog of its flaws. The terms, they charged, mocked worldwide calls for open diplomacy by honoring secret agreements of the sort that sparked the war's outbreak. They violated the principle of national self-determination, granting territory to governments that did not represent the populations involved. Finally, the so-called peace they purportedly secured seemed designed to perpetuate militarism and instability. The Allies were free to stockpile arms and multiply the legions trained to use them, while Germany was saddled with onerous reparations sure to breed hostility among a decimated and impoverished population.[3]

Yet even these acute critics found fruit in Wilson's efforts. Their Zurich manifesto asserted that the "peaceful progress of the world" could "only be assured when the common interests of humanity are recognized in the establishment of a League of Nations," and recorded their "satisfaction" that the League idea had "become so widely accepted." They worried that the League would fail without immediate efforts to democratize its structure. Tellingly, however, they invoked the Fourteen Points peace program, which Wilson himself had announced in January 1918, as their preferred guide for reform. And nowhere did they reject ratification of the Covenant as it stood—League reform, they seemed to suggest, was the next logical stage of an ongoing peace process.[4] For Addams, at least, rejecting the League was never an option. Opposing the war, Addams nonetheless applauded her country's commitment to "lead the nations of the world into a wider life of co-ordinated political activity" and praised her government's promotion of an "international agency" through which the world community could regulate and reform itself. During and after the US Senate's debates on membership she spoke powerfully of the League's potential to alleviate poverty and hunger, dismantle colonial regimes, and prevent war—and of the crucial role the United States could play in realizing that potential. From the moment its shape was revealed, Addams wrote, she saw the League as flawed but full of promise. Though "inevitably disappointed" in several of its features, she was "eager to see what would happen when 'the United States came in!'"[5]

Despite criticisms and misgivings, therefore, Du Bois and Addams saw many of their deepest ethical and political commitments reflected in Wilson's League. Both saw in its covenant the rudiments of an egalitarian, cooperative, adaptive system of international governance, endowed with a deliberative machinery to correct its own defects. The hope they placed in this pending experiment, however, would not be rewarded. The United States did not "come in" to the League of Nations. The Senate twice rejected the Treaty of Versailles that contained the League Covenant—once in November 1919, again in March 1920—thereby excluding the United States from the nascent world body. And though American policy makers spearheaded the creation of a new collective-security system during World War II, the resulting United Nations Organization (UN) was designed to preserve the prerogatives of the United States as much as empower collective action by the international community. In the eyes of the UN's main architects, concludes one historian, Wilson's League "had been simply too democratic and too liberal."[6]

In short, the United States never took up the expansive internationalist experiment it abandoned in the wake of the First World War. It was not Du Bois or Addams but Wilson's Senate nemesis Henry Cabot Lodge who saw his vision of the nation's postwar role fulfilled. Surveying the two years spanning the 1918 Armistice and the 1920 presidential campaign, Lodge concluded that ratification's failure and Republican Warren G. Harding's election had not just "destroyed Mr. Wilson's League of Nations," but shattered the worldview it embodied. The toppling of the League, Lodge pronounced, had "torn up Wilsonism by the roots."[7]

The United States' failure to join the League of Nations has long been recognized as a turning point in the history of American and world politics. Yet inattention to the broader cultural history of this event has obscured its deepest causes and significance. Addams and Du Bois were only two among tens of millions of Americans pondering their nation's global role in the Great War's aftermath. Nevertheless, the support that these committed reformers and anti-imperialists gave Wilson's League presents an important challenge to American historical memory. For decades, Wilson has been remembered as either a paternalistic liberal or reactionary conservative at home, and as a naïve idealist or cynical imperialist abroad. As with most myths, these competing meanings all hold kernels of truth. Du Bois, as an African American, and Addams, as a woman, knew Wilson's paternalist and conservative tendencies firsthand; meanwhile, the millions living in American dependencies in 1919 could be forgiven a healthy suspicion of Wilson's commitment to decolonization. Historians' harsh judgments of Wilson are equally understandable. Wilson won two elections by promising to bring all Americans into a deliberative democratic process ensuring justice for all participants. Later, he prosecuted a war to defend democracy and promote the political empowerment of all peoples. Yet under Wilson, Jim Crow persisted, US interventions in Latin America increased, and a humiliating and economically crippling settlement was forced on Germany. A generation after Wilson raised bright, broad flags of domestic and international reform, stark inequalities and injustices still plagued the United States, myopic nationalism hindered its responsible engagement in world affairs, and a second global conflict, vastly more destructive than the first, threatened the survival of democracy worldwide—leaving many Americans today to wonder what, exactly, the buildings and programs bearing his name are commemorating.[8]

But there is more to the story of Wilson, and the hopes he invested in the League, than these sad truths express. Despite his sins against his own ideals, Wilson formulated a sweepingly democratic vision for the United States and its global role. That role incorporated the familiar trope of Americans leading the world to peace by example, through continual perfection of democracy in a nation forged of many peoples and traditions. But as Wilson explained in his war message to Congress, it also demanded from Americans a new willingness to make sacrifices for a broader democratic project: "for the right of those who submit to authority to have a voice in their own governments, for the rights and liberties of small nations, for a universal dominion of right by such a concert of free peoples as shall bring peace and safety to all nations and make the world itself at last free."[9] This vision for a democratic renewal of the nation's internal and external relations inspired reformers of multiple stripes and Americans of myriad backgrounds to embrace an internationalist experiment bolder than any attempted since.

Power without Victory is the story of this vision and of the cultural moment in which it thrived. Its central claims are two. First, Wilson was not a "Wilsonian," as that term has come to be understood. He did not seek to stamp American-style democracy on other peoples. Rather, he had something simultaneously more radical and more practical in mind: the gradual development of a genuinely global system of governance to maintain justice and facilitate peaceful change. Second, ordinary Americans of the postwar years were hardly the disillusioned isolationists or jealous nationalists of historical lore. Rather, the American people embraced enough of Wilson's program to alarm Senate nationalists and prompt them to launch a massive public campaign against League membership—a campaign that succeeded only through Wilson's acts of self-sabotage.

For some readers this second claim will rank first in importance, for it disputes a historical narrative that has long undermined efforts to advance international governance. Since the mid-1940s, self-styled "realists" among policymakers, political scientists, and historians have invoked the story of Wilson's League to augment their broader argument for the primacy of national interest—defined as conservation and enhancement of power—over all other world-political imperatives. In this view, even were it theoretically possible to reconcile the individual interests of states with an international common good, the US Senate's rejection of League membership confirms the practical futility of the effort. As former diplomat George F. Kennan argued in the early 1950s, Americans, despite their attraction to moral crusades, are too changeable in opinion and parochial in outlook to support responsible membership in the kind of organization necessary to achieve such feats of international accommodation.[10] The concessions of national sovereignty that such a body would demand are inimical not only to American national interests, but to American political culture, which could never sustain such a relationship; for Kennan and his heirs, supranational schemes augur ill for the country and no better for the world.[11] Even for "neorealists" who admit the value of multilateral institutions, the example of Wilson and the League only highlights the wisdom of a later generation. Aware of the "firmness" with which Americans "repudiated" Wilson's League, writes historian John Lewis Gaddis, Franklin Roosevelt shrewdly built the international institutions of the second postwar era so as to "ensure, in all of these structures, the predominance of the United States."[12]

Even among Wilson's sympathizers the League's rejection has informed similarly pessimistic conclusions about the viability of his aims. During World War II some proponents of multilateralism conflated the government's failure to join the League in 1920 with the public's reluctance to intervene in the crises of the 1930s. During closed discussions with Senators in 1944, Roosevelt's Secretary of State Cordell Hull explained that a veto ensuring America's freedom of action was crucial to securing membership in the nascent United Nations. Without it, he warned, public support would plummet to levels no higher "than in 1920."[13] A quarter century later at the height of the Vietnam conflict, political scientist Stanley Hoffmann argued that the same halfway, on-our-terms internationalism still pervaded American political culture, hampering a more responsible engagement in multilateral initiatives and a more prudent acceptance of international restraints. The nation's hearty embrace and abrupt rejection of a global role in the Great War era was for Hoffmann the archetype of this "Wilsonian syndrome."[14] Today even the realists' most formidable critics scruple to discuss a universal, integrative, flexible system of global governance as a reasonable goal, however long-term, toward which work must begin. G. John Ikenberry, perhaps the leading liberal institutionalist and a firm advocate for the importance of multilateral institutions, owes much to the vision that inspired Du Bois, Addams, and millions more Americans during World War I. Yet Ikenberry sees Wilson as a man ahead of his time, and our own; a prophet whose call for significant concessions of sovereignty to a "world democratic order" was—and remains—"a bridge too far."[15]

Yet Wilson was not building on air. Whatever the climate on Capitol Hill, nationwide support for League membership was strong and sustained.[16] Of course Du Bois and Addams did not speak for all their fellow citizens. The American Red Cross, General Federation of Women's Clubs, and Federal Council of Churches of Christ, however, spoke for scores of millions; and all these groups, with many more besides, endorsed participation in Wilson's League. Such endorsements were not confined to fellow Democrats or groups led by them. Wilson's Republican predecessor and 1912 presidential opponent, William Howard Taft, led the League to Enforce Peace, an organization of one hundred thousand members devoted solely to

American participation in a League of Nations. Despite disagreeing with Wilson over details of the League's design, Taft mobilized dozens of voluntary organizations—representing more than twenty million Americans—to demand immediate ratification of the Covenant principally authored by his rival. Nor was support restricted to pacifists, disarmament advocates, or the cosmopolitan urban elite. Membership was endorsed by the American Bankers' Association, the Chamber of Commerce of the United States, the American Federation of Labor, all of the nation's largest agricultural groups, and even Frank D'Olier, head of the American Legion—a newborn veterans' association styling itself the "living force" of "one hundred percent Americanism."[17]

But the question arises: What does it matter if Americans supported a doomed endeavor? If the breadth and even existence of popular internationalism in the United States has been forgotten, the futility of the League is remembered all too well.[18] Yet that memory, too, must be checked against the facts—at the very least against the fact that the League's creators assumed American membership and built in capacities sorely weakened by American abstention. Hence the relevance of this book's primary claim, regarding the thought and aims of the League's major architect, Woodrow Wilson himself. To assess the effects of US absence from the League requires a sense of the role designed for it and thus an accurate understanding of the designer. To that end, *Power without Victory* reinterprets Wilson's intellectual development from his early years as a scholar through the bitter months of the League fight, revealing unfamiliar strands of thinking that were later woven deeply into the fabric of his policies. In the process it recovers the neglected ties between Wilson's internationalist vision and another of the era's most important cultural phenomena: the influence of American pragmatism on a cadre of reformers working toward a more just, egalitarian, and cooperative society.

The goal of these reformers is best encapsulated in a phrase coined by Harvard philosopher William James: an "ethical republic." This vision of the good society was inspired by James's efforts to explain how human thoughts, values, choices, and actions could be meaningful in the world of material forces that science disclosed. "Pragmatism" was the term James used to describe the radical theories of knowledge and truth that emerged from these efforts at the twentieth century's turn to influence two generations of activist intellectuals. James argued that all our ideas are ultimately plans for achieving goals and surmounting the obstacles impeding us. Rather than mental copies of an eternal, changeless reality, true ideas are those that "work" for people by successfully predicting the consequences of their actions and "leading" them to the ends they seek.[19] Pragmatism is an empowering philosophy, asserting that our personal "will to believe" helps make ideas true whenever it prompts actions that fulfill their predictions. It is also a humbling philosophy, asserting that the validity of all our beliefs awaits their testing against experience—including the experience of other people, whose activities our ideas purport to describe or prescribe.[20] And it is a philosophy with profound implications for ethics and politics. If morality, too, is a form of knowledge-guided but experimental action, then all moral beings inhabit an "ethical republic" of obligations imposed, negotiated, and fulfilled with greater or lesser efficiency and satisfaction.[21] The republic flourishes through collective deliberation over the widest possible range of ideals and the demands they entail, by citizens trained to bold thinking, intellectual tolerance, empirical reflection, intentional empathy, and strenuous self-scrutiny. Though James's thoughts on how this pragmatist ethics could be translated into organized structures and established norms of collective action have eluded many, his practical impact on American politics was massive. Several of his students and admirers became leaders in the progressive movement that brought Wilson to the pinnacle of power. At multiple critical moments these pragmatist progressives directly shaped Wilson's policies, affecting the course of national and international affairs for years if not generations.

Historical definitions of "progressivism" proliferate. Those who adopted the label did not share an agenda so much as an impulse to adapt American politics to a changing society outgrowing its laws and conventions. Nearly all those who adopted the label assailed the cult of laissez-faire that they thought dominated and enervated American public life, and nearly all agreed on the basic responsibility of the state to create conditions of economic and social justice.[22] What such conditions were and how to realize them were questions that various avowed progressives answered in diverse and sometimes contradictory ways. The progressives who identified explicitly with James's outlook were distinguished by their commitment to exploiting the fecundity of this fractious critique: interrogating its myriad hypotheses, experimenting with many, and avoiding dogmatic adherence to any. In Jane Addams's formulation, political pragmatism suggested "a new method" of political analysis and action, one that "evolved" as citizens were "driven to realities" and "made to test the validity of their phrases." A pragmatist view of politics implied that the prestige and influence of people, institutions, or ideas must never be "consciously cherished as a possession," for "the complicated conditions of modern life" would remain too fluid for any "*a priori* point of view" to address. A pragmatist method and outlook promised policies that were more *scientific* because more *democratic*—more firmly grounded in the felt and expressed needs of the populace. Pragmatist policies could not please everybody. But they could be formulated on a wide basis of information collected through open and extensive discussion, and to that degree approach "the realization" of public opinion.[23]

Adopting this intellectual posture, Addams and other pragmatist progressives strove to bring methodological coherence to the ideological pluralism of American reform. Indeed, they embraced intellectual and cultural pluralism as both inescapable and salutary. Among this group were several giants of the progressive reform tradition, including Du Bois and Addams; philosopher and educational theorist John Dewey; attorney and industrial reformer Louis Brandeis, as well as his protégé Felix Frankfurter; cultural critics Thorstein Veblen and Randolph Bourne; and journalists Herbert Croly and Walter Lippmann. All shared James's conviction that, among parties committed to open-minded inquiry and critical self-reflection, the exchange of divergent views could generate a range of convergent goals—or at the least a wider understanding of the shared world in which personal goals are pursued. James's concept of an "ethical republic," in which values were shaped and reshaped through such deliberative discourse, inspired the pragmatist progressives to develop a coherent but flexible political ethics, conceived as a general guide for adapting norms and institutions to a diverse, protean polity. It further inspired them to conceive their American ethical republic, in its actual and ideal forms, as enmeshed in an international community, and to articulate their domestic priorities in the context of international and transnational concerns. By the eve of World War I they saw the federal and polyglot United States as a model for a just, peaceful, and prosperous world community, as well as but one of many nodes in a planetary economic, technological, and cultural network. For that reason Americans had a vital interest in global conditions of justice, peace, and prosperity—as well as much to learn from the outside world if they hoped to contribute to such conditions.

This distinctive brand of political analysis helped Wilson develop the nation's first genuinely internationalist foreign policy—and helped him prepare the nation to embrace it. Pragmatist progressives such as Du Bois, Addams, Veblen, and Dewey laid important cultural groundwork for Wilson's policies; others, notably Brandeis, Frankfurter, Croly, and Lippmann, directly shaped them. The resulting relationship was complex. Though blind to the tragedy of racism in America, negligent in his stewardship of political freedoms in wartime, and guilty of imperialist incursions in Latin America, Wilson drew on pragmatist political ethics to develop a radically democratic vision for a peaceful postwar world, embodied in his plan for the League of Nations: a deliberative, remarkably egalitarian international polity, requiring significant concessions of sovereignty from members in order to facilitate cooperative change.

This is not to say Wilson adopted his politics wholesale from students of James or considered himself a "pragmatist." He did not. *Power without Victory* is largely the story of Wilson's intellectual convergence with pragmatist thinkers over time, punctuated by crucial episodes of direct influence. By the time Wilson ran for president in 1912, his political philosophy already exhibited strong affinities with pragmatism. His basic view of legal and political institutions was an amalgam of ideas drawn from the American founders, Edmund Burke, Alexis de Tocqueville, the English constitutional theorist Walter Bagehot, and American gradualist socialists such as Richard T. Ely. He interpreted all these thinkers, including Burke and the founders, as advocates of a functionalist rather than positivist or originalist view of political institutions. In his opinion, these great minds grasped the fundamentally organic and dynamic nature of societies and states. Wilson's early papers and long-neglected personal library also demonstrate his early sympathy with social democratic theory, as well as his belief that participatory deliberative democracy was the political imperative of the social ethics central to his personal Christian faith.

Nevertheless, at several points from the 1890s forward, self-consciously pragmatist thinkers made important contributions to Wilson's evolving political thought. Sometimes they gave Wilson a new vocabulary through which to express, and frequently refine, his ideas; at other times, they helped him formulate policies congruent with their consciously pragmatist sensibilities. Either way, pragmatism left multiple marks on Wilson and his presidency. Between 1895 and 1905 Wilson encountered James's ethical writings, adopting James's defense of religious faith and his concept of the "will to believe." From 1912 to 1914 candidate and then president Wilson collaborated with Brandeis to construct the New Freedom legislation that established the Tariff Commission, Federal Trade Commission, and Federal Reserve to make policy more responsive to rapidly shifting conditions. And from 1916 forward Wilson and his close advisers relied frequently on the judgment, and several times on the policy planning, of Croly and Lippmann, who had caught the administration's attention through their work as editors of the *New Republic* and had themselves been struck by the pragmatist character of Wilson's developing internationalist vision.

The League of Nations became both the focus of that vision and its unifying theme. As both Wilson and the *New Republic* pragmatists imagined it, the League would inaugurate and sustain a grand international project, resembling the American project they traced from the founders, through Lincoln's war for the Union, and finally to the democratic, pluralistic, yet highly integrated and adaptive polity they considered the goal of progressive politics. As Wilson explained in his famous "Peace without Victory" address of January 1917, the war taught that states must eschew the "balance of power" for "a community of power," promoting cooperative striving for the global good and recognizing that governments exercised legitimate power solely by consent of the governed. Only a democratic peace, reflecting the whole world's input, could sustain these relations of equality and solidarity within and among states. To last, such peace required that the belligerents prioritize stability and justice over spoils of victory; it also required Americans to accept that they belonged to a world community to which they were responsible. "We are provincials no longer," Wilson informed his fellow Americans, but rather "citizens of the world."[24]

This radical vision entailed radical means to achieve it. From the war's beginning Wilson tried to mediate the conflict by appealing to the benefits peace would bring to all. Over and again he was frustrated by both sides' attachment to traditional, aggrandizing national interests. During a period of remarkably fruitful dialogue with Croly and Lippmann from mid-1916 through early 1918, Wilson and his close adviser, "Colonel" Edward M. House, made a crucial conceptual leap. They concluded that just as the states of the Union had ceded powers to the federal government in return for long-term security and growth, the states of the world must formally abandon their claims to absolute national sovereignty, authorizing and equipping a deliberative organization to resolve their conflicts. In short, Wilson embraced a drastically transformed world order, anchored by a body combining deliberative, legislative, judicial, and enforcement organs, and charged with improving human life, not just responding to crises that threatened it.

This pragmatist blueprint for international organization is more than a historical curiosity. Since the discipline of international relations (IR) emerged in the 1920s, its central problem has been to determine the potential and formulate the mechanisms for organizing interstate affairs. The contentious debates occupying proponents of several theoretical approaches to that problem would benefit from a fresh examination of Wilson's pragmatist internationalism in the clarified historical context that *Power without Victory* provides.

Among the schools challenged by the book's historical arguments is realism, including the major formulations of the mid-twentieth century and more recent neorealist offshoots. Surveying the history of organized states, realists insist that the price of the security states provide individuals is a Hobbesian anarchy among states themselves. This "security dilemma" persists because for states, the lure of power is stronger than the benefits of a global security guarantee. Unlike individuals, states can remain perpetually alert. They can also defend against and recover from significant mutilations through the deployment and regeneration of their populations. Consequently, the theoretical greater good promised by cooperation is practically diminished by the constant threat of rogue states exploiting the cooperators, which in turn diminishes the degree to which any state can reasonably surrender its fortunes to the system.[25]

The views of the realists' most frequent dueling partners, the liberal institutionalists and other "neoliberals," share slightly more in common with Wilson's pragmatist internationalism—despite the fact that the term *neoliberal* was coined to distinguish the approach from the "liberal" tradition inspired by Wilson himself. Unlike realists, neoliberals insist that states do at times sacrifice relative power for absolute gains achieved through cooperation, and contend that multilateral institutions can ameliorate the consequences of anarchy by facilitating such cooperation. Nevertheless, neoliberal theorists tend to share the realists' belief that international anarchy is a natural and permanent condition; few entertain the possibility of a supranational authority bringing order to the interstate system the way that states bring order to the regions they control.[26]

Closer to Wilson's thinking is the more recent wave of "constructivist" theory. Contrary to "positivist" realists and neoliberals, constructivists deny that the persistence of anarchy reflects objective laws of international relations. Rather, anarchical conditions reflect the prevalence of two assumptions: that the security dilemma is intractable and, therefore, that pursuit of power above all else is rational. Constantly describing and redescribing the world as anarchical, positivist theorists work to construct it as such in the minds of people whose actions contribute to its character; and because their outlook is particularly attractive to policymakers whose interests are entwined with the power of the state, their work has been effective.[27] But although forceful in its critique of positivism, constructivist theories have yielded little in the way of constructivist practice or prescriptions for it. The same is true of one of the discipline's newest schools, an offshoot of constructivism whose adherents in fact adopt the label "pragmatist." Appropriately, these newer pragmatists turn to the work of early pragmatists Charles S. Peirce, John Dewey, and James himself for inspiration, asserting that knowledge production is both socially constructed and practically oriented toward solving real-world problems. But much of the relatively small amount of work in this vein has focused on reforming the discipline's conventions of scholarly communication and research design. Among the exceptions, only a small share exhibit the classical pragmatists' attention to the lessons of concrete historical experience, including James and Wilson's historically inspired awareness of the transformations that desires, commitments, and ideals can effect in realms of experience shaped by human practices. Likely for these reasons, no clear or compelling policymaking ethos or grand-strategic vision has emerged.[28]

More effectively than any of the theories just discussed, Wilson's pragmatist internationalism facilitates a direct response to anarchy and the security dilemma by acknowledging the simultaneously real and constructed nature of each. Wilson knew that interstate relations were anarchical and presented barriers to cooperation. Yet he viewed these interstate relations and their aforementioned characteristics as historical rather than natural facts, perpetuated largely by statesmen acting as though they were eternal. Now the Great War's immense and unexpected costs had revealed to millions of people the irrational risks of ostensibly rational self-serving policies. With competitive norms thus discredited, Wilson strove to enhance the prestige and efficacy of cooperative norms through structures that embodied and promoted them. Specifically, he argued that a deliberative system of international policymaking, backed by the power to enforce its writ, could restrain the anarchical tendencies of states while gradually eradicating incentives to indulge them. The collapse of the old order and the assumptions supporting it had cleared the ground for the cornerstone of a new one: the relinquishment, by every state, of its absolute right to the use of force. By submitting the world's most powerful nation to this constraint, Wilson meant to seize an unprecedented psychological moment. In doing so he hoped to create, for the first time, conditions in which the will to believe in an ordered, cooperative, peaceful international life stood some prospect of vindication.

"There is only one power to put behind the liberation of mankind, and that is the power of mankind," Wilson stated in an address in Pueblo, Colorado, on September 25, 1919—just days before suffering the stroke that crippled him. "It is the power of the united moral forces of the world, and in the Covenant of the League of Nations the moral forces of the world are mobilized." Among those forces, he insisted, were the American people, who had sent their loved ones to fight for a new international order in which their government would freely accept the role of partner rather than master. That sacrifice had impressed upon the world the magnitude of the change the war had wrought, when the strongest of nations, its peace breached by

distant wrongs, was ready to define victory as justice instead of power—
and its fellow nations were ready to assent by treaty to that standard. An
ineluctable logic of global interdependence had led Americans, and peoples
worldwide, to believe a transformation was at hand. And yet, Wilson cautioned, that same logic revealed the outcome as eternally contingent upon
human choice: "The arrangements of justice do not stand of themselves."[29]

Wilson was under no illusions that belief alone could create a new international life, or that even the deepest and widest commitment to peace
could entirely obviate the threat, and consequent need, of force. After all,
it was Wilson's powerful vision for peace that guided his decision for war.
When Germany's leaders resumed unrestricted submarine warfare, then
were caught plotting to foment a second Mexican-American War, the president became convinced of their disdain for international norms and lack
of interest in the mediated settlement his government offered to broker.
He chose to go to war before the next outrage dragged his nation into its
breeding madness, transforming Americans' hopes for peace into the same
bloodlust prolonging the slaughter in Europe. Aware that all wars stoked
nationalist fires, he insisted on Americans' duty to see themselves as partners in a campaign for more democratic international relations. He called
on Americans to be nonpartisans, seeking not to advance their own nation's
interests but to establish methods for discovering common interests and
formulating the means to achieve them.

As 1918 unfolded, events seemed to vindicate those with the will to
believe in such great possibilities. In January Wilson's Fourteen Points address challenged the Allies to accept anti-imperialism, open diplomacy, self-
government, and international cooperation through a League of Nations as
the bases of their postwar policies, and over several months this program
gained the overwhelming endorsement of world public opinion. In November, Germany signed an Armistice based on the program, as interpreted in
a memo by Lippmann—who eleven months prior had drafted most of the
points for Wilson's address. Yet the seemingly unanimous acceptance of
the Fourteen Points played an ironic, catalytic role in the firestorm that
engulfed American politics over the peace terms agreed at Paris. Wilson's
program was interpreted in contradictory ways at home and abroad, and
while all parties recognized the League's centrality, the larger settlement
it was to enforce was fuzzier. Millions of people invested hopes in Wilson
that he was neither prepared nor inclined to fulfill. Most damaging was the
confusion surrounding "self-determination," a term Wilson used rarely and
nearly always as a synonym of "self-government": the right to a voice in
the management of public affairs. Enabling and protecting that voice, he

believed, would require different arrangements for different contexts, and his ideas about them reflected his racial and cultural prejudices. Yet Wilson envisioned all arrangements as subject to future revision by a League whose function was to help international society adapt, cooperatively, to changing circumstances—including the increasingly obvious injustice and anachronism of colonialism.

Wilson could have worked harder to make this essential—and essentially pragmatist—feature of his program clear. Instead he let confusion flourish. In hopes of bringing maximum international pressure to bear on his counterparts at Paris, he never corrected those who conflated his politically integrative internationalism with contrary schemes. The result was epidemic disappointment in treaties that audiences had been free to assume would solve whatever problems they cared about most, by whatever mechanisms attracted them most. The damage was compounded by Wilson's near-total exclusion of Republicans from the peace delegation and poor public communication during the negotiations—a failure to manage expectations that also smacked of hypocrisy from the world's top advocate of open diplomacy. Wilson's peacemaking tactics eroded a support base already weakened by wartime hardships and civil liberties abuses. Select senators took this opportunity to complicate US entrance into the League, which they feared infringed their foreign policy prerogatives and curtailed the nation's diplomatic freedom. Though Wilson made early concessions to Senate rivals led by Lodge, the controversy over "self-determination" and its applications dogged him. Nationalists, isolationists, and jaded internationalists read Article 10 of the Covenant—which pledged to maintain the territorial integrity of signatories against aggression—as binding American soldiers to preserve an unjust status quo.

Fearing that the linchpin of lasting peace was slipping, Wilson embarked on a grueling speaking tour in August 1919, urging Americans to demand what he was certain they desired from the Senate: League membership. He explained that the Covenant did not make Americans foot soldiers of empire, but it did demand a moral commitment, embodied in Article 10, to resist unilateral force as a mechanism of change. He was met by enthusiastic crowds, but public annoyance at both sides in the League fight was growing. Americans cared little about the hairs being split in Washington. They had accepted the League as a war aim from the start, and the vast majority supported membership on whatever terms their leaders could agree.

The chance for such agreement vanished when Wilson suffered a massive stroke in the midst of his tour. A healthy Wilson might eventually have accepted qualified membership, hoping the relationship (like all political arrangements) would evolve with the League itself. The stroke rendered him incapable of such pragmatism. Before the final Senate vote in March 1920, he ignored the inclinations of most Senate Democrats and ordered them to reject the Republicans' compromise terms of membership. Many defied him; a handful more could have secured their nation's place in the League. Though public desire for membership persisted, Democrats had lost control of the issue. A postwar recession gave electoral advantage to Republicans divided over the League but determined to roll back Wilson's domestic reforms and thus to block any policy that might rehabilitate his and his party's reputation among voters. The Republican leadership stalled, theorizing alternative leagues and promising various avenues of cooperation that always seemed to close. Within a few years the booming stock market and absence of any major military conflict had pushed League membership to the back of the public mind.

Though contingent, the derailment of the American internationalist experiment had drastic consequences. American absence destroyed French confidence in the League's security function and hardened French resolve to keep Germany prostrate indefinitely. Britain, by contrast, feared that military sanctions would burden its navy while economic sanctions would forfeit enemy trade to the United States. Thus treaty revision—to restore Germany's prosperity, smooth its return to the family of nations, and prevent its recapture by aggrieved nationalists—became the aim of British statesmen. With France and Britain at loggerheads, the United States exacerbated tensions by pushing both countries for treaty revision yet refusing to cancel the war debts they financed with German reparations. Even as the League resolved several minor crises and global markets boomed, political and economic nationalism once again gained traction in the world's most powerful governments. The United States emerged as the greatest power of the postwar decade. But the system it dominated was dangerously unstable, built on the sandy rubble of its own most important wartime aim.

Power without Victory relates this Pyrrhic turn. It frankly narrates the American internationalist experiment as a tragedy. The story's tragic elements, however, should not draw attention from its contingent course. By 1919, with Europe's leading powers in physical and financial ruins, the United States was bound to occupy a dominant position in world affairs. It was not, however, bound to choose autonomy over cooperation, sovereignty over equality, and power over peace. The League of Nations that Wilson envisioned, though in many respects primitive and to modern eyes unjust, was not destined to fail. Its fate proves no natural law against powerful states submitting to powerful international organizations. Wilson's pragmatist League was never tested; we know only that a very different League did fail and that its very different successor is gravely impaired by the recalcitrance of its strongest members. It is worth considering how we might combine the wisdom gained from these later trials with the boldness and imagination of a previous generation—without repeating the mistakes, ignoring the blind spots, or absorbing the prejudices of an earlier time. This book is written on the assumption that we must better understand that time if we hope to be wiser, bolder, and more creative than those who lived it and those who followed.

CHAPTER ONE

The Ethical Republic

Upon William James's death in 1910, John Dewey neatly explained one of the most ironic and important of the deceased philosopher's legacies. "William James did not need to write a separate treatise on ethics," Dewey claimed, "because in its larger sense he was everywhere and always the moralist." Two years later, James's former student Walter Lippmann made a similar claim about the political character of pragmatism, the philosophy James espoused and popularized. Unlike Dewey, James wrote no treatise defending his theory of democracy or explicating the nature of the state. Nevertheless, Lippmann asserted, James was certain pragmatism had "tremendous consequences" for politics.[1]

History would vindicate their claims—especially the history of American and world politics that both men helped make during the presidency of Woodrow Wilson from 1913 to 1921. Immersed in the reformist ferment of the early twentieth century, Dewey and Lippmann believed that the political implications of James's ethics were progressive in the very ways Wilson understood the term. They would expand government's functions, increase and equalize its accountability to citizens, and encourage intellectual and institutional flexibility, to meet the changing needs of a diverse population as fairly as possible. Pragmatism in politics meant "increasing acquaintance with the varieties of political experience," Lippmann explained. "The statesman's imagination would be guided and organized" by such exposure; familiarity with the range of his fellow citizens' material needs, social ideals, and political opinions "would give him a starting-point for his own understanding of human beings in politics."[2] In short, James's pragmatism provided the ethical basis and methodological thrust of a practical and perpetual reform politics—a movement that was not tied to any particular ideology or program but sought both a government and a culture more attuned to life's variety and flux.

Dewey and Lippmann were not alone in perceiving pragmatism's political import. A host of their contemporaries drew on James's ideas in developing a distinctive political ethics that guided their activism in the late nineteenth and early twentieth centuries. This general guide to evaluating, criticizing, and re-imagining political and social institutions did not result in uniform interests or agreement among those who shared it. It did, however, unite adherents around a few basic—and radical—propositions. Pragmatist progressives asserted that policies and institutions, like the ideas behind them, were historical, fallible, and improvable; politics, they believed, always would and should be an experiment. Identifying interdependence as the hallmark of modern society, they touted participatory deliberative democracy as the fairest and most empirically grounded process for setting political goals, assessing political achievements, and learning from political failures. Finally, pragmatist progressives argued that all people granted full participation in the deliberative process must accept any outcome preserving its open-ended character and capacity to fa-cilitate peaceful change, lest they forfeit their role in the process or gravely damage its function.

These ideas were forged in the decades preceding the First World War, and their influence during those years was clearest in the domestic sphere of American politics. Yet the pragmatist progressives' sensitivity to the intercon-nectedness of human endeavors led them to apply their ideas to world affairs as well, resulting in their embrace and articulation of a bold but nuanced inter-nationalism. Considering relations among states as interdependent and as im-provable as those within them, they began to imagine an international system more egalitarian, deliberative, and responsive to change than that bequeathed by Europe's religious wars, imperial conflicts, and nationalist movements. By the time some of these activist intellectuals got the chance to shape govern-ment policy, their views had acquired a compelling coherence. Pragmatism, progressivism, and internationalism were closely related states of a dynamic political ideal. That ideal would direct Wilson's efforts to relate the world's states more closely, through an adaptive polity embodying the pragmatists' egalitarian, deliberative, experimental ethos. Somewhat as James predicted, his ideas proved "epoch-making" in a manner "quite like the protestant refor-mation." They changed the world in enormous, controversial, and unforesee-able ways.[3]

The basic elements uniting the thought of the pragmatist progressives orig-inated in James's theories of knowledge and truth—theories that gained collective renown as "pragmatism." *Knowledge*, in James's view, arises from attempts to surmount problems impeding achievement of goals. *Truth*

measures the degree to which knowledge solves problems while accommodating the rest of experience—that is, the rest of what has proven useful in
navigating our physical and social worlds.[4]

James's understanding of those worlds complicated what otherwise might
seem a warrant to do whatever works, regardless of the object in view. Paradoxically, James thought human beings were both liberated and constrained
by the fluidity of experience and contextual character of truth. Extending the
arguments of his friend Charles Peirce—who challenged the assumption that
beliefs, to be valid, must exactly copy reality—James claimed there *was* no
static reality that beliefs could once-and-for-all describe. A self-proclaimed
"radical empiricist," he described the universe as "pluralistic": The only humanly accessible reality was multifaceted and constantly changing, not least
through the ceaseless flux of human consciousness—itself a fact as real as
any stone or sunrise. This merging of the world of the mind and the world
beyond it underpinned an even more radical claim: namely, that ideas did
not just *demonstrate* their meaning through the purposes to which people
put them but also *derived* both meaning and value from their origins and
verification in human activity. As James explained, an idea "*becomes* true,
is *made* true by events"—that is, by the "consequences" of acting on it in a
world that both responds to and restricts our actions.[5] Crucially, that world
is not just physically but socially dynamic. Because humans are immersed
in culture, the verification of their beliefs is irreducibly social; it always involves a multiplicity of thinkers and actors, though sometimes at distant
remove. Consequently, "social experience" rather than personal preference
forms "the base" of truth. For the pragmatist, then, our personal and soci-
etal histories explain what we know, our present experience sustains what
is true, and the collaborative inquiry of an "intellectual republic" can best
promote an active but reflective "mental freedom" that advances individual
and collective wisdom.[6]

These pragmatist theories of knowledge and truth had profound implications for ethics and politics. Indeed, they cannot be understood apart
from the ethical and political challenges posed by the upheavals of the middle and late nineteenth century in the United States—upheavals that also
shaped the style and content of Woodrow Wilson's thinking. The American
Civil War had cost the lives of some six hundred thousand Americans and
the political faith of many more. The climactic event of the nation's history
impugned the Jeffersonian ideal that individual freedom bred social harmony, suggesting instead that freedom, however one defined it, entailed a
struggle for power over those who defined it differently. These doubts were

exacerbated by the rise of an industrial economy that glorified the subjec-
tion of the material environment, seemed partial to the self-regarding and
unscrupulous, and accelerated so quickly after the war that resistance appeared a futile and even asinine attempt to evade the laws of nature.[7]

Alas, the sciences seemed to confirm this suspicion. Charles Darwin's
epochal *On the Origin of Species* (1859) demonstrated that all animals had
evolved by a process of natural selection, in which inherited characteristics
of certain organisms favored their survival over others—whether of different species or their own. Hardly creatures of divine design, human beings
were merely accretions of such random advantages, owing their existence to
forbears who outcompeted rivals for scarce resources. Of course, not everyone believed or even thought about Darwin's conclusions. Many who did,
moreover, embraced them as confirming the English social theorist Herbert
Spencer's doctrine of "survival of the fittest" and thus affirming the extant
social order. If the struggle of all, suffering of many, and success of a relative
few was not just frequently necessary but also fundamentally *natural*, then
it must be *good*.[8] But for James, Wilson, and many other Americans, a life
determined solely by material laws and biological drives was revolting and
pointless: no God above man, though blind nature ruled him; no fixed order,
though laws of matter bound him; no true community, though neighbors
encircled him. Things changed constantly, but nothing could *be* changed—
nothing, that is, but what nature predetermined.

The ideas James came to formalize as pragmatism sprang from the yearn-
ing of a mordant young man for a new explanation of the world.[9] For James
found the major alternatives unsatisfying. The British empiricist tradition
stretching from John Locke through Jeremy Bentham, Alexander Bain, and
John Stuart Mill reduced morality to environmentally conditioned response:
What we experience as moral interests stem from physiological drives for
sensual pleasure, which in turn stem from evolved survival mechanisms. All
our ideas, on this reading, are constructed solely of impressions made by the
environment on the brain in the course of obeying our biological nature.[10]
The moral anxieties that spurred James's revolt against this "hedonistic"
and "associationist" brand of psychological determinism also led him to reject the idealist tradition, stretching from Immanuel Kant and G. W. F. Hegel
to British and American moderns purporting to reconcile freedom, God, and
evil in one of various logical syllogisms. In the version of James's friend and
colleague Josiah Royce, for example, the free but erroneous thought of human beings causes evil, the recognition of which intimates the existence and
character of genuinely true alternatives. These further imply an "Absolute"

thinker comprehending both the truths of eternity and the errors of finite minds; a universal consciousness whose completeness made it rational and therefore good.[11]

James remained throughout his life open to the possibility of a universal consciousness. But he could not accept that this consciousness, if it existed, lent access to a "totality" beyond the immediate universe of particular realities and emerging novelties that made genuine thought (as opposed to mere automation) possible. A world with its ultimate character and destiny set—a world in which every experienced evil was necessary and every moral exertion fated—was the kind James needed to escape, whether God's will or atomic forces decreed its movements.[12]

This potential world led James to the brink of suicide, and his decision to oppose it by believing in another was the genesis of his pragmatism. Having "touched bottom" in the early weeks of 1870, he realized that however torturously he cogitated the possibility or impossibility of resisting evil, he was left to conclude one way or another and see what happened. That spring James encountered French philosopher Charles Renouvier's definition of "free will"—"the sustaining of a thought *because I choose to* when I might have other thoughts"—and it crystallized, for him, the paradoxically obligatory voluntarism of consciousness. We cannot think everything at once, so we think selectively. In short, we choose; and even if our options are externally determined, James saw no evidence that our choice among them must be. Science had yet to establish either a world of effective human volition or a world of pure determinism, at least to James's satisfaction, which for the time being left him to choose between them. And how can one choose to deny the existence of choice? "My first act of free will," he declared in his diary on April 30, "shall be to believe in free will."[13]

Despite multiple crises of faith and will over his remaining forty years, James endeavored to maintain the cosmic optimism he chose as a youth, interpreting every evil as evidence that the world, however hard and cold, can be better. Indeed, the very source of his doubts, empirical science, became for him a source of faith in the human capacity for meaningful action. Trained as a chemist and physician, he turned early in his career to psychology, helping establish its scientific footing in his groundbreaking synthesis of experimental research, *The Principles of Psychology* (1890). James's signal contribution to what became known as "functional" psychology reflected his epiphany of 1870: the notion that thinking, even at the basic level of attention, is selective, interested, and idiosyncratic. The human species, he argued, has evolved such that each member's unique mind focuses in unique ways on certain parts of experience rather than others, often in service of entirely unique ends. Put briefly, thinking is a *voluntary act*; indeed, because it is voluntary and because it spurs the other acts for which we are responsible, thinking is perhaps "the only *moral* act."[14] James's pragmatist theories of knowledge and truth emerged from this fundamentally moral conception of cognition. As he explained in 1898, our thoughts, reflecting our unique attentive proclivities, predict "some particular turn to our experience" calling for particular forms of "conduct"—conduct with "consequences" that, desirable or otherwise, make experience different, and to that degree contingent on our original thoughts about it.[15]

This line of argument made James notorious. For if what we know about the world is always dependent to some degree on what we desire from and think of it, what is true about the world is equally utilitarian and contingent. As James explained in *Pragmatism* (1907), *truth* describes neither capricious desires nor eternal objects but simply ideas whose predictions have so far been verified by experience. Their success encourages *belief*, persuading us to act again on their predictions. Due to the dynamism of experience, however, such acts always occur in circumstances different from those initially supporting belief, and result in effects, however small, that alter circumstances further. Hence even verified ideas are only provisionally true, while belief impels their continued verification amid belief's own consequences. Truth, in short, is "the product of a double influence." Facts that verify our ideas create truth, and truth, once acted on, creates new facts. "The 'facts' themselves meanwhile are not *true*," James insisted. "They simply *are*. Truth is the function of the beliefs that start and terminate among them." More simply, truth describes those ideas that lead us unproblematically from one fact to another.[16]

Thus a man doubting his capacity for meaningful action drew comfort from a world of inherent uncertainty. For James, a world in which experience is in flux, truth evolves, and belief has consequences for good or ill is a world that can be different, and potentially better, than we find it; a world "really malleable, waiting to receive its final touches at our hands." That world precludes certainty about what is good and true but preserves the possibility that goodness and truth might be achieved. As James wrote near the end of a life spent exploring it, "No one can deny that such a role would add both to our dignity and our responsibility as thinkers."[17]

If moral questions were central to the emergence of James's pragmatism, his pragmatism was equally crucial to his moral philosophy. Pragmatically viewed, moral knowledge, like all knowledge, is a product of unceasing experience and activity. Moral truths, like other verified beliefs, are working plans of action to be revised in response to shifting environments. It was largely to explain this moral realm that James developed his famous doctrine of the "will to believe": the notion that belief in an idea often creates the conditions necessary to confirm it, by inspiring actions that bring them about.

Famously, James offered this doctrine as a means to defend religious faith from the charge that there was no scientific proof of God's existence.[18] But the relevance of James's doctrine was not restricted to religion. The will to believe meant simply "readiness to act in a cause"—any cause—"the prosperous issue of which is not certified to us in advance." As his language of "cause" implies, James considered the will to believe most potentially powerful when an idea's agreement with reality depends not on the existence or occurrence of objects or events but on the meaning or importance people accord them—that is, when agreement depends on values.[19] This was not to say that mere belief in values—or, synonymously for James, "ideals"—guarantees their truth. Experience often reveals incompatibilities among our values or between our values and others' values. The "vast majority of our moral perceptions" are not derived from ancient survival instincts or inferred from physical laws but are "brain-born," located and meaningful only in idiosyncratic, highly contextualized, ever-adapting human minds. They often conflict with other aspects of experience—especially social experience—and consequently demand some alteration of our thinking, others' thinking, or both. Examining this dilemma, James concluded that every community must deliberate over the widest possible range of *individual* values—and their likely consequences—if it hopes to formulate *social* values that maximize collective satisfaction.[20]

This method for determining the moral bases of action in a dynamic social environment is an ethics in the purest sense: a practical guide to conduct proceeding from a general conception of the good. James expressed its character in terms of its purpose: an "ethical republic." Rather than a fixed program or ranking of ideals, the ethical republic is itself an ideal, of private and public interests converging—an ideal derived from experience yet suggesting at every moment the terms and consequences of its own realization. In James's view, it is an empirical fact that all individuals have unique ideals, requiring cooperation or acquiescence from other individuals for realization. Thus all individuals, through their ideals, impose hypothetical obligations on others. The *practical* validity of ideals and obligations, however, can be established only in the course of moral life, as their consequences are considered and judged by the community.[21]

Thus while *an* ethical republic is a given, *the* ethical republic of each day depends for its scope and character on its members' interventions and interactions. The purpose of ethics is to help individuals examine, test, and revise their freely embraced ideals to accord with the republican reality of moral life, while also helping them alter that reality to accommodate as many ideals as possible. "We all help to determine the content of ethical philosophy so far as we contribute to the race's moral life," James asserted. "In other words, there can be no final truth in ethics any more than in physics, until the last man has had his experience and said his say."[22]

James's ethical republicanism entails two major implications for political life. The first is that freedom and solidarity are related dialectically. Second, it follows that careful consideration of social consequences is the rational course for those who value their freedom. To gain fullest and most favorable recognition of ourselves and our ideals, we must in our strivings account for the responses we elicit from the human environment that defines our "social self." In short, we must account for others; for like all human concepts, ideals acquire meaning and value in the context of "social experience."[23] Consequently, despite rejecting a stable scale of ideals, James identified several generic virtues that social experience, as he read it, had thus far proven vital to a healthy ethical republic.

One was experimentalism: the willingness to reflect on personal and social values in light of the goals they embody, and then alter or discard those falling short. Experimentation can cause conflict, but it also can spur moral discourse and test, refine, or displace conventional and suboptimal means of maximizing freedom. The good ultimately to be achieved by humanity's collective "say" depends on experiment, for our "hypotheses" and the acts they "prompt" are among "the indispensable conditions which determine what that 'say' shall be." Given the stakes, James deemed conscious and reflective experimentation preferable to blind stumbling or feckless obstinacy.[24]

In that vein, James also saw virtue in historical wisdom. Awareness of the practical needs and contingent factors that have driven and constrained moral action in the past can discipline ethical innovation, James believed, without discouraging it. Over generations, societies perform "an experiment of the most searching kind," and therefore ethical reflection should begin with "the customs of the community on top." James never insisted that the way things are is the way they should be; at any time, deeply rooted as society's norms might be, the "revolutionary thought or action" of an innovator "may bear prosperous fruit." Still, such fruit withers in a social and historical vacuum; it is harvested "only through the aid of the experience of other men."[25]

Of similar import to historical wisdom in James's view is empathy, a virtue rooted in consciousness itself. Again, other people's values are among the facts of experience against which all of us, as social beings seeking working truths, must test our own. Moreover, each individual's experience of his or her needs, desires, and ideals suggests that all such projected goods must feel similarly pressing to the mind that harbors them.[26] Still, empathy requires cultivation, as James argued poignantly in the context of US counterinsurgency efforts in the Philippines. He judged that campaign an extreme example of a debilitating "blindness" affecting all human beings: a nasty, navel-gazing habit of ignoring the meanings that others accord their ideals and experiences. When indulged, this habit has the damaging effect of shrinking moral horizons even while encouraging moral license. Its breaking requires a form of emotional radical empiricism: a willingness to search out alien ideals, and thus help realize the potentially greater goods that creative inquiry might reveal or create.[27]

Finally, James emphasized cultivating the "strenuous mood," which demands two things. First is a commitment to ongoing reflection, deliberation, and reconciliation (or working compromise) amid moral conflict. Second is the acceptance that all moral decisions entail sacrificing some ideals to realize others, and that the ideals to be spared are the more "organizable"—those that meet the most widely compelling demands, preserve the deliberative process for formulating common interests, and expand that process to include the widest range of individual experiences.[28] These principles should inspire us to toss "even the dearest" of our personal ideals "impartially in with that total mass of ideals which are fairly to be judged," in a collective running experiment to "satisfy at all times *as many demands as we can*." Put briefly, a strenuous ethics involves accepting the dialectic of freedom and solidarity. "*Invent some manner* of realizing your own ideals which will also satisfy the alien demands," James wrote; "that and that only is the path of peace!" James was aware that most ethical systems are designed to *provide* the manner by which value conflicts are resolved, and for many people his experimentalist ethics will never do. But if James was certain about anything, it was that the moral life is a hard life, and its problems are ours to solve.[29]

James never considered himself a political theorist. Yet his moral philosophy is pregnant with political implications. As his language of conflict, compromise, and continual adjustment suggests, the ethical republic both depends on and nurtures the kinds of deliberative, provisionally dispositive processes for weighing and harmonizing interests that democracies attempt to institutionalize.[30]

Regarding the institutional forms that should house those processes, James never clearly recorded his views in a single, accessible treatise.[31] He once claimed to abhor "bigness in all its forms" and to distrust all varieties of social organization that did not emerge from direct interactions among members. "Only in the free personal relation is full ideality to be found," he wrote in 1899. A decade later, however, freedom and fullness seemed to James so dependent on cooperation and compromise that "utopia" could only mean "some sort of a socialistic equilibrium."[32] In the interim he described himself to a friend as "an anarchist" so far as his "ideas" were concerned, but he applauded her "socialistic work" as more "practical."[33]

Such appreciation for the practical purposes of politics is the common thread uniting James's statements. James saw immense constructive potential in organized social action, and he assumed no inherent conflict between such action and authentic individualism. Late in 1900 he blamed the war in the Philippines for making him "more and more an indiv[id]ualist and anarchist," only to suggest that "*les intellectuels* of every country ought to bond themselves into a league for the purpose of fighting the curse of savagery that is pouring into the world."[34] Around that time James aligned himself (grudgingly) with the progressive wing of the Democratic Party, and though vague regarding the comprehensive agenda he wished would supplant their "very mongrel kind of reform," he was clear on the importance of organizing behind it. "When you get a lot of pure idealists together," he wrote in 1902, "they don't show up as strong as an equal lot of practical men."[35]

To be sure, James's pluralistic worldview made a "democratic respect for the sacredness of individuality" as central to his political thought as to the rest of his philosophy. In his view the sociopolitical innovations of "great men" provide crucial raw material for social evolution. Nevertheless, the mechanism of such evolution is the education and collective action of the community, whose evaluations, endorsements, and imitations of a given innovation determine its survival and influence. "Our better men *shall* show the way and we *shall* follow them," James wrote in 1907, and he considered this capacity to identify and empower an "aristocracy" to spearhead change an advantage rather than a failure of democratic communities. After all, such an aristocracy is empirical rather than hereditary, comprising citizens widely observed to use their "critical sense and judgment" in service of the whole. Moreover, it is an open aristocracy, whose duty is to see that as many people as possible develop the "higher, healthier tone" that defines membership. Finally, the aristocrats of a democracy must count themselves students of those they seek to teach, for as James wrote in *Pragmatism*, all philosophers and philosophies of any sort must "ultimately be judged" by the community, and the "finally victorious way of looking at things will be the most completely *impressive* way to the normal run of minds."[36]

Far, then, from a philosophy for "misfits, mystics, and geniuses" (as one scholar puts it),[37] James's pragmatism yielded a political ethics for social individuals struggling with the innumerable, concrete manifestations of a transcendent dilemma: how to balance personal freedom and the public good. Prefiguring Wilson, James castigated the impulse toward "aggrandizement" in American economic and political life yet sought to counter its "brute instinctive power" through appeal to the nation's "historic and hereditary principles" of popular government and civic obligation. "In a democracy the country belongs to each of us," James jotted privately in 1901, but in the United States it seemed only "the selfish interests" had "organized." "Shall not the ideal ones"?[38] James's "ebullitions of spleen" against bigness were ultimately provoked by "the more brutal, the more mendacious" arrangements of life; by violence to the particular truths of experience. He decried homogenization, not integration. With experiment and interpersonal discourse so crucial to the clarification of interests, resolution of conflict, and expansion of freedom in James's thinking, it is no wonder he was attracted to a method of social analysis he once described as "anarchy in the good sense": a method assuming that "the smaller and more intimate" units of society gave the "truer" insights into its realities and possibilities. Yet in the same breath of praise for "anarchy" James equated its "good sense" with "democracy"— and strikingly, with his "*graft*-theory" of how the "common life is realized" through struggles for "order."[39]

Like his ethics, then, James's political thought was both individualistic and communitarian. Not surprisingly, it also reflected the uncertain and often tragic world that made life morally meaningful. "The abstract best would be that *all* goods should be realized," he told his students in the late 1880s. "That is physically impossible, for many of them exclude each other."[40] Even the most reasonable compromises confirm this tragedy, for the very need to prioritize divergent demands is proof that with every moral choice, "part of the ideal must be butchered." The best that can be done is to seek "the *best whole*, in the sense of awakening the least sum of dissatisfactions," James concluded. "Since victory and defeat there must be, the victory to be philosophically prayed for is that of the more inclusive side,—of the side which even in the hour of triumph will to some degree do justice to the ideals in which the vanquished party's interests lay."[41]

Despite his slippery phrasing here, James was not lapsing into a crude system of accounting that treated all demands as equal; he was certain that demands carry varying weights. Rather, because demand has no existence outside the changeable minds of those who experience it, the community's task is to seek "the maximum of satisfaction to the thinkers taken altogether"—*thinkers*, not demands. The task, in other words, is to be as democratic as possible. The "best system" is not that which accommodates the most ideals, but the most *people* holding ideals; people who want their few, highest demands satisfied before their far more numerous trifling ones.[42] The ethical republic is predicated on the existence both of conflicting demands and the need to reconcile as much demand as possible, with no absolute measure of any one demand's importance. Democracy—under which demand is registered, gauged, and addressed by the very minds that create it—is the only way that each day's extant ethical republic can be understood and its ideal ethical republic approximated. For James, this democratic imperative was implicit in his radical empiricism: each person's experiences of the world are undoubtedly as real as anything else it contains, whatever meaning we find in them; and when attached to a political dilemma, they are facts of the case and deserve a hearing. As James told a colleague late in life, "the moment one *thinks* of other thinkers at all," the crucial leap from "solipsism" to what James called "reasoned faith in radical democracy" has been made.[43]

Fittingly for a radical empiricist, the most revealing expression of James's democratic commitments was an extended reference to historical experience. On Decoration Day in 1897, in a speech dedicating Boston's Robert Gould Shaw Memorial, James eulogized Colonel Shaw, along with the all-black Massachusetts Fifty-fourth regiment he commanded in the Civil War, as models of the boldness, circumspection, empathy, and sacrifice that genuine democracy requires of citizens. Shaw and most of his regiment were slaughtered in an assault on South Carolina's Fort Wagner, but James was not interested in the Fifty-fourth's record in battle. He recounted the regiment's tale as a lesson in the virtues of the ethical republic and as a reminder of the highest object of political life: securing freedom through enhancing solidarity. That object was "embodied" in the "constitution" of the Fifty-fourth, a battalion of the oppressed marching not merely for their own freedom but as "champions of a better day for man." From its beginnings, the republic they fought for had been an "anomaly," a "land of freedom" with "slavery enthroned at the heart of it." Though slaveholders claimed liberty to organize their communities without Northern interference, any liberty so wholly destructive of others' freedom imperiled what James considered the nation's defining faith: that "common people can work out their salvation well enough together if left free to try."[44]

To save this faith required imagining what better form it could take, reflecting on what that new form required, and acting to bring it about, and it was just such an experiment in ethical republicanism that James meant to commemorate. The term *experiment* may seem unromantic, but it is exactly the term James used to describe the decision, by Massachusetts Governor John Andrew, Colonel Shaw, and the soldiers of the Fifty-fourth, to fight for a more integrated society with a more integrated army.[45] Praising the virtue of this experiment, James also noted the historical rationale behind the larger cause. Recalling that decades of "policy, compromise, and concession" had failed to resolve the slavery issue, he acknowledged the cruel wisdom of choosing war when "law and reason" were mortally threatened by "delusion or perversity."[46] Finally, James took pains to convey Shaw's empathy for the enemy, the solidarity he shared with his troops, and the moral unity that their experiment in expanding freedom achieved. He quoted a Confederate officer who praised the gallantry of the "negroes" even as his very uniform denied their humanity. Describing the mass burial of the Fifty-fourth's dead in a "common trench" with their colonel, James explained how this callous act of a scornful enemy in fact "bore witness to the brotherhood of Man," as Shaw's body was "united with the forms" of his comrades.[47]

Throughout his tribute to these fallen warriors, James was careful not to exalt destruction along with the destroyed. Instead of glorifying the martial exploits of his subjects, he suggested that their highest virtues, those of the ethical republic, could have prevented war had more Americans shared them. These virtues instilled the "lonely courage" to act not for oneself only but for a greater good; "civic courage," he called it a sentence later. Perhaps no passage in James's writings better encapsulates both the ambiguity and the power of his political ideal than this equation of "lonely" with "civic," of "courage" with "saving day by day." For James, the patriot is the citizen committed to "speaking, writing, [and] voting reasonably," maintaining "good temper between parties," and resisting the influence of "rabid partisans and empty quacks." Through such daily acts the deliberative citizens of healthy democracies can reduce conflict and realize the ethical republic. "Such nations," James wrote, "have no need of wars to save them."[48]

Nevertheless, war had come—and shown that democracy could fail. Democracy is a method for solving and managing the problems of associated life, not a set of fixed and eternally effective answers to them. The Fifty-fourth's story attests to the burden it thus imposes on citizens: the duty to decide, with no sure knowledge of the consequences, when the forms of democracy have failed the ideal and the deliberative process has exhausted its use. Shaw and his soldiers had no formula for making that decision, nor do we; as James put it, "Democracy is still upon its trial." Certainly we can enhance the robustness of democracy by cultivating the habits of "civic courage": showing "disciplined good temper" toward those who adhere to democratic processes and "fierce and merciless resentment" toward those who subvert them. By breaking the first habit, James contended, "the Slave States nearly wrecked our Nation"; by holding to the latter, "the Free States saved her life."[49] Yet in the end these remain habits, not precise formulas. Reasonableness is not superior to justice; on the other hand, any specific decision to seek justice through coercion entails great risk, with no certainty of righteousness or reward. In the end, as James stated elsewhere, "it is at all times open to any one to make the experiment, provided he fear not to stake his life and character upon the throw."[50]

Thus deliberation and democratic institutions are means of achieving the ideal ethical republic, not ends in themselves. Sometimes other means are necessary. When, and of what sort, James did not say. He warned against judging radical measures solely by the moral fervor they excited; everyone, it seemed to him, is "ready to be savage in *some* cause." Just as dangerous, however, is deferring the ideal to a distant, impossible future free of uncertainty. As James complained to Robert Shaw's sister in 1903, "success" in the United States had come to mean a life in which "making an impotent row" against the system was never a concern. The American faith had degenerated into the Hegelian assumption that this imperfect world will pass naturally into its opposite, and progress will thereby be assured. In contrast, true democracy, as James understood it, implies a contingent kind of progress, its standards subject to revision and achieved through trial and error. "We want people who are willing to espouse failure as their vocation," he insisted. "I wish *that* could be organized—it would soon 'pass into its opposite.'"[51] When to screw up the lonely courage for a political row and how to act so that failure might, for a spell at least, "pass into its opposite" are questions James did not answer; for to answer would forever be the right and obligation of all.

Knowing that his ethical republicanism yielded no rigid formulas for moral conduct, James usually conveyed its lessons through concrete examples. His writings abound with praise for historical and contemporary figures whose responses to specific situations exhibited the general sensibility and deportment that could move each day's ethical republic toward a "newer and better equilibrium." In his own life he took seriously the personal obligations his philosophy implied, opposing the brutal suppression of the

Philippine independence movement and decrying the hideous practice of lynching in the Jim Crow South.[52] Still, James made his strongest impact on politics indirectly, through interventions in the lives of students, acquaintances, and admirers who became leading exponents of the progressive impulse in the United States. James practiced his ethical republicanism on an interpersonal level, giving moral and often material support not only to other heterodox thinkers but also to ambitious women, Jews, and African Americans who later overcame the prejudices of their society to make notable and lasting contributions to it. Several who knew this quality in James sought to build on his example as well as his philosophical achievements, drawing on his pragmatist ethics to guide them in redressing the stark social and political inequalities of industrial American society. The presidency of Woodrow Wilson would owe many of its signal initiatives to their efforts.[53]

Among these pragmatist progressives was Wilson's fellow doctoral student and sometime classmate at Johns Hopkins University, the philosopher John Dewey. Though others spent more time in the reform trenches, Dewey became the sage of the progressive movement that peaked between James's death in 1910 and the US declaration of war with Germany in 1917. He would also become one of the most visible and controversial supporters of Wilson's decision to defend and promote democracy through military means. Like James, Dewey built a case for deliberative democracy on the radical uncertainty of the moral life, the creativity it affords us, and the responsibility it imparts. Having begun his philosophical career as a Hegelian, Dewey credited James's *Principles of Psychology* with sealing his turn away from the Absolute and toward experience as the source of truth.[54] After James's death, Dewey became the main proponent of a pragmatic "recovery of philosophy," by which the study of experience and belief would cease to be "a device for dealing with the problems of philosophers" and become instead "a method, cultivated by philosophers, for dealing with the problems of men." This meant conceiving knowledge and belief as "active adjustments and readjustments" to fluid experience, and truth as the degree to which such "attitudes of response" actually make the "differences" they promised to make. "If the pragmatic idea of truth has itself any pragmatic worth," Dewey wrote the year after James died, "it is because it stands for carrying the experimental notion of truth that reigns among the sciences, technically viewed, over into political and moral practices, humanly viewed."[55]

Dewey never doubted that participatory democracy was the logical political and moral manifestation of pragmatism. True democracy, he asserted in 1908, consists essentially in the opportunity for all individuals to realize as many of their ideals as possible, which in turn requires the expansion of their collective tolerance through "the experiments and tests of men" seeking "intelligent methods of improving the common lot." The same year he drew explicitly on James's theory of the social self to argue that human beings' full self-realization depends on the practical and acknowledged public value of their activities, and thus on the congeniality of their ideals to those of other individuals. Participatory democracy is the only form of social organization providing citizens with "the trained powers of initiative and reflection" that facilitate this vision of the good life. Better than any other system, it encourages individuals to test their private ideals against a range of human experience, thereby fostering a "free preference" to act upon "far-seeing desires" that serve the personal *and* the common good.[56]

In the 1890s Dewey's main contribution to advancing this participatory ideal was through his innovations in educational theory and practice. Convinced that democracy depends less on particular institutions than on the habits of inquiry, communication, and social action that make them effective, his pedagogy aimed at training children to view learning not as the passive reception of facts but as the active solution of problems, revealing ways to employ their unique talents for the benefit of the community that sustains them. By the early 1900s he was advocating changes outside the schoolroom, criticizing power relations that impeded the learning and practice of democracy both within and beyond its walls. When economic and social stratification puts too much power in the hands of too few, he warned, political democracy is largely ineffective and widely despised, for the common good must reflect a common effort. No single person or group of people can identify the interest of a wider community without consulting those involved, or pursue it without enlisting "the freely cooperative activities" of those affected. "This cooperation," he wrote, "must be the root principle of the morals of democracy."[57]

By the end of Wilson's first term, Dewey was among the nation's most prominent advocates of government action to secure the material basis of such cooperation, including improved conditions for workers and their joint control with owners over the industrial process. The fewer the opportunities for "free and equitable social intercourse" among classes, he argued as Wilson faced reelection, the less they encounter the "novelty" prompting moral inquiry, personal growth, and discovery of common interests. According to Dewey, the insufficient autonomy of the disadvantaged atrophies character, the artificial autonomy of sequestered elites stunts and twists it, and the result "makes for rigidity and formal institutionalizing of life." By contrast, communities committed to the "Democratic Ideal" value the multiplication of common interests and attempt "continuous readjustment" to the changes they imply. Through such "diversity of stimuli," Dewey maintained, members of democracies enjoy "a liberation of powers" which would otherwise "remain suppressed." The supreme advantage and obligation of democracy, therefore, was to enhance the "social efficiency" of individuals by cultivating the "natural endowment" of each, rather than forcing them into "feudally organized" roles valued in economic terms. For "if democracy has a moral and ideal meaning," he wrote, "it is that a social return be demanded from all and that opportunity for development of distinctive capacities be afforded to all."[58]

Dewey often worked to effect the changes he called for, lecturing to adult-education classes for immigrants and workers, helping to found the National Association for the Advancement of Colored People (NAACP), and joining his wife, Alice, to campaign for women's education and suffrage. Prior to World War I, however, he focused his reformist energies on education. Meanwhile, two generations of pragmatist progressives made their marks on American social politics and positioned themselves to shape the course of Wilson's presidency.

Among Dewey's contemporaries, Louis D. Brandeis and Jane Addams were the most visible and important to apply a pragmatist sensibility to the socioeconomic and political problems of their day. Brandeis had recorded passages from James's writings while a law student at Harvard, befriended James as a young lawyer in Boston, and stayed closely connected through mutual friends and reformist causes until James's death.[59] Before becoming the architect of Wilson's first-term legislative agenda, Brandeis gained fame as the "people's attorney," championing local communities, small businesses, trade unions, and consumer groups against big-business power. A hero to proponents of small-producer economies and decentralized government, Brandeis himself sought to lay legal foundations for a democratic culture both experimental and solidaristic: a "truly American" culture committed to "development of the individual through liberty" and "attainment of the common good through democracy and social justice."[60] Contemporary industrial conditions, in his view, stunted such a culture by denying citizens, and especially workers, a voice in the organization, conditions, and ultimate purpose of their daily activities.[61] But while suspicious of large, centralized institutions and organizations, he did not consider their disaggregation universally imperative. He believed that communities of all scales thrive when their ability to adapt to change and formulate new goals is maximized. Thus for all his worry about "the curse of bigness," Brandeis affirmed the federal government's responsibility to promote conditions favoring a free and egalitarian culture. If local solutions were ideal, their effectiveness was nonetheless the concern,

and ultimate responsibility, of the national government. As a people's government, it had a duty "to fit its rulers for their task," maintaining an "American
standard of living" permitting citizens to learn, appreciate, and perform their
duties as well as enjoy their freedoms. Otherwise, he warned, "our great experiment in democracy must fail."[62]

Brandeis's sensibility thus closely resembled that of James. He was an
empiricist and democrat in the Jamesian fashion, believing the only "true"
ideas were those suggested by and tested against the widest possible range of
experience. "Experience of life has made me democratic," Brandeis explained
in 1913, for it taught "that many things sanctioned by expert opinion and
denounced by popular opinion are wrong."[63] This pragmatist belief in the
complementarity of empiricism and democracy inspired his pioneering
method of "sociological jurisprudence": the collection, analysis, and courtroom deployment of data demonstrating the social effects of laws, coupled
with insistence that such concrete consequences are as pertinent as doctrine
or precedent to law's interpretation.[64] The animating principle of the so-called
Brandeis brief was that representative governments have a duty to adjust laws
to social needs, and courts to uphold a constitution maximizing latitude for
adapting law to life. In sum, Brandeis affirmed the crucial role of broad epi-
stemic communities in adjusting institutions to experience. As he wrote years
later from the Supreme Court bench, the American system was built for "political change" and founded on "confidence in the power of free and fearless
reasoning applied through the processes of popular government."[65]

Perhaps the only person to surpass Brandeis's fame and influence as a
reformer was Jane Addams, who helped shape Wilson's vision for a League
of Nations and whose support was crucial to his reelection just five months
before the United States entered World War I. Addams counted both James
and Dewey among her major intellectual inspirations, and specifically credited Dewey's ideas with guiding her activities at Hull House, the Chicago
social settlement she founded in 1889.[66] Hull House was indeed run on
pragmatist principles. Addams viewed it not as a philanthropic but rather
a collaborative enterprise: it was assumed that the immigrants and workers seeking education, health care, and recreation at Hull House gave as
much as they received, forming a community in which settlement workers, stymied by middle- and upper-middle-class norms, found fulfilment
through service and broadened their moral imaginations through immer-
sion in the polyglot culture of Chicago's ghettos. The settlement workers in
turn helped Hull House's largely poor and foreign-born clientele understand
society's response to their growing presence and needs, with the aim of better informing it. In short, all parties were preparing themselves through

their daily interactions for fuller participation in the cooperative process of self-government.[67]

Addams inspired as much admiration in James and Dewey as they inspired in her, and for good reason: she was deeply committed to the philosophical principles and cultural project of pragmatism. She was an empiricist, collecting hard data on conditions in factories, slums, saloons, brothels, and what passed for recreational spaces in Chicago's grimmest quarters.[68] And she was an ethical republican through and through. Saturating her writings and motivating her work was the belief that solidarity across social factions would enhance satisfaction and freedom for all of them—a belief congruent with James's teaching that empathy and tolerance enrich the individual moral life. As James himself wrote, her great service to the "religion of democracy" was to encourage "sympathetic interpretation to one another of the different classes of which society consists."[69]

Addams's whole career exhibited her pragmatist belief that such solidarity across classes and interests would both promote and depend on enhanced freedom for all of them. Frustrated by the continuing exclusion of women from many realms of public life, she fought ardently for women's full citizenship, arguing that it was not only just, but would bring to politics the nurturing attitude and empathy for the powerless necessary to expand the rights and opportunities of all and give each American a sense of purpose.[70] To demonstrate that claim, she contributed her boundless energies to scores of progressive campaigns, including for the eight-hour workday, pensions and unemployment insurance, child labor laws, housing regulations, union rights, and programs to combat prostitution and alcoholism. And along with women's suffrage, Addams lobbied for African Americans' civil rights, helping to organize the NAACP in 1910 and fighting (unsuccessfully) to include a plank on racial justice with the other social-justice planks she helped insert into the Progressive Party platform of 1912. Still, Hull House was the major expression of Addams's pragmatism, at least in the domestic sphere. Fully embracing James's empathic experimentalism, she insisted that the settlement be a site of tolerant, deliberative, creative social exchange and activity. There, she asserted in 1892, all "propagandas" must find "the warm welcome of an inn, if perchance one of them be found an angel"; residents, she insisted, must ever and always "be ready for experiment."[71] This commitment to integration through deliberation saturated Addams's social and political thought, and her vision of an ethical republic organized at the smallest social scale would be projected onto a global canvas in her advocacy of a League of Nations.

Although antimaterialistic in ethos, Dewey, Brandeis, and Addams would influence Wilson's policymaking precisely because they knew that most of the problems they tackled boiled down to the distribution of resources. Among their contemporaries, however, it was Thorstein Veblen whose pragmatist critique most thoroughly impugned the economic system that Wilson, as president, would implicate in the breakdown of democracy and outbreak of war. Veblen was a founder of "institutional economics," a historicist analysis of the economic and social conventions regulating human relations. His discipline-spanning, genre-defying, morbidly arresting vivisections of the national social organism earned him a reputation as America's most incisive native critic.[72] But as demonstrated in his signature work, *The Theory of the Leisure Class* (1899), Veblen's target encompassed the formal and informal institutions of the whole industrialized West. Prime among these was "ownership," including its associated habits of "pecuniary emulation," "conspicuous consumption," and "exploit"—the envious veneration, theatrical display, and sociopathic pursuit of wealth. In the West, Veblen argued, humanity's naturally altruistic "instinct of workmanship" had been diverted into covetous, "invidious" habits esteeming consumption over production. Whereas workmanship is an evolved practical impulse to "further the life of the group," ownership is a historical convention under which labor is distasteful yet consuming its products honorable—enough to make virtues of waste, swindle, and extortion.[73] Veblen traced this perversion to ancient demographic expansions, when male social worth grew tied to "prowess" in the struggle to wrest resources from competing groups. During this "barbaric" phase, to create or conserve goods came to signal inability to steal them, and their casual disposal, power to replace them. As technological advances obviated material justifications for exploit, ancient religious apologetics morphed into modern social dogmas of property rights and laissez-faire. The resulting economic system was a wasteful, predatory fraud, stifling the growth of a truly efficient and humane society.[74]

The Jamesian psychological doctrines underlying this critique also explain Veblen's pragmatist progressive politics. It was reading James that provided Veblen an alternative to the classical economists' view of the mind as a "lightning calculator" of pain and pleasure, emphasizing instead all people's "desire to think that their life is of some use" in the material and moral enrichment of their community.[75] Citing James and affirming the "pragmatic" character of all learning, Veblen explained that our "idle curiosity"—an essentially aesthetic impulse to gather all experience under one thematic umbrella—helps generate "a more and more comprehensive system" of social knowledge that, in turn, guides our goal-driven "naïve pragmatism." In the hardscrabble environments of primitive times, these attitudes converged with the instinct of workmanship in socially productive activity.[76] Under the convention of ownership, by contrast, the domestic and foreign predations of "vested interests" are emulated by individuals, tolerated by society, and facilitated by the state. Thus barbaric mental habits perpetuate modern political circumstances fostering economic exploitation, social stratification, and war. Yet however grim his analysis, Veblen was no determinist. Even a state firmly in the grip of vested interests boasts capacities that can be turned against them if enough people imagine and demand different values and practices. Break the habits, change the circumstances, and the instinct of workmanship might yield more egalitarian institutions better adapted to modern conditions of abundance and interdependence.[77]

Veblen even accorded Western civilization an advantage in this work. The "machine process" of modern industry attuned "the workman" to empirical relations of cause and effect, eroding the quasi-religious assumptions legitimating the predations of "business enterprise" and instead encouraging workmanlike judgments based on "tangible performance."[78] In effect, the machine process bred the pragmatic turn of mind that moral freedom and social efficiency required. As mechanized conditions spread beyond the factory to pervade "the modern community," an egalitarian and peaceful culture of workmanship would encourage the exploratory and instrumental inquiry of all members, individually and collaboratively. "Pragmatism" was among Veblen's terms for such variegated mental activity, and the same word could describe the political course implied in his works—a course not dissimilar to that which Wilson would try to chart. Indeed, despite his notorious radicalism and cynicism, Veblen's goals were exactly those that his otherwise more romantic contemporary brought into the American political mainstream: to expose the contingency of institutions, and reform them to promote "free movement of the human spirit."[79]

Dewey, Brandeis, Addams, and Veblen were all born within five years of one another: Brandeis in 1856, Veblen in 1857, Dewey in 1859, and Addams in 1860. As children of the mid-nineteenth century, they helped jump-start the progressive movement's early stages while promoting a Jamesian mode of imagining, implementing, and evaluating reform. In the early 1900s they were joined by a younger generation of reformers equally eager to apply pragmatist methods to the task of social reconstruction and destined to emerge as some of the most influential political and social theorists of the Progressive Era.

Perhaps the most brilliant of these young Jamesians was W. E. B. Du

Bois, whose relationship with Wilson would poignantly demonstrate the impressive yet finite capacity of a pragmatist ethics to reconcile differences. As an African American, Du Bois felt painfully his exclusion from full citizenship and early on turned to pragmatism as an intellectual and political resource in his struggle against it. A student of James's at Harvard, he considered himself a "devoted follower" during the years he was developing what one scholar has called his "Afrocentric pragmatism."[80] His pragmatist sensibility taught him that race was not a fact of biology but an artifact of history and that the natures and roles of races were negotiable. Du Bois believed simple justice demanded that African Americans help shape the social and political institutions that shaped their lives in turn. But he also argued that their "double consciousness" as both African *and* American could yield special insight into the ways that African and European American cultural forms could challenge, alter, and enhance each other—provided each race, as he wrote in *The Souls of Black Folk* (1903), was "a co-worker in the kingdom of culture."[81]

Du Bois had made his name with the publication of *The Philadelphia Negro* (1899), among the first American works to employ statistically based sociological analysis. Du Bois credited James's "realist pragmatism" as a major factor in his turn to social science as "the field for gathering and interpreting that body of fact" on which a positive program for civil and economic equality must be based. That program involved recognizing the fallibility of any single method of inquiry—and any single inquirer—without absolving individual citizens of their personal responsibility for solving social problems.[82] White and black, state and citizen; all were implicated in the American race problem, and all were obligated to promote freedom generally by enhancing solidarity. The nation had a duty to ensure that African Americans no longer served as a convenient distraction from the "deeper national problem" eroding the republican fabric: the entrenchment of "caste." Conversely, blacks had to act with the whole nation in mind—even the racist South—if they wanted to keep and profit from their stake in it. "It is not enough for the Negroes to declare that color-prejudice is the sole cause of their social condition, nor for the South to reply that their social condition is the main cause of prejudice." Humility, reciprocity, and adaptability would serve black and white America alike. "Both must change," Du Bois insisted, "or neither can improve to any great extent."[83]

To that end, Du Bois joined an interracial group of reformers to found the NAACP in 1910 and promptly assumed editorship of its journal, the *Crisis*. From that perch he exhorted African Americans to resist both the pressure to accommodate a racist society and the urge to abandon the American democratic project. He also wrote widely and fearlessly of white Americans' moral and civic duty to welcome blacks' equal participation in the national life they shared. Du Bois would later doubt the prospects for the interracial reinvention of the United States. But during the Progressive Era he exuded an optimistic faith in the constructive power of critical inquiry like that which others had imbibed from James. As he wrote James in 1906, "You must not think I am personally wedded to the 'minor key' business—on the contrary I am tuned to a most aggressive and unquenchable hopefulness." At least through World War I, Du Bois viewed race the way James viewed all reality, as simultaneously constraining and corrigible. The fact that race was interpretable did not make it escapable or ignorable. It made it usable. Indeed, the whole promise of racial equality lay in preserving what was most valuable in black and white racial consciousness and adapting and synergizing those cultural resources to meet shared needs and create shared goods.[84]

The persistent prejudice of average Americans and leaders including Wilson helped keep race at the center of Du Bois's critique throughout the Progressive Era. Meanwhile, a similar lens was trained on the whole panoply of American cultural identities by another pragmatist whom the people and the president were destined to disappoint. A college senior at the start of Wilson's presidency, the budding cultural critic Randolph S. Bourne credited his reading of James with providing the "philosophical basis for a dynamic, creative attitude toward life," while the multiethnic milieus of Columbia University and, later, Greenwich Village amplified James's call for moral tolerance and syncretism. As Bourne wrote in his first book, *Youth and Life* (1913), "Life is a laboratory to work out experiments in living. That same freedom which we demand for ourselves, we must grant to every one." Within a few years Bourne was promoting Dewey's progressive classroom as both basis and model for the inclusive, reciprocal social laboratory he thought could produce a truly democratic culture—diverse yet solidaristic, experimental yet rich in traditions, free yet constrained by bonds of fellowship.[85]

Bourne's communitarian ideal would factor heavily in his opposing American intervention in World War I, which he correctly expected to inflame the nation's class and ethnic tensions. While some theorists, notably James's philosophical mentee Horace Kallen, thought the best way to maintain a fruitful variety of perspectives in the United States was to preserve its many distinct subcultures, Bourne considered such "cultural pluralism" impotent to reconcile freedom and solidarity in an interdependent society.[86] Agreeing that ethnic diversity was the great advantage of American culture, he saw no reason to preserve such diversity in exactly the form it took at some arbitrary point in history. Rather, Americans' heterogeneous experiences and traditions afforded an opportunity for "democratic cooperation in determining the ideals and purposes and industrial and social institutions of a country"—a chance to enhance social relations by experimenting with the rich array of cultural materials available to a nation of immigrants. That pragmatist ethic could both anchor a common culture and direct its growth, through the constant "cross-fertilization" of ideas and ideals. Bourne's "Trans-National America" would be cosmopolitan *and* nationalist, and therefore distinctly American.[87]

To Bourne's consternation, his transnational ideal was shared by several pragmatists who disputed the necessity of his strict pacifism to its realization, especially in the face of global upheaval. Among the most brilliant was Felix Frankfurter, who was also among those who most deeply infiltrated Wilson's policymaking circle. Born in Vienna in 1882, Frankfurter immigrated to New York City in 1894, acquiring a bachelor's degree from the College of the City of New York, a law degree from Harvard, and a keen awareness of the legal elite's anti-Semitism before seeking a civic outlet for his ambitions. He found it in the office of Henry Stimson, recently appointed US attorney for the Southern District of New York by President Theodore Roosevelt. Thus began a career of public service that would shape some of Wilson's most important policies and eventually lead Frankfurter to the bench of the Supreme Court.[88]

Frankfurter's move into public service was partly inspired by Brandeis, whom he first heard speak at a 1905 meeting of the Harvard Ethical Society founded by his roommate—and William James's doctoral student—Morris Cohen. Cohen, too, influenced Frankfurter through his theory of law's interdependence with changing ideals of social welfare. Both influences dovetailed with the legal historicism of his Harvard professors to convince Frankfurter that "facts are changing" and "the law cannot be static. So called immutable principles must accommodate themselves to facts of life"—especially the facts of social inequality, political corruption, and economic inefficiency.[89] Thus in the district attorney's office he fought for the habeas corpus rights of immigrants and against fraud in the customs office. Drawn to Roosevelt's charismatic progressivism, Frankfurter followed Stimson into politics and eventually the War Department, where as special assistant to then Secretary Stimson he worked to advance autonomy for the Philippines and social equality in Puerto Rico.[90] In Washington he also became "half brother, half son" to the inveterate lobbyist Brandeis, each reinforcing the other's concern for the balance of expert inquiry and popular influence necessary to "social advance" in a modern democracy.[91] Returning to Harvard as a law professor in 1914, Frankfurter began to articulate that concern through a jurisprudence modeled on Jamesian epistemology. In a signature article of 1916, published one month after requesting a memorandum on "The Will to Believe" from Brandeis, he identified judicial attitudes toward "the validity of the experience and beliefs of others" as among "the most dynamic factors in the actual disposition of concrete cases." Consequently, "government," which both enacts and prompts these political turns to the law, "necessarily means experimentation." The result, Frankfurter concluded, is a constitution subservient rather than superior to government's evolving responsibilities; a rule of provisional law, under which "opportunity must be allowed for vindicating reasonable belief by experience."[92]

The congeniality of these ideas to those of Wilson and his close advisers combined with a juggernaut personality to give Frankfurter a voice in policy, and thus an influence on politics, that Du Bois and Bourne never had. Not that these three exhausted the list of young pragmatists committed to effecting change in the Wilson era. Du Bois himself was recruited to the NAACP by William English Walling, a student of Dewey's and Veblen's who endorsed pragmatism as "a Socialist philosophy" implying "science and industrial democracy" as prerequisites to justice under modern conditions. And Bourne's commitment to cultural transformation was easily matched by Max Eastman, another student of Dewey's and Veblen's who found in pragmatism a warrant for women, minorities, and workers to communicate through arts and letters, as well as "drastic action," their intention "to take their blessings of civilization" from the white men who monopolized them.[93] Measured by the dual yardsticks of popular and political influence, however, few reformers of any stripe approached the triumvirate of Herbert Croly, Walter Weyl, and Walter Lippmann, founding editors of the *New Republic* and major architects of Wilson's strategy for peace after World War I.

Croly, the senior member in age and editorial rank, had absorbed James's belief in the pervasiveness of change, importance of adaptation, and interdependence of individuals during two aborted stints at Harvard. Pondering the industrial crises of the 1880s and 1890s, he concluded that the nation was undergoing a socioeconomic revolution it was unequipped to handle. The polity seemed divided among traditionalists defending an outmoded laissez-faire; radicals preaching an uncritical, impractical socialism; and those lying in between but lacking coherent alternatives. Determined to fill the gap, Croly staked out a middle route between unrestrained capitalism and dogmatic socialism in his landmark work, *The Promise of American Life* (1909). His achievement was to give familiar practical experiments such as secret ballots, unionization, industrial regulation, and graduated taxation a coherent theoretical grounding: a "New Nationalism" revealing his thorough internalization of James's teachings. Croly historicized the American

democratic ideal, describing fundamental changes in the relationship between its original "promise" of autonomy, equality, and opportunity and the
current socioeconomic context impeding its realization. In his 1914 encore,
Progressive Democracy, he explained the promise as a function of faith in
the Jamesian sense, defined by citizens' active belief in "the ability of the
human will, both in its individual and its collective aspects," to fulfill it.
Imagining and demanding a more equal society, a more active and popularly accountable government, and a deeper cultural commitment to tolerance and empiricism would encourage the public and its servants to devise
more effective and flexible approaches to common goals, even before their
demands were fully met. Indeed, the demands of "progressive democracy"
would never be fully met. Like the pragmatism inspiring it, progressive democracy was a mode of inquiry, recognizing nothing permanent or sacred
save the flux of experience and "the creative power of the will."[94]

Before they gained him entrée into Wilson's circle, Croly's ideas inspired
Roosevelt's 1912 presidential platform and put him in the ranks of Dewey,
Brandeis, and Addams as a theorist and publicist of progressivism. He was
soon joined in this pantheon by Walter Weyl, an economist by training whose
reading of James's *Pragmatism* forever discredited, in his eyes, the "Cosmic
Verities" upholding the established order. Weyl was a valued if occasional
adviser to Roosevelt, Brandeis, and Wisconsin's insurgent Republican Senator Robert M. La Follette even before his first book, *The New Democracy*
(1912), made him a hot commodity among progressive office seekers and
editors.[95] A former labor organizer and associate of Addams's at Hull House,
Weyl preached stricter regulation of business and expanded rights and protections for workers. Weyl was most insistent, however, that the middle
classes use their newfound power as consumers to demand changes that the
poor could not, and the rich would not, effect by themselves. Convinced that
the "social surplus" of an industrial economy could support the downtrodden with minimal sacrifice from the wealthy, Weyl urged reform-minded
Americans to abandon sympathy for all purely theoretical rearrangements
of society and instead embrace gradual, commonsense methods of economic
and political pressure to improve the system they inhabited. "The mortal
defect of Utopias is that they are too static," Weyl wrote. Compared to blueprints for "heaven on earth," he continued, "our present society, with all its
imperfections, is vastly superior."[96]

Weyl's book, ranked by Roosevelt with *The Promise of American Life*,
earned him a spot on Croly's *New Republic* editorial team and thus a voice
in the most politically influential journal of the Wilson years.[97] Round-
ing out the trio was the even more precocious Walter Lippmann, whose

influence on the journal and its thousands of readers was matched only by Croly himself—and in the case of Wilson, matched by none. Like Croly, Lippmann had studied with James at Harvard. His first book, *A Preface to Politics* (1913), employed Sigmund Freud's psychology of irrationality and James's philosophy of uncertainty to attack the intellectual underpinnings of a laissez-faire political economy.[98] His sophomore effort of 1914, *Drift and Mastery*, revealed a firmer commitment to pragmatism and its constructive implications for politics, and made him a star in progressive circles. Lippmann's notion of "drift" struck a chord with Americans tired of government waste, business corruption, and social strife but no longer certain who, what, or how many factors to blame. The "mastery" Lippmann urged readers to exercise was the application of Jamesian pragmatism to the social, economic, and political ills that both reflected and perpetuated this systemic failure of self-government, which in order to thrive required reflection, deliberation, and "a country in which everyone has some stake and some taste of its promise." Toward that end, Lippmann proposed a reform program similar to Croly's: centralizing and enhancing government through increased regulation, broader political participation, and expert consultation to ensure effective legislation. Even more than Croly, however, Lippmann insisted that vigorous pursuit of a broadly conceived agenda did not imply permanent commitment to any of its details: "The only rule to follow, it seems to me, is that of James: 'Use concepts when they help, and drop them when they hinder understanding.'"[99]

Applying this rule to American politics, the *New Republic* editors, especially Croly and Lippmann, became factors in its world-altering course. Collaborating closely with Dewey, Brandeis, and Frankfurter and immersed in a discourse shaped by Addams, Veblen, and Du Bois along with Bourne, Walling, and Eastman, the *New Republic* pragmatists played a formative role in the development of Wilsonian internationalism, including its important but poorly understood legacies. Their commitment to a positive American international policy of political integration across national borders was not simply mashed into James's political ethics after war in Europe made front-page news of world affairs. Rather, it emerged naturally from their commitment to the ethical republic.

James's own writings evince a similar logic. Like his protégés, James took an interest in international affairs and analyzed them in a framework of international interdependence. American imperialism, the major foreign policy issue of his day, was in his view as portentous for the nation's internal development as for its external legacy. Not only was the Philippines campaign "crushing out the sacredest thing in this great human world"—the spirit and experience of self-government—but it also threatened to destroy the "ancient soul" of America. For several years before 1898 James had worried that a seductive rhetoric of power was undermining the reasoned argumentation, fair-minded consideration, and responsible appeal to facts that were essential to self-government. Yet James did not focus solely on the injustice and danger of assertive foreign policies. He believed Americans could and should play a constructive role in international affairs. Initially he even suggested that the Spanish-American War might finally bring the nation to a sense of its international responsibilities. Such moments of optimism regarding the US government's global role were rare, but their scarcity by no means reflects belief in the virtue of isolation, which he labeled an "absurd abstraction." On multiple occasions James denied any sharp division between national and international affairs, describing all politics as part of humanity's eternal struggle for practicable freedom, practically distributed. "Political virtue does not follow geographic divisions," he declared; it followed each country's "internal division" between those who employed "main force" to reach their goals and those who maintained the "critical conscience" to inquire after justice. The latter trait, James argued, characterized the "great international and cosmopolitan liberal party," whose "American section" was but one battalion in a global "campaign for truth and fair dealing."[100]

By the time they emerged on the national scene, Croly and Lippmann had begun to think in similar terms. "Association is a condition of individuality," Croly wrote in *The Promise of American Life*. "International relations are a condition of nationality." There could be no "universal nation," sufficient unto itself, any more than there could be a "universal individual." This lesson was impressing itself on peoples worldwide, Croly asserted, and implied the need to embody some measure of the world's interdependence in "some set of international institutions." Lippmann struck a similar note in *Drift and Mastery*. However one defined it, he admitted, "internationalism" was undoubtedly still "a very distant dream." But it was not so distant as to be impossible, or even invisible to waking eyes. "Patriotism itself has gained a new dignity by its increasing alliance with democratic reform," he wrote, "and there is actually ground for supposing that love of country is coming to mean love of country and not hatred of other countries." Indeed, there were signs that an international "public spirit" was spreading, one that might acquire the power to transcend "mere clashing self-interest" both abroad and at home.[101]

Croly and Lippmann followed this intellectual path to the highest levels of power. But other pragmatists helped pave it for them. Veblen had explicitly linked exploit at home to exploit abroad. Du Bois had long argued that the problem of racism was a problem not only for the United States but for an entire world threatened by the globe-spanning collisions of racist empires.[102] Above all, Jane Addams had built much of her reputation as a social critic on her holistic analyses of domestic and international tensions. Her *Newer Ideals of Peace* (1907) attributed the alienation, lawlessness, and forceful suppression of immigrant and working-class communities in the United States to the pervasive "militarization" of American society, a dynamic linked in turn to the failure of ostensibly civilized nations to foster deliberative relations and achieve lasting peace. In a happy irony, the disfranchised were developing in response what James had called "the moral equivalent of war": a cooperative ethos channeling the "heroic" instinct for strenuous living into constructive social action. Addams wondered that this "new cosmopolitanism" remained subordinate in American public affairs to an individualistic ethos forged in the republic's early decades and increasingly abstracted from the social realities of industrial life. She insisted that the failure to cultivate the social spirit of the ghetto prevented the United States and other modernized nations from pursuing "positive peace": domestic and diplomatic initiatives that would not just prevent war between nations but promote "the nurture of human life" within them.[103]

Like her fellow pragmatists, Addams was convinced that our view of the world affects the way we act in it and thus the way we help shape its present and future. The belief that reality is unchanging, that individuals are biological automata, that social structures are natural rather than historical, and that intercultural clashes are inevitable and irremediable can only encourage resignation to what is unsatisfying, disturbing, or repugnant in life. By contrast, the belief that change is real and that people can consciously order their lives to direct it, however imperfectly, should inspire a sense of responsibility for the present and accountability to the future. That belief in change and in the responsibility it implies lay behind the pragmatists' commitment to a democratic ideal that was both radical and expansive. As Dewey explained, democracy, understood as continuous and cooperative self-government, makes sense only in "a world which in some respect is incomplete and in the making, and which in these respects may be made this way or that according as men judge, prize, love and labor." Conversely, such a pluralistic universe demands a democratic sensibility: a recognition that "where discovery is genuine, error is an inevitable ingredient of reality"; that "good fortune and bad fortune are facts" rather than excuses; and that to affix "certain grades of value" to all things at all times serves primarily to locate authority and entrench power. In the case of human beings, assigning such values is also an absurdity. Each individual life is "a manifestation of something irreplaceable." Each is impossible even to classify, for it becomes "forceful or actual only in relationship with other like beings." Because (rather than in spite) of each soul's singular capacities, "democracy is concerned not with freaks or geniuses or heroes or divine leaders but with associated individuals in which each by intercourse with others somehow makes the life of each more distinctive." For the same reason, the forms and even the meaning of democracy itself are impossible to fix. The former must continuously justify itself through "better institutions of life," and the latter must be gleaned from those "philosophers" who seek less to explain the world than to inspire people to their freest, most generous, and most earnest strivings for the common good.[104]

When Dewey shared these thoughts with a Berkeley audience in late November 1918, an imperfect but nonetheless impressive record of reform marked Woodrow Wilson as just such a democratic philosopher in action. With hostilities ended by an Armistice embodying his program for peace, Wilson seemed ready to inspire whole populations across the world to build better institutions of life. It would be some months before Dewey, like many others, lost faith in Wilson's abilities. Yet even when Wilson still seemed capable of leading history's most ambitious democratic experiment to fruition, Dewey invoked another name to inspire his listeners, "one through whom this vision of a new mode of life has already spoken with beauty and power—William James."[105]

CHAPTER TWO

Common Counsel

On March 4, 1913, Woodrow Wilson—duly elected and officially installed as the twenty-eighth president of the United States—was still looking forward to victory. Delivering his inaugural address to the American people, Wilson hailed the historic victory that he and his party, the long-suffering Democrats, had won. Then he set his sights on the larger triumph that the people could achieve with his party as their instrument: the triumph of progressivism in national politics. His party would commit itself to restoring equality and justice by shielding citizens from "great industrial and social processes which they cannot alter, control, or singly cope with." It would derive the policies of this progressive agenda not from elegant theories but from close observation of "facts as they are." In short, Wilson forecast the ascendancy of a humane empiricism in policymaking. "We shall deal with our economic system as it is and as it may be modified, not as if it might be if we had a clean sheet of paper to write upon," he announced, "and step by step we shall make it what it should be in the spirit of those who question their own wisdom and seek counsel and knowledge."[1]

Wilson's injunction against drawing-board reforms sounds like the creed of a conservative, while his rejection of ideological rigidity placed him at a safe distance from the "radicals" of his day. Nevertheless, Wilson's legislative accomplishments in office mark him as one of the most radical reformers to occupy the presidency. In the first two years of his first term in office he surpassed the total accomplishments of most of his predecessors and successors, establishing an independent tariff commission to equalize the costs and benefits of foreign trade; the Federal Trade Commission to interpret and enforce several strengthened provisions of national antitrust law; and most consequentially, the Federal Reserve System, to prevent financial panics and democratize access to credit for a nation of entrepreneurs. Later

Wilson capitalized on the exigencies of war to weave the graduated income tax, the eight-hour workday, and collective bargaining into the basic fabric of American politics. Clearly Wilson's was not a pure radicalism of the root-and-branch variety but something closer to radical empiricism: careful interrogation followed by purposeful reorganization of the relations ordering the national experience. Put briefly, the sweeping changes he effected in office are best understood as the product of a skeptical and deliberative yet creative and adaptive mind—as the work of a pragmatist in politics.

Wilson did not consult William James's works in drafting his address, nor did he ever label himself a pragmatist. But James's pragmatism had already shaped Wilson's political thought and practice—and would do so again. Regardless, several of James's admirers found a kindred spirit in Wilson. The majority of Wilson's political career, from his governorship of New Jersey through his work at the Paris Peace Conference after World War I, comprises a series of experiments of the sort that James's reformist followers had long endorsed: experiments aimed at restoring popular influence over government, yet recognizing the complexity of a pluralistic society and the need for continuous adaptation to its fluid conditions. James's theory of "corrigible" truth and vision of a deliberative "intellectual republic" had taught these reformers to challenge outmoded political ideas, while his writings on ethics suggested how to replace those ideas in an interdependent society with democratic aspirations.[2] To many of these activist intellectuals, Wilson— especially during the six-year period from the spring of 1913 through the spring of 1919—appeared to be applying similarly pragmatist principles to political values and the institutions enshrining them. In the president's domestic and international policies they descried an effort not only to achieve specific reforms of which they often approved, but also to perpetuate the experiment in interventionist yet deliberative government that was the essence of progressivism as they understood it.

Too often Wilson did not experiment boldly enough for these pragmatist progressives. Indeed, though James was dead by the time Wilson rose to political prominence, it is easy to imagine him, too, growing impatient with the latter's presidency at times. In many ways Wilson was conservative, skeptical of reforms for which large sectors of the public were unprepared and sharing many of the prejudices that kept them that way. But James, too, had recognized that changes in thinking were typically incremental, constrained by a social environment shaped in turn by the past. "Truth," he explained in *Pragmatism*, develops "much as a tree grows by the activity of a new layer of cambium." Wilson took a similarly organic view of the institutions embodying America's political ideas. "The noble charter of fundamental law given us by the convention of 1787 is still our Constitution," he wrote in 1885, but it is "only the sap-centre of a system of government vastly larger than the stock from which it has branched."[3]

Though entirely his own, Wilson's conception of the state as an organic expression of political values in creative tension with the social environment was eminently Jamesian. And though Wilson's direct encounters with James's ideas were intermittent, the vocabulary of pragmatism is particularly suited to explaining the political philosophy and practice of a remarkably elastic thinker—especially one who came to adopt (and adapt) ideas from some of James's most prominent students and admirers. Indeed, Wilson's consistent promotion of a powerful yet flexible and more truly representative national government largely embodied the pragmatist-progressive ideal: a process of continuous political and social reconstruction through broadly inclusive, deliberative discourse—or as Wilson called it, government by "common counsel."

Wilson's thinking changed much over his life, but some of his most persistent ideas were his most important. Prime among these was the superior importance he accorded contingency over determinism in human affairs, and history over theory in explaining them—including theories about God's will and work in the world. The common view of Wilson as a rigidly moralistic theocrat is mistaken. This minister's son and deeply religious man did not deny God's ultimate direction of human events. But neither did he ignore the unpredictability of history as humans experienced and made it, nor dismiss the fallibility of human judgments about God's ends and means.[4]

Wilson's fatalism entailed neither apathy nor certainty. His father, a Presbyterian minister, taught him to view life through the biblical prism of God's covenant with humanity, which demanded constant service to others and vigilance over oneself lest God's blessings be repudiated. Perfection, he taught his son, was always the goal, though rarely, if ever, achieved. This fallibilistic lens led Wilson, like his father, to see tolerance of religious diversity and respect for secular values as means of testing and strengthening faith and to view humans' constant exploration of their changing world, and search for their proper roles in it, as the solemnest of obligations. As young Wilson wrote his fiancée, Ellen Axson, in 1884, any faith that meant "letting things drift, in the assurance that they would drift to a happy result," contravened his view of "*how* all things work together for good—through the careful performance of our duty."[5] As he matured, Wilson came to view life as a series of interlocking covenants of this complex sort. In his student days he wrote several constitutions for campus groups, translating his basic covenantal ideas into practical guides for human relationships. Importantly, all were amendable, on the theory that relationships changed, even if their animating principles remained constant. While away at graduate school he even solicited Ellen's ratification of a two-member "inter-state Love League," permitting adoption of new "bylaws . . . as they become necessary."[6] In short, Wilson's was not a dogmatic faith. It was a backdrop throwing events and choices into relief, a reminder that each day's challenges make unique demands on the moral imagination.

Wilson's writings as a student and scholar reflect a complementary view of politics, which he considered a secular attempt to reconcile the perennial ideal of order with the universal experience of change. In his first book, *Congressional Government* (1885), Wilson described the US Constitution as a "root, not a perfect vine"; in his second, *The State* (1889), he argued that governments of modern industrial societies must expand their "ministrant" functions to provide citizens time, education, and opportunity to participate in adapting institutions to their needs. In future years Wilson would express frustration with the Democratic Party's populist wing and other reform movements that seemed, to him, dogmatic and rash in their particular demands for government intervention. But even in such moods Wilson consistently endorsed a constitutional theory allowing the state maximum flexibility to adapt to social change. As he argued in his last academic work, *Constitutional Government* (1908), the task of the twentieth century was to "bring the active and planning will of the government into accord with the prevailing popular thought and need."[7]

An early source of this concern with the harmonization of order and change was Wilson's reading of the *Federalist* essays. Marginalia in his law school edition of the *Federalist* indicate that, by 1880 or so, he reached a conclusion he would often restate as a scholar and statesman: that the framers' genius lay in making *explicit* the dynamism *implicit* in all social organization, so as to lubricate the institutional modifications that social change required. Wilson took special note of the following from *Federalist* 34, by Alexander Hamilton: "Constitutions . . . are not to be framed upon a calculation of existing exigencies; but upon a combination of these with the probable exigencies of ages. . . . Nothing therefore can be more fallacious, than to infer the extent of any power proper to be lodged in the national government, from an estimate of its *immediate* necessities. There ought to be a CAPACITY to provide for future contingencies . . . and as these are *illimitable* in their nature, so it is impossible to safely limit that capacity." Wilson never abandoned this Hamiltonian view of constitutional government's purpose and character. Nearly thirty years later he would insist that a genuinely "constitutional" government "was one whose powers have been adapted to the interests of its people" and that the US Constitution, especially, was designed to facilitate such adaptation over time—not "to hold the government back to the time of horses and wagons."[8]

Another early influence on Wilson's political thought was his deep admiration for Britain's unwritten constitution, which he considered entirely consistent with the dynamic strain he admired in the American founders. The wisest among the founders, he believed, had thought states were healthiest when policy and institutions were consciously and continuously molded, through strenuous debate among representatives directly responsible to public opinion. Power in such states should be vested in leaders adept at interpreting public opinion, crystallizing it, and mobilizing support behind a program embodying it. By the time he entered graduate school at Johns Hopkins University in 1883, Wilson considered the British system of parliament and cabinet, not its American cousin, the paragon of such vigorous, efficient self-government. Indeed, Wilson believed that American government had become dangerously dysfunctional, ruled by a factional legislature that completely marginalized the most nationally representative branch, the executive.[9]

Wilson did not trace the problems of the United States to the ideas of the *Federalist*. Rather, much like Croly a quarter century later, he blamed subsequent abstractions of those ideas and the simultaneously constrained yet untended growth of the constitutional "tap-root" that resulted. Inspired by Walter Bagehot's evolutionary analysis of the British system in *The English Constitution* (1867), Wilson aimed to discover how the American system of his day had developed and thus begin the process of determining how to fix it.[10] In *Congressional Government*—submitted as his dissertation at Hopkins—he argued that Americans' fetish for the separation of powers and fear of centralization had, ironically, sequestered all "motive and . . . regulative power" in a splintered oligarchy of congressional committees. It was natural that as the nation expanded, the federal government would gain control over matters too complex and far-reaching for states or localities to manage efficiently or fairly. Yet instead of coordinated legislative programs thoroughly vetted by debate, policy was made piecemeal by committees behind closed doors. Nor, given the weakness of the executive, could another institution act with the "responsibility" that would make it truly representative, simultaneously speaking the people's will, educating their conclusions, and superintending their common affairs. The average citizen was shrewd in "esteeming government at best but a haphazard affair, upon which his vote and all his influence can have but little effect."[11]

This critique of the American system made Wilson's name as a scholar. It is also crucial to understanding a major feature of his mature political thought: the centrality of strong party government and executive power to the accountable leadership that self-governing polities demand. Wilson's attraction to British politics reflected his intense admiration for oratorical masters such as Edmund Burke and William Ewart Gladstone and the legislative initiatives their talents underwrote. He grew convinced that their skills were honed in debates of a sophistication and importance no longer seen in American politics. The reason, Wilson argued, was the structure of British government, in which the executive was drawn from the ranks of the legislature and the party in power could be deposed any time. Under that system, unified party action was the only means of realizing legislative goals. And the only way to create such unity was to convince the party that its goals were achievable, valuable, and politically expedient. That convincing occurred in the course of open debate in Parliament, where opposing views demanded recognition, prompted compromise, and—most important—publicized the lawmaking process. These circumstances also helped ensure that the party in power pursued genuine legislative *programs* reconciling multiple interests through complementary measures—thus increasing the efficiency and democratic character of legislation.[12]

The contrast with the American system was striking. "Congress is a deliberative body in which there is little real deliberation; a legislature which legislates with no real discussion of its business," Wilson wrote four years before arriving at Hopkins. In *Congressional Government* he repeated the charge. Even as Congress developed "the habit of investigating and managing everything" through a proliferation of standing committees, strict separation of powers had prevented American Gladstones from rising among the people's representatives and unifying them under a national program in the public interest. National parties under strong leaders were the only way to hold members of Congress accountable to anyone but themselves—yet the obvious means of consolidating and exercising such influence, the presidency, was rendered useless by the weakness of the office.[13]

Here again Americans were shamed by the British system, where strong executive leadership was encouraged and shown to advantage. Because the British executive was a subset of the nation's legislators, it could introduce legislation representing the national policies of its party and remain involved at every stage of the lawmaking process. In the United States, such interbranch cooperation would require that the heads of executive departments hold seats in Congress—a radical constitutional overhaul. Extreme as it was, Wilson believed this "cabinet government" solution would end the executive's isolation from the lawmaking process and thereby democratize the latter—not merely because the president was nationally elected but also because of the double-edged nature of power in a representative democracy. Giving an administration "opportunity and means for making its authority complete and convenient" would give the people a basis on which to judge performance, assign responsibility for successes and failures, and hold government's bunglers or obstructors accountable at the ballot box. *"Power and strict accountability for its use* are the essential constituents of good government," Wilson declared in *Congressional Government*. "The best rulers" are entrusted with "great power," conscious that they will be "abundantly honored and recompensed for a just and patriotic use of it" but receive "full retribution for every abuse of it."[14]

Contrary to popular belief, Wilson never considered himself a prophet. Still, in hindsight, these words seem an eerie portent of their author's fate three decades in the future and practically a world away.

Congressional Government was a smash in the still-emerging field of political science. Disappointingly, however, it offered nothing resembling the "well-considered expedients" for making "self-government . . . a straightforward thing of simple method, unstinted power, and clear responsibility," which its author deemed necessary.[15] One thing is clear, however: Wilson's loyalty to the Democratic Party did not entail sympathy with the strict constitutional construction embraced by its intellectual leaders. The roots of Wilson's thinking ran to Hamilton, Burke, and Bagehot, not Justice Field, and its scholarly fruits would tell their origins.

In fact, over time Wilson's synthesis of his heroes' views yielded a functionalist, evolutionary outlook that exceeded them all in progressive character and democratic scope. In Wilson's mature theory, the ideal polity, comprising leaders and public alike, would explicitly acknowledge and embrace the organic nature of its institutional apparatus, the state. The state in turn would accommodate the evolving character and changing needs of its subjects, for no stable state, not even an absolute monarchy, persists through mere imposition of norms upon a people. "Government is merely the executive organ of society," Wilson explained in 1889, "the organ through which its habit acts, through which its will becomes operative, through which it adapts itself to its environment and works out for itself a more effective life."[16]

This organic ideal of the state in no way implied a passive populace, content to watch political nature take its course. Rather, the reciprocal influence of history, habits, and institutions informed Wilson's correlative *civic* ideal of the state: in its highest form, a complex of adaptive political formations that simultaneously foster and depend on a culture of self-government. As the sociopolitical organism grows in complexity, Wilson reasoned, new problems arise, requiring new solutions, along with new ideals inspiring new goals and encountering new obstacles. In the healthiest polities such solutions and goals are informed by cultural commitments to both individual freedom and the common good, for only citizens who see beyond their private interests can sustain the stable yet flexible institutions a plural, protean society demands. Through this civic commitment to private and public flourishing the polity develops the capacity for self-government. Inhering in the people, not the state, self-government in essence comprises both the right and the habit of deliberative decision making in public affairs. More than free speech and accountable representatives, it implies the broad social practice of a critical, tolerant, discursive political ethics. "Self-government is not a mere form of institutions," Wilson declared. "It is a form of character. It follows upon the long discipline which gives a people self-possession, self-mastery, the habit of order and peace and common counsel."[17]

Two rarely noted features of Wilson's training at Hopkins likely encouraged these experimental and deliberative inclinations. One was the mentorship of economist Richard T. Ely, whose mix of Christian socialism and hardheaded empiricism infused Wilson's earliest efforts to outline a normative theory of the democratic state. Few scholars acknowledge that Wilson studied economic history with Ely, or that he was recruited by the latter to cowrite a historical treatise on American political economy.[18] During that period Wilson sketched an essay submitting that the charge of modern democracies is literally sacred, though necessarily secular in method. Its ultimate purpose, he asserted, is to propagate "the supreme and peaceful rule of *counsel*," drawing humanity toward "kinship with God" by affirming "reason over passion." After reading Ely's *Labor Movement in America* (1886), Wilson drafted another essay, adopting Ely's interest in nonrevolutionary socialism as a source of experimental methods for reviving the "rule of counsel" in Gilded Age society. Genuine democrats should not reject such methods a priori, Wilson admonished, for "in fundamental theory socialism and democracy are almost if not quite one and the same," resting together "upon the absolute right of the community to determine its own destiny."[19] Wilson disdained dogmatic socialism, but he also disdained dogmatic laissez-faire. By the time he published his second book, *The State* (1889), Wilson was endorsing the major protective and regulatory reforms

that would characterize Ely's "Wisconsin Idea" of progressivism, justifying such "socialism" (as Wilson called it) by government's duty to see that
"individual self-development" be made "to serve and to supplement social
development."[20]

Wilson's intellectual affinity with Ely was lasting. His organic theory
of the state was far less teleological than that of the Swiss and German
scholars whose works studded his syllabi. Like Ely, he adopted an empiricist's version of historicism, arguing that despite its organic relationship to
the society it served and regulated, the state must never be confused with
the social organism itself. Rather, the state and its laws constitute "the
historical form of the organic common life of a particular people"—those
associations, relationships, and widely shared convictions that the majority
has found it "expedient" to formalize. This argument that a state's forms
and functions reflect historical conditions and are sacred only in proportion to their expediency framed his political thought for the rest of his life,
eventually informing his vision of a League of Nations designed to evolve in
unforeseen ways amid unforeseen changes.[21]

A second factor illuminating this trajectory in Wilson's thinking is his
interest in modern philosophy, specifically the "new psychology" introduced to Hopkins by the future president of Clark University—and William
James's doctoral student—G. Stanley Hall. As an aspiring young philosopher, Hall was drawn to James's search for an account of mental life more
coherent with biological evolution than the dualistic Cartesian and Kantian
schemes yet friendlier to free will than alternatives postulating a universe
governed entirely by material laws or absolute thought.[22] Significantly, it
was during Hall's Harvard years (1876–1881) that James laid foundations
for what he later popularized as "pragmatism." During that span James
first stated in print that mind is not passive but acts upon interests—many
linked to survival, but many subjective and idiosyncratic.[23] During the same
years he also argued that the knowledge we acquire and truths we discern
are never complete or certain but reflect a course of experience profoundly
shaped by our interests and daily modified by events. Thus we believe in
ideas that *work* for us so long as they successfully predict the outcomes
of our actions. More controversially, James argued that we also often believe in ideas not yet thoroughly tested, and we do so justifiably if (1) belief
alone can spur the actions likely to confirm or disconfirm them; and (2) confirmation would yield some desired consequence.[24] Finally, James was already spreading the ethical gospel of his nascent pragmatism. He urged
his early readers to cultivate and discipline their natural experimentalism
by taking a skeptical attitude toward abstraction and tradition, a tolerant

attitude toward diversity and novelty, and an existential attitude toward the power, limits, and uncertain outcomes of their freely exercised wills.[25]

Eventually Hall and James diverged on several metaphysical implications of functionalist psychology. In Hall's early years at Hopkins, however, his teaching and scholarship emphasized those aspects of his thought most hospitable to James's belief in free will, moral responsibility, and the potential of science to affirm and serve them. During that same period Wilson took Hall's yearlong course in philosophy and education, deeming his instructor "one of the most interesting and suggestive men at the 'Varsity.' "[26] Meanwhile Hall was so struck by the consonance of Wilson's constitutional analysis with his own functionalist, historicist account of human psychology that he twice asked Wilson to assist with his undergraduate courses. Wilson declined, citing ignorance, but grew close enough to Hall to consider (albeit briefly) completing his studies under the philosopher's direction.[27]

Exactly which (if any) of James's works Wilson read for Hall or at his suggestion is unclear.[28] Yet his thinking in the mid- to late 1880s exhibits fascinating congruencies with James's. Along with his organic conception of the state, Wilson intensified two other intellectual commitments reflecting deepening interest in the power and limits of human agency. The expansion of self-government, in both reach and meaning, was one. Although Wilson's fixation on self-government is familiar, his abiding commitment to what is now termed *deliberative discourse* needs emphasizing. Indeed, such discourse became as central to Wilson's ideal of political democracy as to the cultural ideal that James, John Dewey, and other future exponents of philosophical pragmatism were drawing from their insights into the social and provisional character of knowledge. Public deliberation, Wilson wrote in 1885, allows individuals to serve both a higher interest and themselves by freely serving society as "a *thinking member* of the body politic." When functioning properly, this self-coordination of social organs is both autonomous and contingent; securing the "benefits of political cooperation" requires that mechanisms be "found by experiment, as everything else has been found out in politics." States equipped for such democratic experimentation are likeliest to grow in "organic wholeness & all-round adjustment," he wrote in 1888, for "all interests will have representation & a voice." In consequence, the polity need not "depend for its progress upon the eye or upon the limited knowledge of a 'Government'" distant and abstracted from popular experience. Instead it could "itself direct, from many sides . . . its own course of conduct & development."[29] In sum, Wilson concluded that the highest, freest, most constructive form of inquiry was radically empirical and thus *social*. Despite his scare marks in the preceding quotation, his was no dream

of a world without "Government." Like the pragmatist-progressives, he saw
government as a natural product of deliberative discourse, a crucial facilitator
of its expansion and refinement, and an essential guarantor of its necessary
conditions.[30]

Wilson's interest in improving these conditions explains his reputation
as a champion of efficient administration, a second intellectual commitment that deepened in the late 1880s. Some careless phrasing in his seminal
article, "The Study of Administration" (1887), has led some scholars to consider him a naive proponent of apolitical technocracy. Yet Wilson not only
denied that administration *could* be insulated from politics, he insisted it
should not be. Instead it must be guided by science and politics both. The
public's opinion on "constitutional questions" should set goals, which naturally would raise "administrative questions" requiring study and experiment. Given the impracticability of referenda on every government task,
administrators should have broad powers to make specific *policies* for the
state reflecting the general *politics* of the public. Meanwhile, for both policies and politics to serve the common good, scientific administration must
be accountable to a public that is itself scientific in formulating goals. That
criterion depends not upon expert manipulation but upon public institutions that foster a deliberative, experimental culture; institutions, Wilson
wrote, that complement American society's "interdependent" character.[31]
Lecturing on public law, Wilson further emphasized the constructive, even
expressive, functions a people can exercise through efficient administrative
tools. "Government does not stop with the protection of life, liberty, and
property," he insisted, but "goes on to serve every convenience of society."
Its administration should be businesslike, but "it is not business. *It is organic life.*" That statement expressed in a nutshell Wilson's primary theoretical aim in *The State*: to identify and analyze the central "elements of
historical and practical politics," or in other words, the experiential ground
from which to launch a controlled experiment in cooperative existence.[32]

Whether or not he succeeded on that score, Wilson's *Habilitationsschrift*
secured a more immediately precious goal. Within a year of its publication
he was appointed Professor of Jurisprudence and Political Economy at his
alma mater, Princeton. Wilson was elated, but his ambition was hardly sated.
"Evidently I am 'writ down' in the category of 'successful men,'" he wrote
to his father. "I suppose I ought to feel an immense accession of personal
satisfaction,—of pride; but somehow I can't manage it." As he had earlier
written in his confidential journal, Wilson envisioned a career as dynamic as
the institutions he studied, and nearly as significant. "Why may not the present age write, through me, its political *autobiography*?"[33] Why not indeed?

Scholars convinced of the classically liberal, politically conservative, or even reactionary character of Wilson's thought typically mine his Princeton years for evidence. One reason is Wilson's increasing respect for the eighteenth-century Irish politician and political philosopher Edmund Burke, a hero to Anglophone conservatives across eras. Another is Wilson's disapproval of the populist movement and its adherents in the Democratic Party, including (and particularly) the party's perennial leader, William Jennings Bryan. Like many thoughtful Americans, Wilson spent much of the 1890s and early 1900s searching for an adequate intellectual framework in which to place and understand his rapidly changing society. At no point, however, was resistance to the novel, or restoration of the past, among the alternatives he explored.[34]

From 1890 forward Burke was Wilson's favorite example of the statesmanship he thought Americans needed. He knew that Burke praised the slow processes of legal and institutional development as the best responses to social change.[35] But Wilson admired Burke for other reasons. The Burke he applauded was an empiricist, his thought "immersed in matter," his judgment "steadied" by contact with real life. He was "the apostle of the great English gospel of Expediency"—the same "expediency" Wilson endorsed in *The State* (using that very term) to justify the catalog of regulatory responsibilities he thought modern society demanded of government. As a historian, Wilson commended Burke's anti-ideological rejection of "speculative" for "practical politics," his effort to treat affairs not "as they are supposed to be" but "as they are found at the moment of contact." In short, Wilson discovered a Burke that even a pragmatist could love.[36]

Events lent further shine to Burke in Wilson's eyes. In the 1890s, affairs were not as they were "supposed to be." As violent conflicts flared at the Homestead steel plant, the Pullman Palace Car plant, and elsewhere—conflicts frequently exacerbated by forceful state intervention against labor—Wilson found in Burke's "practical politics" the essential elements of leadership for an efficiently administered but popularly accountable government. An essentially artisanal exercise, such leadership was simultaneously conservative and radical. Its task, Wilson explained in a popular public lecture, was to prepare the "major thought of the nation" for whatever changes its growth and health demanded, while respecting the centripetal force of tradition and accounting for practical constraints. That task required insight into what stirred the masses, discrimination between their "firm" and "whimsical" desires, and persuasion to direct their energies constructively—all while recalling that leaders who reach too far ahead of society risk leaving it "deformed" by their amputation. In short, democratic leadership was an exercise in "interpretation," with all of the evaluative, communicative,

subjective, and socially constructive connotations the word can carry. But it
was also an exercise of power, a "sympathy" that both humanized and facilitated "command."[37]

Such leadership needed fostering, and Burke also reinforced Wilson's
conviction that parties, despite their evils, fostered it best. Again, it was
Burke's emphasis on expediency that appealed. Parties, in Burke's opinion,
not only coordinated political action but also often checked corruption, as
Wilson noted in his copy of Burke's collected works:

> Whilst men are linked together, they easily and speedily communicate
> the alarm of any evil design. They are enabled to fathom it with common
> counsel, and to oppose it with united strength. Whereas, when they lie
> dispersed, without concert, order, or discipline, communication is un-
> certain, counsel difficult, and resistance impracticable. Where men are
> not acquainted with each other's principles, nor experienced in each oth-
> er's talents . . . it is evidently impossible that they can act a public part
> with uniformity, perseverance, or efficacy.[38]

Burke's reference to "common counsel" may have inspired Wilson's adoption of the phrase, which to the end of his career expressed his ideal of
party dynamics and politics generally. Not that Wilson or Burke denied the
tendency of parties to adopt a "narrow, bigoted, and proscriptive spirit," as
Burke put it. Still, "party" was the best method yet devised for negotiating political values and achieving political goals. *"Party is a body of men
united for promoting by their joint endeavors the national interest upon
some particular principle in which they are all agreed,"* Wilson underlined
in Burke's *Works*, marking the rest of the paragraph with a line along the
margin. "For my part," Burke continued, "I find it impossible to conceive,
that any one believes in his own politics . . . who refuses to adopt the means
of having them reduced into practice. It is the business of the speculative
philosopher to mark the proper ends of government. It is the business of
the politician, who is the philosopher in action, to find out proper means
towards those ends, and to employ them with effect."[39] This is the message that drew Wilson to the premier Anglophone critic of the French Revolution as his own nation seethed with discontent. Change would happen,
and should be directed as much as possible toward high ideals, but always
with care that the means did not destroy the ends purportedly served. As
such, party government was not a necessary evil but an essential element of
popular government. The collective inquiry, cooperative action, and public

debate facilitated by broad-based, adversarial parties made secret subversion of government harder and thoughtful innovation in government possible.[40]

Clearly, Wilson greatly admired the man he once described as "the Master."[41] But to make too much of this epithet is to misconstrue the character of Wilson's "conservatism," which bears little relation to that of the Burke most historians know. For Wilson, conservatism meant looking to experience for guidance through change. In short, it meant pragmatism, and Wilson chided Burke for his failures to practice it. Burke's mistrust of the masses precluded carrying the requisite support to achieve his "high purposes." He "erred" in supposing "that progress can in all its stages be made without changes which . . . go even to the substance."[42] Briefly, Burke often failed to practice the expediency he preached, and the failures Wilson identified—mistrust of the masses, fear of radical change—would top the sin lists of few conservatives of any era.

Nor was Wilson being hypocritical. It is true that in the 1890s and early 1900s his party's repeated electoral failures led him to censure its "radical theorists" and assail their campaigns for populist utopias. In these years he frequently invoked the "spirit" of Jefferson, venerated by party conservatives as a laissez-faire individualist. Yet he also declared Jefferson's extreme individualism and fear of government outmoded. In an age of industrial organization, the question was how to organize *citizens*. His answer in the early 1900s was to begin locally. But instead of invoking theories of laissez-faire or states' rights, he evoked the writings of the French philosopher Alexis de Tocqueville, which had impressed him in the 1880s. "It is easier to apply morals in limited communities than in vast states," he wrote for a 1906 Jefferson Day address, and long training in this communal moral practice had developed the habits of deliberation, negotiation, and adaptation that were democracy's lifeblood. But still it was *training*, in Wilson's view: the conditioning to sustain a larger, nobler movement toward unified national life among "the general mass of the people."[43]

That movement needed strong leaders and parties to accelerate it. Although society's development depends on its members, crafting policies enhancing its "self-command" requires careful study of past and present—and time that few citizens consistently can spare.[44] It also requires a culture-wide commitment to "the general development," which organized parties can broadly promote. Still, even at the height of his antipopulism, Wilson never questioned the majority's ultimate authority to establish the priorities and shape the policies of government. Rather, he asserted in 1906, he "would *turn again*, and turn with confidence, to the *common people* of the country,"

who "speak in their judgments the true and simple spirit of all just law."
No one person or faction can ensure the health of a free political system, he
reminded a group of conservative Democrats. "I cannot make Democratic
theory out of each of you, but I could make a Democratic theory out of all
of you."[45]

Wilson's legislative records as a governor and president would demonstrate the power of his belief in democratic (small *d*) party government.
Only late in life would he let it submerge his parallel belief in the frequent
necessity of compromise. Unfortunately, it would prove the undoing of a
body devoted to promoting such compromise among the world's nations—a
community without the luxury of elections to fall back on.

Wilson's first opportunity to put his political ideas into practice came not
in public office but as president of a storied private institution, his beloved
Princeton. Assuming office in 1902 with intent to reform the institution,
he consciously approached the job in prime-ministerial fashion. Conceiving
broad and bold programs to be vetted by faculty, he delegated responsibility for particular features to capable lieutenants. He believed deeply in the
importance of universities to the civic life of the nation, whose increasingly "complex" affairs required "efficient and enlightened men" to manage them. His plan to make Princeton a school for such leaders belies, to
an extent, the remark's elitist tone. True, the leaders he envisioned stream-
ing from Princeton's gates were all of one gender and monotonously hued.
Still, each of his reforms—from modernizing the curriculum, to encouraging seminars, to reorganizing the school's institutions and campus—was
designed to make Princeton a more meritocratic, egalitarian, and tight-knit
community of inquiry. If Princeton failed to become such a place, Wilson
warned his comrades in orange, it would fail a nation likely to be called to
lead the world through the dawning century.[46]

Granting this civic vision, Wilson's Princeton leadership is less important for the insights it lends into his political thought than for the role it
played in his political career. Despite a string of successes, Wilson in 1910
met defeat in a divisive and highly publicized contest over the location of
Princeton's new graduate school. The affair culminated a series of bitter controversies, convincing Wilson to resign the role he had come to consider his
calling. His university presidency's demise was due partly to happenstance,
partly to vicious academic politics, and partly to his neglect of the collegial,
deliberative leadership that underwrote his successes. Its memory elicited
painful feelings of betrayal and failure for the rest of his life.[47] Nevertheless, Wilson's rise and fall at Princeton brought him an opportunity he had

dreamed of as a young man but treated as only a dream since: a political career. As if to make up for lost time, that career would begin with the governorship of New Jersey.

The opportunity was presented by two unlikely characters: George Harvey, conservative editor of *Harper's Weekly*; and former US Senator James Smith, boss of the New Jersey Democratic machine. Harvey had long admired Wilson's oratory, and Wilson's disaffection from the populist wing of his party led Harvey and Smith to recruit him as a candidate for senator in 1906, with hopes he might challenge William Jennings Bryan for the 1908 presidential nomination. Wilson, deeming the plan half-baked, declined.[48] His defeats at Princeton, however, made him receptive to outside opportunities. Despite their reputations, his suitors seemed amenable to a high-profile academic reformer exploiting the rising tide of progressivism to win New Jersey back to the Democrats. Strong party men, aware of growing popular interest in reformist candidates nationwide, they perhaps decided it better to have a moderately reformist Democrat in the governor's seat—and if all went well, the White House—than a Republican.[49]

Wilson's initial association and, later, unpleasant falling out with these backers has encouraged the view that he embraced progressivism only belatedly and opportunistically.[50] It is possible that Wilson's antipopulist comments led Harvey and Smith to consider him a conservative of their ilk. More likely, they bet on their ability to manipulate a middle-aged academic with no political experience. For Wilson's writings in the half decade preceding his run display total confidence in the rightness and expediency of strong government measures to restore the voice of a growing, changing people to policymaking—or, as he put it in his 1908 book *Constitutional Government*, to "bring the active and planning will of the government into accord with the prevailing popular thought and need." Since the Spanish-American War, moreover, the rapid expansion of presidential power accompanying the growing world role of the United States had created new "opportunities for constructive statesmanship" open to a bold but reflective executive—a change Wilson thought could put *Congressional Government* "hopelessly out of date." Whatever Harvey and Smith thought of him, Wilson had decided that American politics needed the leadership of one who squared his "thinking" with "facts" and dispensed with "antiquated" theories—the leadership, as he put it, of "a modern radical."[51]

An array of evidence indicates that this intensifying commitment to a strong, experimental state was encouraged by Wilson's continuing exposure to William James's ideas. The two men often moved in the same circles and impressed the same people. Both, for instance, had long-standing intellectual and personal relationships with Felix Adler, leader of the "Ethical Culture" movement and organizer of a series of summer institutes James and Wilson attended in the early 1890s.[52] Meanwhile, the man who hired Wilson and preceded him as president at Princeton, Francis L. Patton, was well aware of James's psychological work, commenting in the faculty-edited *Princeton College Bulletin* on the "brilliant" exposition and analysis of interior life found in *The Principles of Psychology*.[53]

More significantly, Wilson worked with, befriended, and hired several Princeton faculty who knew James's work and considered him a friend. They ran the gamut from outright critics to open partisans of James's ideas. But all engaged James frequently in their scholarship and teaching.

Take John Grier Hibben, professor of logic and Wilson's closest friend until they fell out during the graduate school affair. Prior to that, the Wilsons and Hibbens dined together several nights a week.[54] Hibben refused to accept James's notion that *no* truths can be assumed as universal.[55] But this fact did not preclude Hibben's deep respect for James, consistent interest in his work, and the occasional endorsement of some of his major doctrines. In 1896 Hibben sent James his newly published *Inductive Logic*, which despite asserting the existence of universal principles drew on James to illustrate how the power of inference exceeds mere association of experiences.[56] In the *North American Review* of January 1898 Hibben went so far as to insist, à la James, "that there is a will to believe that is not solely the result of reasoned analysis, that there are intimations of truth which are not demonstrative," and "that the heart has its reasons which the heart alone can understand."[57] Hibben continued to engage James's work as the latter developed his pragmatism, acknowledging the importance of James's contribution to philosophy even as he found it increasingly unacceptable personally. In 1904 he lobbied James (unsuccessfully) to contribute a book to his series on "epochs in philosophy," and in 1910 he gave a course of twenty public lectures at Princeton on "Trends of Philosophical and Scientific Thought" that culminated with "The Doctrine of Pragmatism."[58] Even in warning students against fully embracing the pragmatist "creed of change," Hibben endorsed its primary epistemological tenet, admitting with James that "we must be prepared to find false to-morrow what is true to-day."[59]

Closer to James personally and intellectually was James Mark Baldwin, appointed professor of experimental psychology at Princeton in 1893. Baldwin referred to James's *Principles of Psychology* as "a *vade mecum* to psychological inquirers" and in his first major work endorsed James's "stream-of-consciousness" argument that "our minds never have just the same contents twice over."[60] In his most important work, *Social and Ethi-*

cal Interpretations in Mental Development (1897), Baldwin argued along Jamesian lines that social and physiological spurs to human action are constantly interacting, so that while individual "genius" is due to "variations in intellectual endowment," its "limitations" reflect "the reciprocal character of social relationships." The individual's "estimate of things and thoughts," Baldwin continued, gets applied "to himself and to his own creations," so that despite "particular" exceptions, the "essential thing comes to be the reflection of the social standard in the thinker's own judgment." In other words, "the individual's private 'selective thinking' proceeds under the social tests involved in his personal growth," to the benefit of individual and society both. The echoes of James's arguments for the empirical and normative ethical republic are less startling, but no less clear, for the fact that Baldwin was paraphrasing James's own analysis of individual and social development in "Great Men and Their Environment" (1880).[61]

Baldwin had his disagreements with James, particularly over the "throwing-of-dice" attitude he associated with James's will-to-believe doctrine.[62] Baldwin's main complaint, however, was that James exaggerated the differences between his purported "discoveries"—the stream of thought; a distinct, continuous, yet social and relational self; the selective function of attention; the spontaneity of will—and the views of others like himself. Still, Baldwin considered the metaphysical implications of James's work nothing short of epochal: a defense of the free, spontaneous, creative, efficacious character of consciousness that heralded the ultimate demise of psychological associationism and metaphysical determinism.[63] This enthusiasm spilled from Baldwin's scholarship into Princeton's classrooms and lecture halls. Baldwin was hired to establish a much-anticipated program in experimental psychology, and, as the *Daily Princetonian*'s front page reported, he adopted James's works among the major texts for his courses. From that moment through the end of Wilson's university presidency, James's writings remained central to the Princeton psychology curriculum, as Wilson's own reporting to the Board of Trustees makes clear.[64] Meanwhile, Baldwin's were among several lectures on James's thought, many public, advertised in the *Daily Princetonian* during Wilson's tenure. In a 1902 address on "Faith" before Princeton's Philadelphian Society, Baldwin even set aside his dice-throwing qualms and endorsed James's "will to believe" as "one of the most important principles of ethical life."[65]

Indeed, at times there seemed as much interest in James around Wilson's Princeton as at James's own Harvard. Taking just the years of his Princeton presidency, Wilson might have heard Baldwin speak on "Pragmatism" to the Philosophical Seminary, or dropped in on William Brenton Greene's course on "Pragmatism" at next-door Princeton Theological Seminary.[66] He might have started upon hearing the Reverend Dr. William H. Oxtoby of Philadelphia's Tabernacle Presbyterian Church invoke James as authority "that prayer is one of the divine facts of life," or Hibben praise Augustine for discerning that "the will to believe" was "the root of religion."[67] During the same years Wilson certainly would have known that "The Method of Pragmatism" was the topic of the annual Princeton-wide Dickinson essay prize in 1909–10, and that "Pragmatism" was the topic of the philosophy department's McCosh essay prize in 1908–9, 1909–10, and 1910–11. These and other notices were published in the *Princetonian*, which Wilson, a proud former editor, read almost daily.[68] Wilson may even have fostered this campus interest in James. In 1903 he appointed Horace Kallen instructor in English, and in 1904, after long consultation with Hibben and a two-day interview, he hired Frank Thilly to replace Baldwin (who had gone to Toronto).[69] Kallen, James's student, was a self-identified pragmatist. Thilly had liberally cited James and endorsed his notion of an active yet practically bounded intellect in two major works, and he later drew on James's account of the mind's synthetic as well as selective functions in his effort to bridge the free will–versus–determinism divide.[70]

Finally, Wilson directly encountered James, in print and in person, multiple times during his Princeton tenure. James was on campus for the 1894 meeting of the American Psychological Association, where he was elected president for the fourth straight year and gave a public address emphasizing the practical import of concepts and concatenated character of experience. Perhaps Wilson missed James at the meeting, as well as at President Patton's reception for the guests.[71] But he could not have avoided him two years later at the Princeton sesquicentennial celebration in October 1896, where James received an honorary degree for his contributions to morals and letters. Not only did Wilson deliver the sesquicentennial oration, "Princeton in the Nation's Service"; he also served on the subcommittee that selected James as an honoree, processed with James during the ceremony, and sat at James's table during dinner.[72] And Wilson doubtless knew that James—with G. Stanley Hall—was elected that week to Princeton's American Whig Society, the debating club that Wilson himself had joined as an undergraduate and officially represented in his role as sesquicentennial orator.[73]

Physical proximity does not prove intellectual affinity. But Wilson also owned numerous volumes reprinting James's work or referring to his ideas. These include Wilson's two favorite periodicals, the *Atlantic Monthly* and the *Century*, entire runs of which he collected from the early 1890s through his Princeton presidency. In volumes inventoried with Wilson's papers at the Library of Congress, *Century* writers quoted at length the passage in James's Shaw Oration explaining the character and necessity of "civic courage" (August 1897); praised his defense of indeterminism and vindication of faith (June 1899); quoted his essay "Is Life Worth Living?" to the effect that beliefs must align with needs (July 1902); and invoked his work in arguing that religious experience can make new truths accessible (July 1903).[74] Meanwhile, the *Atlantic* published glowing reviews of James's *Principles of Psychology* and *Varieties of Religious Experience* in 1891 and 1902, respectively—the former noting the originality of James's argument for the stream-like character and selective function of consciousness, the latter referencing "The Will to Believe" and doctrine of "pragmatism" in emphasizing the practical functions and fruits of religion as James conceived it.[75]

The *Atlantic* did not just peddle James secondhand. From February through May 1899, it serialized ten of the first fifteen chapters of James's *Talks to Teachers*. Wilson saved all four issues.[76] The selections offer perhaps the most succinct and accessible overview of James's psychological doctrines and their epistemological and moral implications that he ever published. The first selection introduced both the stream of consciousness and the basic pragmatist principle that thoughts are consequential for conduct, and conduct alone.[77] Subsequent selections argued that humans are instinctually social, experimental, and practical in their thinking; that thinking involves attentive effort, directed largely by subjective interests; that objects of thought draw meaning and interest from the relations among them rather than inherent qualities; that we are attracted to novelty yet seek in the new its most useful relations to previous experience; and that empathy and co-recognition impel the enlargement and refinement of the human race's intellectual and moral life. Indeed, the final selection alone contains nearly all the elements of James's pragmatist epistemology and ethics. Thinking, James explained, is a moral act, for our attention to certain experiences over others yields consequences. To the extent such attention is voluntary, the nature of its consequences depends on free will. The ultimate goal of intentional learning, therefore, should be to tame this experimental will through reflection and exercise it "as if our free action in this regard were a genuine critical point in nature, a point on which our destiny and that of others might hinge."[78]

Did Wilson actually *read* James in these years, and did it make any impression? Almost certainly. Between 1890 and 1910, Wilson not only subscribed to periodicals that published or discussed James's work but also wrote for them, including five articles for the *Atlantic* in the twenty-four months preceding its serialization of *Talks to Teachers*.[79] The two men, moreover, were more than once featured in the same magazine, and in ways likely to catch Wilson's eye. In one, a profile touting soon-to-be Governor Wilson as "One of the Men Needed by the People" was followed twelve pages later by an article on "The Common Sense of William James: Why His Thought Has Become the Thought of the People." In another, a story on the "New Democratic Governors," headed by a three-quarter-page portrait of Wilson, was followed by an article on "Great American Universities" in which Princeton was treated, and which was followed in turn by a piece on "The American Academy" discussing both men—and opening with a portrait of James.[80] Whatever the channels, James indisputably impressed himself on Wilson's consciousness at some point: Wilson purchased the full version of *Talks to Teachers* sometime after 1910, and a small volume reprinting "On a Certain Blindness" and "What Makes a Life Significant" sometime after 1913.[81]

The primary evidence of James's influence on Wilson in the 1890s and early 1900s, however, is in the latter's writing and speaking. Nine months after the sesquicentennial and six months after James's *Will to Believe* brought his work to a popular audience, Wilson composed an essay, "On Being Human" (1897), echoing James's exhortations to think and act with a sense of personal power, social responsibility, and empathic curiosity. The "truly human man," wrote Wilson, exhibits a "balance of faculties, a catholic sympathy,—no brawler, no fanatic, no Pharisee," yet "ardent and full of definite power." If truly human we "will study the world . . . to school our hearts and tastes, broaden our natures, and know our fellow men as comrades rather than as phenomena." Not "bodies of critical doctrine," but "experiencing natures" distinguish human freedom from bestial instinct. Amid "innumerable" standards of thought and action we must make choices, and we are wisest and freest when choosing from "a comparative point of view." Our privilege and duty is to seek a society in which all have leisure and capacity for such choice; for "the gain of being human accrues in the choice of change and variety of experience far and wide, with all the world for stage,—a stage set and appointed by this very art of choice,—all future generations for witnesses and audience."[82]

Other post-sesquicentennial writings also find Wilson echoing James. Despite defending his nation's tutelary role in the Philippines, Wilson's widely read essay "The Ideals of America" (1902) frequently evokes James's Shaw Oration, extolling a civil religion of deliberation, experimentation, and civic courage. "Not battles," wrote Wilson, "but the slow processes by which we grew and made our thought and formed our purpose in quiet days of peace" best embody the "spirit and mission" of the republic's founders. The object of their faith was "no abstract point of governmental theory" but "the plain right of self-government, which any man could understand": the right of all people "to live their own lives according to their own genius."[83] The task of combining "liberty" with "government," Wilson continued, is both empirical and normative, demanding "clear experimental knowledge" of individual and social needs along with "sufficient equality of social and economic conditions" to foster "community of feelings" across differences.[84] The nation's "greater statesmen" have recognized "that the best polity is that which most certainly produces the habit and spirit of civic duty," a polity "which shall make men seek honor by seeking service. These are the ideals which have formed our institutions, and which shall mend them when they need reform."[85]

Other hints of James's influence emerge when comparing versions of addresses Wilson delivered more than once and revised over time. His Princeton inaugural address, for instance, reprised his triumphant sesquicentennial effort, but with significant changes. The original, "Princeton in the Nation's Service," articulated a critique of science far exceeding James's in "The Will to Believe," warning, "Science has bred in us a spirit of experiment and a contempt for the past," including the humanistic values and Christian morals that built and defined Western civilization.[86] Six years later, in "Princeton for the Nation's Service," Wilson again defended a liberal, Christian education, but now as an aid in harnessing science to the cause of social improvement—to imbue "efficiency" with "the energy of a positive faith." "We are not put in this world to sit still and know," he concluded in a Jamesian register; "we are put into it to act."[87] Wilson's 1905 revisions of a lay homily first delivered in 1895 yield further evidence of James's influence in the years following the sesquicentennial, while clarifying at least one textual source. Unlike Wilson's original, his revised version addressed the same cultural tensions between religion and science examined in "The Will to Believe," and mounted a defense of religious faith that echoed James's. In fact, Wilson titled the later version "The Profit of Belief," and in explaining humans' power to shape their personal and social realities, even used the phrase "wills to believe."[88]

In sum, although Wilson might not have labeled himself a "pragmatist" when recruited to run for governor, he had much more in common with James than with suitors Harvey and Smith. Whatever the exact lines and force of James's influence, it showed—including in his most considered thinking on politics. Written three years before Wilson became governor,

Constitutional Government—his last major academic work—exhibited a striking affinity with the pragmatist progressivism of John Dewey, Jane Addams, and other Jamesian advocates for more participatory, plastic, and powerful government. Writing in late 1907, Wilson argued that individual liberty was both supreme and dependent on "common counsel" to socialize it, a paradox he resolved by affirming the basic premise of pragmatist ethics: the contingency of values. "The ideals of liberty cannot be fixed from generation to generation," he wrote; "fixed" liberty was "no liberty at all." Like the pragmatists, Wilson invoked Darwinian science to explain the evolution of values and the policies embodying them. Again like the pragmatists, his political Darwinism was prescriptive as well as descriptive. "Living Constitutions," Wilson asserted, "must be Darwinian in structure *and* in practice." This conviction obliged experimentation in government, on grounds that human actions shape human constructs, and deliberate action might shape them to our liking.[89]

The latent radicalism of this updated organicism justified what became the major themes of Wilson's political career: the legitimacy of interventionist government and the necessity of an activist yet popularly accountable executive to direct it. *Constitutional Government* simultaneously revealed the pragmatist habit of mind that led Wilson, in light of changes witnessed since graduate school, to see new promise in an American system he once dismissed as impotent and aimless. Certainly the federal government must avoid any "mere act of will," usurping powers not implied by the Constitution. But Wilson saw nothing wrong with the states granting new powers to Washington if circumstances required. Categorically prohibiting such grants while ignoring the practical alignment of ends and means was to hew to an "old theory of sovereignty" that had "lost its vitality."[90] The nation was a complex organism, and to focus its diffuse interests into political will and action required a center of power responsible to and for the mass.

In the years since *Congressional Government* was published, "evolution" had selected an unlikely coordinating organ: the president. Mass communications and the increasing importance of foreign affairs had created an office almost entirely distinct from the one Wilson dismissed as a young dissertator. "His is the only national voice in affairs," Wilson now wrote of the president. "If he rightly interpret the national thought and boldly insist upon it, he is irresistible." By performing an epistemological function like that which James ascribed to human minds, the president could truly be the head of government: registering, interpreting, and acting upon the stimulus of public opinion to facilitate informed and efficient collective action. Like a central nervous system, simultaneously directing and responding to the body's activities, constitutional government under strong executive leadership could and should be a faculty of "synthesis, not antagonism"—and as persistent labor unrest, economic inequality, and political corruption revealed, the nation needed it.[91]

If oversimplified, of course, this view of the president's connection to the people can distract from the mundane politicking that clears paths for big ideas. Such oversimplification and distraction marked the last years of Wilson's presidency. Still, it is appropriate that in his last major work before assuming public office, this professor of politics once again argued that a hale body politic needs brains at the top.

From 1908 to 1910, Wilson consistently affirmed government's duty to devise better ways to effect the people's will. Now standing as candidate for governor, he determined to run on a platform embodying his view of power as "a thing not negative, but positive."[92] First, however, he needed his party's nomination.

The nomination was hard-won. In previous years Wilson had publicly scolded labor leaders for tolerating production limits, which he thought could only drag good workers down. Recalling these statements, the state's progressive newspapers portrayed him as the pawn of bosses and businessmen. Having renounced campaigning as a token of his disinterestedness, Wilson abandoned silence only once, in August 1910, when the American Federation of Labor officially denounced him as antagonistic to their cause. Asked by the editor of the *Labor Standard* to respond, he replied that it was not just "legitimate, but absolutely necessary that Labor should organize if it is to secure justice from organized Capital." His profession of "hearty support" for accident insurance, just wages, and reasonable hours, however, won few converts among workers. Furthermore, though he and Harvey had devised a platform tailor-made for his party's progressives, he could not reveal it until nominated lest he break his pledge of silence. The task of securing the nomination fell to Boss Smith, who would not rest—and on the eve of the convention did not sleep—until he had convinced the major cogs in his sprawling machine to deliver their delegates' votes, and the nomination, to Wilson on September 15, 1910.[93]

Wilson promptly declared independence from his sponsor. "I shall enter upon the duties of the office of Governor, if elected, with absolutely no pledge of any kind to prevent me from serving the people of the State," he told a roomful of doubtful delegates. "Government is a matter of common counsel, and everyone must come into the consultation with the purpose to yield to the general view." Good government, while averting all-out "warfare of interests," nevertheless entailed the sacrifice of some interests to others more pressing. Just as James had argued that "there is always a *pinch* between the ideal and the actual" requiring that "some part of the ideal must be butchered," Wilson asserted that "strong purpose, which does not flinch because some must suffer, is perfectly compatible with fairness and justice and a clear view of the actual facts." He then explicitly and forcefully endorsed a Democratic platform incorporating almost every plank in the progressive shed. It demanded stricter corporate regulation, a public utilities commission, broader employer liability, an eight-hour workday for government employees, a corrupt-practices act, an expanded civil service, and electoral reforms. The goal was nothing less than to reconstruct both "economic society" and "political organization" for New Jersey and, through force of example, the nation. "This reconstruction," he predicted, "will be bigger than anything in American history."[94]

The subsequent campaign revealed the sharpening of Wilson's progressive vision and, in hindsight, its continued convergence with pragmatist ethics. In a late October exchange with the editor of the *Trenton True American*, Wilson reiterated his commitment to the Democrats' sweeping proposals. Then, pledging to abolish bossism through "pitiless publicity," he began the process immediately, "denouncing" efforts by his patron Smith and others to maintain machine control. On the stump, meanwhile, Wilson admitted that healthy polities required "poise, patience, and the ability to make progress by these virtues." But "progress" was his emphasis: "If any part of the body politic were to lose its impulse for progress," he insisted, "it would die." Progress depended on "respect for the law," but only such law as preserved the people's "free determination to change it." Though Republican candidate Vivian Lewis pledged to be "a constitutional Governor" who would never "coerce the Legislature into doing anything simply because it was in the interests of the people," Wilson promised to be "an unconstitutional Governor" who would do just that. Such, after all, was the true purpose of politics: to maintain order *through* rather than *against* the changes endured and demanded by citizens, through public discussion of needs, open efforts to meet them, and frank assessment of consequences. In touting such general "methods of right" as heavily as his specific policies, Wilson echoed James's ethical writings throughout his campaign. He also demonstrated to great effect the interpretive and persuasive methods he ascribed to "leaders of men": on November 8, 1910, he won a plurality of almost fifty thousand votes and carried fifteen of twenty-one counties, many going Democratic for the first time.[95]

In office, Wilson gave substance to the image in which he had cast himself during the campaign. He first pushed an electoral reform bill through the legislature that threatened boss control of the nominating process at every level. Bills on corrupt practices, utility regulation, workers' compensation, municipal reform, and public-education standards followed, all becoming law within two months of Wilson's inauguration. Observers in New Jersey and nationwide were simply astonished at the scope, scale, and speed of his legislative accomplishments. Remarkable, too, were the means of their achievement, though perhaps not so remarkable to Wilson. He simply practiced the disciplined yet deliberative brand of party government he had long deemed essential to bold but wise policymaking. He set the tone with the electoral reform bill, ignoring all precedent by personally visiting the Democratic legislative caucus and urging the shocked assemblymen to support the bill as a party measure. Wilson convinced them that their political future depended on his ability to deliver on the promises he had made in their party's name, which in turn depended on their united action. His party in line, Wilson took his measures to the public to explain their significance, describe their place in his larger program, and encourage debate of their merits. He also built bridges with Republicans, especially in the less machine-dependent Senate—a body that passed Wilson's bills on electoral reform, corrupt practices, public utilities, and worker compensation unanimously. When the legislature adjourned on April 22, Wilson could review a ninety-day period in which he had personally propelled the type of coordinated, deliberative policymaking he first theorized a quarter century earlier. As biographer Arthur Link wrote, the governor "was truly a prime minister in the state."[96]

In the eyes of many observers, however, Wilson was looking more like a president. His impressive electoral victory generated presidential murmurs even before he took office in Trenton. His legislative victories in the session of 1911 made him a top contender for the Democratic nomination. Although further reform in the following session was stymied by a cross-party alliance of bosses, Wilson had caught the imagination of a public increasingly placing its hopes for change in the presidency. The spectacle of a governor spearheading the formulation and passage of an entire legislative program was not only novel but revolutionary in the eyes of a nation taught to view his office as executive in its strictest sense. And Wilson, it seemed, was just warming up. Compared with other presidential prospects, opined the *Nation*, Wilson was "much the more radical" when it came to the "social program" he articulated. "If we interpret Gov. Wilson's attitude correctly," the editor continued, cleaning up government was "only a first step. He is deeply aroused by the failure of representative institutions to represent, and he is prepared to go far, it may seem to many too far, in his desire to make these institutions over."[97]

Wilson was hardly a shoo-in for the Democratic presidential nomination in 1912. Progressives saw Harvey as an incubus, the machines backed House Speaker Champ Clark of Missouri, and the nomination came only after Ellen Wilson shrewdly facilitated a personal rapprochement between her husband and Bryan, who one last time was the dominant figure at the national convention. Ultimately Wilson's progressive credentials convinced the party factions that he could attract reform-minded independents, and their faith was rewarded—despite Theodore Roosevelt's defection from the Republicans to head the new Progressive Party's ticket and the additional challenge of charismatic Socialist candidate Eugene Debs. Indeed, once the election became a four-way race, in which he alone had a major party's full support, 1912 was Wilson's year.[98]

All four candidates paid homage to change. Rhetorically, at least, they were also in surprising agreement over the ends toward which to direct it. Even incumbent William Howard Taft, the candidate of the Republican "stand patters," proclaimed that "the best government, the government most certain to provide for and protect the rights and governmental needs of every class, is that one in which every class has a voice." Theodore Roosevelt could have spoken these words to the Progressives at "Armageddon," as he dubbed the electoral battle of 1912, and even "Red" Eugene Debs could not have painted a rosier political picture. The question was not whether or whither to change, but how—a question of method. "We need no revolution," Wilson declared in accepting the Democratic presidential nomination. "We need only a new point of view and a new method and spirit of counsel." What that method should *be*, however, was a question both for voters and for Wilson. How could New Jersey's democratic restoration be replicated nationally? How could Wilson articulate his answer so that voters found it a proposition worth testing?[99]

Wilson consciously asked himself these questions, but it was only after meeting Louis Brandeis that he realized how central the question of method would be to his message. This meeting occurred relatively late in the game. It was not until August 28, 1912—two months before the election—that Wilson called Brandeis to Sea Girt, New Jersey, in hopes that the "people's attorney" could help him reach the people. Wilson was lucky; unbeknownst to the candidate, Brandeis had been preparing to help him for weeks and developing means to do so for years—means distinctly pragmatist. By 1912 Brandeis was both mentoring and frequently consulting the young pragmatist Felix Frankfurter and was soon to develop similar relationships with Walter Weyl and Walter Lippmann. Like Wilson, Brandeis had for years theorized a more empirical approach to organizing American society, but as a lawyer and activist, he had gained vast experience devising detailed solutions to concrete problems. In the process Brandeis learned to identify not only the facts most pertinent to his own analytical tasks and ethical goals but also those most convincing to whoever was positioned to endorse or reject his ideas. After examining the facts in 1912, Brandeis, hero to reformist Republicans and Democrats alike, announced that "progressives, irrespective of party affiliations, should in my opinion support Woodrow Wilson for the Presidency. He is thoroughly democratic in spirit."[100]

Brandeis ranked Wilson's nomination as "among the most encouraging events in American history." Although Wilson's dry acceptance speech was not the triumph its gubernatorial counterpart had been, it did somewhat clarify his conception of the next president's political tasks. While endorsing his party's platform generally, he outlined no specific economic policies, asserting instead that each party's platform was but a stab at answering "great questions of right and of justice" pertaining not just to the role of business in society, but to "the development of character and of standards of action" in many spheres of associated life. The salient question was, "*How* do we expect to handle the great matters that must be taken up by the next Congress and the next administration?" It was a question of means more than ends; or rather, one of means *as* ends. For years, "great matters" had been "handled in private conference" by "men who undertook to speak for the whole nation." Some had done so "very honestly it may be, but very ignorantly sometimes, and very shortsightedly, too." The point was that no matter how honest the men or noble their objects, government by the few would always be "a poor substitute for genuine common counsel."[101]

Thus it was an *idea*, the idea that "common counsel" was the best method of government, that—if Wilson had anything to do with it—would be voted on in November; an idea, he hoped, that would distinguish his Democrats from the rivals they so resembled: the Progressive Party and their candidate Roosevelt. "No group of directors, economic or political, can speak for a people," Wilson declared, alluding to the "paternalistic" methods he attributed to the Progressives. "They have neither the point of view nor the knowledge." Wilson proposed, in effect, to make politics more pragmatist by stimulating broader deliberation over public affairs. But declaiming "common counsel" as "the meaning of representative government" was a far cry from describing how it worked. Wilson needed a policy hook, an example of how common counsel might look in action, to catch the public's attention; but tariff reform, the oldest weapon in the Democratic armory, turned to rust in his hands. For the first three weeks of the campaign, there was no blade in Wilson's rhetorical scabbard—a mortal disadvantage against the oratorical onslaughts of a Roosevelt.[102]

Brandeis armed Wilson with "principles" to parry "personalities." Theirs was a meeting of like minds. "I am for Wilson because I found him in complete sympathy with my fundamental convictions," Brandeis told reporters. Wilson, meanwhile, found his hook: "Both of us," he told the press with newfound clarity, "have as an object the prevention of monopoly." Brandeis briefly outlined that object. "We must undertake to regulate competition instead of monopoly," he said, alluding to Roosevelt's proposal to place trusts under government control, "for our industrial freedom and our civic freedom go hand in hand and there is no such thing as civic freedom in a state of industrial absolutism."[103]

Along with a motto—"To Regulate Competition Instead of Monopoly"—both men found renewed purpose at Sea Girt. Brandeis left determined to garner Wilson the vote of every reform-minded journalist, editor, social worker, businessman, and politician he knew—a considerable number. Wilson immediately hurled the fruits of his encounter with Brandeis at Roosevelt, lauding his rival's social goals but dissenting from his "central method"—the paternal. The Progressives, he alleged, had determined on "acting as a Providence" for the people, as if understanding their needs implicitly. "I have never known any body of men, any small body of men, that understood the United States," Wilson countered. "And the only way the United States is ever going to be taken care of is by having the voices of all the men in it constantly clamorous for recognition of what is justice as they see the light."[104]

Wilson's biggest breakthrough came in a letter from Brandeis dated September 30, 1912, indicating both the specific antitrust measures the Democrats should promote and the principles of social analysis and political experimentation inspiring them. Essentially Brandeis's advice was that the Democrats propose to learn from experience—including failure—promising both to use it constructively in the near term and keep the learning process going in future. The social harm resulting from the Sherman Antitrust Act's failure, for instance, although revealing that statute's "defects," also "established the soundness" of the policy it was meant to embody. Effectively implementing that policy required examining the economic experience of the whole nation, legislating accordingly, and institutionalizing the process, making future legislation an empirical exercise. "Experience," Brandeis wrote, had revealed many forms of economic combination that suppressed competition unreasonably, and it was time "to utilize that experience and to embody its dictates in rules of positive law." Yet experience also showed that *any* method of dominating markets, barring pure "efficiency," was unreasonable, necessitating protections against methods yet unknown. Thus "an administrative Board" was needed, with "broad powers" of investigation and legislative initiative that could evolve "as we learn from experience."[105]

Wilson initially intended to publish the letter under his own name, and both his stylistic emendations and his subsequent policies suggest significant internalization of Brandeis's arguments. Yet the emendations also reveal important differences. Where Brandeis wrote of measures "by which existing trusts might be effectively disintegrated," Wilson crossed out the last word and substituted the phrase "deprived of their domination and illicit power." He also deleted a paragraph proposing retroactive punishment of combinations that, though declared illegal by the courts, had not had to pay reparations. Clearly, Wilson never believed as deeply in the intrinsic superiority of a small-producer economy as did Brandeis, or in the need to wreak vengeance upon the trusts. Nevertheless, he was sufficiently convinced of the dangers of concentrated economic power to fear both trust- and government-dominated industry as graveyards of material and social growth. Wilson's dog-eared and underscored copy of Brandeis's *Scientific Management and Railroads* (1911), which he read around this time, evinces the degree to which he embraced Brandeis's basic logic: Competition bred experimentation; experimentation, efficiency; efficiency, prosperity; and prosperity, the opportunities for personal development that self-governing citizens required. If competition flagged, government must restore it, find a substitute, or risk its own stagnation.[106]

Brandeis did more for Wilson than point his lance at the soft underbelly of Progressive Party trust policy. Brandeis articulated a pragmatist method for preserving self-government in perpetuity, not merely restoring it in 1912. The fact that Wilson came during his presidency to find Brandeis's proscriptions of bigness increasingly simplistic shows how thoroughly he appropriated Brandeis's method, and perhaps hints at the wider range of facts to which he applied it. Meanwhile, anchoring the issues in Brandeis's social and economic empiricism gave Wilson's campaign messages the intellectual coherence and political substance they had lacked. "We talk, and we talk in very plausible phrases, indeed, about returning the government of this country to the people of this country," he told an Indianapolis audience three days after reading Brandeis's letter. But *how?* Not simply by voting for a "Progressive." As president, Roosevelt had tolerated "the very conditions we are trying to alter," and now sought to "assuage" rather than change them by placing monopolies under government stewardship. Roosevelt and Taft both, claimed Wilson, sought simultaneously to preserve monopoly power and restore lost freedoms, an impossible denial of "what the whole country knows to be true": economic freedom and monopoly power were incompatible, and to restore lost freedoms required a "new freedom"—a freedom from the *power* of the trusts, no matter where it resided.[107]

More than just the New Freedom's central policy promise, breaking the power of the trusts was a critical symbolic step toward reconstituting government on Wilson's long-imagined model: responsive to the people's will and efficient in carrying it out. Restoring government to the people meant restoring prosperity to the mass of them, giving them time and energy to participate in public life. And restoring prosperity meant opening the economic laboratory to as many enterprising souls as possible.[108]

Herein lay the difference between Wilson's and Roosevelt's progressivism. As Wilson realized, their immediate objects, similar or dissimilar, were less important than the "engineering principles of liberty" each applied to politics. Whereas Roosevelt's emphasis on national unity as the repository of national strength led him to define citizenship as self-sacrifice and leadership as the ability to elicit it, Wilson defined citizenship as self-government, in which obligations and interests played complementary roles. The task of a leader was to encourage the search for compatible interests, facilitate the mooting of the sacrifices entailed, and suggest public policies embodying the conclusions—to promote, in short, "a common understanding and a free action all together." Ultimately Wilson's was a vision of democracy a plurality of Americans shared on Election Day.[109]

Wilson is recalled as one of the most partisan US presidents, and rightly so. To lead a unified party pursuing coordinated measures was his aim from the beginning. For twenty-five years he had thought such leadership the only means of consolidating power, and thus locating responsibility, in government. "He must be prime minister," Wilson wrote of the president in February 1913, "as much concerned with the guidance of legislation as with the just and orderly execution of law." A month after he wrote those words, his premiership began.[110]

Wilson's first act was a reprise of his performance in the New Jersey legislative caucus. "With a sweep of decision that shattered precedent," Wilson appeared personally before both houses on April 8—the first such appearance since Jefferson abandoned the practice in 1801—to introduce the first item on his legislative agenda, tariff reduction. Wilson informed his new associates that he was "not a mere department of the Government hailing Congress from some isolated island of jealous power," but "a human being, trying to cooperate with other human beings, in a common service."[111] His legislative program, in turn, was an attempt to institutionalize government by common counsel as he defined it: responsive to the broadest possible array of interests, coordinated and efficient in accommodating those it could, and open to future challenge by the partisans of those it could not—so long as such challenges respected the limits, and were not obviously destructive of, the democratic process that permitted them.

Tariff revision was a logical start. It was a venerable Democratic priority, and progressives considered the existing rate schedule a prop of monopoly power. Wilson advised chair Oscar W. Underwood of the House Ways and Means Committee as the latter drafted a rate-slashing bill. Wilson also initiated a public investigation into lobbying that led a chastened Senate to cut rates even further than Underwood proposed. Meanwhile, Wilson's solution to recouping the lost tariff revenue—a graduated income tax—demonstrated a key feature of his pragmatist progressivism: its mix of radicalism and restraint. The original Underwood bill incorporated a slightly graduated tax for revenue purposes, but a bipartisan band of Senate radicals led by Robert La Follette demanded a drastically increased surtax, endangering the bill's passage. Wilson intervened, supporting compromise rates that were eventually approved with the rest of the bill in October. The result was successful passage of a milestone piece of legislation: for while choosing to "begin upon somewhat moderate lines," Wilson had nonetheless facilitated the first national legislation for redistributing wealth in American history.[112]

Wilson's handling of Congress during the tariff bill debates firmly established his leadership of the party, paving the way for the rest of his New Freedom program. The development of the Federal Reserve, which rationalized the nation's chaotic banking and credit system, exhibits Wilson at the height of his leadership—moderating, compromising, seeking a middle road, and boldly taking it despite attempts to block his path. Faced with demands ranging from a centralized, privately controlled reserve system and currency to a loose confederation of treasury note warehouses—demands pressed with a vehemence that portended a party split—Wilson had to lay his political middle road on sound economic bedrock, with little or no personal knowledge of finance.[113]

On June 11, 1913, Wilson called Brandeis to the White House for the answers he needed. Brandeis solved Wilson's problem by collapsing the economic and the political: "The beneficent effect of the best conceivable currency bill will be relatively slight," he wrote in a memorandum for Wilson, unless it "curb the money trust" and "remove the uneasiness among businessmen due to its power." Within three days, Wilson met with the main Democratic antagonists to lay out a compromise embodying Brandeis's advice. The government would exercise sole control over the Federal Reserve Board (a nod to demands that government ensure access to credit), but not branch banks (a nod to creditors seeking to retain some control over inflation), and would be exclusively liable for Federal Reserve notes (giving it primary control over the money supply but also primary exposure to the risks of expansion). This met both sides' minimum demands—if only barely. After placating the party's farming interests with an agricultural-credits amendment, Wilson signed the Federal Reserve bill on December 23—establishing a system that has done as much to transform the political economy of the United States as any legislative innovation in the century since.[114]

Wilson's antitrust program, the central plank of the New Freedom campaign, took longest to pry from the platform and nail down into law. Throughout the process Wilson combined adherence to broad principles with a willingness to compromise, assimilate new ideas, and adapt to changes in the political environment. Wilson first took a vigorous statutory approach to regulation, modeled on New Jersey's so-called Seven Sisters legislation (passed toward the end of Wilson's governorship) and embodied in a bill drafted by Congressman Henry Clayton of Alabama. Many of Brandeis's policy suggestions were incorporated into the Seven Sisters and the Clayton bill. In the latter case they included a provision declaring decisions in government-initiated suits applicable to private suits (so that plaintiffs had merely to prove damages rather than retry massive antitrust cases), as well as a list of antitrust practices specifically prohibited by law and thus precluded from defense under the Supreme Court's "rule of reason" doctrine—a doctrine that, in Brandeis's opinion, eviscerated the Sherman Antitrust Act that was then the foundation of federal antitrust law.[115]

The Clayton bill provoked immediate opposition, and not just from the trusts. Labor leaders were furious that unions were not exempt from prosecution under the proposed legislation, and they threatened to take their votes elsewhere. Wilson refused a blanket exemption, claiming that the bill was meant to attack special privileges for all industrial combinations, not grant them to unions. He gave ground, however, suggesting an amendment restricting injunctions, guaranteeing jury trials for union members or leaders charged with contempt, and prohibiting unions not practicing illegal methods of industrial warfare from being designated a combination in restraint of trade. Meanwhile, at Brandeis's suggestion, Wilson sought to reassure workers by appointing prominent labor lawyer and activist Frank P. Walsh as chair of the recently established Commission on Industrial Relations. (Brandeis, Wilson's first choice, had declined the position.) Though rejected by Samuel Gompers of the American Federation of Labor, Wilson's compromise bill was accepted by labor's congressional allies in a White House conference on May 26, 1914. Later Gompers himself came around, profusely thanking Wilson for giving him the pen with which the bill was finally signed into law on October 15, 1914.[116]

But labor was not the only Democratic constituency with misgivings about the Clayton Act. Wilson-friendly business interests complained that the law threatened jail time for socially conscious executives who experimented with self-regulatory agreements designed to preserve rather than destroy competition. Conversely, reformers worried that the specificity of the law's prohibitions would encourage the invention of other anticompetitive practices the courts might allow. Brandeis, sympathetic to both concerns, was dismayed that the Clayton Act failed to incorporate his most characteristically pragmatist suggestion: an independent commission equipped to administer the law under variable circumstances. As Brandeis conceived it, such a commission should have power to investigate practices not foreseen (and thus not specifically prohibited) by the architects of the law, hold public hearings on them, and issue injunctions against any found demonstrably restrictive of trade or harmful to consumers. The commission should also collect and publish data on the daily operations and effects of American business, to encourage public and professional deliberation over its consequences. Brandeis even suggested establishing "industrial experiment stations" where small firms could test new ideas and products as readily as large concerns. Finally, the commission should be accountable to the people. Commissioners should be appointed by the president and confirmed by the Senate, with a mandate to act not only in the general interest, but "at the request and for the benefit" of anyone injured or potentially injured by the law's infraction. In Brandeis's view, such a commission was the only way to ensure that the law would serve, over time, to "prevent oppression and injustice" in an economy both dynamic and prone to stratification.[117]

Eventually Wilson himself came to consider the Clayton Act deeply flawed. Even as its New Jersey analog was still being lauded as a progressive triumph, Wilson absorbed Brandeis's critique of the Clayton Act's underlying philosophy, concluding by late 1913 that statute alone was unequal to the task of both moralizing and energizing business. As in 1912, Wilson was attracted to Brandeis's empirical, experimental approach and impressed by the political traction it gained. After a bill modeled on Brandeis's plan and drafted by his close friend George Rublee passed the House in early June 1914, Wilson summoned Brandeis, Rublee, and bill sponsor Raymond B. Stevens of New Hampshire to the White House, informing them that a trade commission would thereafter be the focus of his antitrust program. In adopting yet another of Brandeis's empirically oriented policies, he also signaled, once again, his thorough assimilation of the method behind it. As early as January 1914, Wilson had parried charges that he was fighting the trusts with Roosevelt's armory, explaining his tactical change in pragmatist terms: "Constructive legislation, when successful, is always the embodiment of convincing experience, and of the mature public opinion which finally springs out of that experience." That summer and fall, Wilson brought both public opinion and talents of persuasion to bear on Congress, and the result was the Federal Trade Commission Act, signed into law on September 26, 1914.[118]

Directly inspired by Brandeis, the new Federal Trade Commission (FTC) clearly reflected the pragmatists' vision of iterative and constructive social inquiry. Due largely to Brandeis's influence, its mandate included both the duty to collect and publish the data on which an informed public opinion depended and the authority to issue advisory opinions on trade practices. This latter function soon came to include dissemination of best-practice analyses and promotion of self-regulating trade associations. Finally, the FTC's investigatory and injunctive powers, under constraint of judicial review, allowed it to preserve competitive space for small and midsize concerns without dissolving all large firms or controlling their operations. An executive agency uniting responsiveness to consumers, businesses, and their shared environment with a positive power to effect change, the FTC Act embodied the pragmatist thrust of Wilson's New Freedom politics and marked a watershed in the development of the American administrative state. As Herbert Croly remarked, the FTC "contained the possibility of a radical reversal of many American notions about trusts, legislative power, and legal procedure. It may amount to historic political and constitutional reform." Croly's analysis was perceptive. Moving well beyond the sector-specific Interstate Commerce Commission that preceded it, the FTC was the first national agency with a broad and elastic mandate to promote the public interest through direct legal and economic intervention in a wide range of private-sector affairs. Despite a rocky start, it became a template for many other agencies that followed.[119]

In explaining Wilson's first-term legislative successes, sheer personal drive must loom large. Equally important, however, was Wilson's personal application of the common-counsel method he sought to institutionalize. In Congress, in caucuses, at White House conferences, and in personal encounters with the nation's representatives, Wilson followed a consistent pattern: frankly stating his views, soliciting feedback, compromising when he felt he could, and firmly invoking his authority as leader of his party and spokesman of the nation when compromise proved elusive. Wilson explained his method to the press in November 1913, insisting: "I haven't had a tariff program. I haven't had a currency program. I have conferred with these men . . . and then have gotten back what they sent to me—the best of our common counsel." A lifetime of political thought lay behind that statement. Yet Wilson was publicly committed to bringing all Americans into the process of common counsel, and it would take two years and a much more radical domestic agenda before he convinced most of the pragmatist progressives— and other proponents of participatory, deliberative democracy—that he could do so. Wilson's New Freedom efforts had abolished private monopoly over credit in the United States, extended benefits to farmers and other Americans far from Northeastern financial centers, established means to provide an elastic yet stable currency for a growing and changing economy, and introduced the first graduated income tax in American history. The pragmatist and gradualist socialist William Walling claimed Wilson had opened the door to a democratic, liberating collectivism combining the best American traditions with the keenest insights of modern social science. On the other hand, Wilson's vaunted antitrust measures failed to restructure the economy as thoroughly as many progressives desired, while his appointment of prominent businessmen to the Federal Reserve Board led some observers, such as Senator Robert M. La Follette, to criticize him for "Legalizing the 'Money Power.'"[120]

Nor does that exhaust the list of Wilson's failures in his first half term as president. Paralleling the narrative of Wilson's quest for greater economic equality and wider political participation is a different story of the New Freedom years: a story of indifference to racial and gender injustices at home and chauvinism toward peoples pursuing their own quests for new freedoms abroad. Among those who followed this story line closely were most of James's students and admirers—including Croly, who in late 1914

warned Wilson to avoid "extravagant claims" about the gains made for democracy under his leadership, lest he demonstrate a gross ignorance of both
"the meaning and the task of American progressivism."[121] Social problems
that no tariff, trade, or monetary commission could fix still plagued a nation divided by race, sex, and class. By that time, moreover, it was clear
that Wilson confronted international problems as volatile as any faced
by his predecessors. His handling of those that emerged before the war in
Europe, especially involving Latin America, was not calculated to inspire
perfect confidence—at least not among Americans like Croly, his fellow
pragmatist progressives, and other cosmopolitan reformers, whose belief in
the symbiosis of national and international affairs was cardinal by the time
the strains of neutrality made their support invaluable.

CHAPTER THREE

A Certain Blindness

Anticipating the presidential inauguration on March 4, 1913, W. E. B. Du Bois dared to hope that his vote for Woodrow Wilson, and those of half a million other African Americans, represented "a step toward political independence" for Americans of all colors excluded from the nation's prosperity and public life. Five thousand miles south, in Buenos Aires, the editors of *La Prensa* also took courage, predicting "a new era" of imperial rollback under a president whose enmity toward monopolists and reactionaries logically implied friendship toward their victims, wherever they might reside. Such hopes were short-lived. A year into Wilson's term, white posses had murdered scores of black men with impunity, and US marines had occupied the Mexican port city of Veracruz. The Argentine anti-imperialist Manuel Ugarte expressed the opinion and anger of millions north and south by explaining that Wilson, purported herald of change, had upheld his nation's hoariest and goriest traditions. "The United States invented the Monroe Doctrine and the lynch law," he snarled in an April 1914 interview. "The lynch law serves to assassinate men, and the Monroe doctrine to assassinate nations."[1]

Racism and its frequent partner, imperialism, are central to every chapter of American history. Despite the United States' founding on principles of equality, its leaders and citizenry have been as badly afflicted as any in the world with what William James called "a certain blindness in human beings"—a tendency to ignore the value and meaning that others attach to experience. Few of the mostly white men who have monopolized political and economic power throughout American history have escaped this affliction or avoided making decisions reflecting its morally disabling effects—decisions with grave consequences for Americans and other peoples. This sad statement holds as true for presidents as for anyone else, and undoubtedly so for Wilson—a president who, more than most of his peers, has come to symbolize the ironies and hypocrisies of his nation's ostensibly democratic project.[2]

Wilson's reputation as a racist, imperialist, and hypocrite raises two questions. First, what explains it? And second, what does it explain? The first is more easily answered than the second. Wilson was elected president on a platform promising fuller freedom to Americans excluded from effective participation in public life. His commitment to the cause seemed sincere, and would continue to find reinforcement through pragmatist social thought. Indeed, sometime before May 1915, Wilson read James's 1899 essay, "On a Certain Blindness in Human Beings," perhaps the philosopher's most eloquent case for tolerance, empathy, and inclusive deliberation in moral and social affairs. The papers of Wilson's second wife, Edith, reveal that the couple discussed and admired the piece. Yet by then Wilson had acquiesced in a highly publicized effort by cabinet members to segregate their departments. Meanwhile, the landing of marines at Veracruz exemplified a larger intention to teach Latin Americans to "elect good men," as Wilson haughtily stated in 1913. Within two years he would likewise land troops in the predominantly nonwhite states of the Dominican Republic and Haiti to impose order on what he (along with most Americans and Europeans) viewed as dangerously unruly populations. In short, Wilson's reputation as a racist, imperialist, and hypocrite is explained by several actions that were racist, imperialist, and hypocritical.[3]

But what do these actions explain? The instinctual answer for historians conditioned (by hard historical facts) to be skeptical of white male power is, "Everything." Multiple critics conclude that Wilson's brand of American liberalism was fundamentally rooted in racist thought and essentially dependent on the imperialistic subordination of peoples whose societies and cultures diverged most widely from his own. From segregated government to a color-coded League of Nations, everything associated with Wilson's presidency, in this view, is of a piece.[4] Even scholars who credit Wilson's rhetoric with sparking the anticolonial nationalist movement, or his League of Nations with enabling its development, emphasize the irony of a racist helping unleash such forces.[5]

Wilson's prejudice does indeed explain several of his administration's policies and their tragic consequences: the frustration of blacks treated as second-class citizens by their government employers; the psychic and physical trauma of those victimized by a lynching epidemic Wilson was reprehensibly slow to condemn; the death and destruction visited upon Caribbean and Central American peoples by soldiers he deployed in their lands.

These actions and consequences also explain his reputation as a hypocrite. But that reputation itself is a reminder that something about Wilson does not square with his chauvinist image. The something in question is the larger political vision of common counsel he so fervently promoted—a vision inspiring him to a host of actions that racism but poorly and awkwardly explains. For all the blind spots marring it, that vision informed policies designed to extend the pragmatists' ideal of deliberative democracy, first to greater numbers of Americans inhabiting an increasingly interdependent nation, then to the relations among states in a shrinking world. Prejudice led Wilson to deviate from this pragmatist vision when he lacked the energy, empathy, or wisdom to pursue it—whether at home, in the face of far more determined racists than he; or abroad, amid circumstances that often bewildered and frustrated him. Frequently blind to the significance others attached to their experiences, Wilson at times failed to see how cruelly they could mock his democratic and internationalist pretensions. For many vulnerable people the results were tragic, and it is right that the weight of responsibility should diminish Wilson's standing.

Such moral breakdowns, however, were products of Wilson's worst flaws rather than his best ideals. Moreover, as several of the pragmatist progressives came to recognize, he learned from some of them. In particular, the development of Wilson's Latin American policy exhibits a shift in his conception of self-government, one crucial to his later plans for a more just and cooperative world order under the League of Nations. A clear view of Wilson's mature internationalism and its relevance to contemporary affairs depends, therefore, on a clear understanding of his stumbling efforts to apply pragmatist political ethics to diplomatic practice in Latin America and Asia before Europe consumed his attention.

In dark contrast, Wilson never recognized his apathy toward his own nation's race problem for what it was: a moral and political failure of terrible consequence, one that perpetuated injustice and violence and undermined the ideals he treasured most. A sober assessment of his record on this score is essential to understanding—and critically evaluating—the reflexive and ironic dismissal of his political thought by many inheritors of his cosmopolitan vision.

No region of the United States is more closely associated with racism than the South; and the South's overriding importance to Wilson's identity and worldview has never been a secret—except to Wilson himself.

Wilson's parents were not southerners. His father was born to Irish immigrants in Ohio, his mother emigrated from England, and neither lived in the South until shortly before Wilson's birth in Staunton, Virginia. True, "Tommy" spent most of his childhood in Georgia and South Carolina—prompting a conscious, methodical effort to rid himself of his southern accent.[6] Still, several otherwise able interpreters have explained Wilson's thought and character, especially regarding race, by his southern birth and upbringing during the American Civil War and Reconstruction. The political chaos and sense of humiliation that led so many white southerners first to resist Reconstruction, then replace slavery with the Jim Crow regime, is assumed to have set the pattern of Wilson's thinking, too.[7] There is a prima facie logic to this argument, and Wilson's obvious racial prejudices lend it plausibility. As a whole, however, the record simply does not sustain the interpretation of Wilson as southern redeemer in progressive costume.

To be sure, Wilson's father was an ardent states'-rights secessionist, and from young adulthood the future US president expressed "regrets" about the course of southern history since secession. But as twenty-four-year-old Wilson wrote on Confederate Decoration Day in 1881, his were "not of the same sort of regrets that are supposed to engage the thoughts of others" in Dixie. "*My* regret is, that there should be any such ceremonious decoration of these graves. I think that anything that tends to revive or perpetuate the bitter memories of the war is wicked folly." This was neither a plea to let sleeping dogs lie nor a moral indictment of southern racism. It was rather a defense of national over sectional politics as the path to democratic advancement. As he later wrote, "the South would have been ruined by success" in the Civil War; "preservation of the Union" was "politically right," and "secession was wrong." But while dismissing the increasingly popular view of secession as a noble though misguided cause, Wilson also declined to condemn secession as "morally wrong." To modern ears, such silence on the moral abomination impelling secession—slavery—is deafening. For Wilson, however, moral judgments of secessionists, passed with the benefit of hindsight and social progress, were self-indulgent and ahistorical. "It is easy and cheap now to point out that the war was a mistake," he insisted, yet "perfectly plain" that many latter-day critics would repeat it if placed "in the same circumstances."[8]

This is not to say Wilson excused slavery or denied its malignancy. He insisted that abolition was a blessing in which any true lover of the nation, and especially the South, should "rejoice." Americans were too interconnected, their economic relations too complex, the ideals of the majority too sharply at odds with the patrician ethos of a slave society for a Southern nation, built on outmoded states'-rights doctrines and feudal social arrangements, to thrive. Slavery, he wrote while studying law at the University of

Virginia, was "enervating" and "exhausting" the South long before the Confederacy's foolish effort to secede. "Even the damnable cruelty and folly of Reconstruction was to be preferred to helpless independence."[9] Nine years later, writing from Middletown, Connecticut, to a southern friend, Wilson warned that the editor of his forthcoming book would insist on his "doing justice to those abolitionist rascals and other characters of ante-bellum and post-bellum times"—in other words, those who sought, cruelly or bunglingly or otherwise, to realize freedom and equality more completely across the polity. "And I am afraid I *shall* do them justice!" he warned further. "I am getting most unreasonably impartial in this latitude." Indeed, when accepting the commission for the volume—eventually published as *Division and Reunion* (1893)—he had pledged "impartiality" toward all causes treated but one. "Ever since I have had independent judgments of my own," he averred, "I have been a Federalist(!)"[10]

Thus Wilson's views on the South were complex but clear—at least to him. Born there, raised there, he was keenly aware of both the difficulty and the necessity of its integration into the larger national fabric. In that sense it would always be, in his words, "the only place where nothing has to be explained to me."[11]

Wilson's racial views were far more complicated, due largely to his own lack of interest in race as a moral, political, or even an intellectual problem. That his racial views included many rac*ist* views is undeniable. His low opinion of Reconstruction was rooted in prejudice, reflecting his belief in the incapacity of newly enfranchised and elected blacks to become anything but pawns of "unscrupulous adventurers" from the North. That prejudice ran deep enough to preclude critical analysis of the racist scholarly consensus he peddled secondhand in *Division and Reunion* and his notorious *History of the American People* (1901). In the latter work Wilson even empathized with the white vigilantes who formed the Ku Klux Klan, portraying their efforts to reestablish the social order that had crumbled around them as understandable and predictable.[12]

Empathy, however, is not sympathy. Wilson found the Klan comprehensible, not reasonable. Their vigilantism reflected the "disorder and upheaval" of Reconstruction, but did not and could not redress it. To the contrary, the Klan's violent insistence that change and its agents were inherently evil brought "a reign of terror" to the South, "and society was infinitely more disturbed than defended."[13] Nor was Wilson simply advocating a more orderly rollback of the postwar civil rights revolution. In *Division and Reunion* he blamed southern legislatures for bringing radical Reconstruction upon themselves by enacting laws to keep blacks "in virtual slavery." As early as 1881 he welcomed the rise of black landowners in the South, applauded what he viewed as a growing trend toward independent political action among southern blacks generally, and argued that schooling for black children (as for whites) should be compulsory to encourage such hopeful developments. Six years later, in an article foundational to the discipline of public administration in the United States, Wilson wrote that government could not remain the property of Anglo-Saxons but must become a government "of Irishmen, of Germans, and of negroes" if order and freedom both were to flourish.[14]

Wilson also knew better than many outside the South how far away that goal remained—and how much his southern brethren impeded it. Encountering a British author's claim that the Fourteenth Amendment had erased most differences in the voting rights bestowed by the several states to their citizens, Wilson was incredulous. "This amendment can hardly be said to be in this respect practically operative," he scribbled in the margin. Living briefly in Atlanta, he rued his move to the "ignorant" backwater of Georgia and despised the Jim Crow men, including future Democratic Senator Hoke Smith, who came to dominate its politics. His discomfort with southern life doubtless factored in his refusal of the region's most prestigious academic post, the presidency of the University of Virginia, years before the Princeton presidency was on the table.[15]

That discomfort included his admitted lack of "ease" with "coloured people."[16] But it also reflected his sense that "the perfect and easy adjustment of each man to his fellows" in which "freedom" consists had been abandoned in the South by all but the lowly. As he told the faculty and students of Virginia's Hampton Institute, Booker T. Washington's alma mater, "In a community where all men are not equal under the law, there is no liberty." Granted, he continued, anyone expecting "to bring the millennium by a sudden and violent effort at reform, is fit for a lunatic asylum." Nevertheless, those who would "rouse the world" merely "by blowing the horn" should not distract others, like his listeners, from the duty to "take your swords, and do your fighting, and that before you and not behind." Wilson was not reciting boilerplate. Ironically, his tone-deaf theme of gradualism and dismissal of past conflicts suggest a message consciously tailored to a black underclass ripe for radicalization. Still his sympathy and admiration for his audience was genuine. "I do not know when an audience has so moved me," he told Ellen privately. Discovering that the school struggled annually to meet expenses, he refused his honorarium and reimbursements, noting, "I did not feel that it was in the least an act of generosity."[17]

The point is not to paint Wilson as an advocate of social equality between races. He was anything but. But neither was he particularly exercised by those who were. Perhaps most remarkable in the documentary record is how little Wilson thought about racial matters at all. When prompted, he shared opinions more typical of a northern than a southern racist, exhibiting none of the deep, personal investment so common below the Mason-Dixon Line. Responding in 1884 to a certain Dr. Taylor's endorsement of widespread "miscegenation" as a solution to the American racial problem, Wilson predictably denounced the idea as "utterly unsound." Curiously, in light of his own background, however, he thought a union between "a fine African" and "a callous Scotch girl"—presumably inured to social degradation by her own experience—might prosper. Years later, prompted by a potential African American applicant to Princeton, Wilson wrote from the president's office that "the whole temper and tradition of the place are such that no negro has ever applied for admission, and it seems extremely unlikely that the question will ever assume a practical form." Princeton was dominated by sons of Southern white gentlemen, and Wilson had scant interest in forcing racial tolerance upon them. Yet two years earlier he caused a stir—and scandalized Ellen's Georgia relatives—by inviting Booker T. Washington to march in the academic procession and speak at the gala dinner afterward. Granting Washington's accommodationist stance toward race relations, Wilson's lavish praise for his oratory—most treasured of Wilsonian talents—suggests genuine respect for the Wizard of Tuskegee. It also exemplifies his disbelief in innate racial inferiority. As he declared in 1909 before an African American church in Princeton, "the so-called 'negro problem' is a problem, not of color, but of capacity; not a racial, but an economic problem."[18]

In sum, however ignorant and chauvinistic, Wilson's racial views were far from "white supremacist."[19] He simply was not that interested, as even his historical works attest. Any claim to originality in Wilson's analyses of the Civil War and its aftermath consists in his preponderant emphasis on the political rather than moral economy of slavery and secession. Of course slavery had to go; though usually benign (in Wilson's view), its legal and constitutional defenses crumbled before an antislavery movement built "upon obvious grounds of moral judgment." But Wilson himself devoted little space to the moral case against slavery. His interest lay in the economic backwardness and political myopia it encouraged in the South. Because of the South's commitment to slavery, Wilson deemed it "impossible that the industrial revolution, elsewhere working changes so profound, could materially affect the structure of her society." Instead, slavery bred among whites a habit of "resolutely, almost passionately, resisting change" that resulted, ironically, in cataclysm. In their "compulsion" to preserve the institutional cornerstone of their society from inexorable erosion, Southern whites effectively abdicated the responsibilities of self-government and abandoned that society to fate, "until change and even its own destruction were forced on it by war."[20]

For Wilson, therefore, the essential narrative of the Civil War and Reconstruction was not the failure and revival of white supremacy in the South. It was the failure and revival of his pragmatist constitutional ideal—an ideal having much to do with deliberation and adaptation among citizens but little to do with the domination or liberation of racial groups. That ideal was neither a final expression of universal values nor an ultimate guarantor of eternal social arrangements but rather a framework for managing change in an orderly, cooperative fashion. Change, Wilson argued, is inevitable, and each free citizen of a self-governing polity has the duty and privilege to help shape its course. Yet "change which breaks roughly with the common thought will lack the sympathy of that thought, provoke its opposition, and will inevitably be crushed by that opposition." The first lesson was lost on the antebellum South, the second on the architects of secession and Reconstruction. In each case zealots ignored the moral of organized human history: "Society, like other organisms, can only be changed by evolution."[21]

Though not without progressive implications, in the absence of empathy this conclusion meant apathy. The "race problem of the South will no doubt work itself out in the slowness of time," Wilson wrote in 1897. "Time is the only legislator in such a matter."[22] Even spoken at the height of his antipopulism, such words are starkly discordant with the ethos of active idealism he was rediscovering in the writings of William James. They would prove a dark foreshadowing of his apathy toward his nation's race problem as president.

The most notorious example of Wilson's racism is the segregation of federal offices under his administration. For decades historians have blamed Wilson for introducing segregation into the federal government, despite the fact that many African Americans voted for him in protest against the segregationist policies of his Republican predecessors. The best recent work is more nuanced, downplaying Wilson's direct personal efforts to "bureaucratize" racism while arguing that the process was congenial to his political philosophy and goals.[23] The truth is, Wilson considered his subordinates' segregation schemes *irrelevant* to his political philosophy and goals—at least until the fallout among white liberals convinced him to countermand the initiatives. His deficit of empathy for African Americans did not translate into militant segregationism. Rather, it translated into political meekness and dereliction of his duty, as chief executive, to promote just treatment of all citizens under the law.

To call it a lost opportunity for Democrats would be an understatement. For years, articulate opponents of Washington's "Tuskegee Machine" had called for a new dispensation: No more trading the dignity of equality for a few Republican political offices. W. E. B. Du Bois, William Monroe Trotter, and other founders of the Niagara movement in 1905 refused to accept that the summit of black politics was to serve as a living practical joke played by Republicans on white southern Democrats. In 1912, though long since riven by internal tensions, the movement's former leaders agreed on the need to oust the Republicans. William Howard Taft had curtailed the offices provided blacks through the Tuskegee Machine while tacitly encouraging segregation and voter suppression in the South to lure white votes. Segregation in federal buildings, begun under Theodore Roosevelt, accelerated under Taft. From 1910 forward the president himself indulged his substantial appetite in a segregated White House dining room.[24]

"I was and had been for years utterly disgusted with the treatment which the Republican Party had meted out to its Negro supporters," Du Bois recalled a quarter century later. Nor could he vote Roosevelt's Progressive Party ticket. Despite the support of fellow pragmatists including Jane Addams, Herbert Croly, Felix Frankfurter, and Walter Weyl, Roosevelt lost Du Bois when he "flatly" refused to support racial equality. This refusal proved a boon for Wilson. Du Bois knew Wilson's academic work, found his account of Reconstruction no worse than every other study (barring Du Bois's own), and respected his constitutional and political theory. In *The State*, especially, Du Bois saw a flexible and farseeing mind at work.[25] But it took more to overcome his misgivings.

First, Wilson earned the support of Trotter and other black progressives who saw a natural harmony between his attack on economic privilege in New Jersey and their own campaign for social justice nationally. Wilson sealed the deal in mid-July 1912, personally promising Trotter and several allies that he would "know no white or black" as president but serve the whole nation. The following month, several of Du Bois's colleagues in the National Association for the Advancement of Colored People (NAACP) extracted similar pledges. As Wilson assured Bishop Alexander Walters, who also headed the National Colored Democratic League, his "earnest wish" for African Americans was "to see justice done them in every matter." Second,

Wilson benefited from some hard political math. Du Bois concluded that a vote for his true favorite, Eugene Debs, was wasted—and black America had no votes to waste. Resigning his membership in the Socialist Party, Du Bois informed *Crisis* readers that among the candidates likely to win, Wilson alone had yet to fail them. "On the whole, we do not believe that Woodrow Wilson admires Negroes," Du Bois admitted, but "he has brains." Given the changing demography of the United States and Wilson's insight into the protean nature of political institutions, it was not entirely vain to hope for "farsighted fairness" from him. That November Du Bois dared readers to advance the ideal of a "Democratic" party for all by voting to make it so, through Wilson. For such an ideal, he wrote, "We are willing to risk a trial."[26]

The sheer height of the hopes Wilson raised explains much of the disappointment over their dashing—a disappointment which, at least in historical accounts, appears cataclysmic compared to the aftermaths of so many similar injuries and betrayals.[27] It was certainly a rapid descent. In the March 1913 issue of *Crisis*, Du Bois, a Jamesian as well as a student of the president's writings, reminded Wilson that to make a people both "servile and dignified, docile and self-reliant, servants and independent leaders" was immoral and futile. Ensuring "a reasonable chance for life, liberty, and happiness" to African Americans was not just the "sane and practical solution of the race problem" but also "the bedrock of a just solution of the rights of man in the American Republic." In the same issue Jane Addams was quoted to similar effect, arguing that to muzzle and smother any substantial minority drains national "capacity" and "must finally result in a loss of enthusiasm" for the whole democratic project.[28] Yet by the second week of April Wilson was getting his first taste of the medicine mixed by his southern partisans. Support for his progressive agenda was contingent on patronage for white southern Democrats who in most cases could barely imagine much less accept serving under black supervisors. That same week Wilson's postmaster general and chief liaison to southern congressional Democrats, Albert Sidney Burleson of Texas, informed him in cabinet of plans to segregate the postal rails. Indeed, Burleson was "anxious to segregate white and negro employees in all Departments," assuring Wilson that he had "talked with Bishop Walters and other prominent negroes and most of them thought it would be a great thing to do."[29]

Thus began Wilson's near total abdication of responsibility for protecting the rights of African Americans during his presidency. Without directly approving Burleson's departmental plan, he tacitly permitted its implementation. He was far more skeptical of Burleson's universal plan to segregate blacks. He insisted that regardless of their physical working arrangements, he had promised "to do them justice" and wanted no reduction in jobs available to them. Burleson pushed back, declaring it "wrong" in principle to place white workers under black supervision. Warming to Burleson's theme, Treasury Secretary William Gibbs McAdoo "doubted whether the Senate would confirm a negro" in authority over whites "even if the President appointed one." No official action was taken, and the matter dropped out of Wilson's sight. That evening, and through the following month, he turned attention to his main patronage strategy: replacing party-machine hacks with vetted progressives. Anxious to conserve his remaining political capital to leverage his economic program, he was largely oblivious to Burleson's rapid and methodical segregation and elimination of African American workers in the US Postal Department, a practice soon mimicked in the Census Bureau, Bureau of Engraving and Printing, and Treasury.[30]

Others noticed. Oswald Garrison Villard, NAACP cofounder and prominent liberal publicist, had been among those who extracted Wilson's promise in the summer of 1912 to do blacks justice. Certain that Wilson would be scandalized by his subordinates' actions, Villard secured an Oval Office meeting on May 14, 1913. He left convinced that Wilson would soon establish full control over his party and secure enough allies to withstand its "reactionary" southern contingent. He also left with Wilson's assurance, or so he thought, that some systematic inquiry into the American race problem was imminent, and might even result in a "National Race Commission" to address racial injustice.[31] He was sorely disappointed. Wilson took no action to roll back segregation or to launch a larger inquiry into the nation's race relations. Reminded by Villard that the New Freedom was purportedly a movement for all Americans, Wilson replied, "It is as far as possible from being a movement *against* the negroes." By segregating their departments, his subordinates merely sought to reduce discomfort for everyone—a goal, he assured Villard, which several black leaders approved. Meanwhile, by lowering tariffs, expanding credit, and taming trusts, Wilson would lift all downtrodden Americans—among whom blacks were overrepresented—to a higher and wider plane of opportunity.[32]

These exchanges turned concern for Wilson's reputation among African Americans into exasperation and anger over his abandonment of their interests. On August 15, 1913, Villard cosigned and published a letter with Du Bois and others demanding that Wilson uphold African American constitutional rights. Its effect was noticeable even to Wilson. Over the next two weeks, worried and angry letters to the White House reported plummeting support among African Americans in states they helped deliver in 1912.[33]

Du Bois penned another open letter, published in the September 1913 *Crisis*, describing the chasm separating the common counsel Wilson preached as a candidate and his current failure to preserve a role for blacks in the nation's deliberations. Echoing Wilson's own arguments about slavery's effects on the Old South, Du Bois implied that by abetting discrimination against blacks, Wilson endangered order and progress for the nation. "There are foolish people," he warned, "who think that such a policy has no limit. . . . Have we assumed too great and quick a growth of intelligence in the party that once made slavery its cornerstone?"[34]

As pressure mounted, Wilson gestured toward change—too little, too late. He informed Villard that a race commission was impossible while his economic policies hung in the balance. Hoping to mollify his critics, however, he granted a rare private meeting at the White House to a delegation led by Trotter in November 1913. The twenty thousand signatures on the antisegregation petition they presented may have humbled Wilson. His calm was almost eerie as Trotter, after excoriating his appointees' segregationist policies, practically ordered the president to action: "Wipe out the blot, apostle of 'New Freedom,' put no limitation on any being for race." Wilson, pleading ignorance of details, admitted that "mistakes have probably been made" and assured Trotter that they could be "corrected." Indeed, Wilson soon launched an inquiry. Within a month, the *Boston Daily Advertiser*, an erstwhile critic, reported that segregation had been "effectually checked" and was "being rapidly disintegrated." Yet over the following year, more black Democrats lost their positions or saw appointments blocked, while southern Democrats in Congress attempted to make federal segregation compulsory. When the Civil Service Commission began requiring photographs from applicants in May 1914, it seemed segregation might yield to outright exclusion.[35]

In late 1914, Wilson's relations with African Americans approached their nadir. Trotter, who had done as much as anyone to deliver black votes to Wilson, lost patience. In a second White House meeting, he demanded "an executive order against any and all segregation of government employees because of race or color." Wilson's response revealed his pathetic ignorance of the black lives his decisions affected. Taken aback by Trotter's bluntness, he whined about the presidency's burdens and then grew defensive, insisting that Burleson and company's sole purpose in segregating their departments was to make life easier on everyone. Absurdly, he asserted that Americans "as a whole" wished success to "the Negro race," then superfluously reminded Trotter that despite such goodwill, "friction" was an all-too-frequent outcome of "intercourse" between the races. Wilson assured Trotter that he personally viewed race merely as a marker of geographic extraction, but cautioned that "generations" would be required to overcome more prevalent and "embarrassing" racial ideas. Although he could, theoretically, take executive action to meet Trotter's demands, progress would "come quickest if these questions aren't raised." Instead, men like Trotter should work to ensure "that the race makes good" and try not to view purely administrative measures as a "humiliation"—an erroneous interpretation causing inordinate distress. If, instead, "you should take it in the spirit in which I have presented it to you, it wouldn't have serious consequences."[36]

Wilson's blithe, almost avuncular tone set Trotter off. "We are not here as wards," he protested. "We are here as full-fledged American citizens, vouchsafed equality of citizenship by the federal Constitution." Segregation was clearly a "humiliation," and Wilson should know it. Caught entirely off guard, Wilson was so offended by Trotter's show of anger that he turned the equality argument against him. "You are an American citizen, as fully an American citizen as I am," he retorted, and to repay calm engagement with angry demands—in the Oval Office—was a grievous breach of republican etiquette. Trotter explained that his anger stemmed both from the injustices faced by his people and from his branding, with others, "as traitors to our race" because of their support for Wilson in 1912. Wilson was unmoved: Trotter had turned a discussion of complex moral and practical issues into an act of "blackmail," threatening to rescind political support due to disagreement over what was "the right thing at the right time." Oblivious to the naïveté and sheer absurdity of this last complaint, Wilson declared that he would "resent" such treatment "from one set of men as from another" and concluded the conversation.[37]

Wilson immediately regretted the episode, which was widely reported. "I was damn fool enough to lose my temper and show them the door," he told Navy Secretary Josephus Daniels. Had Wilson listened quietly and promised to consider the petition—as "of course" he would—"no more would have been heard."[38] Few of Wilson's statements so succinctly capture his particular form of racism. He regretted not his blindness to the experience of African Americans but rather his failure to avoid the issue deftly. And although the episode did mark a slight shift in his attitude toward racial injustice, his ignorance and overwhelming interest in other matters made it a distinction without much difference. A month later, in a blissful marriage of ignorance and paternalism, he insisted that "the heart of the South desires the good of the Negro," while his own "object" was to "help him in every way that is possible." To his credit, he did make some

moves in that direction. That spring he signed a bill to incorporate the Ellen Wilson Memorial Homes, a project to provide sanitary housing in one
of the capital's worst and most densely black ghettoes, and one for which
Ellen—despite her own frequent expressions of racism—had lobbied hard
before her death in August 1914. Later, in July 1915, Wilson publicly urged
businesses, local governments, and private citizens to support a national
exhibition commemorating "the achievements of the negro race."[39]

Unfortunately, Wilson's southern constituents had no interest in rebuilding his relationship with African Americans. In February 1915, Wilson
met with Thomas F. Dixon Jr., an acquaintance from Johns Hopkins who
asked to arrange a White House showing of D. W. Griffith's new film, *Birth
of a Nation*. Although the film was partially based on his 1905 novel *The
Clansman*, Dixon did not inform Wilson of its content, including its scur-
rilously racist account of Reconstruction. "Of course, I didn't dare allow
the President to know the *real big purpose back of my film—which was to
revolutionize Northern sentiments by a presentation of history that would
transform every man in my audience into a good Democrat!*" Dixon wrote
weeks later. "What I told the President was that I would show him the birth
of a new art—the launching of the mightiest engine for moulding public
opinion in the history of the world."[40]

Wilson agreed to a showing on February 18. The only eyewitness on
record recalled him appearing preoccupied and leaving without comment as
soon as the film ended. He certainly did not utter the infamous words, "It is
like history writ with lightning," attributed without citation by a journalist
decades later. They do not even appear in Dixon's memoirs. Wilson's name
appears in none of the film's publicity materials, otherwise festooned with
endorsements from congressmen and celebrities. Indeed, Wilson later called
the film "a very unfortunate production." Still, Dixon and Griffith used the
showing to great promotional effect, giving the public the impression of an
official White House endorsement. The fact that they embroidered their
silent narrative with carefully selected (and manipulated) quotations from
Division and Reunion rendered White House protests to the contrary futile.
From then on, Wilson would be identified in the minds of blacks and whites
alike with the movie that inspired the modern Ku Klux Klan.[41]

It was also at that point that the little interest Wilson had shown in racial politics evaporated. The apparently irretrievable loss of African American support, continuing hostility from aggrieved southern politicians, and
above all, the war in Europe pushed and pulled his attention in other directions. His pattern of failure in addressing racial injustice would be replicated
throughout his presidency. Its consequence was just what the pragmatist

critiques of Du Bois and Addams predicted: an erosion of the habits of self-government that Wilson deemed crucial to democracy's success. Southern congressmen continued to hold administration policy hostage to a white-supremacist agenda. Meanwhile, as the 1916 election approached, Du Bois concluded that no vote at all was better than a Wilson vote. He suggested that blacks who could not vote Socialist or Republican simply stay home on polling day.[42]

It is hard to imagine a clearer indictment of Wilson's record on race: a fellow historian and political scientist, sharing his deep belief in the social, cultural, and individual wellsprings of political democracy, suggesting that the best course for millions of citizens was to abstain from choosing their leader. But for that very reason the racial injustices marring Wilson's record should be viewed as contradictory rather than essential to his most considered thinking. His acts of narrow prejudice were deviations from a broader vision, which emphasized the moral and practical necessity of expanding rather than sealing off the democratic sphere. Racial justice was not antithetical to this vision but obstructed from it by multiple factors, including his felt need for southern Democratic cooperation with his reform program, his assumption it would redound to the benefit of African Americans, and the racial prejudice that facilitated such rationalizations.

Federal segregation is a perfect example. Burleson, its instigator and major architect, was Wilson's liaison to southern Democrats leery of his interventionism and ready to mutiny at the smallest threat to Jim Crow. Wilson's substantial prejudices made him susceptible to Burleson's inane argument that both black workers and "prominent negroes" thought segregation best for all. But neither Wilson's turn to segregation as a political expedient nor his blindness to its degrading effects proves he intended to build an impregnable fortress of white democracy on a permanent foundation of black oppression. Few southerners credited him with such a plan; they were too furious over his repeated appointment of blacks to offices desired by whites, or granting authority over them. The real fire-eaters were in a constant lather: Mississippi Senator John Sharp Williams warned that Wilson's "best friends" in Congress felt "slapped in the face" by such appointments, while Williams's Magnolia-state colleague James K. Vardaman, along with Georgia Senator Hoke Smith and South Carolina's Ben Tillman, threatened to abandon the New Freedom over the appointment of a single black man to the treasury department.[43]

In short, Wilson was a racist, but not the racist of white supremacists' dreams or many historians' imaginations. The Klansman's vision did not inspire but instead repelled him, as his historical writings and response to

Birth of a Nation show. At times he displayed empathy for blacks and, in rare instances, even acted on it—as when he moved to investigate and miti-gate the "mistakes" of federal segregation or, during World War I, publicly condemned the "disgraceful evil" of lynching.[44] Yet even these efforts were crippled by indifference—one too lazy to secure lasting justice for black federal workers, the other too tardy to save the lives, or even honor the passing, of far too many victims. No one can deny the enormity of Wilson's failures or the responsibility he bears for them. But that is the point: Wilson bears that responsibility not because he was incapable of thinking outside a racist mind-set but because he could, however infrequently, recognize such affronts to his own ideals.

How could he have ignored so many others? Unfortunately, he left few clues to his mind, except that it was generally elsewhere. The daily injus-tice and terror facing African Americans was almost impossibly remote to him. When he thought about it, its worst manifestations troubled him; he knew they violated his highest ideals. But like the majority of white Ameri-cans at the time—and before, and long after—he rarely did think about it. It was not real to him.

One reality Wilson could not escape was that his nation sat within a web of economic, cultural, and political networks spanning the world—and that parts of that world were on fire. In the years preceding Wilson's 1913 in-auguration, coalitions of peasants and urban reformers in both China and Mexico had deposed their governments and subsequently disintegrated into warring factions. Wilson's first term witnessed political upheavals in the Dominican Republic, in Haiti, and across Europe, where nationalist vio-lence in the Balkans became the pretense for a war spanning the continent and beyond.

Wilson's insensitivity to the lived experience of millions within his na-tion's borders helps explain his uneven responses to the complex affairs he encountered beyond them. Once again James's notion of "a certain blind-ness in human beings" captures Wilson's difficulty in empathizing with people whose experience was foreign to his own. In contrast to his domes-tic record, however, Wilson's diplomatic record demonstrates his ability, in major instances, to overcome such blindness and adopt a broadened vision—one modern-day cosmopolitans should not summarily dismiss. That vision was only fully developed near the Great War's end, when its essence was embodied in Wilson's plan for the League of Nations. Its roots, however, stretch back to Wilson's prewar efforts to align his domestic and international policies. Indeed, they reach further, to his days as a student and analyst of politics.

Granted, many of Wilson's prepresidential writings on foreign affairs sit awkwardly beside his pragmatist-progressive theory of politics. Wilson deemed annexation of foreign territories unwise.[45] But when his nation emerged from war with Spain to assert its authority over the Philippines, Guam, and Puerto Rico, he affirmed Americans' duty to train their wards in the "principle and custom" of self-mastery before imposing self-government and independence on them. One source of this conviction was his organic theory of political development, which proscribed the abrupt transplantation of living institutions to foreign soils. The success of American government, "like every other government," depended largely "on qualities and conditions which it did not itself create, but only obeyed." Another source was his confidence in the advanced political development of the United States and the privileges it entailed. To impose "full-fangled institutions of American self-government" on peoples "in the childhood of their political growth" would be "a curse." It was the United States' duty to instill in its wards "the drill and habit of law and obedience" learned through "strenuous processes of English history," and thus encourage "the natural development which shall make them at last equal members of the family of nations."[46]

Clearly, Wilson's assessment of international society in his day was hierarchical. But as the passage just quoted suggests, his *ideal* of international society was not. Nor did it resemble the particularistic vision of "self-determining" polities historically linked to his name. Rather, Wilson's was a modified Kantian vision of self-*governing* polities striving for mutual understanding and negotiating the terms of their common life. In the mid-1890s he explained that "the mind of man, *whatever his race, whatever his religion,*" recognized "vital principles of right" furnishing a feasible basis for positive international law. He did not describe those principles as explicit precepts of a fixed ethical code. Instead he spoke of a "universal conscience," such as Kant perceived in the ability of culture-bound individuals to conceptualize humankind in toto.[47] International order depended on the degree to which this "moral sense" of shared humanity could be embodied in "a community among states," for like the laws of free nations, international law must proceed "from those *upon* whom it is enforced." A perfected world order would protect and serve the interests of "independent states" on the model of individuals in civil society—that is, "states responsible for their actions."[48]

At this point Wilson diverged from Kant, whose belief in the moral independence of states precluded a "world republic" and limited his vision to
"a federation" averting war.[49] Wilson thought that in the course of ordering
peaceable relations, the international community might develop patterns of
interaction analogous to the self-governing habits of its healthiest members—
perhaps eventually generating a supranational democratic body. As early as
1887, Wilson discerned a "tendency" toward "confederation" in the world:
the integration, "first, of parts of empires like the British, and finally of great
states themselves." Distinct from the aggressively expansionist agendas of
certain ethnic nation-states, this was a movement "towards the American
type—of governments joined with governments for the pursuit of common
purposes, in honorary equality and honorable subordination."[50]

In the wake of the Spanish war, Wilson hoped to see this movement advanced by an American nation whose citizens accepted the reality of international interdependence. For Wilson the prizes of empire were not economic or
geopolitical but epistemological and moral. As he explained in 1902, building
a self-governing Philippines would require an "experimental" attitude and a
willingness to let the Filipinos "teach us, as our critics." Such "freedom of
opinion" did not preclude the Filipinos' duty to submit to the authority of the
US government. But it did permit their contribution to a fund of knowledge
and experience that would shape their country's future as well as advance the
democratization of the United States—"a task but half done."[51] Ironically,
the anticipated fruits of the national project Wilson described resemble those
of the anti-imperialist James's "Moral Equivalent of War." Confronting challenges of domestic and international progress, Americans would learn that
personal freedom and responsibility entail social freedom and responsibility:
"the duty to lift other men."[52]

In the context of his government's brutal suppression of insurrection in
the Philippines, Wilson's statements evince willful ignorance rather than
cosmopolitan foresight. Even so, the *philosophy* of world politics he developed in the decade after 1898 was, in its essentials, genuinely cosmopolitan.
As he argued in 1907, technology, enterprise, and cultural exchange made
splendid isolation impossible. "Peace itself becomes a matter of conference
and international combination," he wrote. "Cooperation is the law of all action in the modern world."[53] That philosophy would ultimately be embodied
in the League of Nations Covenant. First, however, it would be sorely tried—
and extensively refined—through painful efforts to put it into practice.

Wilson's unique vision for the world and his nation's role in it made him an
anomaly among presidents, but not a freak. Like all presidents, he hoped to

further American economic interests abroad. He saw no reason why such interests could not also benefit the nations in which Americans did business—as long as Americans were willing to do business on equal terms. "All trade is two-sided," he told the Commercial Club of Omaha late in the 1912 campaign, and both sides must benefit. Confident in the returns of such "two-sided" trade, the administration made improved and expanded economic relations a priority.[54]

Yet economics were never paramount for Wilson. Invariably he viewed world politics through his pragmatist-progressive domestic lens. Unsurprisingly, his few statements on foreign affairs as a presidential candidate echoed his domestic rhetoric of broad development over narrow profit. Every democratic government's duty is "to develop a whole people," he wrote on the eve of the election, keeping them "free and alert and unhampered" while framing policies of "common use and purpose." For powerful democracies such as the United States, this duty was expanded. Americans must "think of the progress of mankind rather than the progress of this or that investment, of the protection of American honor and the advancement of American ideals rather than always of American contracts, and lift our diplomacy to the levels of what the best minds have planned for mankind." Wilson hinted at the nature of those plans after his election, telling an audience of seminarians that "service of humanity" was not only "the best business of mankind," but was best directed *by* mankind—or rather, "by governments which mankind sets up."[55] In sum, Wilson believed that American diplomacy ought to be every bit as democratic as American domestic policy, and work just as hard to expand its scope.

Among the non-European challenges of Wilson's first term, those in East Asia were most easily converted into opportunities for pragmatist statesmanship.[56] The new Republic of China, established on fragile foundations in early 1912, presented the first. Following his inauguration, Wilson withdrew support for an international loan consortium that US bankers had joined at Taft's behest—the latest effort to maintain an "open door" for US economic interests in China. In Wilson's view, a government commitment to press for repayment of American loans was certain, at some point, to elicit demands for "forcible interference" in a nation "just now awakening to a consciousness of its power and of its obligations to its people." Unfortunately, his blow for Chinese independence was awkwardly struck: the weakening of US influence over Chinese economic policy increased the relative power of less scrupulous foreign governments.[57] Nevertheless, Wilson's stand enjoyed the support of his cabinet and a wide swath of American opinion. Prominent Chinese also hailed Wilson's action, which some thought not wholly fruitless. Future Chinese president Li Yuan-hung would credit Wilson with "delivering China from domination by a hard and fast combination of capital."[58]

Thus Wilson rejected the economic coercion that had long enabled Western powers to dictate to China's rulers. In that spirit of common counsel, his government also became the first in the West to recognize the Chinese republic. Wilson tried to rally other Western governments to his cause beforehand, hoping to avoid roiling the bad blood created by his unilateral withdrawal from the loan consortium. After a month of futile entreaties, however, he recognized the Republic of China on May 2, 1913. American pundits praised Wilson's decision on practical and ethical grounds, as a means to recoup the influence lost by withdrawal from the consortium and a warning to Britain, Russia, and Japan that China was not a vast, international scrimmage field. The Chinese response was overwhelmingly positive, and overall Wilson's early diplomacy in China created a lasting reserve of goodwill. As President Li observed in December 1916, looking forward to a second Wilson term in the White House, "whenever agreements concerning China were made, the American Government had taken steps to safeguard the rights of China and the principle of equal opportunity."[59]

In the Philippines Wilson saw and grasped another opportunity to translate pragmatist political ethics into foreign policy practice. As late as 1911 Wilson had reiterated that the Filipinos were not yet "prepared for independence" but should "*be* prepared for independence by a steadily increasing measure of self government." Early in his presidency he sent an old Princeton colleague, Henry Jones Ford, on a fact-finding mission to test that assessment. A few weeks later he received a memorandum from Secretary of War Lindley M. Garrison recommending a sharp advance toward autonomy. Under Garrison's plan, the US governor-general would conform all administrative decisions to the will of the Philippine legislature; replace Americans in the appointive upper chamber with Filipinos; and take Filipino counsel in all matters affecting the islands, including preparations for independence. Garrison's memorandum was prompted by Felix Frankfurter, who had remained with Henry Stimson in the War Department after Wilson's election. Now, via Garrison, he urged Wilson to apply the pragmatist-progressive logic of the New Freedom to the Filipinos, who faced dangers similar to those facing average Americans—and from the same source. "In the name of self-government," Frankfurter declared, "we cannot allow government to fall into the hands of a small, masterful, highly-educated, wealth[y] minority, who have on the whole, but little community of interest and little sympathy with the great masses."[60]

In the Frankfurter-Garrison plan Wilson recognized the force of two entwined arguments that he himself had been making for twenty-five years: first, the input of the governed is crucial to the integrity of government; and second, only self-governing people can foster self-governing institutions. In August, Wilson appointed former New York congressman and Philippine independence advocate Francis Burton Harrison as governor-general, eliciting the ringing endorsement of the islands' delegate to Congress, Manuel Quezon.[61] In October, after Ford submitted a report echoing Frankfurter's analysis, Wilson announced the appointment of a native majority to the upper chamber of the Philippine legislature. The elective lower chamber promptly resolved that "happily the experiments of Imperialism have come to an end."[62]

That judgment was premature. It was not until August 1916 that Congress finally passed the Philippine Autonomy Act, and this act provided only that independence be granted once stable political institutions were in place. Delayed by American intervention in Europe, the indifference of Wilson's Republican successors, and Japanese occupation during the Second World War, full independence arrived only in 1946.[63]

Nonetheless, the United States' Philippine experiment in imperialist foreign policy had entered its long unwinding phase—a change encouraged by Wilson's effort to see Filipinos as they might see themselves. Not once did the islands' racial makeup give Wilson pause. To the contrary, Wilson recognized the blindness of a course in which one people determined when another could make its own decisions. As Ford reported before the Frankfurter-Garrison plan was implemented, the preponderant influence of Americans in Philippine officialdom meant that fitness for self-government was measured by "adherence to American political traditions in a country where they have no historical basis and are incompatible with social conditions." Wilson's decision to put all affairs short of independence more firmly under native control was taken to resolve this contradiction. He did not promise immediate independence; that decision rested with Congress. But he did promise to make Filipinos genuine partners in the process. "Every step we take," Wilson wrote in Harrison's official introduction to the Filipino people, "will be taken with a view to the ultimate independence of the Islands and as a preparation for that independence. After each step taken experience will guide us to the next." Over the next several years, "experience" as Wilson interpreted it pointed clearly toward self-government: among his final statements as president was a forceful (though unheeded) call for Congress to grant Filipinos the independence "they so honorably covet."[64]

While enjoying success in China and the Philippines, Wilson fumbled the thorniest problem of his prewar Asian diplomacy: Japan. Relations with Japan were bedeviled by grievous discrimination in the United States against Asians generally and Japanese specifically. When Wilson took office, Japanese officials were particularly incensed by a California bill, endorsed by Governor Hiram Johnson, to prohibit Japanese and other "Orientals" from owning land in the state—a sop to white tradesmen, shop owners, and farmers threatened by the competition. The Japanese government protested, and the bill became a major diplomatic irritant.

Compared to his Chinese and Philippine policies, Wilson's response to the Japanese protests was politically and ethically lame. Publicly he ducked the issue, claiming "no right" to interfere with "the undoubted constitutional powers of the State of California." Though willing "to seek counsel out there" and "give intimations" of what he considered just, to speak strongly against the California bill would imply a "promise" to Japan that he could not deliver.[65] In private Wilson was even more deferential to California's supposed "sovereign" right to make or destroy national foreign policy. Conscious of the state's electoral significance, he politely asked its legislators to soften the bill's language and contrive a subtler mechanism for excluding Japanese land ownership.[66] Instead, leaders in Johnson's Progressive Party and among the state's Democrats pressed for versions singling out the Japanese in humiliating fashion. Briefly finding his mettle, Wilson urged the governor and citizens of California not to "embarrass" the United States by impairing its treaty obligations and besmirching its "honor and good faith." But beyond such moral suasion Wilson refused to go. Though worried about relations with Japan, he feared that concerted opposition to the California bill would surrender huge "political capital" to the state's Progressive Party.[67]

The Californians rewarded his indulgence with a strongly exclusionary bill passed on May 9, 1913. It elicited an immediate formal protest from Japan, where public anger reached such a pitch that the US Navy brass feared a surprise invasion of the Philippines. On May 14, the Joint Board of the Army and Navy requested authority to transfer three gunboats to the archipelago. This was too much for Wilson. He finally took a measure of control and quashed the Joint Board's proposal. Bryan issued a series of notes assuring the Japanese that his government was eager to negotiate a friendly resolution. Public rancor soon subsided in both countries. Still, from the Japanese perspective no remotely satisfactory resolution of the California land-ownership issue was ever reached.[68]

Perhaps Wilson justified his refusal to coerce the State of California and his efforts to compromise with its leaders in terms of his "common counsel" code. If so, he was fooling himself. His deference to one state's racial politics smacked of a parochial indifference not only to Japanese sensitivities but also to the larger international community to which he claimed all Americans bore responsibility. Indeed, as the *Outlook* argued, Wilson had failed even the narrower test of nationalism, rightly conceived. "Who may come to America, who may settle in America, who may become citizens of America, who may enter into the trade and commerce and life of America, are questions to be settled for America by America, not by the people of any one State for the Nation."[69] In later years Wilson came to see petty assertions of sovereignty and disregard for the general welfare as among the deadliest threats to peace and prosperity, and he would battle his own countrymen to establish bulwarks against their destructive effects. In these early months, however, the best that can be said for Wilson's dealings with Japan is that he refused to consider fear and rumor cause for war. The worst is that he lacked what James called the "lonely courage" to defend more fiercely the equality of persons against avowed democrats who violated that ideal.

Despite falling short in Japan, Wilson's early Asian policy generally aimed and mostly served to nurture democracy in various indigenous forms. His Latin American policy was similarly motivated but often disastrously prosecuted, wreaking destruction both physical and diplomatic. Nevertheless, it was the failure of his unilateral efforts to promote democracy in Latin America that first pushed Wilson to conceive, in practical terms, a whole new structure for the regulation of international society that would not only promote democracy but also embody its principles.

For many Latin Americans, of various political persuasions, the prospect of a Wilson presidency was initially a hopeful one. After his election, *El Diario* of Mexico City bade farewell to the chauvinism of past administrations and heralded the arrival of a true statesman, determined "to convert his presidential armchair into a throne of justice." Rival *El Pais* opined that while time alone would tell whether Wilson's election was good for Mexico, his critical mind, personal virtues, and campaign statements condemning the Yankee chauvinism of years past boded well.[70]

At the start of his presidency Wilson seemed poised to fulfill those hopes. In his first foreign policy address as president, he declared that the United States must stop treating its sister republics as political subordinates and economic raiding grounds. It must reject paternal domination for fraternal cooperation in protecting freedom and independence for all American peoples and governments. Declaring "that just government rests always upon the consent of the governed, and that there can be no freedom without order based upon law and upon the public conscience and approval," Wilson pledged "to make these principles the basis of mutual intercourse, respect, and helpfulness between our sister republics and ourselves."[71]

A noble goal. But the converse of Wilson's principle was unnerving. Given the hemisphere's interdependence, "disorder, personal intrigue and defiance of constitutional rights" in one place threatened the "common life and common affairs" of all—a principle implying its own guidelines for action. As "friends of peace," the people of the United States would *prefer* those who act in the interest of peace and honor, who protect private rights and respect the restraints of constitutional provisions."[72] This logic of preference would soon be tested, most severely in Mexico, the Dominican Republic, and Haiti. The logic failed, and in the process revealed the dangers of an internationalist vision obstructed by prejudice.

Some of the administration's early forays into Latin American affairs were benign, even fruitful—including several small but significant successes racked up by Secretary of State William Jennings Bryan. Bryan's Christian pacifism inspired him to negotiate a series of so-called cooling-off treaties between the United States and thirty other countries, the majority Latin American, committing signatories to submit disputes to nonbinding arbitration before commencing hostilities—a time out, as it were, "during which passion could subside."[73] Often derided as utopian flummery by historians, Bryan's initiative garnered international praise. Eventually twenty-one treaties were ratified, helping legitimize the still radical notion that wars of aggression threatened the interests of the entire international community, including the aggressor—a principle later enshrined in the League of Nations, Pact of Paris, and United Nations.[74]

Unfortunately, Bryan's other efforts to build regional trust fell flat. In fact, it was often those very efforts that perpetuated the view of *Yanquis* (Yankees, denoting the people of the United States generally) as callous imperialists. Take for example Nicaragua, where in June 1913 the destitute and despised regime of Adolfo Díaz proposed a treaty tying its survival to US interests. Drafted by an American lawyer (and friend of Bryan's) retained by Díaz, the proposed treaty barred Nicaragua's government from declaring war, granting territorial concessions, or contracting large debts without US approval. It also asserted the right and duty of the United States to intervene in case of domestic turmoil, permitted US building of a naval base at Fonseca Bay, and guaranteed a US option (in exchange for three million

US dollars) to construct and control any interoceanic canal carved through Nicaraguan territory.[75]

Bryan grasped Díaz's selfish motives. Still, he saw the treaty as a means to draw down US forces previously deployed (at Díaz's request) by Taft, while allowing his government to moderate a regime otherwise destined for violent overthrow or European capture. Wilson, giving little attention and even less thought to the matter, gave Bryan permission to pursue it with the Senate.[76] Absent a community of trust and cooperation, however, the Bryan-Chamorro Treaty signed in August 1914 appeared to regional observers as just another deal between the United States and a reactionary puppet—even after the Senate Foreign Relations Committee deleted the most offensive provisions. Wilson, by this point thoroughly distracted by events in Mexico and Europe and happy to see the treaty's most brazenly interventionist bits removed, publicly urged ratification to get it off the Senate docket, and the Democratic majority obliged.[77]

Wilson now headed a government with an official financial stake in Nicaragua, presaging decades of meddling in that country's affairs.[78] More important, Bryan's commitment to stability in Nicaragua set a larger pattern in US-Caribbean relations. Wilson had pledged to protect and serve all American peoples, but his administration had established no new instruments for shaping events. The Dominican Republic and Haiti soon joined Nicaragua on the US State Department's list of "trouble" nations whose citizens' safety and liberties needed preserving. But as in the past, financial and military pressures were the only tools available. And as in the past, their use by a single dominant power allowed misjudgments and created resentments that the "common counsel" of multiple nations might have avoided.

Conditions in the Dominican Republic worried Bryan from his first days in office. In 1905, Roosevelt had established an American receivership of the Dominican customs to prevent bankruptcy and preempt European intervention. Stability prevailed until 1911, when the assassination of President Ramón Cáceres led to civil war and the subsequent installation—by the US State Department—of a neutral government in 1912. A year later, when a member of the powerful *Horacista* faction (named for its top man, General Horacio Vásquez) was elected president by the Dominican Congress, provisional president José Bordas Valdés refused to step down. By the time Bryan took office, civil war loomed.

In September 1913, Bryan informed the *Horacistas* that the United States would withhold recognition and customs from any government established by force. At first the *Horacistas* seemed to comply. But Bordas's regime weakened, prompting *Horacistas* and other malcontents to form a powerful new coalition, the *Legalistas*, bent on overthrowing it. The State Department, determined to see Dominican troubles settled by free and fair elections, had propped up an unpopular president just long enough to see every alternative but revolution evaporate. Or every alternative except one: direct interference. In late July 1914, Wilson stepped in, drafting what came to be called the "Wilson Plan." He informed the various factions that his government demanded an immediate cease-fire, free elections under American supervision, and cessation of "revolutionary movements." Cooperation, if withheld, would be compelled by force.[79]

Initial results were promising. The threat of intervention elicited Bordas's resignation, the *Legalistas'* agreement on an interim president to oversee elections, and the subsequent installation of General Juan Isidoro Jiménez on December 5, 1914.[80] That, however, was the extent of the Wilson Plan's success. Bryan undermined the fragile peace by pressuring Jiménez to entrust state finances and public works to US experts and officials. Jiménez's efforts to oblige caused a popular backlash leaving him entirely dependent on the US State Department. Bryan's successor, Robert Lansing, deemed the Dominicans incapable of governing themselves and in September 1915 communicated a demand that the republic become a US protectorate in all but name. Jiménez objected, and when the clouds of revolution broke again in May 1916, Lansing urged intervention. Wilson complied. Despite their failures, the US State Department and Navy remained his only guides through a situation he had largely ignored aside from his rash threat of force should it deteriorate. Eventually they convinced him that conditions had in fact deteriorated, to such a degree that US military government was the only means of rebuilding the country and preventing a humiliating failure of US policy. Wilson, expressing deep reluctance, agreed, and US Navy Captain Harry S. Knapp decreed martial law on November 29. It would be a lengthier occupation than Wilson ever imagined: US forces were not withdrawn until 1924.[81]

The precedent set in the Dominican Republic proved all too easy to follow in neighboring Haiti, which attracted American attention later but intervention sooner. In the first half of 1914, as Haiti's traditional cycle of revolutions intensified, Bryan grew concerned for its people's lives and freedoms as well as suspicious of French and German designs on the strategic port of Môle-Saint-Nicolas. As he cast about for means to stabilize the country's politics and finances, Americans connected to both the State Department and the National Bank of Haiti suggested a customs receivership on the Dominican model. Wilson approved a plan for Haitian consideration just as President Oreste Zamor's government collapsed. When Zamor's successor Davilmar Théodore broached the idea, the public backlash fueled yet another rebellion. By March 1915 Théodore's former ally, Vilbrun Guillaume Sam, had taken up residence in the presidential palace.[82]

Along with complicating diplomatic relations, the continuous and rapid change of regimes at Port-au-Prince reinforced assumptions about the Haitians' political immaturity on the part of US State Department officials and the president. Still, Wilson was caught off guard when on July 27 and 28, 1915, a truly gruesome orgy of violence erupted, culminating in the dismemberment of President Sam's body and the distribution of its pieces to a cheering crowd. Rear Admiral William B. Caperton landed a contingent of marines in Port-au-Prince to restore order and protect foreigners. After some hesitation, Lansing, now secretary of state, bowed to pressure from his subordinates and urged a full-scale occupation allowing US administrators to establish a working constitutional government and long-term stewardship of Haiti's finances.[83]

Any competent student of American history would have expected such advice from one quarter or another. Anticipating such pressure on the president, Du Bois wrote to the White House urging creation of a bipartisan, biracial commission to "co-operate with a Commission of Haytians" in planning "the establishment of peace and order." Such a "high-minded move" would bolster "the moral hegemony of the United States" in hemispheric affairs while combating its "reputation for studied unfairness toward black folk." Certainly "the only independent Negro government in the World" deserved friendship, not wardship.[84]

Wilson reasoned otherwise. Troubled by the fact that "we have not the legal authority to do what we apparently ought to do," he was equally alarmed at the prospect of renewed chaos were American forces to withdraw prematurely. Fatefully, as famine loomed over Port-au-Prince, he concluded on August 4, 1915, that there was "nothing for it but to take the bull by the horns and restore order." Within a week he had instructed Caperton to oversee the "election" of a handpicked president. Just five weeks after that, on September 16, the new government signed a treaty giving the United States control over Haiti's finances, its constabulary, the reorganization of its government, and its foreign relations. The alternative, Caperton informed the Haitians, was US military rule. Yet despite their cooperation, the Haitians would endure a longer, more extensive, more brutal occupation than their Dominican neighbors. Haitians did not regain full sovereignty for their nation until 1934, after nearly two decades of harassment and oppression by US forces rife with racism.[85]

What Du Bois condemned as "the outrage of uninvited American intervention" in Haiti is the most obvious and scarring failure of Wilson's vision for a pragmatist diplomacy of common counsel.[86] His ideal of a hemispheric community implied each member's assumption of a basic responsibility for the welfare of others. Unfortunately, he shut his eyes to the fact that the absence of multilateral institutions or authority deprived his government's efforts of critical legitimacy and salutary scrutiny. In Haiti, as throughout the Caribbean, Wilson was not even directing those efforts, leaving them to the State Department until crises resulted. Oblivious to the Haitian people's vigorous participation in their nation's tumultuous politics, Wilson promptly assumed that they were helpless victims of tyrants and cabals and that in time they would welcome their nation's liberation and political modernization. He never spoke of Haiti's subordination to the United States as a function of race, instead referring repeatedly to Haiti as a "small republic" with potential to develop all the capacities the term implied.[87] Yet he imposed an alien authority on its people and, pushing them from his mind, left them suffering under its yoke. It is hard to imagine him treating a similarly chaotic but largely white republic with the same combination of chauvinism and lack of interest. In sum, Wilson's record in Haiti was one of gross negligence and ignorance. Sadly, it was not the only time he stumbled blindly into a situation that contradicted his ideals and left him, apparently, with no way out.

For a time Wilson's Mexican policy seemed destined for the same outcome.[88] In 1911 the thirty-five-year dictatorship of Porfirio Díaz had collapsed, a casualty of agrarian and urban middle-class resentment toward the land magnates, corporate tycoons, army officers, and clerics who had brokered the country's vassalage to foreign creditors. This resentment had united an array of reformist and radical elements under Francisco I. Madero, who succeeded Díaz in mid-1911; but with Díaz gone, the coalition splintered. In February 1913, agents of foreign interests (with, it was later revealed, the blessing of US Ambassador Henry Lane Wilson) backed a military coup led by General Victoriano Huerta, aimed at reestablishing the status quo ante. Despite reports of Madero's summary execution, Huerta's regime was recognized by the major European powers and Japan. No sooner had he declared himself "provisional" president than he was faced with an armed rebellion of loyal *Maderistas*, now calling themselves "Constitutionalists," pressing the original cause.

Wilson could not have ignored Mexico had he wanted to. A populous nation sharing a two thousand-mile border with the United States, its troubles threatened US citizens in border states and in Mexico itself. Wilson's own daughter Eleanor was briefly "lost" amid the chaos in Mexico while vacationing there in 1910. Indeed, Mexico was home to thousands of American expatriates and millions of dollars of American assets. It was also the destination of around $30 million of US exports annually, a number that would more than triple in the next five years to more than $100 million, or roughly $1.6 billion in 2015 dollars.[89]

Yet Wilson weighed American economic interests in Mexico lightly compared to freedom for its people and security for its neighbors. He refused to recognize Huerta's "government of butchers," heedless of Ambassador Wilson's insistence that cooperation was crucial to safeguarding American assets. "Cooperation" with governments founded on "arbitrary or irregular force," the president affirmed, was impossible. State Department veterans disagreed, noting that the United States had always recognized governments "as existing or not existing" rather than legitimate or illegitimate. But President Wilson had the support of most of his cabinet, who agreed that they should not encourage regional instability—and facilitate European coercion of cash-hungry dictators—by "winking at revolution."[90]

The subsequent barrage of protests from Ambassador Wilson and State Department lawyers was mere nudging compared to the pressure from American businessmen, landholders, and investors demanding a "strong policy" toward Mexico. Meanwhile the Hearst galaxy of papers provided a forum for the voluble band of Americans convinced that only military intervention could prevent Mexico's deadly free-for-all from spilling into the backyard of the United States. Simmering since the revolution's outbreak, such heated rhetoric was dangerous nonsense to President Wilson, who would countenance neither recognition nor preemptive war.[91]

Liberal and progressive organs applauded Wilson's stand. Villard's *Nation* praised his restraint, dubbing him "the mouthpiece of civilization" in Mexican matters. *La Follette's Weekly* likewise lauded Wilson's refusal to let "Wall Street bankers" and "sordid commercialism" dictate diplomacy. But if Wilson's disdain for Americans seeking profit over justice in Mexico was obvious, his attitude toward the Mexicans themselves was more ambiguous. Repulsed by Huerta's brutal methods and reactionary politics, Wilson the Burkean remained wary of the Constitutionalists' plan for immediate and wholesale redistribution of land. Despite his critics' assumptions, he was also deeply worried by the ever-present threat of violence crossing the border, and could not dismiss the possibility of intervention to prevent loss of life in the United States. Still, he tended to assume, in a pragmatist-progressive vein, that the question of which party received his government's recognition would be determined in Mexico, by Mexicans. "We don't decide that," he answered a reporter's query as to whom or what he regarded as the Mexican government. "That is decided between brawls!" Americans could only wait, and watch for signs that the Mexicans had begun finally "to constitute a constitutional government."[92]

Unfortunately for US–Mexican relations, Wilson found "watchful waiting" (as his policy became known) easier said than done. During the spring of 1913 his thoughts rarely strayed from the trouble to the south. He soon concluded that despite its economic dimensions, the Mexican crisis was fundamentally political, as were the dangers it posed. Accordingly, he set his mind on a political settlement. In mid-May he informed Huerta of his strong desire for a "constitutional settlement of affairs in Mexico by means of a popular election," kindly offering to "assist in the process." That summer, though reiterating his commitment to open-minded, "diligent inquiry," he ramped up pressure, certain that success would benefit Mexicans, Americans, and the region.[93] Via special emissary John Lind, the president informed both Huerta and his Constitutionalist rival, General Venustiano Carranza, that it was time to grow up. The United States, read his instructions to Lind, could not "stand inactively by" as the prospect of stable popular government in Mexico continued to recede. In the interest of Mexican "sovereignty and independence" as well as "the maintenance of tolerable political and economic conditions in Central America," a settlement was imperative—and US "counsel and assistance" were available to facilitate it. The conditions of settlement included a "definite armistice"; a "free election" in which Huerta disavowed candidacy and all parties agreed to participate; and a promise from both *Huertistas* and *Carrancistas* to respect the results and "cooperate" in building a new government. Wilson's own government was not only eager to assist in each phase but could "conceive of no reasons" to justify declining its "offices of friendship." Carranza protested the total redaction of Mexico's economic problems from Wilson's blueprint. Huerta rejected its "humiliating" terms out of hand.[94]

Wilson's first gambit for a constitutional settlement in Mexico induced anger and suspicion that colored his future actions in the eyes of all parties. This result was doubly unfortunate, for against all appearances, Wilson knew that his administration could not dictate Mexico's fate. However committed to "enlargement of the field of self-government," he told Congress, the United States must "exercise the self-restraint of a really great

nation" and allow "the people of Mexico to set their affairs in order again."
Certain that "the consent of mankind" endorsed such "forbearance," he
predicted that "moral force will before many days break the barriers of pride
and prejudice down, and we shall triumph as Mexico's friends sooner than
we could triumph as her enemies."[95]

Here was Wilson at his best and worst. As observers noted, the president
had shown willingness to cooperate in solving a neighbor's troubles and,
rebuffed, resisted pressure to coerce it.[96] Moreover, events soon suggested
that Lind's ostensible failure might prove a sleeper success. Huerta scheduled elections for October, committed himself to a constitutional transfer
of power, and endorsed foreign minister Federico Gamboa for president,
pledging not to stand himself. American opinion swung heavily to Wilson
as September seemed to herald the springtime of Mexican–American relations. To Ellen he allowed that "moral pressure has, after all, proved pretty
powerful," and he dared look forward to "a new era in the Latin American states."[97] But this rosy view was riddled with blind spots. Declining to
impose a government on another country was hardly an act of "patience
and forbearance." Wilson's assumption that "the consent of mankind" was
behind him conveniently ignored the large portion of Mexican humanity
that resented his meddling. And to suggest that "the barriers of pride and
prejudice" impeding happy relations were all on the south side of the border
revealed an utter failure to comprehend or empathize with his Mexican
interlocutors.

This failure proved tragic after the autumn honeymoon with Huerta
ended. In late September Huerta moved to cement his position by capital-
izing on the intransigence of Carranza's Constitutionalists, who refused to
support elections unless all sides pledged economic reforms—an arrangement requiring long negotiations through neutral intermediaries under
conditions of armistice. Refusing an armistice and rejecting foreign meddling, Huerta arrested 110 dissenters in the Chamber of Deputies. Cancel-
ing the October elections, he made himself dictator in all but name. In turn
the *Carranzistas* declared their intention to secure land reform first and
free elections second—which they would run without American assistance,
gracias.

Frustrated by the Constitutionalists' deferral of constitutionalism, Wilson finally began to grasp their logic. Never totally blind to the economic
roots of Mexico's troubles, he began to recognize just how damaging the legacy of economic imperialism in Latin America had been—and how deeply
the United States was implicated. In a note to governments worldwide he
wrote that the arrests in the Mexican Chamber of Deputies revealed the

slim popular basis of Huerta's power and its near total reliance on owners of "foreign capital"—among whom he pointedly included Americans. Days later, in Mobile, Alabama, he gave the most important address on foreign affairs of his presidency to that point, articulating what pundits soon called "the New Monroism." Admitting that Americans had not only failed to protect the hemisphere from economic predation but engaged in it themselves, he challenged his compatriots to assume toward Latin Americans the main obligation of pragmatist ethics: that of "comprehending their interest, whether it squares with our own interest or not." Such comprehension was the moral "soil" from which "human rights, national integrity, and opportunity" would spring, and its cultivation was crucial to external and internal relations alike. "We have seen material interests threaten constitutional freedom in the United States," Wilson reminded his listeners. "Therefore, we will now know how to sympathize with those in the rest of America who have to contend with such powers, not only from within their borders but from outside their borders also."[98]

The Mobile address was historic and recognized as such.[99] It reversed the proprietary implications of the Monroe Doctrine, redefining the US government's responsibility for regional affairs in terms of a larger, hemispheric interest in justice, freedom, and democratic processes that all American nations must cooperate in promoting. It also marked a major stage in Wilson's increasingly cogent critique of the world-political system generally and traditional US policy specifically, emphasizing the continuity of domestic and foreign affairs and the value of a pragmatist political ethic to navigating them.

The origins of this shift are traceable to the summer of 1913, when Wilson began seriously to consider formal Pan-American cooperation. Argentina and Chile set the tone, indicating readiness to withhold recognition from Huerta and thus lend legitimacy to Wilson's overall policy in the eyes of an excitable US public. Late in July, John Barrett of the Pan American Union urged Wilson to spearhead a more formal arrangement and thereby express his reinterpretation of the Monroe Doctrine in stronger form as a "Pan American Doctrine." Effectively, Barrett suggested a solution to the dilemma Wilson encountered throughout the Caribbean: a means to promote democracy democratically. Giving "a Pan American tone to mediation" would "strengthen Mexican confidence in your good intentions and gain the lasting sympathy of the rest of Latin America," he told Wilson. Diplomatic inquiries soon revealed that Argentina, Brazil, and Chile—the so-called ABC countries—were eager to participate in formal, multilateral mediation of the Mexican Civil War.[100]

Wilson's Mobile address, therefore, embodied not just his developing theory of global interdependence but also his emerging ideas about putting it in practice. In succeeding weeks and months, however, his theory grew muddled and his practice proved inept. Still leery of intervention in Mexico, he was also increasingly eager to see Huerta go. This cognitive dissonance was exacerbated by a rapid conversion to the Constitutionalist cause that, unfortunately, did not entail a complementary insight into the Constitutionalist mind. A stream of reports from Wilson's unofficial emissary William Bayard Hale conveyed Carranza's deep commitment to radical revolution and reinforced the economic analysis of Wilson's Mobile address. Other advisers had meanwhile grown convinced of Carranza's ultimate military triumph.[101] Wilson might be forgiven the assumption that the "First Chief" would welcome direct American efforts to accelerate his victory—except that Carranza repeatedly stated otherwise. He was quite clear in mid-November 1913, after Wilson proposed a harebrained scheme to "declare war" without "armed entrance"—thus legally justifying a naval blockade of *Huertista* ports, assuring Constitutionalist victory, and paving the way for free elections. Carranza responded that the United States should scrap any plans to export troops or advice to Mexico, and simply recognize the Constitutionalists' belligerency in order to legalize the sale of arms to them. Wilson could not squeeze Mexico into a neat constitutional framework, and US troops deployed under that or any other pretense could expect no welcome but the whizz of bullets.[102]

For a time it seemed Wilson got the message. On February 3, 1914, he lifted the arms embargo, informing the British Ambassador to Washington that Mexico's inequalities were far more entrenched than those of the United States and "radical revolution was the only cure."[103] Subsequent gains by Constitutionalist armies should have encouraged Wilson to let matters take their course. Unfortunately, their advance on the port city of Tampico foretold a crisis. A major oil hub, home to numerous American and European expatriates and huge sums of foreign capital, Tampico was jealously guarded by Huerta's forces. Nervous American residents called on Rear Admiral Henry T. Mayo, commander of the United States naval squadron assigned to the area, for protection. Hundreds of foreigners from surrounding towns soon sought refuge in Tampico, and tensions mounted between their American protectors and Huerta's soldiers. On April 9, a Mexican patrol arrested some American sailors, at gunpoint, for steering their whaleboat into a restricted zone. The local commander ordered their release and apologized to Admiral Mayo, but the latter demanded an official apology and a twenty-one-gun salute as penance for the "hostile act." Huerta refused, prompting Wilson to send every US battleship in the North Atlantic to the Tampico harbor behind a message cautioning against the "grave consequences" of further contempt.[104]

Wilson had ignored far more egregious affronts to American citizens, security, and honor. Not two months prior, a US citizen pasturing horses on a contested stretch of the Texas–Mexico border had been arrested by *Huertistas* and peremptorily hanged.[105] Why the president chose to elevate the kerfuffle at Tampico into a pretext for intervention is not entirely clear. His eagerness to inaugurate a new era of "emancipation" through close cooperation with democratic neighbors was surely part of it: Lind, Bryan, and Wilson's close personal adviser Edward M. House (known by the honorary nickname "the Colonel"), had for months encouraged him to press any opportunity to realize that vision. Strategic considerations also certainly factored: Unlike the anarchical border towns of Sonora, Chihuahua, and Coahuila states, Tampico was far from US territory and, along with nearby Veracruz, collected customs revenues that Huerta could ill afford to lose. More worryingly, a burgeoning power struggle between Carranza and the charismatic Francisco "Pancho" Villa raised the specter of metastasizing conflict, even should they manage to cooperate in toppling Huerta.[106] More than ever, American intervention seemed the straightest, quickest road to peace and freedom for ordinary Mexicans.

Still, Wilson had repeatedly been told that American power could not clear such a road. He himself told the British Ambassador that foreign intervention would unite "all the patriotism and all the energies" of the country against the invaders and any Mexicans who dared cooperate.[107] The dilemma of Wilson's new diplomacy was starkly revealed: Was it better to promote democracy within polities, demanding self-government for their citizens; or among them, respecting the equality and sovereignty of their governments? With no official deliberative body or cohesive community of nations to advise or endorse a course of action, Wilson was relegated to either promoting his democratic ideal through unilateral coercion or abandoning it entirely.

Thus Wilson had already planned to request congressional authorization to establish a blockade and seize the Tampico and Veracruz customs when he learned that the German steamer *Ypiranga* was bound for Veracruz, laden with arms for Huerta. To prevent their transfer, all forces that had mobilized for the original plan converged on Veracruz, disembarking on April 21. Facing unexpectedly heavy resistance from *Huertista* soldiers and local patriots, Admiral Frank Fletcher's troops went beyond seizing the arms and customs and moved to secure the city. By midday on April 22, a score of marines and at least six times that number of Mexicans were dead—and Huerta had ordered reinforcements.[108]

Politically, the Veracruz invasion was the most disastrous of all Wilson's actions in Latin America. Personally, it proved the greatest moral shock of Wilson's first term, and perhaps his presidency.

The invasion ignited the ire of the Mexican people, who burned American flags and mobbed US consulates in cities across the country. Similar riots broke out in Chile, Costa Rica, Ecuador, Guatemala, and Uruguay. The Latin American press exploded in anti-*Yanqui* editorials, castigating "the bellicose attitude of the grand republic of the north." In Europe the consensus was that Wilson was reaping the fool's harvest sown by withholding recognition from Huerta and swallowing the rhetoric of Carranza's faithless mercenaries.[109] At home, most of the nation's major papers expressed shock and grief over the hostilities but resolved to support the president and the American soldiers now in harm's way. The labor press and major liberal and progressive journals, however, were almost uniform in denouncing the president.[110] Indeed, Wilson's haphazard path to intervention united implacable congressional skeptics and potential philosophical allies in common bonds of consternation. In the Senate, Roosevelt allies Elihu Root and Henry Cabot Lodge joined Robert La Follette and William E. Borah in deriding the flimsy casus belli of Wilson's original force resolution, which the House had approved before Fletcher's impromptu sprint to Veracruz. Outside Congress, Du Bois intoned that the government's "blunder into murder and shame" was not "war" but "crime." Months later, his fellow pragmatists Herbert Croly and Walter Lippmann were still condemning the Veracruz invasion as a dark "comic-opera" encapsulating the absurdity and futility of Wilson's "Mexican problem": "Mr. Wilson has no Mexican policy, yet Mr. Wilson has interfered in Mexico."[111]

More than any political fallout, however, it was the guilt of sending Americans to kill and die that led Wilson to regret his course in Veracruz. Assuming a show of force would cow the *Huertistas*, Wilson had never really confronted the possibility of serious casualties. When that possibility materialized, it "seemed to affect him like an ailment," a friend recalled. "He was positively shaken."[112] The facts support this recollection. Despite pressure from Senate Republicans, border state interests, and his own secretary of war, Wilson prohibited expansion of the Veracruz campaign. Instead he accepted a joint offer from the ABC nations to mediate—not just between the Huerta and Carranza factions but between them and his own government. In negotiations in Niagara Falls, Ontario, Wilson still lobbied for a constitutional settlement. But he also shared Carranza's economic analysis of Mexico's ailments, and he finally understood that Mexicans must administer the cure. When the long-stalled negotiations adjourned on July 2, 1914, the United States agreed to recognize whatever government emerged from the civil war. Within two months, Huerta abdicated, Carranza's army occupied the capital, and the "First Chief"—husky, bearded, but with a professorial air recalling his Washington counterpart—was installed at the National Palace as president of the Provisional Government of Mexico.[113]

Wilson learned two lessons from the American misadventure in Veracruz. The first involved Mexico as a problem of international relations. He still believed that a mutuality of interest united the peoples of the Western Hemisphere and that the United States must work to ensure that "no one shall take advantage of Mexico" in its hour of distress. What changed was his appreciation of the nature and limits of such work in an anarchical society of states. He now saw that although political chaos might spread contagiously, stability and advancement were difficult to achieve without a community of states occupying some sort of level ground. It was not that Washington had nothing to teach or learn from Manila or Mexico City. But without a roughly symmetrical forum for discussion, Washington's teaching would always be at risk of becoming mere dictation, and its learning might not happen at all. For these reasons, in the second half of 1914 Wilson would renew his push for a Pan-American system that could not just organize and equalize hemispheric relations but also model such cooperation for the world at large.[114]

Profound though it was, the extent of this change in Wilson's thinking should not be exaggerated. He remained convinced that in some cases, as during the American Civil War, otherwise lamentable actions were justified if taken to halt or prevent larger evils. But the need for such painful compromises, he now emphasized, would diminish drastically once "tasks of peace are performed in a similar spirit of self-sacrifice."[115] Though Wilson did not know it, that statement reverberated with echoes of James's Shaw Oration, and in coming years Wilson would not forget that force is sometimes necessary to defend the deliberative processes that ultimately minimize its use. But nor would he forget that, for just that reason, commitment to cooperation is as vital as aversion to conflict in securing peace.

The second lesson involved the Mexican people as what James would call "psychological quantities." After Veracruz, Wilson finally realized that the Mexicans were not political children wanting a teacher. They had their own political thoughts, and mere dissimilarity from Wilson's did not render them valueless. "The principle that I am going on is that we ought studiously to seek to leave the settlement in their hands and that our only part is to see that they get a chance to make it," he told George Record during the ABC negotiations. After Huerta's abdication he went even further, telling Garrison that while "things may happen of which we do not approve," he could imagine "no conceivable circumstances which would make it right for us to direct by force or threat of force the internal processes of what is a profound revolution, a revolution as profound as that which occurred in France." A year later he was drawing analogies between Mexico's "failures" and his own nation's divisions and inequities. Both nations suffered from the depredations of an "educated, privileged, and propertied class, who are, as with us, owning and running everything, the reactionary class. Hence the wedge in our own domestic politics." Wilson's equation of a poor, largely nonwhite failed state with his own United States suggests a new capacity to empathize with a people he merely pitied before Veracruz. The resistance and resentments elicited by his interference in Mexico's affairs opened his eyes not only to the concrete reality and complex humanity of its inhabitants but also to the fact that self-government, whether in Mexico or the United States, must often precede self-mastery.[116]

That revelation informed Wilson's effort to create an international deliberative forum through which the international community—despite its members' demonstrated incapacity to master their worst inclinations—could learn to govern itself. In the meantime, no such deliberative forum existed. The United States still had its parochial interests, developed in that deliberative vacuum, and no structure for negotiating them with neighbors whose troubles seemed chronic and potentially metastatic. As a result, Veracruz was not Wilson's last use of force in the region, as the Dominican and Haitian occupations attest. It was not even his last use of force in Mexico: in 1916 a series of border raids by bandits beyond Carranza's control would spark a crisis that again threatened war. But these incidents only confirmed, for Wilson, what he took to be the verdict of Veracruz. As Europe's powers decided and proceeded to destroy one another, that verdict became axiomatic to his theory of the collective life of nations: "Separated they are subject to all the cross currents of the confused politics of a world of hostile rivalries; united in spirit and purpose they cannot be disappointed of their peaceful destiny."[117]

CHAPTER FOUR

Trials of Neutrality

A large and motley brood of American pacifists, jingoes, isolationists, military expansionists, and unidentifiable mongrels was spawned by the outbreak of war across the Atlantic in 1914—a brood conceived and born in what seemed a single instant of horror at Europe's madness. "When news came to America of the opening of hostilities which were the beginning of the European Conflict," Jane Addams later recalled, "the reaction against war, as such, was almost instantaneous throughout the country." Though tensions had been brewing for years and the so-called July crisis boiling for weeks, Americans were astonished that "such an archaic institution"— war—"should be revived in modern Europe."[1]

Astonishment soon gave way to conviction, indignation, anxiety, or in some cases lassitude. The war was the impetus behind the Woman's Peace Party, founded by Addams and others to promote "organized opposition to militarism" in the United States. By contrast, the New York *World* declared annihilating "German autocracy" on the battlefield to be imperative, crucial to "the emancipation of the German people themselves as well as the salvation of European republicanism." Most German Americans thought differently. "You cannot separate the German Kaiser from the German people," asserted the New York *Staats-Zeitung*. The United States, the editor warned, ought to "avoid any permanent disarrangement of the friendly relations between the German and American people."[2] Some analysts, including Wilson's close adviser Edward M. House, thought it wise to mobilize a "reserve force," lest the war cross the ocean and catch a sleeping America unaware. Others saw the war as Europe's own tragic fate. In words he later put in Wilson's mouth, Theodore Roosevelt declared he was "not taking sides one way or the other" in Europe's "death wrestle." Roosevelt soon changed his tune, becoming the loudest advocate of a more "heroic" stance against Germany after the kaiser's army overran neutral Belgium. The clash of opinions on the US response to the war intensified over the following months and years, as the US government was drawn—through coercion, conscience, and national interest—into the conflict. Knowingly or not, Walter Hines Page, US Ambassador in London, anticipated both the diplomatic and domestic trials ahead when he wrote to Wilson, "Be ready; for you will be called upon to compose this huge quarrel."[3]

Still, for the first eighteen months of the conflict, the majority of Americans agreed that military intervention was inappropriate. Certainly, some leading figures believed that the threat of an organized military response, with US backing, would have prevented the German aggressions that most Americans considered the immediate cause of Europe's suffering. Harvard president and erstwhile Wilsonian A. Lawrence Lowell joined William Howard Taft and several other public figures in criticizing Wilson's response to the war's precipitating tensions and events. Constituting themselves a League to Enforce Peace (LEP), they demanded that future administrations adopt—and act on—the maxim that "violence must be met by force." Yet they remained leery of leaping into the war then raging. Their official platform, adopted in Philadelphia on June 17, 1915, asserted that the United States should join a "league of nations" pledged, in future, to compel member states to arbitrate disputes before resorting to hostilities. There was no call for intervention in the current war. Indeed Taft, the LEP's president, explicitly denied any intention to influence or even end the present conflict.[4] In Congress, too, most members in both parties supported neutrality, in harmony with prevailing public opinion. According to a contemporary analysis of the press, "there was but one opinion" of Wilson's neutrality policy in the war's first months: "approval." Even when violations of neutral rights by belligerents elicited calls for action, there was no "appreciable demand" to join the fighting. The Democrats, then, were canny in choosing the official slogan for Wilson's 1916 reelection bid: "He kept us out of war with honor."[5]

As his interventions in Mexico, Haiti, and the Dominican Republic attest, Wilson had repeatedly sent Americans into conflicts abroad, and he himself harbored doubts that he had brought honor to the nation in doing so. Wilson had, however, avoided full-blown war with Mexico and any military involvement at all in Europe's fratricidal orgy. This diplomatic poise, as much as his legislative success, won him his second term in the White House. Of course, many observers saw the two achievements as intertwined. Reform politicians, from Democratic Secretary of State William Jennings Bryan to Republican Senator Robert M. La Follette, saw war as a threat to the progressive state now under construction, the aim of which was to provide security, prosperity, and freedom rather than bring danger, privation, and conscription upon its citizens. As La Follette argued regarding intervention in Europe, it was "as brutal and irrational" for a nation "to draw the sword" as for any of its citizens "to 'pull a gun.' "[6]

Prominent pragmatists such as Jane Addams and Randolph Bourne also insisted that strict neutrality and mediation were the only rational, productive approaches to the European crisis. War, in their view, totally inverted their pragmatist ethic of deliberative discourse, empathetic reflection, and mutual concession—both among and within nations. As Addams recalled, it was war's "reversal of human relationships" that revolted her most: the substitution of "curbed intelligence" and "thwarted good will" for the "free mind and unfettered kindliness" through which individual and collective well-being were harmonized. Throughout the neutrality period, Randolph Bourne deemed the "preparednessers" calling for expanded defense capabilities "madmen." Like Addams, he believed joining or even readying for the conflict would not just sanction the militarism that sparked it but import it to the United States, squandering the moral authority and resources that might help the nation mediate peace. For Addams, Bourne, and other intellectual and spiritual heirs of William James, the pursuit of justice through war was inherently unpragmatic: destructive rather than creative; coercive rather than deliberative; antagonistic rather than cooperative.[7]

But there was no necessary reason to assume the congruence of neutrality and pacifism with pragmatism. Several of James's admirers, equally devoted to a more just and peaceful world, put neutrality and pacifism to the pragmatist test and found both wanting. W. E. B. Du Bois was one. Condemning all the belligerents as imperialists, Du Bois saw racist nationalism as more deeply embedded in Germany's foreign policy than in the policies of Britain and France. German victory, he warned in November 1914, would mean "the triumph of every force calculated to subordinate the darker peoples." He urged the US government to lend moral and material support to the Allies—and urged African Americans to lend *their* support to any such policy, as a step toward dismantling colonialism and a demonstration of their value to the American democratic project.[8]

Several of Du Bois's fellow pragmatists viewed the rank injustices and dangerous consequences of worldwide racism as symptoms of a deeper problem, affecting the whole structure of Western and global society. Herbert Croly, Walter Lippmann, and John Dewey thought the war signaled both the need and the opportunity to reconstruct *all* human relationships— including those among nations—on a social rather than self-regarding basis, and they insisted that the United States consider all possible means of bringing that revolution to pass. Croly, in fact, had been sounding an internationalist strain since 1909, when he linked the national to the global commonweal in *The Promise of American Life.* "The American nation," he wrote, "just in so far as it believes in its nationality and is ready to become more of a nation, must assume a more definite and a more responsible place in the international system." Croly's teacher James had believed that empathy and curiosity regarding the experiences of others enhance the universal freedom on which personal freedom depends, and James had promoted a more egalitarian society to foster those traits. Applying James's pragmatist political ethics to international society, Croly argued that the strength of Americans' commitment to a free and unified nation must be measured by their willingness to extend, beyond their borders, the organizational principles and humanitarian ideals that drove egalitarian reform at home. "The will to play that part for all it was worth," he declared, "would constitute a beneficial and a necessary stimulus to the better realization of the Promise of our domestic life."[9]

Certainly, peace was an element of that promise, one not to be sacrificed lightly. But as Croly explained later, when tensions with Germany were peaking in early 1917, peace—like all elements of a wholesome national life—depended on a hospitable "international community" to thrive. "The life of a nation would be just as much stunted and frustrated by arid or wholly predatory international surroundings as the life of an individual would be frustrated by arid or anarchical social surroundings."[10] By the time Croly wrote those words, he found himself among many pragmatists who concluded, ruefully, that Americans could either accept the dangers and deprivations of war on their own terms or wait for events to thrust those evils upon them. Two years of collateral damage and near escapes had convinced them that in an interdependent world, peace and prosperity must be widely shared among all nations, or it must be fleeting for even the strongest.

More than anything except the events of the Great War itself, this strain of pragmatist internationalism determined the course of Wilson's presidency, dovetailing with his domestic thinking, clarifying the lessons of his early diplomacy, and providing both a theoretical underpinning and an influential constituency to support his own burgeoning internationalism. The uncontainable nature of the war in Europe convinced Wilson it was time to toss the old diplomatic chestnuts into the fire. From the ashes he raked a philosophy of democracy as an ethical ideal extending beyond the domestic to the international sphere, requiring robust yet flexible institutions within and among nations through which to negotiate—and enforce—common codes of conduct. Wilson's program for achieving that ideal first took practical shape during debates over military preparedness and intervention, when Croly and Lippmann were brought directly into the administration's counsel. Important facets, however, began emerging earlier, as the *New Republic*'s criticisms of Wilson's neutrality policy and his own reflections on its virtues and failings slowly merged into a vague but common vision by the middle of 1916. That vision recognized force as a tool of order. Yet even through war's dense fog, it descried new political and moral implements with which nations, working in common fields, might sow and tend a common peace.

Despite the burdens of official correspondence, Wilson read a wide range of unofficial material through most of his presidency. He kept large files of articles and editorials clipped from his favorite papers or received from friends and aides, so that publications from across the country and the world contributed to his trove of ideas. Still, the *New Republic* has a special importance for the study of Wilson's internationalist thought. The journal populated the universe of liberal discourse with many of its most distinctive ideas during the Wilson years, and powerful figures in the administration, including the president, read its articles and other works by its staff. Over the first eighteen months of the *New Republic*'s existence, Wilson's thinking and that of its editors converged in striking ways, setting the stage for contacts between them that would directly shape policy from mid-1916 on. Most important, the *New Republic* editors were self-conscious pragmatists. Comparing their evolving thought to Wilson's is therefore crucial to understanding the policies he developed after they entered his circle—policies projecting his maturing pragmatist ethics on a global scale.

The *New Republic* was founded in 1914, by millionaires Dorothy and Willard Straight, to advance the "New Nationalist" agenda Croly proposed in *The Promise of American Life*.[11] With Croly at the helm, the journal soon became the nation's leading organ of progressive political analysis. Joining Croly on the editorial board were two other leading minds who shared his admiration for William James: Walter Weyl and Walter Lippmann. Both attracted Croly's attention through their talent for promoting pragmatist-progressive ideas much like his own. Weyl's "New Democracy" resembled Croly's new American nation: a political democracy that was "compromising in action" yet "uncompromising in principle," and a "socialized democracy which conceives of society as a whole and not as a more or less adventitious assemblage of myriads of individuals."[12] As for Lippmann, *Drift and Mastery* had made him an intellectual star that would lend a shine to any masthead. Lippmann's notion of "drift" could not but appeal to Croly, who had used the same word in *Promise* to describe the piecemeal reformism that served as foil to his comprehensive New Nationalism. Meanwhile, Lippmann's exhortations to develop "mastery" through conscious and cooperative experimentation in political life had channeled Croly's own most Jamesian instincts, in prose that would make a veteran editor's mouth water.

Unsurprisingly, a distinctly pragmatist sensibility infused the *New Republic* from issue one. "The New Republic is frankly an experiment," read its opening lines on November 7, 1914. It was an experiment along the lines Croly, Lippmann, and Weyl had laid out in their earlier works: driven by "faith" in the potency and resilience of "trained intelligence" when subjected "to ruthless criticism." Theirs was essentially a faith in the creative power of rigorous communal inquiry in the United States—in the potential of a self-governing people to exercise mastery over their affairs. But it was a faith not yet realized, as the nation's willingness to drift aimlessly along the edge of Europe's maelstrom made clear. "We in America are not immune to what some people imagine to be the diseases of Europe," wrote the editors. "We, too, have our place in the world. We have our obligations, our aggressions, our social chasms, our internal diseases. . . . We are committed to responsibilities we do not understand, we are the victims of interests and deceptive ideas, and nothing but our own clarified effort can protect us from the consequences. We, too, can blunder into horror."[13]

To avoid such blundering required a nonpartisan, pragmatist political philosophy the editors came to call "constructive American radicalism." Politics should be a science, with experiment its method, government its tool, and a more human and efficient society its object. It was a philosophy that attracted Randolph Bourne and Felix Frankfurter as unofficial staff writers—indeed, Frankfurter, newly appointed to the Harvard Law faculty, had been Croly's first choice as coeditor. But perhaps the greatest testament to the journal's pragmatist orientation was the almost immediate enlistment of John Dewey as a regular contributor. Although a coup for Croly, Dewey's association with the *New Republic* was unsurprising: His conviction that deliberative democracy was the logical political and moral manifestation of pragmatism was, if anything, stronger than his editor's and even clearer than his old friend James's. "If the pragmatic idea of truth has itself any pragmatic worth," he had written the year after James died, "it is because it stands for carrying the experimental notion of truth that reigns among the sciences, technically viewed, over into political and moral practices, humanly viewed."[14] Reaching such pragmatic truths, as Croly and company hoped to help Americans do, required a delicate balance of original thinking, reflective inquiry, and reasoned argumentation. Throughout the war years, therefore, the journal reiterated its mission to "preserve its independence, seek indefatigably for new light and try to communicate to others such light and faith as it has."[15]

Sparkling with such leading lights as Croly, Weyl, Lippmann, and Dewey, the *New Republic* became a powerful shaper of elite and administration opinion. Wilson had already encountered two explicit political adaptations of James's psychology that harmonized with the journal's pragmatist voice: Graham Wallas's *Human Nature and Politics* (1908) and Lippmann's own *Preface to Politics* (1913). Whether or not Wilson noticed these connections, he became an early and regular reader of the *New Republic*, finding its value increasing as his interest in the war deepened.[16] For their part, the journal's editors did not regard Wilson as the man to advance a pragmatist foreign policy until well into 1916, when he appeared to abandon what they deemed an impracticably evasive stance toward Europe. Nevertheless, from August 1914 onward, the spirit and vocabulary of philosophical pragmatism increasingly pervaded Wilson's public, private, and diplomatic communications, while his efforts to maintain both neutrality and national honor reveal a pattern of reflection, deliberation, and experimentation remarkably similar to that which Croly and company urged the world's statesmen to follow. Committed to fostering "common counsel" in international relations as well as domestic politics, Wilson sought to show the world that a nation could balance its principles and interests with charity toward the priorities, idiosyncrasies, and (to an extent) unpleasantries of its neighbors. With circumstances changing like mercury, he took more than a few pages from the pragmatists' manual to meet them.

Wilson first responded to the war by urging an attitude of "impartiality and fairness" on Americans. From the start, that appeal linked national interest to international responsibility. Heated divisions among American citizens, most of whom felt ties to the various peoples at war, would impede their nation's ability "to play a part of impartial mediation and speak the counsels of peace and accommodation." Although Wilson's "thought" was "for America," his America was a nation among nations, not apart from them. With most of Europe convulsed by war, his was also the nation "fit beyond others to exhibit the fine poise of undisturbed judgment, the dignity of self-control, the efficiency of dispassionate action" that a just and early settlement would require. In sum, it was a pragmatist nation, a kind which "neither sits in judgment upon others nor is disturbed in her own counsels" but "keeps herself fit and free to do what is honest and disinterested and truly serviceable for the peace of the world."[17]

From the war's beginning, then, Wilson promoted a distinctly active form of neutrality, designed to keep peace at home and foster it abroad. Theoretically, this was also the *New Republic*'s stance. The United States should remain "independent," the editors wrote, but not "in the sense of being isolated"; in the modern world, nations were inherently *inter*dependent. Americans should not attempt to control their destiny by avoiding the world's problems but by keeping "the relation between our democratic national ideal and our international obligations" in proper perspective. That perspective required not just detachment but also sympathy and humility. It required Americans to condemn global imperialism, European militarism, and German violations of neutrality without ascribing to any party, including themselves, a martyr's virtue or seer's vision. Finally, as one first-issue contributor wrote, it required a double attitude of caution and readiness; for though none could augur the ironies of history, "we can all be pardoned for believing we have some part to play in it."[18]

Wilson, too, knew the war was not reducible to "invasion," "encirclement," or similar populist precipitates swirling around Europe; that no one could predict its phases or transformations; and that Americans must recognize their own catalyzing potential in the conflict. It was thus in a pragmatist rather than passive spirit that Wilson urged Americans to remain "impartial in thought as well as in action."[19] That was a tough prescription to follow. The majority of Americans could say exactly which side was the right side; it simply depended on the American asked. In the nation's Irish American and German American communities ran deep hostility toward the Allies, reflecting Irish nationalist resentment of Britain and ethnic German attachments to the homeland. Moreover, a slew of prominent American progressives cited "German collectivism" (to use Bourne's phrase) as the stimulus of their efforts to socialize American democracy.[20] Others reminded Germanophiles that Britain's parliamentary government had survived the growth of empire, while German social democracy had been hijacked by "Prussian militarism." It was not the number of wars, declared Oswald Garrison Villard's *Nation* in early September, but the preparation and excitement for them that marked a nation as "militarist." It was no coincidence that Germany was "universally so classed."[21]

This perception of German hypermilitarism, and even archaic barbarism, drew the majority of Americans to the Allied cause—especially as telegraphs wired news of the German war machine's unparalleled destructiveness. There arose in the minds of Americans an image of Germany as acutely foreign in contrast to Britain (cousin in language and culture) and France (sister republic and midwife to independence). Many Americans referred to Germans as "Huns," the Turkic invaders of early medieval Europe. Sacking towns, ravaging swathes of French and Belgian countryside, impressing civilians into work camps; the Germans had placed themselves beyond the pale of the very civilization they helped build. This view occasioned much scoffing at Wilson's call for impartiality, and not just on moral grounds. Failure to "denounce such sordid and infamous cruelty," wrote one *Nation* correspondent, could only strike the Allies as "so unjust that any offer of our services as mediators would be rejected." Though admitting the folly of military intervention, the *New Republic* too warned of the wages of silence. Should a move toward settlement suddenly materialize, wrote the editors, the country would "be treated as we deserve to be treated, as a nation of well-meaning people who run no risks, and build their faith upon their simple and uncritical desires."[22]

Despite official silence, several members of Wilson's administration shared such concerns. Most were decidedly pro-Allied, with Secretary of State Bryan, a principled pacifist, the major exception. Most important, House worked assiduously, and often furtively, to further the Allied cause. House was for several years Wilson's closest adviser on foreign affairs: "my second personality," the president allegedly once described him, "reflecting my opinion by whatever action he takes." That assessment—which House, not Wilson, recorded—is so drastic a simplification of their relationship as to squeeze it nearly dry of truth. From the start of the war and through its settlement, House's goal was a new balance of power with an Anglo-American alliance as fulcrum—a stark contrast to Wilson's internationalist vision. In general, House's consistent endeavors to "reflect" Wilson's opinion—at least in conversation with the latter—cast more doubt than light on the extent to which he shaped it.[23] Still, House's stance and those of his colleagues were important, for they reinforced Wilson's own sympathies. Though he harbored no illusions about France's and Britain's roles in the war's deep causes, those nations represented, to him, the closest approximations of genuine self-government in Europe and a bulwark of democracy everywhere—including the United States. If Germany triumphed, he told the British ambassador, "we shall be forced to take such measures of defence here as would be fatal to our form of Government and American ideals." In sum, Wilson's was a measured rather than an amoral or apathetic response to the war—a war that his government, while he headed it, would not permit the Allies to lose.[24]

That did not mean they had to win it. To the contrary, Wilson's ideal outcome was an early draw. With effort, therefore, he suppressed his partiality to the land of Bagehot and Gladstone. Doing so was made easier by his frequently intense frustration with the Allies, and the British especially. Thanks to them, the Great War, while a great boon to American trade, was also a great hazard to neutrals sailing under what soon became a type of mar-itime martial law, imposed by a British government determined to starve the enemy of income and resources. In any case, Wilson was convinced that a conflict attaining such proportions was impossible to pin entirely on Germany or any single nation. It was the logical result of a diplomatic con-sensus deeming conflicts of national interest unavoidable and use of force to resolve them rational. As long as Europe's statesmen thought in such terms, Wilson concluded, the present conflict was intractable and "future calamities" inevitable.[25]

So he set to work changing minds. Given his impositions of will in Latin America, it is ironic but fitting that among his early strategies for reform-ing the Old World was to set an example in the New. Wilson had mulled the benefits of Pan-American cooperation since July 1913, and memoranda regarding an official Pan-American Pact crossed his desk that November. But it was not until House revived the idea in December 1914 that Wilson undertook his first effort at international organization. The Mexican situ-ation was (temporarily) resolved, thanks largely to the friendly offices of Argentina, Brazil, and Chile. Meanwhile, instability in other Latin Ameri-can states raised fears of Europe's chaos expanding across the Atlantic. Re-suming the pursuit of hemispheric unity thus seemed more possible and more necessary to regional security than previously, while a Pan-American union might also, as House put it, "play a great and beneficent part in the European tragedy" by providing "a model for the European Nations."[26]

House did not mention the *New Republic* in recording that discussion with Wilson, but he would have found strident support for his suggestion in its pages. Days before, the editors had opened their December 12 issue with an argument for just such an initiative. Clearly, they opined, in a chaotic international climate, the interest of Latin American states lay in forging ties with the United States. The traditional US policy of "protection," how-ever, must give way, not only to a new doctrine of "cooperation" (as Wil-son suggested at Mobile), but to "a larger measure of official Pan-American organization." This idea was hardly original. As recently as September, the industrialist and philanthropist Andrew Carnegie had written to Wilson on the topic. In late autumn 1914 House twice spoke in vague terms about the importance of "welding together" the hemisphere, cultivating "friendli-ness," and relinquishing "the big stick"; while in early December, Wilson made equally vague appeals for expanding commerce with trade-starved Latin America. But neither suggested any steps toward these ends, much less a formal organization to achieve them. Only after the *New Republic* endorsed a Pan-American Pact did House push Wilson in that direction.[27]

Whether through influence or coincidence, Croly and company were suddenly thinking in harmony with the administration. At House's suggestion, Wilson drafted two articles embodying the essentials of a hemispheric organization: one guaranteeing territorial integrity and "political independence under republican forms of government" for all members, the other mandating each to nationalize munitions in their jurisdictions. While House opened exploratory talks with the Argentine, Brazilian, and Chilean ambassadors, Wilson completed his draft Pan-American Treaty.[28] The first and third articles resembled the two he had typed out for House, but much else was new. The second and longest article established that all territorial disputes among aspiring signatories would be settled, before the pact's incorporation, by "final and conclusive" judgment of a cooperatively appointed tribunal. That primeval commitment to deliberative methods was the "condition precedent" to the treaty's territorial and political guarantees, lest they be interpreted as barriers to contestation and change. A fourth article extended this logic, pledging signatories to submit "all questions" to a "permanent international commission" for mediation and, should that fail, binding arbitration, providing the issue did "not affect the honour, independence, or vital interests" of the parties involved. The draft was sent to the ABC governments on February 1, 1915.[29]

Wilson's Pan-American plan has been aptly described as "a kind of mutualization of the Monroe Doctrine," an effort to institutionalize the principles of sympathy, solidarity, and cooperation he first articulated at Mobile in 1913.[30] His draft treaty also captured a democratic shift in emphasis since that time, from solicitude for his nation's long-oppressed neighbors to the "great advantage of intermixture" with them.[31] The pact's greatest significance, however, lay in its *transatlantic* purpose of facilitating Europe's rehabilitation through practical demonstration of political cooperation. Its outline places Wilson among the earliest statesmen of his era to ponder the necessary elements of a more integrated postwar order. It also reveals that he had much to learn. Mandating arbitration of major disputes and prohibiting violence toward those abiding its outcome doubtless are essential to any organized community. Excluding questions of "honour" and "vital interest" from these requirements, however, creates a loophole the size of Veracruz—or all of Europe. "We are not pushed on by the desire of conquest," Kaiser Wilhelm had averred as German armies trampled through Belgium into France. "We are moved by the unbending desire to secure for ourselves and those coming after us the place on which God has put us."[32]

Croly, Lippmann, and Weyl saw this difficulty more clearly than did Wilson, and addressed it more boldly. Though recognizing that the "experimental" nature of an initial Pan-American convention would require conserving "the foundation of national interest," they believed that no workable system of international cooperation could evolve without significant curtailment of its members' "independent political action." Should its members accept that condition, a Pan-American Pact "might grow until it converted the world to a pacific system of public law," sublimating the nationalism of local cultures into the internationalism of global citizens keener on mutual prosperity and cultural enrichment than economic competition and physical devastation.[33]

Eventually, Wilson would conclude that a narrow regard for honor and interests was war's major cause, and a collective conception of honor and interests its best prophylactic. The Pan-American plan marked a seminal moment in that intellectual development. But it never set down institutional roots. Engaged in a long-standing territorial dispute with Peru and determined to avoid arbitration, Chilean officials sidetracked the discussion with complaints about the threat to national sovereignty posed by the guarantee of republican institutions. Over the next two years, no treaty alterations short of total evisceration could convince the Chileans to open their boundary claims or domestic institutions to the scrutiny of a hemispheric organization. When Brazil, in the spring of 1917, proposed a new treaty making the guarantees of both territory and republican institutions enforceable only on request of the relevant nation's government, Wilson called off negotiations.[34] Having just decided to intervene in Europe, the president had no time for symbolic gestures of regional comity; he had long since determined that a much more radical reorganization of international affairs was his nation's top duty and the world's best destiny.

If Wilson saw Pan-Americanism as an active but indirect strategy for reforming Europe's politics, he soon found himself involved more directly— and far less constructively. In late 1914 and early 1915 it was the British who harried him most. Britain's wartime naval strategy placed enormous strain on American neutrality during the first two years of war in Europe. After it became clear that war against Germany could only be won at sea, Britain began mining North Sea shipping channels and disrupting neutral trade, seizing food and other nonmilitary necessities as contraband under the doctrine of "continuous voyage"—the doctrine that goods bound ultimately for enemy destinations could be seized at neutral ports. Wilson partly sympathized with Britain's predicament but faced pressure to enforce American shipping rights from merchants and from cotton and mining industries depressed by the disruption of trade. Southern interests, crucial to his control of Congress, were particularly distressed, leading the editor of the *Progressive Farmer* to write Tumulty in October warning of "political disturbances that may imperil party supremacy in the South." Wilson's Senate advisers warned that inaction risked open debate and likely denunciation of his policy on the Senate floor. In December 1914, Wilson authorized an ambassadorial protest of British search and seizure as an "infringement upon the right of American citizens."[35]

Wilson was loath, however, to take too hard a line. His reasoning was both vulgarly practical and philosophically pragmatist. By the time he authorized the protest, Allied war orders were enriching American farmers and manufacturers, facilitated by short-term banking credits that helped make Britain the nation's largest trading partner.[36] Though some sectors struggled, Allied trade was too valuable to the nation's economy to sacrifice on the altar of neutral rights. But Wilson also had deeper reasons for treating Britain gingerly. For much of the fall he had described his philosophy of neutrality in active terms—as a willingness "to fight, not with cannon, but with light," as he told the Young Men's Christian Association in October 1914. But light, he reminded his audience, revealed new things daily—at least to those who paid attention. However careful the thought and good the faith behind an action, he admonished, "you are a fool if in the back of your head you don't know that it is possible you are mistaken."[37] If Wilson ever thought neutrality meant treating all belligerents the same, by December 1914 he began to realize it could not be applied like whitewash on the fence of foreign affairs. Each nation was stuck in its own posthole, exposed to different elements, occupying a unique geographical and economic position vis-à-vis the United States. Maintaining neutrality meant assuming different postures in different situations.

Thus the president decided it was not fair for a neutral United States government to deprive Britain of its maritime advantage when Germany controlled most of northwestern Europe. Besides, Wilson saw a marked difference, with concrete consequences, between illegally boarding ships and illegally invading countries—a difference great enough to make any European settlement depend on Germany agreeing to "fundamental change in her military policy."[38] The editors of the *New Republic* agreed on both counts. "That the British Government should wish to increase in every way the military advantage which it enjoys from control of the sea is natural," they wrote, though they supported Wilson's protest of Britain's search-and-seizure methods. Whereas many parties were "responsible" for the war, concluded the editors, Germany's invasion of Belgium had actually begun the affair. Like other pragmatist-progressives and the majority of Americans, they increasingly viewed Germany as both emblematic of Europe's cultural implosion and uniquely problematic. As Thorstein Veblen explained in 1915, feudal values seemed to have persisted longer and stronger in Germany than in its industrial rival Britain, allowing an archaic warrior caste to mobilize the state and economy with remarkable ease for what amounted to a war over status.[39]

The president, accused by some of abetting this insane course, made clear that his policy reflected no hostility toward the British government nor any intention to impede its prosecution of the war against Germany. After all, American merchants, to "the great embarrassment" of the US government, had hidden contraband under noncontraband cargoes, understandably raising British suspicion of the entire merchant fleet. On the other hand, there was "no debating" that Britain's methods violated international law. A firm but temperate protest had been necessary, and that, agreed observers in and outside Washington, was what Wilson had delivered. As the *New Republic* stated, "Our note to Great Britain in regard to shipping is a frank and self-respecting performance"; the editors only wished such a principled, measured statement had been issued to Germany following the violation of Belgian neutrality.[40]

For his part, Wilson believed he had done all he could, from the moment war broke out, to balance principle and prudence in maintaining American neutrality, which to bear fruit at the peace table would have to inspire both respect and trust in all the major belligerents. He carefully considered the views of extreme Anglophiles such as former Harvard president Charles William Eliot, as well as such leading German American intellectuals as Harvard's Hugo Munsterberg.[41] To the monarchs of all belligerents he immediately offered his services in mediating peace, and in early 1915 he sent House to Britain, France, and Germany with a letter emphasizing his desire to act as a mutual friend through whom the powers might communicate frankly and confidentially. When asked by House if he himself would sail to Europe to preside over a future peace conference, Wilson answered yes. He thought that "the American people would desire it" as a sign of the nation's commitment to a constructive world role.[42]

In these early peacekeeping efforts Wilson at times seemed torn between the desire to establish a new, demilitarized order in Europe and the suspicion that the only hope for an early peace was reversion to the status quo. Certainly House tried to convince the European governments that peace was vital to the system of global economic interdependence that had made their nations wealthy before the war; and some scholars have interpreted Wilson's diplomacy as geared toward securing the postwar economic

primacy of the United States through extension of a liberal-democratic economic regime.[43] Yet there is little evidence that Wilson's neutral policies
were ever dictated primarily by economic interests. Early in the war he
declined to permit American firms to build and ship sections of submarines
to the British government, for fear of "violating the spirit of neutrality."[44]
On the other hand, in January 1915 he approved Bryan's decision to permit American munitions firms to ship arms to belligerents—which, due to
the British blockade, meant the Allies. He was well aware that the money
earned from arms sales to Britain far surpassed any potential profits from the
sale of submarine components. Was neutrality to be construed technically
only when it promised significant American economic gain? In fact, Wilson
was primarily persuaded by Robert Lansing's very different argument that
an embargo would actually benefit the side that had been more militarized
before the war and thus required fewer imported arms. As Wilson stated in a
public response to Austro-Hungarian protests, restricting arms sales by neutrals to belligerents "would inevitably give the advantage to the belligerent
which had encouraged the manufacture of munitions in time of peace,"
handicapping less militarized opponents. Such a precedent, by encouraging
nations to stockpile arms, "would force militarism on the world and work
against that universal peace which is the desire and purpose of all nations
which exalt justice and righteousness in their relations with one another."
The Central Powers were hardly satisfied. But the American public was persuaded, and congressional support for an embargo evaporated.[45]

Wilson's decisions regarding the sale of submarine parts and the traffic
in munitions exemplify the moral and grand-strategic logic of his neutrality
policy rather than any economic motives. Neither was made for economic
gain. Both were made in hopes of legitimating the United States' role as an
impartial advocate of peace. More and more, Wilson viewed the international situation as a manifestation of what Lippmann had called the "chaos
of new freedoms" confronting his nation. The war was full of potential for
the United States, promising both economic growth and a chance to lobby
for a more democratic world order when the guns were lowered. But how
to realize this potential? What were the "neutral" principles that justified
its fulfilment? What did "impartiality" mean in action—and what were the
results, real or ideal? Few precedents of international law pertained to this
wholly new experience of war. Wilson was beginning to realize that "strict
neutrality" was meaningless dogma. Like Lippmann—or James in "The
Will to Believe"—he saw that not choosing was a choice, and not acting an
action with consequences.

Meanwhile, the president's pragmatism was put to a sterner test. In early 1915 Wilson was frustrated in an effort to legalize the purchase of foreign merchant ships interned in American ports, most of which were German vessels. US shipping capacity was strained to the limit, and purchasing the redundant ships would help meet the demands of trade, reduce rates, and increase trade further. Wilson intended the ships for use in direct trade with Latin America, realizing full well "the complications" of setting them back on routes to and from Europe.[46] Nonetheless, these purchases would have put money into German hands for ships the Germans were not using, and which might have been captured by British vessels had they not found haven in American ports. The British were furious over Wilson's bill to legalize their purchase, as were American Anglophiles. Massachusetts Senator Henry Cabot Lodge led the Republican opposition in Congress, introducing an amendment to ban purchase of belligerent ships under any circumstances—negating, in effect, the original bill.[47]

Wilson refused to accept the amendment. The administration was upholding a "vital American right" with international implications—the right to freedom of commerce. More practically, by restricting the ships' use to coastwise rather than transatlantic trade, the bill affirmed the nation's right to determine its own foreign economic relations without directly challenging the Royal Navy's blockade. Wilson's foes in Congress, he complained, clearly did not understand the pragmatic aims of this compromise. To "preserve" a "vital right" did not mean that it "must be asserted" with no thought for its wider consequences. But it did require the United States to take seriously its role as "chief representative and trustee of neutral rights." Wilson would not "pay for the passage of the shipping bill" by renouncing the international rights it was designed to assert.[48]

Wilson also saw the fight for the shipping bill as a test of his leadership, on both the party and national levels. Multiple opposition organs accused him of initiating a socialist revolution by financing and controlling a government merchant fleet, and though support for the bill was at least as strong, Wilson worried that defeat would start a cascade that could "destroy" his presidency "and bring back the days of private influence and selfish advantage." He was convinced that the opposition was beholden to powerful shipping firms fearful lest "control of ocean carriage and of ocean rates pass out of their hands." Nothing less than a principled stand by a united Democratic Party, he concluded, could "break the control of special interests over this government and this people."[49] The *New Republic* editors grasped this logic while doubting its applicability. An "extreme special measure" embodying

138 CHAPTER FOUR

the principle of government ownership and operation would be beneficial if it was one "upon which the party was united, and for which a clear preponderance of favorable public opinion could be obtained." Wilson's ship-purchasing program, however, was no such measure; too many in Congress and the public at large thought this particular "experiment" more "dubious" than "necessary." The shipping industry was booming, and if the government, without clear public support, were to enter such a highly competitive industry and then fail to perform, the whole project of pragmatic nationalism for which the *New Republic* stood might be compromised.[50]

The agitation over shipping was exacerbated by the *Dacia* affair, a plan hatched by a Michigan businessman to purchase interned ships privately, for the purpose of delivering cotton to the Netherlands for German and Austrian purchase. As a test case, the *Dacia* was bought and loaded, and clearance to sail to Rotterdam was requested from the State Department. Bryan, in turn, instructed Ambassador Page to ask the British Foreign Office for its consent, stressing that the *Dacia* scheme was only an experiment in solving the export problem, one that need not be treated as a "precedent" thereafter. A diplomatic row ensued when the British foreign secretary, Sir Edward Grey, facing a torrent of anti-American sentiment in Britain, vowed to seize the ship if it approached the Continent. He then telegraphed to the British ambassador in Washington a protest against the peculiar US version of neutrality: The Wilson administration had forbidden the sale of submarine parts to Britain; Congress was voting on a bill to purchase "German" ships and effectively compensate the kaiser for their loss; and now the administration sought British acquiescence in an explicit attempt to short-circuit their blockade. Ambassador Cecil Spring-Rice detailed the charges in a telegram to Bryan on January 21 and in a memorandum to House on January 22, presenting the case in no mild terms.[51]

With the battle over the ship purchase bill heating up, Wilson could not capitulate outright to the British regarding the *Dacia*. But he was willing to compromise. Regarding "the principles" of neutral rights, he asserted in a draft note to the British Foreign Office, the two governments were doubtless in "agreement." All they lacked was "some practical method" for reducing specific disputes "to a negligible minimum," and the United States "would not only welcome but earnestly desire practical suggestions looking to that end."[52] Meanwhile, Wilson was trying to cut deals with Congress. Now that the fight was about the influence of special interests in Washington, he even entertained Lodge's idea to prohibit government purchase of interned belligerent vessels, so long as government control of an expanded merchant fleet was secured. On February 11, however, the Senate voted, forty-eight to forty-six, to adjourn without voting on the bill. Wilson staged a final two-pronged attempt to regain control, first masterminding an amended bill providing for time-limited government control of purchased ships and then vowing to call a special session of Congress if the bill was not approved before the lame-duck session ended on March 4. But although the amended bill passed the House by a large majority on February 17, it had no chance of passing the Senate: seven Democrats who had previously pledged to oppose it renewed their vows, while the compromise over government control stripped the bill of any lingering appeal to Republican progressives. Told as much by Senate Democratic leaders, the president accepted defeat.[53]

Wilson reacted with a mix of pragmatic equanimity and righteous anger. He did not punish Congress with a special session, and was gracious toward House Democrats who voted against the bill, assuring one that his opposition had "made me question my own judgment more than it made me question your confidence in me or your loyalty to the party."[54] Wilson found it harder to forgive the "Seven Rebels" in the Senate. He drafted a statement blaming their "unnatural and unprecedented alliance" with the Republicans for having "fastened the control of the selfish shipping interests on the country." But he did not issue it. Instead, on March 5 he publicly praised the Congress for its historic domestic achievements—tariff reduction, the Federal Reserve system, and a new antitrust regime—and attempted to revive a sense of national unity infused with the spirit of his burgeoning internationalism. "A great Congress has closed its sessions," he stated, whose work would "prove the purpose and quality of its statesmanship more and more the longer it is tested." Every "patriotic man" should now direct his efforts toward ensuring that the nation maintained "a just and tempered judgment in the face of perplexing difficulties." Both the strength and the honor of the nation depended on its people's "power to think, to purpose, and to act with patience, with disinterested fairness, and without excitement, in a spirit of friendliness and enlightenment"—a spirit that would help the United States "firmly establish its influence throughout the world."[55]

There were lingering hard feelings, however. As Wilson explained to one of the Seven Rebels, their defection was more than a personal slight. "I can form no working idea of the successful operation of popular institutions," he wrote Georgia's Thomas Hardwick on March 15, "if individuals are to exercise the privilege of defeating a decisive majority of their own party associates in framing and carrying out the policy of the party." Certainly, "personal convictions" should be "candidly and earnestly presented" in party conference, as in any democratic process. But there was no "surrender either of personal dignity or of individual conviction in yielding to the determinations of a decisive majority" after deliberation had run its course. If minorities, despite ample opportunity to participate in the decision-making process, consistently frustrated its outcomes, no party could hope "to be serviceable to the country as a governing agency." Wilson hoped the rebels understood that their president would continue to press this view of party government upon his Senate colleagues "with the earnestness of a conviction which underlies all others." In so many words, Wilson insisted that his party respect, cultivate, and practice the habit that William James had declared essential to democratic ethics and government: "the habit of trained and disciplined good temper towards the opposite party when it fairly wins its innings."[56] In that spirit, Wilson determined to consolidate his losses on neutral trade and settle the *Dacia* affair with Britain as gracefully as possible. When the vessel was seized by a French ship off Brest on February 27, 1915, and later condemned, the US State Department encouraged its owner to appeal through the French civil courts; just like that, the *Dacia* ceased to exist as a diplomatic issue.[57]

All in all, Wilson showed a great deal of humility in accepting the outcomes of the ship purchase and *Dacia* controversies. As the *New Republic* had advised just days before the climax of February 17, he abandoned his insistence on either the private or the national right to purchase German ships. But the journal also praised Wilson for setting an important standard. Though still bemoaning the lost opportunity to protest the invasion of Belgium, the editors supported the president's subsequent efforts "scrupulously to safeguard neutral rights" for purposes transcending national self-interest. "It may later be possible for us to aid in converting neutrality into a positive principle," they wrote, entailing responsibilities and opportunities to foster international stability through cooperative adaptation to change. Yet the advent and implementation of such a principle depended on potential aggressors knowing that "established neutral rights" would be defended against wanton violations.[58] Wilson, the message went, was learning that the maintenance of order and pursuit of change were not only compatible but often mutually reinforcing. Indeed, by early 1915, despite the editors' dismay over some of the president's actions—or lack thereof— the picture of the world presented in their journal as often as not resembled sketches from Wilson's Oval Office window.

As tensions with Britain were peaking in early February 1915, relations with Germany took an ominous turn. On February 4, the German government, its belt tightening daily after months behind the Allied blockade, declared the waters surrounding the British archipelago a war zone and warned that enemy ships there would be sunk regardless of the lives of neutral passengers. If submarine commanders had reason to believe a neutral flag was a cover for an Allied vessel (a common British tactic), they were authorized to attack.[59]

Wilson immediately instructed Lansing to draft a reply. The United States, it declared, "would be constrained to hold the Imperial German Government to a strict accountability" for any loss of American life or property resulting from a German submarine attack, and was prepared to "take any steps it might be necessary to take" to secure freedom of the seas for Americans. Yet the note did not directly threaten to sever relations and made no mention of military retaliation. Wilson altered Lansing's original reference to "the critical situation in the relations between this country and Germany which would arise" in the event of American casualties, so that the finished note read "might arise." He also substituted "deliberately unfriendly" for Lansing's "hostile" to describe how his government would interpret such an incident. Finally, he agreed to protest the misuse of American flags by British vessels. As he hoped, the Germans were shaken but not inflamed, and on February 17, they promised to limit attacks to belligerent vessels and respect neutral colors legitimately flown.[60]

American citizens were less cooperative. They continued to book transatlantic passage on Allied liners—regardless of the colors flown. Wilson urged Americans not to take such a risk: it was no secret that many liners carried munitions representing thousands of potential casualties to the German government. Still, Wilson did not believe he had authority to ban American passage on belligerent vessels outright. The result was tragic, but perhaps inevitable. On May 7, 1915, the Cunard liner *Lusitania* was sunk by a German submarine. It took to the bottom a massive cargo of munitions bound for Allied armories, as well as almost 1,200 lives, including 128 Americans. House, in Britain at the time, thought it might mean war, and he welcomed the prospect. "The question must be determined either now or later," he wrote Wilson, "and it seems to me that you would lose prestige by deferring it." For Theodore Roosevelt, "murder on so vast a scale" permitted but one response: "to do the duty imposed on us" and directly aid the Allied war effort.[61]

Wilson, like his nation, was shocked but torn. He realized that Roosevelt's jingoistic outrage was shared by many Americans, but not as many as the Hero of San Juan Hill liked to believe. Revulsion against Germany increased a week later after publication of a report, by the respected former

British ambassador to the United States, Viscount Bryce, on the German army's conduct during its initial sweep through Belgium and France. But the response to its catalog of (sometimes fictional) German atrocities revealed that most Americans were more horrified by the prospect of war than by collateral damage such as the *Lusitania* sinking. A survey of reaction to the report in the American press revealed indignation, disgust, and some persisting incredulity, but not one call for intervention.[62]

Wilson, for his part, decided that while the United States had received an errant blow, there was nonetheless "such a thing as a man being too proud to fight." Nations, like individuals, were in society with one another, and a civilized nation must sometimes set an example for its peers by "being so right that it does not need to convince others by force that it is right."[63] Rational, deliberative discourse was the long-tempered tool with which civilization must replace the crude, blunt instrument of war to preserve itself. Joining in this belief were the nation's leading pragmatists. Addams had recently founded her Woman's Peace Party on the assumption that "the savage spirit in man," so susceptible "to the primitive appeal," was "unworthy of modern civilization." Du Bois, interpreting the *Lusitania* sinking as further proof of white civilization's failure, preferred abstention from its latest murder spree. The constellation of pragmatists at the *New Republic* also counseled restraint. Clearly, if no "definite assurance of safety for the future" was secured, the US government must "convey a threat" sufficient to elicit one. That might mean severing relations. But there was no call for war. The *New Republic* pragmatists contended that American belligerence must remain secured behind a series of diplomatic doors, emerging only if Germany insisted on kicking them in. Meanwhile, Wilson's government should sign those doors clearly and determine "before each step in the negotiations, just what action it will take if Germany is obdurate." "We can proceed slowly," they concluded. "No 'military necessity' need stampede our diplomacy. We must if at all possible avoid war, or steps which make war inevitable."[64]

These suggestions aligned both with Wilson's convictions and with public opinion. When New York newspapers polled editors nationwide, only six of nearly one thousand respondents deemed war a reasonable option. As even the hawkish Lansing recalled, Wilson's "determination to preserve our neutrality" and "the doubtful state of public opinion" together "prevented 'putting teeth' into the notes sent to Berlin."[65] Yet teeth can be bared without biting. Wilson sent three strong protests in an effort to translate Americans' collective snarl into terms the German imperial government could understand. He hoped to convince both the kaiser and the American people that neither technicalities of international law nor injury to national pride were as impor-tant as the vital link between human rights and international justice. "The sinking of passenger ships involves principles of humanity which throw into the background any special circumstances of detail," he wrote to Berlin. "The Government of the Unites States is contending for something much greater than mere rights of property or privileges of commerce. It is contending for nothing less high and sacred than the rights of humanity, which every Gov-ernment honors itself in respecting and which no Government is justified in resigning."[66]

This rhetoric of human rights was lost on Secretary of State Bryan, who resigned in June to protest Wilson's animus toward Germany and turned his considerable energies toward drying up the country. (It may well be that prohibition—though alas, not the nation—was saved by Bryan's break with the president.)[67] Public reaction, however, was largely favorable across the American political spectrum. The president received a particular boost when his former opponent, William Howard Taft, drafted an approving telegram endorsed by nearly a thousand lay Methodist leaders whom he happened to be addressing in New York.[68] Unfortunately, the negotiations following the *Lusitania* sinking did not go smoothly. Under Bryan's replacement Lansing, they dragged on for months. On July 21, the administration reiterated the importance of "freedom of the seas" and called for "the practical co-operation of the Imperial German Government" in maintaining it. Though Wilson and Lansing were obviously referring to the renunciation of submarine warfare, Johann Heinrich von Bernstorff, the German ambassador, disingenuously in-terpreted their language to imply a joint protest against the British block-ade. Despite this show of diplomatic guile, Bernstorff pressed the kaiser to abandon unrestricted submarine warfare, as did Chancellor Theobald von Bethmann-Hollweg. The influence of high-ranking naval officers over the kaiser, however, delayed official response to the American note. Such was the situation in August when the British liner *Arabic* was torpedoed, with a reported four Americans among the casualties.[69]

This latest affront threw the *Lusitania* negotiations into a tailspin. House urged a diplomatic break, insisting that "some decisive action upon our part is inevitable; otherwise we will have no influence when peace is made or afterwards." Still, Wilson reckoned that international peace depended on American neutrality, telling his future wife Edith Galt that the "worst thing that could possibly *happen to the world* would be for the United States to be drawn actively into this contest,—to become one of the belligerents and lose all chance of moderating the results of the war by counsel as an outsider."[70] American opinion, by contrast, was growing hot. Roosevelt's preferred organ, the *Outlook,* printed a special supplement calling for the severance of relations with Germany, and even the staid *Independent,* although urging calm, described the sinking as just the sort of "deliberately unfriendly act" Germany had been told might cause a break.[71] On August 22, Wilson vowed to sever relations with Germany if its government did not apologize for the sinking, and he backed Lansing's official demand for a categorical disavowal of unrestricted submarine warfare from Berlin. To Bernstorff, Lansing gravely predicted that, given the state of public opinion, his government would soon be giving the ambassador his passports.[72] This communication finally elicited from Germany a pledge, on September 1, to halt attacks on unresisting passenger liners, give fair warning of any impending attack, and take measures to preserve the lives of those on board. While maintaining that the commander of the offending U-boat in the *Arabic* case had fired in anticipation of attack, the imperial government offered its apologies and promised to pay indemnities. It seemed a triumph of pragmatist diplomacy: the United States had spoken its piece in support of a "vital principle," and the ensuing conversation, however heated, had prevented conflagration.[73]

The *Arabic* incident's apparent resolution led Oswald Garrison Villard, disgruntled racial democrat and pacifist editor of the New York *Evening Post,* to laud Wilson as the man who "without rattling a sword, won for civilization."[74] Many internationally minded progressives joined the huzzah. The *New Republic* offered a contrasting assessment. "Respect for some kind of public law, belief in its value, and willingness if necessary to fight for its maintenance, must lie at the foundation of any worthy and enduring international structure," the editors wrote on September 4, 1915.[75] Germany's promise to submit questions of liability to arbitration should future "mistakes" occur did little to bolster that foundation, leaving it "much as it was on the day after the sinking of the Lusitania." Then it was right to restrain the fighting instinct, giving Germany a chance to modify its behavior. Now Wilson must demand "more satisfactory explanations" than the excuses of rogue or frightened U-boat commanders. Germany must know that its next violation of American rights would mean the severing of diplomatic relations, which in turn might bring war. But a war "precipitated by further German aggression" would garner "a sufficient consensus of public opinion" behind Wilson to protect and even advance his domestic and diplomatic goals. Indeed, Wilson seemed to grasp the connection between a principled stance for neutral rights and the "security of pacific social democracy." But he had failed to convey its importance to Americans and thus failed to guide the debate over the nation's diplomatic future. The editors did not envy the president his position. Yet if defending principles of humane conduct meant "risk of war," Wilson must accept it with the same clear conscience with which Lincoln, "at a moment of still graver crisis and still deeper division of public opinion," accepted "the danger of civil war rather than compromise with the South."[76]

Wilson soon discovered how little diplomatic traction the apparent resolution of the *Arabic* incident left him. No sooner had Germany made its promises than the British and Italians stepped up efforts to arm their merchant marines and passenger liners, with the explicit intention of attacking German U-boats. This action prompted the Wilson administration to suggest a modus vivendi to the Allies and Germany in early February 1916: if Germany agreed "to adhere strictly to the rules of international law in stopping and searching merchant vessels, determining their belligerent nationality, and removing the crews and passengers to safety before sinking the vessels," then the Allies should agree to prohibit their merchant and passenger vessels "from carrying any armament whatsoever."[77] The move failed. Both sides eventually rejected the proposal, but the German government's response was most galling. Though styling itself a reluctant dragon, starved into snapping at neutral vessels plumped with goods for its tormentors, it celebrated publicly over every sinking. Wilson's patience ran out on February 10, 1916, when the German and Austro-Hungarian governments invoked his proffered compromise in a public declaration of intention to sink any merchant vessel that refused to disarm. This cynical misrepresentation of the American proposal was far more frustrating than the Allies' outright rejection and erased what little progress had been made in settling the *Lusitania* and *Arabic* affairs.[78]

After Germany announced it would resume firing on armed merchant ships, Wilson followed the course the *New Republic* had suggested in the wake of the *Arabic*'s sinking, informing House Democrats that if an armed merchant ship were sunk by a U-boat and Americans killed as a result, diplomatic relations with Germany would be severed and war would likely follow. Reactions were intense. Strict neutralists of his party's Bryanite wing staged a minirebellion, introducing House and Senate resolutions to restrict American travel on belligerent vessels. Equally distressing for Wilson was a highly publicized speech of February 15, 1916, in which former Republican Senator Elihu Root of New York, onetime head of both the War and State Departments, decried the timidity of Wilson's response to German aggression. Root, "bristling with censure," argued that Wilson's record of conciliation, beginning with his refusal to condemn Germany's invasion of Belgium, had encouraged Americans' failure to recognize duty as "correlative" to rights—a charge that the isolationist rebels in Wilson's party threatened to make stick. Rebellion or no, stated the *New Republic*, Root's speech set a "higher standard of international responsibility" than Wilson had offered.[79]

Newspapers across the country credited Root with landing the first blow in the 1916 campaign battle.[80] Wilson, however, responded deftly to the crisis, and did so by positioning himself as just the type of active internationalist Croly and company called for: one ready to defend American honor not for its own, abstract sake, but as a bulwark of international security. Through tireless lobbying of individual congressmen, he scuttled the resolutions restricting travel. "I shall do everything in my power to keep the United States out of war," Wilson wrote in a public letter to Senator William Stone, chair of the Foreign Relations Committee, on February 24. But that power was limited, and its exercise now would curtail it further in future. "To forbid our people to exercise their rights for fear we might be called upon to vindicate them" would not just mean "deep humiliation" but "acquiescence in the violation of the rights of mankind everywhere. . . . Once accept a single abatement of right," he concluded, "and the whole fine fabric of international law might crumble."[81] The *New Republic* pragmatists had been waiting for such a statement from the president, and they applauded his poise and discernment. Not only had he "smashed a rebellion" in Congress that threatened his ability to negotiate effectively, he had finally recognized that "the nation's desire for peace" must be "mixed with the intention to save general principles."[82]

In fact, Wilson had made the logical connection between peace and general principles a year earlier, in defending the ship purchase bill. Moreover, and unknown to Lippmann, the president had come to agree that the Allies were the likeliest partners in achieving a principled yet practical peace, and worth treating as such. Though Wilson could not make it public during the rebellion in Congress, he had already conditionally approved a secret agreement negotiated between British Foreign Secretary Grey and Colonel House, who ostensibly was touring all belligerent capitals to sound out a mediated peace. In his initial instructions to House, Wilson insisted that his government was "concerned only with the future peace of the world and the guarantees to be given for that," including "military and naval disarmament" and "a league of nations to secure each nation against aggression and maintain the absolute freedom of the seas." There was to be no talk of American intervention on behalf of either side; rather, if either would consent to a conference negotiating such a peace, it would "clearly be our duty to use our utmost moral force to oblige the other to parley."[83] House disregarded these instructions and instead proposed a plan, first to the French and then the British, to bring the United States into the war on the side of the Allies by year's end. His visit to Berlin had convinced him that Germany would soon mount an all-out offensive on the blockade and that neutral ships with American passengers would be sunk. He intimated to the Allies that if a sinking were to occur after Germany refused a public offer of mediation from Wilson, the United States would intervene against the Central powers with the full backing of American public opinion. House and Grey drafted a memorandum embodying this scheme on February 17.[84]

In its final form, the "House-Grey Memorandum" read: "President Wilson was ready on hearing from France and England that the moment was opportune, to propose that a Conference should be summoned to put an end to the war. Should the Allies accept this proposal, and should Germany refuse it, the United States would *probably* enter the war against Germany." With the exception of adding the word *probably* to the text, Wilson received the House-Grey Memorandum warmly.[85] Why? It hardly accorded with his instructions to House. All the Allies had to do was request a conference at a moment when, as the memorandum stated, "it would secure peace terms not unfavorable to the Allies." The French and British naturally saw this as a way to continue strangling German trade until Germany either submitted to a harsh peace or lashed out at the United States. But the president was unaware of this attitude. House made it sound to Wilson as if the Allies were eager for his mediation, not for total victory. In the meantime, House told Ambassador Spring-Rice that the British should step up the blockade and continue to tighten the screws on the Germans.[86]

House's dissembling had a profound impact on Wilson's policy toward Germany. The president now thought he had "allies" in his quest for a negotiated peace, an assumption that made a firm stand against German submarine warfare not merely possible but desirable. If an American-mediated conference was truly at hand, the German government would have less time to grow frustrated with the Allied blockade and break its pledges to the United States. If the Germans refused to attend such a conference now or in the near future, with the powers locked in a grinding stalemate, they would prove themselves the main aggressors, bent on total victory whatever the cost. In such circumstances, a German provocation might very well justify the breaking of relations and, ultimately, intervention. Nevertheless, the insertion of *probably* signaled Wilson's sympathy for the Allies without committing the United States irrevocably to war. And if matters stood as House presented them, the Allies would at least give Wilson a chance to bring Germany to the table before such a crisis arrived. In the light in which House had cast them, the Allies appeared the party of reason.

On this score, Wilson again found himself in familiar pragmatist company. Frankfurter, almost in spite of his administration ties, was among those coming to appreciate Wilson's grasp of the slippery mess spreading outward from Europe. He had often found Wilson's diplomatic solutions more verbal than practical, as in the case of Germany's *Arabic* pledge. By early 1916, however, he was even surer than Veblen that the German aristocracy's "demand for mastery, their intoxication about *das Deutsch*" was the criterion of their nation's foreign policy and the major threat to future peace. "Only German jingoism is the prevailing danger," Frankfurter asserted.[87] His friends at the *New Republic* agreed. Denouncing both sides at the start of the war, the editors had come to support the Allied cause and accept that direct US resistance to German victory might be necessary to securing lasting peace in Europe. In a world system where "reason and goodwill" had repeatedly failed to stem violence and destruction, they wrote in February 1915, a decisive strike at its militarist core had to be considered. Again drawing a parallel to the American Civil War, they stressed the need to resolve the "irrepressible conflicts" that might spawn future wars instead of simply condemning war in the abstract.[88] By November the journal's prescriptions had become more definite. A just peace depended for practical and moral purposes on an Allied victory, and specifically on a strong postwar alliance between Great Britain and the United States, which "by virtue of an unassailable maritime supremacy" would form the nucleus of a viable peacekeeping organization. The following March, the journal proposed a "system of reciprocal guarantees" to build an "entente of the British Empire, the French Republic, and Pan America," and thus "create the largest area of unified liberalism the world has ever known."[89]

When that same month a German U-boat sank the unarmed French steamer *Sussex*, injuring (though not killing) several Americans, it seemed the United States had been given a decisive shove straight into the Allied camp. In the ensuing diplomatic crisis, Wilson had to deal not only with the Germans but with increasing numbers of Americans vaguely but angrily demanding "action" against them.[90] Wilson refused to play the Rooseveltian warrior and treat the sinking of the *Sussex* as an affront to national honor tantamount to an act of war; the public, he believed, was not ready for it. Yet Wilson himself thought war "probable." He could not ignore this blatant violation of the kaiser's *Arabic* pledge. His only hope was in the House-Grey Memorandum. To Grey he proposed "acting at an early date on the plan we agreed to"—that is, calling a peace conference to forestall further provocations by Germany. Otherwise, "this country must break with Germany unless the unexpected happens." In fact, the unexpected did happen. Grey, after claiming to have conferred with his Allied counterparts, rejected Wilson's proposal, asserting that "war must yet continue to have any chance of securing satisfactory terms from Germany."[91] By contrast, German Chancellor von Bethmann-Hollweg initialed a cable to Washington stating his government's intention "to conduct submarine warfare with due regard to neutral rights," reiterating its purely "defensive" war aims, and expressing its readiness to conclude peace. Meanwhile, Bernstorff admitted to House that "if passenger ships were torpedoed without warning and American lives lost," Wilson would have "no alternative" but severing relations with Germany. On April 17, Bernstorff received instructions to suggest a joint "commission of inquiry to establish [the] facts" of the *Sussex* case. It seemed the kaiser was scared, and the civilian leadership was supplanting the high command in his counsels.[92]

In a message to Congress on April 19, 1916, Wilson pressed his advantage in an ultimatum to Germany: "immediately declare and effect an abandonment of its present methods of submarine warfare" or see all diplomatic relations with the United States severed. Wilson spoke less like the head of a nation than the herald of civilization. Americans were "by the force of circumstances the responsible spokesmen of the rights of humanity" and had an obligation to themselves and the world to fulfill. "We owe it to a due regard for our own rights as a nation, to our sense of duty as a representative of the rights of neutrals the world over, and to a just conception of the rights of mankind to take this stand now with the utmost solemnity and firmness." Yet Wilson was still unwilling to expunge Germany from the rolls of civilized nations. He concluded with the hope that "the Imperial German Government, which has in other circumstances stood as the champion of all that we are now contending for in the interest of humanity, may recognize the justice of our demands and meet them in the spirit in which they are made." Perhaps the power of persuasion, crackling between the poles of anger and conciliation, could be harnessed once more.[93]

Wilson's middle way worked, at least for the moment. On May 5, Germany, unwilling to risk war with the United States, pledged that no unresisting merchant vessels would be sunk unless warned and given evacuation assistance. As an attempt to save face and salvage some diplomatic advantage, the German government insisted that in return the United States pressure the Allies to abandon the blockade that was starving the German people. But Wilson would not budge. He "accepted" the response he desired, rather than the one he received, replying that as far as the government of the

United States was concerned, Germany's pledge was not "in the slightest degree . . . contingent upon the conduct of any other government."[94]

Thus, as with the *Arabic* negotiations, future collisions were postponed rather than prevented. Yet Wilson had no choice but to ignore the German conditions. He could not convince Britain to abandon the naval blockade; in fact, Anglo–American relations had already begun a precipitous decline. In April the British government's bloody reaction to the Irish rebellion inflamed American opinion and led many Americans, including the *New Republic* pragmatists, to question the democratic credentials of what was supposedly the most liberal of European governments.[95] As for persuading the British to give up the blockade, the United States could not even secure the maritime rights of its own citizens. State Department protests of continued British infringements—opening American mail, seizing cargoes, even blacklisting firms rumored to trade with Germany—were sometimes angrily rebutted by Whitehall, usually arrogantly dismissed. Ironically, then, after the *Sussex* sinking, German–American relations improved, while popular support for the Allies eroded in the United States during 1916. By December of that year, the *New Republic* was forced to admit that the Allies were no longer fighting a defensive war but were attempting "to alter in their favor the European balance of power." Wilson too wrote to the Colonel as early as July that, "I am, I must admit, about at the end of my patience with Great Britain and the Allies."[96]

Unfortunately, Wilson's strong line with Germany, while immediately necessary to maintain peace and principle, threatened his experiment in neutral diplomacy by effectively making Whitehall the arbiter of American policy. Wilson knew that in the face of the continuing British blockade, the Germans would eventually feel forced to resume unrestricted submarine warfare. Then, who could tell what act of ruthlessness, carelessness, or desperation might ignite a blaze of public fury that Wilson could not control? What act might take the last life of an American nation at peace?

CHAPTER FIVE

Trojan Horsemanship

From the spring of 1916, Wilson's thoughts turned increasingly to the possibility of war. On the surface, the period stretching from May to December was one of relative quiet in German–American relations. But it was a quiet pregnant with danger. Great Britain's strangulation of the Central powers made resumption of submarine warfare a near certainty. After the *Sussex* exchange, the dark, scimitar silhouette of the U-boat hung like a sword of Damocles above the United States and Germany, ready to drop and sever relations at any moment. Finding a way to prepare the nation for this contingency while doing everything possible to avoid it became Wilson's top priority.

Meanwhile, controversy raged over the state of America's armed forces. "Preparedness" advocates insisted that US forces must expand in case future outrages made war unavoidable. Many of these advocates, including prominent "patrician progressives" such as Theodore Roosevelt and Henry L. Stimson, argued that universal military training would create a more disciplined, cohesive citizenry, while others argued that a larger army and navy would deter Europe's belligerents from actions demanding a military response. These views were vehemently challenged by a smaller group of pacifists and antimilitarists, who warned that preparedness would increase not only the nation's capability for war but also its propensity for it, by tying economic interests to defense and militarizing public psychology. For their part, the more radical elements of the American reform movement feared that preparedness would siphon resources and attention from pressing social issues while providing a profit incentive for war. Among these reformers were several pragmatists, notably Jane Addams, Randolph Bourne, and Max Eastman, the latter declaring it nonsense to "denounce 'German Militarism' in one breath, and advocate 'Military Preparedness' in another. These two things are one and the same."[1]

Other pragmatist progressives rejected this "passivist" interpretation of "pacifism," as the *New Republic* editors termed it. Herbert Croly and Walter Lippmann especially came to believe that prudent expansion of military resources and forces presented a golden opportunity for both progressive reform and international peace. Government management of the nation's armaments production, they argued, was the perfect "Trojan Horse" for smuggling both industrial democracy and the full nationalization of the arms industry into the realm of political possibility. Ironically, moreover, it was only as a viable military power that the United States could help prevent the triumph of Germany's militarist autocracy and achieve lasting peace in Europe. Wilson was a fool to accept the sincerity of Germany's "concessions" in the wake of the *Sussex* crisis, argued the editors. Unless the United States could "force" Britain to relax its blockade—which happened to be northwestern Europe's main defense against German conquest—the kaiser's government would resume submarine warfare, and a clumsy slide into war would follow. Wilson's proper course was therefore obvious: "abandon the pretense of neutrality" once and for all, and declare his government's intention to intervene on the side of the Allies unless Germany categorically renounced submarine warfare and evacuated its forces from Belgium and France. Otherwise, readers were warned, the United States would "drift into the war" in a "handicapped" state, "without a constructive policy calculated to promote our own security and wellbeing or that of other nations."[2]

Through the winter of 1915–16, Croly and Lippmann despaired of Wilson's ability to halt such a drift. Yet in the ensuing months, the tone of their journal shifted—haltingly, erratically, but seismically—from criticism to approval, and even admiration, of the president's diplomacy. Reflecting as the 1916 election approached, Croly and Lippmann began to think the spume of the sinking *Sussex* had washed the scales from the president's eyes. They discerned a promising pattern in Wilson's evolving policy: active neutrality, designed to maximize his nation's mediating influence, was followed by prudent military preparedness designed to maintain that influence—whether as the only unspent power at the peace table or, should war be thrust upon it, as the decisive force in battle.

This pattern of convergence first struck the editors only two weeks after they levied their charge of "hypocritical neutrality" against the president. On May 27, 1916, Wilson publicly endorsed the idea of a league of nations, which the *New Republic* had advocated since the previous spring.[3] In wedding national interest to organized internationalism, the editors claimed,

Wilson had "broken with the tradition of American isolation in the only way that offers any hope to men."[4] Soon the editors were approached by Wilson adviser "Colonel" Edward M. House, who sought both to clarify and promote the administration's positions and to pick the brains of men who, despite particular reservations, were publicly articulating the practical idealism guiding Wilson's course. In response to this infiltration the editors began their own game of Trojan horse, interlacing policy analysis and proposals with warm expressions of support in private messages conveyed by House to the president. Although numerous plans for a league of nations informed Wilson's thinking from mid-1916 forward, his developing synthesis most resembled that of Croly and Lippmann, who insisted that an effective league must have force to respond to aggression, a deliberative body to defuse its causes, and authority to make binding but revisable decisions that facilitated orderly change. Meanwhile, Wilson's strong but calm responses to a string of German provocations and to violent chaos at the Mexican border helped win him reelection in 1916, as the man voters thought best equipped to keep the United States out of war. Yet for Croly, Lippmann, and other like-minded pragmatists, the president's stances against Germany, belief in the interdependence of international society, and commitment to its collective security all made Wilson himself a potential Trojan horse: the peace candidate who would not shrink from a war against war if other strategies failed.

Wilson began to think seriously about national security in July 1915, when he instructed the navy and war departments to formulate programs for expanding the armed forces. House was the catalyst, arguing that preparedness was essential to American national defense and diplomatic leverage.[5] Secretary of War Lindley M. Garrison's army-expansion plan was published in November, and the "Garrison plan" raised a storm of protest from pacifists across the country, who found little irony in the name. Garrison proposed expanding the regular army and creating a "Continental Army" of reservists—leading some Americans to predict their nation's transformation into a "Garrison" state. The plan would relegate the US National Guard to domestic police duties, horrifying those who cherished the nation's state-militia heritage. Former Secretary of State William Jennings Bryan folksily expressed the antipreparedness case, insisting that the United States "should not be a pistol-toting nation unless it is going to adopt pistol-toting ideas."[6]

Despite these objections, Wilson was confident of ample congressional support for preparedness, and took to the road to convince the public.[7] He first propounded what he termed "reasonable preparedness" in an address to the Manhattan Club in New York City on November 4, 1915. In this early plea lay the seeds of three ideas that already echoed the pragmatist political philosophy expounded in the pages of the *New Republic* and would grow clearer as the president's case for preparedness evolved.

First, refuting charges of militarism, Wilson denied any distinction between the domestic and external obligations implied in the American democratic ideal. "We believe in political liberty and founded our great government to obtain it," he declared. For that reason, all Americans should agree that their nation must "never again take another foot of territory by conquest" or "make an independent people subject to our dominion." Second, Wilson asserted the need for conscious adaptation to changes that might otherwise derail the pursuit of established goals. The nation's domestic peace and freedoms, for a century threatened only from within, now required means to repel the armies of once-distant nations, lest they stunt the growth of democracy in its richest soil. That an American army might be used to impose political change on American citizens was unthinkable; its sole charge was to defend rights and principles that thrived "only in the kindly and wholesome atmosphere of peace." Third, Wilson asked all Americans to view themselves as united in a common pursuit, facilitated by a government they ultimately controlled. In promoting preparedness, he asked for "hearty support" from "the rank and file of America," not as "a private individual" with particular interests but "as the trustee and guardian of a Nation's rights." Finally, Wilson brought his message full circle, once again situating national honor and freedoms in the larger, shifting matrix of international obligations. In its foreign relations, the United States must show itself "too big and generous to be exacting, yet courageous enough to defend its rights and the liberties of its people wherever assailed or invaded."[8]

Many preparedness advocates applauded Wilson's message, and some erstwhile critics were appeased. But as the *New Republic* saw it, the speech's "platitudes" about defending political liberty were inadequate to "educate opinion," much less "crystallize it." Wilson had conjured a castle in the air with no blueprint for its construction. How would preparedness be funded? How would the "waste in our present military establishments" be reduced? The editors predicted trouble for Wilson's program, and they were right. His ambiguous exhortation—a call to arms for purposes of peace—whipped up a tornado of antimilitarist bellowing that cut a swath through Wilson's progressive base. Supporters in Congress grew timid, some even recalcitrant. Seizing on the discord among Democrats, Wilson's nemeses in the Republican Party launched an offensive against his record of "shuffling" in foreign affairs and "failure to lead" at home. Their epigones in private life were more vicious. Owen Wister, the cowboy novelist and close friend of Roosevelt, wrote and published a sonnet calling upon "Dead Washington" to "wake and blast [Wilson's] soul" for having sacrificed the nation's security and honor to his own "complacent dream."[9]

Support for the administration plan fully evaporated when Garrison told an already skeptical Military Affairs Committee of the US House of Representatives that the only alternative to a "Continental Army" was conscription. Garrison had proved himself an alarmist, and the president was forced to change tack. He told James Hay, head of the House Military Affairs Committee, that the plan was only a suggestion, that he would support enlargement of the National Guard if it could be federally controlled, and that he was firmly opposed to compulsory military service. Garrison, refusing to endorse any program "based on State forces," offered to resign. Without immediately accepting the offer, Wilson started planning for a post-Garrison military policy. Admitting that he saw "insuperable constitutional obstacles" to direct federal control of the National Guard, he nonetheless assured Hay that he was not "dogmatically committed to any one plan." He would consider any means toward "genuine nationalization of the reserve forces" that Hay's committee or anyone "thoroughly acquainted with the subject matter felt ready to propose."[10] In the meantime, he planned a public speaking tour with a double focus on the necessity of preparedness and the desirability of compromise.

By distancing himself from Garrison's plan yet reiterating his commitment to national security, Wilson hoped to convert pacifists to his cause and keep progressive nationalists in his tent. Still, international obligation remained his touchstone. His "Western Tour" opened in semantically incongruous New York City, where he carefully thanked James R. Mann, the Republican House minority leader, for a recent speech expressing willingness to "forget party lines" and "act with a common mind and impulse for the service of the country." Preparedness, he explained, was a means for Americans to preserve "the principles upon which their political life is founded": the democratic principles of freedom and justice, "ideals which are the staff of life of the soul itself" and which Americans had always held "for others as well." These principles were foundational to lasting peace, and with the "circumstances of the world" changing daily, it was the duty of the United States to amass the power to defend them "against every contingency."[11] Rather than careen into militarism, a prepared America would retain its democratic balance as the surrounding earth convulsed.

As his tour progressed, Wilson focused more and more on the unpredictability of events—and on preparedness as insurance against them. As he told a Cleveland audience, "peace is not always within the choice of the nation." The chaos of external events might force Americans to fight for the freedoms they stewarded for all nations. That stewardship was the source of the nation's honor, and despite the president's "double obligation" to maintain peace and honor both whenever possible, the two were not coterminous. "Do you not see," he asked his listeners, "that a time may come when it is impossible to do both of these things?" Though dreading such a time, it was clear to Wilson where his choice would lay. The "real man," he declared (in the gendered language that both opponents and advocates of preparedness used against their respectively bestial or effeminate foes), "believes that his honor is dearer than his life; and a nation is merely all of us put together." The United States, Wilson concluded, must strive to maintain peace. But to set peace above honor would cost Americans the respect and confidence of a world that looked to them as "the champions of humanity and of the rights of men."[12]

Wilson's rhetoric in New York, Cleveland, and other stops on his preparedness tour echoed his speech to the Manhattan Club before the Garrison plan fiasco. Still, two new and substantive ideas, again congruent with philosophical pragmatism, gained salience as the tour progressed. The unpredictable nature of international relations, and thus the contingent character of American policy, was one. The other was his insistence on the compatibility of conviction and compromise. In Saint Louis, the last stop of his tour, Wilson hammered both points home with a fervor that drew repeated bursts of applause from his audience. "The peace of the world, including America, depends upon the aroused passion of other nations, and not upon the motives of the nation itself," Wilson declared. National and global security thus depended on American preparedness in its broadest sense: on citizens highly trained not only in the arts of war but also in the arts of industry, commerce, and cooperative political action. Such preparedness merely applied, in the context of global interdependence, "the ancient American principle that the men of the country shall be made ready to take care of their own government." As for the specific details of preparedness, true Americans need not fear for their conscience. Deliberative discourse would win the day for anyone willing to engage in it: "I am not jealous, and you are not jealous, of the details. No man ought to say to any legislative body, 'You must take my plan or none at all'—that is arrogance and stupidity. But we have the right to insist . . . on the essential thing, that is to say, a principle, a system, by which we can secure a trained citizenship." Conversation, not calumny; discourse, not diatribe; these were basic to the mode of self-government that Wilson urged Americans to preserve for the world. The true "voice of America" was not the bluster of a Roosevelt or the homily of a Bryan; it was the "very still" but "very powerful voice" of a people speaking firmly after careful reflection. In urging military preparedness on practical and humanitarian grounds, Wilson believed he had heard that voice and spoke its common counsel. "I believe," he closed, "that that voice has brought me, in unmistaken accents, the resolution of this country to do whatever is necessary and essential to do, in order that no man might question the honor and perfect integrity or disregard the rights of the United States of America."[13]

The tour was a triumph in many respects. Audiences across the western heartland of antipreparedness welcomed Wilson warmly and even excitedly. The president had "resumed control of the situation," opined the *New Republic*, and provided "a wonderful example" of the bold leadership the presidency could afford.[14] But Wilson's troubles soon reasserted themselves. Garrison, almost impossibly, had further alienated the military affairs committee during his absence, again scorning federalization of the National Guard and insisting on his continental army plan. Hay informed Wilson that his committee would never endorse a continental army as big as Garrison demanded and that Congress as a whole overwhelmingly favored federal control of the National Guard as a solution to the nation's lack of reserve forces. Any attempt to expand the regular army would have to involve serious consideration of this proposal.[15]

For the second time Garrison offered to resign, and this time Wilson accepted. He too had hoped for a continental army, but he had meant what he said about compromise on his tour. "The one obvious thing," he wrote Garrison, "is the necessity for calm and deliberate action on our part at this time when matters of such gravity are to be determined." This meant more than just careful thought; it meant "action which takes into very serious consideration views different from our own." Wilson was not convinced that the National Guard could be federalized, but he felt "in duty bound" to remain "open to conviction on that side." No bill had yet been drafted, and Wilson thought it "a very serious mistake to shut the door" on a "good faith" effort by Congress to meet the nation's security needs "in a way of their own choosing."[16] Such a politically charged issue, Wilson reasoned, required the method of common counsel for its resolution.

Others thought Wilson's deliberative political ethics had blinded him to more immediate practical dangers. "I cannot bring the President to realize the importance of making ready to meet the crisis which may fall upon him any day," wrote House privately.[17] House misjudged the keenness of his friend's weather eye. But his forecast of a storm blowing in from the Atlantic, and hitting Wilson with particular force, would prove accurate.

When Garrison officially resigned, much of the support Wilson had garnered among preparedness advocates, including the *New Republic* editors, evaporated. "Mr. Garrison's resignation exposes a condition which close observers of Congress have suspected for some time," Lippmann wrote on February 19, 1916. Only Garrison had approached the army expansion plan "as a whole," Lippmann continued, "for to think of the plan as a whole was to think in terms of the nation, and few Congressmen do." Hence the desire to expand the National Guard: "No matter that forty-eight separate militias are an absurdity for a nation. It promised to open another pork barrel." Garrison had courageously opened his national "horizon" to Wilson, who, in Lippmann's view, had weakly capitulated to the myopic provincialism of the states. But the problem was greater than Wilson's cowering before "little Congressmen," Lippmann wrote. "It arises because our vivid interests are still local and private in scope. . . . The evil of localism is a radical evil, so radical that it frustrates practically all effort to reform anything." Many Americans felt "out of sorts" with their "straggling democracy": shamed by a "freedom without high purpose," a Congress that was nothing more than "a convention of local interests," and a diplomacy that "uses words without underwriting the costs." Yet Americans themselves were the problem. Wilson's failure to secure a truly national program of military preparedness was symptomatic of "the general slouchiness and distraction of the public morale"—just one more instance of the politics of fission precluding the progressive goal of an "integrated America."[18]

Whether Lippmann's fellow Americans were indeed such a "scattered people" as he claimed, his assessment of their congealing discontent with their president's foreign policy was accurate.[19] In mid-February and again in early March, members of the propreparedness National Security League staged enormous rallies in New York City to protest Garrison's resignation and promote both a continental army and compulsory military training. By the summer of 1916, despite his recent *Sussex* success, Wilson was taking constant fire for failing to defend Americans against the encroachments of Europe's belligerents. Roosevelt was especially shrill, raining oaths upon pacifists and blaming Wilson personally for American deaths at sea.[20]

The president knew he must regain control of the preparedness issue. But far less bellicose voices than Roosevelt's informed his change in policy. Instead he drew from the marginally less critical but appreciably more coherent suggestions of pragmatist nationalists such as Lippmann. Deeply worried about the nation's defenses yet loathing "militarism" as the midwife of autocracy, Wilson determined to transform the debate by linking preparedness not only to internationalist foreign policy but also to domestic progressive reform.

The editors of the *New Republic* had already laid out a somewhat twisting yet trailblazing path toward such a policy. They had taken a proarmament stance almost immediately. Seeing no need for immediate intervention in Europe, they denied that the decision to remain at peace precluded preparing for war: "Pacifism must, then, be sharply distinguished from passivism. The newer ideal of peace, whether in domestic or foreign policy, has to be actively and intentionally promoted. . . . Passivism merely makes it easy for militarism. It repeats in the larger realm of international politics the error which the advocates of *laissez-faire* used to make in domestic politics."[21] As early as December 1914, the editors were applying Lippmann's pragmatist progressive logic of "mastery" to foreign affairs. International "passivism" was a species of "*laissez-faire*"; domestic and foreign policy were continuous. In a series of editorials throughout the summer of 1915, the journal developed this position as it bore on the question of preparedness, asking in pragmatic fashion, " 'Preparedness' for What?" The editors proposed a radical reply: preparedness promised not only the power to encourage democratic change in international relations but also a means to increase the pressure for democratic social control at home.[22]

By autumn Croly, Lippmann, and Walter Weyl had fully fleshed out their idea. In the November 6, 1915, issue, they described preparedness as an ironic "Trojan Horse," a seeming monument to militarism containing the machinery of domestic peace. War had forced Europe's governments into breaking up inefficient monopolies, streamlining factories, and marshaling resources to stave off unemployment and starvation. Most important, as the British case demonstrated, war had forced recognition of labor's power and its right to a voice in national policy. Did this mean all good reformers should demand immediate American intervention? No; the improvisational measures forced on Europe by war involved painful contortions of government and society. "Preparedness," by contrast, "would mean that these measures had been planned ahead." Planning the efficient deployment of society's resources before a crisis occurred would prevent much waste, anxiety, and domestic strife. Indeed, the scientific pursuit of economic and military preparedness would be an exercise in "social organization" on the vast scale that genuine industrial democracy required. In this sense it prepared a nation for much more than foreign wars. To be unprepared for conflict abroad was to be unprepared for conflict at home as well. "A planless society cannot suddenly become purposeful," wrote the editors; "a nation corrupted by bitter feuds, by rankling injustice, by thoughtless education will reveal itself hideously in time of war. Those who are complacent about the [social] horrors of peace will have to admit this. If they have not the courage and the intelligence to deal with the problem for its own sake, they may at least be ready to deal with it for the sake of military preparedness."[23]

The plan to "integrate America" that Lippmann proposed after Garrison's resignation described even more explicitly the relationship between a policy of preparedness and a "vision of a purposeful America."[24] This vision once seemed to belong to Roosevelt, who had tried to articulate a "conception of the state and of the obligations of citizenship" that cohered with "the general feeling that the United States can no longer be irresponsible in the world." Lippmann traced this feeling to the analogous conviction that "industrial life must be organized from out of its chaos and waste, that the population cannot be allowed to disintegrate into its European elements, that citizenship is a much firmer duty than it ever was, and that in general there must be an end to the slack and thoughtlessness and drift of our national life." In short, Roosevelt aimed "to draw Americans out of their local, group, class, and ethnic loyalties into a greater American citizenship." Viewed correctly, this was not a nationalist vision merely, "for every time we increase the area of vivid and practical loyalty we take a step toward decreasing the friction of mankind." An "integrated America" was the precursor to an integrated world. "We shall learn world-citizenship, if at all, in the school of graded experience," Lippmann wrote, "when the object of loyalty is constantly being enlarged."[25]

Tragically, this "impulse" for integration had been diverted from constructive channels by Roosevelt himself. His "revolutionary conception" of nationalism was now fully eclipsed by "his contempt for Mr. Wilson and his command of epithets of scorn." His single-minded commitment to "compulsory military training" as the nation's best hope to "redeem its spiritual life" was equally misguided, a "mechanical solution for a real problem." Taking a page from John Dewey's book, Lippmann wondered how, "at the very moment when teachers are discovering that discipline and responsibility cannot be produced by blind obedience to superiors, military enthusiasts are in haste to embrace the discarded theory and to educate a people through the drillmaster." Such "conscriptionists" subordinated reason to ideology, insisting "that if the idea is a good one men ought to stand for it whether it is practical or not." They failed to see that the successful implementation and positive benefits of compulsory service hinged on the very virtues it was meant to promote. Its adoption required that Americans "grasp the vision, realize their own faults, and have the collective energy to change their whole traditional view of life. If they could do that, compulsion would hardly be necessary." At least at the present stage of American political culture, compulsory service was not an impractical but a *useless* idea; it could only be implemented after its object had been achieved. And for a pragmatist like Lippmann, there was no such thing as a good, useless idea.[26]

In any case, Lippmann asserted, consent, not compulsion, is the fundamental "good" of a democracy; and Americans would not consent to a more highly organized national order until the government seeking it earned their sympathy and trust. "Our government is weak in the affections of the people because it is a weak government, because it rarely touches their lives, because it does not protect them, because it is still something distant and unimportant," Lippmann lamented.[27] In his view, no compulsory sacrifice could induce large numbers to serve such a government or their fellow citizens beyond their mandate. Instead, a plan to forge a stronger civic nation must begin by identifying and taking all existing opportunities to make the national government a positive presence in citizens' lives. Just as Hamilton secured the Union by wedding an array of financial and commercial interests to its survival, twentieth-century nationalists must "wed larger and larger masses of Americans to the federal government."[28]

The railroads offered a starting point. Nationalizing the industry would help secure the gains of its unions and create a staging ground for further advances in industrial democracy. Conversely, the lack of a unified rail service precluded mobilization and coordination of military, industrial, and other resources in case of a national emergency. Finally, a federally controlled rail service would create "a very large class of bondholders, employees, shippers, executives, whose immediate interests were national rather than local." To the objection that government was "too inefficient" for such an undertaking, Lippmann replied that "efficiency grows from practice and need. Give a great enough number of people a vital interest in railroad efficiency," and "they will develop that efficiency." Here as elsewhere, Lippmann articulated the classic pragmatist theory of democracy as a running experiment in civic education, in which policies were not merely goals in themselves but pedagogical tools. Only "great enterprise" could teach Americans "their most needed lessons: that a successful democracy must have a powerful government, that it must be a government that touches their lives if they are to cherish it, that it must be the custodian of interests so great that inefficiency and waste and the lack of public spirit are crimes against the state."[29]

If this last clause awakens in modern readers a reflexive fear of the Nazi and Soviet police states, the second phase of Lippmann's plan traces a wholly different, though perhaps equally radical, trajectory. "A statesman interested in the integration of America must realize some proposal which will give human warmth to the national government," Lippmann wrote. Industrial efficiency was not enough; if "the people are to weave their affections into the structure of the nation the government must be able to reach them in sickness and in sorrow, in misfortune and in old age." A truly united citizenry required what few Americans had then seriously considered, and few have since: a full-fledged welfare state. Prefiguring Franklin Roosevelt's "Four Freedoms" of a quarter century later, Lippmann called for a "nation-wide system of health, accident, maternity, old age and unemployment insurance" to give all Americans, and especially its millions of struggling workers, "greater security, greater share in the government, a discipline in cooperation, and a sense that they lived in a nation which did not ignore them."[30]

Lippmann was not so naive as to argue that personal investment in national affairs would arise spontaneously from a healthier, wealthier work force. The key to his system of social insurance was its focus on the active cultivation of habits of self-government. Like Brandeis, Lippmann envisioned a system of production and protections that workers helped direct in cooperation with other interests. "If such a system were cooperatively administered," it would generate "so much experience in self-government, so much good-will, and provide so great a demonstration of what the state means and might mean, that a real impulse would have been given towards efficiency and discipline and a synthesized people." With such experience behind them, Americans might finally be willing to nationalize education, to ensure preparedness "not merely for military responsibilities but for all other necessities which are frustrated by the chaos and suspicion of our life." It was a bold plan, and Lippmann offered just as bold a challenge to any statesman who would channel the "impulse" behind preparedness into a truly radical program of social reconstruction. "Mr. Roosevelt and the Progressives would have to do more than 'come out' for such a program," he wrote. "They would have to see to it that it was not a plank in a platform, but the essence of their best vision. They would have to make it their own with the same fervor that they are now pouring into military preparedness alone. This is the dwelling of which armament is merely a façade."[31] It was not Roosevelt, however, but Wilson who would come to picture this dwelling as one in which Americans could and should reside. It was Wilson, too, who would discover firsthand how difficult it was to build it in the midst of a global earthquake.

After the *Sussex* incident, the editors of the *New Republic* called even more fervently for military preparedness, both as a means of protection and as an engine of democratization. This is not to say they abandoned their critical attitude toward the "hotter" sorts of preparedness advocates. Nor did the journal ignore the fine and dangerous line between social reconstruction and social engineering. In articles that made the cover page twice in four weeks, John Dewey warned readers that to channel all social energy into "highly specialized divisions of labor" would create a "habit of mind . . . as incompatible with democracy as is sheer militarism." Rather, the key to preparedness was "a combination of a scientific and a humanistic education," cultivating the human instinct to refine and expand knowledge through a "wide and free range of human contacts." When Americans learned "to interpenetrate this human sense of one another with thorough training in scientific method and knowledge," he asserted, "we shall have found ourselves educationally." Public schools, not drilling fields, were the proper training grounds for instilling this rigorous humanism, an ethos crucial to the conduct of domestic and foreign affairs alike. As Dewey informed his fellow Americans, their contacts were expanding; "we are part of the same world as that in which Europe exists and into which Asia is coming."[32] Meanwhile, because the manner and goals of preparedness had such momentous implications, Dewey's *New Republic* editors challenged Wilson to lead the cause before its potential to effect "democratic organization" and shape "an adequate foreign policy" was lost.[33]

The journal's position evolved partly in response to Lippmann's increasing contact with the Wilson administration. Lippmann was spending more and more time on Capitol Hill researching his "Washington Notes" column for the *New Republic*, and he often dropped in to chat with Wilson's cabinet members (as much to share his opinions as to gather information).[34] His conversations after the *Sussex* sinking led him to believe that "there wasn't one of them who had looked beyond the possibility of a rupture with Germany and had tried to think out a policy in case things became still more acute." The *New Republic*'s first major editorial after the president's "so-called ultimatum to Germany" aimed to address that problem at the source.[35] In "An Appeal to the President," the editors made one of their most impassioned pleas for adopting an explicitly anti-German "neutrality."[36] It was true, Lippmann wrote for the staff, that to "declare war now in the old-fashioned way" and "join the Allies" would make Americans the accomplices of British and French imperialists covetous of enemy territories. But the lack of any clear American policy increased the risk of drifting into the war with no say in the peace—surely no formula for a just and lasting settlement. The situation required more radical action: The United States "must abolish the old doctrine of neutrality." If Americans truly cherished justice and fairness, they could not remain "neutral between the violator and his victim" but must call on their government to exercise "its moral power, its economic resources, and in some cases its military power against the aggressor."[37]

The editors submitted their "suggestions" to the president "with all due respect"—and might have been surprised at the respect with which he received them.[38] Wilson clipped and filed the "Appeal," but not before highlighting Lippmann's call to define Germany as the aggressor and "aid her enemies" until the high command abandoned submarine warfare, evacuated occupied territories, and accepted that to flout arbitration was to invite the wrath of the international community.[39] In fact, Wilson had already begun to approach the issue of preparedness in terms of the editors' earlier question: "Preparedness for what?" He too knew that neutrality was frangible and that "mental and moral preparedness" for the *why* of war was as important as physical preparedness for the *when*.[40] Multiple factors contributed to this convergence of perspective. Most important, war was a distinct possibility. By vigorously protesting the sinking of the *Sussex*, Wilson had indeed led his nation "to the breaking point," as Lippmann put it.[41] Wilson also faced an approaching election, ahead of which pacifists decried his militarism and hawks his spinelessness. He had to take a clear position on preparedness, and in the *New Republic* he found a stance both consistent with his ideals and conducive to his political survival.

Finally, the editors had found an influential spokesman for their views in Garrison's erstwhile "pacifist" successor in the War Department, Newton D. Baker.[42] A reformist lawyer and former mayor of Cleveland, Baker resembled Wilson in his instinctually moderate leanings yet openness to advanced progressive stances. He soon established himself as one of the president's closest advisers, ablest administrators, and warmest supporters both during and after Wilson's term in office. Baker's appointment alone ensured that Lippmann would make his introductions, to be followed by periodic inquiries (or intrusions). Baker apparently viewed their discussions in the first light, for the two became good friends through their many talks in his office. By May 1916, Baker was asking Lippmann for a "schedule" of his regular visits to Washington and for notice of any "irregular comings" so that he could "have a chance to see you when you are here." By late summer Baker had brought Lippmann fully up to speed on the army's preparedness and mobilization plans, and in September described him to Wilson as "the wisest, sanest, and best of The New Republic group."[43]

Though each doubtless shaped the views of the other, Lippmann's influence on his elder was more immediately apparent. Baker was soon echoing Lippmann's concern over the cabinet's post-*Sussex* lassitude over preparedness. At the height of discussion over the proper response to the sinking, he sent Wilson a "Memorandum on Preparedness as a Policy" stating three necessary "elements of national preparedness." Along with a "speedily mobilized" army and a navy "adequate in equipment and personnel," Baker's plan demanded exactly what the *New Republic* had urged for months: "such an organization of the industrial, commercial, financial and social resources of the nation as will enable them to be mobilized, both to support the military arm and to continue the life of the nation during the struggle." Baker went on to endorse the type of political mastery Lippmann propounded, suggesting that the "widespread agitation" around preparedness could be channeled to practical ends. Though causing some discomfort, "this enthusiasm ought not to be allowed to cool" but "should be captured and capitalized into a policy tending to strengthen and consolidate our national life." A concrete statement of the three aims identified could "lead the emotion for preparedness into definite lines and to make of it a national policy."[44]

Baker's suggestions for the content of such a statement reveal further affinities with the ideas of the *New Republic* pragmatists, and specifically Lippmann's vision of an "integrated America." Its "pivotal point" should be that economic and social mobilization were as important as military mobilization in a crisis, and likely more difficult. Given the unsettled state of world affairs, a "new national machinery" was needed to bring "the highest expert acquaintance" with the nation's economic and social resources into contact and coordination. Under such machinery, a national council would award peacetime contracts to firms in exchange for government authority to commandeer their plant and personnel in a "national emergency." In such a case, male employees would be retained "as enlisted men" and owners compensated based on "normal dividends," precluding a "profit interest in war." With worker-soldiers trained in new skills and higher positions filled from among their ranks, converted plants would be continually "reinforced" with both fresh perspectives and the spirit of "voluntary cooperation." In sum, Baker's "third element of preparedness" comprised a suite of legal, political, and economic mechanisms to make industrial mobilization as "automatic" as military mobilization, "and this through sympathetic cooperation between" instead of "coercive action on the part of the Government."[45]

By the time Baker's plan crossed Wilson's desk, the latter had committed himself to an army plan that he hoped would appeal to the moderate security concerns of most Americans. Working closely with Hay's committee, he was won over to the idea of an expanded, federally controlled National Guard, and on March 23 the House voted its overwhelming approval for a bill embodying this idea. When the bill proved unacceptable to the Senate, Wilson steered a compromise bill through the conference committee. The bill passed both chambers in May, providing for a federalized National Guard and limited expansion of the regular army.[46] The Army Reorganization Bill, signed June 3, 1916, met none of Baker's requirements for the "third element of preparedness" and did little to please strident preparedness advocates. And yet the Baker plan was not ignored. In May, Wilson had encouraged Baker to discuss the matter with banker Bernard M. Baruch, who had approached Wilson with similar concerns not long before. Then, in a Memorial Day address to business leaders, Wilson had publicly promoted Baker's "third element," asking listeners if they would "lend a hand" in preparing the nation for danger, to preempt coercion in the event of a crisis. "A bill is lying upon my table now ready to be signed," he told them, "which bristles all over with that interrogation point."[47]

The Army Reorganization Bill, silent on that question, was not the bill he had in mind. Baker had continued to meet with Lippmann since drafting his preparedness memorandum, and on the day Lippmann's "Appeal to the President" was published—April 22—Baker wrote the author asking if they might "arrange to start early some evening and talk late," adding, "there are several sub-surface things about which I am anxious to have your advice." By the time Wilson made his Memorial Day pitch to business leaders, Baker's proposal for a civilian "general staff" had been introduced as a bill in the House of Representatives. Taken with the scheme, Wilson shrewdly convinced Hay to present it to the military affairs committee as an amendment to the army appropriations bill. Baker's "third element of preparedness" was incorporated into the version Wilson signed into law on August 29. Through such Trojan horsemanship, Baker and Wilson secured legal provision for what became the Council of National Defense (CND), the bureaucratic giant that would steer America's economic mobilization upon entry into the First World War. "The Council of National Defense has been created because the Congress has realized that the country is best prepared for war when thoroughly prepared for peace," Wilson told Americans in October.[48] With that statement, Wilson encapsulated the arguments for a unified and rationalized domestic and foreign policy that had filled the pages of the *New Republic* since issue one.

That same spring of 1916, while the editors of the *New Republic* were just glimpsing the magnitude of the shift in their government's military policy, Wilson surprised them again. On May 27, the president first publicly endorsed American involvement in a league of nations. From then on, the creation of a viable machinery of international cooperation was the central aim of Wilson's foreign policy.

That a supranational body of states—part parliament, part court, part police force—would have prevented the war, and that only its incarnation in a postwar order could redeem Europe's descent into hell, was not Wilson's personal inspiration.[49] Political rivals in the Grand Old Party had as much claim to this gospel as he. Republicans including former President Taft, New York Senator Elihu Root, Harvard President A. Lawrence Lowell, publisher Hamilton Holt, and other prominent "conservative internationalists" led the largest American constituency supporting international organization before 1917. Valuing stability over change, their hopes for international order centered initially on a world court establishing legal norms that, slowly but surely, would restrain the bullying and sparring that sparked Europe's general brawl. A subset, influenced by French and British movements and led by former president Taft, went beyond such strict legalism to advocate internationally coordinated measures compelling states to arbitrate disputes before resorting to war. In the summer of 1915, this philosophy was enshrined in the official platform of the League to Enforce Peace (LEP), adopted at Philadelphia's Independence Hall on June 17. The platform called for a postwar organization of states pledged to submit disputes over treaty obligations or international law to a council of arbitration, and "non-justiciable" disputes touching on national honor or national interest to a court of conciliation. Signatory nations would pledge to respond with economic sanctions and military force to any act of war against a fellow signatory by any state—signatory or otherwise—that failed first to submit its case to the international community.[50]

The LEP's "Warrant from History" persuaded thousands of Americans that the security of even the strongest nation depended on collective proscription and punishment of aggression. Yet the LEP's posse commitatus approach to peacekeeping was not the only product on the postwar-policy market, and the group's inattention to the socioeconomic causes of war, skepticism of a mediated peace, and indifference to the lack of democratic control over national foreign policies tarnished its appeal for Wilson. In this regard he was closer to Jane Addams and her colleagues in the Woman's Peace Party (WPP), who not only emphasized the concomitance of social justice and international peace but feared deeply for both should their nation slide into war. Pacifist that she was, Addams nonetheless credited Dewey with helping the WPP find "a foothold in reality" for its program and a "method" for developing and refining it—a method of deliberative engagement rather than polemical denunciation of divergent perspectives. Pragmatist that she was, Addams employed that method rigorously, overseeing the drafting of a "practical solution" to the problem of war and bringing it repeatedly to Wilson's and the world's attention. That solution called for an early, mediated peace; limitation and nationalization of arms manufactures; democratic checks on foreign policy; international free trade; and a "Concert of Nations to supersede 'Balance of Powers' "—including an "international police" to replace "rival armies and navies."[51]

Wilson shared many of these goals and several others that distinguished the WPP from the LEP. Most important was an apparatus that did not just enforce international laws but also worked to eradicate the causes of their infraction—causes including the economic and social inequities that immiserated, marginalized, and radicalized populations. Indeed, Wilson told Addams in January 1916 that the WPP's plan for a new international order was "the best formulation which up to the moment has been put out by anybody."[52]

Yet while welcoming a politically constructive alternative to the LEP's more legalistic, reactive program, Wilson found the WPP's stance against military preparedness naive—especially as successive crises on the high seas threatened to suck the nation into war.[53] Seeking a third way, he soon discovered that Addams was not the only one applying "the Dewey teaching" to the problem of peace. Like Wilson, Dewey's friends at the New Republic considered the LEP's legalism as sterile as the WPP's antimilitarism. Before either group was officially founded, Croly, Lippmann, and Weyl had begun sketching a hybrid plan for peace: an armed "league of neutrals," committed to both collective security and pursuit of shared "ideals"—including expansion or incorporation into a comprehensive world body. The editors argued that a neutrality of simple nonbelligerence bound nations such as Belgium to choose either dependence on or complacence toward the world's great powers. By contrast, a neutrality defined by the "joint interests and ideals" of peaceable peoples would "command a much increased respect" when backed by "the armed support" of multiple nations. To secure "the moral and material cooperation" of such a league, one side in a conflict would naturally lend its assistance if the other violated a member's rights, and such assistance, offered to a collective rather than a single, distressed state, would entail no clientelist expectations. Should neutrality be thus "energized, organized, and charged with positive ideas and purposes," wrote

the editors, the Belgiums of the world "would have earned by common sacrifices a species of joint independence, wholly divorced from offensive belligerency, which would be a new thing under the sun and which might become
the point of departure for a substantial and triumphant league of peace."[54]
Though nascent, this was the journal's first explicit call and detailed
rationale for a collective organization of states "prepared to exercise a very
sharp supervision over the foreign policy of its members"—supervision
sharper than that of any hypothetical league the editors had encountered.
The subordination of national sovereignty to international security became
a defining feature of the postwar order that they and Wilson would so earnestly promote in the coming years. So did another of the editors' early
obsessions: adaptability. The "vice" of other nonpacifist "schemes" in cir-
culation, they argued in March 1915, was a narrow focus on "preventing
wars," to the exclusion of facilitating peace. The "static view of the world"
they embodied typified the "citizens of satisfied powers," for whom keeping the peace meant maintaining the status quo. But a league of peace that
made "no provision for any organic alteration in the world's structure" was
doomed to fail. "We can no more prevent war by organizing a defensive
league than revolution by creating a police. We must deal with causes, must
provide some means alternative to war by which large grievances can be
redressed and legitimate ambitions satisfied."[55]
Despite the LEP's failure on this score, the journal welcomed its formation in June 1915 and consistently praised its work thereafter. The editors'
motives were strategic. Despite its "limitations and dangers," Croly considered the LEP platform "the most promising concrete proposal that has been
made since the war began." Without shying from criticism, he resolved to
support its general mission. With its roster of business leaders, university
presidents, media magnates, and former senators, the LEP was bound to
set down roots in the public imagination; perhaps the *New Republic* could
coax a more complex, multifoliate body from the dicot of a world court and
mutual-defense society.[56]
Acquiescing to this strategy, Lippmann nonetheless took Croly's caveats to heart, echoing Addams, Eastman, and other pacifistic pragmatists in
criticizing the LEP's failure to address "the constructive elimination of the
causes of war." In *The Stakes of Diplomacy*, published in November 1915,
Lippmann adjudged the LEP's panacea of arbitration inadequate to that task.
The disputes drawing nations into conflict rarely involved points of fact or
mutually acknowledged norms, he argued. Rather, "real disputes are matters of policy. They are attempts to say how something shall be done, whose
word of command shall be recognized." Consequently, he concluded, "The

modern substitute for war is not arbitration, but election." As democratic nations had discovered, human beings "see different truths in the same situations, and no pope exists whom we are ready to have pronounce between us." As a shrinking world brought ever greater numbers into shared situations, governments, like individuals, must find an alternative to both the tragedy of anarchy and the farce of absolutism. In short, they must substitute the "political method" for "pretensions to sovereignty." In contrast to Addams and company, however, Lippmann also insisted that governments commit to defend such deliberative processes. Like James in the Civil War's wake, Lippmann in the Great War's midst concluded that such processes offered the best hope but no sure guarantee of peace—and then only if scrupulously maintained against threats and restored after violations. "Peace," he affirmed, "implies not only the construction of machinery for unifying mankind, but the readiness of enough men to defend that machinery."[57] Neither a central legal authority nor an inclusive political forum alone could anchor a lasting new order. Some hybrid would have to be conceived.

The "Appeal to the President" issued after the *Sussex* sinking confirmed the *New Republic*'s commitment to just such a thought experiment—and to seeing it run in the real world. It was necessary, Lippmann wrote, that Wilson "enunciate not only a great aspiration but a great policy," and the editors were ready to help formulate the latter. Synthesizing the journal's long-standing positions on neutrality and national security with the positive proposals of the LEP and WPP programs, Lippmann outlined a scheme incorporating a policy of comprehensive preparedness into a broad system of international deliberation and justice. Of course, he wrote, the United States must be "ready to go in" to a war it might be unable to avoid. But Americans must be equally prepared to make peace. To let the Allies make the terms was unthinkable. Their aims embodied fear, hatred, and vengefulness; the United States must enter the war for the sole purpose of fashioning a new world. This new world would be organized not around the principle of neutral rights but around the imperative "to uphold the law whether your rights are violated or not"; for in an interdependent world, as in an interdependent nation, the "common defense of rights is the only way individual rights can be maintained."[58]

This internationalist critique of the "old doctrine of neutrality" had filled the pages of the *New Republic* since its debut: national honor and interest both demanded resistance to aggression. But in answering the question, "How does one define the aggressor?" Lippmann's "Appeal" first articulated the unifying concept of Wilson's mature internationalism: the

power and sanctity of deliberative discourse among nations. "The aggressor," Lippmann asserted, "is the nation that will not submit its quarrel to
international inquiry, that will not suspend action until the world has had a
chance to pass judgment upon it, or that pursues its quarrel after the world
has decided against it." Whereas the LEP would compel only arbitration of
disputes, Lippmann insisted that the community demand compliance and
hold accountable any nation refusing to show a Jamesian "good temper"
when a rival "fairly wins its innings."[59] That Germany cease torpedoing commercial ships and evacuate occupied territory must remain the immediate
objects of American policy. The ultimate criterion, however, was to establish that in future, "all nations shall use their resources against the Power
which refuses to submit its quarrel to international inquiry"—as Wilson himself noted on the copy of the "Appeal" preserved in his papers. If this objective was clearly announced by the United States and accepted by Germany,
peaceful intercourse between those nations might resume. More important,
by insisting on a pragmatist ethics of inquiry, deliberation, and compromise
in international relations, the president would do "more than anyone else
has ever done to put a sanction behind the law of nations."[60]

    This plan, admitted the editors, could fail. But if successful, it would
codify and operationalize the principle "that an injury to one is an injury
to all," while providing a path "back into the family of nations" for any
German government "ready to acknowledge that there is a greater law than
the law of her own interests." Either way, to endorse such a principle was
to define the meaning of any future "break" with Germany by setting the
terms on which peaceful relations must rest. "Make those terms coincident with an international program," pressed the editors. "Make this crisis
count." Whether war or peace resulted, here was a way of "making the interests of America coincident with the interests of mankind."[61]

    Wilson agreed. Privately, he had desired American participation in an
international body of justice since the beginning of the war; a body whose
transcendence of mere police functions cohered with his other early aim of
a compromise peace.[62] He had viewed the Pan-American Pact as a model for
Europe, and in headier moments as a "light on high for the illumination of
the world." Yet on the issue of a truly global association of states, Wilson
had been publicly silent. He thought it impolitic to voice his enthusiasm
for the idea until public opinion and circumstances warranted. But he had
given it careful thought. House and Sir Edward Grey, the British foreign secretary, had danced around the subject during House's peace mission of February 1915, after Wilson identified an international guarantee of territorial

integrity as essential to any settlement. Embarrassingly, when Grey not only accepted that principle but pressured House to pledge his government to such an arrangement, the latter had to refuse: the tenor of American public opinion was not yet in tune with House and Wilson, and Wilson was loath to raise a ruckus among noninterventionists in Congress.[63]

By December, however—five months before Wilson publicly endorsed the idea—a postwar organization of states had become the pivot of his diplomacy. On the eve of House's second European tour, Wilson informed his emissary that no "rational man could accept" a peace excluding "a league of nations against aggression."[64] The following February, after Wilson's endorsement of a Pan-American treaty, House took the audacious step of inviting Britain (as Canada's sovereign government) into the pact, urging an immediate proposal in Parliament to that effect. Now Wilson could give his public approval. The league movement was in full force, supported in some way or another by Americans of widely varying political persuasions. Despite concerns over how to include an empire in a league of republics, the president hoped that Britain's unequivocal endorsement of Pan-Americanism would catalyze broader European involvement in a world-spanning body.[65]

Wilson was also thinking more systematically about what such a global body might look like. Along with the ideas of the LEP and WPP, he was familiar with several other plans for international organization, including those of the American Socialist Party and the American Union Against Militarism (AUAM), of which Max Eastman's wife, Crystal Eastman, was executive director.[66] Elements of such plans appealed to Wilson, but the *New Republic*'s was closest in substance and spirit to the president's emerging vision. The resonance of Lippmann's "Appeal" with his own thinking is clear from Wilson's "colloquy" with an AUAM delegation just days before he first publicly endorsed the league idea. Deflecting the barb of "pacifism," the delegation's members announced themselves in favor of "reasonable preparedness" but argued that continued expansion of the nation's armed forces would "annul the moral power" so crucial to negotiating a just peace.[67] Wilson disagreed unequivocally: "When you go into a conference to establish the foundations for the peace of the world, you have to go in on a basis intelligible to the people you are dealing with." If a shattered Europe were ever to undertake "a joint effort to keep the peace," it would "expect us to play our proportional part in manifesting the force which is going to rest back of that." Wilson was "just as much opposed to militarism as any man living" and just as committed to reconciling the "family of nations." But any nation or family of nations declaring that it "shall not have any war" better have the chops to "make that 'shall' bite." Happily, a family required smaller "individual contributions" to the force behind that bite than isolated nations were obliged to muster. "Surely," the president asserted, "that is not a militaristic ideal, but a practical one."[68]

Though this was no pitched ideological battle—more a friendly scrimmage—Wilson was well equipped for the engagement.[69] Lippmann had visited the Oval Office only days before his "Appeal" was published, and the young pragmatist made no bones about the need "to invent some kind of coercive policy which would have an actual relation to the submarine issue" that had come to stand for the war in general; in other words, the need for a material complement to moral force. Recounting the episode to his friend Graham Wallas, Lippmann was none too sanguine about his persuasive abilities: "From the talk I had with the President," he wrote on April 21, "I haven't very much hope that any discriminating policy will ever be adopted."[70] He had no way of knowing that Wilson would so carefully read his essay on just that topic, much less deploy his heaviest-gauge arguments for preparedness against the AUAM. When partial transcripts of the colloquy were published, Lippmann and his colleagues were ecstatic. Wilson had expressed "an admirably and completely sound body of doctrine about military preparedness and its relation to democracy," they wrote in the May 13 issue of the *New Republic*. That doctrine was their own: that "militarism" was defined not by the size of a nation's army but "the kind of control" exercised over it. Rather than keep their army weak, Americans should make it "servant" to "a really national policy—one based upon the best immediate adjustment between the national ideals and the important prevailing conditions." In his conversation with the AUAM, Wilson had finally hinted at such a policy: membership in an international body with "bite." Such a "revolution in American foreign policy" would necessitate a national cultural shift. "Yet such is the power over public opinion and the prestige of the American President," the editors concluded, "that an explicit and emphatic statement by him of his intention to use his influence on behalf of such a League would promote it immediately from popular insignificance to popular importance and from the condition of a dubious international experiment into a question of practical foreign politics."[71]

Within days of this challenge, Wilson deemed it time to accept. On May 18, 1916, he belatedly replied to an invitation from William Howard Taft, dated May 9, to address the LEP. Lippmann and company's most recent blandishments and proposals had been fortuitously timed: Having declined a similar invitation from Taft just one month earlier, Wilson was now ready to accept.[72] The president was frustrated with the Allied governments—especially the British, from whom House had led him to expect more. In April, Grey communicated the Allies' refusal to act on the provisions of the House–Grey Memorandum, citing the imperative for "more German failure" on the battlefield "before anything but an inconclusive peace could be obtained." The British also declined to raise the question of the Pan-American Pact in Parliament or curtail their "intolerable" disruptions of American trade.[73] Still, Wilson pushed for peace. On May 10, the day after receiving Taft's invitation, he informed Grey, through House, of his desire to call a peace conference and announce to the world his government's pledge to participate in a postwar association of states. Grey responded with withering candor. A peace conference summoned on Wilson's proposed terms—without proposals for territorial adjustments and indemnities—"would be construed as instigated by Germany to secure peace on terms unfavorable to the Allies while her existing military position is still favorable to her." The belief was "widespread" among Allied observers that the German army, despite its present advanced position, was nearing "collapse." As such, Grey concluded, although "a league of nations may be of the greatest service to humanity," he was not persuaded "as to the desirability of it now."[74]

Time to "get down to hard pan," Wilson told House, and set to work on his speech to the LEP.[75] "We had a little hand in that through Colonel House," Lippmann recalled years later. "I'm not sure I didn't draft the memorandum for House as to what we thought he ought to do."[76] No evidence of such a memorandum exists, but Lippmann was right to recall a clear convergence of administration strategy with his colleagues' suggestions. No longer, resolved Wilson, would he work quietly to convince thick-headed diplomats to blink the war's red haze from their eyes and grasp the chance for peace that shimmered before them. If the Allies would not cooperate in a move for peace, they deserved "the same plain speaking and firmness" from the United States as Germany had gotten. Britain would be alerted by cable that to "do nothing is now, for us, impossible." In the meantime, the administration "must act, and act at once."[77]

It was thus as a spokesman and agent of international change that Wilson appeared before the LEP on May 27, 1916. While "glad to accept" their invitation, he warned his hosts that he did not intend to discuss their program.[78] Rather, as "the desire of the whole world" turned "eagerly" toward peace, Wilson hoped "to give expression to what I believe to be the thought and purpose of the people of the United States on this matter." Though

fought on another continent, the war had affected the United States "profoundly." National interest and "the great interests of civilization" obliged
Americans to hasten its end, and when that end came, to help ensure "that
peace and war shall always hereafter be reckoned part of the common interest of mankind." The war's message to Americans transcended the infernal
roar of clashing armies: "We are participants, whether we would or not, in
the life of the world," Wilson relayed. "The interests of all nations are our
own also. We are partners with the rest."

The importance of this partnership was revealed in the manner of the
war's emergence, "suddenly and out of secret counsels, without warning to
the world." Despite the commonality of interests it threatened, the war came
"without discussion, without any of the deliberate movements of counsel
with which it would seem natural to approach so stupendous a contest." Had
the eventual belligerents acknowledged their implicit partnership, spoken
freely of their fears, and reflected collectively on the possible consequences
of acting on them, they might well "have been glad to substitute conference
for force." The "poignantly clear" lesson of their failure was that "the peace
of the world must henceforth depend upon a new and more wholesome diplomacy." Governments must learn to identify "common interests" and develop
"some feasible method of acting in concert" when they were threatened. The
world's peoples formed a single community, and "must in the future be governed by the same high code of honor that we demand of individuals."

It was a lesson the American people needed as much as any other, having "in the past been offenders against the law of diplomacy which we
thus forecast."[79] And yet, Wilson continued, Americans' convictions were
"rather the more clear" because of it. The time had come to view all peoples
as partners in the republican pursuit of "common agreement for a common object," and to recall "that at the heart of that common object must
lie the inviolable rights of the peoples of mankind." Specifically, Americans must genuinely embrace and unequivocally affirm three core beliefs:
first, "that every people has a right to choose the sovereignty under which
they shall live"; second, "that the small states of the world have a right
to enjoy the same respect for their sovereignty and for their territorial integrity" as the powerful; and finally, "that the world has a right to be free
from every disturbance of its peace that has its origin in aggression and
disregard of the rights of peoples and nations." As a pledge of his nation's
faith, and confident in the support of his fellow citizens, Wilson announced
"that the United States is willing to become a partner in any feasible association of nations formed in order to realize these objects and make them

secure against violation." In a transatlantic riposte to Grey, Wilson offered to "initiate a movement for peace" on negotiated terms, including a "universal association of the nations" charged with upholding neutral rights and preventing "any war begun either contrary to treaty covenants or without warning and full submission of the causes to the opinion of the world—a virtual guarantee of territorial integrity and political independence."

The speech rolled out from the New Willard Hotel like a thunderclap. The *New York Times* deemed it "the most important" delivered by Wilson "since the beginning of hostilities in Europe." The LEP supporters composing the majority of Wilson's audience applauded as if convulsed. Many of their leading lights seemed equally transported. Not a year after the LEP's formation, the president of the United States himself had endorsed American membership in a postwar peacekeeping body. In Hamilton Holt's opinion, the group had abetted and witnessed a world-political coup as epochal as the signing of the Declaration of Independence—in this case, "a Declaration of Interdependence."[80]

Wilson, however, had his own agenda, and it differed greatly from the LEP's. It was an election year, and the LEP had the support of Bull Moose Progressives whose opposition might cost him a second term. Wilson entered the forum of the Willard to sweep the legs of the Republicans, the party most closely linked in the public mind with the LEP's prize of lasting peace. Furthermore, his speech reveals a vision quite different from that of his hosts. In his opening sentence he declined even to discuss, much less endorse, the LEP's program, and what followed was a paean to deliberative discourse and active cooperation, not legal codification and reactive enforcement. The nations of the world, in Wilson's view, shared interests beyond national security, and those interests had to be cultivated. The freedoms of states and the people under them must be protected regardless of whether national security or international peace were directly and immediately affected. As he clearly stated, it was not "alliance" but "common agreement" that was his goal.

Hence Wilson's call for a negotiated peace and refusal to endorse the war aims of the Allies—another divergence from the run of LEP members. Hence also his care to avoid even the slightest implication of German responsibility for the war.[81] These subtleties did not go unnoticed in Europe. The British left was ecstatic over the speech—just the effect Wilson, seeking to put pressure on the Foreign Office, had intended. Viscount Bryce and his comrades in the British league movement were "greatly cheered by the President's recent deliverances on the subject," the like of which they had long hoped to hear.[82] For the most part, however, British opinion was inflamed by Wilson's intrusion in Allied business, especially in the guise of arbiter between moral equals. The hostility of the majority of French commentators to Wilson's mediation offer was surpassed only by their sarcastic mockery of his do-gooder platitudes. German editors, too, dismissed American mediation out of hand.[83] Most disappointing to Wilson were the uniformly negative responses from the major belligerent governments. The Germans evaded the question in hopes that the French and British would bear the ignominy of rejecting peace. They obliged. The French leadership dismissed Wilson's speech as a reelection ploy, while the British Foreign Office, surveying a war map of Europe, was genuinely convinced that immediate peace meant victory for Germany. Thus Grey cabled to House that unless the United States was prepared to ensure, by force of arms, Germany's evacuation of its forces from northwestern Europe and cession of Alsace-Lorraine to France, peace negotiations were futile.[84]

Having chosen his path, the president would not be diverted. Three days after the LEP address, he was rallying crusaders at Arlington National Cemetery. "I shall never, myself, consent to an entangling alliance," he explained to his Memorial Day audience. "But I would gladly assent to a disentangling alliance—an alliance that would disentangle the people of the world from those combinations in which they seek their own private interests and unite the people of the world upon a basis of common right and justice." What the terms of a "disentangling alliance" might be the president did not say, but his vigorous, if vague, support for the idea of a league of nations did much to endear him to liberals and progressives of many stripes. The *New Republic*'s editors thought it "of historic importance," Lippmann told Baker, and hoped they had made that clear to readers.[85]

In fact, they left no doubt as to the significance of "Mr. Wilson's Great Utterance." "President Wilson's declaration on May 22nd [*sic*] at the dinner of the League to Enforce Peace may well mark a decisive turning point in the history of the world," the editors wrote on June 1. "No utterance since the war began" compared with its "overwhelming significance for the future of mankind," while for Americans it marked "the opening of a new period of history and the ending of our deepest tradition." The United States had finally "converted to a program of armament and industrial preparedness which will make our power count." Now the world had an answer to the question, "What does America intend to do with this power?" Monomaniacal calls for a "supreme navy" to cow the fleets of Britain and Japan were the urgings of "madmen," antistrophic echoes of the Old World's suicidal war cry. "Mr. Wilson," on the other hand, had "done some real thinking on the problem of national defense." He had reached the conclusion "of a growing body of people in all the important countries of the world"—namely, that "security cannot be had by any one nation alone" nor "by force divided among 'sovereign' nations. It can be had only by force which is unified under the control of nations that cooperate." A defensive alliance of states retaining individual prerogatives of force gave scant guarantee of security: "Armament cannot defend one *section* of mankind." Rather, "to be of use it must defend an *organization* of mankind."[86]

In the *New Republic* editors' view, the consequences of Wilson's "real thinking" were twofold. First, having "broken with the tradition of American isolation" and "the pernicious doctrine of neutrality," Wilson had effected "one of the greatest advances ever made in the development of international morality." Simultaneously, Wilson had taken "the first practical step towards peace." An American commitment to long-term peace in Europe did not just offer hope to a frightened England, ravaged France, and violated Belgium. It also offered Germany a "choice" between rearming for the future wars that victory would invite or "finding real safety in a league of the Western World."[87] Meanwhile, Europe's liberals could resist calls for a "phantom peace of total exhaustion" with the "vigor of the richest people on earth" behind them. "Let no one suppose that Mr. Wilson made his offer without realizing its significance," the editors closed, repeating, "It may be said at last without any exaggeration that the first move towards peace has been made."[88]

Though their assessment of Wilson's emerging policy was accurate, the editors' rapture had affected their critical thinking. Despite their claims, there were no "definite assurances" from the French or British governments "that such a league is desired."[89] They had also elided their own worries about the League to Enforce Peace, whose program differed from the *New Republic*'s (and Wilson's) more integrative vision. It was true, as the editors wrote, that both the LEP and Wilson sought "not the abolition of force but the improvement of the purposes for which force is used." In attributing to both the general conviction that "force shall be used to defend the community of nations," however, the editors ignored the crucial differences between Wilson's and the LEP's conceptions of that community.[90] In coming years, they would regret Wilson's similar failure to distinguish his conception of collective security and international governance from the myriad permutations his rhetoric inspired.

At this early stage in the public discussion, however, it made some sense to persist in Croly's original LEP strategy. Supporting the LEP's popular version of the league idea allowed the editors to stretch its shape and scope through creative interpretive glosses. This strategy also served another, perhaps more valuable end. Wilson himself read and saved the article from the *New Republic* lauding his speech, and over the next few months the integrationist element the editors had detected in his formula for peace became the key reagent in his own continuing thought experiments.[91] Wilson's "Great Utterance" was a potent fertilizer of the common ground he was coming to share with his erstwhile critics at the *New Republic*, who now saw their president sowing the type of hybrid strain of international governance they were cultivating in their columns. Three weeks after the speech, the editors offered an admiring—and accurate—genealogy of what many modern historians would call "Wilsonianism":

> Bit by bit the President has of late been evolving an imaginative and educative background for the preparedness movement. His speech on the League to Enforce Peace showed that his mind had moved far beyond the mere panic and formless patriotism of the enthusiasts who want to be tremendously prepared for nothing in particular and everything in general. . . . Mr. Wilson declared the truth that armament in America is needed not so much to repel raiding parties from Germany . . . but to give weight to American diplomacy; he followed this by the argument that the only real defense lies in pooling our force with other nations against the aggressor; he met the bogey of militarism with an admirable reaffirmation of civil over military power, of the citizen over the solider; he supplied the honest answer to the sincere pacifist when he insisted that the difference between militarism and democracy lies not in the possession or lack of force but in the political purpose for which force is used.

Wilson, the editors concluded, was thinking broadly and creatively, yet purposefully—a pragmatist's president indeed. "In his treatment of the many-sidedness of the 'preparedness question,'" they concluded, "the President is setting a hot pace."[92]

The pace had been heating up in another field as well, but Wilson was not setting it. By mid-1916 he was again under intense pressure to invade Mexico—not with a small contingent of marines but with a force capable of imposing order on a nation whose revolution threatened to spill its borders.

In fact, the revolution did splatter blood on American soil after Pancho Villa, offended by Wilson's de facto recognition of Venustiano Carranza's regime, determined to destroy relations between the president and the "first chief." Villa committed his first calculated outrage on January 10, 1916, stopping a train in northern Mexico and executing seventeen American engineers. Border-state politicians and the implacably anti-Wilson Hearst papers immediately raised a war cry. But it was not until Villa's bandit army raided the town of Columbus, New Mexico, early on the morning of March 9—looting stores, torching houses, and killing seven American soldiers and twelve civilians—that a military response from the United States became inevitable.[93]

Wilson knew something had to be done about Villa if his Mexican policy, his push for preparedness, and indeed his entire administration were to retain credibility in the eyes of American citizens. He knew, also, that he could not count on Carranza to hunt down and punish Villa. Accordingly, Secretary of State Lansing made clear to Carranza's representative in Washington that US soldiers would likely be sent into Mexico to pursue Villa.[94] Still, Wilson was wary of another Veracruz and adamant to avoid the war that a punitive expedition launched without Carranza's approval was likely to cause. Given the circumstances, the administration's initial solution to the problem was ingenious, if somewhat devious.

First, to assure his American audience, Wilson released a statement on March 11 announcing definite plans to send "an adequate force" into Mexico "with the single object" of capturing Villa. Without consulting Carranza, he gave assurances that the mission would be carried out with the "friendly aid of the constituted authorities in Mexico and with scrupulous respect for the sovereignty of that republic." Before this announcement, on March 10, Carranza had suggested through his Washington envoy, Eliseo Arredondo, a protocol permitting Mexican forces to chase bandits into American territory, and American forces to pursue bandits in Mexican territory, if another incident like that at Columbus should occur. After Wilson's announcement, Carranza warned that any expedition launched without his express permission would constitute an act of war. Wilson and Lansing chose to ignore this warning and instead, in a diplomatic note dated March 13, formally accepted Carranza's suggested protocol of March 10.[95] Eliding Carranza's distinction between past and future raids, the note declared the agreement "complete and in force," praised the de facto government for its "spirit of cooperation," and thanked Carranza for his gracious permission to send troops into Mexico. To further sugar the pill, Lansing issued an additional statement, drafted by Wilson, insisting that Villa's capture was the sole object of American operations in Mexico and repudiating "intervention of any kind in the internal affairs of our sister republic." Carranza, forced to choose between war, capitulation, or apparent cooperation, chose the last; his commanders were instructed to cooperate with the Americans.[96]

Thus Mexico was made to appear an equal partner in the punitive expedition launched on March 15. Wilson's motives, however, were purer than his methods. He shared them with his secretary, Joseph P. Tumulty, who was eager to see American soldiers clean up the national backyard. "Tumulty, you are Irish, and therefore full of fight," Wilson joked. Then he turned serious. "I have to sleep with my conscience in these matters and I shall be held responsible for every drop of blood that may be spent in the enterprise of intervention." True, he continued, "the man on horseback is always an idol," and a Mexican invasion "would mean the triumph of my administration." But in the event, neither he nor "the gentlemen on the Hill who now clamor for it" would have to mount the warhorse. "It is some poor farmer's boy, or the son of some poor widow away off in some modest community, or perhaps the scion of a great family, who will have to do the fighting and the dying." To endure the insults of "coward" and "quitter" was a small price to pay for conserving American and Mexican life, and preserving space for Mexican development. "Time, the great solvent, will, I am sure, vindicate this policy of humanity and forbearance," Wilson predicted. "Men forget what is back of this struggle in Mexico. It is the agelong struggle of a people to come into their own."[97]

Hence his manipulation of the protocol. Unfortunately, catching Villa proved harder than the administration envisioned when it was signed. On March 15, Brigadier General John J. Pershing and thirty-five hundred troops crossed the border with the official, if grudging, blessing of Carranza's government and explicit orders to avoid conflict with the first chief's forces.[98] By April, Pershing's command had swelled to eight thousand and penetrated some three hundred miles into Mexico. Carranza, working through diplomatic channels, renewed his protests, and Wilson's discomfort with the operation grew daily. On April 10, the two governments reached an uneasy, unofficial agreement that Pershing would effect a slow, partial withdrawal by snaking back to the border in ostensible pursuit of Villa.[99] That agreement crumbled on April 13, when Pershing's forces clashed with a "mob" of Mexican civilians—later reported to be Carranza's troops—at Parral, about 180 miles from the US border. The fighting left two Americans and forty Mexicans dead. Coincidentally, Carranza's foreign minister had sent a note to the US State Department the day before demanding the withdrawal of American troops, on the assumption that it was already occurring. The note was published the same day as news of the fighting at Parral, and though it stated merely that it was "now time to treat with the Government of the United States" regarding the expedition's recall, it had the effect of an ultimatum as far as Mexican public opinion was concerned.[100]

Meanwhile, a small but vocal minority of American politicians and citizens, little caring who or what provoked the attack on US troops at Parral, considered it grounds for war. Wilson hardly agreed, but he was determined to avoid the spectacle of US troops expelled from Mexico for bad behavior, or of the US government pleading guilty to trespassing. Stalling for time, he agreed to withdraw troops as soon as recent rumors of Villa's death at the hands of Carranza's forces were corroborated. Meanwhile, Wilson and Baker arranged a conference between Major General Hugh L. Scott and General Alvaro Obregón, Carranza's minister of war, who together agreed on a coordinated hunt for Villa (or his body) and a gradual draw-down of US troops. Tragically, two days later, bandits raided the towns of Glen Springs and Boquillas, Texas, killing three soldiers and a nine-year-old boy.[101] Calls by the jingoistic Hearst papers (and some of more moderate organs) for a Mexican invasion were joined by a savage attack on the administration's weakness by Republican Senator William E. Borah. A small detachment of US cavalry crossed the border, while Carranza sent thousands of troops northward, ostensibly to pursue the Glen Springs–Boquillas raiders and pacify the border regions. Rumors that Carranza was drafting a "new friendly note" to Wilson were quashed, however, by Obregón, who told Scott that the deployment of US cavalry had made the Mexican–American situation "acute."[102]

Indeed, the continued presence of US troops in Mexico had brought anti-American sentiment to such a pitch that Carranza had no choice but to demand a total withdrawal. He instructed his generals to repel any further detachments crossing the border and to use force, if necessary, to prevent Pershing from moving his army in any direction but north. In response, Wilson ordered the National Guard incorporated into the regular army on June 18 and approved a note, dated June 20, informing Carranza's government that American operations in Mexico would continue and that "the gravest consequences" would ensue should American forces be attacked. On June 21, hours after Carranza received the American note, a clash between US and Mexican troops at Carrizal appeared to signal war's arrival. Villa's troops, promised amnesty if they joined in resisting an American invasion, rallied to the *Carrancistas*. Meanwhile, the Wilson administration demanded the immediate release of twenty-three American prisoners captured at Carrizal and the punishment of the incident's Mexican instigators, strongly implying that noncompliance would invite US occupation of northern Mexico. Wilson prepared an address requesting congressional authority for such action, insisting it was not a war against a sovereign and responsible government he contemplated—for no such government existed—but a forced "suspension" of military activity in the border regions until the

Mexican people established a government capable of fulfilling its obligations to its northern neighbor.[103]

Wilson never delivered that message, and war—or whatever he planned on calling it—never came. Carranza deserves much of the credit for this outcome. Despite the tenor of his public pronouncements, he was eager to resolve the differences between the two countries in a peaceful manner. Although the nationalist reaction to the crisis had unified the people behind him and weakened both radical and conservative opponents of his regime, his position was still too precarious to survive the dislocations of a full-scale war. Retreating from the brink, he ordered the release of the twenty-three Americans captured at Carrizal on June 28.[104]

For his part, Wilson was sick at the thought of war with a nation he regarded as painfully but gallantly struggling "to come into its own." His tough talk of recent weeks had been genuine insofar as he considered it his duty to prevent future raids and secure the release of the Carrizal prisoners; but it was directed toward nervous and critical Americans as much as toward the Mexican government. The pressure for war had grown immense. Republican critics blamed Wilson's "watchful waiting" for Villa's continued outrages and Carranza's insolence, and deemed drastic corrective action necessary. Taft declared it Wilson's duty to accept the consequences of his ineptitude and invade Mexico, seizing "every port and city in the entire country." Roosevelt offered to raise a division of twelve thousand men for the purpose. Even some habitually sympathetic editorialists and progressives worried that Wilson's conscientiousness was turning to squeamishness. At some point, they reasoned, it was the government's duty to deliver its citizens, and perhaps Mexico's, from chaos and bloodshed. The president also received pressure to invade from leading advisers, including House, who urged a strong stance against Mexico to enhance the administration's stature in the eyes of Europe's belligerents.[105]

Wilson refused to entertain such suggestions. "INTERVENTION (that is the rearrangement and control of Mexico's domestic affairs by the U.S.) there shall not be now or at any other time if I can prevent it," he declared in a note to House. His draft message to Congress reiterated that stand. However sophistic his distinction between war and not-war, or intervention and nonintervention, Wilson insisted that "the form, the circumstances, and the *personnel* of their government" were the Mexicans' concern.[106] Besides, if the situation in Europe suggested anything to Wilson at that moment, it was to *avoid* war with Mexico. Despite the diplomatic triumph he had gained with Germany's *Sussex* pledge, he was hardly satisfied that his nation's troubles with that country were over. As he earlier explained to Ray

Stannard Baker, he did "not want one hand tied behind him at the very moment the nation might need all its forces to meet the German situation."[107]

Even so, Wilson gave little indication that the German threat was his main reason for avoiding war with Mexico.[108] The primary factors were his ideals of deliberation and cooperation in international relations—ideals that received important moral and practical reinforcement during the last week of June. On June 25, the American Union Against Militarism sent an American officer's eyewitness account of the Carrizal incident to major newspapers. Published widely on June 26, it portrayed another American officer as having provoked the violence. In response, citizens and organizations from across the country flooded the White House mail room with pleas for peace. Among them was a petition from the WPP forwarded by Jane Addams, to whom Wilson replied, "My heart is for peace." In the meantime, Argentina, Brazil, and Chile had offered to mediate the US-Mexican conflict, a proposal initially killed by Washington. After Mexican soldiers had been cleared of blame for the Carrizal clash and Carranza had released the prisoners captured there, however, talk of mediation was revived.[109]

Now it was Wilson's turn to demonstrate his good faith. In a June 30 address to the New York Press Club, he declared himself happy to sacrifice his own and his party's political fortunes if it would preserve the continent's peace and save the nation's honor. "Do you think the glory of America would be enhanced by a war of conquest in Mexico?" he asked. "Do you think that any act of violence by a powerful nation like this against a weak and distracted neighbor would reflect distinction upon the annals of the United States?" Within four days of this "Peace Pledge," Lansing and Arredondo agreed on behalf of their governments to submit all outstanding differences to mediation. In the event, the United States and Mexico declined mediation in favor of direct negotiations, which produced their fair share of tension and lasted several months. Nevertheless, war was averted.[110]

Wilson's handling of the 1916 crisis with Mexico was both more honorable and more pragmatic than many later critics and some contemporary pragmatists allowed. The Veracruz debacle still weighed heavily on him, and if experience had taught anything since Villa's Columbus raid, it was how easily the smallest spark of force could ignite a volatile mixture of mutual suspicion and ignorance.[111] The *New Republic* editors agreed that lighting matches was dangerous, especially in the arid borderlands straddling the Rio Grande. Unlike Wilson, however, they had called for a controlled blaze to burn away the hazardous debris of revolution, only to watch the administration stumble into it. By publicly maintaining the "absurd" pretense that Mexico was a fully sovereign state, they wrote on June 10, Wilson had invited its people's outrage over Pershing's expedition. Any nation with sovereignty "intact" would resist the presence of foreign troops. That Carranza could only protest proved the weakness of the Mexican state; still, he could not back down without seeming to abdicate the sovereignty Wilson had imagined for him. Only Wilson could break the stalemate—by declaring Mexican sovereignty "a legal fiction" irrelevant to American policy. Carranza's government was impotent to protect the lives and property of aliens within its borders or prevent the depredations of marauders beyond them. Its security was dependent upon the Monroe Doctrine, its institutions prey to villains and warlords. "Thus while it is insisting on all the privileges of a sovereign state it is ignoring most of the responsibilities." In the editors' view, maintaining this sham prevented the United States from fulfilling its true legal and moral obligations regarding Mexico, including securing the border, preserving close economic relations, preventing European meddling, and assisting the Mexicans "in the work of recuperation"—in short, obligations to interfere. Given the behavior of the major factions, "it may be necessary to use the familiar Mexican arguments of bloodshed and coercion, in order to make the interference effective," the editors suggested. "And unless it is effective how can it be beneficial?"[112]

It happened that all the objectives just listed were achieved. As American troops withdrew, Carranza's stature grew, the country stabilized, and a new constitution was adopted in early 1917. Most important to Wilson, and due largely to his statesmanship, his fear of thousands of American farm boys dead in the desert or stained with Mexican blood never came to pass. Of course, Wilson did not achieve what each and every American editorialist, investor, entrepreneur, or congressman considered his proper objectives, and he was glad of it. "Very few of those who desire a settlement of Mexican affairs by the force and power of the United States desire it for the sake of Mexico," he wrote in the war address he never delivered. "It does not lie with the American people to dictate to another people what their government shall be or what use shall be made of their resources, what laws or rulers they shall have or what persons they shall encourage or favor."[113]

Lansing, annotating Wilson's draft, queried, "Haiti, S[anto] Domingo, Nicaragua, Panama?" He could be forgiven raising an eyebrow at Wilson's apparent forgetfulness.[114] But it might have been Haiti and the Dominican Republic that Wilson had in mind. He had intervened in both places regretfully, knowing that no legal basis for either action existed. Calm prevailed in Haiti for the moment, but Wilson had been depressed by the deaths of US marines during the occupation campaign and distressed at the far heavier losses among the Haitian *cacos* opposing them. More recently, Wilson had chastised the American military authorities at Santo Domingo for arresting seven Dominican senators and a deputy without cause, and as he drafted his address, the US State Department and Navy still had not managed to compromise with the Dominicans on a president.[115] Was it plausible that a larger force and fuller presidential attention was all it would take to control Mexico—an area twenty-five times larger and vastly more populous than Hispaniola?

In refusing that gamble, Wilson avoided one of the major pitfalls of an unsophisticated pragmatism: the tendency to mistake ignorance for uncertainty and turn a field of inquiry into a forced option prematurely. William James, though recognizing no choices as certain, did insist that choices be informed. And while James had also identified choice as one among many determinants of reality, Wilson knew that his Mexican policy was nowhere near a stage at which believing and acting as if peace could be imposed had any likelihood of creating that fact. In 1916 both popular and official opinion in the United States reflected a significant ignorance of Mexican politics, society, and culture, and any attempt to rearrange its pieces would doubtless have shown it.

It was in their very different attitude toward Mexico—and not, as later critics argued, toward the war in Europe—that the *New Republic* editors flattened pragmatism into what might be called "technicalism."[116] James would have agreed that policies are beneficial in proportion to their effectiveness but would have cautioned that the effective and the beneficial are not identical. Perhaps the United States could have occupied Mexico and established a new government in a highly effective fashion. The long-term benefits for either country, however, were dubious, to say the least.

More coherent than the editors' interventionist position were their musings on international relations, current and future, prompted by Wilson's stance. Was Wilson a Trojan horse of international peace through military preparedness or of international anarchy through diplomatic propriety? Wilson's resistance to intervention, they wrote, was doubtless calculated to appease the governments he hoped to weld into a Pan-American union. Yet those governments had long expounded "a rigid legalistic nationalism" according to which "all states are equally independent and deserve to be kept equally inviolate, no matter how well or ill they use their independence." Recent experience had taught "the danger and futility of any such theories of absolute national sovereignty." A merely legal prohibition of aggression was useless. "International security must be provided by an organization of international force, and the only theory on which such force can be organized is that of qualified national sovereignty for both large states and small." The same logic of sovereignty that rendered weak states "immune from all interference, even though they repudiate their obligations to other nations," granted powerful states "sovereign discretion" to "override the rights and interests" of neighbors. Organized or disorganized, a "community of absolute sovereigns is a contradiction in terms," and the extent of sovereignty enjoyed by a nation such as Mexico must be "justified by its fruits." In light of American citizens' exposure to Mexican chaos as well as the US government's power to contain the damage, the right and obligation to control affairs in Mexico had shifted northward.[117]

These were the facts as the *New Republic* editors saw them in June 1916. A month later, their perspective had changed. Necessary or not, intervention was no solution to the problem of anarchy. The American people, they wrote on July 8, "would go into Mexico only because every other method had failed" and "with every intention of withdrawing as soon as possible," eager to resume the quest for global peace and its commercial and cultural benefits. The nations of the world, however, would little credit such intentions unless the American army was "in actual fact the instrument of some international organization." Unfortunately, no such organization existed, because the peoples of the Western hemisphere—including those of the United States—refused to surrender their "adolescent sovereignty." Outside a "Council of Nations," no moral or physical means "of rehabilitating Mexico" could be legitimate in any sense but the purely subjective. In the early days of July, before the relaxing effect of Wilson's "peace pledge" was obvious, the potential necessity of a technically illegal act of justice and charity seemed a grim paradox indeed. "Never was there a more startling demonstration of the truth that good intentions alone will not keep the peace," the editors wrote. "The underlying lesson of Mexico is that international organization alone can make good intentions effective. . . . If we drift into war, and from war to empire, it will be because the people of this hemisphere have been too lazy, too vain, and too stupid to organize their own safety."[118]

CHAPTER SIX

Provincials No Longer

For all the thought that Wilson gave his Mexican policy, it was not going to win him an election. Among the pragmatist progressives—a group counting several desirable proxies and potential philosophical allies—reactions were mixed. In Jane Addams's view, Wilson had shown "great forbearance to a sister republic" that was "struggling awkwardly toward self-government," but the presence of US marines on Hispaniola dampened any anti-imperialist hopes thus raised. Max Eastman printed statements in the *Masses* from Mexican workers and the American Union Against Militarism (AUAM) warning that further interference in Mexico would cripple a people's campaign against the same international plutocrats that oppressed American workers and corrupted American politics. W. E. B. Du Bois—granted, long since alienated from Wilson—was harshest, denouncing the Pancho Villa chase as "a foolish venture" that, characteristically, entailed a cost in African American lives with no compensatory benefits for African American life.[1] Finally, Mexico put the *New Republic* pragmatists in a skeptical mood. To them, Wilson's strained attempts to reconcile Mexican sovereignty with American interference recalled his early neutrality policies: "a sort of meddlesome *laissez-faire*," muddying his vision of a global deliberative body and undermining his sporadic efforts to practice a new internationalist diplomacy.[2]

Wilson's 1916 reelection campaign made believers of all bar Du Bois. The *New Republic* crowd, particularly Herbert Croly, Walter Lippmann, and their sounding board Felix Frankfurter, were especially impressed by Wilson's resurgent and broadening radicalism. Nearly every plank of the Democratic Party platform adopted in June seemed to resonate with Lippmann's February paean to an "integrated America." Drafted mainly by Wilson, the platform linked mastery of social chaos to preparedness for global conflict, and justified the whole in terms of Americans' moral obligations to humanity. In adopting it, Wilson and his collaborators set the stage for a transformation of the Democratic Party and a wholesale reconstruction of American society. Cementing the support of influential pragmatists, Wilson also initiated the period of their largest contributions to his foreign policy—contributions that structured the world's first great experiment in internationalism before its dismantling by the US Senate in the spring of 1920.

The origins of Wilson's shift toward a more aggressive pursuit of social justice date to late 1914 and early 1915. The Federal Trade Commission Act was the culmination of Wilson's attempt to give common people greater control of their economic lives. But it was not the end of his quest for government by common counsel. Although the 1914 midterm elections shrank the Democrats' majority, House Democrats fought off Progressive Party challengers in the West, while Wilsonians won governorships in several traditionally Republican states.[3] Wilson took these outcomes as signs of a disintegrating Progressive Party rather than a repudiated Democracy and saw bright prospects for further reform. Still, expecting a reactionary counterattack on his New Freedom program, he made a preemptive strike. Two weeks after the elections, in a public letter to Treasury Secretary William Gibbs McAdoo dated November 17, Wilson reminded reformers of the "dangerous ill-humors" of recent decades, which his party's main accomplishments—tariff revision, democratized credit, and trade regulation—were working to dispel. A people plagued by "agitation and suspicion and distrust" were finally "all in the same boat" and could say with confidence, "We know the port for which we are bound." Uniting behind the New Freedom, Americans might soon look upon the recent past as "upon a bad dream."[4]

Wilson's aim was off. Advanced progressives read his letter as a declaration of total victory for reform. But although economic justice might be furthered by the New Freedom (to what degree none yet knew), from where would social justice come? Wilson had opposed federal assistance to farmers as "class legislation," declined to support a woman suffrage amendment on constitutional grounds, and compiled an abysmal record on race. To many progressives, Wilson seemed to live in a different dimension. "Any man of President Wilson's intellectual equipment who seriously asserts that the fundamental wrongs of a modern society can be easily and quickly righted as a consequence of a few laws," wrote Herbert Croly, "casts suspicion either upon his sincerity or upon his grasp of the realities of modern social and industrial life."[5]

Well before the new Congress convened in December 1915, Wilson had come to agree with this assessment of his nation's "fundamental wrongs" (if not the assessment of his character and faculties). Like Croly, he concluded that only a display of reforming zeal as bold as or bolder than the New Freedom could unite the forces for change in what his platform collaborator, Senator Robert L. Owen of Oklahoma, called a "spirit of Progressive Democracy."[6] In fact, *Progressive Democracy* was the title of Croly's most recent book: a work notable not only for its explicit equation of democracy with pragmatism but also for its consonance with Wilson's ideas about the essentially moral, methodological, and mutable character of democracy. Croly described democracy as a cooperative experiment by which a people continuously improved, but never perfected, the conditions of mutual freedom and obligation that maximized personal and social development. Laws and institutions that did not facilitate this mode of life, cultivate its habits, and increase its esteem in the minds of citizens must be repealed or replaced if they could not be reformed—and much of the legal and constitutional structure of the United States warranted disposal. "In this sense," Croly wrote, "democracy is necessarily opposed to intellectualism and allied to pragmatism." Knowingly or unknowingly, Croly explained this pragmatic transformation of the state as driven by the quintessentially Wilsonian habits of self-government—deliberation, cooperation, and the free embrace and discharge of obligation among citizens. Only if these habits were ingrained in American ethics and celebrated in American culture could an adaptive, experimental, and constructive government emerge to effect the democratization of economic and social resources essential to moral and material progress.[7]

In *Progressive Democracy* Croly expressed serious misgivings about "Wilson progressivism." The New Freedom emphasis on restoring competition, he feared, would make progressivism an ideology "supplementary" rather than antagonistic to conservatism. Croly nonetheless acknowledged the precedents Wilson had set for legislative change and their broadening effect on the public's expectations of government. Recognizing the practical restraints imposed by the American constitutional and party systems, Croly credited Wilson with a kind of halfway pragmatism. "He is, I think, by way of being a realist in politics rather than a doctrinaire," Croly wrote. "He can understand the authority of human opinions and social needs which do not fit into antecedent theories." The main problem with Wilson's quasi-pragmatist progressivism was its failure to focus such forces; its incapacity, so far, "to inspire sufficient energy of conviction" for the sacrifices an efficient and egalitarian society required. Wilson, Croly worried, was not preparing the public for several "ultimate results" that were implicit in his politics yet "inimical to institutions and ideas cherished by a large part of his followers."[8]

In short, Wilson's admirable "method" lacked the moral "purpose" that distinguished pragmatist progressivism from artful conservatism. Thus it did not yet breathe what Croly, anticipating Owen, dubbed the "spirit" of progressive democracy. "If progressivism is to be constructive rather than merely restorative, it must be prepared to replace the old order with a new social bond," one "no less secure than its predecessor" but serving "more effectually as an impulse, an inspiration and a leaven." Modern conditions demanded "not merely a new method" of politics "but a new faith, upon the rock of which may be built a better structure of individual and social life." Indeed, for Croly, the method and the purpose of progressive democracy were indistinguishable, both being to cultivate the virtues of William James's ethical republic. Citizens must be "required," he wrote, through "actual experience and unavoidable responsibilities, to develop those very qualities of intelligence, character, faith, and sympathy which are necessary for the success of the democratic experiment."[9]

It is unclear whether Owen had *Progressive Democracy* in mind when he urged a platform of "progressive democracy" on Wilson. It is almost certain that Wilson had not read Croly's book. Yet he was well aware of the similar ideas being expressed in the *New Republic*, alongside criticisms of his failure to adopt and apply them. He was also familiar with the Jamesian ethics behind Croly's politics, having again encountered James's writings more than a year before drafting the Democratic platform. Wilson read James's essay "On a Certain Blindness in Human Beings," and probably also "What Makes a Life Significant," sometime before May 1915. These essays were reprinted together as *On Some Ideals* (1913), and the well-worn copy preserved among Wilson's books at the Library of Congress was read at least once by the president. On May 20, 1915, Wilson's eventual second wife, Edith Bolling Galt, wrote to him asking, "Do you remember Wm. James Essay 'On a Certain Blindness in Human beings'?" Having "read it again" that night, Galt described the passage that spoke to her most clearly: "I mean the fable of the monk who heard the 'bird in the woods break into song'—and then, 'all that is not merely mechanical is spun out of two strands—*seeking* for that bird, and *hearing* him.'"[10]

A rather gnomic passage when taken out of context, Edith's selection nonetheless elegantly expresses a central theme of James's moral philosophy. "On a Certain Blindness" comprised selections from James's favorite readings, stitched together by commentary on the singularity of each individual's perception of value. The passage Galt described is from a tale of a monk so enraptured by what he thought was the short trilling of a songbird that he remained in the forest, listening, for fifty years, unaware of time's passage. This extreme—and to most minds absurd—devotion to birdsong reminded James (and he hoped his readers) that no person's experience of the good is perfectly analogous to another's. If the good, rather, is a matter of "seeking" and "hearing," of striving toward an ideal as well as experiencing its often unexpected and always highly personal fulfillment, then a prescriptive ethics insensible to the variety of human experience—a rule for seeking, heedless of hearing—was misguided. The infinity of human ideals "commands us," James argued, to "tolerate" and even "indulge" the ideals of all who extend us the courtesy; for "neither the whole of truth nor the whole of good is revealed to any single observer, although each observer gains a partial superiority of insight from the peculiar position in which he stands."[11]

Galt's query as to whether Wilson remembered James's essay and her reference to a particular, treasured passage indicate that both had read and discussed it. Such discussion was bound to affect Wilson's thinking: as students of his relationship with Edith note, she almost immediately became his closest confidante in private and public matters—even replacing the ubiquitous Colonel House.[12] The lovers also frequently read to each other, and Wilson's copy of On Some Ideals evinces multiple readings. As he mulled his legislative program for the sixty-fourth Congress, perhaps the president read, or culled from conversations with his fiancée, the closing sentiments of the companion to "On a Certain Blindness": James's "What Makes a Life Significant." In social conflicts over the essentials of "happiness and unhappiness and significance," James wrote, each party too often "pins them absolutely on some ridiculous feature of the external situation" at issue, "and everybody remains outside of everybody else's sight." A "newer and better equilibrium" for society required widespread recognition that any life of "fidelity, courage, and endurance" in pursuit of ideals was meaningful to the person living it, and entitled to empathetic consideration in the disposal of communal affairs.[13]

Perhaps. Regardless, during the Sixty-Fourth Congress Wilson promoted a host of measures designed to close the social distance between Americans; to bring "everybody" back into "everybody else's sight." Rural credits, child labor laws, a government-worker's compensation act, and a more sharply graduated income tax were all passed or in passage before the Democrats unveiled their 1916 platform. That platform included nearly all the social justice planks the Progressive Party had adopted in 1912, making it the springboard of the first national leap toward social democracy in the United States.[14]

The Democratic platform's frankly internationalist foreign policy was as revolutionary as its domestic agenda. Indeed, the platform made the interdependence of domestic and external affairs explicit. "The part that the United States will play in the new day of international relationships that is now upon us," read the "Americanism" plank, "will depend upon our preparation and our character." Echoing Lippmann's "Integrated America," the Democrats urged solidarity among the nation's multitudinous class, ethnic, and racial groups to show the world "the unity and consequent power of America"—a nation not of "partisans" but "patriots."[15] Clarifying the expansive character of such patriotism, the following plank pledged support for economic and military policies adequate to preserve American freedoms and fulfill "the international tasks which the United States hopes and expects to take a part in performing." Reprising a theme from Wilson's preparedness tour—global instability—the platform then endorsed a version of Lippmann's "differential neutrality." The war had "revealed necessities of international action which no former generation can have foreseen," so that national interests and moral imperatives obliged the nation "not only to make itself safe at home," but to "assist the world in securing settled peace and justice." At the same time, the platform appealed to the sympathies of the Woman's Peace Party and the AUAM, affirming the nation's obligation to take "the earliest possible opportunity" for mediating peace in Europe and to promote everywhere the "fundamental principle" that "all men shall enjoy equality of right and freedom from discrimination in the lands wherein they dwell."[16]

The party of Thomas Jefferson and William Jennings Bryan—for generations the party (in theory) of disentanglement from foreign affairs—had pledged itself an active member of the global community. Nothing signaled this pledge more clearly than the party credo of "International Relations," adopted nearly word for word from Wilson's address to the League to Enforce Peace (LEP). "We believe that every people has the right to choose the sovereignty under which it shall live; that the small states of the world have a right to enjoy the same respect for their sovereignty and for their territorial integrity that great and powerful states insist upon; and that the world has a right to be free from every disturbance of its peace that has its origin in aggression or the disregard of the rights of peoples and nations." In light of these rights, the party affirmed "the duty of the United States to join the other nations of the world in any feasible association that will effectively serve those principles, to maintain inviolate the complete security of the highway of the seas for the common and unhindered use of all nations."[17]

Following in the steps of its leader, the Democratic Party had committed itself to the goal of a league of nations.

It was a move both courageous and savvy. Endorsing a league of nations in the context of promoting "equality of right and freedom" removed barriers between Democrats and independents predisposed toward the platform's social justice agenda. The explicit linking of domestic reform and international responsibility was also calculated to restore Wilson's credibility in the eyes of those who viewed the punitive expedition to Mexico as another step in the onward march of imperial capitalism. To this effect, the resolutions committee inserted a tortured explanation of the Mexican situation: blaming Wilson's reluctant use of force on Venustiano Carranza's dangerous and deadly failures of governance and the consequent violations of American territorial integrity, they commended the president's "stubborn resistance" to "every demand" for Mexico's "military subjugation."[18] By contrast, the committee balked at Wilson's generic endorsement of a right to security against invasion. Excised from his original pledge to join an international "association" was the conclusion, which had broadened the body's hypothetical mandate to include "a virtual guarantee of territorial integrity."[19] Perhaps the committee thought Bryanite currents were still too strong to divert the Democratic mainstream so drastically; or perhaps, as with the inserted clause supporting American mediation, they were consciously courting the votes of left-progressives opposed to intervention in Europe. Regardless, Wilson would likely have seen little disadvantage in the change. A "league to enforce the freedom of the seas," though a truncation of his vision, was a historic commitment for an American major party, and if realized would lay the foundation for a larger international edifice casting a longer protective shadow.[20]

In truth, Wilson could not have asked for more. The internationalist principles he had fought for months to defend—even while struggling to define them for himself—were now joined and nailed to the floor of his party's house, which a year before had seemed hopelessly divided over foreign policy. Yet when time came to present the platform at the national convention in Saint Louis, a bizarre concatenation of events conspired to gag the voice of internationalism at its own housewarming. The keynote speaker, former New York Governor Martin H. Glynn, struggled to keep the crowd's interest until he happened upon the topic of Wilson's foreign policy, raising cheers with his praise of strict neutrality and nonintervention as its guiding "self-evident truths." Glynn's warming audience prodded him into a litany of international provocations, the crowd shouting "What did we do?" and Glynn replying, "We didn't go to war!" A scribbled note from convention chair William McCombs, urging Glynn to acknowledge the *limits* of American patience, was to no avail; the crowd craved tales of Franciscan forbearance, and Glynn giddily obliged. In the frenzy's aftermath, an unknown member of the platform committee inserted a sentence that begat one of the best-known campaign rallying cries in American political history: "In particular, we commend to the American people the splendid diplomatic victories of our great President, who has preserved the vital interests of our Government and its citizens, and kept us out of war." From that point on, the slogan "He kept us out of war" was irrepressible. Though the slogan was changed in subsequent literature to read "He kept us out of war *with honor*," the implication of honor's superiority to peace was lost on most Americans—to the chagrin of Wilson, who had orchestrated the convention as a thundering response to slights against his patriotism. As the *New York Times* reported, "The plans which went so wrong" at the convention "were those of President Wilson himself."[21]

Wilson had reason to worry. Louis Brandeis, John Dewey, Frankfurter, and the *New Republic* editors all read the platform of 1916—and its primary author's intentions—more carefully than the delirious delegates in Saint Louis did. They noted that the document concluded by entwining "the enlargement of our National vision and the ennobling of our international relations." Yet they also heard the chants for peace and could not ignore the platform's hurrah for the "splendid diplomatic victories" that "kept us out of war."[22] For a time they wondered what kind of transformation they had witnessed in Wilson.

On the one hand, the platform helped convince them, along with fellow pragmatists Addams, Eastman, and William Walling, that Wilson was committed to radical, systemic reform, fanning a hope first kindled in January when he nominated Brandeis for a seat on the Supreme Court. Even while cheering Wilson's firm support of his nominee against intense conservative and anti-Semitic opposition, the *New Republic* pragmatists could not quite shake the suspicion that in a confrontation between independent liberals and the Democratic old guard the president would "side with his party."[23] Now that party, already pushing a bevy of reforms through Congress, had endorsed a more sweeping social justice agenda than most progressives had dreamed possible outside of a third-party bid. By July it was clear that Wilson commanded a unified Democratic organization bent on "assimilating" reforms they had "condemned" four years earlier—a sign, for the *New Republic* pragmatists, of sensitive, responsive, and intelligent growth.[24]

Wilson had indeed worked to earn the confidence of reformers, and after the convention, he continued to inspire it. A bellwether for many progressives was the income tax measure his administration steered through Congress. Though welcoming the income tax of 1913, several prominent reformers joined John Dewey in calling for more "rapidly progressive rates," and from 1914 on seized on preparedness as a lever for raising the surtax. In early 1916, Dewey's Association for an Equitable Federal Income Tax (AEFIT) petitioned the president and Congress to fund preparedness by a tax of up to one-third on millionaires, and throughout the spring Dewey cosigned public letters on the topic addressed to the administration. In June his group submitted a draft plank on the income tax to the Democratic National Committee in Saint Louis.[25]

Wilson had informed Congress in December that he hoped to raise revenue through income taxation, claiming that "modern governments" everywhere had demonstrated its prudence.[26] Having pushed for an Emergency Revenue Act in 1914 (to offset the economic repercussions of the European war), he had grown uncomfortable with its regressive reliance on consumption taxes, while dwindling trade was shrinking returns. A band of Democrats in Congress sought to capitalize on Wilson's growing (though quiet) interest in progressive taxation by funding military expansion through the income tax, thus redistributing wealth and reducing the profit motive for war. The administration responded with the Revenue Act of 1916, signed September 8. The act's unprecedented estate and munitions tax provisions, both mainly administration creations, were genuinely radical: the first in its highly redistributive structure, the second in the high rates and net profits basis that Dewey's AEFIT promoted. Wilson and McAdoo also lobbied to lower exemptions while halving the basic rate, generalizing the tax while still shifting the burden to the wealthy.[27]

For the editors of the *New Republic*, the revenue bill was yet more evidence of Wilson's capacity for "introducing positive changes in our national politics"—as well as a source of enormous "capital" for the president and other Democrats seeking progressive votes in the 1916 elections.[28] That capital realized its greatest growth, however, through Wilson's handling of the railroad crisis of 1916. Industry managers and employee representatives had wrangled for months over worker demands for an eight-hour workday and overtime pay when, by late summer, a ruinous general strike seemed imminent. On August 13, Wilson intervened, calling both sides to the White House and proposing a solution: concession of the eight-hour workday, temporary suspension of the overtime demand along with any collateral demands from management, and "the constitution, by authority of Congress," of a presidential commission to investigate the consequences of the eight-hour workday and whether the lines might raise rates to offset its cost.

The brotherhoods accepted, but for weeks the managers remained obstinate. Pessimistic and impatient, the brotherhood leaders called a general strike for September 4.[29]

Wilson had prepared for this contingency; legislation was already in committee to prevent the strike and permanently remove its causes. On August 29, Wilson urged Congress to pass an act embodying his compromise, along with provisions for compulsory suspension of strikes pending federal investigation of grievances and presidential power to compel operation of trains in wartime. This solution, Wilson explained, was simultaneously empirical, expedient, and principled. The "preponderant evidence of recent economic experience" commended the eight-hour workday on grounds of "health, efficiency, contentment, and a general increase of economic vigor." Other, muddier issues would ultimately require arbitration. Yet thus far arbitration had failed, and to "stand firm for the principle of arbitration and yet not get arbitration" would be "more than futile," involving "incalculable distress to the country." The "practical and patriotic course" was to concede the eight-hour workday, prohibit the planned general strike, and "lay the foundations" for further compromise in an atmosphere of peace. "This is assuredly the best way of vindicating a principle," he urged; "namely, having failed to make certain of its observance in the present, to make certain of its observance in the future."[30]

The *New Republic* had for months printed calls for a solution along these lines. Indeed, the editors anticipated Wilson's remarks to Congress by three days. "You may believe in 'arbitration,'" they announced on August 26, "but if one party which has the power declares that an issue is not arbitrable, it is useless sentimentality to talk about arbitration." The journal praised Wilson's initial White House proposal for having subordinated "principles" to "facts" when adherence to principles merely invited what they were "designed to prevent." Moreover, Wilson's proposal of empirically and impartially justified overtime pay and freight rates promised to avert "calamity" now as well as prevent it in future. Predictably, wrote the editors in the September 16 issue, Wilson was attacked by Republican presidential candidate Charles Evans Hughes for "abandoning" arbitration and capitulating to the "spirit of force." This charge was obtuse. "Any board of arbitrators would have been obliged to do as Congress did—that is, to indicate a preference." In other words, implied these Jamesians, the good of the larger community required some butchery of private ideals. Happily in this case, the community's representatives responded pragmatically, accounting for the inevitability of change and error, building it into their solution, and accepting responsibility for the experiment.[31] Most important, Wilson seemed finally to have employed pragmatic methods in a genuine "spirit" of progressive democracy, seeking to redefine American politics as a space in which common ends were discovered and pursued. "Mr. Wilson has done what high statesmanship in a democracy must do," they wrote in the wake of the railroad crisis: "he has interpreted the demands, principles, and interests of group interests, and lifted them up into a national program."[32]

But still there was the resounding strain, "He kept us out of war." It drowned out the calls for preparedness and global-mindedness that Wilson had made in the months preceding the convention. This suited Randolph Bourne, still contributing regularly to the *New Republic* but feeling marginalized politically; and to a lesser extent Weyl, who in August took a sabbatical to write a guide for the nation in its potential role as neutral mediator.[33] In the meantime, Croly, Lippmann, Dewey, and Frankfurter increasingly suspected that American intervention would prove not only difficult to avoid, but necessary to ensure the creation of an international league at war's end. The last thing the United States needed was a president lacking the moral will or political capacity to meet that challenge. Yet within a few months of Wilson's pacifist apotheosis in Saint Louis, they were viewing him not as the man who avoided war but as the man who might end it.

The first convert—and proselytizer of the rest—was Lippmann. In August he wrote to Graham Wallas that any hope of meaningful American assistance for the Allies depended on Wilson's reelection.[34] The congruence of Wilson's agenda with Lippmann's own, however, began revealing itself much earlier. Lippmann determined as early as February that Theodore Roosevelt and other critics were "forcing Wilson's hand" toward a less equivocal stance on the war. They were "trying to make him seem afraid of the Germans," he wrote to Wallas on February 21. "This he resents, and you may expect him to act like a good imitation of a bold man as the conventions draw nearer." Wilson's foreign policy, he predicted, would shift in an anti-German direction out of sheer political necessity. A month later, Lippmann got his first sense of the deeper currents in Wilson's thinking. A drawn-out battle with conservatives and anti-Semites dead-set against Brandeis's Supreme Court appointment provided the pretext for his first private interview with the president on March 22. "You've come to work me over," Wilson assumed, and suggested instead that he "show you the inside of my mind." From the brief notes in Lippmann's diary it appears that the president discoursed on nearly every issue, domestic and foreign, that occupied his crowded thoughts.[35] The rhetoric Lippmann had often found vapid in print must have seemed weightier in person; to judge by his succeeding correspondence and articles, Lippmann came away half converted, at least, to the president's cause.[36] When Roosevelt's largely forgotten disavowal of even "the smallest responsibility" for Belgium was brought to his attention, Lippmann was the impetus behind the *New Republic*'s public apology to Wilson for abetting Roosevelt's subsequent smear campaign.[37]

This was a striking turnaround for a journal inspired by Roosevelt himself. Just as significant, however, is Wilson's interest in the editors' ideas. Wilson was actively wooing the journal, eager for the votes of nationalist progressive readers who had voted for Roosevelt in 1912.[38] But he had also learned from the *New Republic* and its leading voices, Croly and Lippmann. He read their journal as often as possible and considered their positions seriously. He also welcomed, and sought, their direct advice. On August 4, Secretary of War Newton Baker forwarded, to Wilson, Lippmann's suggestion that his nomination acceptance speech emphasize "the economic war" that was sure to follow the shooting war unless the problem of "economic alliances" was addressed. Wilson, through Baker, conveyed to Lippmann a request that "as his ideas clarify he will let me have the benefit of them, either directly or in an editorial expression," an invitation already extended through his secretary, Joseph Tumulty.[39] He also took Lippmann's advice, as Tumulty intimated in a letter to Lippmann covering an advance copy of Wilson's speech. "You will doubtless be interested in the President's speech of acceptance," Tumulty teased. And indeed, on September 2, at Sea Girt, New Jersey, Wilson asserted his government's duty "to insist" upon "conditions of fairness and of even-handed justice in the commercial dealing of the nations with one another," conditions requisite to "the peace and ordered life of the world." Equally gratifying to a pragmatist progressive, Wilson reiterated the need for American leadership in securing peace as well as extending the realm of justice. "We can no longer indulge our traditional provincialism," he declared, nor afford the smug complacency toward domestic affairs it often entailed. He insisted that the United States not only promote international guarantees against aggression but also make its domestic jurisdiction "mean the same thing" for continental and insular populations and, strikingly, guarantee a "living wage" and "health and safety" for all workers.[40]

As the election approached, relations between Wilson and the *New Republic* pragmatists, Lippmann especially, grew warmer every week. On July 26, Lippmann wrote Tumulty asking if he might visit with the president "some time before the campaign gets fully underway," to help the group "in making up our minds."[41] At the end of August, Wilson invited Lippmann to Shadow Lawn, his rented summer home, and took the audacious step of confiding to Lippmann his receipt of a dispatch, from the American embassy in Berlin, predicting resumption of unlimited submarine warfare after the elections, regardless of their outcome.[42] Given Wilson's ultimatum after the *Sussex* sinking, such a turn would make war with Germany "almost inevitable," Lippmann remembered later. "Wilson told me so." According to Lippmann, the president feared that intervention might prove the only route to a stable peace and successful international organization. "It's a terrible thing for me to carry around with me."[43]

Directly after his visit to Shadow Lawn, Lippmann wrote to Graham Wallas, "I have talked to Wilson and to all the people closest to him, and there is no doubt that the desire to form a league has grown upon them until it is really their greatest passion." Wilson's nomination acceptance speech contained "a very effective statement about it, going so far even to accept the doctrine The New Republic has been preaching that in the future the United States cannot be neutral in a world war." Wilson had shared with Lippmann in late summer 1916 what he had been thinking since the embargo debates two winters past: impartiality and justice were not synonymous; neither were isolation and security sides of any political coin still current. Both sentiments could have graced the *New Republic*'s masthead. It is no surprise Lippmann had "come around completely to Wilson."[44]

"Now we'll face it," Lippmann told the rest of the staff. "What we're electing is a war president—not the man who kept us out of war—and we've got to make up our minds whether we want to go through the war with Hughes or with Wilson." Ultimately the group concluded that Wilson was the only one with "the imagination and the will" to turn war, should it come, into an opportunity "to make a radical move in the organization of peace."[45] Croly was skeptical at first, and Willard Straight, who had founded the journal in part to promote his hero Roosevelt, winced at the open break with the ex-president, who hated Wilson.[46] But the twisted logic of the Republican campaign made supporting Wilson easier. Hughes, declaring Wilson too timid to defend American rights, sounded by turns anti-British, anti-interventionist, and jingoistic, confusing and alienating pro-Allied independents and internationalist progressives alike. The *New Republic* editors had always tented in the latter camp, and Lippmann especially found it impossible to vote for the planless Republicans.[47]

To characterize their stance as *against* Hughes, however, would be inaccurate; they were *for* Wilson. Through September and October, their efforts on his behalf grew in scope and vigor. Lippmann suggested and wrote speeches for the president—and even gave some himself—trumpeting Wilson's reform record and harping on the incoherence of the Republican message.[48] The cause received a major boost just before the election when

Dewey declared his support. While the Hughes campaign hurled epithets, wrote Dewey, Wilson offered voters a record and a vision. He had "appreciated the moving forces of present industrial life," promoting a roll of progressive measures "in consonance with the social needs of the times." He was, moreover, the only candidate with "some consciousness of the situation to be faced by the world when the war ends." Such praise from the dean of American social thought amplified a chorus of voices inflected with the pragmatist tone. Eastman stumped for Wilson; Walling promised one hundred thousand socialist votes. Addams and Bourne gambled on peace under Wilson and reform under peace. At the last minute, James's friend, protégé, and future biographer Ralph Barton Perry of Harvard announced his conversion to Wilson's cause.[49]

Meanwhile, Lippmann and Croly, though scrupulously commissioning dissenting essays, pursued the dual task of securing and shaping a second term for Wilson. Indeed, Lippmann's "Case for Wilson," published on October 14, essentially urged readers to elect a pragmatist for president: "I shall not vote for the Wilson who has uttered a few too many noble sentiments, but for the Wilson who is evolving under experience and is remaking his philosophy in the light of it." Wilson had not only discarded laissez-faire individualism for a politics "national in scope" and "liberal in purpose." He had defined that purpose in internationalist terms, having recognized that the "cause of the Allies is in a measure our cause."[50] Wilson had changed his positions on many issues since 1912 and would continue "shifting his ground." But this was not "caprice." Rather, his changes reflected his "growth"—rather rapid—"into a constructive nationalist." In Lippmann's view, any sane progressive must welcome such adaptability to change. "The next years will bring us to the settlement of the war, and the infinite difficulties of reconstruction." In such matters, "Wilson's sensitiveness to changing conditions" and "flexibility of mind" would be crucial—as would a party worthy of such an intellect. The party of Hughes was not merely ponderous and chauvinistic, but vacillating and corrupt. Wilson, by contrast, had "mastered" his party. Under his leadership, the world could expect the United States to seek international justice, in whatever form the situation demanded; under Hughes, American policy would be a mystery. To change course now, in the absence of any "real alternative," would be unpragmatic in the extreme. "Mr. Hughes," Lippmann closed, "ought not to be elected in the dark, not today, not in these difficult times." Those who saw the light would vote for Wilson.[51]

Croly, unsurprisingly, was the last to cast his lot with Wilson. Roosevelt had been his hero and friend, the champion of his philosophy, vesting the

"Promise of American Life" with an authority that the shy, awkward theorist could never have wielded alone. It was not until the end of October that Croly banished the ghosts of 1912 and set his mind for Wilson. Even then, there was pain in the parting.

"I shall vote for the reelection of President Wilson on November 7th," announced Croly in the October 21 *New Republic*, though he admitted the choice was difficult. The first two years of Wilson's term had disappointed. From the winter of 1915 forward, however, it became increasingly clear that the Democrats were "assimilating many progressive principles and a few former Progressives," while the Republicans were "assimilating many former Progressives but no progressive principles." Given that choice, he wrote, "I prefer to go with the principles."[52]

Those principles were particularly evident in two of Wilson's most impressive efforts, both characteristically pragmatist. First, Wilson had managed to "resurrect" the Democratic Party by "modifying the Democratic creed." Discarding "party dogmas," he united his party and insisted it govern with "self-control, adaptability, and competence." He had fortified the watery broth of the New Freedom with a potent tonic one could honestly label *progressive*, replacing "incoherent, indiscriminate, competitive, localistic individualism" with "a continuing process of purposive national reorganization." That process, "determined in method by the realities of the task," was defined in substance as the "enhancement of individual and associated life within and without the American commonwealth." Croly could hardly believe the result. "For the first time in generations," the Democrats were the party of "genuinely national democracy." The Republicans, by contrast, comprised "a fortuitous collection of warring ingredients" emulsified solely by "utter intolerance of President Wilson." Its conservative leaders whitewashed the status quo while its liberal dissidents plastered its cracks. Neither could say, or even ask, how to reconcile such contradictions, for fear of splitting the party.[53]

Croly's second reason to vote for Wilson in 1916 was the president's "recovery" in foreign affairs. The president had begun poorly. Wanting "chiefly to keep out of trouble" when the European war broke out, he "talked resolutely" but "acted irresolutely." Yet Bryan's resignation marked a turning point. From the *Arabic* affair, to the Garrison plan, to the *Sussex* sinking, Wilson handled each crisis better than the last. Most important, he had embraced and elaborated the "revolutionary doctrine" of "general security." Once characterized by strict neutrality and willful blindness to the possibility of war, Wilson's was now "an essentially sound and really national foreign policy," combining "benevolent neutrality towards the better cause" with "intelligent support of the plan of international organization"—all backed by enough military power to make the United States a "considerable factor in the politics of the world."[54]

The alternative, in Croly's view, was "the abstract and undiscriminating legalism" of the "inveterate lawyer," Hughes. Insisting monotonously on defense of American neutral rights, Hughes showed no appreciation of the patient, prudent, trial-by-error diplomacy lately enhancing the nation's stature. Nor did he realize that the same diplomacy had finally instilled "some sense of international responsibility" in a people unaccustomed to the feeling. Americans were "listening" to their president, wrote Croly, because he was listening to them—even as his critics betrayed "sheer impatience" with such "wholesome processes of democracy." Not even the most "courageous, resourceful and imaginative leadership" could easily force a democracy "into premature action," Croly wrote in Wilsonian prose. The president's method of "conscious national preparation" had proven effective, achieving "a huge increase in governmental power" while keeping "class opposition" manageable—a coup, opined Croly, which his Republican critics could not have effected even were there any chance of their trying. Voters faced a choice between supple pragmatism and nerveless dogmatism—between mastery and drift. It was a choice between a party "trying"—however fallibly—"to shape itself into a better servant of the collective interest" and one trying hardly at all.[55]

On November 7, Croly, Lippmann, and Weyl went to the polls to vote, so they hoped, for a very different Woodrow Wilson than had won the presidency four years earlier. They were joined in that hope by many of their philosophical allies, whose collective efforts helped swing progressives to Wilson in an election where every vote counted; droves of Bull Moose registered the same change of heart.[56] That the candidate himself had undergone a complementary transformation remained, however, a working hypothesis.

Lippmann's efforts on Wilson's behalf caught the administration's attention; and in Lippmann's view, attention was but a channel to influence. Invited to a White House dinner on December 12, 1916, Lippmann wasted no time grabbing the president's ear. That day Washington had gotten word that German Chancellor Theobald von Bethmann-Hollweg had proposed terms for a compromise peace to the Allies, and Lippmann asked the president point-blank what he intended to do about it. Wilson was convinced the Allies would reject the offer on grounds that only total defeat could prevent German hegemony in Europe. The result would be renewed U-boat attacks and thus war with Germany. The Europeans simply could not be left to themselves. "If they don't let me mediate," he told Lippmann, "we'll be drawn into war." He was determined to work for peace, if only to control, as best he could, the terms on which his country would go to war. The drift of affairs was intolerable: "We've got to stop it before we're pulled in."[57]

The German note disoriented Wilson, for it arrived only three days before he had planned to send his own peace note to the belligerents. Bethmann, sensing growing war weariness in Germany despite recent victories, concluded that even a futile effort at settlement with one enemy might avoid making another. The influence of the German high command and the impatience of Admiral Alfred von Tirpitz were bound to result in the scenario Wilson described to Lippmann unless Bethmann gained control of the kaiser's script. Even if the Allies refused Bethmann's proposal and U-boats were again unleashed on Atlantic bottoms, Germany's pacific overture might at least restrain American anger. By such reasoning the chancellor convinced Kaiser Wilhelm, Field Marshal Paul von Hindenburg, and even Tirpitz that it was time to paint the flag white—at least on one side.[58]

Initially the German note seemed to leave the United States no place at the negotiating table. But on December 13, Ambassador Johann Heinrich von Bernstorff sent a letter to House conveying the chancellor's intention "to meet the wishes of the President" and his "hopes for the President's cooperation." The same day, Lansing received a communication from the American embassy in Berlin relaying Bethmann's "formal and solemn offer" on the part of Germany and its allies "to enter immediately into peace negotiations."[59] Encouraged, Wilson drafted notes to the belligerent governments and a cable to the American embassy in London. He instructed the American envoys to "intimate quite explicitly" that "this Government is deeply interested in the result of these unexpected overtures" and would "presently have certain very earnest representations to make on behalf of the manifest interests of neutral nations and of humanity itself." These pending representations were not to be construed as "associated" with those of the Germans. The latter had "created an unexpected opportunity" for discussion, "but the United States would have itself created the occasion had it fallen out otherwise."[60]

Wilson, in other words, was endorsing a proposal the Germans had happened to make, not "the German proposal." The note as received by the Allies, with revisions suggested by Lansing, jumbled matters further. Though his original draft had called for a peace conference, the final note was merely an appeal to the belligerents for specific war aims. Wilson "took the liberty of calling attention to the fact" that both sides' general aims were "virtually the same": each expressed the desire to secure "the rights and privileges of weak peoples and small states" along with their own," and "each was ready to consider the formation of a league of nations" to do so. It remained for each, however, to avow "the precise objects which would, if attained, satisfy them and their people that the war had been fought out." Only such "interchange of views" could "clear the way for a conference" and thus make peace "a hope of the immediate future."[61]

Wilson's note shrewdly challenged the belligerents to act on the humanitarian aims they publicly professed. His labored nonendorsement of Germany's "overture," however, sapped the note of any emollient effect on the Allies. The editors of the *New Republic* offered a more coherent response. "The German peace proposals," they wrote in the December 16 issue, were not the "sign of weakness" many Britons and French descried, but nor did they herald the peaceable kingdom. By "moving for peace" on "terms that look moderate to the Central European peoples," they continued, Germany "strengthens herself at home and throws upon the Allies the burden of continuing the war." In the meantime recent victories put Germany in "position to operate freely both on a peace front and on a war front." In short, although the German note belonged "to the diplomacy of war rather than to the diplomacy of peace," outright rejection would be "costly and dangerous." Conversely, the only risk negotiations posed was to "the vain hope of a peace dictated to an utterly beaten and humiliated enemy"—a hope both sides would do well to abandon. Here was a chance "to substitute, if not peace for war at least the methods of peace for the methods of war." The editors hoped "for the sake of the French and British peoples that the French and English governments will not refuse."[62]

They did not—not officially. Wilson's note outraged the majority of "the French and British peoples," but their governments could fume only privately. Agreeing that outright refusal was unwise, however, they stalled while searching for some alternative response.[63] They were still searching when news came of an extraordinary statement by US Secretary of State Robert Lansing at a press conference on December 21. Without consulting Wilson, Lansing asserted that the purpose of the president's note was to acknowledge "the possibility of our being forced into the war," which "ought to serve as a restraining and sobering force" on any belligerent tempted to ignore "American rights." Offering a perfunctory hope that the note might bring "an earlier conclusion of the war," Lansing emphatically denied collusion with the Germans in seeking a negotiated peace.[64]

Nothing could have relaxed the squirming bodies at Whitehall and the Quai d'Orsay as thoroughly as this particular pill from Lansing's private cabinet—nor sent the president into such an apoplectic state. The American press had reacted to Wilson's note with renewed hope for negotiated peace; now his secretary of state was talking of intervention and abjuring anything smacking of support for Germany's proposal. Wilson, infuriated by Lansing's act of sabotage, considered demanding his resignation. But practicality prevailed. Rather than reveal fissures within the administration, Wilson directed Lansing to disavow to the press their "radically misinterpreted" versions of his statement. Grudgingly, Lansing consented.[65]

Still, the damage to the president's plan was done. German nationalists seized on Lansing's statement as evidence of an Anglo-American conspiracy to negotiate for peace while preparing a united assault. Kaiser Wilhelm received Wilson's peace note and Lansing's two statements on the same day and erupted in a noxious cloud of anger, self-pity, and confusion. The members of his high command were strengthened in their belief that only the submarine could bring peace to Germany—through victory. Chancellor von Bethmann-Hollweg, meanwhile, was despondent even before Lansing's statement. Wilson's demand to publish peace terms was impossible for a man keeping his country together through vague encouragements to its weary citizens and tailored assurances to their fractious representatives. As for Wilson's mediation offer, Lansing had confirmed for Bethmann's constituents (if not for Bethmann himself) that American economic and cultural prejudices were too strong to expect impartiality. On December 26, the German government cabled its reply to Wilson, thanking him for his suggestion and promising, "after the ending of the present conflict," to cooperate in the "sublime task" of preventing future wars. The Allied governments now felt free to publish war aims at their leisure, which they eventually did on January 12, 1917. These aims included restoration, with indemnities, of Belgium, Serbia, and Montenegro; evacuation of France, Russia, and Romania; and "liberation" for Italians, Romanians, Slavs, and other European ethnic groups oppressed by alien powers—in effect, the dismantling of the Austro-Hungarian and Ottoman Empires.[66]

Obviously these aims were not calculated to encourage negotiation. The multiethnic Austro-Hungarian and Ottoman Empires would never acquiesce in their own dissolution, and Germany would never pay indemnities for glories dearly gained on the battlefield. The Allies' aims could only be achieved on those same battlefields—or at sea. Wilson's note, or Lansing's gloss, or both, had drawn the scimitar of submarine warfare closer.

They also, however, indirectly sired one of the most famous phrases and inspiring ideals in modern history. While the belligerents were considering their responses to Wilson's peace note, the *New Republic* was making a pragmatic case for a negotiated peace. Focusing on the British, by this point clearly the senior partner among the Allies, the editors explained the hesitant response to Wilson's note. It was "difficult for the official spokesmen of Great Britain to say what they were fighting for" because they were "fighting for victory, not for terms." They had not gone to war to gain territory but to preserve "prestige." Were they to accept a negotiated peace, "no matter how moderate," their empire would emerge diminished. This was a political threat on multiple levels: prestige was "the life of a successful empire," and to "retrieve" it was the mandate of David Lloyd George's new government. No wonder "imperial Britain" was loath to accept Germany's "inconsiderately liberal offer"—an offer of "peace without victory."[67]

The Germans were wise to offer such a peace, even if it cost every foot of conquered territory. "A restoration of the status quo ante," wrote the *New Republic* editors, would preserve "Germany's greatest and most enduring conquest in this war"—"Middle Europe," comprising the vast tracts and populations "which she has led and organized from Hamburg to Bagdad." Though "welded" by war, this emerging empire's foundation was economic, and the Germans were doubtless anxious to build on it while bricks yet remained. Thus there was "statesmanship and not merely propaganda" in the kaiser's "liberal" turn. "The organization of Central Europe requires a peaceful world."[68]

Not that the editors assumed a peaceful world would accommodate "organized Central Europe." Even half-formed, the phenomenon "destroys completely the British theory of continental politics," they admitted. The British Empire had not maintained equilibrium among its rivals; it was arbiter of Europe no longer. If Britain and its Allies were certain of destroying Middle Europe at "bearable cost," they should reject Germany's offer. "But if they are once again underestimating the strength of the central alliance, if through vanity or stubbornness they are unable to face the facts, then a refusal to negotiate is an abominable waste of life." Should war drag on, with British bodies piling up in France and the German overture lingering in the public consciousness, Lloyd George would face "the staggering task of explaining to the British people the politics of prestige."[69]

Whether or not their analysis of British motives was accurate, the *New Republic* editors completely misread the Germans. Their proposal *was* a sign of weakness; the fruitless, ten-month battle of Verdun and the recent, costly repulse of the Allied Somme offensive had required titanic efforts that brought the country near to exhaustion. Chancellor Bethmann was losing control. At an August conference in Pless, he had agreed to consult the high command in making his final determination on submarine warfare. Now Hindenburg insisted on a U-boat campaign against all merchants engaged in trade with Britain, armed or otherwise, and threatened to resign as field marshal if his plan was not effected by January 31, 1917. He and Ludendorff had acquired such heroic proportions in the eyes of the German public that the kaiser could little afford to back his chancellor against them. As soon as the Allies published their response to the peace proposal (which appeared in German papers on January 13), the chancellor's failure was inevitable.[70]

Inevitable, but undisclosed. The German government kept its decision secret, and throughout January 1917, Wilson worked for a mediated peace. He was encouraged by the Germans' official reply to his note. Ignorant of ongoing communications between a solicitous (and duplicitous) Lansing and the French and British foreign ministries, he had no idea how soon events would sink the paper ships passing between Washington and the European capitals. While sending secret feelers to the main belligerent governments, Wilson began to craft a speech explaining "what, in his opinion, the general terms of the settlement should be, making the keystone of the settlement arch the future security of the world against wars." So confident was Wilson in the prospects for settlement that he snapped at House for worrying aloud about the nation's military preparedness. "There will be no war," he told the Colonel. "We are the only one of the great white nations that is free from war to-day, and it would be a crime against civilization for us to go in."[71] This was not an expression of racial paranoia. Since the 1880s, *nation* had been Wilson's term for the organic complex of a particular culture and the institutional apparatus evolved to express and regulate it. Like many in his day and after, Wilson considered self-government the crowning achievement of the European diaspora, and deemed its spread the criterion of global security. American intervention threatened to corrupt the last peaceable nation reared to its habits, ending the "domination" of "white civilization" by destroying its most valuable asset and most precious contribution to the world.[72]

Croly and Lippmann shared Wilson's optimism over the German reply to his note, though for different reasons. "Its weakness," they wrote in the *New Republic* for December 30, "is his opportunity." The promise to consider "prevention of future wars" *after* settling the current conflict "completely missed the point," but it also gave Wilson a chance to reiterate that a moderate peace depended on all parties subordinating victory to the goal of "a safer Europe." The Allies, too, had been given an opportunity. A statement that "organization of security" was primary and "territorial details" secondary "would constitute a perfectly adequate reply" to Wilson's note. For both sides, it was a test that would show their true colors even through the haze of war.[73] Meanwhile, developments appeared to justify Wilson's hopes.

Ambassador Bernstorff, awaiting his government's official response to Wilson's peace feeler, nonetheless led House to believe the kaiser was tired of war and genuinely committed to internationalist principles. He assured House that Germany would join a league of nations, cooperate toward a general disarmament, work to restore Belgium, and even accede to an independent Poland. "To my mind," House wrote Wilson, "this is the most important communication we have had since the war began and gives a real basis for negotiations and for peace." Wilson, initially suspicious, soon caught House's enthusiasm. He instructed House to prepare a statement outlining Bernstorff's terms, "as you get them in writing," for transmittal to Lloyd George. "But hold it until I can consult Lansing," he enjoined, "and until the address I am about to make to the Congress has had time to sink in a little."[74]

That address, as he shared with Herbert Croly in the days immediately afterward, was composed with more than a little help from the *New Republic*. "I was interested and encouraged when preparing my recent address to the Senate to find an editorial in the New Republic which was not only written along the same lines but which served to clarify and strengthen my thought not a little," Wilson wrote to Croly on January 25. "In that, as in many other matters, I am your debtor." On the front page of Croly's journal, Wilson had found a phrase that encapsulated his ideas and soon captured the public imagination: "Peace without Victory."[75]

The landmark address was delivered with a heavier heart than that with which it was written. Two days prior, Bernstorff had received his instructions from Berlin and was obliged to renege on his commitment to a Wilsonian peace. "They are slippery customers," House wrote to the president; at least the British, however "stubborn" and "stupid," could be trusted.[76] Wilson's spirits dropped. The German high command had all along been maneuvering toward resumption of unrestricted submarine warfare. Still, there remained a glimmer of hope. Perhaps his speech—already in the dossier of every American ambassador in Europe, ready for publication the moment he spoke its closing syllable—could marshal the forces of peace. It would not be the last time he put his faith in the public opinion of the world.[77]

"In every discussion of the peace that must end this war," Wilson addressed the Senate on January 22, "it is taken for granted that that peace must be followed by some definite concert of power which will make it virtually impossible that any such catastrophe should ever overwhelm us again." It was "inconceivable that the people of the United States should play no part in that great enterprise," for it was the fulfillment, on a world stage, of "the very principles and purposes of their polity." But before Americans could do their part, certain questions must be asked and answered. The first was that "upon which the whole future peace and policy of the world depends"; namely, "Is the present war a struggle for a just and secure peace, or only for a new balance of power?" If the latter, the desire of Americans and other peoples for peace was trivial, for no power or powers could stabilize such an arrangement. The answer to the first question was therefore simple. "There must be, not a balance of power, but a community of power; not organized rivalries, but an organized common peace."

The next question was more specific and its answer more controversial. What did the terms "community of power" and "organized peace" imply in practice? "They imply, first of all, that it must be a peace without victory." It was a sore test for the millions who had suffered through the war to abandon the end for which all other wars were fought. But Wilson sought "only to face realities." This was a new war, and victory was not its end. In the victor's shadow, "humiliation" and "intolerable sacrifice" would leave their bitter deposits, "upon which terms of peace would rest, not permanently, but only as upon quicksand." A new war and a new world required a new peace, "a peace the very principle of which is equality and a common participation in a common benefit." Second, therefore, a collectively organized and guaranteed peace implied a "peace between equals," affirming the practical kinship of interests among nations. "Right must be based upon the common strength, not the individual strength, of the nations upon whose concert peace will depend." Finally, anchoring these aspirations was a "deeper thing," the foundation of equality and cooperation in any polity, national or international: self-government. "No peace can last, or ought to last, which does not recognize and accept that governments derive all their just powers from the consent of the governed, and that no right anywhere exists to hand peoples about from sovereignty to sovereignty as if they were property." Rather, the "inviolable security of life, of worship, and of industrial and social development should be guaranteed to all peoples who have lived hitherto under the power of governments devoted to a faith and purpose hostile to their own."

This call for the internationalization of self-government was the first of many to elicit "all kinds of double interpretations" (as the *New York Times* put it) regarding Wilson's ideas about postwar political arrangements, ideas which the next three years saw him fail, in crucial moments, to clarify for the American and world public. Wilson's brand of what would come to be called "self-determination" was a far cry from the simple carving up of continents into ethnically homogeneous territories. He understood that political, religious, and social freedoms were just as likely to suffer as thrive if global politics were reduced to the `ɪprinciple of "one nation, one state."[78] As he told the Senate, none of the conditions of peace Wilson laid before them were derived from "abstract political principle." Self-government, universal access to the sea, worldwide arms reduction; all reflected observed "realities" of human nature through history. For the benefit of skeptical Americans, Wilson explained that to implement these measures was merely to adopt "the doctrine of President Monroe as the doctrine of the world: that no nation should seek to extend its polity over any other nation or people." Reprising a theme from his LEP address, he insisted that commitment and cooperation to promote self-government, equal rights among nations, and arms reduction were not "entangling alliances" but "American principles, American policies," and Americans "could stand for no others." More important, they were "the principles and policies of forward looking men and women everywhere, of every modern nation, of every enlightened community. They are the principles of mankind," he closed, "and they must prevail."[79]

Though a paean to peace, Wilson's address revealed him irrevocably committed to an internationalist vision that, under pressure of events, came to mean war. "We are provincials no longer," he told the country in his second inaugural address on March 5, 1917. The shock waves of a distant tumult had made Americans "citizens of the world." By that date, the president was gripping his plowshare with white knuckles. On January 31, not ten days after his dramatic refusal to countenance the Allies' campaign for Germany's destruction, Ambassador Bernstorff communicated his government's intention to resume unrestricted submarine warfare.[80] Still, Wilson began his second term determined, if at all possible, to see the American people "play the part of those who mean to vindicate and fortify peace." Preserving that possibility while "staying true" to the principles avowed in his "Peace without Victory" address consumed his energies for two months after the German high command threw down the gauntlet, until finally, grimly, he took it up.[81]

For a day or two in January, however, Wilson was electric. The "Peace without Victory" speech was shortly known around the world. It was recognized by his audience in the Senate, regardless of agreement or approval, as one of modern history's epochal public utterances.[82] The overwhelming majority of progressive organs praised what the *Independent* (recycling its eulogy of Wilson's LEP address) called his "Declaration of Interdependence."[83] The *New Republic*, unsurprisingly, was among them. Indeed, upon reading the address, Croly immediately left his West Twenty-First Street offices for House's East Fifty-Third Street apartment, where he proclaimed it "the greatest event of his own life." Wilson was less effusive, but more penetrating, in assessing his work: "I have said what everybody has thought impossible. Now it appears to be possible."[84]

It was, to that point, Wilson's finest speech: a noble sentiment, and a noble effort toward a lasting peace. He would soon outdo it, bequeathing yet another immortal phrase to posterity not ten weeks later, in an April 2 address to a special session of Congress. That day, as cherry trees bloomed in the capital, Wilson too forecast a blood-hued future: the future of a free people, provincials no longer, whose world must be made safe for democracy.

CHAPTER SEVEN

The Will to Believe

In January 1917, a week before Wilson's "Peace without Victory" address, the *New Republic* ran an editorial titled, "The Will to Believe." Readers for whom William James's identically titled essay evoked the woolly notion that what *ought* to be *can* be, if wanted badly enough, were likely confused by the article's hardheaded analysis of peace scenarios. Editors Herbert Croly and Walter Lippmann, however, knew that the cosmic uncertainty James found so rich in possibilities made consequence, not preference, the acid test of any proposition. In this vein, they argued that despite liberal hopes for a diminished German empire, the very ideals inspiring those hopes made serious consideration of alternatives necessary. A "moderate peace now," for instance, would likely result in a German-dominated "Middle Europe." But the current carnage would end. The exhausted German people, moreover, would not lightly suffer future leaders threatening to resume it. And the world would surely prefer an integrating Middle Europe, tended by a chastened Germany, to a political swamp slowly choked by the spread of Russian autocracy. Certainly, neither outcome was "a permanent or hopeful solution" for the world at large or the peoples most affected. "But suppose Allied statesmanship could rise high enough to offer these peoples internationalization of the trade routes and of the chief strategic points as the basis of a protected Balkan confederation," the editors hypothesized. Such a commitment from the Allies "would probably fulfill their own desires," for the "liberal enthusiasm" awakened in the region would render German hegemony "infinitely difficult."[1]

Here the editors revealed their essential argument as well as their subtle understanding of James's philosophy. Liberalism is good; good enough to fight for. Imperialism is bad; bad enough to fight against. But those were the premises, not the conclusions, of the debate that was needed. What would it take to crush Germany? What would it cost to negotiate? What actions and commitments might alter the answers? Was the "awful gamble" on victory worth it?[2]

The editors thought it might be. But that was not their point. Once again they were urging their readers to be critical idealists, to distill the essential objects of their beliefs from the accidents of their formulation. To predicate peace on Germany's destruction without deliberating over the consequences would be foolish. At some point Germany would have to buy into the peace; a settlement calibrated for democracy must itself be democratically calibrated. Meanwhile, a concrete commitment to the autonomy of smaller nations might increase their chances of attaining it. The will to believe in a democratically organized world and act as though it were possible was a necessary condition for its emergence. Though Croly and Lippmann's attitude toward the kaiser's regime would harden during the course of the war, "The Will to Believe" encapsulated the pragmatist politics they espoused and urged on their president for its duration—right until the Paris Peace Conference convinced them their advice had fallen on deaf ears.

Wilson's view of the war was more fearful, anguished, and tragic than Croly's or Lippmann's. But it was no less rooted in the will to believe that the world's idealists could shape its outcome—perhaps foolishly or negligibly, perhaps wisely and substantially. As Wilson confided to journalist Frank Cobb on March 19, two weeks before asking Congress to declare a state of war with Germany, intervention would likely produce "a dictated peace" in Europe. Worse, it could herald a moral catastrophe at home. "Once lead this people into war and they'll forget there ever was such a thing as tolerance," he predicted. "To fight you must be brutal and ruthless, and the spirit of ruthless brutality will enter into the very fibre of our national life, infecting Congress, the courts, the policeman on the beat, the man on the street."[3] He might have added "my administration" to his list. During wartime, several executive departments and agents fed public hysteria, curtailed civil liberties, and ignored mob violence, making their chief complicit in his own nightmare.

Yet Wilson overcame his fears for the American soul and accepted its trial by fire. He did so not in a flight of naive optimism but in a spirit of stoic pragmatism. His worries about intervention and its consequences were matched by the fear, equally burdensome, that some grievous insult or shocking atrocity would provoke the American people to lash out blindly; to fight for no reason but that they were injured and afraid "and saw no remedy but to risk still greater, it might be even irreparable, injury," to end the threat and settle the score. Balancing that fear was relief that war fever had not yet spread among Americans; that repeated injuries had not conditioned them to violence but committed them to seeing it "eliminated as a means of attaining national ambition"; and that the seemingly inevitable conflict could still be engaged by a nation thirsting for justice, not vengeance.[4]

How this clear-eyed yet faithful democrat lost his moral and political bearings on the home front is difficult to say. The record makes clear that for Wilson, the war was paramount. Winning it meant winning the chance to give the world what Americans often took for granted: the freedom and opportunity to "speak, act, and serve together."[5] Perhaps when some of these lucky Americans refused to cooperate, he thought they needed a lesson. Perhaps when the subordinates to whom he entrusted American liberties failed him, he had no strength left to act. Perhaps the quest for a democratically united world took too much from him, especially when the democratically united America that was to bear its standard grew fractious and unruly. The only certain conclusion is that, ultimately, Wilson was not strong enough to drag a great, hesitating democracy onto the world stage without doing it violence.

For all his hopeful efforts toward settlement in the month preceding his "Peace without Victory" speech, Wilson was not surprised by their collapse. Europe had become a vast mass grave. In 1916 the western front saw well over 2 million killed or wounded in the battles of Verdun and the Somme alone. On the eastern front, Russia's massive Galician offensive produced another 1.4 million casualties in just two months. These stupendous losses only encouraged a desperate drive to redeem them on both sides. The Somme proved Britain's bloodiest and most embarrassing engagement, but it cost Germany more—perhaps as many as 500,000 casualties, on top of 300,000 to 400,000 at Verdun—and the resultant stalemate produced doubts in the Reich that a land war was winnable. Submarine attacks against British shipping increased even as the German chancellor, Theobald von Bethmann-Hollweg, formulated his peace strategy; six American crewmen of the British merchant vessel *Marina* lost their lives to a German torpedo on October 28, 1916. Wilson, according to his secretary, Joseph Tumulty, foresaw "an inevitable crisis with Germany" over the submarine issue but insisted on trying "every means" to avoid it.[6]

Wilson stayed this course even after Germany's announcement of renewed, unrestrained submarine warfare. "This means war," he stated upon reading it—but not yet. Wilson announced the severance of relations on February 3. Against the advice of his secretary of state, Robert Lansing, and most of his cabinet, however, he did not ask Congress to declare a state of war. Promising more drastic measures should the peaceful pursuits of Americans be impeded, Wilson nevertheless stated that only events at sea could convince him of Germany's genuine hostility. German Ambassador Johann Heinrich von Bernstorff had insisted, however disingenuously, that Allied obstruction of his government's peace move had precipitated the new submarine policy, and Wilson was determined not to make war under circumstances rendering it "impossible to save Europe afterward." If the United States was to intervene and yet maintain its moral authority at the settlement, there must be no question that Germany had summoned the whirlwind upon itself.[7]

Rather than a war message, therefore, Wilson set to work on a draft constitution for a league of neutrals, bound by mutual guarantees of political independence, arms limitation, and economic cooperation, which he envisioned as a forum for negotiating peace among the belligerents. Meanwhile, he agreed to meet a delegation representing twenty-two American peace societies that had resolved in favor of the government handling all diplomatic disputes through "peaceful means alone." Jane Addams was among the four delegates scheduled to meet the president at the White House on February 28. She intended to assure him that no such "hyper-nationalism" as had goaded Europeans to their deaths would spread widely enough through the "cosmopolitan" United States to trouble his pacific course. She would also warn him that his common-counsel domestic agenda would certainly be "sidetracked or destroyed by leading the country into a military means of settling disputes."[8]

By the time Addams saw Wilson, however, his options had narrowed sharply. On February 25, a German U-boat sank the British liner *Laconia* without warning; an American mother and daughter were among the dead. That same day the British released an intercepted telegram from German Foreign Minister Arthur Zimmermann proposing to the ruling Mexican general Venustiano Carranza that Mexico ally with Germany (and perhaps Japan) against the United States, in return for economic aid and recovery of territory lost in the Mexican–American War. It was a clear sign of hostile intent. Still, Wilson sought to stave off the inevitable, asking Congress on February 26 to authorize the arming of American merchant vessels as a final alternative to war. The House of Representatives promptly passed an armed ship bill, and seventy-six senators voiced support for the same. Eleven of their colleagues, however, were determined to block any step toward armed conflict. Led by Robert La Follette, James O'Gorman, and James K. Vardaman, they filibustered the bill for two days until the Sixty-Fourth Congress elapsed at noon on March 4.[9]

Wilson was apoplectic. Amid a crisis as difficult and dangerous as any in American diplomatic history, he fumed to the press, a "little group of willful men" had paralyzed the government, profaning the deliberative process and shackling a majority "ready for action." The result could only destroy their purposes. The "Zimmermann Telegram" had hit papers on March 1, causing an outrage. The public was still seething when German U-boats sank three American ships in one day on March 18. Three days prior, a major barrier to intervention had fallen when Russian Emperor Nicholas II of Russia abdicated power to a provisional government endorsing a liberal constitution. The German threat was now real, and the moral contrast between the Central and Allied Powers was now stark. Wilson's cabinet unanimously endorsed war on March 20. Navy Secretary Josephus Daniels assented through tears.[10]

There was no question in Wilson's mind that "war had become inevitable." He had told Addams so on February 28. In light of German provocations, he could only expect "a seat at the Peace Table" (much less a voice in the world's future security) as head of a belligerent nation; if the Allies thought his government incapable of responding to aggression, "he could at best only 'call through a crack in the door.'"[11] How remarkable, then, that he forced himself to think about it, revolving the problem in his mind for ten long days after his March 20 cabinet meeting. As he had confided to Cobb the day before, he knew that US intervention would shift the remaining balance of global economic and political power "off a peace basis and onto a war basis," and when the fighting ended, his would be among many governments forced to "reconstruct a peace-time civilization with war standards."[12] Yet for that very reason he determined that if war was imminent, its standards must be molded, at the outset, into standards of selflessness, clear thinking, and hope, rather than selfishness, passion, and cynicism. That act of national self-definition depended on the conscious choice of the American people and an ordered state of mind in which to make it. Thus, on March 30, Wilson wrote an address to Congress asking the country to choose war on its own terms, before the chance was lost. Just after eight o'clock on the evening of April 2, he arrived at the Capitol to deliver it.

Wilson entered the House Chamber to applause from Congress, the justices of the Supreme Court, nearly the entire ambassadorial population of Washington, and some fifteen hundred reporters and invited guests. The irony of such a warm reaction visibly pained the president. He was asking for war, with "a profound sense of the solemn and even tragical character of the step" he was taking.[13] Yet rather than surrender to war's horrors, he urged Americans to adapt this evil means to noble ends as best they could. "I have exactly the same things in mind as when I addressed the Senate on the twenty-second of January last," Wilson asserted: "to vindicate the principles of peace and justice in the life of the world as against selfish and autocratic power and to set amongst the really free and self-governed peoples such a concert of purpose as will henceforth insure the observance of these principles." Though these were now war objectives, their attainment required a different type of war than the belligerents had waged the past thirty-one months. Americans must "fight without rancor" and "without passion." They must "observe with proud punctilio the principles of right and fair play we profess to be fighting for." The tragedy of leading a "great and peaceful people into war" was inescapable but not final: it was an opportunity for the United States to help restore "the right" that was "more precious than the peace," and it must be grasped. "God helping her," Wilson concluded his address, "she can do no other."

The invocation of Martin Luther, defending his beliefs at the Diet of Worms ("God helping me, I can do no other"), was surely conscious. As a historian and a man of faith, the scion of Protestant clergymen, Wilson knew he was asking his country, in Luther's words, to "sin boldly."[14] He understood that any war effort or peace program, however generously undertaken and carefully conceived, would be fraught with risk, and corrupted to greater or lesser degree by ignoble interests. The duty of a people facing such hazards was to strive as best they could for the best ideals they could imagine, while remaining as humble and self-critical as possible; in short, to adopt a pragmatist ethic, harnessed to the practical vindication "of human right, of which we are only a single champion." Perhaps no sentiment uttered by Wilson has ever been so thoroughly ignored. In the interconnected and uncertain world he perceived, the risks, rewards, and responsibility of action and inaction, by persons or nations, were social and global. Hence this obsessive stylist did not promise "to make the world safe for democracy," as tradition has it. Rather he averred, "The world *must be made safe* for democracy"—with the help, he reiterated, of an American nation working as "*but one of the champions* of the rights of mankind."[15]

Never did so motley a collection of minds and hearts thrill in such unison to a presidential address than in the House Chamber that evening. Then and later, no eyewitness could recall a single dissenter from the ovation that met its closing save La Follette, who alone remained silent. Alone, that is, aside from Wilson. Only on returning to the White House did he speak of the address and its import. "Think of what it was they were applauding," he told Tumulty. "My message to-day was a message of death for our young men. How strange it seems to applaud that."[16]

Wilson was wise to remind himself that the human sacrifice of war, however laudable, was hardly applaudable. And yet the war had other consequences that even many of his pacifist challengers in progressive-nationalist circles did applaud. Above all, it vastly expanded the role of the federal government in citizens' lives. Military, financial, and industrial mobilization involved assertions of federal power vis-à-vis the states, corporations, and individuals that seemed, to supporters and skeptics alike, revolutionary.[17]

Wilson left military strategy to the generals. In getting them the men and means to carry it out, however, the administration took its own bold course, viewing the fight against militarist autocracy abroad as a chance to advance progressive democracy at home. The Selective Service Act of 1917 made the war a truly national responsibility. It required all males aged twenty-one to thirty (later eighteen to forty-five) to register for wartime (not necessarily military) service and banned the hiring of proxies that had made the American Civil War a poor-man's war. Meanwhile, in accordance with his war address, Wilson was determined to finance the war, as far as possible, through "equitable taxation" rather than borrowing. The War Revenue Act of 1917 quadrupled the income tax on multimillionaires (to 67 percent) and levied an "excess-profits" tax on corporations to prevent profiteering. The Revenue Act of 1918 again raised the top rate (77 percent) and expanded the bracket to include incomes of one million dollars or more. As tools of income redistribution and revenue generation, these acts were astoundingly effective: only 5 percent of the population paid income taxes in 1918, but the associated revenue covered one-third of war expenses. The rest of the cost was covered by the sale of Liberty Bonds—advancing, in a small way, Lippmann's "integrated America" by making average citizens creditors to the state.[18]

In fact, several of the administration's boldest measures benefited from the support and input of pragmatist progressives. In the war's early days, the paragon of progressive interventionism was the Council of National Defense (CND) that Lippmann and Secretary of War Newton Baker had first conceived a year earlier. Charged "intelligently to coordinate diverse industrial factors and to direct their activities to the definite needs of the Government," the CND oversaw twenty-five divisions, scores of committees, and hundreds of local and state subcommittees coordinating deployment of the nation's material, financial, and human resources. Technically an advisory body, its membership, including the secretaries of all major executive departments excluding State, gave it a voice in every aspect of wartime domestic policy. Although its work was initially hampered by its multilevel organization, diffuse mission, and utter lack of institutional precedent, Baker, the national chair, was free to experiment with increasingly functional (versus geographical) approaches that nevertheless maintained local connections. In his first annual report, Baker described a dynamic "organism," developing novel supply chains, organizing labor–employer collaborations, coordinating the win-the-war efforts of the several states—in sum, an organism "in process of evolution rapid enough to keep abreast with the changing current of the times." According to advisory committee member Bernard Baruch, the CND "served as a great laboratory devoted to discovering and making articulate the new administrative problems which the war was to involve."[19]

As Baruch well knew, the dialectic of invention, obsolescence, and reinvention characterizing the CND's operation spawned far nimbler bodies. These included the War Industries Board, to coordinate munitions and defense manufacturing and chaired, from March 1918, by Baruch; a War Labor Board, to formulate wage, hours, and working conditions standards and arbitrate disputes between labor and management; a Food Administration, to maximize production of vital foodstuffs and ration their consumption; a Fuel Administration to do the same for coal; and a Railroad Administration to bring that most logistically critical of industries under federal control. With such powerful agencies helping to secure rights and benefits for millions now effectively in government employ, workers' power, wages, and confidence grew. Unsurprisingly, labor progressives and mainstream labor leaders were among the greatest champions of Wilson's mobilization efforts, joined by business owners profiting from government contracts. Yet it was frequently to pragmatist progressives that such efforts owed their conception and character.[20]

All the aforementioned organizations began as CND committees, under Baker's ultimate supervision.[21] To relieve his burden, Baker recruited Frankfurter from Harvard and Lippmann from the *New Republic* as his principal civilian advisers. (They were eventually joined in government service by Weyl, whose economic expertise and labor connections recommended him to Baker; and Thorstein Veblen, whose radical solutions to the farm labor shortage were rather less popular with the Food Administration.[22]) Frankfurter soon developed a reputation as the War Department's éminence grise. His earliest official job was to devise labor contracts for the textile industry (soldiers require uniforms) that somehow protected the eight-hour workday, collective bargaining, and equal pay for women and minorities, all while eliciting voluntary cooperation from employers and convincing American Federation of Labor (AFL) president Samuel Gompers that the government's practical need for labor trumped his principled commitment to the closed shop. He was remarkably successful.[23]

A larger and more thankless task came with Frankfurter's transfer to the Labor Department and appointment as secretary and counsel for the President's Mediation Commission (PMC), established to resolve increasingly violent labor conflicts in western extractive industries. Arizona was a flashpoint. Its copper barons had long denied an ethnically and ideologically diverse labor force the right to organize, driving miners into the arms of the anticapitalist (and antiwar) Industrial Workers of the World (IWW). Frankfurter gamely attacked the problem as a litmus test of "our American striving to realize the democratic faith—here." Ultimately, however, industry resistance, AFL (and Labor Department) prejudice, and Frankfurter's hardnosed conclusion that the necessity of efficient production limited time for negotiations combined to produce settlements far more conservative than he initially hoped.[24] Authoring the PMC's final report of January 9, 1918, a frustrated Frankfurter recommended correctives, including guaranteed collective bargaining rights, a standard eight-hour workday, permanent arbitration machinery, and a "single-headed administration" to direct US labor policy for the war's duration.[25]

The last suggestion foreshadowed Frankfurter's heftiest wartime service. It began with a boost from Justice Louis D. Brandeis, whose Supreme Court duties—and residence in Washington—made him more rather than less accessible to the administration. Convinced to stay in DC throughout the Court's summer recesses, Brandeis met often with Baker's two pragmatist lieutenants, all three parties regularly encouraging the administration to avail itself of the others' advice and talents.[26]

Their collusion bore fruit. It was a memorandum from Brandeis, requested by House in early January 1918, that convinced Wilson of the need for independent, functionally defined boards to rationalize the mobilization effort—the failings of which were "imperiling success abroad and also the ascendancy of the Democratic Party upon which we must rely for the attainment of our ideals at home." Brandeis recommended that all munitions-related industries be directed by an administration "with a single head" and "full powers of delegation," a suggestion later embodied in Bernard Baruch's War Industries Board. He also recommended that a similar administration be created "to deal with labor problems for all departments of the Government." This suggestion found institutional form in the War Labor Administration, which eventually included Frankfurter's War Labor Policies Board (WLPB). Frankfurter had in fact prepared Brandeis for House's request, having just submitted a detailed recommendation for the CND's reorganization to

Baker. Appointed WLPB chair in May 1918, he found his allegations of waste and injustice daily confirmed. With little formal power, he coaxed and cajoled industrialists, union leaders, and officials at every level of government to standardize wages, protect unskilled laborers, and match worker aptitudes to sectoral needs—in short, to democratize war prosperity as well as optimize war production. Achieving several industry-specific and regional successes but falling short of his systemic goals, Frankfurter garnered the scorn of employers (who resented wage minima and regulated shops) and trades unions (who feared wage ceilings and open shops), while his sometimes propagandistic methods—including public oaths to support federal policy—turned stomachs among civil libertarians. Still, his radical reputation and formidable political skills grew so notorious as to give another activist labor lawyer, National War Labor Board cochair Frank P. Walsh, cover to develop one of the most radical Washington agencies to that point in history—in partnership with William Howard Taft, no less.[27]

Lippmann navigated similarly rough and narrow straits in government service. He would not be excluded from what seemed a great campaign to integrate America and institutionalize a politics of mastery. Determined to work in Washington, now the buzzing center of national activity (and a more fitting arena for his talents, he decided, than a boot camp or a battlefield), he deemed the War Department his best chance. He had long presumed to advise its secretary, and mobilization presented opportunities actually to do things he had only written about. Baker was "happy" to agree to the "experiment," and though it pained Croly, the *New Republic* was soon under that committed journalist's sole editorship.[28]

Like Frankfurter, Lippmann was initially assigned a labor relations dossier. His first official role was government representative to the Cantonment Adjustment Commission, which mediated disputes between employers and workers building training camps for the rapidly expanding army.[29] Lippmann's major contribution to mobilization, however, began before war was declared, when he first sketched the outlines of the selective service program. Wilson and Baker both were on record against conscription when Lippmann wrote to each on February 6, 1917, urging reconsideration. Raising an all-volunteer force, he warned Baker, would require "a newspaper campaign of terrible lying and misrepresentation," fueling "organized hatred" against German Americans and anyone else presumed insufficiently "patriotic." Such "manufactured hatred," he reiterated to Wilson, would pervert the entire war effort. Better a draft, with exemptions for conscientious objectors, than an indiscriminate flood of propaganda.[30]

Baker responded coolly at first, but Lippmann persisted. The day after Wilson's war address, Lippmann reminded the president of the "war psychology"—and Baker of "the poisoning of the public mind"—that a recruitment campaign would induce. Instead he proposed a "register of all men of military age," recording each registrant's "present occupation and alternate abilities" and letting the government decide whom to retain in "essential industries" and whom to exempt from military service.[31]

By that date, Baker and Wilson had seen the light. Baker recalled convincing the president in March to authorize the drafting of a conscription bill, if only as a fail-safe should volunteers prove scarce. Moreover, several days before Wilson's war address, Theodore Roosevelt had informed the administration of his desire to raise and command a volunteer regiment. Gently rebuffed by Baker, Roosevelt shared his scheme with the press.[32] Roosevelt's verbal lacerations of all persons and causes not committed to Germany's destruction had drawn blood aplenty in peacetime. Who more likely to realize Lippmann's nightmare predictions for wartime? In this context, Baker responded to Lippmann on April 4, with assurances that "the program that the War Department is going to recommend" would be "to your liking." The president's answer three days later was clearer: Lippmann's "interesting and important suggestion" regarding the "registering all men of military age will necessarily, I take it, be part of the plan."[33]

It was, and largely in the form and for the reasons Lippmann suggested. Eventually registering twenty-four million men, the Selective Service Administration exempted conscientious objectors from military service and, as Wilson put it, facilitated the "assigning of men to the necessary labor of the country" without hatemongering or browbeating—at least in theory.[34] In practice, the program disappointed. Its reliance on local draft boards staffed by community volunteers was one of many channels through which the acids of "the war psychology" corroded its machinery; Justice Department collusion with self-appointed "slacker" police was another.[35] But Lippmann spent little mental energy on the draft's moral fallout. He was not an administrator. With encouragement from Baker, he interpreted his duty to consist largely in brainstorming ways to fight and win the war properly, leaving implementation to others. Nor was he a loyal bureaucrat. His thinking was rarely confined to War Department business. He had always cared less about the war's military aspects than the apparent opportunities it provided to transform international relations. And of course, he continued his correspondence with House. As a result, Lippmann soon followed the stream of his own ideas out the door of the State, War, and Navy building in

Washington and back to New York City, where House was putting one of the best of them into operation. Meanwhile, the larger landscape of ideas saw violent convulsions.

Crucial to the overall mobilization effort in a country with a weak state and voluntarist culture was the mobilization of public support for the war being waged—and an odd war it was. Its objects were simultaneously limited and expansive: limited in seeking settlement, not victory; expansive in that the only acceptable settlement amounted to a revolution in international relations. This was a difficult war to sell.

It was not for lack of buyers. Before Wilson made his case for war on April 2, few Americans grasped the extent of the German government's provocations. Almost overnight a sizable number concluded they were beyond the pale.[36] An overwhelming majority in Congress, including several critics of Wilson's internationalist war aims, concurred. And while the president's abhorrence of war did not prevent what John Dewey described as "the immense moral wrench" of its arrival for his pacifistic supporters, it did permit the compensatory hope that "the pacific moral impulse retained all its validity," and in some cases the conclusion that its "full fruition" depended on German defeat. Many who regretted the war shared Dewey's enthusiasm for the vast experiments in "public supervision and control" that its waging made possible: some, like Addams, desperate to maintain the momentum of the prewar years; others, like Dewey himself, eager to see complacency banished and "the public aspect of every social enterprise" revealed by the light of crisis. Both of these venerable progressives welcomed the "international state" that, in Dewey's words, seemed "on its way," as did theorists from across the socialist spectrum, including pragmatists William English Walling (who supported intervention to achieve it) and Max Eastman (who did not). Even W. E. B. Du Bois accepted Wilson's challenge to transform the war, through will and work, into a global fight for the human rights his own government denied to millions. "War! It is an awful thing! It is Hell," he wrote in May 1917. But "slavery is worse; German dominion is worse." Fourteen months later he was still urging African Americans to "close ranks" with all citizens determined to eradicate "military despotism" and "inaugurate the United States of the World."[37]

The support of diverse and prominent shapers of opinion, however, did not alter the facts that Woodrow Wilson was president of the United States and that the United States was, institutionally and culturally, feebly equipped for concerted national action. Its population was heterogeneous, and its reigning political ideal one of consensus through appeal to higher motives. The various ethnic and cultural loyalties already appealing to those motives, combined with traditions of circumscribed government and aloofness from European politics, made for a war president's nightmare. How could Americans of all extractions be convinced that this was a war against German autocracy, not the German people? How could such a fight be reconciled with rapid and unprecedented centralization at home? And how could "supporters" such as Senators Henry Cabot Lodge (for whom war meant restoring the balance of power and punishing German aggression) or William E. Borah (who sought "no alliances" but only to defend his "countrymen and their rights") be prevented from hijacking public opinion and diverting the war effort from Wilson's supreme objectives of negotiated peace and a league of nations?[38]

Some critics denied that the war effort could be controlled at all. Randolph Bourne was aghast at "the relative ease with which the pragmatist intellectuals" had "moved out their philosophy, bag and baggage, from education to war." His disappointment in Wilson paled in comparison to his sense of betrayal by the pragmatist interventionists—most wrenchingly, John Dewey—who had drawn the curtain over the wizard in the White House. In Bourne's view, supposedly great thinkers nourished by a rational, humane political ethics were now slurping an intellectual and moral porridge warmed over the garish fire of events. What Dewey declared a "plastic juncture" in history was in truth a "slackening" in the pragmatists' own amorphous thinking, an excuse to abandon the difficult, boring work of reform for the more exciting game of dreaming up ways to make peace out of war. Granting, for the sake of argument, their genuine desire to make the best of a bad situation, Bourne posed an uncomfortably practical question: "If the war is too strong for you to prevent, how is it going to be weak enough for you to control and mold to your liberal purposes?" Any opportunity so to shape the war evaporated, Bourne argued, when the United States failed to make intervention "conditional" upon adoption of specific, liberal war aims by the Allies.[39]

In truth, Bourne denied that war under any circumstances could bring about the changed world that liberals awaited. "War is just that absolute situation which is its own end and its own means, and which speedily outstrips the power of intelligent and creative control." Dewey, failing to realize this, had let his pragmatism degenerate into a purely technical instrument, and he was not alone. Too many "war intellectuals" had immersed themselves in Europe's torrent of madness hoping to control its "current forces," calling Wilson captain and seeking a commission in his great campaign. They would see, Bourne prophesied, "how soon their 'mastery' becomes 'drift,' tangled in the fatal drive toward victory as its own end; how soon they become mere agents and expositors of forces as they are."[40]

The targets of this last salvo were, of course, Lippmann and the *New Republic* army, from whose ranks Bourne claimed to have been summarily dismissed. (In fact, Croly continued to print Bourne's letters and reviews, complete with jabs at the journal's official agenda).[41] Contrary to the ballistics analyses of later generations, however, Bourne fired blanks. Aiming to scatter a cloud of moral moths from the flames of adventure, power, and glory, his only ammunition was the empty shell of armed neutrality, which he claimed could secure Allied shipping lanes, force a starved Germany to the peace table, and position the United States to mediate terms of relief. Leaving aside the idea's recent death in Congress, Wilson—along with the *New Republic* editors—had considered and ultimately rejected the notion that armed merchant ships could keep American casualties to politically acceptable levels. Wilson, especially, feared that the shoot-on-sight approach sure to be adopted by merchants and submariners alike would simply spark the vindictive war he was determined to avoid. As for a nonbelligerent United States mediating peace, that outcome depended on one of two highly unlikely scenarios: either both sides would have to accept mediation offers already repeatedly rebuffed; or the belligerents would have to fight to a draw, the wait for which risked either an Allied victory imposing a punitive settlement on Germany or a German victory marking the triumph of militarist statecraft in Europe.[42]

Granted, Bourne's more famous advice was that his twilit idols abandon such niceties of the "war-technique" and rekindle the "poetic vision" that had delivered their apostle James from the temptation to place "executive ordering of events" above "idealistic focussing of ends." Yet such advice revealed a cursory attention, at best, to the developments in John Dewey's thought that so disgusted Bourne. On the eve of intervention, Dewey wrote that were he a "poet," his "ode" would be to the "national hesitation" over war, the courageous capacity of a people to question the "doing" even of deeds "imperatively demanded." Events might force immediate decisions and actions, he explained, without permanently binding the nation's "will as to what to be." A pragmatist's decision for or against intervention would be made not with ease and certainty "but in the light of the confronting situation," Dewey asserted. "And that situation is dark." Germany had revealed dangerous capacities and purposes to which Americans could no longer be "passive accomplices." But their "deeper hesitation" would and should persist until the Allies embraced "democracy and civilization" as their aims; only with such tonic skepticism could those ideals be massaged into action.

That Bourne saw so much less poetry and pragmatism in this risky effort to secure lasting peace than he did in the equally risky choice to preclude its potential failure might well have confused Dewey, Lippmann, and the other students of "The Will to Believe" whose political aesthetics he impugned. That these men refrained from condemning the moral as opposed to merely strategic probity of their detractor is a credit Bourne cannot share.[43]

Bourne was right about one thing, however: Wilson could count on the *New Republic* pragmatists to promote his goals of war without malice and peace without victory. In a remarkable letter to House, written even before the "Peace without Victory" speech, Croly gushed over the president's efforts to ensure a stable settlement and pledged his and Lippmann's support. "Both Mr. Lippmann and I," he wrote, "are only too glad to give whatever ability we have and whatever influence the paper may have to presenting to our public the underlying purposes of the President's policy." He asked that House "let us know whether or not we are misinterpreting what the President is trying to do, or whether we are under-stating or over-stating the real motives of his policy." The editors wished "merely" that their journal might "be the faithful and helpful interpreter of what seems to us to be one of the greatest enterprises ever undertaken by an American president."[44]

These were foolish things for a responsible journalist to say to the president's closest adviser, who was encouraged in assuming that he had yet another powerbroker in his palm. Nevertheless, the *New Republic* mostly maintained the critical distance solemnly pledged upon its debut. As Croly, Lippmann, and Weyl would have contended, critical and objective thinking are distinct: one is possible, the other impossible; one productive, the other either stultifying or self-deluding. The editors believed that Wilson's program, as they understood it, was worth trying. For that reason, to report it accurately, without "under-stating or over-stating the real motives" behind it, was their job as journalists, their wont as pragmatists, and their best hope as idealists.

Indeed, Wilson found they had not shaken their annoying habit of asking discomfiting questions. As the strains of mobilization increased, an arrhythmia developed between their journal's steady drumbeat of support for Wilson's diplomacy and its fretful foot tapping over his government's failure to fulfill the domestic end of the nationalist-internationalist bargain.[45] The *New Republic* had outlined a "War Program for Liberals" even before Wilson's war address, and Croly hewed to that basic program thereafter. "It is the business of liberalism to insist by the most drastic criticism that 'defense' shall not become the mask for a mere process of running amok and refusing to think," he warned on March 31. Hence the need for

clear domestic goals to complement the nation's international objectives—
goals including full unionization of labor, reform and extension of public
education, expanded social assistance programs, and aggressive social justice legislation. Americans would not make sacrifices to maintain a just
and secure international order if their experience under its major national
champion was one of injustice and insecurity. Similarly, Croly insisted that
the limited public censorship and government secrecy essential to national
security should "under no circumstances" suppress "inconvenient" political discussion: "The nation cannot do its work if it depends merely on a
'patriotic' press." That work, as Croly drove home month after month, was
to create a centralized yet democratic government adapted to an interdependent society and integrated world; a government capable of mediating
and promoting the common goals of empowered citizens and committed to
a similarly vigorous yet deliberative framework for balancing the needs of
people worldwide.[46]

Weyl and Lippmann, now officially in Wilson's corner, kept their eyes
on the same prize. "We leave behind our old Americanism to find abroad
a new and broader Americanism; an Internationalism," Weyl wrote during
1917. "We are going abroad to protect our own American democracy, as an
emigrant may fare forth to earn the wherewithal to protect his own home."
To return from this epic journey's first stage only to find the family circumstances declined might end the whole adventure. Reform at home must
proceed apace. Still, the world had grown so closely knit that no domestic gains were safe without international guarantees. Only "faith in a new
world society, in a new unity and a new concert" could give the conflict and
American participation in it "a rational and moral base."[47]

Among pragmatist progressives, Lippmann took the most optimistic
view of the war from the start and remained the most confident of its constructive issue for the duration. Certainly Lippmann relished proximity to
power and the chance to influence global affairs. But that very drive to direct policy into channels of mastery made him allergic to toadying. Bourne's
aspersions notwithstanding, Lippmann's desire to manage circumstances in
light of rather than in spite of his ideals explains far more than does his
personal egoism, including the relief (not fever) that war brought when it
finally came. That relief stemmed from months of worry that it would come
in the wrong way, destroying all chance of its ending justly. Weeks before
Congress declared war, Lippmann concluded that the power-worshipping
militarists making German policy would not negotiate in good faith until
cowed by superior force. Equally important, the example of America's voluntary "Defense of the Atlantic World" would do more than anything else

to "make the organization of a league of peace an immediately practical object of statesmanship."[48]

Lippmann was hardly insensitive to the immediate difficulties or potential consequences these conclusions entailed. In a March 11 memorandum to Wilson, he clearly outlined the dilemma that intervention posed. Prefiguring Wilson's war address, he explained that the German government's outrages betokened "aggressive ambitions which if achieved would render the future peace of the world unstable." Halting such outrages was therefore crucial to the "victory of international order over national aggression" that was the hope of all nations. Yet war, he continued, posed great dangers to American society. Many Americans were not ready for war, and many who were expressed disturbing ideas regarding its purpose. Pacifists failed to connect the "peace program" and the "warlike measures" necessary to achieve it, while "jingo elements" sowed public doubt that "belligerency" could "remain subordinate to liberal policy."[49]

Lippmann had previously warned that preventing a national fracture along these lines would require a massive and perilous propaganda campaign. Lest it degenerate into a witch hunt, censors would have to ignore the "conventionally unpatriotic" and crack down on those who "persecute and harass and cause divisions among the people." The war effort must be popularized not by manufacturing public support but by earning it through democratic deliberation of its merits. Admittedly, he wrote to House, the task of such a "press bureau" would be exceedingly difficult. It would have to drum up enthusiasm for a "gigantic" industrial and military operation while stamping out jingoism and promoting "objects" and "methods" wholly new to warfare. Meanwhile, domestic objects and methods must suit an effort "to make a world that is safe for democracy." The public should "supply ideas and criticisms" even as the bureau sought to "advise and warn" the press regarding the government's purposes and expectations. Rallying Americans to the president's standard would be a particularly trying exercise in the democratic art of leading while learning.[50]

These arguments, echoed (not coincidentally) by Frankfurter and Baker, convinced the president to establish a government information agency giving citizens "the feeling of partnership that comes with full, frank statements concerning the conduct of the public business."[51] The Committee on Public Information (CPI) was thus founded on the muckraker's principle that the simple facts of any case, disclosed widely and repeatedly, could inform and inflame enough individual consciences to spur and direct public action. Unfortunately, the CPI was therefore also susceptible to the sensationalism that had often characterized journalistic campaigns for reform.

Wilson's choice to handle the beast of public opinion was a respected veteran of those previous campaigns, George Creel. Committed to waging an "American" war, Creel declared informed consent his creed, and censorship anathema. Wilson, too, preferred information over obfuscation. He thought it "a public mistake to create an instrumentality exclusively for the purpose of propaganda," judging "simple means of explanation and discussion" more effective as well as more palatable.[52]

Initially the CPI reflected these priorities. Its *Official Bulletin* provided a day-by-day record of operations in every government department, and thousands of "Four-Minute Men" were instructed to promote the US effort across the country through short speeches conveying simple facts rather than fear or hate. The CPI also worked with the Bureau of Education to combat the influence of nationalistic organizations waging their own propaganda war against Germans and other immigrants in American schools. In attempting to save Americans from the nativists and jingoes in their midst, however, the CPI soon adopted many of their adversaries' tactics. By early 1918, CPI officials, often under pressure from other agencies, were instructing citizens to report pessimists and radical pacifists to the authorities, feeding the Four-Minute Men stories of German barbarism, and abandoning film projects lionizing American soldiers for those demonizing the kaiser and the German officer corps. Creel, increasingly obsessed with achieving uniform support for the war, inadvertently energized an "Americanization" campaign in which the drive to integrate society was overwhelmed by the desire to purify it of alien elements. Already in February 1917, Congress had passed, over Wilson's veto, a bill subjecting immigrants to literacy tests and barring most Asians from entry. By the early 1920s, the spirit of "100-percent Americanism" had fed so richly on wartime passions that Congress restricted even European immigration to a bare Teutonic minimum.[53]

The failure to direct "patriotism" into productive channels did not affect just immigrants. Most government officials counted American workers among the most crucial assets on their books—until work stoppage or antiwar agitation moved them to the liabilities column. International and domestic factors both encouraged such shifts. Europe's workers provided a restive example that frightened American employers, who often fed their conspiracy theories to local, state, and federal agencies. As the cost of living soared and demand for labor increased, workers grew simultaneously squeezed and strong, and strikes became epidemic. In this climate, the occasional anarchistic or antiwar pronouncement of a lone radical or local "Wobbly" (i.e., IWW) chapter allowed tightfisted employers to tar anyone even threatening a strike as a saboteur of the military machine. These slanders in turn stoked fears that all workers were potential dupes of the American Socialist Party (ASP), which loudly condemned the war as a Wall Street venture. To counteract the ASP's appeal, Creel and Gompers orchestrated a national campaign to convince American workers that their welfare depended on the war and the war depended on them. Unfortunately, labor and capital alike frequently interpreted this message as equating agitation with disloyalty, especially after the Justice Department raided and indicted scores of Wobblies for seditious conspiracy. With an odd mix of cynicism and naïveté, Wilson, encouraged by Attorney General Gregory, hoped the raids might prevent strikes in war-critical industries, mollify conservative employers and trade unions, and substitute courtroom for vigilante justice. Predictably, the raids did nothing for labor–capital relations, and the jury box cured few citizens of antiradical hysteria. More potent were the president's occasional and irresponsible expressions of "contempt" for pacifists, which encouraged those already equating pacifism with socialism, and socialism with immigrant labor, to damn the lot as traitors. In a gruesome twist on Wilson's voluntarist theme, the more excitable among such patriots dispensed with curses and chose to beat, hang, or shoot their way to "100 percent Americanism."[54]

Perhaps inevitably in a culture so inured to racial violence, African Americans, too, were scorched by the torches of intolerance. Though in this case the administration was not actively fanning the flames, Wilson again proved fatally negligent in the face of injustice and murder. A rash of lynching blotted the South, then crept northward as the war brought jobs, high wages, and huge influxes of southern blacks to the nation's industrial centers. Cities like Chicago and East Saint Louis became cauldrons of racial tension that boiled over into mob violence.[55] Elsewhere, black men seeking to earn the respect of their white fellow citizens through military service were despised, abused, and attacked by those who encountered them. On the night of August 23, 1917, Houston became a literal battlefield on which African American soldiers confronted armed white civilians in a clash, leaving four of the former and fifteen of the latter dead. Black soldiers received less deadly but equally degrading treatment from the US Army itself. As Du Bois discovered on an investigatory visit to France, they were typically relegated to hard labor and rarely given commands above corporal. Ironically, many whom he canvassed described their Gallic tour as an almost magical idyll in a paradise of tolerance—except when on base.[56]

Wilson did not entirely ignore these grim manifestations of the war psychology and the deeper pathologies it revealed. He backed Frankfurter's efforts to bring antilabor vigilantes to justice, despite a foot-dragging attorney general and an uncooperative Supreme Court. He conferred with black leaders disturbed by the violence at East Saint Louis, expressed his disgust, and authorized Gregory to exploit "any instrumentality of the Government" that might "check these disgraceful outrages." In July 1918, he released a "Statement to the American People" charging vigilantes, mobs, and all who abetted their travesties of justice with endangering the war effort and betraying their country. "How shall we commend democracy to the acceptance of other peoples, if we disgrace our own by proving it is, after all, no protection to the weak?"[57]

Almost invariably, however, Wilson's efforts were too little, too late. Behind his indictment of lynch rule lay a year's worth of pressure from racial democrats, including white "war intellectuals" such as Walling and Croly.[58] Yet missing from his statement was any specific condemnation of violence against blacks, crucial in a country that had long denied them equal protection under the law. Meanwhile, Wilson accepted at face value the War Department's claim that segregated black soldiers would enjoy "full opportunities" for advancement—though in transmitting this assurance to black leaders, he deliberately changed the phrasing to "*fullest possible* opportunities." As he informed a National Race Congress delegation, "Human nature doesn't make giant strides in a single generation"—a Burkean claim that would have earned his rebuke had the issue been class (or international) relations rather than race relations.[59] Once again, Wilson seemed paralyzed in matters touching race. In private correspondence he expressed his desire to stand up for blacks, but only "with the likelihood that it will be effective." Part of him knew he had failed black Americans, but mostly he blamed circumstances. "I have never had an opportunity actually to do what I promised them I would seek an opportunity to do," he lamented to Creel. Yet Wilson had made a career of creating opportunities where none presented themselves. Unfortunately, when it came to racial justice, opportunity almost always meant action without cost.[60]

If Wilson's wartime stance on racial justice was by turns craven and cavalier, his stance on censorship was simply baffling. His previous political career, close relationships with liberal journalists, and faith in freely formulated public opinion all suggested that while activities hampering the war effort might be disallowed, analyses of its wisdom would be welcomed, or at least tolerated. Meeting with his cabinet on the day war was declared, Wilson quashed proposals from Postmaster General Albert Sidney Burleson and Secretary of State Lansing to ban "critical" material from the mails and outlaw German-language papers. Reflecting his correspondence with Lippmann, he concurred with Baker and Secretary of the Navy

Josephus Daniels that "there should be no censorship of opinion or comment," only suppression of "military news that would aid the enemy." A good sign: House thought Burleson "the most belligerent member of the cabinet," fiercely pro-Allied and violently antipacifist, antisocialist, and anti-immigrant. Yet a few weeks into the war, Wilson effectively appointed Burleson sheriff of the press, turning his own attention almost exclusively to diplomacy. "I must admit that I haven't been able to read all of the enclosed," he wrote Burleson regarding the proposed "rules of procedure" for censorship, "but you know that I am willing to trust your judgment after I have once called your attention to a suggestion."[61] That indeed was the pattern characterizing nearly the whole of Wilson's record on censorship, a record marred with appalling and absurd assaults on free speech that proved devastating to his internationalist agenda.

One of the earliest such episodes involved Max Eastman and his socialist review of arts, events, and politics, the *Masses*. The Espionage Act passed in June 1917, banned all incitements to "insubordination, disloyalty, mutiny, [or] refusal of duty, in the military or naval forces," and authorized the postmaster general to identify offending periodicals and revoke their mailing privileges. For Burleson, socialism was inherently disloyal—even the moderate socialism of those, like Eastman, who supported Wilson's war aims (if not his war). Despite Eastman's earnest attempts to keep his statements about the war within legal bounds, the *Masses* was declared "unmailable" several weeks after Congress declared war. When the Second District Court invalidated that decision, Burleson revoked Eastman's mailing privileges on grounds that his periodical's "continuity" had been "interrupted—it having been interrupted," Eastman explained exasperatedly to Wilson, "at the request of the Post Office." Eastman had "repeatedly" asked Burleson's department how to make the magazine "mailable"; Burleson's response was to haul Eastman before the Senate and charge him with instigating draft resistance. Such pointless abuses of bureaucratic power, Eastman warned, would not only prevent patriotic socialists from playing their part "in the further democratizing of the world" but also erode the support of "radical-minded people the country over"—support Wilson had painstakingly earned.[62]

Was Wilson ignorant of just how crucial such support would be? When the *Masses* was first attacked in July, he received a letter from Eastman, Amos Pinchot, and John Reed—all of whom had voted for Wilson—imploring that he defend "the Anglo-Saxon tradition of intellectual freedom." The president duly forwarded the letter to Burleson, describing the writers as "very sincere men" whom he "should like to please."[63] He did not work very hard to do so. "I think that a time of war must be regarded as wholly exceptional and that it is legitimate to regard things which would in ordinary circumstances be innocent as very dangerous to the public welfare," Wilson wrote in response to Eastman's letter. Tortuously, he explained that "the line is manifestly exceedingly hard to draw and I cannot say that I have any confidence that I know how to draw it. I can only say that a line must be drawn and that we are trying, it may be clumsily but genuinely, to draw it without fear or favor or prejudice."[64]

"*We* are *trying* . . . ." That was the closest Wilson came to describing his philosophy of civil liberties in wartime. Straining his pragmatist principles and theory of leadership beyond their limits, he seemed to imply that protecting rights was an experiment which it was his deputies' responsibility to supervise. As he told Creel in November 1917, "it would be extremely difficult to state correctly and wisely my views about free speech just now, and I think I had better seek a later occasion."[65] Such occasion never came, leaving less distracted pragmatists to attempt to solve his conundrum for him. In October 1917, Lippmann alerted the administration to the "sullen mood" of prominent liberal interventionists over Burleson's "brutally unreasonable" censorship. Abjuring any "doctrinaire belief in free speech" and allowing its necessary restriction in wartime, Lippmann tried to focus Wilson's attention on "the method now being pursued," which was dividing the country into "fanatical" jingoes and pacifists, just as he had warned. Having united a powerful but fragile coalition of liberal intellectuals, labor groups, and even many socialists behind the war, Wilson could not afford to abandon it to the "heresy hunting" of subordinates. Why should the government bother with what "an obscure and discredited little sheet says about Wall Street and munition makers"? Suppression merely imbued such froth with the substance it lacked. Meanwhile, most of the war's radical critics could still be won over, "simply by conserving the spirit of the President's own utterances" regarding its democratic purpose. Above all, the "delicate task" of wartime censorship "should never be intrusted to anyone who is not himself tolerant, nor to anyone who is unacquainted with the long record of folly which is the history of suppression."[66]

Croly, too, urged the substitution of Wilsonian method for Burlesonian madness. The latter was "really hurting the standing of the war," he wrote to Wilson on October 19. The rumor of government–capitalist conspiracy that had prompted Burleson's latest crackdown was "sufficiently silly" that Croly could imagine only one thing "which would give it any plausibility": Burleson's latest crackdown. Suppression of socialist propaganda was the one "plain fact" upon which the story of a war to eradicate socialism could be based. Why not take the same voluntarist approach to the mails as to industry? Surely it was possible to "negotiate," establishing "certain limits" on agitation without "forcing" journalists to betray their convictions. Leaving even "unreasonable" sorts to discredit themselves was preferable to Burleson's heavy-handed tactics, which were dividing the public into dogmatic anti-interventionists suspicious of Wilson's peaceful objectives and fanatical jingoes who ignored or disclaimed them. Such a climate made it "extremely difficult" for responsible interventionists to promote "the pacific and constructive purposes which underlie American participation." Invariably such level heads appeared "half-hearted," especially "as compared to the war propagandists."[67]

The political as opposed to merely ideological force of these arguments makes their failure to move Wilson all the more mysterious. In the half apology concluding Croly's letter lay a clear warning: "There is no public object in which I more profoundly believe than the object for which you are waging this war," he assured the president, but propaganda and censorship gave him "the utmost difficulty in writing about it from week to week without making an appearance of opposing what our government is trying to do." Unfortunately for Croly, his difficulties would increase. Though Wilson deemed Burleson "inclined to be most conservative" in the use of his powers, the postmaster general's inclinations sloped steeply in the opposite direction—reaching a minor peak of absurdity with his investigation of the New Republic itself. On that occasion and several others, Wilson urged moderation. Still, in all such cases he seemed more afraid of offending his postmaster general (who repeatedly threatened resignation) than turning the liberal press against the war.[68] Lippmann, Croly, and other pragmatists invested in Wilson's international program understood his impulse to act vigorously rather than parse principles in time of crisis. But what Dewey called "conscription of thought" was a rotten way promote the "social solidarity" that a war to destroy autocracy required. In a pluralistic society, solidarity depends on the deliberate cultivation of understanding that pragmatists defined as "reason." By late 1917, that once valued commodity was trading at a discount. "The appeal is no longer to reason," Dewey lamented, "it is to the event."[69]

Wilson's efforts to instruct citizens in the collective art of autocracide were, as Dewey charged, often unreasonable, sometimes constitutionally dubious, and generally ham-handed. Above all, they were shortsighted, a fact explained in part by his focus on the international scene. Wilson was not so dense as to think the American public alone needed educating. The Allied peoples, for instance, would have to support his vision of peace if it were ever to materialize. Hence the CPI waged a massive propaganda campaign across Europe to distinguish the American government's aims as an "Associated Power" from those of the Allied governments.[70] Equally if not more decisive would be Wilson's success in educating, or at least overwhelming with information and argumentation, the Allied statesmen who would join him at the peace table—men who as yet had shown scant interest in a rehabilitative settlement. The key to this effort, in turn, would be to educate himself and his delegation about the war aims of the belligerents and their historical, strategic, and ideological rationales, "that we may formulate our own position either for or against them." This was the origin of the Inquiry, a group established in September 1917 to devise and justify settlement terms on a scientific basis. House, charged with overseeing the group, chose Lippmann as its general secretary—one of four "chiefs" who effectively led the operation and the one who became its primary conduit to the administration.[71]

That Wilson and House looked to Lippmann in staffing the Inquiry was unsurprising. For one thing, he and Croly had suggested just such an operation to Baker and House before its creation.[72] The *New Republic* editors had also spent two-and-a-half years trying to educate the president on the nature of the current international order and the prospects for replacing it, and at crucial points the president had paid attention. House's prewar relationship with the editors had grown closer and their "weekly talk" habitual. Lippmann watered the roots of the relationship in Washington, sprinkling notes and memoranda across the wide fields Baker opened to him. In New York, Croly did his part to sustain House's assumption that the journal was both at his service and under his influence, requesting in July, for instance, "an outline of the foreign situation, so that he and his staff might write intelligently and not conflict with the purposes of the Government." The *New Republic* had just condemned the "petty and ineffectual tyranny" of that same government's censorship policy. Nevertheless, Croly consistently reminded his readers that Wilson's war, despite its risks, was the best long-term bet for the nation and the world.[73]

But Croly, painfully shy and devoted to his journal, was never in the running for the Inquiry job. Lippmann, socially as well as intellectually precocious, had during his War Department tenure turned an already extensive web of administration connections into a policy forum as effective as his journal ever was. That web included the president. Since drawing on the *New Republic*'s editorials to clarify his general stance toward the war in January, Wilson had talked only in generalities of the "peace without victory" he sought. He was nonetheless intent on defining its major features, and Lippmann's writings remained a favored resource. Five days after his speech, Wilson requested a copy of Lippmann's *Stakes of Diplomacy*, which urged "enlarging the areas within which force takes a more civilized form" rather than abjuring force altogether, and suggested that a federation of self-governing nations—given a representative legislature, strong executive, and mechanisms for expanding its writ and membership—might gradually but practically secure peace by substituting elections for war, as in the federal system of the United States. Within weeks of requesting the book, as his mediation effort was collapsing, Wilson received Lippmann's March 11 memorandum on the rationale for intervention and its necessity to lasting peace. Lippmann's arguments were so congruent with those of Wilson's war address that if they did not directly influence the latter, they surely increased the president's appreciation for such lucid explications of ideas mirroring his own.[74]

In fact, Wilson relied on Lippmann's bold thinking and clear expression to get out of one of his first diplomatic jams as a war president—an episode that redefined America's strategy for the war, clarified the peace that was its object, and prompted the Inquiry's founding. By midsummer 1917, a German military resurgence, rumors of secret Allied treaties carving up Central Europe and the colonial world, and Russia's descent into civil war raised a clamor among American liberals and war-weary Europeans for definite moves toward an early peace. Surveying a scene set for the triumph of atheistic Bolshevism, Pope Benedict XV called publicly on August 1 for a negotiated peace resolving territorial disputes by plebiscite, hoping to take the anti-imperialist wind out of the Bolsheviks' sails. This direct challenge to Wilson's moral leadership posed a dilemma. To ignore or clumsily deflect the pope's appeal might dissipate the force of opinion that Wilson hoped to concentrate, through his person, on his counterparts at the peace table. To second the appeal at a moment of Germany military ascendancy, however, would alienate the Allies and similarly compromise his influence.[75]

Wilson knew what the essence of a negative reply must be. The "present German Imperial Government" could not be trusted to negotiate honestly, he told House, and any settlement leaving it in power would put the world's peace "upon quicksand."[76] Yet such a reply must be phrased to satisfy international liberals and Allied statesmen alike, while reminding the latter of the war's proper object. In a memorandum submitted to Wilson via Baker, Lippmann solved the dilemma. He clarified the connection between continuing war and securing peace by restating the purpose of both: not to destroy Germany but to dismantle its militarist autocracy and clear the ground for democracy in Central Europe. Yet the Germans could only be "weaned from their governing class" if convinced of a "safe, prosperous, and respected" existence in its absence. In rebutting the pope, therefore, Wilson

must emphasize the *"method of settlement"* rather than its terms, reminding both Germans and the Allied peoples that unless determined democratically, by legitimate representatives of their interests, no settlement would
prevent another catastrophe. Sad as it was, the very contingency that prevented peace at present made it possible in future. "We are at war with the
German procedure," wrote Lippmann. "We go on the assumption that it is
possible to deal in good faith with a democracy."[77]

"Lippmann is not only thoughtful, but just and suggestive," Wilson wrote
Baker on August 22. He had prefigured Lippmann's argument in certain of
his speeches in the months before the pope's appeal.[78] Wilson, however, had
argued that an acceptable settlement depended merely on the German high
command's fear of losing. Lippmann, by contrast, identified its actual demise
as a precondition for peace. Convinced, Wilson composed a reply to Benedict,
insisting that the war's supreme object was "to deliver the fine peoples of
the world from the menace and the actual power of a vast military establishment controlled by an irresponsible government." Peace could be had only if
"the masters of the German people" were deposed, and their victims, within
and beyond Germany's borders, delivered from autocracy. Until that outcome
was assured, there would be no armistice.[79]

"I have not thought it wise to say more or to be more specific," Wilson remarked upon completing his reply. Ten days later, however, he asked
House to assemble a team of experts to turn his generalities into clear objectives. Wilson had called the pope's bluff: the reply had its desired effect,
eliciting favorable reports from Europe and praise from Max Eastman, of
all people, for giving "concrete meaning" to talk of a "war for democracy."
But Wilson had also raised the stakes in tying German rehabilitation so
closely to international reconstruction. At the peace table he would need a
strong hand and a psychological edge to stare down the seasoned gamblers
bent on soaking the Germans. The massive research program Lippmann
oversaw was in this sense a giant card-counting effort, aimed at predicting
and controlling a game that, sooner or later, would decide the future of international relations.[80]

The Inquiry job was one for which Lippmann had "dreamed" since war
was declared. It seemed the perfect mix of learning, thinking, and application, a chance to extrapolate from the smallest details policies of the largest
importance. It was, he wrote to Baker, a "real application of the President's
idea" requiring "inventiveness and resourcefulness"—an exercise in mastery.[81] Lippmann was surrounded by men of ability, including fellow "chiefs"
David Hunter Miller, an expert on international law; James T. Shotwell, a
Columbia historian recommended to House by Croly; and Isaiah Bowman,

director of the American Geographical Society. The group was secret, non-partisan, staffed by civilians, and worked independently of the State Department to maximize objectivity and flexibility. This "scientific" operation, however, had a distinct philosophical cast. The directorate trained an implicitly pragmatist lens on world affairs, through which the constantly shifting emotions, perceptions, ideas, and desires of human beings were studied as closely as populations, land formations, and economic resources.[82]

For Lippmann this approach was conscious, and he queried his fellow pragmatists for suggestions to improve it. Veblen advised "discovering and presenting the lowest terms and the most neutral claims" by which the Allied–American partnership—the most viable kernel of international organization—could be "held together as a going concern." Weyl asserted the need for "a free competition" of ideas within the Inquiry itself. Fusing both ideas, Lippmann suggested a division assigned the "continuous task" of critiquing the Inquiry's own plans as well as those it studied—a task he ultimately performed himself. With House, Lippmann also facilitated a remarkably open dialogue with the Inquiry's British and French counterparts, even suggesting near war's end that operations move to France, to ensure more "intimate knowledge" of European affairs and thinking. The American peace program would be a product of the pragmatic method, at least ideally.[83]

Lippmann imposed a correspondent philosophical and political shape on the Inquiry's massive output, sifting the work of its myriad specialists, synthesizing the best of it, and presenting it clearly and concisely in memoranda submitted directly to House and Wilson. These often concerned discrete subjects such as arms control or economic reconstruction, but Lippmann kept his attention on the bigger postwar picture. Accepting the importance of open diplomacy, arms reduction, and compulsory arbitration—generic pillars of the "liberal peace program"—Lippmann considered a broader foundation to support them paramount. In his view, lasting peace depended on advancing the global psychological shift the war had already prompted, on converting mere recognition of international interdependence into an ethos which would inspire and sustain institutions for managing it.[84]

Lippmann and other pragmatist progressives had long argued that traditional conceptions of individual right and sovereign prerogative impeded the maintenance of order amid change. Germany's autocrats had, ironically, confirmed this proposition. The war, Lippmann believed, was initiated and exacerbated by Germany's brutal application of the "doctrine of unlimited national sovereignty": a "policy which began by denying that a quarrel in the Balkans could be referred to Europe," proceeded "to destroy the internationalized state of Belgium," and then "culminated in indiscriminate

attack" on neutral nations. Yet by demonstrating *"ad nauseam* the doctrine of competitive nationalism,'' Germany had elicited pioneering experiments in "cooperative nationalism." The democratic revolution in Russia,
the movement toward genuine federation of the British Empire, and the
intervention of the United States all showed that the peoples of these nations expected more than German defeat from their governments' alliances.
"They have learned that they cannot be free unless they cooperate" and
"cannot cooperate unless they are free." The logical application of this
lesson was not arbitration, a treaty of disarmament, or an economic accord.
It was a "Federation of the World" that would alter the internal politics of
nations, including the United States. "We shall turn with fresh interests to
our own tyrannies—to our Colorado mines, our autocratic steel industries,
our sweat-shops and our slums," Lippmann concluded. "We shall call that
man un-American and no patriot who prates of liberty in Europe and resists
it at home."[85]

These basic themes ran throughout Lippmann's Inquiry work. With circumstances changing daily, he wrote in March 1918, "no treatise planned
now" would likely remain "pertinent to the actual negotiations" for peace.
Rather, as he had argued but a month into his duties, a viable settlement
depended on "keeping alive the picture of a reunited peaceful world."[86] That
picture was one in which governments pursued their objects through discussion, not aggression, and submitted to the will of an international majority. To make the world's peoples believe in that possibility required beating
Germany's army and forcing reform of its government; specific peace terms
were "inevitably secondary" to discrediting "nationalist absolutism." Certain general terms, however, were crucial to the latter's demise and must be
conceded before any negotiations commenced. These included restoration
of Belgium, consensual settlement of territorial claims, an end to colonial
exploitation, and the establishment of a league of nations whose authority
"should be regarded as an infringement neither of sovereignty nor of national
honor."[87]

Though Lippmann's personal quest remained, as before the war, to promote the symbiosis of national and international interests to influential
audiences, the secretary of the Inquiry could not ignore the specific understandings and mechanisms that would convert those interests into world
policies. Indeed, he and his codirectors oversaw production of literally thousands of reports on such matters at the local, regional, continental, and
global scale. Still, Lippmann insisted that the American program remain
"flexible": that negotiators focus on "the needs and purposes which inspire the claims put forth by the Powers," rather than the claims alone, and

have enough "alternative suggestions" at hand to "give an accommodating and experimental character to American purpose." Moreover, he continued to believe that no program, however flexible, had any chance of success unless ultimate political sovereignty was vested in a "new fellowship" modeled on the American political ideal: an organized community of states committed to democracy within and across borders.[88] That, after all, was the central theme of pragmatist internationalism. It was "plain that the peace will be secure in direct proportion to the measure in which national discrimination and prestige are allowed to pass into nothingness and be forgot," Veblen had written in *The Nature of Peace* (1917). To accomplish this at a stroke during peace negotiations was impossible; hence the need for a legally and practically sovereign league, empowered "to enforce peace by overmastering force, and to anticipate *any* move at cross purposes with the security of the pacific nations"—both during the risky period of reconstruction and over the generations required to build a global culture of democracy.[89]

This was the contribution of the pragmatist progressives to twentieth-century internationalism: the notion that the old model of sovereignty was deadly inefficient, and even uncertain experiments in pooling sovereignty were preferable. As Dewey wrote in August 1917, the United States was fighting for "the beginnings of a public control which will cross nationalistic boundaries and interests." Agreeing on the goal if not the method, Addams and colleagues from the Woman's Peace Party published a revised peace program demanding "autonomy and democratic government" within political jurisdictions and a suite of institutions for adjusting relations among them, including an international court, permanent international legislature, and permanent administrative commissions handling "matters of common international interest." As Weyl explained in defending his similar proposal, the world required "machinery" analogous to that "by which a nation, composed of conflicting classes and economic groups, manages to secure a degree of common interest and action among such groups." That such machinery would never "work perfectly," would "repeatedly break down," and could be "perfected only through trial and error" were "facts, which though in themselves discouraging, need not lead to the abandonment of the effort." Indeed, as early as 1913, Randolph Bourne had argued that "world-federation" required no huge leap of imagination, but merely "recognition of the fact that war is world-suicide."[90]

These were Lippmann's own convictions. As secretary of the Inquiry, however, he faced a dilemma. On the one hand, specific endorsement of such radical terms might open fissures between right and left that German propagandists could exploit. On the other, the ultimate success of Wilson's

program required "placating the moderate left" in Britain, France, and the
United States, in order to maximize public support and avoid "moral dis-
union"—especially as American democracy groaned under the strain of mobilization and world liberalism gasped at rumors of Allied plans to carve up
Europe. The task, then, was to formulate a statement of war aims specific
enough to pin the belligerents down, flexible enough to permit some wig-
gling, and liberal enough to bring the clamor for a new diplomacy to a cre-
scendo; or in Lippmann's words, to express a "catholic idea" of the war,
inspiring "consent" to its highest purpose and continued prosecution despite ambiguities and disappointments.[91] That task became imperative in
December 1917, and though it fell to Wilson, it became a collaborative effort
that produced the most important state paper of his presidency: a fourteen-
point template for peace that steeled the world's will to believe in its
possibility.

CHAPTER EIGHT

The Fable of the Fourteen Points

In July 1918, President Wilson received an impassioned but shrewd memorandum by the British political analyst, prominent league of nations advocate, and frequent *New Republic* contributor Norman Angell. The most pressing task of statesmanship, Angell declared, was consistently to remind the world that the catastrophe of the last four years was not the product of natural laws or objective forces but of human ideas and actions. For decades, the widespread belief that a nation's security was a function of its "individual power" had fostered a competitive system of international politics, "which could only give security if each unit could be stronger than any of the others—a mathematical absurdity." Despite its horrific consequences, belief in this system was so ingrained, and had produced so much evidence of humanity's belligerency, that a cooperative alternative could "only become operative as the result of an 'act of faith'—the conviction, that is, on the part of statesmen and public that the risks involved in the newer policy are less than those involved in the old." Citing William James's essay "The Will to Believe," he ventured to remind the administration that "the one factor necessary to make a policy or method practical, is just the general decision that it is practical." Only if enough people believed in the possibility of a safer, freer world under a system of cooperative internationalism could the first experiments in creating that world commence. "And that," Angell concluded, "is the moral for the Western World at this moment": its people must decide, in light of their common history, whether "better policies can be made to produce better results than in the past."[1]

Angell wrote to the administration because the president had for years promoted the internationalist faith he described. Just six months prior, Wilson had outlined the "better policies" that faith suggested in one of the twentieth century's great state papers, his "Fourteen Points" address of

January 8, 1918. Unfortunately, Wilson was so identified with the idea that nations could cooperate, and might even do so given proper guidelines and inducements, that when he failed to live up to its various and conflicting interpretations, he nearly bankrupted all of them. Yet the number and diversity of people who invested their hopes for a new world order in Wilson reflected more than just the confusion he sowed in the months following his address. Throughout 1918, Wilson and his close advisers expanded the Fourteen Points into a pragmatist program for global governance, one just radical enough to be practical—or at least to seem so to tens of millions worldwide who had borne the burden of nationalist rivalry and political oppression far too long.

The glimpses that Wilson afforded the global public could not convey his plan's sophistication, including its tough proposed compromises and built-in abatements of its inevitable imperfection. Seeking to shield his program from early and crippling attacks, Wilson hid it away and left its development to public imagination, where it took a host of fantastical forms. Monstrous and beautiful alike, these forms came to bedevil his efforts and ruin his peace—but not yet the world's. The faith he had labored to spread proved remarkably resilient to the slings of fate and politics, and stolid in the face of his own human frailty. By war's end, the president was still, despite his errors, in a position to lead the broken and frightened nations of the world to mutual asylum.

"Do we have a co-belligerent or an umpire?" Britain's King George V asked about the United States at war. From April 1917 through October 1918, the American government provided his empire and its allies the financial assistance; then the naval, air, and material support; and finally the two million troops that, taken together, turned the tide against Germany. Nonetheless, the "Allies" had cause to resent their "Associate," as Wilson pointedly distinguished the United States. Though relations with Germany were severed in February, the administration resisted cutting diplomatic contacts with the other Central powers. Congress waited eight months to declare war on Austria-Hungary, and it never declared war on the Ottoman Empire or Bulgaria. Arthur Balfour, Sir Edward Grey's replacement as British foreign secretary, had rewarded the American declaration against Germany with news of secret treaties divvying enemy territories among the Allies; and though Wilson never read them, their mere existence convinced him that for America's enemies and associates both, the "main object" remained "aggression and conquest." Persuaded that Britain fought primarily for German colonies in Africa and Asia, France for colonies and control of the European continent, and Italy for chunks of Austria and other orts from the Allied galley, Wilson refused public discussion of their objectives throughout 1917, so as not to legitimate them by the honor of his attention—or betray his own heading to the pirates at Whitehall and the Quai d'Orsay. Instead, he steered a course for the diplomatic center-left, navigating by the bright but nebulous polestar of a "liberal peace."[2]

In the summer, fall, and winter of 1917, however, developments in Britain, France, and above all Russia sucked the United States' associates into its political wake. In Britain, liberal and labor elements grew restive, perhaps even "anxious," as Prime Minister David Lloyd George feared, "to break down the national nerve and then rush us into a premature and disastrous peace." In France, fear and hardship encouraged a sharp rise in antiwar and antigovernment propaganda from the Left, prompting assaults from the Right on the government's political timidity and military incompetence. By late November, confidence in the French government was so low that President Raymond Poincaré invited Georges Clemenceau, a personal enemy and caustic critic, to assume the premiership.[3]

Most important were events in Russia. The Bolsheviks' seizure of power on November 7, their moves toward a separate peace with Germany, and the consequent collapse of the eastern front all guaranteed that American intervention would be the decisive factor preventing Allied collapse. France was still recovering from the previous spring's disastrous Nivelle offensive and the mutinies it sparked; the Italians had been annihilated at Caporetto just as the Bolsheviks seized power; and the pointless Third Battle of Ypres, or Passchendaele, had decimated the British army just as the Germans were redeploying eastern forces westward. US Army General Tasker H. Bliss, after a month of strategizing with Allied military leaders, predicted that "without great assistance from the United States," the Central powers would "have the advantage" by the spring of 1918, probably for good.[4]

Grim as it was, this was not unwelcome news to Wilson. The president wanted a firepower advantage over friend and foe alike before stating his terms for peace. As it happened, the American Expeditionary Force was then nearing 170,000 men, with two more divisions on the way. Since July, the US Navy had helped the Allies cut their shipping losses dramatically while doubling the number of U-boats destroyed. All this provided just enough of an advantage over Germany to demonstrate the centrality of US power to Allied victory. In short, the Allies' mortal peril gave Wilson a macabre version of his wish.[5]

The Russian civil war was the hinge of this diplomatic swing. But the swing was not precisely in Wilson's direction. While increasing his leverage over Lloyd George and Clemenceau, the Bolshevik triumph also spawned an ideological beast with which he would wrestle until, ironically, the beast and its would-be breaker were fused like a chimera in the world's consciousness. The creature in question was "national self-determination," and its homeland was Soviet Russia. In April 1917, the Russian provisional government had declared "the self-determination of peoples" among the essentials of any peace settlement. By the time the Bolsheviks seized power in November, Vladimir Lenin had come to view ethnic nationalism as a powerful solvent of existing state structures that would help spread proletarian revolution across Central Europe. The "Declaration of the Rights of the Peoples of Russia," issued by Lenin on November 15, promised all "non-Russian nationalities in Russia, full freedom, including freedom of secession."[6] One week later, Leon Trotsky announced his government's intention to negotiate a "democratic peace" with Germany "on the basis of self-determination of nations," and on December 6, he challenged the Allies to accept these arrangements or "openly state before the world . . . in the name of what purpose must the people of Europe bleed during the fourth year of war." By then the Bolsheviks had published secret treaties, agreed between the czarist and Allied governments, exchanging territory in return for a generation slaughtered. What other gifts had the Western "democracies" in store? Did they include "self-determination" for the peoples of Central Europe, and those "of Ireland, Egypt, India, Madagascar, Indo-China"? The longer the invitation to join Trotsky's proposed general peace went unanswered, the clearer it became that the Allies were motivated by a "cynical imperialism" making them the common enemy of the stateless peoples they oppressed and the working classes they exploited. Audiences in colonized regions across the globe were listening to the Bolsheviks, urging the Allies to answer the charges levied. Above all, they turned to Wilson for assurance that the governments in his coalition were ready to accept as partners peoples whom they had long sought to control as subjects.[7]

The Treaty of Brest-Litovsk, signed by Russia and Germany in March 1918, has been called the "catalyst" of a diplomatic and ideological revolution.[8] But the catalytic effect of Russia's exit from the war began months before. Initially, at an inter-Allied conference convened just days after the secret treaties were published, Lloyd George, Clemenceau, and Italian foreign minister Sidney Sonnino refused to discuss their import or prudence except in purely military terms, despite the insistence of Wilson's adviser, Edward M. House, on regaining the psychological advantage with a statement of liberal war aims. Even Wilson's public charge that British, French, and Italian covetousness had driven Russia from the war was ignored by the Allied leaders, who acknowledged only his call, in the same address, for the kaiser's deposition. But in late December, the Allied Left was aroused, when Russian proposals at Brest-Litovsk for a peace of no annexations, no indemnities, and self-determination for subject nationalities were met by the Central powers' cagey endorsement of "immediate general peace without forcible annexations of territory and without indemnities." In Britain the pressure culminated on December 28, when the Labour Party published a "Memorandum on War Aims" demanding an avowedly Wilsonian program, including "a supernational authority" comprising an international legislature, world court, and mediation council to settle "non-justiciable" disputes. The role of the French Left was more complicated. Still, even when imploring their Russian counterparts to abandon the separate peace with Germany, French Socialists insisted that the Allied governments revise their war aims to reflect the "international justice" for which they claimed to fight.[9]

Signs like these emboldened Wilson. The peace propaganda from the Bolsheviks and Central powers said nothing about a "supernational authority" such as British Labour invoked and Wilson championed. In the Bolsheviks' bid for global moral leadership and the Central powers' second annual call for peace, Wilson saw an opportunity to bring the Allied leaders to heel. Discredited by the secret treaties, fearful of political collapse or revolution, they would have no choice but to align themselves with a pragmatically internationalist program—a program anti-imperialist and unselfish enough to shore up liberal support for the war, draw the Russians back into it, and encourage the war-weary German people to seize control of their affairs and end it. On Wilson's instructions, House put the Inquiry to work drafting a list of those objectives most crucial to postwar stability and to countering the effect of the "cynical" secret treaties.[10]

That *New Republic* editor Walter Lippmann would have a strong hand in organizing Wilson's thoughts on the settlement was a foregone conclusion. The president had long solicited his views on its immediate and long-term essentials. Since the declaration of war with Germany, Wilson had discussed Lippmann's *Stakes of Diplomacy* with US Secretary of War Newton Baker, read Lippmann's July article demystifying sovereignty and endorsing global governance, and called on Lippmann to draft his reply to Pope Benedict XV.[11] Since September, House had relied on Lippmann to digest and synthesize the Inquiry's work in dozens of memoranda for discussion with the president. Thus Lippmann found himself working around-the-clock between December 18 and January 2 to outline a concrete program for a Wilsonian peace—first on a memorandum written with Inquiry colleagues

Sidney Mezes and David Hunter Miller, dated December 22 and expanded circa January 2; then alone, on a December 31 memorandum clarifying the program's philosophical framework. In the latter—embodying his contributions to the expanded joint memorandum—Lippmann explained that Germany's leaders, having renounced annexations, seemed finally convinced that the "mad dream" of continental domination had failed. Now they must recognize that their country would never recover until "those who have learned to distrust her" were "fully convinced that the diplomacy of intrigue and force is abandoned" and normal commercial and political intercourse could resume. "They are not yet convinced," Lippmann stated curtly. Neither the structure nor the proposals of the present German government were compatible with "enduring peace." Through freely chosen representatives, the German people must agree to restore Belgium, northern France, Serbia, and other victims of the "lawless spirit" that so imperiled the cause of "justice among nations." They must also recognize that "the formula of no forcible annexations" could not be applied "with such literalness as to preclude the righting of wrongs" which would "remain to trouble the peace of the world." Lippmann acknowledged that the Central empires were likely to lose some territory in a pragmatic settlement striking a "just balance of nationalistic and economic considerations." Regardless, he asserted, "oppressed peoples" and "national minorities" in all states must be assured "the right to live and grow in peace and security." Only after these basic terms were embraced in good faith could "the present league of nations against Germany and her vassals . . . be expanded to include the Central Powers," and a new chapter in world history commence.[12]

Reviewing the Inquiry materials on January 4, 1918, Wilson and House finally outlined a response to Brest-Litovsk: a proposal for an international political superstructure, geared toward global stabilization but cast in the deliberative, democratic, anti-imperialist mold Lippmann suggested. On January 8, before a joint session of Congress, Wilson revealed his "Fourteen Points" to the world. The program included eight solutions to specific territorial and political problems that had caused or arisen from the war: evacuation of occupied Russian territory and freedom for Russians to determine their own institutions; evacuation of Belgium; the return of Alsace-Lorraine to France; adjustment of Italy's borders with respect to the nationality of affected majorities; political equality for nationalities within the Austro-Hungarian and Ottoman Empires; and a Polish state guaranteed access to the sea. These specific suggestions were anchored in six general propositions embodying the larger goals for which the United States fought: open diplomacy, freedom of the seas, abolition of trade barriers, arms reduction, colonial reform, and most important, an "association of nations" to maintain "the political independence and territorial integrity" of "great and small states alike"—a league of nations.[13]

The league was Wilson's criterion. It provides the lens through which his program should be viewed, and it alters some familiar historical pictures. Most important, Wilson did not endorse the Bolsheviks' ethnonationalist (and disingenuous) ideal of "self-determination" for all cultural groups seeking political independence—not privately, and not in his address.[14] Rather, the organizing principle of the Fourteen Points was the same that had organized his political thought for decades: the civic ideal of self-*government*, or as he phrased it in connection to Hapsburg and Ottoman subjects, "autonomous development." To emphasize the distinction is not to endorse the view that Wilson's address was a "countermanifesto" to Lenin's. The program was inspired by ideals he had trumpeted since 1914, and each of its specific elements had peppered Inquiry memoranda and Wilson's own speeches for weeks and months; if anything, Lenin had cribbed from Wilson's "Peace without Victory" address. The ideological appeal of Bolshevism concerned Wilson only to the extent that it hampered the war effort, and at this point Wilson still saw both "the Bolscheviki" and their rivals as potential allies in the fight for a liberal peace.[15]

Nevertheless, Wilson's entire philosophy of government was antithetical to the Bolsheviks' pronouncements that every ethnic-nationalist aspiration must be realized in a sovereign state. Dogmatic adherence to that notion affronted Wilson's civic-nationalist ideal of variegated communities forming common purposes through "common counsel"—an ideal he considered so critical to peace that he took his country to war to promote it. As he explained to the Russian provisional government that first made "self-determination of peoples" a war aim, Americans too desired "the liberty, the self-government, and the undictated development of all peoples" but sought to secure these through a "common covenant" organized to reflect the "brotherhood of mankind." Had Wilson thought the integrity of this covenant depended on statehood for any and all fractions of the human race who desired it, he certainly would not have trusted Lippmann to help him express it. Yet that prolific nemesis of national sovereignty and its deadly pretensions was given that very task—with "no instructions" for completing it. His characteristic response was to emphasize a "just balance" of economic, nationalist, and strategic considerations in resolving all territorial questions. Even for Poland—cause célèbre of European political nationalism—Lippmann's drafting group stressed the need for boundaries reflecting "a fair balance of national and economic considerations" and governance on a "democratic basis" to prevent "internal friction" among its diverse ethnicities. If ethnic Poles were to have a state, they must share it nicely with others—and the international community must see that they did so.[16]

Consequently, the term *self-determination* appears nowhere in the Fourteen Points. Wilson knew that the principle the phrase described could never be applied universally, even in a universe as small as Europe. "Pushed to its extreme," he confided to the British ambassador on January 4, 1918, "the principle would mean the disruption of existing governments to an undefinable extent."[17] Instead Wilson's entire address evinced his pragmatic focus on fostering self-government through idiosyncratic, tailored arrangements. "What we demand in this war," he told Congress, was a world "made safe for every peace-loving nation which, like our own, wishes to live its own life, determine its own institutions, [and] be assured of justice and fair dealing by the other peoples of the world." The polyglot, patchwork United States was Wilson's general model, and the right of all people to an accountable government, unthreatened by hostile powers, was his object.[18]

In this spirit, the eight points addressing specific territorial questions (6 through 13) were designed prevent depredations by governments operating solely on the principle of force: the fundamental characteristic, as Wilson saw it, of the "Imperialists" leading the Central powers. In addressing the vexed question of Russia, Wilson studiously cultivated the friendship of the Bolsheviks. He knew that "the part of wisdom," as House put it, was to keep as many Russians as possible fighting the war.[19] Yet in point 6 of his address, Wilson applauded the Bolshevik negotiators at Brest-Litovsk for their efforts to secure justice from the "Central Empires." He urged evacuation of all occupying forces from Russia, to permit "the independent determination of her own political development and national policy." This was not the ruse of a bourgeois or reactionary, bent on converting Russia to "liberal capitalist democracy" or clearing a field for "open-door imperialism." Rather, Wilson explicitly condemned interference in Russia's affairs, offering instead "a sincere welcome into the society of free nations under institutions of her own choosing."[20] Wilson's sincerity on this score would later be undermined by his deployment of troops to northern Russia and Siberia in order to protect Allied assets, help reestablish an eastern front, and counterbalance much heavier deployments planned by an expansionist Japanese government. All three objectives entailed support for the Bolsheviks' White Russian enemies and severely compromised the "independent determination" of Russian affairs by Russian citizens. At the time of his address, however, Wilson was "struck by the good sense of the Russian proposals" at

Brest-Litovsk, despised the Central powers for dismissing them, and sympathized with the aspirations of the Russian people toward self-government—even if he had doubts about the men claiming to represent them.[21]

Reconciling his sympathies for common Russians with his desire to keep them in the war was a genuine struggle for Wilson, who wrangled little over his other territorial points. That Belgium should be "evacuated and restored," for instance, was perhaps the sole item on which nearly everyone outside Wilhelmstrasse agreed. As point 7 stated, the security of a peaceful, established, and in this case multiethnic state was crucial to "the whole structure and validity of international law." The remaining territorial points, though addressing issues in which nationalist aspirations played larger roles, also demonstrate Wilson's belief that self-government within and between states was the best remedy for conflict-prone regions. On the advice of Lippmann, Mezes, and Isaiah Bowman, Wilson rejected Miller's plank explicitly demanding full restoration of Alsace-Lorraine to France. World-political rather than ethnic or historical considerations might make a different settlement desirable, Wilson determined, "in order that peace may once more be made secure in the interest of all."[22] Point 9, calling for "readjustment" of Italy's borders along "clearly recognizable lines of nationality," was formulated by the Inquiry to "meet the just demands of Italy" while denying the "larger ambitions" revealed in the secret treaties, which reduced multiple populations to mere spoils of war.[23] Points 10 and 12, endorsing "autonomous development" for ethnic minorities under Austro-Hungarian and Ottoman rule, were formulated to encourage "federalism" in those empires and thereby end their "vassalage" to Germany. Again, the destruction of autocracy within and between established states took precedence over breaking them apart. (Wilson's later recognition of the protostates emerging from the Austro-Hungarian Empire was largely the recognition of a fait accompli.)[24]

In discussing the Balkans, Wilson again subordinated nationalist aspirations to deliberative politics, regional stability, and freedom from foreign intrigue. Point 11 stated that the "relations of the several Balkan states to one another [should be] determined by friendly counsel along historically established lines of allegiance and nationality." The task, in other words, was to settle borders between these existing political entities, not to establish new nation-states. Indeed, only "Rumania, Serbia, and Montenegro" were mentioned, for they were the only states extant. As for other Balkan territories, the Inquiry memorandum stated that their "ultimate relationship . . . must be based upon a fair balance of nationalistic and economic considerations applied in a generous and inventive spirit after impartial scientific inquiry." The ultimate goal was to discourage "the meddling and intriguing of Great Powers" that had destabilized the region for generations, and to this end, a settlement ensuring "economic prosperity" was "most likely" to last. Without dressing Wilson in the ill-fitting garb of a racial democrat, it must be said that his acceptance of this logic, not to mention his refusal to promote Irish and Baltic nationalism, challenges the notion that a racially exclusive principle of statehood for Europeans shaped his theory or practice in any determinative way.[25]

Wilson's point 13, calling for a Polish state comprising "the territories inhabited by indisputably Polish populations," was the only outright concession to national self-determination. Still, the Inquiry's caveats about the new state's multiethnic character, imprecisely ethnological borders, and imperative need for a democratic constitution suggest that Polish nationalism was not the cause but merely the most salient circumstance of the proposal. Wilson believed that centuries of partition and ethnic persecution by conquering powers entitled the Poles to a state of their own. For the same historical, situational reasons, Polish independence would be a symbolic killing stroke against autocracy and balance-of-power politics. As Wilson would argue at Paris, the best means of establishing Poland's boundaries was "to consult the people. All told, it would be a question of ascertaining, not what the race and the language of the people are, but under which regime they prefer to live."[26]

In any event, neither point 13 nor any of the territorial proposals Wilson adopted from the Inquiry was intended as a microcosm of the ideal future. Some concrete program of territorial adjustment was necessary to start and shape the discussion of peace. Nevertheless, all the territorial proposals save those regarding Russia and Belgium were formulated with an eye toward flexibility, as comparison of Wilson's original drafts with the final product shows: every imperative "must" or "shall" was replaced by Wilson with "should." The territorial points were designed to identify the major problems that would face peacemakers at war's end, and to exemplify rather than codify pragmatically internationalist solutions.[27]

Not all points were created equal, however. Drafting and revising the speech with House, Wilson determined on "placing the general terms first and territorial adjustments last," making the general terms a prolegomenon to the rest. The exception was the call for a league of nations, which Wilson thought "should come last because it would round out the message properly."[28] The crux of that message was that deliberative discourse within and among nations must replace force and repression as the primary guarantor of both domestic and international order, and that only a radical experiment in international governance could possibly achieve that goal.

Thus, "Open covenants of peace, openly arrived at" were necessary to ensure that the external affairs of states were conducted "frankly and in the public view" (point 1). Many analysts considered a secretive alliance system the major cause of the present war. For his part, Wilson believed that no people anywhere, if aware of and involved in their government's affairs, would sanction the types of treaties that had drawn a whole continent into war with a single assassination as pretext. At House's urging, he rearranged his first typed draft so that this point came first, "to lay deep stress upon it."[29] Wilson's call for "freedom of the seas" (point 2) also resonated with concerns both specific to the current war and applicable to world politics generally. The disruption of American shipping had involved the United States in the conflict, and true freedom of the seas might have prevented a transatlantic war. Moreover, as Lippmann and other advisers repeatedly impressed on the administration, an "outlet to the sea" was crucial to a nation's economic development and thus its mutually productive relations with neighbors.[30] Even so, Wilson's caveat that the seas could be "closed" through "international action" reinforced his ideal of a cooperative and deliberative political order striving not only for fairness but also for flexibility.

A similar logic inspired Wilson's call for "removal" of "all economic barriers" among nations (point 3). The struggle for autarky was a powerful motor of the expansionism that brought the belligerents into conflict. Conversely, Wilson agreed with many contemporaries that commerce was a unifying and pacifying force. Still, only "equality of trade conditions among all the nations consenting to the peace," giving each democratic nation a say in how such conditions could best be maintained, would ensure that trade served to unite rather than stratify and divide the world's peoples.[31] Wilson also invoked a deliberative paradigm of international relations in his call for disarmament (point 5). He could not but acknowledge that the war had been fought with weapons, whose very proliferation seemed to have demanded their use—as peace advocates long had warned.[32] Disarmament, however, was a thorny issue. No peace program could fail to call for arms reduction. Yet Wilson had often stated that the contemplated league of nations depended on a "concert of power" to protect member states.[33] Moreover, a state required enough force at its disposal to maintain internal order. Hence Wilson endorsed "guarantees . . . that national armaments will be reduced to the lowest point consistent with domestic safety"—affirming disarmament while inviting discussion over the specifics of a devilishly complex issue.

If disarmament was a tightwire, colonialism was the third rail of world politics. Nothing reveals more clearly the complexities of Wilson's desire to foster self-government in the various ways—and at the various rates—he thought a heterogeneous world demanded, than point 5: a demand for "free, open-minded, and absolutely impartial adjustment of all colonial claims," stipulating that "the interests of the populations concerned must have equal weight with the equitable claims of the government whose title is to be determined." Wilson's decision to include point 5 was his own. It was not suggested in the Inquiry memorandum or by House. Indeed, Wilson and House both worried over the Allies' reaction to it.[34] Despite its equivocal wording, Wilson's call to weigh natives' "interests" against foreigners' "equitable claims" reflected his deliberative conception of self-government and genuine belief in the right of everyone to it. More important, it was a direct challenge to the imperial order of the day. "Imperialism," in the Wilsonian lexicon, implied self-interested, autocratic, violent interference in politics, not territorial sovereignty over large regions. Thus the British, whose (white majority) territories constituted "a union of free peoples acting on free impulses," administered a radically different sort of empire than the Germans did. As long as a people's expressed interests were served by their government, that government was legitimate—a standard to which the Allied and Central powers alike would be held under the new international order Wilson envisioned.[35]

How to meet that standard was far less clear than the obligation to do so. It did not, in Wilson's view, entail immediate decolonization. He still conceived self-government as a habit arising from long practice under hospitable conditions. And yet the tragedy of the war, as well as his own botched attempts to bring democracy to Mexico, had shaken his belief that white men trained in the arts of self-government were competent to instill such habits in others. As his later advocacy of the mandate system would demonstrate, Wilson simply did not know how or when long-oppressed peoples would reach their potential for full self-government. His stomach for postponement was stronger than that of most postcolonial liberals, but not because he considered oppression a matter of racial destiny. As he later revealed at Paris, he considered the "adjustment" of colonial conditions to self-governing principles a problem to be solved case by case, under the auspices of an impartial, international body in which every community would enjoy—or look forward to enjoying—responsible representation.[36]

Thus the exact degree to which the injustices of colonialism could be alleviated by the unknown men who would negotiate peace was a murky matter for Wilson. Nevertheless, it was a matter he had considered at length, along with other uncertainties his program entailed. He knew that no peace would be perfect. Mistakes would be made in even the most judicious settlement, and the world community would change over time.

That the call for a league of nations was the finale of Wilson's peace overture suggests his grasp of these facts and the strength of his commitment to a pragmatically internationalist peace. Despite its "guarantees of political independence and territorial integrity," the league he imagined was a flexible, amendable, evolving forum for international discussion and adaptation to the flux of international relations—a compromise between the legalistic posse commitatus devised by the League to Enforce Peace (LEP) and the pacifistic mediatory body envisioned by groups such as the American Union Against Militarism. As he would tell the American peace delegation en route to Paris, the league idea "implied [not just] political independence and territorial integrity," but "alteration of terms if it could be shown that injustice had been done or that conditions had changed." "In fact," recorded one listener, Wilson "could not see how a treaty of peace could be drawn up or how both *elasticity* and *security* could be obtained save under a League of Nations." The same theme ran through the Inquiry materials that House supplied Wilson for the drafting of the Fourteen Points. Ironically but fittingly, therefore, and in contrast to the territorial proposals, point 14 was constructed in the imperative: "A general association of nations *must* be formed." As House recorded, Wilson hoped the world would note the distinction. Disposal of common affairs by methods of common counsel was the sole principle he sought to inscribe in the law of nations.[37]

"An evident principle runs through the whole programme I have outlined," Wilson concluded his Fourteen Points address. "It is the principle of justice to all peoples and nationalities, and their right to live on equal terms of liberty and safety with one another." *With* one another, not independent of one another; that was how Wilson envisioned the world's peoples living freely. It was a vision inspired by the achievements and failures of an American democracy still awaiting the triumph of civic unity over cultural division but working steadily toward it.

The Fourteen Points thrilled Americans devoted to that work—not least those pragmatists lately disturbed by the unpragmatic, illiberal course of Wilson's domestic policy. Jane Addams, forwarding a Woman's Peace Party resolution praising the speech, expressed her "personal appreciation" of the president's "courage and far-sightedness in thus making so clear the great principles of a democratic peace." She demonstrated that appreciation by enlisting with the Committee on Public Information (CPI) as an educational speaker. Herbert Croly, writing in the *New Republic*, praised Wilson's program as the first of note "based on a correct diagnosis of our international maladies" yet "infused with the red blood of a binding, a healing and a leavening faith." Lippmann was simply ecstatic over the president's direct adoption of ideas and verbiage from the Inquiry memoranda. "This is the second time I have put words into the mouth of the President!" Lippmann pompously exclaimed to his annoyed—and envious—Inquiry colleague Bowman.[38]

To be sure, the speech's importance inhered as much in Wilson's own inimitable rhetoric as in the proposals, and above all in his ringing endorsement of a League of Nations. Still, shrewd observers noted how deftly each specific term balanced practical considerations with ideal desires, while exemplifying both the firmness and the flexibility that a settlement hospitable to a successful League required. "A durable peace for the world does not depend upon the acceptance of the President's programme without the changing of a word," opined the New York *World* on January 9, "but it does depend upon unyielding adherence to the principles of justice and right that he has enunciated." As Max Eastman reflected some months later, Wilson's Fourteen Points had brought to statesmanship "some of the same thing that Bergson and William James and John Dewey have brought into philosophy—a sense of reality of time, and the creative character of change. . . . It is the expression of a wisdom which is new and peculiar to our age."[39]

That wisdom was lost on many others who adopted the Fourteen Points as their gospel—a confusion due, in part, to the immediate circumstances surrounding their delivery. Wilson was not the only statesman seeking to salvage some advantage from the Bolsheviks' accord with the Central powers. To his dismay, the day he finished drafting his address—January 5, 1918—Lloyd George delivered his own manifesto for peace at Caxton Hall, before the British Trades Union League. The speech seemed to anticipate so much of Wilson's program that the president nearly canceled his address. In fact, he soon realized, the differences were major. Attempting to woo both the British Left and the world's neutral powers, Lloyd George criticized Austria-Hungary's refusal at Brest-Litovsk to entertain "suggestions about the autonomy of subject nationalities," then collapsed Lenin's and Wilson's terminologies, insisting that the disposition of territories must respect "the right of self-determination or consent of the governed." Most confusingly, he extended the right of "self-government" to colonial "natives" living "under chiefs and councils . . . competent to consult and speak for their tribes and members," asserting that the "general principle of national self-determination is therefore applicable in their cases as in those of occupied European territories."[40]

Clearly, Lloyd George's various permutations of the "general principle of national self-determination" precluded a strict construction accommodating political independence for ethnic groups alone. Nonetheless, it was at Caxton Hall that Lenin's centrifugal concept of ethnic self-determination first exerted its pressure on Wilson's centripetal concept of civic self-government. As far as many thousands worldwide were concerned, Wilson's address, which House predicted "would so smother the Lloyd George speech that it would be forgotten," simply amplified it.[41] A year later, as Wilson battled to enshrine the spirit and substance of his address in the treaties ending the war, George Harvey of the *North American Review* published a widely read (and highly critical) article identifying Lloyd George's speech as "The Genesis of the Fourteen Commandments."[42]

The confusion, however, was immediate. Viscount Bryce, former British ambassador to Washington, publicly praised Wilson's "broad, clear assertion of the right of a nationality to self-determination." In their enthusiastic response, British Labourites called for "Self-Determination for India." By June, Stephen Paneretoff, the Bulgarian ambassador in Washington, was declaring that "Wilson's formula for the self-determination of nations" was "alone capable of a lasting solution of the Balkan problem." Long before Wilson went to Paris, "national self-determination" had become the insidious shorthand by which his ideas for peace were translated into something at once greater and less profound in the consciousness of the world.[43]

These immediate misunderstandings were not Wilson's fault. That the incubus of self-determination was left to grow until it burst from the host of public opinion was. Wilson began laying the traps that would ensnare him barely a month after his address when, again before a joint session of Congress, he first uttered the phrase *self-determination* on February 11, 1918. Already the careful language of the Fourteen Points had begun to disappear. " 'Self-determination' is not a mere phrase," he told Congress, upon receiving Germany's disappointing reply to his previous address. "It is an imperative principle of action, which statesmen will henceforth ignore at their peril." The speech was hardly an unequivocal endorsement of territorial sovereignty for ethnic groups. "Self-determination" in the form of ethnic nationalism was indeed a force acting in Europe; one did not have to embrace it fully to recognize its power and, in many cases, justice. Besides, "national self-determination" was not the phrase Wilson used, nor the idea with which he was centrally concerned. He immediately explained that it was Germany's insistence on "individual understandings between powerful states" rather than a peace "submitted to the common judgment" that was most intolerable. As he stated earlier in the address, one continent's problems "each and all affect the whole world" and must not be "discussed separately or in corners."[44]

Still, Wilson's address was irresponsible. Mixed with his indictment of the old diplomacy was the insistence that Europe's problems be approached "with a view to the wishes, the natural connections, the racial aspirations, the security, and the peace of mind of the peoples involved." Further confounding the distinction between ethnonationalism and self-government, he declared, "National aspirations must be respected; peoples may now be dominated and governed only by their own consent." Wilson clarified that his government desired only to prevent another war, not "to act as arbiter in European territorial disputes," and noted that the territorial program of the Fourteen Points provided only a "sketch of principles and of the way in which they should be applied." But he then reprised the theme of "national aspirations," stating that the war's "roots" lay in "the disregard of the rights of small nations and of nationalities which lacked the union and the force to make good their claim to determine their own allegiances."[45]

Between February 1918 and his return from the Paris peace negotiations nearly eighteen months later, Wilson's nice distinctions between self-government and self-determination were known only to his closest advisers—and even they saw but dimly into his mind. Consequently, the world's peoples, who Wilson hoped would ratify his charter of international democracy, were left to make of his words what they would. Though Wilson spoke later of his "anxieties" over the false hopes he raised worldwide, he never stated publicly that he had been misunderstood.[46]

Indeed, as waging the war and planning the peace consumed him, Wilson betrayed his own deep convictions regarding democratic leadership. He had long viewed the duty of the democratic statesman as a complicated mix of boldness and circumspection, of educating and acquiescing to public opinion. "Whoever would effect change in a modern constitutional government must first educate his fellow citizens to want *some* change," he wrote in 1887. "That done, he must persuade them to want the particular change he wants." In the 1890s, Wilson elaborated this theme, writing that "no reform may succeed for which the major thought of the nation is not prepared" and that "the instructed few may not be safe leaders, except in so far as they have communicated their instruction to the many." By the first decade of the twentieth century, Wilson was convinced that the president, if he could "rightly interpret the national thought," might "form it to his own views," which of course would reflect the thought he had studied. Whether interpreting or shaping opinion, however, the democratic statesman must never forget "the rule of entire frankness and plain speaking that ought to exist between public servants and the public whom they serve."[47]

It was just such frankness and plain speaking that Wilson began to abandon after January 1918. A host of factors likely precipitated this decline in his leadership. His eagerness to have the weight of world opinion backing his assault on the old diplomacy might explain his failures to distinguish the internationalism he embraced from the ethnonationalism he inspired. Then again, after *self-determination* gained currency, he might simply have found the phrase convenient—perhaps as a propaganda tool, more likely as an occasional substitute for his preferred terms *self-government, autonomous development,* and *common counsel,* which gained far less traction in international discourse. Even Croly, while attempting to explain the delicate experiment in world democracy that he considered the true objective of Wilson's policy, invoked "national self-determination" in the pages of the *New Republic.*[48]

By that time, Wilson had contributed as much as anyone to the confusion over the new world order he championed—and his contributions continued. Even as military fortunes improved in August, Ray Stannard Baker wrote to House from London of "the need of strong constructive leadership from Mr. Wilson." Lippmann, writing from France, worried that "the old liberal leadership of the President has not been exercised sufficiently in the last few months."[49] With a few important exceptions Wilson continued to disappoint such informed believers in his vision, largely by refusing to disappoint anyone else. His willingness to ride the global wave of support for a disintegrative principle in which he did not believe, rather than frankly defend the integrative policy he meant to pursue, was symptomatic of a growing contempt for the pragmatic methods his theoretical commitment to common counsel implied. From the spring of 1918 forward, the trajectory of Wilson's leadership would demonstrate with growing frequency and poignancy the costs, and ultimate futility, of a politics divorcing democratic ends from democratic means.

Events hardly ordained such misfortunes. Granted, the war dragged on for ten more miserable months after the Fourteen Points address. During that time, however, Wilson capitalized on its course, adding crucial refinements to his vision for peace. Although the Austro-Hungarian foreign minister, Count Ottokar Czernin, eventually communicated his government's openness to the president's proposals after an unusual two-week delay, the equally delayed but far more "equivocal" reply of his German counterpart, Georg von Hertling, seemed to Wilson but one more instance of the old diplomacy of deception. Peace conversations were futile, Wilson told Congress, unless the parties explicitly affirmed four principles: that all disputes should be arbitrated; that peoples and territories were not pawns in geopolitical games; that territorial questions should be resolved in the best interests of the populations concerned; and that long-standing ethnonationalist aspirations should be satisfied to whatever extent was coincident with international order.[50]

Despite its attendant confusions, the last point marked an important moment in the evolution of Wilson's internationalism. His acknowledgment of the irredentist sentiment roiling Europe revealed his expanding awareness that lasting order and peace would depend as much on the world's response to conflicts within states as between them. Typical of his pragmatist sensibility, Wilson avoided dogmatic pronouncements on how nationalist aspirations should be satisfied. It was Hertling's unwillingness to respect the *fact* of self-determination that was troubling, indicating the German government's stubborn resistance to the realities of an interdependent age. Knowing it would not be the last to resent "international action and international counsel," Wilson grew increasingly certain that an effective League of Nations must have power and authority to intervene in the internal affairs of states if the need were acute.[51]

Military setbacks in the spring and summer of 1918 gave Wilson further opportunities to promote his program. When Russia withdrew from the war permanently on March 3, under harsh terms imposed by the German high command, Wilson concluded that despite liberal sentiment in the Reichstag, the militarists were in control of Germany and likely to remain so. A peace without victory, elevating all rather than trampling the powerless and vanquished, now depended entirely on crushing defeat for Germany's militarist master class. "Force, Force to the utmost, Force without stint or limit, the righteous and triumphant force which shall make Right the law of the world, and cast every selfish dominion down in the dust"—this, Wilson told a Baltimore audience in April, was now the ironic but fatefully ordained means of achieving stable peace. With Russia out of the war, Allied forces were being driven like dust before the full force of the German military. To leave any vestige of the enemy's old order intact after such victories, he reiterated in July, would invite a resurgence of falsely confident militarism, dooming democracy in Germany and all Europe. Elaborating this theme, he articulated four additional points he now declared crucial to the settlement first sketched in January: the destruction of every arbitrary power threatening the world's peace; the settlement of all international questions with the explicit consent of the people involved; the pledge of the world's states to be governed, in their mutual relations, by the same principles governing citizens under rule of law; and "an organization of peace" empowered not merely to protect its members, but to "check every invasion of right" through a "tribunal of opinion to which all must submit." To defeat the German Empire was to clear ground for a global republic, embodying "the organized opinion of mankind" and the "hope for justice and for social freedom and opportunity" that all peoples shared.[52]

Wilson's Independence Day address coincided with a change in Allied fortunes. Just days after its delivery, the German onslaught stalled short of Paris. With American forces approaching full strength, Supreme Allied Commander Ferdinand Foch launched a counteroffensive that by late September had reversed Germany's costly gains and driven Bulgaria out of the war.[53] As early as August 9, Lippmann, having probed Britain's head of political intelligence, Sir William Tyrell, conveyed the latter's warning that as the German threat receded, so would European interest in the League of Nations. To prevent the idea growing "stale," Lippmann opined to House on August 21, a "breath of fresh air" from the president was needed. Writing to House again on September 2, Lippmann explained the stakes. "Each nation in its claims to strategic security assumes it is likely to be involved in war with its neighbors, that economic self-sufficiency is necessary to national safety, that no alliance is permanent," he wrote. These assumptions, combined with the vengeful emotions inflamed by war, created a vicious tautology. "Wherever you go people tell you in one breath that Germany will be beaten to a point where her militarism will be destroyed and in the next that it is necessary to raise up all sorts of dams against Germany after the war, in order to prevent German militarism from making another assault upon the world." The cycle of dynastic war, vindictive peace, and revisionist aggression was so familiar as to limit the imagination to cosmetic updates of the alliance system. "Now if the idea of the League of Nations means anything," Lippmann asserted, "it means that a new set of conceptions are introduced into diplomacy." The time to follow up those introductions had arrived.[54]

Wilson, sensing that Germany's resources and morale were nearly exhausted, agreed. On September 27, he devoted his fourth Liberty Loan address to explaining, once again, the philosophy that must guide the imminent settlement. "*The common will of mankind has been substituted for the particular purposes of individual states,*" he emphasized. The war's "sweeping processes of change" had made people of every imaginable standing conscious of their shared fate. These were the *"facts"* of the war, and they dictated that those who would gather to end it properly come "ready and willing to pay the price": a pledge to subordinate national interest to "impartial justice," through creation of a "virile" League of Nations and submission to its authority. To make of this "thesis" a "practical programme," Wilson supplemented his previous pronouncements with five additional "particulars": first, that the equal rights of victors, vanquished, and neutrals be recognized; second, that the special interests of nations be subordinate to "the common interest of all"; third, that exclusive alliances among League members be prohibited; fourth, that economic combinations and boycotts not approved by the League be likewise banned; and finally, that all international agreements be published in full for the world's scrutiny. In an unequivocal affirmation of pragmatist internationalism, Wilson declared his nation's readiness to interpret Washington's proscription of "entangling alliances" in the light of "a new day," embracing a "general alliance" to obviate the opportunism and liabilities of the old diplomacy. In the meantime, only victory over those opposing such an object could bring it into being; *"nothing else can,"* Wilson thundered.[55]

In fact, Wilson had recently hammered out an elaborate scheme for his long-theorized "general alliance." Ever since the Fourteen Points address, Lippmann and Mezes had urged the administration to confer with the Allied governments, if not the American and Allied peoples, about the League's organization.[56] House pressed the issue throughout the spring, but still Wilson resisted. Finally House showed him a watered-down "alliance" plan that the British cabinet had considered publishing, and pleaded that Wilson take the initiative. Wilson relented, and House went to work. He asked David Hunter Miller, the Inquiry's top international lawyer, to draft a constitution, and then modified Miller's draft. In the process, he added what would become one of the most important features of the League that Wilson would champion at Paris: a flexible territorial guarantee allowing for future adjustments "pursuant to the principle of self-determination"—that is, the Wilsonian principle that governments must promote "the welfare and manifest interest of the peoples concerned" and that "the peace of the world is superior in importance to every question of political jurisdiction or boundary."[57]

Wilson embraced this expansive yet pragmatic conception of collective security and altered the rest of House's rather anemic draft in the same spirit. Where House suggested a weak plank on sanctions, for example, Wilson insisted that arbitration be compulsory and binding. He also rejected House's plan for a League comprising the great powers alone, insisting that the equality of all states be acknowledged, and the rights of small states protected, by the latter's full participation. While House intended to appease Allied leaders and US senators jealous of national prerogatives, Wilson was adamant that the international community's most powerful members be answerable to the whole. Certainly, some would make greater material contributions to the League than others. In Wilson's view, it was the moral and practical obligation of the privileged to sustain the community that ultimately sustained them. Like his earlier Pan-American plans, but to a magnified degree, the so-called Magnolia Covenant (drafted at House's vacation home in that north-shore Massachusetts town) was a global projection of the constitutional order Wilson hoped to cultivate at home.[58]

Wilson's faith in the acuity of public opinion honed by open debate should have encouraged him to publish the Magnolia Covenant and assume true leadership of the League movement. Instead, the divergence between his theory and practice of pragmatist politics continued. He refused to publish his plan or engage seriously with the British in formulating a consensus. As such, he squandered an opportunity to give substance to the spreading illusion that the Allied governments shared his war aims—an illusion and opportunity his Fourteen Points had created. Perhaps Wilson thought his best chance of extracting liberal terms from Allied leaders was to bring the full weight of world opinion on their heads at the peace conference, rather than dissipate its force beforehand. But he knew the settlement would be imperfect. As such, a clear popular mandate for the type of League that could fix its own flaws was the single most valuable asset he could have brought to the negotiations.

He did not invest in that asset. Instead, he needlessly alienated the League to Enforce Peace, many of whose members were friendly with both conservatives in Congress and Wilson's progressive-internationalist supporters. Consequently, Taft and Roosevelt, newly reconciled, collaborated during the midterm elections to portray the Republicans as both the party of the League and the party of American self-reliance.[59] In the meantime, Wilson's reticence lost him the support of many progressive internationalists, allowed others to invest his program with their own dreams, and made it impossible for the pragmatist progressives who were his ablest exponents to keep his vision front and center.

His reticence was not entirely unreasonable. "My own conviction . . . is that the administrative constitution of the League must *grow* and not be made," he shared with House in March 1918. The League "must *begin* with solemn covenants," he continued, but "the method of carrying out those mutual pledges should be left to develop of itself, case by case." Philosophical considerations aside, the Senate "would never ratify any treaty which put the force of the United States at the disposal of any such group or body.

Why begin at the impossible end when there is a possible end and it is feasible to plant a system which will slowly but surely ripen into fruition?" By
August he had changed his mind about the possibility of getting a powerful
League through the Senate, but not about how to approach it. The Magnolia
draft would incense "Senators of the [Henry Cabot] Lodge type," he told the
Colonel. He preferred to give them as little opportunity as possible to slash
it apart.[60]

Had Wilson endeavored to explain this reasoning to the public, he might
have remained strategically coy and still cemented the support of American internationalists—especially those of a pragmatist bent. The philosophy
Wilson brought to the League issue was clear enough that a modicum of
frankness regarding his worries would probably have earned the trust even of
pickier sympathizers, while getting them thinking about the rather different
obstacles faced by presidents versus pundits. Instead, he made his allergy to
details so palpable that even Paul Kellogg's League of Free Nations Association (LFNA)—a Wilsonian counterweight to the LEP, founded in the spring
of 1918 with Croly, Dewey, Addams, and Felix Frankfurter as charter members—dared not approach him until after the Armistice.[61] At the least Wilson
should have forthrightly explained his understanding of "self-determination"
and its significance to his postwar program. Clearly distancing himself from
the ethnonationalist version of the principle would have preempted much
criticism from conservatives fearful of its anarchical implications, and
might have encouraged progressive internationalists to view this fissiparous
idea more critically in light of Wilson's integrative vision.

Instead, Wilson's credibility as a champion of international democracy
suffered its first big blow in July 1918, when he authorized military intervention in Russia after concluding that Japan sought an expansionist foothold there. Ten thousand US troops were deployed to the Trans-Siberian
rail terminus at Vladivostok, soon outnumbered by a Japanese contingent
that grew to seventy thousand troops spread across eastern Siberia—almost
sixty thousand more than the US and Japanese governments had agreed.
Another five thousand US troops were deployed to reinforce the British at
Murmansk, to protect Allied weapons caches and launch a rescue mission
for a legion of Czech soldiers stranded in the Russian interior. Though Wilson feared that Allied intervention would mean "interference in the right of
Russians to choose their own form of government," he decided that, for that
very reason, the United States had to restrain its associates' anti-Soviet activities. Unfortunately, clashes between Bolshevik armies and US forces under British command at Murmansk, as well as Japan's massive presence in
Siberia, made Wilson look complicit in an imperialist venture sprung upon

an American public oblivious to his long holdout against Allied pressure. Given these circumstances, the harsh criticism Wilson received from many progressive-internationalist allies was largely justified. Wilson did not fail to uphold the principle of self-government in Russia so much as fail to convince Americans that US troops were there for that purpose. That failure was partly due to his reliance on the Czech legion's plight as pretense for intervention. Mostly, however, it reflected his larger failure to familiarize the public with a version of "self-determination" in which political freedoms rather than political frontiers were sacred.[62]

Indeed, by the end of 1918, Wilson was hard-pressed to convince progressives that he cared for political freedoms at home. The suppression of free speech under Burleson and Gregory had proceeded apace. After his trial returned a hung jury, Eastman was tried a second time for the same violation of the Espionage Act. Another hung jury kept him out of prison, but Eugene Debs, tried in September on similar charges, received ten years. That same month, Burleson lit a stick of dynamite under Wilson's progressive bandwagon when he barred the September 14 issue of Oswald Villard's venerable *Nation* magazine from the mails because of an editorial protesting the infringement of civil liberties. This was too much even for Wilson's staunchest progressive allies. Frank Cobb of the New York *World* condemned the administration for undertaking "the Prussianization of American public opinion," earning kudos from the *New Republic* for his stand.[63]

Wilson was playing into the hands, but not the hearts, of conservatives. War had siphoned profits from businesses engaged in the manufacture and retail of nonessentials, while wartime taxation had cut those of industries grown lucrative during the period of neutrality. The salaried middle classes saw the cost of living rise faster than their incomes while workers' wages rose as much as 20 percent in some industries, engendering a reaction against Wilson's progressive labor policies. Farmers benefited more than any other group during wartime in terms of real income, but the Food Administration's decision to peg the price of wheat alienated midwestern and Great Plains farmers, adding to the ranks of the disgruntled in regions with large German American populations traumatized by their treatment during a war their president was supposed to avoid. Among such groups, Republican critics of governmental overreach in domestic and foreign affairs found open ears: Wilson had championed an interventionist government for the United States and the world, and attacks on either program implicated the other.[64]

Wilson's pragmatist-progressive supporters appreciated the domestic and international stakes of America's postwar transition, and had kept up a chorus about the need to begin "reconstruction" before the gains of wartime planning and opportunities of wartime dislocation were lost. "We are not entitled to assume that automatically there is going to be a desirable reorganization and reconstruction after the war," John Dewey wrote in the fall of 1918. It was time to devise a "not too rigid" program to do what most needed doing, while "trusting to the experience which is got in doing them to reveal the next things needed." Accordingly, the new *Dial* magazine he edited with Thorstein Veblen adopted reconstruction as the standing subject of its editorial page, beginning with the October 5 issue.[65] Months before, in a memorandum for the Inquiry submitted in January 1918, Veblen had explicitly identified domestic reform as essential to international reform, insisting that lasting peace required dislodging the vested interests who fattened on war and its causes. Above all, he explained, the "economic penetration" of "backward countries" must be strictly controlled, so as to benefit the native inhabitants and global good rather than further the "commercial enterprise" of plutocrats and the "national ambitions" they manufactured. These imperatives, like Wilson's entire internationalist program, demanded an "extensive surrender of powers" by individual nations that the distribution of power within them could only impede.[66]

The administration was familiar with such concerns. Even before receiving Veblen's memorandum, Lippmann had suggested to House that an Inquiry-style organization undertake "a disinterested analysis and forecast" of the postwar scene and prepare "a number of alternative programs" for the president's consideration. Clearly worried at the reactionary climate of opinion, Lippmann repeated his suggestion the following May, emphasizing that until it was time to introduce reconstructive measures to the American people as bills in Congress, they should be formulated secretly, by "an expert staff with liberal sympathies."[67] Croly also feared that Americans' critical faculties had grown flaccid during the war, but his solution was to exercise them. Soon after Wilson's Fourteen Points address, he urged "genuine reconsideration" of the president's economic policies, allowing "sufficient time for their exhaustive and prolonged public discussion." Though salutary, Wilson's "measures of state socialism" brought "new difficulties" obliging the public and its representatives to devise means of "balancing and, if necessary, of resisting the political leviathan," without reinstating the "confusion between public and private interest" that reigned when the latter had controlled the labor, resources, and services essential to society.[68] Indeed, by mid-October, it seemed clear to Croly that "the Congress about to be elected" would "probably deal more with questions of reconstruction than with war problems"—a notion directly communicated to House via Frankfurter.[69]

By then Wilson, too, had turned attention to the coming elections, but it was far too late to influence them—except to his disadvantage. On October 25, he appealed to the American people to return a Democratic Congress and thus demonstrate their support for his peace program to leaders "on the other side of the water."[70] Wilson failed to recognize that the election would turn on the domestic issues that had arisen out of the war, and not matters of high international policy. He also failed to recognize that a mandate from the American people was unlikely to weigh heavily in Allied leaders' calculations at the peace conference, though a rebuke of his administration might. Meanwhile, Democratic lawmakers pressured him to make the appeal to save their own seats in Congress, and Wilson, committed to party government, was susceptible to their entreaties. Voters, however, were not susceptible to *his* entreaty. Republicans made hay out of Wilson's embrace of the partisan politics he had ostentatiously "adjourned" in May 1918 in the interest of wartime unity. They captured both houses of Congress under the banner of the party's most reactionary members, who indeed came to represent a popular American repudiation of the Fourteen Points in the eyes (or at least the negotiating strategies) of Wilson's more nationalist European counterparts. Nothing could have demonstrated more clearly the inextricability of domestic and foreign policy, and of political means and ends, that Wilson had so often emphasized. Through its suppression of civil liberties, his administration muzzled articulate supporters of Wilson's stance on the socioeconomic issues most deeply dividing the United States—a stance rooted in the same principles, and attracting the same supporters, as the foreign policy monopolizing his attention, including the comprehensive League of Nations at its center. Consequently uncertain of *his* League's purchase on the public mind, Wilson discouraged a national conversation about *any* League's scope and structure, clearing the stage for conservative soliloquies on the supremacy of independent action over international organization and the conjoined iniquities of domestic and international "Wilsonism," as Lodge called it. Thus, explained the *New Republic*, a nation voting "in the dark" had declared itself "wholly unprepared to deal with the new responsibilities to which it is committed as the consequence of its own acts and the convulsions of the world."[71]

And yet the next few weeks brought diplomatic triumph for Wilson and vindication for those who had cheered and guided his efforts. On September 29, the German high command informed Kaiser Wilhelm that the war was unwinnable. A cease-fire would allow German forces to regroup and prevent an outright Allied victory, while giving the kaiser time to liberalize his government and prevent revolution. Some of the generals, particularly General Erich Ludendorff, seem to have reckoned that if armistice terms proved unacceptable, a rested and regrouped army might reopen hostilities; regardless, all agreed that the fighting must stop or the army and government both would crumble. The imperial government duly asked Wilson to broker an armistice on the basis of the Fourteen Points and his subsequent elaborations. Over the next five weeks, Wilson spoiled any German plans for a comeback, manipulating the kaiser's representatives into acknowledging defeat while dampening popular German resentment by convincing the Allies publicly to accept a lenient peace. He insisted on negotiating only with a civilian German government, which enjoyed no say in the terms of evacuation and disbandment of forces. At the same time, he curried official and popular German trust, publicly repudiating the calls for "unconditional surrender" filling the halls of Congress and the columns of dailies and working assiduously for an armistice denying Britain, France, and Italy the intoxication of "too much success or security."[72]

The president was not the only one working hard for a pragmatic peace. His adviser House, sent to Paris to negotiate terms with the Allies, was desperate for a detailed interpretation of the Fourteen Points to guide him. Lippmann, lately transferred to Europe to propagandize a Wilsonian peace through the army's intelligence unit, was the obvious choice to provide such a gloss. "You'll have to write me a memorandum on each of the Fourteen Points," Lippmann recalled House saying on October 28, "and I'll have to have it by tomorrow at ten o'clock."[73] There was a problem, however: Lippmann had fallen from Wilson's good graces in September, after frankly criticizing the administration for failing to educate public opinion on "the character of the peace."[74] Fortunately for House, Wilson's trusted friend Frank Cobb was available to "direct" the project, and Wilson approved the "Lippmann-Cobb Memorandum" on October 30. It proved invaluable to House. For each point, Lippmann provided both preliminary negotiating positions and the absolute minimum demands by which the political, strategic, and economic criteria of lasting peace could be met. The exception was the League of Nations, the structure of which, in Wilson's view, could not be exposed to contentious debate before its basic existence was certain. At the time, however, the League was of far less concern to the parties involved than were the territorial and economic points Lippmann elucidated. "It has been stated that many of the Fourteen Points were so vague and so general that they were practically meaningless, and the Entente could very well refuse to interpret them in the way they were meant," House recalled. "This is not true. . . . These interpretations were on the table day after day when we sat in conference in Paris while the Armistice was in the making. Many times they asked the meaning of this or that point and I would read from the accepted interpretation."[75]

House recalled correctly. Indeed, after the Treaty of Versailles was concluded, the Armistice was often employed by outraged Germans and scandalized liberals to illustrate a genuine Fourteen Points peace. From October 29 through November 4, House relentlessly pressured the Allies to accept the minima set by Lippmann and Cobb, at one point conveying the president's threat of a separate peace if they balked. Finally, he suggested that the Allied premiers submit their gravest reservations as possible amendments to be discussed and decided at the peace conference. Whether shrewd or foolish (the Allied reservations would prove almost as troublesome for Wilson as their more notorious Senate counterparts), this gambit ended the stalemate. On November 4, House, Clemenceau, and Lloyd George agreed on a settlement embodying most of the Lippmann-Cobb Memorandum's terms, qualified by France's demand that Germany assume liability for civilian damages and by Britain's reserved right to challenge unqualified "freedom of the seas" at the conference. Foch's military terms, including joint Allied-American occupation of the Rhineland during peace negotiations, were also agreed. These were significant concessions on House's part, especially to German eyes. But the German chancellor, Prince Max von Baden, had been abandoned in the midst of revolution by a high command eager to hang defeat on the new civilian government. He had no choice but to accept the arrangements. House, meanwhile, was "glad the exceptions were made," for they affirmed "acceptance of the Fourteen Points" overall. Wilson, who rated the political terms of his program higher than the economic or military, agreed. Thus the so-called Pre-Armistice Agreement became the Armistice itself when signed by Germany's representatives on November 11, 1918.[76]

Though its flaws would become apparent at the peace conference, the Armistice, when published, was rightly recognized as a landmark of internationalist diplomacy. "Every ancient right of princes or castes or classes to dispose of the wills of other men is on the table for liquidation," Croly assured his readers. "At this instant of history, democracy is supreme." Yet confusion challenged democracy's reign from the moment of its ascension. Both the popular mood in the Allied countries and the record of the statesmen representing them augured ill for a democratic peace, Croly argued. The promise of the Armistice only reinforced the necessity of a "genuine" League of Nations, to "act as a corrective of possible future mistakes and as a test of future decisions."[77] But while clarifying the scope and power of the body he envisioned, Wilson had left its actual shape in doubt, leaving the increasingly formidable transatlantic League movement without a single program to inform and consolidate opinion. Lippmann, who had been shipped off to France expressly to promote a Wilsonian peace, was at a loss, as he shared with the LFNA's Learned Hand. "I've been rushing around trying to act as midwife to a baby that was conceived in the dark and in danger of being disowned."[78]

Even so, for weeks after November 11, internationalist spirits were high. Wilson had won a great victory, and despite his recent silences projected the will to win an even greater one. The growth of the LFNA suggested many Americans were ready to join him. A League of Nations embodying the president's Fourteen Points was the world's best hope for a "sounder future international order," the group announced on November 30. Close political cooperation and equality of economic opportunity were crucial to security and prosperity for all nations, and neither would be viable unless governments relinquished sovereignty in myriad contexts—or, rather, reconceived sovereignty as a communal good. Effectively exercising this novel, social sovereignty required "a universal association of nations based upon the principle that the security of each shall rest upon the strength of the whole," and Wilson, they averred, knew and sought the same.[79]

In sum, not everyone missed the point of the Fourteen Points. The most visible champion of American pragmatism saw it clearly. As Dewey wrote for the *Dial*, Wilson's "New Diplomacy" was the logical extension of pragmatist political ethics from the domestic to the international realm—a call for nations to employ their natural or cultivated advantages "in behalf of a public interest." Appropriately in light of Wilson's domestic experiments, his Fourteen Points had outlined an "administrative" rather than "merely judicial" League.[80] The social upheavals of recent decades, Dewey wrote, "demonstrated that more is needed to secure freedom and equality of conditions between individuals than to declare them legally all free and equal," and the same held for "equality among nations." Just as federal bodies with constructive mandates were needed to counter economic tyranny at home, "powerful international commissions" with control over labor standards, trade rights, and even access to credit and capital were necessary curbs against economic imperialism.[81] Cynics might interpret Wilson's economic plank as nothing more than "an academic proclamation of the principle of free trade" or assume his appeal for equitable colonial adjustments applied "merely to the German colonies" lately seized. But such cynical interpretations simply did not square with the president's repeated calls for reliable, deliberative alternatives to conflict in an interdependent world.[82] In short,

Wilson had greatly clarified the "thesis" propounded by the pragmatist progressives: that social peace and justice require political and economic integration. Now thoughtful citizens were obliged to help him elaborate the mechanisms for achieving those goals.[83]

The optimal design and continuing efficacy of such mechanisms, of course, depended on open, vibrant inquiry within and among the communities sustaining them—something the president had done little to encourage recently. Still, the moral of Wilson's failure to communicate and model his ideals was not fully manifest by the end of 1918. Despite the "great difficulties" beleaguering critical idealists including Croly, the *New Republic* editor was encouraged by the political and economic transformations Wilson had wrought in the United States and applauded the greater transformations he seemed set to launch worldwide.[84] Lippmann's enthusiasm over the Armistice led him, briefly, to fantasize that the rest was mere formality. "This is the climax of a course that has been as wise as it was brilliant, and as shrewd as it was prophetic," he wrote House. "The President and you have more than justified the faith of those who insisted that your leadership was a turning point in modern history."[85] Surely this pragmatist and major architect of Wilson's vision suspected that the very faith he invoked had worked for its own justification. Whether experience would continue to confirm the power of that faith, and thus affirm the right to hold it, remained to be seen.

CHAPTER NINE

A Living Thing Is Born

"He had no plan, no scheme, no constructive idea whatever for clothing with the flesh of life the commandments which he had thundered from the White House," wrote the young British economist John Maynard Keynes of Woodrow Wilson's performance at the Paris peace conference. Though widely copied, Keynes's caricature of a priggish neophyte, "bamboozled" by his counterparts and choking on his own thin broth of principles, is ludicrous.[1] Wilson did have a plan for the peace conference, and his very presence there was part of it. "I'm going to Europe because the Allied governments don't want me to," he told a Swiss peace activist on November 22, 1918. The heads of those governments knew and feared his plan to "extend the Monroe Doctrine" into a policy both global and democratic: "Not a big-brother affair, but a real partnership."[2] He had laid its diplomatic groundwork through a series of public maneuvers—calling for a peace without victory, rejecting the pope's compromise with autocracy, and articulating a principled yet provisional program for settlement—all of which established a pragmatist standard for peacemaking that other statesmen might resist but could not ignore. Wilson's accomplishments at the conference bespeak his leverage as author of its framing terms, while the record of deliberations shows the wisdom, skill, and purpose with which he pressed his advantage. The British foreign secretary, Arthur Balfour—privy to most of the "Big Four" meetings of Wilson, Britain's David Lloyd George, France's Georges Clemenceau, and Italy's Vittorio Orlando—thought Wilson "as good round a table as he was on paper." General Jan Smuts of South Africa declared him "the noblest figure, perhaps the only noble figure in the history of the war."[3]

Though truer than Keynes's, these kinder assessments are incomplete. In Paris Wilson continued to alienate supporters at home and abroad. He treated his own delegation as clerks of his private diplomatic realm, a kingdom he weakened by effectively exiling the Republican Party and the press. No figure better dramatizes the self-inflicted damage of Wilson's bridge burning than Walter Lippmann. Excluded from Wilson's counsel, Lippmann resigned from the staff of Wilson's longtime adviser, "Colonel" Edward M. House, and left Paris in low spirits on January 23, 1919, less than two weeks after the conference opened. Back at the *New Republic*, he joined editor Herbert Croly in chastising Wilson for choosing "the lone hand" over "the effort of building up an informed and energetic public opinion." Eventually, this major architect and lucid exponent of the president's peace turned against him—but not before trying to turn him around. "You know as well as I do the resentment which has been aroused by the President's failure to explain what he is doing," Lippmann wrote to House in March. Press reports were too thin on facts to be trusted, while official reports were "about as interesting as a railroad time-table." As the "temper of the country" cooled toward Wilson, his task was both obvious and critical: "The president has only to explain clearly and definitely why each move he makes is related to a programme of permanent peace in order to win over all the opposition that counts."[4]

To Wilson, in the wake of the Armistice and on the threshold of a new world, such criticism could only sound like carping. For months—years—he had drawn from the wells of public wisdom fuel for a political revolution. He was not just prepared but determined to see his and every nation take up the responsibilities of the new world order illuminated by its fires. He knew that the Allied leaders' recalcitrance and the American electorate's rebuke were dark specters menacing his program's success. For that reason, he broke all precedent and traveled to Paris to negotiate personally on behalf of his nation—and, he believed, the world.

The initial reward could not have been more gratifying or narcotizing. From the time Wilson arrived at Brest, France, on Friday, December 13, 1918, until the day the conference opened one month later, the demons of politics seemed banished by the dawn of peace. The only otherworldly phenomena crossing his path as he wound through London, Rome, Paris, and countless towns and villages in between were the thronging, adoring, transported souls pouring tears and roses at his feet and haunting their leaders with literal hallelujahs to his name.

But finally it came time to parley, mortal to mortal. He correctly predicted a great but human achievement. He did not anticipate the physical and mental toll that would lead him to squander it.

Wilson enjoyed few unvarnished successes at the conference but suffered fewer outright defeats. Above all, he succeeded in his major task: the creation of a League of Nations, a solemn "covenant" of states providing both moral motive and democratic mechanisms for addressing the settlement's inevitable imperfections. The League was the foundation on which a global ethical republic would be built, and it was laid primarily by Wilson. He insisted that the League be the first order of business at Paris, assumed the chair of the League of Nations Commission (LNC) charged with constructing it, and succeeded in tying ratification of the settlement's several treaties to ratification of its covenant.[5]

Three basic schemata for the League were presented at Paris. The French backed the plan of longtime League advocate Leon Bourgeois, the distinguishing features of which were an international army under a general staff with extensive authority. Wilson suspected, however, that these radical features were meant to advance the reactionary goal of a new balance of power in Europe, with French continental hegemony at its fulcrum. Rather than accuse the French of such motives, he argued that with no prior experience of global governance, few countries would accept a supranational military command, while Americans were constitutionally bound to reject it. In contrast to the French, the British backed a plan submitted by Lord Robert Cecil that could have been written by an American sovereignty hawk such as Theodore Roosevelt or Henry Cabot Lodge: a loose alliance system in which the five major powers (Britain, France, Italy, Japan, and the United States) would have preponderant influence as sole members of an executive directorate. This plan proved harder to dismiss, and several of its conservative features infiltrated the final Covenant.[6] Still, through wise compromise, tough negotiation, clever leveraging of small-state concerns, and strategic retreats, Wilson managed to counterbalance most of those features with articles restating the central terms of the Magnolia Covenant and thus reasserting the activist and egalitarian character of the League.

Indeed, contrary to Keynes, it was the Magnolia plan and Wilson's subsequent Paris drafts that provided the basic skeleton and much of the "flesh" for the League Covenant. Granted, Wilson had many collaborators. But it was he who worked most tirelessly and successfully to ensure that the League assumed as "virile" and democratic a form as possible. His efforts demonstrate that regardless of his shortcomings as a domestic leader during this period, he still approached his role as world statesman pragmatically. He eagerly adopted novel extensions of the Magnolia Covenant's terms. At the suggestion of US Army General Tasker H. Bliss, for instance, he altered both the preamble and the collective security article of his "First Paris Draft" to indicate that internal revolutions were outside League jurisdiction unless they posed a manifest threat to international order—a provision escaping those who later impugned the League as a bulwark of the status quo or an anticommunist alliance in disguise. Additionally, and again at Bliss's suggestion, Wilson clarified the supreme obligation of mandatories to foster self-government in their mandates, thus giving his "Second Paris Draft" an unmistakable anti-imperialist cast.[7] Wilson also incorporated useful suggestions from Allied counterparts while resisting others as best he could. He knew, for example, that the British feared an imbalance between official authority and effective responsibility in a League dominated numerically by small states. Thus, in his First Paris Draft, he adopted Smuts's proposal for a bicameral structure, assigning parliamentary functions to an Assembly of equally represented states and executive functions to a nine-member Council granting permanent members Britain, France, Italy, Japan, and the United States a bare majority. This arrangement did much to appease the British, and Wilson, too, thought it accommodated geopolitical reality: after all, the five great powers would be the League's major financial and military sponsors. At the same time, Wilson's plan preserved the internationalist ideal of great-power accountability by vesting veto power in *any three* of the executive *nine*—certainly more democratic than Cecil's vision of a great-power club in which small states would "not exercise any considerable influence."[8]

Wilson's Paris drafts also reveal his efforts to anticipate the trepidations of conservative nationalists at home while fulfilling the expectations of internationalists with more expansive visions of the League's role. To meet conservatives halfway, Wilson took Bliss's advice and altered his original article on enforcing the results of arbitration: His Second Paris Draft read that noncompliant members would "*ipso facto* be deemed to have committed an act of war," rather than "*ipso facto* become at war with all the members of the League"—a tactical effort to align the document with the US Congress's constitutional authority to make or not make war.[9] With his progressive-internationalist constituency in mind, Wilson devised articles requiring all League members to guarantee "humane conditions of labor" and the rights of "racial or national minorities," while working to include provision in the territorial guarantee for readjustments "pursuant to the principle of self-determination" and crucial to "the peace of the world."[10]

Neither the national-minorities article nor the readjustment clause of what became Article 10 appeared in the final Covenant. Their fate reveals the practical limitations Wilson faced at Paris and the value of his least appreciated skill: strategic retreat. Wilson simply could not have exactly the League he wanted, and he was forced to compromise to gain one broadly beseeming his rhetoric and principles. Just before the LNC's first session, Wilson discovered that his chief international lawyer, David Hunter Miller, along with Cecil and the British delegation's chief counsel, C. J. B. Hurst, had eviscerated his Second Paris Draft of its pragmatist-internationalist character in the course of redrafting it for discussion. The four small-power seats were eliminated from the executive body, and the provision for future boundary adjustments was excised from the guarantee of territorial integrity. Incensed, but aware of the British delegation's shaky support for the League, Wilson agreed to let the so-called Hurst-Miller draft serve as the basis of the LNC's deliberations.[11] Subsequently, however, he used his position as LNC chair to guide discussion so that the small-state delegates were alerted to its departures from his version. As predicted, these delegates successfully recast the Covenant in a more internationalist mold, restoring small-power representation in the Council (Article 4) and demanding a strong guarantee of collective defense in place of Cecil's weak pledge of abstention from war (Article 16).[12] Not only could Wilson join in these small-power victories, he could do so without worrying that Lloyd George, Clemenceau, or Orlando would demand tit for tat when his next disagreement with them arose.

Still, Wilson could not regain all the ground he ceded by allowing the Hurst-Miller draft. The article protecting minorities was not restored, nor was the collective-security article's proviso for territorial change. But Wilson did not abandon either of the objectives they served. Rather, he sought them by alternative and sometimes stealthier routes. One was inserting protections for national and religious minorities in all treaties between victors, vanquished, and new states.[13] Another was granting the Assembly power to propose changes to existing treaties (Article 19). Still another was a little-remarked section of Wilson's Second Paris Draft that survived the Hurst-Miller pruning to be enshrined eventually as Article 11. Wilson's original version declared "any war or threat of war, whether immediately affecting any of the Members of the League or not," a potential cause for League action "to safeguard the peace of nations"; it also reserved the right of every League member to call the body's attention "to any circumstances anywhere which threaten to disturb international peace," later changed to read "any circumstance whatever affecting international *relations*."[14] Wilson drew little attention to this article during the drafting process, but it became, for him, a repository of the expansive League functions he failed to get explicitly enumerated elsewhere. In his view, the clear meaning of Article 11 was "that every matter which is likely to affect the peace of the world is everybody's business." Under its provisions, he told an Indianapolis audience, "there is not an oppressed people in the world which cannot get a hearing," assuming their "cause is just." Ethnic minorities, irredentist nationalists, and native peoples of mandated territories had only to gain the ear or spark the concern of a single League member to receive Council attention. On this reading, Article 11 fulfilled Wilson's intention that the League supersede the particular interests it comprised, for it provided "that the peace of the world transcends all the susceptibilities of nations and governments."[15]

Of course getting a hearing and getting redress are two different things, and Wilson knew that the latter, as well as the League's overall democratic functioning, would be impeded by one of the Covenant's defining features: its general rule of unanimous decision (Article 5, paragraph 1). Though Wilson pushed hard against British and French officials demanding unanimity (and thus national vetoes over international initiatives), their insistence, combined with pressure from nationalists in the US Senate, forced his capitulation. But here, too, Wilson clawed back ground, uniting with small-state representatives to achieve several exceptions to the rule. Article 15, for instance, stated that in case of dispute between members, the Council "by a majority vote shall make and publish a report" recommending a "just and proper" resolution (paragraph 4). It further stated that should any such report receive unanimous agreement *exclusive of parties to the dispute*, no member—including disputants—could go to war with any party "which complies with the recommendations" (paragraph 6). Lest a party fear general collusion among the Council, it could request referral to the Assembly, which then inherited the Council's Article 12 prerogative of insisting on arbitration and a three-month prohibition of war, as well its Article 15 prerogative to report recommendations and prohibit attack on compliant parties, provided the concurrence of an Assembly majority and unanimous Council exclusive of disputants (Article 15, paragraphs 9 and 10).

The importance of these exceptions lay in Articles 12, 13, and 16, which, respectively, obliged members to avail themselves of League arbitration in any dispute, abide by the results of the processes described in Article 15, and acknowledge that "resort to war in disregard of its Covenants under Articles 12, 13, and 15" would ipso facto constitute "an act of war against all other Members" (Article 16, paragraph 1). The result (Article 16, paragraphs 1 and 2) would be automatic economic, financial, and diplomatic sanctions, and potentially a military response, to be determined with reference to other duties as outlined, for instance, in Article 10.[16] Thus, despite the lack of a unanimity exception in Article 11, members with serious concerns about conflicts or injustices dangerous to international peace were afforded multiple, if difficult, avenues by which to pursue League action on even highly sensitive or divisive matters—provided they had the will to traverse them, and enough fellow members had the will to respond. In this light, the

Covenant appeared to Wilson neither an entangling alliance nor a stanchion of the status quo but a practical guide to addressing, in deliberative fashion, issues of common concern to the international community.

To be sure, the Covenant did not provide formulas to solve all possible problems of peace. In Wilson's opinion, such wide scope for interpretation was intentional and salutary. There was a reason that the League of Nations Covenant, like the US Constitution, specifically provided for its future amendment (Article 26). Its "elastic" nature was a practical imperative, a realistic accommodation to the limits of political foresight and the value of continued experiment. "The simplicity of the document," he told the plenary session that adopted it at Paris, "seems to me to be one of its chief virtues, because, speaking for myself, I was unable to see the variety of circumstances with which this league would have to deal. I was unable, therefore, to plan all the machinery that might be necessary to meet the differing and unexpected contingencies. Therefore, I should say of this document that it is not a strait-jacket but a vehicle of life."

"A living thing is born," Wilson then announced. Like other living things, the League would both shape and evolve with its environment, according to the ideals of its members and "the changing circumstances of the time." Its Covenant was thus "a practical document and a humane document," identifying problems and attempting to solve them, yet representing above all the will to believe that peoples once mutually "suspicious" could "now live as friends in a single family," aware of their "common purpose." That purpose was, in a basic sense, identical to the means of attaining it. As the president told a Montana audience many months later, "The League of Nations substitutes discussion for fighting."[17]

When Wilson disembarked the *George Washington* at Boston on February 23, 1919, eight days into a monthlong respite from the Paris negotiations, he had reason to believe he returned to a nation brimming with enthusiasm for a League.[18] To be sure, prominent Republicans had picked up the trumpet of nationalism after its virtuoso, Roosevelt, died on January 6. Most notable were Senators William E. Borah of Idaho, Philander C. Knox of Pennsylvania, and Henry Cabot Lodge of Massachusetts, the powerful chair of the Senate Foreign Relations Committee. Borah was a true isolationist, "irreconcilably" opposed to a League, while Knox adhered to "a new American doctrine" which did not "dogmatize against any possible entente" but only "the ignis fatuus of the theorists"—that is, Wilson and other supporters of a powerful League. Lodge's views were probably similar to Knox's, though his determination to carry Roosevelt's legacy—and destroy Wilson's—makes them hard to discern.[19]

Wilson attempted to compromise with these critics and their allies in a White House meeting on February 26. Retreating from his earlier critical stance toward the Monroe Doctrine, he praised it as worthy of global extension across the globe through a League counting the United States as senior partner. He also downplayed the likelihood of the US government having to accept any League decision it had not helped make through representatives in both the Assembly and the Council. But he would not prevaricate on the main issue: the military obligations imposed by Article 10. Like any legal person consenting to government, the United States must "willingly relinquish some of its sovereignty" and work cooperatively to replace anarchy with order. The League Covenant was not a "usurpation" of power, but an "agreement" on how to use it under circumstances the agreement itself helped prevent. If "the objection of sovereignty was insisted upon by the Senate," Wilson declared, the League would be doomed, and the nation more rather than less likely to find itself at war again.[20]

The meeting revealed that despite months of poor communication with the American people, Wilson had returned from his first stint in Paris a pragmatist. He was willing to converse frankly with rivals whose worldviews differed significantly from his own. He was willing to entertain contrary ideas and make substantial concessions to achieve compromise in the interest of Americans and the world—including agreeing to renegotiate portions of an internationally approved document in which he had invested more time, thought, and emotion than any person on earth. But he was not willing to undermine efforts to extend an analogous ethic of deliberation and mutual obligation to the international society of which his nation and its representatives, willingly or not, were members. It was not trivia but questions of moment that required collective wisdom, and the most momentous questions facing nations involved the mutual rights and responsibilities of force. The integrity of the League, and the future peace of the United States, demanded that the country's government and people respect the common counsel of the world.

Such slander against sovereignty was all Lodge needed to hear. Late in the evening of March 3, he introduced a "Round Robin" signed by thirty-seven senators—enough to defeat a treaty in the Senate—which declared that the League Covenant in its present form "should not be accepted by the United States" and that no covenant should be considered until peace was concluded.[21] Wilson's will to believe that compromise between antagonists was possible had encountered an uncooperative reality, as Lodge's intensifying anti-League campaign confirmed over subsequent weeks and months. It was a dispiriting episode that hardened Wilson's attitude toward his Senate critics. Months later, after his stroke in October 1919, that attitude would become as sclerotic as the arteries silently plotting against his brain.[22]

The severity and publicity of the opposition Wilson faced on Capitol Hill made his return to Paris even more unpalatable. To mollify his domestic critics, he was forced to seek changes to a document he had fulsomely praised. Most significant was a new Article 21, specifically recognizing the Monroe Doctrine's "validity" as a "regional understanding" facilitating "maintenance of peace." Though insisting to the LNC that the Monroe Doctrine would not preclude League action in the Western Hemisphere and that he had always considered it compatible with the Covenant, the president was now in the Entente's debt. Worse, the Round Robin revealed the extent of his domestic vulnerabilities. Most of the concessions to selfish and vindictive nationalism for which Wilson has since been blamed were extracted thereafter. Even so, the majority of Wilson's compromises approximated his ideals to a degree that few others could have achieved in the atmosphere of fear and hatred created by the war. The result was a treaty that he knew would disappoint many parties and that Germans especially would resent, but which nonetheless struck him as fair—especially given the "machinery of adjustment" at its heart.[23]

A central and controversial part of that machinery was the "mandate system," adopted to facilitate the colonial "adjustment" comprehended in the fifth of the Fourteen Points. Wilson could not convince Europe's victorious powers to abandon their colonies. Nor could he dislodge Allied armies from their enemies' former possessions. But he did prevent the distribution of colonial spoils foreseen in the secret treaties, ensuring through long and bitter negotiation that each captured colony would not be annexed by its occupier but governed under a "mandate" to foster its progress toward self-government and, theoretically, League membership.[24] The system was hardly satisfactory to anticolonialists, nor entirely satisfactory to Wilson. Borrowing from a plan first circulated by Smuts, it left France and Britain to govern most of the Middle East under mandates envisioning independence within a few decades, while South Africa and other British dominions assumed wardship of African and Asian-Pacific territories deemed to require several generations of tutelage. Typically, Wilson regretted the system's concessions to French and British imperialism, having argued first for direct League supervision of mandates and then for supervision by small states unused to power and easily policed. Also typically, he blithely accepted the racist logic of the system's tiered structure. Nonetheless, the colonial system received a heavy blow at Wilson's hand. Their hopes of annexation stymied, the mandatory powers were politically tied and legally responsible to an international community bound, by treaty, to prevent exploitation of native peoples and ensure their opportunity for political advancement—a community in which colonial powers were a minority.[25]

Italy's retention of territory in the German-speaking South Tyrol was another blow to Wilson's reputation among idealists. Later he, too, would question the wisdom of his acquiescence. At the time, however, he thought it justified on security grounds, which he had pledged to consider as carefully as demographic factors, and necessary to maintain Italian confidence in a League expected by millions to compel disarmament. Meanwhile, Wilson famously and publicly denounced the Italian delegation for demanding the Adriatic port of Fiume, declaring it economically and strategically critical to the new Yugoslavia and insisting that polls of residents were all "unfavorable to Italy." After driving the Italians from the conference in a huff, he eventually extracted their commitment to resolve the issue through direct, League-supervised negotiations with Yugoslavia. By the end of the conference, Wilson had thwarted most of Italy's other territorial ambitions—which included almost the entire Dalmatian coast—while drawing them back, at least officially, into the internationalist fold.[26]

More disappointing to Wilson, and liberals everywhere, was Japan's retention of the former German concession in China's Shandong Peninsula. Wilson's long-standing sympathy for China and personal view of "what is just and right" made his decision to support Japan's claim over Chinese objections among the hardest of the conference. That decision was complicated by another outcome for which he still is vilified: the rejection of Japan's move to insert a clause affirming the "equality of Nations" in the League of Nations Covenant. Though initially receptive to the proposal, Wilson concluded after conversations with Allied representatives that its implication of ethnic and racial equality would scuttle the whole League project by stoking Anglo-French fears of revolt in Ireland, Africa, and South and Southeast Asia. Thus, to the fury of Japan and several smaller states, he effectively vetoed the clause through parliamentary procedures requiring its unanimous endorsement by the League of Nations Committee, where only Britain and Poland opposed it. The result was to trade the potential defection of Britain or France for that of Japan, whose participation in the postwar political and security architecture Wilson deemed critical to its success—especially since Italy's participation was in doubt. Shandong was the price demanded and paid. Of course, Wilson confided to his future biographer, he was certain to be "accused of violating his own principles—but never-the-less he *must* work for world order & organization against anarchy." To advance and partially redeem that work, he helped secure a pledge from Japan to relinquish the territory peacefully at a later date—a pledge duly honored in 1922.[27]

Despite this effort to draw its sting, the Shandong controversy would haunt Wilson's campaign for Senate consent to the peace. His greatest handicap in that endeavor, however, was the financial and moral burden the settlement imposed on Germany.[28] Few at the conference or elsewhere outside Germany objected to stripping the country of its armed forces as punishment for ransacking Belgium. But the Treaty of Versailles that ended the war with Germany went further. Clemenceau and Lloyd George were driven by conscience, strategic calculation, and constituent opinion to foist the entire cost of the war on those they sincerely held responsible. Article 231, the "war-guilt clause," assigned full liability for the war to Germany and provided the legal basis for reparations. The Armistice had limited indemnities to "civilian damages," but under intense pressure, Wilson agreed to expand that term's definition to include pensions for millions of Allied veterans. Wilson's other controversial concessions in this realm included France's right to occupy the Rhineland if reparations went unpaid; French ownership of the Saar Valley's coal mines as indemnity for the German army's destructive retreat; and a twenty-year, League-supervised French occupation to protect the mines. Less controversially, Germany returned Alsace-Lorraine to France, relinquished three small enclaves to Belgium, and ceded ethnically heterogeneous Prussian territory to newly independent Poland.

Wilson made these concessions with the understanding that an international commission would calculate a reparations schedule based not on Allied claims but on Germany's ability to pay, subject to revision or even cancellation as German economic conditions dictated. When Wilson fell ill in early April, however, House undermined his position. Eager to play world statesman, he conciliated and prevaricated on the issue, prompting the Big Three to assume (or pretend to assume) that Wilson himself had accepted a schedule ratifying Allied claims and enforceable regardless of circumstances. Upon recovering, Wilson felt deeply betrayed, his work undone by a diminished éminence grise whose sympathy for the Allies and their great-power pretensions had already cooled one of his warmest adult relationships. That relationship never recovered.[29] Nor has Wilson's reputation recovered from his resignation to the situation. And yet, despite the reparations fiasco, Wilson managed mostly to fulfill his promise of averting a Carthaginian peace. Along with preventing France's outright annexation of the Saar, he prevented the dismemberment of the German Rhineland into French-controlled Rhenish republics as well as France's alternative to occupy the region permanently. Ultimately, after Wilson implied a threat to abandon negotiations, the French accepted a limited occupation followed by permanent demilitarization on the condition—suggested by Wilson—that the United States and Britain join France in a mutual treaty of defense against Germany, in concurrent effect with the Versailles Treaty. In this way Wilson brought both the security-obsessed French and the commercially minded British together in support of a settlement that salvaged some chance of Germany's rehabilitation as the economic engine of Central Europe. Equally important, the peace conference survived to meet its remaining challenges.[30]

Most of those challenges were met in ways that realized both Wilson's and the world public's ideals of self-determination, despite the differences between them. An independent Poland with access to the sea was established, and a plebiscite was called to allow the people of Upper Silesia to choose between Polish and German jurisdiction. Those nations that had gained independence from Austria-Hungary were recognized and compelled to sign treaties guaranteeing the rights of ethnic minorities. Throughout the negotiations on these and hundreds of other matters, Wilson resisted efforts led by Field Marshall Ferdinand Foch of France and Britain's secretary of state for war, Winston Churchill, to make the conference the cradle of an Atlantic alliance against Bolshevism. "My policy regarding Russia is very similar to my Mexican policy," he asserted shortly before the conference began. Russia, like any other nation in the Wilsonian cosmology, had the right "to settle her own affairs in her own way"—so long, he added, "as she does not become a menace to others."[31]

That comment on Russia encapsulated Wilson's entire approach to the conference. It also expressed his hopes for the work it had done and his confidence that those hopes could be realized given time and the good-faith efforts of nations far safer than they had ever been to make them. At the end of June 1919, with the Treaty of Versailles at the printers, Wilson faced his first press conference in six months squarely and proudly. "I didn't say it adheres to the Fourteen Points," Wilson admitted. "But really, I think it adheres more closely to them than I had a right to expect."[32]

Many Americans disagreed. Cruelly, they included some of Wilson's staunchest pragmatist-progressive supporters. "THIS IS NOT PEACE," shouted the cover of the May 24 *New Republic*. Croly and Lippmann had undergone a fantastic transformation since the Armistice. They had already urged readers to "Defeat Article X"—not because it infringed on US sovereignty but because it bolstered the status quo. Nonetheless, they had accepted Wilson's contention that "final justice" could not be achieved at Paris and in the early spring counseled patience: Regardless of its details, they argued, the League of Nations would promote whatever ideals its members held dearest, and as such the basis for judgment must be the general tone and implicit priorities of the German treaty. Well before its official publication, however, the editors had seen enough. The League's members-to-be had shown quite clearly what they could do together. "It would be the height of folly to commit a great people as the guarantor of a condition which is morbidly sick with conflict and trouble," they concluded: the United States should reject the treaty—and the League.[33]

Walter Weyl, who had only just rejoined the editorial staff, thought the break with the administration long overdue; from Europe he had watched American liberalism "crumbling," and his faith in Wilson had crumbled with it.[34] The decision was searingly painful for Croly, who agonized over the question all pragmatists face: What is the lesson of failure—to fix or to forsake what it has wrought? Depressed by the vicious humor circulating in the United States, he saw the treaty as proof of its similar prevalence in Europe, and concluded that spiritual renewal must precede political reconstruction across the Western world.[35] Lippmann tried taking a more clinical view. "The bottom fact of the whole failure was a failure of technique," he wrote to Felix Frankfurter. "The intentions were good enough," but "you cannot in ignorance improvise a structure of good will." Yet Lippmann, too, saw tragedy in the treaty, and more ahead for Wilson. "For the life of me I can't see peace in this document," he wrote to Ray Stannard Baker on May 19, "and as the President has so frequently said, statesmen who cannot hear the voice of mankind are sure to be broken."[36]

Lippmann—and the president—were right. As groups of "mild reservationists," "strong reservationists," and "irreconcilables" coalesced in the Senate to oppose Wilson's League on various grounds, the public, long since exiled from his counsel, returned to haunt him. Many, if not most, progressives and moderates understood that the only way to mitigate the settlement's evils was through some type of League. What they did not understand were the many interrelated ideological and practical factors that made this *particular* League so precious in Wilson's eyes, for during the conference the president had hidden the painful process of its birth from public view. In the meantime, he had alienated the most articulate propagandists for the type of League he thought he had created. Whereas in February the *New Republic* had lauded the Covenant as, on balance, the humane document he claimed, his subsequent unexplained capitulations to Allied national aggrandizement confirmed their worries that Article 10 would prove the bulwark of a victor's settlement, while discrediting the president's promises of pragmatic adjustment under American leadership.[37] Equally demoralizing for the editors was concluding that what they had criticized as a dangerous inconsistency between national and international policy was a sadly ironic illusion. For two years they had kept their faith in Wilson's fight for world democracy despite the "suppression of criticism in which he so weakly acquiesced" at home, only to see the same disdain for public participation yield, in their view, lousy results at Paris. Lippmann, inspired perhaps by some simplistic conception of poetic justice, covertly revealed to the League's most powerful opponents in the Senate Wilson's early knowledge of the Allied secret treaties, information used by irreconcilables to portray the Covenant as another example of common counsel among imperialists.[38]

The *New Republic*'s volte-face, however, was unpopular. Thousands of readers cancelled their subscriptions, apparently agreeing with the majority of liberal journals—and, if the editors of the nation's dailies are any guide, the majority of Americans—that the nation's best course was to ratify the treaty and join the League of Nations.[39] Yet when the "League Fight" finally ended in March 1920, that course was closed. Wilson had left Paris tired of making concessions, and his change of attitude since his February visit to Washington inflamed resentment among senators. Initially he signaled confidence in the prospects for compromise, indicating to the press that he would consider the "complicated problem" of reservations. But there was an edge to his optimism. *"The Senate is going to ratify the treaty,"* he told reporters on July 10, the day he presented it formally to that body—and there would be no abridgment of Article 10. In the Senate chamber, after Republicans pointedly abstained from the applause with which Democrats and the gallery greeted his entry, Wilson "informed" the body that the time for *discussing* their nation's duty had passed and the time for *doing* it had come, lest the nation "break the heart of the world." To spearhead a union of nations was the fulfillment of America's historical mission, "disclosed," he insisted, by "the hand of God who led us into this way." One need not invoke dubious theories of a "messiah complex" to realize that exhaustion, frustration, and a grasp of the stakes involved produced a major rhetorical shift on Wilson's part: instead of an attempt to live in peace *as* God willed, the League was an expression *of* God's will.[40]

The absolutist turn foreshadowed in this speech ultimately destroyed Wilson's cause. But failure, despite the adage, has many fathers. Immediately after the speech, Wilson told Democrats and reporters of his regret over Shandong, perplexity over Ireland, and conviction that Article 10 fully preserved Congress's war-making authority. In the last half of July, he held twenty-two hour-long, one-on-one meetings with Republican senators. But his guests were unmoved and his energies drained by the effort. Former President William Howard Taft's abrupt decision to break ranks with his colleagues in the League to Enforce Peace (LEP) and propose yet another set of reservations exacerbated the effects of declining health on Wilson's judgment.[41] That summer and fall, Wilson's tendency to lump even "mild reservationists" with the "irreconcilable" minority relinquished the middle ground to Lodge, who argued that limiting American obligations under Article 10 was the nationally *and* internationally responsible course: not only would it keep American soldiers out of unimportant wars, it would also allow their government to cooperate in improving the treaty without enforcing its objectionable features. Meanwhile, most of the "mild" reservationists proved hotter than advertised, especially after Lodge staged a series of artfully packed and seemingly interminable hearings before the Committee on Foreign Relations. A last-ditch effort to compromise on interpretive rather than formal reservations was uncharitably received by Lodge and his committee partisans, who responded by moving formally to amend the Covenant and thus trigger another round of international negotiations. Wilson's fury prompted a final, herculean labor in support of unqualified membership. Despite a grueling Western Tour, however, Wilson could not prevent Lodge from reporting a resolution of consent with reservations. He could only instruct Democrats to defeat it—as they did on November 19, 1919, and again on March 19, 1920, finally rejecting the Treaty of Versailles and, with it, US membership in the League of Nations.[42]

Wilson could have prevented this outcome in three ways. First, and most obviously, he could have compromised earlier and more extensively on reservations. His refusal to do so seemed to contradict his rhetoric of common counsel, and perhaps he should have compromised, trusting in the adaptability of his nation's and the League's constitutional governments. But Wilson had cogent reasons for rejecting both the individual reservations proposed and the idea of reservations in general. Reservations demanding independence for Ireland and full Chinese sovereignty in the Shandong Peninsula threatened chances of ratification by other powers, as did the notion that a treaty drafted by a constituent assembly of nations could be altered by the United States alone. Most important, the reservation to Article 10 portended an entirely illusory collective security to which the world's greatest power admitted no obligation. "That we should make no general promise, but leave to the nations associated with us to guess in each instance what we were going to consider ourselves bound to do," Wilson explained to a Wyoming audience, was "a thing unworthy and ridiculous."[43] Given that the fundamental principle of Wilson's League was the supremacy of international over national interests, claims that he "slew his own brain child" by resisting special exemptions for his own government ring hollow, even as they reverberate across generations.[44]

Still, Wilson had helped sow the whirlwind he reaped. On the day Wilson asked Congress to declare war, his friend Thomas Brahamy, pegging Lodge as a student of international affairs whom the president should "consult freely and frequently," nonetheless rued in his diary: "In most things the President is his own counselor."[45] Brahamy's comment foreshadowed Wilson's second missed opportunity to mitigate the disaster that befell his work: the selection of the American peace commission. Wilson spurned not just Lodge himself but all of his peers and copartisans, inviting no senators to join the commission and only one obscure, nonpolitical Republican, ex-diplomat Henry White. This decision, following two years of struggle with Congress over war powers and the previous month's spurious but damaging "referendum" on foreign policy, ensured that most Republican senators would oppose any treaty Wilson secured.[46] Instead of building bridges to internationally minded Republicans, Wilson built a wall.

The case could be made that any commissioner satisfactory to Lodge's powerful faction was likely to undermine Wilson at Paris. Yet by most accounts, the members of the handpicked group that did accompany the president to Paris were little closer to the action for their travel. Only days before the *George Washington* berthed at Brest, France, former Inquiry member Charles Seymour described a meeting between Wilson and the commission as "really a historic occasion because it is absolutely the first time the President has let anyone know what his ideas are and what his policy is." It seemed things were changing: Wilson "explained that he could not know the details of all the questions" that would arise in Paris and "would be forced to rely on the information we gave him." Wilson said "that he wanted us to come to him freely and that we must expect him to call on us. One phrase sticks in my head—'You tell me what's right and I'll fight for it.'"[47] William Christian Bullitt recorded the same promise in his diary—perhaps explaining some of the bitterness soaking his letter to Wilson five months later, tendering his resignation from the peace delegation:

> That you personally opposed most of the unjust settlements [at Paris] . . .
> is well known. Nevertheless, it is my conviction that if you had made
> your fight in the open, instead of behind closed doors, you would have

carried with you the opinion of the world . . . and might have established
the "new international order based upon broad principles of right and
justice" of which you used to speak. I am sorry that you did not fight our
fight to the finish and that you had so little faith in the millions of men,
like myself, in every nation who had faith in you.[48]

Croly had foretold the costs of such faithlessness the moment the Armistice was signed. Democracy, he reminded the coming settlement's architects, did "not consist in popular approval of policies" forged in secret. "If
democracy is to be only less perilous than autocracy it must decide with all
possible knowledge of the case upon which it is passing judgment."[49] This
warning went unheeded. At Paris Wilson sought to establish open diplomacy in camera. At home he too often sought approval through the plebisci-
tary methods that Croly, and many others, considered grotesque caricatures
of democracy.

   Thus, by abandoning pragmatist methods in his personal politics, Wilson missed his greatest opportunity to infuse them into the law and life of
nations. Could Americans have followed his reasoning through the treaty
negotiations, they might better have understood both the concessions he
made and the dangers he saw in Lodge's alternative. Even amid the public
revulsion against the Treaty of Versailles, Wilson's Western Tour promoting League membership drew enthusiastic crowds, proving once again his
skill as an educator of public opinion—before a massive, nearly fatal stroke,
suffered on October 2, 1919, left him bedridden and totally isolated. From
that moment on, all hope of Wilson's engaging the public in a constructive dialogue about the League vanished. Unfounded rumors that wife Edith
was deciding policy while Woodrow himself was descending into insanity
caused public confidence in the president's leadership to plunge. Indeed, his
leadership *was* impaired by the behavioral consequences of his brain trauma,
exacerbated by a severe prostate infection that almost killed him. Typical of
the pathology of stroke, Wilson lost concentration and emotional control.
The stubborn, "promethean" aspects of his character were magnified until
he became, in the words of the League fight's premier historian, "literally
incapable of compromise."[50] After his stroke, Wilson's chance of rapprochement with the Senate was even lower than that of renewed rapport with
the people.

   Yet despite his health—despite *himself*—Wilson came far closer than
historical memory admits to bringing his stereotypically isolationist country into an incipient system of global government. The votes cast November 19, 1919, reveal that 85 percent of the sitting senators supported some

form of League membership. Next March, the Senate voted 49–35 to consent to the Versailles Treaty as parsed by Lodge's reservations—*after* Wilson ordered twenty-three Democrats to vote against. Had seven of those twenty-three followed the pragmatist who pronounced the Fourteen Points rather than the dogmatist delivering their orders, the treaty would have been ratified, creating at least a primitive form of international organization with potential to mature over time. Many thousands, scandalized by Wilson's role in the trampling of that seedling, would have found tragic irony in his reported assessment of its demise: "Doctor," he told White House physician Cary T. Grayson, "the devil is a very busy man."[51]

Granted, the fact that a majority of senators supported League membership reveals no more about the thought of the American people than the fact that a majority of senators voted against it. How, then, to tell whether US membership would have proved acceptable to enough Americans to stay on the books, much less make any meaningful impact on international affairs?

The press offers some clues—especially the Republican press. In early 1919, several Republican papers announced support for League membership, as did the majority of independent and Democratic organs. During the election of 1920, Republican editors were as likely to explain away Warren G. Harding's frequent equivocations on the League issue as they were to endorse its rejection. In September, the pro-Harding and pro-League New York *Globe* insisted that Harding's opinion on the League, though maddeningly confusing, was inconsequential: He would be compelled by public opinion to accept membership. The New York *Tribune*, admitting that Harding's failure to endorse ratification was "disappointing to many Republicans," implied that he was merely avoiding specifics until he could assess the balance of power in the Senate. The Denver *News* argued that League membership was an economic necessity and that after the election, Republican leaders were "likely to take a broader view" of the country's "international relations." To vote Harding, the editor opined, was to vote against Wilson's form of "personal government," not to vote against the League.[52]

The Republican press had reason to apologize for its party. It is remarkably difficult to find major interest groups that did not support the League, or at least accept it as the logical outcome of a war explicitly fought to establish it. Despite its conservative-internationalist heritage and Republican leadership, the League to Enforce Peace, with its one hundred thousand members, was recognized at the time as the most broadly financed and eclectically constituted single-issue advocacy organization in American history to that point. The LEP provided logistical and financial support to hundreds of national and local bodies staging referenda and lobbying state and national officials for treaty ratification. Despite some waffling on reservations, William Howard Taft made heroic efforts to rally tens of thousands in cities nationwide to the highest cause of the man who took the presidency from his party—under his watch.[53]

But the LEP is only part of the story. Today, when religion is so often equated with conservatism in public discourse, it is instructive to recall how overwhelmingly the nation's religious bodies supported Wilson's radically internationalist agenda. Most prominent was the Federal Council of the Churches of Christ in America—a conglomeration of thirty church bodies representing 150,000 congregations and perhaps thirty million American Protestants. This highly organized and politically connected organization promoted the League as a means to extend the operation of Christ's golden rule across the earth.[54] At its annual convention in the spring of 1919, while Wilson was still in Paris, the council passed a resolution demanding ratification of the Covenant without alteration, with affiliates including the Presbyterian General Assembly, Northern Baptist Convention, Methodist-Episcopal Bishops, and Unitarian Association all following suit at their own spring gatherings.[55] Ahead of the first Senate vote, the council blitzed the mails with hundreds of thousands of pamphlets and created a thousand "Local Committees of Cooperation," reported to have spoken to more than ten million Americans about the League.[56] In October 1919, a petition signed by 16,450 clergy was presented to the Senate urging ratification "without amendments," and in December, after the Versailles Treaty's initial rejection, the council passed another resolution urging immediate ratification with only those changes explicitly required by the US Constitution. In June 1920, three months after the final Senate vote, the council sent a group of forty clergy across the Atlantic to convince Europeans that Americans were shocked by the government's failure to join the League and determined to redress it.[57]

League support was not simply a Protestant phenomenon. The National Catholic War Council was founded in part to unite the nation's Roman Catholic organizations behind promotional activities like the Federal Council's, and the first page of its *Handbook* quoted Wilson pledging US participation in a League of Nations.[58] In January 1920, the *Biblical World* described the League as an institutional extension of Catholic teaching and of the fundamental message uniting the Christian and Hebrew scriptures.[59] The nation's most prominent Jewish organizations agreed. In April 1919, the Central Conference of American Rabbis passed a resolution assuring Wilson of American Reform Judaism's "fullest support" in his "strivings" to establish a League and make a "just peace." As Rabbi Samuel Schulman stated that same spring, in his opening sermon to the Union of American Hebrew Congregations, "The vision of our Prophets foresaw the time when the whole world would be bound together by a real league of peoples, who consented to be governed by a higher law than their own will to power."[60] In 1919, B'nai B'rith awarded Wilson its Gold Medal for Services to Humanity, and the National Federation of Temple Sisterhoods assisted the LEP in lobbying the president and Senate to compromise on membership terms before the whole League project was lost.[61]

The Sisters of the Temple were typical of most female voluntary organizations. Given women's traditional prominence in peace activism (and the widespread belief that it was woman's special role to preserve life), it is not surprising that an organization designed to curb aggression and prevent mass destruction enjoyed wide support among women's groups. As the League fight heated up, the president of the General Federation of Women's Clubs introduced Wilson to a Los Angeles crowd by declaring, "The League of Nations must and will become the bulwark of a war-weary world for all time." Apparently, she spoke for more than her organization's two million members. In January 1920, the General Federation, National Council of Women, and Woman's Christian Temperance Union joined twenty-three other organizations representing some twenty million Americans to present a manifesto to Wilson and the Senate demanding swift ratification of the Covenant. That same year, the National American Woman Suffrage Association resolved in support of League membership at its fiftieth-anniversary convention.[62]

The most important American relief, social work, and social justice organizations also supported League membership. In January 1919, Eliot Wadsworth, acting chair of the American Red Cross (ARC) War Council, quoted a recent Wilson speech endorsing the League before expressing his own hope that the ARC's war service had "served [even] in the smallest way to bring about the end for which our President is striving." In March the council's official head, Henry P. Davison, announced the ARC's intention to join an international league of Red Cross societies, whose coordinated relief work would be a "vital factor" in the League of Nations' peace-building efforts but could not, as he clarified later that spring, replace intergovernmental cooperation. At that point, the ARC claimed more than thirty million adult and junior members—around one in four Americans.[63] In keeping both with its outreach and its evangelizing traditions, the Young Men's Christian Association (YMCA) also pursued a League-friendly program, cooperating with the armed forces to educate soldiers awaiting discharge on the purposes and necessity of the world body. Its head, John R. Mott, was among the nation's most visible League supporters for years following war's end.[64] The National Consumers' League made Secretary of War Newton Baker its president, and the National Conference of Social Workers petitioned the executive and legislative branches in favor of speedy ratification.[65] Two of the three largest organizations promoting justice for African Americans, the National Association for the Advancement of Colored People (NAACP) and the National Race Congress (NRC), also petitioned the government to join the League of Nations, specifically to ensure "the protection and development" of African peoples. Surprisingly, the NRC requested that the notoriously segregationist US government assume mandatory oversight of Germany's former African colonies, to shepherd them to self-government.[66]

But what about the "interests"—that is, the economic interests that unsentimental Americans of the twenty-first century (like many Americans in Wilson's day) tend to suspect really determine politics in the United States? Most major economic interest groups appear to have embraced, or at least expected, League membership. Labor—which, after all, saw a special body created within the League, the International Labor Organization (ILO), to investigate and improve working conditions worldwide—was generally supportive, although the more radical groups dissented. The American Federation of Labor (AFL)—by far the largest labor organization of the day— overwhelmingly approved a resolution supporting immediate ratification of the peace with Germany, and thus the League Covenant, at its June 1919 convention: 93 percent of its 32,000 delegates voted in favor. In December, after the Senate rejected League membership for the first time, 118 of the 200 trade union presidents affiliated with the AFL approved a declaration including demands for immediate ratification; only eight voted against. The AFL unions were more divided by the following year's convention, but a pro-League, no-reservations platform again won the day.[67]

Most agricultural organizations were also pro-League. In February 1919, the National Board of Farm Organizations adopted a program calling for a special League of Nations body to deal with international agricultural questions, much like the ILO. The next month, after Wilson had been greeted on his brief return from Paris by senators demanding alterations to the League Covenant, five of the largest farmers' organizations pledged support for the president.[68] Again, in May, nearly two hundred agricultural organizations representing what the *New York Times* described as "an overwhelming majority" of the nation's twelve million farmers endorsed US entry into the League. In June, the Agricultural Press of the United States found that sixty-two of sixty-six leading farm journals concurred.[69]

Price volatility due to continued political chaos was a primary factor spurring farmers' support for the League of Nations. For similar reasons, major commercial and financial interests also supported League membership—global stability meant global markets and repayment of loans. The Chamber of Commerce of the United States publicly endorsed treaty ratification while spearheading the creation of an International Chamber open only to representatives of League members. Director and Boston department store mogul Edward A. Filene was among the most prominent League advocates in the United States, and the Chamber distributed pro-League literature in several US cities.[70] Bankers also lent support to the cause. Indeed, Senators Hiram Johnson of California and William Borah of Idaho repeatedly charged US banks with financing the League movement for their own selfish purposes, prompting an investigation by the Senate Foreign Relations Committee. After the treaty failed in March 1920, the American Bankers Association strongly endorsed League membership and sent a delegation to the International Chamber of Commerce in Paris to cooperate with the international business community to bring it about.[71] Civic boosters tended to support membership, too, on moral as well as economic grounds. Despite an "unwritten law" precluding public positions on divisive issues, for instance, the National Civic Federation staged nationwide educational meetings widely seen as pro-League due to the obvious sympathies of the organizers and speakers. The *Rotarian*, meanwhile, routinely published resolutions of support for League membership from local Rotary chapters.[72]

In fact, significant pockets of support for the League could be found in several places likely to surprise historians conditioned to view its defeat as a conservative cause. In September 1919, the head of the militaristic American Rights League endorsed the League of Nations, insisting that Teddy Roosevelt (who died earlier that year) would have wanted the United States to join. His organization followed suit in January 1920.[73] Throughout the League fight, several local and state chapters of the American Legion endorsed membership, including the New York, New Jersey, and Georgia Legions. In the heat of the 1920 campaign, the national head of the Legion, Frank D'Olier, gave his endorsement. Harking back to the purpose of the Legion's founding, he also called for the creation of an international veterans' organization under League auspices—not merely to secure veterans' benefits, but more importantly to unite war's firsthand witnesses in cooperative pursuit of "world peace."[74]

Perhaps most telling of the climate of opinion were the thousands of town meetings, city councils, and other local government bodies—including thirteen state legislatures in just the first four months of 1919—that petitioned

Congress or adopted resolutions in support of ratification.[75] Seventeen legislatures had passed similar resolutions before the peace conference, including in Lodge's home state, Massachusetts. Indeed, the cases of Massachusetts and California—the latter home to one of Wilson's fiercest "irreconcilable" opponents, Senator Hiram Johnson—illustrate just how disconnected from public opinion the Senate votes were. The vast majority of Lodge's constituents who signed their names to a position took the side of ratification and League membership, and in the wake of Lodge's Round Robin on reservations, the two houses of the Massachusetts legislature resolved concurrently in favor of a swift conclusion of peace and "establishment of a League of Nations."[76] In California, nearly every informed observer deemed the state pro-League—including Senator Johnson himself, who was willing to risk his career by defying the "eighty percent" of Californians he thought supported League membership in order to keep the nation out.[77]

None of this is to say there were not deep misgivings about the Treaty of Versailles and the League of Nations, or to argue that the postwar program Wilson helped construct was either entirely consistent or assured of success. Even before it failed the Senate, Wilson's League had been altered by the pressures of peacemaking at home and abroad, and the result fell far short of what he and other pragmatist progressives envisioned. Still, several of the latter agreed with the majority of Americans that significant steps in the right direction had been taken. Though "inevitably disappointed in the newly formed League," Jane Addams was nonetheless "eager to see what would happen when 'the United States came in!'"[78] W. E. B. Du Bois condemned the peacemakers' failure to dismantle colonialism, but he nonetheless considered the League "absolutely necessary to the salvation of the Negro race": It would provide a forum in which "the Negro nations" could talk sense into "the selfish nations of white civilization" before their outrages sparked a "Great War of Races."[79] Even Lippmann, a decade after the League fight, admitted, "If I had it to do over again, I would take the other side." In the 1950s, he was even more certain of his error in having "submitted" to Croly. "I knew more about the details of why the treaty was an unworkable treaty," he recalled, "but I would have accepted it, nevertheless, so that we could have joined the League."[80]

Years of reflection had arguably sharpened Lippmann's judgment but indisputably dimmed his memory; his opposition to ratification was just as adamant as Croly's in 1919 and 1920, and his faith in pragmatist political ethics as rudely shaken.[81] Still, rejecting a flawed League tied to a problematic treaty did not require discarding the ideas it imperfectly embodied. John Dewey opposed the Versailles settlement because it sanctioned "secret treaties and secret diplomacy," but he also believed its problems could only be solved by a "genuine League of Nations—one with some vigor."[82] As for America's postwar global role, the "national dilemma" Dewey identified was familiar to pragmatists: "isolation is impossible and participation perilous." The solution was equally familiar: craft policies reflecting the *reality* of circumstances without assuming their *finality*, and hope to make participation safer. With the German threat ended, there was no immediate reason to make "general commitments" to states that had sought victory over peace at Paris, and good reason to avoid "contamination through contact." Dewey, however, was not expounding a *doctrine* of disengagement, only a *policy*, to be altered as Europe democratized and Americans gained both "greater knowledge of foreign and international politics" and "sure means of popular control."[83]

Dewey's faith that American diplomacy might soon be driven by an educated, engaged public in firm control of its government went unrewarded, but it was not misplaced. The isolationist mood that gripped the nation in subsequent years has obscured the fact that in 1920, by all available measures, most Americans thought their government should play a constructive role in world affairs. Of course, reasonable people disagreed over the exact duties that role entailed, and Wilson's final failure was refusing to accept a compromise putting to the test those hypotheses he deemed inferior and presumably proving the need for bolder experiments. Under the unfavorable circumstances he had helped create, a compromise on membership with mild reservations was the best he could expect from powerful senators jealous of national sovereignty and institutional prerogatives. It was also the most plausible means of winning back skeptical pragmatists like Dewey, who embraced Wilson's ideal of international self-government but counseled caution until conditions for its realization improved. For pragmatism offers no universal answer to the general dilemma Wilson and Dewey faced: When to base action on conditions, and when to change conditions by action? Wilson argued ably that his plan changed certain deciduous conditions of international law to accord with the defining condition of international life: its interdependence. He refused, however, to accept an equally salient condition of democratic debate: namely, that some arguments carry, and some fail. Rather, in the heat of battle he chose defeat for his League and for the deliberative process it embodied, instead of a strategic compromise that might, eventually, have secured victory for both.

Contemporary commentators knew it was not the American people who squandered that victory. As the editor of *Searchlight*, the organ of the National Voters League, argued in October 1919, "public sentiment" was thwarted by "Big politics." The same editor, after the League's second de-feat, opined that Lodge had "many times" been on the verge of compro-mise, but each time "had his back stiffened rather unceremoniously" by certain "irreconcilables" positioned to threaten his leadership. The follow-ing month, however, the *Searchlight* placed the lion's share of blame on the president. "Without Wilson's unyielding opposition to reservations the whole question would have been settled long ago."[84]

Americans had reason to hope that the election of 1920 would finally settle the question—and bring their government into the League of Na-tions. Democrats had lost control of the issue, becoming the party of war and recession rather than peace and reconstruction, and Republicans pushed their advantage by endorsing membership—membership on qualified terms, but membership nonetheless. Their presidential candidate had twice taken that position in the Senate and shortly before his election pledged again his desire for American participation in "an association of nations." Because Harding's "association" would be "inspired by ideals of justice and fair deal-ing, rather than of power and self-interest," it would for that very reason advance a world order to "a great extent intertwined" with Wilson's best achievements at Paris. Europe's governments would surely welcome efforts to see the League "changed for the better," and Harding pledged, if elected, "to improve, to save and build upon whatever is good rather than to abandon the good there is and repudiate the world's aspirations for peace."[85] Though Harding's subsequent presidency saw a few weak gestures in that direction, his inaugural address foreshadowed the confusion and ultimate disappoint-ment that broadly defined his tenure: as the *New York Times* editorialized, his characterization of Republican victory as a referendum on "internation-ality" versus "nationality" was "an unhappy partisan left-over, grotesquely wide of the facts"—indeed, the speech itself contained as many paeans to the "new world order" as repudiations of "world super-government."[86] Harding even appointed pro-Leaguers to two of the four top foreign policy cabinet positions, naming the LEP's Charles Evans Hughes secretary of state and the pro-League Herbert Hoover secretary of commerce. When the administra-tion called an international conference on naval disarmament to Washing-ton in 1921, many League advocates took it as a first step toward American integration into some system of international governance.[87]

The nation's major peace groups and other large voluntary, civic, and pro-fessional organizations continued to lobby for League membership, while others pursued World Court membership or disarmament and free-trade pacts with League members—initiatives widely understood as opening wedges toward membership or, at minimum, de facto participation in the League.[88]

By the mid-1920s, however, it was clear that the Republican leadership was dominated by nationalists paying mere lip service to such Wilsonian gestures and dead set against any movement toward the League. Some, like Lodge, could not conceive of handing Democrats the prize for which they had sacrificed power, and through which they might regain it. Others were purer in their opposition to any and all limits on the nation's freedom of action. Meanwhile, returning prosperity, the League's early political successes, and—ironically—increasing US cooperation with its scientific and cultural activities combined to sap the sense of urgency from many who supported formal membership.[89] Rather than a babe strangled in the cradle, the living League that Wilson midwifed at Paris was more like a maimed and neglected child, deprived of the sustenance and security necessary to thrive and, ultimately, survive.

Power without Victory and the
Right to Believe

In 1901, William James responded with exasperation to a friendly critic—one of scores—who had misapprehended his most important idea. "It seems to me absurd to make a technical term of the 'Will to Believe,'" he wrote to James Mark Baldwin. "Would to God I had never thought of that unhappy title for my essay." Three years later, he complained that the essay "should have been called by the less unlucky title the *Right* to Believe." Few documents better express James's view of the complementary and even mutually constitutive character of right and obligation—the essential double helix of moral life. In choosing among visions of the good, whether from a private or public perspective, James deemed it "a necessity for individuals" to consider the possible as well as the proven, "because the total 'evidence,' which only the race can draw, has to include their experiments among its data." Of course belief per se could not create any reality an individual or community desired. But belief in specific possibilities, grounded but not mired in experience, could open doors "into a wider world" than the incomplete and partially comprehended version known to history. Given the modern "polemic" against the "dangers" of such belief, James's own polemic emphasized "the right to run their risk."[1]

The ten years between James's death in 1910 and Woodrow Wilson's political demise in 1920 showed just how risky the exercise of such a right can be. The pragmatist progressives' will to believe in a more democratic nation and deliberative world order did not make either of those things real, at least in the forms they initially envisioned. None of them was shaken more deeply by this fact than Wilson's erstwhile adviser and champion Walter Lippmann. On the eve of intervention, he believed that educated citizens, given adequate institutions and opportunities, were the best source of counsel for those called to govern them and steward their relations with the rest of humanity. By the close of peace negotiations at Paris, he was lamenting the failure of this ideal in every nation that had been party to the conflict. Over subsequent years, his disappointment sapped his will to believe it could ever succeed, even in the world's most advanced democracy. The vision of a citizenry comprising individuals "inherently competent to direct the course of public affairs" was a "false ideal," he wrote in *The Phantom Public* (1925). It was not "undesirable" but "unattainable," he explained, "bad only in the sense that it is bad for a fat man to try to be a ballet dancer." The tragedy of Lippmann's requiem for the "omnicompetent citizen" belied his arch tone. Its consequences reached beyond the pervasive American pretensions to horse sense, know-how, and enlightened self-interest to strike at the very foundations of democracy. For if it was false to believe that the private citizen could ever have "opinions on all public affairs," it was equally false to think "that the compounding of individual ignorances in masses of people can produce a continuous directing force in public affairs." Citizens for whom self-government ranked far below health, prosperity, and entertainment had little time to concern themselves with the process of policymaking. Rather, they could only look to their own condition, "support the Ins when things are going well," and "support the Outs when they seem to be going badly."[2]

With typical acuity, Lippmann isolated the central question facing democratic theory in a highly complex society: Is it possible for citizens to exercise a tolerable amount of control over their governments, with tolerable effects? None of his fellow pragmatists could escape it. Not even John Dewey could deny that the American public exhibited little awareness of its common affairs and exercised just as little control. But Dewey spied a flaw in Lippmann's argument that undermined his indictment of democratic participation in policymaking. Lippmann ignored the fact that the state in its current form was contingent on other social organizations: a diverse array of bodies animated by specific ideas, interacting in specific ways at specific times, to become a public. His theory of "democratic realism" naturalized the historical product of an outmoded political and economic system—the bewildered public—and in a neat tautology cited it as evidence in the case against changing that system. "The old saying that the cure for the ills of democracy is more democracy" did not mean that the cure was simply "introducing more machinery of the same kind as that which already exists," Dewey wrote in *The Public and Its Problems* (1927). Rather, it implied "the need of returning to the idea itself, of clarifying and deepening our sense of its meaning to criticize and re-make its political manifestations." A broken system did not prove its inevitability merely by its existence. It simply set the tasks of politics for the generation burdened with it. The first task was to imagine a new system, "by which a scattered, mobile and manifold public may so recognize itself as to define and express its interests"; the next was to test and perfect it until a "genuinely shared interest in the consequences of interdependent activities may inform desire and effort and thereby direct action."[3]

It is tempting to assume that the pulping of Wilson's global covenant of common counsel by the political system that most inspired it had cleared Lippmann's head, while leaving Dewey's as muddled as his prose. But in the fall of 1920—after the anti-German and antiradical orgies that disgusted him, after his disappointment over the Versailles treaty, after his government's arrogant and spiteful abstention from an international organization he nevertheless thought unworthy of his own massive efforts—Lippmann agreed with Dewey. As the League of Nations launched its career with the United States on the sidelines, Lippmann extolled the "happiness of creating, and of enhancing, of inventing, of exploring, of making—and finally, of drawing together the broken, suspicious, frightened, bewildered and huddling masses of men. To be excluded from that happiness," he continued, "is tragic as no suffering and no calamity are tragic. To exclude oneself because of embarrassment and timidity is pitiable forever. . . . It is to stumble through life without sharing in the beginning of knowledge that man can, if he wills it, become the master of his fate. . . . He need not forever drift helplessly," Lippmann concluded. "He can, if he will dedicate himself to the task in an inquiring and tolerable and reasonable spirit, go a very great way towards closing the gap between his experience and his ideals. For history, although almost every page is stained with blood and folly, is a record also, not perhaps of ideals realized, but of opportunities explored and conquered, by which ideals can ultimately be realized."[4]

When he wrote these words, Lippmann had already decided that neither Woodrow Wilson nor the scattered, primitive tribes of American liberalism had been inquiring and reasonable enough to "close the gap"—to explore and conquer the opportunities war had presented for bridging ideals and experience. What, then, gave him the right to believe that they might have been so inquiring and reasonable had they tried harder or with greater wisdom? What had he seen to suggest that others might be in future?

One thing Lippmann saw was a surge in humanity's erstwhile creeping awareness of its interdependence—an awareness enhanced by a localized conflict's unexpectedly global ramifications and the rapidly improving communications that brought their connections into high resolution. He also witnessed the powerful influence of public opinion on President Wilson's response to the challenges of domestic and global interdependence and the development of his thinking about the future structure of American and world politics. Finally, Lippmann watched the president exploit the sentiments, arguments, and consequences of interdependence to rally millions in the United States and around the world behind truly radical change—only to see him fail to explain what that change should (eventually) and would (initially) look like, then fail to put his personal ideals in perspective and embrace the best immediate outcome of a messy deliberative process.

Those failures were no more inevitable or total than the storied "failure" of the League of Nations, which despite American obstruction hobbled gamely along for its first decade of existence. Nevertheless, their consequences for American and world politics were and are severe, due in no small part to the myths of inevitability and totality surrounding them. For nearly a century, these myths have clouded the historical memory of Wilson, the war, and the League so completely that those who dare seek peace, order, and justice *among* nations through means resembling those that work *within* them labor on the borders of respectable opinion.

Perhaps the most pervasive myth is that regardless of Wilson's health (or character) and its impact on the outcome of the American treaty fight, the world's nations were just not ready at the Great War's end to relinquish enough of their sovereign independence to make an international security and governance organization effective—and if not ready then, likely never will be. At least in the case of the United States, this myth exists in a fantastical space created by the total historical erasure of the public's support for the League. Whether measured by editorial opinion; the assessments of religious leaders; the public stances of civic, professional, and trade organizations; or even the sentiments of the majority of the people's representatives in the body that sent it to defeat, opinion favoring some version of League membership significantly outweighed opinion opposing it. It was Wilson's obvious culpability for his government's failure to join the League that cost the Democrats control of the issue and helped sweep Republicans into office in 1920. Alert to this fact, the Republican leadership strained for several years to appear sympathetic to the League idea in some form. Peace groups and several large voluntary organizations continued to lobby for membership, while other mass organizations devised and demanded other arrangements to achieve the same practical effect. These persistent Wilsonians were not found only among the untutored, idealistic millions who identified with the nation's largest religious and peace organizations. They were represented across the spectrum of American trades and professions, including

politics and, notably, academia: throughout the 1920s, an apparent majority of American political scientists, international lawyers, and historians continued to view Wilson's original project as essentially valuable and
salvageable.[5]

That consensus was ultimately overturned by a revisionist challenge
that continues to shape the study and practice of US foreign policy. As the
war receded into memory and most Americans, both League supporters and
opponents, busied themselves with mundane concerns, an intellectual revolt shook the lettered classes. The release of official documents in the early
1920s enabled British and French critics to dissect their governments' prewar policies and establish their roles in provoking the war. These damning
works prompted a modest but influential number of American writers to
pose an uncomfortable set of questions. If the United States had not fought
solely on the side of good, why had it fought at all? And might it unknowingly have fought on the side of evil?[6] The war's unfinished economic business reinforced this suspicion and bred a creeping cynicism. The assignation
of total war guilt to Germany, and the consequent reparations demanded by
Britain and France, convinced several highly quotable liberals that Wilson
had been the tool of foreign imperialists and their American financiers. By
the early 1930s, with the world mired in economic depression, these cynics
saw the same transatlantic vampires calling for international cooperation
to rejuvenate the zombie system they had desiccated. As the world's most
visible site of such cooperation, the League evolved in their minds from a
failure to a danger—a ship skirting the edge of another violent maelstrom.[7]
And indeed, within a few years it was engulfed, leaving nothing for League
supporters to support. Thus commenced the transubstantiation of cynicism
into "realism."

The cynics were correct, strictly speaking, in predicting the League's
demise. Where they erred was in explaining it. Their problem was the same
one afflicting their so-called realist successors: their utter failure to grapple
with American absence from the League.[8] This failure is nothing short of
astounding given that for nearly two decades, from the League's debut at
Geneva to Hitler's appeasement at Munich, the relationship of the United
States to the international body it abandoned was possibly the single most
important issue in world politics, and undeniably implicated in every other
issue with claims to surpass it. It seems almost impossible that subsequent
generations of political scientists in the dominant tradition of international-
relations scholarship could ignore that an organization designed to include
every significant state in its deliberations and activities excluded the most
economically, culturally, and (initially) militarily powerful state the modern

world had seen. And yet the story that a structured, mutual subordination of the world's major states was *tried* by Wilson's generation, only to explode in humanity's face, remains central to most empirical cases for realism's central claim: namely, that the world's states form an inescapably anarchical system in which they usually act to enhance their relative material power, and always should.[9]

This is not to say that American participation would have guaranteed the venture's success. It is only to recall that especially in the crucial early years, when the norms of the fledgling regime required practical reinforcement, American abstention discouraged and thwarted them. Just two examples should suffice. First, Anglo–French cooperation in the League was premised on the credibility of its collective-security function, which once enhanced by the Anglo-Franco-American defense pact had elicited French acquiescence in Germany's rehabilitation. The US Senate's defeat of the Versailles treaty negated the tripartite pact, leaving Britain seeking a stable, wealthy Germany to revive Europe's economy and France seeking a prostrate, eunuch nation incapable of future aggression. Consequently Germany's financial, economic, and military status festered. Second, the American anomaly undermined the sanctions system critical to deterring and punishing aggression worldwide. Were a nation to face League sanctions, the United States would be in position to receive its trade, enriching the American economy while sustaining the aggressor. With the United States not only rejecting collective security but raising tariffs and refusing to renegotiate war debts, it is no surprise that sanctions were rarely imposed and even more rarely effective.[10]

Again, the fact that American abstention effectively aborted the League experiment designed at Paris cannot prove that a full and fair trial would have succeeded. Yet there is little controversy regarding the consequent problems of Anglo–French divergence and generalized sanction aversion. The first exacerbated the economic and social crises in Germany that helped bring Hitler to power. The second encouraged the course of appeasement that culminated in his unleashing hell on the world once again.

Granted, the internationalist experiment seemed to get its "second chance" after World War II—and the results have disappointed. When Japanese air forces bombed Pearl Harbor on December 7, 1941, the Wilsonian remnant suddenly regained its voice in American public discourse, and the popular image of Wilson shifted from clay-footed idol to unheeded prophet. From 1941, when the United States declared war on the Axis powers, to the end of 1943, when US President Franklin Delano Roosevelt, British Prime

Minister Winston Churchill, and Soviet Premier Josef Stalin first met together in Tehran, Iran, American postwar planning was directly shaped by
Wilsonians recruited by US Secretary of State Cordell Hull and Undersecre-
tary Sumner Welles. For a time, it appeared that the Wilsonian experiment
would get its fair trial.[11]

During this period, the State Department produced two blueprints for a
collective-security organization that would likely have made Wilson proud.
The first obligated all members to resolve disputes peacefully—if necessary,
through the organization's own mediating machinery. Failure to comply in
this process or with its outcome would be interpreted as intent to violate
international peace and automatically elicit any diplomatic, economic, or
military measures necessary to maintain or restore it. The second blueprint
retained these features while establishing the general membership's authority over regional organizations. To be sure, both plans catered to Roosevelt's
insistence on an outsize role for the United States, Great Britain, the Soviet
Union, and China—the "Four Policemen" he presumed would carry the
weight of global responsibilities. Still, both also restricted the policemen's
veto, barring its use in cases of threats to peace and thus compelling deployment of national forces should two-thirds of the Executive Council, including three of the four policemen, conclude on it.[12]

By 1945, this second chance for a Wilsonian peace had been wasted.
The architecture ultimately agreed on by the United States, the Soviet
Union, and Great Britain replaced the deliberative yet expedient schemes
just described with one granting each permanent member of an ironically
named "Security Council" an absolute veto over all substantive decisions,
including application and enforcement of sanctions. It is tempting to assume the veto was the price of great-power participation in any successor to
the League. Indeed Stalin, and more tactfully Churchill, presented obstacles
to a Wilsonian organization. But American anti-Wilsonians were equally
responsible for the now familiar constraints on the United Nations' political and peacekeeping functions. Roosevelt often seemed as skeptical as his
counterparts toward an organization hinging on the Wilsonian principle of
deliberation. When relations with the Soviets were warmest, he made no effort to establish its importance, assuming the alignment of interests and coordination of action achieved during wartime could be managed informally
in time of peace. Later he came to favor the veto, anxious to preserve total
control over deployment of US forces. Meanwhile, the dominant attitude
of Republican leaders had not changed much from the days of Henry Cabot
Lodge: prominent "internationalist" power brokers such as Senator Arthur
Vandenberg made support for US membership in a postwar organization

contingent on a veto. Hull, knowing Roosevelt's inclinations and recalling the League's defeat, arranged to stall congressional resolutions endorsing clear derogations of national sovereignty, even while urging Roosevelt to accept procedures permitting permanent Security Council members to refuse participation in enforcement actions without preventing them entirely.[13]

But Roosevelt was committed to great-power unanimity, and thus the privilege of great-power unilateralism—the antithesis of Wilsonian internationalism. Perhaps the dynamics of the US–Soviet relationship would have precluded another course. Regardless, if a new American consensus on international engagement had indeed emerged to shape the future of US foreign policy, it was not a Wilsonian consensus. Nor were conditions favorable for a Wilsonian peace. After Roosevelt's death in April 1945, his territorial concessions to Stalin—and the latter's intention to keep them—raised the specter of a communist Europe among Americans, while American nuclear diplomacy (which included Westminster and excluded the Kremlin) confirmed Stalin's fears of capitalist encirclement.[14] From the moment the charter of the United Nations Organization was ratified in October 1945, even its promising capacities in cultural diplomacy, world health, and disaster relief have been undermined by the competitive nationalism and political unilateralism it was intended to constrain.[15]

And yet, for many commentators, "Wilsonian" is the descriptor of choice for American foreign relations in the postwar era, and even the twentieth century as a whole.[16] Certainly, particular diplomatic initiatives evoking Wilson's internationalist efforts might be identified, but compiling a balance sheet of genuinely and speciously Wilsonian policies is a poor means to assess his place in historical memory. It is simpler—and more revealing—to consider just a few of the major policies under subsequent US presidents which have acquired the "Wilsonian" sobriquet. Harry S Truman's militarization and globalization of communist containment; Dwight D. Eisenhower's support of right-wing coups in the third world; John F. Kennedy's adventurism in Cuba; Lyndon B. Johnson's escalation of military involvement in southeast Asia; Ronald Reagan's reprise of Eisenhower's policies; George W. Bush's invasion of Iraq; all are routinely described as "Wilsonian," yet none involved or credibly advanced the multilateral resolution of disputes or cooperative pursuit of international goals. Each may share other features—good, bad, and ugly—with several of Wilson's policies, but unless every direct intervention by the United States in world affairs since 1776 is also to be labeled "Wilsonian," it is hard to see how these later policies deserve the name.

Like so much else, this eclipse of Wilson by "Wilsonianism" is partly explained by the brain-addling effects of the Cold War. Increasingly alarmed at the prospect of a worldwide, open-ended conflict with communism, realists constructed a narrative of American history in which idealism and moralism trumped prudent calculations of national interest, drawing parallels between Wilson—the last president to mobilize the nation against a distant rather than immediate threat—and the Cold Warriors of the 1950s. Almost simultaneously, a new band of "revisionist" historians adopted their predecessors' argument that the ultimate drivers of intervention in 1917 were commercial. Also alarmed by the Cold War, including their government's multiplying efforts to impose anticommmunist governments on postcolonial peoples, they constructed a narrative in which the quest for markets and resources consistently outweighed democratic scruples abroad and at home—a balance tipped further, in both cases, by racism.[17]

Meanwhile, the full consequences of Wilson's failure to distinguish his internationalist vision from the ethnonationalism preached by the Russian communist leader Vladimir Lenin were being felt throughout the global south. Disillusion with the Peace of Paris had inflamed anticolonial nationalism in the provinces of Europe's remaining empires. The half-built League of Nations was not the facilitator of negotiated reform and evolving autonomy that many African, Asian, and South Asian activists had hoped, and revolutionary independence movements gained momentum. As the French and British empires crumbled in the decades after 1945, a proliferation of purportedly ethnic yet empirically heterogeneous "self-determining" nation-states transformed the international order, tying the concepts of political freedom and autonomy more tightly than ever to that of sovereign independence.[18]

The persistent conflation of Wilson's politically integrative vision with these politically fissiparous developments finally brought it into full eclipse. It simultaneously reinforced the realist narrative of Wilson (builder of fancy sand castles) and the revisionist narrative of Wilson (Trojan horse of embattled empires)—both of which gained plausibility as Americans came to see their government's postwar interventionism as either aimless or misguided. In the writings of many historians the narratives merged, cementing the consensus on Wilson's wrongness, the League's hopelessness, and the ideological invulnerability of national sovereignty. Certainly few US policymakers, and even fewer of the hardheaded sorts who monopolize their counsel, give much thought to the possibility and potential benefits of pushing the international order toward a configuration, in Wilson's words, of "the American type—of governments joined with governments for the pursuit of common purposes, in honorary equality and honorable subordination."

In that sense Wilson's Wilsonianism has been an utter failure, and mostly forgotten.

The fate and implications of the American internationalist experiment cannot be understood apart from the nation's domestic politics and public philosophy, and specifically their deterioration.

Despite the increasingly obvious disjuncture between his campaign for democracy abroad and his tactics of repression at home, few distinguished Wilson the so-called internationalist from Wilson the so-called progressive when the Treaty of Versailles was signed. As one scholar notes, "In an emerging age of personal politics, the discrediting of Wilson meant the discrediting of progressivism." With a fledgling and still vulnerable institutional basis, and only the sullied banner of common counsel uniting the disparate interest groups it comprised, progressivism fragmented in the 1920s. Joining internationalism and progressivism in the boneyard of postwar American social thought was pragmatism, the perversion of which by behavioral psychologists, scientific managers, and advertising executives mirrored its steady decline in respectable intellectual circles and its near erasure from the field of professional philosophy.[19]

To be sure, progressivism, including the pragmatist strain that characterized so much of Wilson's policy, was not without its legacies. Franklin Roosevelt drew on the ideological and human resources Wilson had marshaled, as demonstrated by the massive enhancements of federal power, expansion of social programs, and proliferation of administrative instruments planned and staffed by former Wilsonians under the New Deal.[20] Like Wilson, Roosevelt insisted that modern economic conditions rendered political rights alone inadequate to guarantee the freedom of opportunity and basic level of economic security that a peaceful, prosperous, just society requires. Still, Roosevelt's heartier embrace of class and ethnic politics obscured the most important and powerful part of Wilson's political message: the pragmatist notion that personal freedom and social unity were mutually reinforcing ideals, achieved most effectively through the *civic* participation—creative, collaborative, self-disciplined and self-governing—of all society's members. During the 1930s, what remained of this spirit of civic democracy all but evaporated, even as some of the structural changes it inspired in Wilson's day—notably the shift in accountability from party machines to administrative bureaucracies—abetted the rise of a pluralist politics in which corporatized interest groups lobbied rather than deliberated, and competed rather than cooperated.[21]

The effects have been long-lasting. After decades of fiscal and social policy promoting the entrenchment of wealth and desiccation of public services, and after multiple undeclared, unfocused, unpopular wars breeding suffering and insecurity at home and abroad, Americans in significant numbers have only just begun, once again, to suspect that their personal freedoms and advantages depend on a culture in which everyone values and enjoys a basic level of social and economic equality, and a political system in which all have opportunity and incentive to invest. If the successes and failures of pragmatist progressivism tell us anything, it is that this trend, hindered as it is by countervailing forces, will have to be powerful and long-lasting if diversity and solidarity are again to become complementary forces for orderly change. It will also have to be channeled by responsible leaders who can promote radical progressive change without disdaining its incremental tasks and phases or demonizing its honest skeptics. Whether liberal or conservative, policies designed to make government the tool of the people will fail if the people are disinclined to order themselves as a community.[22]

The same is true for diplomacy. Putting the world on a path toward the kind of cooperative internationalism Wilson and his pragmatist supporters envisioned depends not on treaties and institutions alone but on a cultural shift—a shift that has yet to occur. This is not to deny the shift toward engagement, and even a fitful multilateralism, that the cumulative effects of the Depression and World War II initiated.[23] It is simply to assert that even in its multilateralist phases, the engagement of the post-1945 era is not the internationalism Wilson had in mind. Perhaps the opportunistic multilateralism that now passes for internationalism will prove a stage toward his more expansive and practical vision of a global community, governed like any other viable, complex society. But it could have been reached much earlier. The American people were ready for it. By no means were all Americans ready to embrace unreservedly the communal sovereignty of nations and peoples, nor did the League yet require it. But the majority were ready to begin a journey that led in that direction, through an organization designed to blaze the trail; and if Wilson thought a greater change in their view of themselves and their place in the world was imminent, he should have taken them that one step closer. Due to ill health or weakness of character, he decided instead that the shift must be complete, the ideal embraced with no further qualifications, if a new reality embodying it was ever to emerge. In this he forgot Edmund Burke's lesson, that it is not the leader's job to force a nation's will but to bend it, in directions in which it has power to grow. He forgot, too, what James's students tried to teach him (and which some forgot themselves at the end): that to wait for an ideal to realize itself is to consign it indefinitely to the realm of hypothesis, where long-term residence earns it the status of myth.

Wilson's ideal that the "liberty of the world" could survive and prosper if the "powers of all" would secure and promote it has for too long functioned as such a myth, imparting the moral that politics is and always will be solely a function of the will to power.[24] As a myth—a rationalization of the way things seem—it does not so much compel belief as prevent belief in anything different. Perhaps it is time to examine Wilson's internationalist vision once again as an ideal, in the pragmatist sense—a morally inspired but rigorously tested and contested plan for improving the world. Those saddened by the mythic status of a more egalitarian, cooperative world politics may or may not have the will to believe in the ideal: to weigh it against the others that define their culture, criticize and revise their conceptions of its benefits, and act to make the desirable possible. The history of American thought and politics during the era of William James and Woodrow Wilson does not tell us what today's Americans will believe and do, and it certainly does not tell us what their beliefs and doings will accomplish. Only the future can vindicate the will to believe in a more progressive democracy and constructive diplomacy. Still, the record of an era in which both ideals had begun to make real differences before they were abandoned should vindicate the right to believe in them—at least until it is proven that national cultures and the states that reflect them are frozen in their current pattern of relations.

ACKNOWLEDGMENTS

I began my journey with Woodrow Wilson and the pragmatist progressives more than a decade ago, while still a graduate student. It has now taken almost as long for me to trace the routes of their reciprocal influences and to characterize the stages—and consequences—of their tangled relationships as it took them to blaze the trails and set the markers in the first place. During that time my own path through the academy and the world has taken me through three academic and two nonacademic positions, four cities and towns, a marriage, a first book, and the birth of a child. At every stage, my work on this project was supported, tolerated, enriched, and advanced by countless colleagues, friends, and family members. Like the book they helped make possible, the following effort to thank them will no doubt fall short in many respects. But it remains the best I can do.

My academic mentors and colleagues have been many and magnificent. As members of my dissertation committee, Akira Iriye and Erez Manela supported my project with consistently sage advice despite its initially inadvisable scope. Jim Kloppenberg began as my committee chair and ended up a treasured friend. As I have stated elsewhere, Jim has not merely encouraged but propelled my pursuit of William James's psychological and philosophical ideas into the realms of politics and international affairs. To the benefit of my scholarly development and luckily for his scholarly reputation, his is a generative rather than replicative intellectual force. The same can be said for John Cooper, whose acknowledged status as dean of Wilson scholars and frank skepticism of a pragmatist connection never impeded but rather only abetted my efforts to disseminate and substantiate my heterodox interpretations. Tom Knock and Lloyd Ambrosius join him on the list of senior scholars whose works on Wilson, World War I, and the League of Nations proved indispensable to my own, and whose incisive but generous criticism improved this book immensely, regardless of appearances. This book would not carry the Chicago imprint, nor be worthy of it, if not for the efforts of Jona Hansen and David Hollinger, who recommended it; David Milne and, again, John Cooper, who reviewed it; and Liz Borgwardt, who was as zealous and effective a promoter as she was a reader of this project. For additional valuable contributions and for providing opportunities to receive them I also thank the following friends and fellow scholars: James Axtell, Brooke Blower, Bob Bonner, Angus Burgin, Leslie Butler, Chris Capozzola, Charlie Capper, Frank Costigliola, Nancy Cott, Evan Dawley, Ted Delaney, Ron Edsforth, David Engerman, Adam Ewing, Niall Ferguson, Elizabeth Hoffman, Daniel Immerwahr, Julia Irwin, Sam Jacobs, Andy Jewett, Andrew Johnstone, Chris Jones, Amy Kittelstrom, Ruth Mandel, the late Ernest May, Phil Mead, Chris Nichols, Richard Pells, David Redlawsk, Emma Rothschild, Daniel Sargent, Sam Schaffer, Moshik Temkin, Dan Wewers, Ann Wilson, Chris Wohlforth, and Bill Wohlforth.

Several institutions and their staff members made this project possible through generous gifts of time, money, and expertise. Harvard University and the Harvard History Department provided financial support and a stimulating community of inquiry for six years of graduate school and another four as a faculty member. The John Sloan Dickey Center at Dartmouth College, along with Dartmouth's History and Government departments, provided support for some of the research behind this project as well an intellectual home for a fondly remembered year. For practical assistance I am grateful to the staffs of the Houghton, Langdell, and Schlesinger Libraries at Harvard; the Mudd Manuscript Library at Princeton University; the Library of Congress; the National Archives (I); the New York Public Library; the Presbyterian Historical Society; and the special collections departments of the Carleton College, Columbia University, Rutgers University, Stanford University, and University of Chicago library systems. For financial as well as logistical support I am grateful to the American Catholic History Center, American Jewish Archives, Hagley Museum and Library, Huntington Library, and Rockefeller Archive Center. I also received generous funding for my research from the Charles Warren Center and the Center for American Political Studies at Harvard University; the Eagleton Institute of Politics at Rutgers University; the George C. Marshall Foundation; and the Society for Historians of American Foreign Relations. Finally, I am fortunate to have worked with the University of Chicago Press, where I have been treated by every employee and affiliate with delectable professionalism: sweetened by patience and unadulterated by pedantry. Special thanks are due to Robert Devens, who launched this project, and Tim Mennel, who saw it through.

Before I left teaching I used to tell my students that historical research is an exercise in wish fulfillment that depends for success on adaptable wishes: you start out looking for something and, if you're lucky and careful, find something else that makes more sense. Such has been the case for this book and such has been the case for the life of its author. I did not seek to leave academia. Yet I find myself thriving in a different profession while maintaining my scholarly agenda and identity. I am grateful to Mari Carlson at Mount Olivet Lutheran Church and especially to Dean Jean Quam, Lynn Slifer, and my colleagues at the University of Minnesota College of Education and Human Development for opening new doors without closing others. I did not seek to move back to the Twin Cities, either, but I find it once again feels like home. I thank all the friends—old and new, here and across the country—who have helped me adjust and flourish. They are too many to list; if you suspect you are one of them, you are. Above all I thank my family, which has grown in size and importance since I began this book. My parents, Mark and Carol, are moral anchors and inspirations, and the source of much of what this book contains and represents. My brother Trevor is my best friend and (often) my wisest counselor, and Polly and Charlie are ever brightening lights in my life. The same is true for the generous, compassionate, still growing, and forever entertaining family I legally acquired when making the one decision that undermines my general doctrine of fallibilism: namely, marrying my wife Kate. Kate's support, advice, and gentle reminders of what really matters in life helped bring this book to completion, and on more than one occasion helped prevent its author from collapsing. Her love and friendship are almost as valuable to me as the care, education, and example she provides for our son Peter, who is the most important person in the world to me and the most wonderful I have ever known. As I write this I am eager to meet his only conceivable equal: another boy who is already proving my adage about wish fulfillment. Louis, you will enter this world and our lives facing, and bringing, unexpected challenges. But those challenges are not unwelcome. They are exactly those that will make you, and us, the only people it will ever make sense for us to be. For that reason this book is dedicated to you.

ABBREVIATIONS OF NAMES AND
SOURCES USED IN THE NOTES

CER	William James. *Collected Essays and Reviews*, edited by Ralph Barton Perry. New York: Longmans, Green, 1920.
CWJ	*The Correspondence of William James*, edited by Ignas K. Skrupskelis and Elizabeth M. Berkeley. 12 vols. Charlottesville: University Press of Virginia, 1992–2004.
EMH	Edward Mandell House
EMHmss	Edward Mandell House Papers, Yale University, New Haven, CT.
FF	Felix Frankfurter
FFmss	Felix Frankfurter Papers, Library of Congress, Washington, DC—microfilm.
FRUS	*Papers Relating to the Foreign Relations of the United States*
HC	Herbert Croly
IDNA	Inquiry Documents (Special Reports and Studies), RG 256.2, National Archives, College Park, MD—microfilm M-1107.
JA	Jane Addams
JAmss	Jane Addams Papers, Swarthmore College, Swarthmore, PA.
JD	John Dewey
JPT	Joseph Patrick Tumulty
LDB	Louis Dembitz Brandeis
LDBmss	Louis Dembitz Brandeis Papers, University of Louisville, Louisville, KY—microfilm.
MW	*The Middle Works of John Dewey, 1899–1924*, edited by Jo Ann Boydston et al. 15 vols. Carbondale: University of Southern Illinois Press, 1976–83.
NDB	Newton Diehl Baker
NR	*New Republic*

NYT	*New York Times*
PWW	*The Papers of Woodrow Wilson*, edited by Arthur S. Link et al. 69 vols. Princeton, NJ: Princeton University Press, 1966–94.
RB	Randolph Bourne
RBmss	Randolph Bourne Papers, Columbia University, New York, NY.
RSB	Ray Stannard Baker
RSBmss	Ray Stannard Baker Papers, Library of Congress, Washington, DC—microfilm.
TV	Thorstein Veblen
UP	University Press
WB	William James. *The Will to Believe, and Other Essays in Popular Philosophy*. New York: Longmans, Green, 1897.
WEBD	W. E. B. Du Bois
WEBDmss	W. E. B. Du Bois Papers, University of Massachusetts–Amherst, Amherst, MA—microfilm.
WJ	William James
WJmss	William James Papers, Harvard University, Cambridge, MA.
WL	Walter Lippmann
WLmss	Walter Lippmann Papers, Yale University, New Haven, CT.
WW	Woodrow Wilson
WWLLC	Woodrow Wilson Library, Library of Congress, Washington, DC.
WWmss	Woodrow Wilson Papers, Library of Congress, Washington, DC—microfilm.

INTRODUCTION

1. WEBD, "An Open Letter to Woodrow Wilson," *Crisis* 5 (March 1913): 236–37.

2. WEBD, "The League of Nations," *Crisis* 18 (May 1919): 10–11.

3. "The International Congress of Women," *Searchlight* 4 (August 1919): 22–24.

4. Ibid.

5. JA, "Patriotism and Pacifists in War Time," *City Club Bulletin* 10 (June 16, 1917): 184–90, esp. 187; JA, *Peace and Bread in Time of War* (New York: Macmillan, 1922), 189. See also JA, "Feed the World and Save the League," *NR* 24 (November 24, 1920): 325–27; JA, "The Potential Advantages of the Mandate System," *Annals of the American Academy of Political and Social Science* 96 (July 1921): 70–74; JA, "Why the League Limps," *Christian Century* 39 (January 19, 1922): 72–74.

6. Paul Kennedy, *The Parliament of Man: The Past, Present, and Future of the United Nations* (New York: Random House, 2006), 27. On the UN's antidemocratic structure and operation, see Robert Keohane, *After Hegemony: Cooperation and Discord in the World Political Economy* (Princeton, NJ: Princeton UP, 1984); John G. Ruggie, *Winning the Peace: America and World Order in the New Era* (New York: Columbia UP, 1996); Ian Johnstone, "Legislation and Adjudication in the UN Security Council: Bringing Down the Deliberative Deficit," *American Journal of International Law* 102 (April 2008): 275–308.

7. Henry Cabot Lodge to Vance C. McCormick, November 13, 1920, Henry Cabot Lodge Papers, Massachusetts Historical Society (microfilm), reel 67.

8. Wilson's best-known biographer, Arthur S. Link, was frequently kind to his subject, notably in *Wilson: Campaigns for Progressivism and Peace* (Princeton, NJ: Princeton UP, 1965); and *Woodrow Wilson: Revolution, War, and Peace* (Wheeling, IL: Harlan-Davidson, 1979). More recently others have discovered much of merit in Wilson's thought and policies: Thomas J. Knock, *To End All Wars: Woodrow Wilson and the Quest for a New World Order* (New York: Oxford UP, 1992); Erez Manela, *The Wilsonian Moment: Self-Determination and the International Origins of Anticolonial Nationalism* (New York: Oxford UP, 2007); John Milton Cooper Jr., *Woodrow Wilson: A Biography* (New York: Knopf, 2009). Studies emphasizing Wilson's conservatism and/or chauvinism

include Richard Hofstadter, *The American Political Tradition and the Men Who Made It* (New York: Knopf, 1948); Eldon J. Eisenach, *The Lost Promise of Progressivism* (Lawrence: UP of Kansas, 1994); and Stephen Skowronek, "The Reassociation of Ideas and Purposes: Racism, Liberalism, and the American Political Tradition," *American Political Science Review* 100 (August 2006): 385–401. Critiques of Wilson's diplomatic naïveté include Roland N. Stromberg, *Collective Security and American Foreign Policy: From the League of Nations to NATO* (New York: Praeger, 1963); Lloyd E. Ambrosius, *Wilsonian Statecraft: Theory and Practice of Liberal Internationalism during World War I* (Wilmington, DE: SR, 1991); and Ross A. Kennedy, *The Will to Believe: Woodrow Wilson, World War I, and America's Strategy for Peace and Security* (Kent, OH: Kent State UP, 2009). Works stressing Wilson's imperialism include William Appleman Williams, *The Tragedy of American Diplomacy* (New York: Dell, 1959); Lloyd Gardner, *A Covenant with Power: America and World Order from Wilson to Reagan* (New York: Oxford UP, 1984); and Joan Hoff, *A Faustian Foreign Policy from Woodrow Wilson to George W. Bush: Dreams of Perfectibility* (Cambridge: Cambridge UP, 2008).

9. WW address to Congress, April 2, 1917, *PWW*, 41:526–27.

10. George F. Kennan, *American Diplomacy* (1951; repr., Chicago: University of Chicago Press, 1984), 68–74. On realist assessments of American public opinion and international affairs, see Oli R. Holsti, "Public Opinion and Foreign Policy: Challenges to the Almond-Lippmann Consensus," *International Studies Quarterly* 36 (1992): 439–66.

11. See John J. Mearsheimer, "The False Promise of International Institutions," *International Security* 19 (Winter 1994–95): 5–49. Challenging the theory that narrow security and economic interests explain the course of twentieth-century American foreign policy is John A. Thompson, *A Sense of Power: The Roots of America's Global Role* (Ithaca, NY: Cornell UP, 2015).

12. John Lewis Gaddis, *Surprise, Security, and the American Experience* (Cambridge, MA: Harvard UP, 2004), 43, 53.

13. Cordell Hull memorandum, May 2, 1944, Cordell Hull Papers, Library of Congress, Washington, DC (microfilm), reel 52. Senator Guy M. Gillette (D-IA) recalled of UN planning efforts, "everyone was convinced that we could not get anything through the United States Senate that did not maintain for the United States a veto power." *Review of the United Nations Charter: Hearing before a Subcommittee of the Committee on Foreign Relations, United States Senate, Eighty-Third Congress, Second Session, Part 2, February 12, 1954* (Washington, DC: GPO, 1954), 280.

14. Stanley Hoffmann, *Gulliver's Troubles; or, the Setting of American Foreign Policy* (New York: McGraw-Hill, 1968).

15. G. John Ikenberry, "Woodrow Wilson, the Bush Administration, and the Future of Liberal Internationalism," in *The Crisis of American Foreign Policy: Wilsonianism in the Twenty-first Century*, by G. John Ikenberry, Thomas J. Knock, Anne-Marie Slaughter, and Tony Smith (Princeton, NJ: Princeton UP, 2009), 1–24, esp. 15. George C. Herring's contribution to the Oxford History of the United States similarly concludes: "Americans were simply not ready to undertake the huge break from tradition and assume the sort of commitments asked of them." *From Colony to Superpower: U.S. Foreign Relations since 1776* (New York: Oxford UP, 2008), 434.

16. Cf. Adam Tooze, *The Deluge: The Great War and the Remaking of Global Order*

(London: Penguin, 2015), arguing that the United States had the power and influence to sustain a League-centered order but lacked popular or elite support.

17. *American Legion Weekly* 1 (November 14, 1919): 12.

18. George Scott, *The Rise and Fall of the League of Nations* (London: Hutchinson, 1973); Elmer Bendiner, *A Time for Angels: The Tragicomic History of the League of Nations* (New York: Knopf, 1975); F. S. Northedge, *The League of Nations: Its Life and Times, 1920–1946* (Leicester: Leicester UP, 1986); Sally Marks, *The Illusion of Peace: International Relations in Europe, 1918–1933*, 2nd ed. (Basingstoke: Palgrave, 2003). A masterly review of efforts to recover the League's successes as well as failures is Susan Pedersen, "Back to the League of Nations," *American Historical Review* 112 (October 2007): 1091–1117.

19. WJ, *Pragmatism: A New Name for Some Old Ways of Thinking* (New York: Longman's, Green, 1907), 80.

20. WJ, "The Will to Believe" (1896), in *WB*, 1–31.

21. WJ, "The Moral Philosopher and the Moral Life" (1891), in *WB*, 198, 184.

22. Most mid twentieth-century studies of progressivism defined it as an attempt by one social group or another to maintain or advance its material and cultural interests. Others claimed there was no progressive "movement," merely a swarming succession of issue-oriented alliances. In 1982, Daniel T. Rodgers described progressivism as a series of shared "languages" defining the limits of political discourse. Subsequent overviews have interwoven earlier narratives without taking clear interpretive stances. Peter G. Filene, "An Obituary for the Progressive Movement," *American Quarterly* 22 (Spring 1970): 20–34; Daniel T. Rodgers, "In Search of Progressivism," *Reviews in American History* 10 (December 1982): 113–32; Michael McGerr, *A Fierce Discontent: The Rise and Fall of the Progressive Movement, 1870–1920* (New York: Oxford UP, 2003.

23. JA, "Pragmatism in Politics," *Survey* 29 (October 1912), 11–12, quoted at 12.

24. WW inaugural address, March 5, 1917, *PWW* 41:334.

25. This characterization draws on Robert Jackson and Georg Sørensen, *Introduction to International Relations: Theories and Approaches*, 3rd ed. (Oxford: Oxford UP, 2007), 66.

26. Examples include Ernst B. Haas, *Beyond the Nation-State: Functionalism and International Organization* (Stanford, CA: Stanford UP, 1964); Robert O. Keohane and Joseph S. Nye, *Power and Interdependence: World Politics in Transition* (Boston: Little, Brown, 1977); Robert O. Keohane and Lisa L. Martin, "The Promise of Institutionalist Theory," *International Security* 20 (Summer 1995): 39–51; and G. John Ikenberry, *After Victory: Institutions, Strategic Restraint, and the Rebuilding of Order after Major Wars* (Princeton, NJ: Princeton UP, 2001).

27. Alexander Wendt, "Anarchy Is What States Make of It: The Social Construction of Power Politics," *International Organization* 46 (Spring 1992): 391–425. See also Andrew Moravscik, "Taking Preferences Seriously: A Liberal Theory of International Politics," *International Organization* 51 (Autumn 1997): 513–53. Pitched as an alternative to positivism and constructivism, Moravscik's "new liberal theory" is more a refinement of constructivism urging greater attention to internal, "state-society" factors (versus external, "state-state" interactions) shaping policymakers' worldviews and goals.

28. On pragmatism as corrective to academic tribalism, see Jörg Friedrichs and Friedrich Kratochwil, "On Acting and Knowing: How Pragmatism Can Advance International

Relations Research and Methodology," *International Organization* 63 (Fall 2009): 701–31. The exploratory collections edited by Harry Bauer and Elisabetta Brighi, *Pragmatism in International Relations* (London: Routledge, 2009) and Shane J. Ralston, *Pragmatism and International Relations: Essays for a Bold New World* (Plymouth, UK: Lexington, 2013) contain stimulating applications of pragmatist epistemology and ethics to real-world problems, but a generalizable attitude toward international affairs remains elusive. Shiping Tang's recent case for a "social evolutionary paradigm" (SEP) of international-relations theory echoes James's historicist analysis of social institutions but arbitrarily privileges material over ideational factors in explaining them. Moreover, SEP offers no normative or predictive guidance other than to assert that no future theory can supersede it. Shiping Tang, *The Social Evolution of International Politics* (Oxford: Oxford UP, 2013).

29. WW address in Pueblo, CO, September 25, 1919, *PWW* 63:500–513, esp. 503, 513.

CHAPTER ONE

1. JD, "William James" (1910), *MW* 6:92; WL to Graham Wallas, October 30, 1912, WLmss. For a survey of major interpretations of James's ethics, analysis of its elements, and discussion of its implications for political theory and history, see Trygve Throntveit, *William James and the Quest for an Ethical Republic* (New York: Palgrave, 2014). Among relatively few comparable treatments, see Ralph Barton Perry, *The Thought and Character of William James*, 2 vols. (Boston: Little, Brown, 1935), 2:250–322; James T. Kloppenberg, *Uncertain Victory: Social Democracy and Progressivism in European and American Thought, 1870–1920* (New York: Oxford UP, 1986), chaps. 4–5; George Cotkin, *William James, Public Philosopher* (Urbana: University of Illinois Press, 1994).

2. WL, *A Preface to Politics* (New York: Mitchell Kennerley, 1913), 114.

3. WJ to Henry James Jr., May 4, 1907, *CWJ* 3:339.

4. On the development and complexities of these doctrines, see Throntveit, *Quest for an Ethical Republic*, chaps. 1–2.

5. WJ, "Does Consciousness Exist?" (1904), in *Essays in Radical Empiricism*, ed. Ralph Barton Perry (New York: Longmans, Green, 1912), 37; WJ, *Pragmatism*, 201 (see intro., n. 19). On Peirce and James, see Perry, *Thought and Character* 1:533–42 and 2:221–24; Hilary Putnam, "James's Theory of Truth," in *The Cambridge Companion to William James*, ed. Ruth Anna Putnam (Cambridge: Cambridge UP, 1997), 166–85; Louis Menand, *The Metaphysical Club: A Story of Ideas in America* (New York: Farrar, Straus and Giroux, 2001), 226–30, 347–58.

6. WJ, *The Meaning of Truth: A Sequel to Pragmatism* (New York: Longmans, Green, 1909), 218; WJ, "The Will to Believe," (1896), *WB*, 30.

7. On the memory and psychological effects of the Civil War, see David W. Blight, *Race and Reunion: The Civil War in American Memory* (Cambridge, MA: Harvard UP, 2001); and Drew Gilpin Faust, *This Republic of Suffering: Death and the American Civil War* (New York: Knopf, 2008). On the disorienting economic, social, and cultural changes toward the nineteenth century's end, see Alan Trachtenberg, *The Incorporation of America: Culture and Society in the Gilded Age* (New York: Hill and Wang, 1982).

8. Herbert Spencer, "A Theory of Population, Deduced from the General Law of Animal Fertility," *Westminster Review* 57 (1852): 468–501, esp. 499–500. On Spencer's

American "vogue," see Richard Hofstadter, *Social Darwinism in American Thought* (Philadelphia: University of Pennsylvania Press, 1944), chaps. 1–3 and 5. The narrative of a coherent "social-Darwinist" movement inspired by Spencer is challenged in Robert C. Bannister, *Social Darwinism: Science and Myth in Anglo-American Social Thought* (Philadelphia: Temple UP, 1979).

9. James's depressive youth is recounted in Linda Simon, *Genuine Reality: A Life of William James* (New York: Harcourt Brace, 1998), chaps. 5–6; and Robert D. Richardson, *William James in the Maelstrom of American Modernism* (Boston: Houghton Mifflin, 2006), chaps. 11–12, 17.

10. Even John Stuart Mill, James thought, failed to expunge these hedonistic and associationist premises from his liberal theory of self-development. For James's early reactions to British empiricism, see Perry, *Thought and Character*, 1:543–72. On Mill's "higher utilitarianism," see Henry R. West, *An Introduction to Mill's Utilitarian Ethics* (Cambridge: Cambridge UP, 2004).

11. Josiah Royce, *The Religious Aspect of Philosophy: A Critique of the Bases of Conduct and Faith* (Boston: Houghton Mifflin, 1885). For James's struggles with and against idealist and rationalist metaphysics, see Perry, *Thought and Character*, 1:573–85, 711–30, 797–824; James B. Conant, "The James/Royce Dispute and the Development of James's 'Solution,'" in R. A. Putnam, *Cambridge Companion to William James*, 186–213; Thomas Carlson, "James and the Kantian Tradition," in R. A. Putnam, *Cambridge Companion to William James*, 363–83.

12. WJ, "On Some Hegelisms" (1880), *WB*, 263–98, esp. 279.

13. WJ diary entries, February 1 and April 30, 1870, WJmss (4550). As of the April entry, James had just read Charles Renouvier's *Essais de critique générale* (Paris: Librairie Philosophique de Ladrange, 1854).

14. WJ, *The Principles of Psychology*, 2 vols. (New York: Henry Holt, 1890), 2:566 (emphasis added).

15. WJ, "Philosophical Conceptions and Practical Results" (1898), *CER*, 406–37, esp. 411–12.

16. WJ, *Pragmatism*, 224–25.

17. Ibid., 257.

18. WJ, "Will to Believe," esp. 2–3, 25–29. Compare WJ, *The Varieties of Religious Experience: A Study in Human Nature* (New York: Longmans, Green, 1902), 475–516.

19. WJ, "Will to Believe," 90.

20. WJ, "The Moral Philosopher and the Moral Life" (1891), *WB*, 184–215, esp. 186–87; see also Throntveit, *Quest for an Ethical Republic*, 87–92.

21. WJ, "Moral Philosopher," 198.

22. Ibid. 184.

23. WJ, "What Makes a Life Significant" (1898), *Talks to Teachers on Psychology; and to Students on Some of Life's Ideals* (New York: Henry Holt, 1899), 293–97 ("social self"); WJ, *Principles of Psychology*, 1:293–96; WJ, *Meaning of Truth*, 218 ("social experience"). The dialectic of freedom and unity in James's thinking is central to John K. Roth's *Freedom and the Moral Life: The Ethics of William James* (Philadelphia: Westminster, 1969).

24. WJ, "Moral Philosopher," 184.

25. Ibid. 206, 208–9.

26. WJ, *Principles*, 2:672–74.

27. WJ, "On a Certain Blindness in Human Beings" (1899), *Talks to Teachers*, esp. 240–45.

28. WJ, "Moral Philosopher," 210. On the generic human capacity for the strenuous mood, see WJ, *Principles*, 2:679; WJ, "Is Life Worth Living?" (1896), *WB*, esp. 51, 54–56.

29. WJ, "Moral Philosopher," 205. See also Gerald E. Myers, *William James: His Life and Thought* (New Haven: Yale UP, 1986). Myers (398–99) argues that James's goal of maximum individual satisfaction destroys the "alleged sciencelike progress" of humanity's "ethical experiment" through interminable subjective "checks." Yet James never envisioned a moral experiment with "predefined aims" progressing toward final "moral order." The individual checks ostensibly derailing the experiment are instead inescapable aspects of experience and vital tests of morality's relevance to it.

30. James's long-neglected political ideas are now the subject of a growing philosophical and political-theory literature, including Joshua I. Miller, *Democratic Temperament: The Legacy of William James* (Lawrence: UP of Kansas, 1997); Andrew F. Smith, "Communication and Conviction: A Jamesian Contribution to Deliberative Democracy," *Journal of Speculative Philosophy* 21, no. 4 (2007): 259–74; Kennan Ferguson, *William James: Politics in the Pluriverse* (Lanham, MD: Rowman and Littlefield, 2007); and Colin Koopman, *Pragmatism as Transition: Historicity and Hope in James, Dewey, and Rorty* (New York: Columbia UP, 2009). Intellectual historians recognizing the political implications of James's pragmatism include Perry, *Thought and Character*; Kloppenberg, *Uncertain Victory*; Cotkin, *William James, Public Philosopher*; and Throntveit, *Quest for an Ethical Republic*; see also James Livingston, *Pragmatism and the Political Economy of Cultural Revolution, 1850–1940* (Chapel Hill: University of North Carolina Press, 1994); Jonathan M. Hansen, *The Lost Promise of Patriotism: Debating American Identity, 1890–1920* (Chicago: University of Chicago Press, 2003); and Christopher McKnight Nichols, *Promise and Peril: America at the Dawn of a Global Age* (Cambridge, MA: Harvard UP, 2011). It is now hard to state credibly that James's philosophy is apolitical or, as Cornel West described it, a philosophy of "political impotence." Cornel West, *The American Evasion of Philosophy: A Genealogy of Pragmatism* (Madison: University of Wisconsin Press, 1989), 60.

31. There is substantial evidence that James did accord demonstrated efficacy to certain elements of democratic infrastructure, including broadly representative government, social equality, rule of law, an educated citizenry, and the opportunity and elevation of citizen service to the national community (Throntveit, *Quest for an Ethical Republic*, 128–36).

32. WJ to Sarah Wyman Whitman, June 7, 1899, *CWJ*, 8:546; WJ to William M. Salter, September 11, 1899, *CWJ*, 9:41; WJ, "The Moral Equivalent of War" (1910), in *Memories and Studies*, ed. Henry James Jr. (New York: Longmans, Green, 1911), 285, 286.

33. WJ to Pauline Goldmark, January 30, 1903, *CWJ*, 10:191. Contrast Deborah J. Coon, "'One Moment in the World's Salvation': Anarchism and the Radicalization of William James," *Journal of American History* 83 (June 1996): 70–99.

34. WJ to William Dean Howells, November 16, 1900, *CWJ*, 9:362.

35. WJ to Grace Norton, July 6, 1900, *CWJ*, 9:249–250; WJ to Henry Pickering Bowditch, November 12, 1900, *CWJ*, 9: 357; WJ to Katharine Sands Godkin, March 14, 1902, *CWJ*, 10:12.

36. WJ, "Great Men and Their Environment" (1880), *WB*, 216–54; WJ, "The Social Value of the College Bred" (1907), in *Memories and Studies*, 313, 318–19, 320, 323; WJ, *Pragmatism*, 38.

37. Menand, *Metaphysical Club*, 372.

38. WJ to Carl Stumpf, August 6, 1901, *CWJ*, 9:526; WJ, loose leaf in ca. 1901 notebook, WJmss (4476).

39. WJ quoted in Perry, *Thought and Character*, 2:383 (emphasis in original).

40. WJ, "Ethics Course, 1888–89," WJmss (4427).

41. WJ, "Moral Philosopher," 202–3, 205 (emphasis in original).

42. Ibid., 188, 206.

43. WJ to Ralph Barton Perry, July 17, 1909, *CWJ*, 12:291.

44. WJ, "Robert Gould Shaw" (1897), in *Memories and Studies*, 39–40, 42–43.

45. Ibid., 45.

46. Ibid., 41–42 (quotations reversed).

47. Ibid., 46–55, esp. 54.

48. Ibid., 40–41, 46–50, 54, 57–58.

49. Ibid., 57, 60–61.

50. WJ, "Moral Philosopher," 206.

51. WJ to E. L. Godkin, December 24, 1895, *CWJ*, 8:109; WJ to Josephine Shaw Lowell, December 6, 1903, *CWJ*, 10:339.

52. WJ, "What Makes a Life Significant," 298–99. For detailed discussions of James's political interventions and activism, see Throntveit, *Quest for an Ethical Republic*, chap. 4.

53. James's immediate and lasting influences on American social thought and reform are surveyed in James T. Kloppenberg, "James's Pragmatism and American Culture, 1907–2007," in John J. Stuhr, ed., *100 Years of Pragmatism: William James's Revolutionary Philosophy* (Bloomington: University of Indiana Press, 2010), 7–40.

54. See JD to WJ, May 10, 1891 and June 3, 1903, in Perry, *Thought and Character*, 2:517, 520; also JD, "From Absolutism to Experimentalism" (1930), *The Later Works of John Dewey, 1925–1953*, ed. Jo Ann Boydston et al., 17 vols. (Carbondale: Southern Illinois UP, 1981–90), 5:157–58. Dewey had his quibbles over James's conception of truth; see Robert B. Westbrook, *John Dewey and American Democracy* (Ithaca, NY: Cornell UP, 1991), 130–32.

55. JD, "The Need for a Recovery of Philosophy" (1917), *MW*, 10:46; JD, "A Short Catechism Concerning Truth" (1909), *MW*, 6:3–5; JD, "The Problem of Truth" (1911), *MW*, 6:31.

56. JD, "Intelligence and Morals" (1908), *MW*, 4:39, 44, 45; JD and James H. Tufts, *Ethics* (1908), *MW*, 5:277, 292 (James cited at 85).

57. JD and Tufts, *Ethics*, *MW*, 5:276. See Westbrook's excellent overview of Dewey's educational writings and activities from the mid-1890s to the early 1900s in *Dewey and American Democracy*, 93–113.

58. JD, *Democracy and Education* (1916), *MW*, 9:90–93, 128–29.

59. Brandeis's interest in James's pragmatism is noted in Philippa Strum, *Louis D. Brandeis: Justice for the People* (Cambridge, MA: Harvard UP, 1984), 45, 417; and Melvin I. Urofsky, *Louis D. Brandeis: A Life* (New York: Pantheon, 2009), 109. For evidence of

the James–Brandeis relationship, see Alice Howe Gibbens James to WJ, January 1, 1883, *CWJ*, 5:372; WJ to Elizabeth G. Evans, July 29, 1897, and to Pauline Goldmark (Brandeis's sister-in-law), April 18, 1899, *CWJ*, 8:288, 515; WJ to Goldmark, November 17, 1903 and June 30, 1904, *CWJ*, 10:330, 426; WJ to Alice Howe Gibbens James, August 30, 1906, and to Margaret Mary James, September 1, 1906, *CWJ*, 11:263–64; Elizabeth G. Evans, "Memoir," typescript, Folder 1, and correspondence of Elizabeth G. Evans and LDB, 1886–1934, Folder 37, both in Elizabeth Glendower Evans Papers, Schlesinger Memorial Library, Harvard University, Cambridge, MA; Allon Gal, *Brandeis of Boston* (Cambridge, MA: Harvard UP, 1980), 10, 60–61, 150.

60. LDB, "True Americanism," (1915), in Solomon Goldman, ed., *Brandeis on Zionism: A Collection of Addresses and Statements by Louis D. Brandeis* (Washington, DC: Zionist Organization of America, 1942), 5.

61. Philippa Strum, *Brandeis: Beyond Progressivism* (Lawrence: UP of Kansas, 1993); David W. Levy, "Brandeis, the Reformer," *Brandeis Law Journal* 45 (Summer 2007): 711–32.

62. LDB, "True Americanism," 5. For Brandeis's wariness of large organizations, see LDB, "A Curse of Bigness" (1913), *Other People's Money, and How the Bankers Use It* (New York: Stokes, 1914), 162–88.

63. LDB interview reprinted in Philippa Strum, ed., *Brandeis on Democracy* (Lawrence: UP of Kansas, 1995), 35.

64. Brandeis debuted this approach in *Muller v. Oregon* (1908), arguing successfully before the Supreme Court for the constitutionality of an Oregon minimum-hours law for working women. Brandeis submitted ninety-five pages of research showing that strenuous workdays endangered women's health, compromised their childbearing and child-rearing roles, and generally threatened the nation's welfare. LDB, with Josephine Goldmark, *Women in Industry* (New York: National Consumers' League, 1908), esp. 47.

65. *Whitney v. California*, 274 US 357 (1927) at 377 (Brandeis, J., concurring); see also Philippa Strum, "Brandeis: The Public Activist and Freedom of Speech," *Brandeis Law Journal* 45 (Summer 2007): 659–709, esp. 696ff.

66. JA, "A Toast to John Dewey," *Survey* 68 (November 15, 1929): 204–5. On Addams's relationship with James and Dewey, see Daniel Levine, *Jane Addams and the Liberal Tradition* (Westport, CT: Greenwood, 1971), 95–96; Allen Freeman Davis, *American Heroine: The Life and Legend of Jane Addams* (New York: Oxford UP, 1973), 140–41; Katherine Joslin, *Jane Addams, a Writer's Life* (Urbana: University of Illinois Press, 2004), 82–89, 171–72, 221, 226; Victoria Bissell Brown, *The Education of Jane Addams* (Philadelphia: University of Pennsylvania Press, 2004), 4, 87, 130, 285, 292, 296.

67. See JA, "A Function of the Social Settlement," *Annals of the American Academy of Political and Social Science* 13 (May 1899): 323–55, invoking Dewey's definition of knowledge as problem solving and citing James's pragmatic principle as inspiration. On working with rather than for the disfranchised, see JA, "Ethical Survivals in Municipal Corruption," *International Journal of Ethics* 8 (April 1898): 273–91; JA, "Social Settlement," *Chautauqua Assembly Herald* 25 (August 13, 1900): 2.

68. Exemplary is the now little-studied volume by JA et al., *Hull-House Maps and Papers* (New York: Thomas Y. Crowell, 1895).

69. WJ to JA, September 17, 1902, JAmss, reel 4.

70. JA, *Twenty Years at Hull-House* (New York: Macmillan, 1911), 64. See also JA, "Woman's Conscience and Social Amelioration," in *The Social Application of Religion: The Merrick Lectures for 1907–8* (Cincinnati: Jennings and Graham, 1908), 41–60; JA, "Why Women Should Vote," *Ladies' Home Journal* 27 (January 1910): 21–22.

71. JA, *Twenty Years*, 126 (quoted).

72. Veblen's status as pragmatist is established in Trygve Throntveit, "The Will to Behold: Thorstein Veblen's Pragmatic Aesthetics," *Modern Intellectual History* 5 (November 2008): 519–46. For overviews of Veblen's life and career, see John Patrick Diggins, *The Bard of Savagery: Thorstein Veblen and Modern Social Theory* (New York: Seabury, 1978); Stephen Edgell, *Veblen in Perspective: His Life and Thought* (Armonk, NY: M. E. Sharpe, 2001); Rick Tilman, *Thorstein Veblen and the Enrichment of Evolutionary Naturalism* (Columbia: University of Missouri Press, 2007).

73. TV, *The Theory of the Leisure Class: An Economic Study of Institutions* (New York: Macmillan, 1899), esp. 15–16.

74. Ibid., chaps. 1, 3–4, 8–10, 12, esp. 27–30; TV, "The Preconceptions of Economic Science," I-III (1898), *The Place of Science in Modern Civilization and Other Essays* (New York: B. W. Huebsch, 1919), 82–179; TV, *The Theory of Business Enterprise* (New York: Scribner, 1904); TV, *Absentee Ownership and Business Enterprise in Recent Times* (New York: B. W. Huebsch, 1923), esp. 438–39.

75. TV, "Why Is Economics Not an Evolutionary Science?" (1898), *Science in Modern Civilization*, 73; TV, "The Instinct of Workmanship and the Irksomeness of Labor," *American Journal of Sociology* 4 (September 1898): 189–90. For Veblen's reading of James and its influence on his psychological assumptions, see his 1896 edition of James's *Principles of Psychology*, Veblen Collection, Carleton College, Northfield, MN, esp. 1:166–68, and 2:638–40; see also Throntveit, "Will to Behold," 527.

76. TV, "The Place of Science in Modern Civilization" (1906), *Science in Modern Civilization*, 5–15 (citing WJ, *Principles*, 2:633–71); TV, *The Instinct of Workmanship and the State of the Industrial Arts* (New York: Macmillan, 1914), 37. Some scholars have quoted these works to paint Veblen as hostile to pragmatism; e.g. John P. Diggins, "Thorstein Veblen and the Literature of the Theory Class," *International Journal of Politics, Culture, and Society* 6 (Summer 1993): 481–90. This interpretation is refuted in Throntveit, "Will to Behold," 530–31. Veblen's positive interest in pragmatist psychology and epistemology, fanned by acquaintance with Dewey, is especially clear from TV to Sarah Hardy, January 23, 1896, Thorstein Veblen Papers, University of Chicago, Chicago, IL; Andrew Anderson Veblen to Joseph Dorfman, October 1, 1926, Andrew Anderson Veblen Papers, Minnesota Historical Society, St. Paul, MN; and Becky Veblen Meyers (stepdaughter), "Becky's Biography" (unpaginated typescript), Veblen Collection.

77. TV, "Neglected Points in the Theory of Socialism" (1891), *Annals of the American Academy of Political and Social Science* 2 (November 1891): esp. 57–59, 74; TV, *Instinct of Workmanship*, 38–39. On the centrality of power to Veblen's thought, see Sidney Plotkin and Rick Tilman, *The Political Ideas of Thorstein Veblen* (New Haven: Yale UP, 2011).

78. TV, *Instinct of Workmanship*, 303–27, esp. 303, 310; TV, *Theory of Business Enterprise*, 374; TV, *The Vested Interests and the Common Man* (New York: B. W. Huebsch, 1919), 178.

79. TV, *Instinct of Workmanship*, 303, 310, 320–21, 331–34 ("pragmatism" at 331n).

80. WEBD, *The Autobiography of W. E. B. Du Bois: A Soliloquy on Viewing My Life from the Last Decade of Its First Century* (New York, 1968), 133; Richard Cullen Rath, "Echo and Narcissus: The Afrocentric Pragmatism of W. E. B. Du Bois," *Journal of American History* 84 (1997): 461–95. On Du Bois's pragmatism, see also Nancy Muller Milligan, "W. E. B. Du Bois's American Pragmatism," *Journal of American Culture* 8 (Summer 1985); 31–37; C. West, *American Evasion*, 138–49; Ross Posnock, "The Distinction of Du Bois: Aesthetics, Pragmatism, Politics," *American Literary History* 7 (Autumn 1995): 500–524. The authoritative biography of the young Du Bois is David Levering Lewis, *W. E. B. Du Bois: Biography of a Race, 1868–1919* (New York: Henry Holt, 1993).

81. WEBD, *The Souls of Black Folk: Essays and Sketches* (Chicago: A. C. McClurg, 1903), 4.

82. WEBD, *The Philadelphia Negro: A Social Stu*dy (Philadelphia: University of Pennsylvania Press, 1899); WEBD quoted in C. West, *American Evasion*, 139.

83. WEBD, *Souls of Black Folk*, 168–69, 188.

84. WEBD to WJ, June 12, 1906, WEBDmss. Cf. WEBD, *Souls of Black Folk*, 3: "The American Negro . . . would not Africanize America, for America has too much to teach the world and Africa. He would not bleach his Negro soul in a flood of white American-ism, for he knows that Negro blood has a message for the world."

85. RB to Prudence Winterrowd, January 16, 1913, in *The Letters of Randolph Bourne: A Comprehensive Edition*, ed. Eric J. Sandeen (Troy, NY: Whitston, 1981), 66; RB, *Youth and Life* (Boston: Houghton Mifflin, 1913), 244–45 (quoted); RB, *Education and Living* (New York: Century, 1917), esp. v–vi. Studies noting Bourne's attraction to prag-matism include Bruce Clayton, *Forgotten Prophet: The Life of Randolph Bourne* (Baton Rouge: Louisiana State UP, 1984); Casey Nelson Blake, *Beloved Community: The Cultural Criticism of Randolph Bourne, Van Wyck Brooks, Waldo Frank, and Lewis Mumford* (Chapel Hill: University of North Carolina Press, 1990); and Leslie J. Vaughan, *Randolph Bourne and the Politics of Cultural Radicalism* (Lawrence: UP of Kansas, 1997).

86. Horace M. Kallen, "Democracy *Versus* the Melting Pot" I–II, *Nation* 100 (Febru-ary 18/25, 1915): 190–94/217–20. A sense of James and Kallen's close relationship can be gleaned from WJ to Horace Kallen, September 9, 1906; August 6 and September 4, 1907; April 5, April 14, and May 11, 1909; and March 29, 1910; all in Horace Meyer Kallen Papers, American Jewish Archives, Cincinnati, OH.

87. RB, "Trans-National America" (1916), in *The Radical Will: Selected Writings 1911–1918*, ed. Olaf Hansen (1977; repr., Berkeley: University of California Press, 1992), 248–64.

88. Michael E. Parrish, *Felix Frankfurter and His Times: The Reform Years* (New York: Free Press, 1982), chap. 1.

89. Melvin I. Urofsky and David W. Levy, introduction to *"Half Brother, Half Son": The Letters of Louis D. Brandeis to Felix Frankfurter*, by LDB, ed. Melvin I. Urofsky and David W. Levy (Norman: University of Oklahoma Press, 1991), 4; Joseph P. Lash, "A Brahmin of the Law," in *From the Diaries of Felix Frankfurter*, ed. Joseph P. Lash (New York: W. W. Norton, 1975), 10–11 (re: Cohen); Parrish, *Frankfurter and His Times*, 15, 19, 20–23, quoted at 54.

90. Parrish, *Frankfurter and His Times*, 30–38, 42–50.

91. Urofsky and Levy, introduction to *"Half Brother, Half Son,"* 5–6; Parrish, *Frankfurter and His Times,* 54–59; LDB to FF, January 28, 1913 ("social advance"), and FF to LDB, January 30, 1913, FFmss, reel 15.

92. Lash, "Brahmin of the Law," 12–13; LDB to FF, March 17, 1916, LDBmss, reel 41 (the memorandum was drafted by Brandeis's law partner Ernest R. McLennen); FF, "The Constitutional Opinion of Mr. Justice Holmes," *Harvard Law Review* 29 (April 1916): 683–702, quoted at 686, 691–92.

93. William English Walling, *Larger Aspects of Socialism* (New York: Macmillan, 1913), quoted at 5; William English Walling, *Progressivism—And After* (New York: Macmillan, 1914), esp. 297; Max Eastman, "Knowledge and Revolution," *Masses* 4 (December 1912): 1. See also Jack Meyer Stuart, "William English Walling: A Study in Politics and Ideas" (PhD diss., Columbia University, 1968), esp. 30–33; William L. O'Neill, *The Last Romantic: A Life of Max Eastman* (New York: Oxford UP, 1978), chap. 1.

94. HC, *The Promise of American Life* (New York: Macmillan, 1909); HC, *Progressive Democracy* (New York: Macmillan, 1914), quoted at 378, 424. On Croly's debts to pragmatism, see Kloppenberg, *Uncertain Victory,* 314–16; David W. Noble, *The Paradox of Progressive Thought* (Minneapolis: University of Minnesota Press, 1958), 66–77; Charles Forcey, *The Crossroads of Liberalism: Croly, Weyl, Lippmann, and the Progressive Era, 1900–1925* (New York: Oxford UP, 1961), 155–160. The completest studies of Croly's life and thought are David W. Levy, *Herbert Croly of "The New Republic": Life and Thought of an American Progressive* (Princeton, NJ: Princeton UP, 1985) (more skeptical of pragmatism's influence); and Edward A. Stettner, *Shaping Modern Liberalism: Herbert Croly and Progressive Thought* (Lawrence: UP of Kansas, 1993).

95. Ernest Poole, "Exploration," in *Walter Weyl: An Appreciation,* ed. Howard Brubaker (Philadelphia: Maurice N. Weyl, 1922), 33–53, esp. 37; Walter E. Weyl, *The New Democracy: An Essay on Certain Political and Economic Tendencies in the United States* (New York: Macmillan, 1912). For detailed analysis of Weyl's thought and career, see Forcey, *Crossroads of Liberalism;* Samuel P. Jacobs, "Walter Weyl and the Progressive Mind: The Promise and Problems of the New Democracy" (honors thesis, Harvard University, 2009).

96. Robert W. Bruère, "An Attempt at Appraisal," in Brubaker, *Walter Weyl,* 141–42; David W. Levy, "Weyl, Walter Edward," *American National Biography Online,* last modified February 2000, http://www.anb.org/articles/14/14-00764.html; Weyl, *New Democracy,* 354.

97. Theodore Roosevelt, *Theodore Roosevelt: An Autobiography* (New York: Macmillan, 1913), 25.

98. For James's influence on Lippmann's *A Preface to Politics,* see WL to Graham Wallas, July 31 and October 30, 1912, WLmss, reel 32. On Lippmann and pragmatism generally, see Forcey, *Crossroads of Liberalism,* esp. chaps. 3, 5; Ronald Steel, *Walter Lippmann and the American Century* (Boston: Atlantic-Little, Brown, 1980), chap. 1; David A. Hollinger, "The Problem of Pragmatism in American History," *Journal of American History* 67 (June 1980): 88–107, esp. 103–4.

99. WL, *Drift and Mastery: An Attempt to Diagnose the Current Unrest,* ed. William E. Leuchtenburg (1914; repr., Madison: University of Wisconsin Press, 1985), 142, 144, 160.

100. WJ to William M. Salter, April 8 and 21, 1898, *CWJ*, 8:355, 360; WJ, "Address on the Philippine Question" (1898/1904), *The Works of William James: Essays, Comments, and Reviews*, ed. Frederick Burkhardt et al. (Cambridge, MA: Harvard UP, 1987), 83–84.

101. HC, *Promise of American Life*, 264; WL, *Drift and Mastery*, 167.

102. WEBD, "The Future of the Negro Race in America," *East and the West* 2 (January 1904): 4–19; WEBD, "The Color Line Belts the World," *Collier's* 38 (October 20, 1906): 30; WEBD, "Race Friction between Black and White," *American Journal of Sociology* 13 (May 1908): 834–38; WEBD, "The Present Outlook for the Dark Races of Mankind," *Church Review* 17 (October 1910): 95–110.

103. JA, *Newer Ideals of Peace* (New York: Macmillan, 1907), 24, 238. Although James's essay "The Moral Equivalent of War" was first published in February 1910, it drew on ideas presented at the 1904 Universal Peace Congress, where James and Addams shared the dais, and from a 1906 address entitled "The Psychology of the War Spirit," cited by Addams in *Newer Ideals*.

104. JD, "Philosophy and Democracy" (1918), *MW*, 11:41–53, esp. 50–53.

105. Ibid., 53.

CHAPTER TWO

1. WW, inaugural address, March 4, 1913, *PWW*, 27:151.

2. The descriptions of truth as "corrigible" and a discursive community as an "intellectual republic" are from WJ, "The Will to Believe" (1896), *WB*, 14, 30.

3. WJ, *Pragmatism: A New Name for Some Old Ways of Thinking* (New York: Longman's, Green, 1907), 64; WW, *Congressional Government: A Study in American Politics*, 15th ed. (1885; repr., Boston: Houghton Mifflin, 1901), 7.

4. On Wilson's religious upbringing, personal faith, and political thought, see John M. Mulder, *Woodrow Wilson: The Years of Preparation* (Princeton, NJ: Princeton UP, 1978). Influential caricatures of Wilson as a prudish, narrow-minded child of the manse include those in John Maynard Keynes, *The Economic Consequences of the Peace* (London: Macmillan, 1919); Alexander L. George and Juliette L. George, *Woodrow Wilson and Colonel House: A Personality Study* (New York: J. Day, 1956); and Sigmund Freud and William C. Bullitt, *Woodrow Wilson: A Psychological Study* (New York: Houghton, Mifflin, 1966).

5. WW to Ellen Louise Axson, May 25, 1884, *PWW*, 3:191–92. For Joseph Ruggles Wilson's influence on his son, see Mulder, *Years of Preparation*, chap. 1; John Milton Cooper Jr., *The Warrior and the Priest: Woodrow Wilson and Theodore Roosevelt* (Cambridge, MA: Harvard UP, 1983), 17–19.

6. WW to Ellen Louise Axson, July 15, 1884, *PWW*, 3:248; also Mulder, *Years of Preparation*, xiii, 7–8, 82–83, 102, on Wilson's penchant for covenanting.

7. WW, *Congressional Government*, 9; WW, *The State: Elements of Historical and Practical Politics*, 15th ed. (1889; repr., Boston: D.C. Heath, 1909), 613–15, 623–25, 631–32; WW, *Constitutional Government in the United States* (New York: Columbia UP, 1908), 23.

8. [Alexander] Hamilton, [James] Madison, and [John] Jay, *The Federalist, on the New Constitution, Written in 1788* (Hallowell, ME: Masters, Smith, 1852), 147, WWLLC; WW, *Constitutional Government*, 2, 169; cf. WW, *Congressional Government*, 284, 332–33.

The *Federalist* passage is marked by two vertical pencil lines in the margins; italicized text represents Wilson's underscoring. Internal markings indicate Wilson first read the book in 1880 while studying law at the University of Virginia.

9. On Wilson's earliest thinking along these lines, see John Milton Cooper, *Woodrow Wilson: A Biography* (New York: Knopf, 2009), 28, 30–32.

10. "His book has inspired my whole study of our government," Wilson wrote. WW to Ellen Louise Axson, January 1, 1884, *PWW*, 2:641.

11. WW, *Congressional Government*, 9, 11, 280–81, 331–32.

12. WW, "Cabinet Government in the United States" (1879), *PWW*, 1:493–510.

13. Ibid., 1:495; WW, *Congressional Government*, 46, and chaps. 2 and 5, passim.

14. WW, *Congressional Government*, 284. Oddly, Wilson did not explicitly suggest the "cabinet government" remedy, despite having again proposed it in an article—"Committee or Cabinet Government?"—published in January 1884, the month he began *Congressional Government* (*PWW*, 2:614–640).

15. WW, *Congressional Government*, 332–33. On the response to *Congressional Government* and its merits as political science, see Arthur S. Link, *Wilson: The Road to the White House* (Princeton, NJ: Princeton UP, 1947), 12–19; Henry W. Bragdon, *Woodrow Wilson: The Academic Years* (Cambridge, MA: Harvard UP, 1967), 124–40; Cooper, *Warrior and the Priest*, 49–51.

16. WW, *The State*, 575–76.

17. WW, *Constitutional Government*, 23. A deeper account of Wilson's early political thought is Trygve Throntveit, "The Higher Education of Woodrow Wilson: Politics as Social Inquiry," in *The Educational Legacy of Woodrow Wilson: From College to Nation*, ed. James Axtell (Charlottesville: University of Virginia Press, 2012), 207–43.

18. For Wilson's enrollments in Ely's courses, see *Johns Hopkins University Circulars* 3 (November 1883): 26, and *Johns Hopkins University Circulars* 3 (March 1884), 69; see also WW, draft contribution to Richard T. Ely et al., "The History of Political Economy in the United States," ca. May 25, 1885, *PWW*, 4:631–63. For Wilson's admiration of Ely's methods and moral commitments, see WW to John Bates Clark, August 26, 1887, *PWW*, 5:565. Exceptions to the neglect of Ely's influence on Wilson include Niels Aage Thorsen, *The Political Thought of Woodrow Wilson, 1875–1910* (Princeton, NJ: Princeton UP, 1988), 69–76; Thomas J. Knock, *To End All Wars: Woodrow Wilson and the Quest for a New World Order* (New York: Oxford UP, 1992), 6; and Robert Adcock, *Liberalism and the Emergence of Political Social Science: A Transatlantic Tale* (New York: Oxford UP, 2014), 213–25. Though silent on Ely, Martin J. Sklar finds socialistic strains in Wilson's thinking in *The Corporate Reconstruction of American Capitalism, 1890–1916: The Market, the Law, and Politics* (Cambridge: Cambridge UP, 1987), chap. 6.

19. WW, "The Modern Democratic State," ca. December 1–20, 1885, *PWW*, 5:90; WW, "Socialism and Democracy," ca. August 22, 1887, *PWW*, 5:561–62; also accompanying editorial notes, *PWW*, 5:54–58, 563. Wilson's copy of *The Labor Movement in America* (New York: T.Y. Crowell, 1886) is preserved in WWLLC, along with Ely's *French and German Socialism in Modern Times* (New York: Harper, 1883).

20. WW, *The State*, 631–32; cf. J. David Hoeveler Jr., "The University and the Social Gospel: The Intellectual Origins of the 'Wisconsin Idea,'" *Wisconsin Magazine of History* 59 (Summer 1976): 282–98. A comprehensive picture of Ely's political thought and activism

is Richard T. Ely, *Ground under Our Feet: An Autobiography* (New York: Macmillan, 1938).

21. WW lecture notes, ca. July 2–10, 1894, *PWW*, 8:597–608, esp. 599–600. Wilson never adopted the Hegelian political philosophy of his professor, George Sylvester Morris. Nevertheless, the study of German political thought was more important to his own than is often recognized. See Robert D. Miewald, "The Origins of Wilson's Thought: The German Tradition and the Organic State," in *Politics and Administration: Woodrow Wilson and American Public Administration*, ed. Jack Rabin and James S. Bowman (New York: Dekker, 1984), 17–30.

22. Dorothy Ross, *G. Stanley Hall: The Psychologist as Prophet* (Chicago: University of Chicago Press, 1972), 62–68. James considered Hall an ally against "priggish English Hegelism" and once had to assure Hall he was not abandoning the "empiricism" they shared. WJ to G. Stanley Hall, September 3, 1879, January 16, 1880, and March 16, 1880, G. Stanley Hall Papers (B1-3-2), Clark University Archives, Worcester, MA.

23. WJ, "Remarks on Spencer's *Definition of Mind as Correspondence*" (1878), *CER*, 43–68; WJ, "Are We Automata?" *Mind* 4 (January 1879): 1–22; WJ, "The Sentiment of Rationality" (1881), *CER*, 83–136.

24. WJ, "Remarks on Spencer's *Definition of Mind*," esp. 67, 65; WJ, "Reflex Action and Theism" (1881), *WB*, 111–144.

25. WJ, review (unsigned) of G. H. Lewes's *Problems of Life and Mind* (1875), *CER*, 4–11; WJ, "Great Men," 216–54 (see chap. 1, n. 36); WJ, "Sentiment of Rationality," esp. 82, 90–91, 97, 102; WJ, "Reflex Action and Theism," esp. 116, 137, 139–41, 143–44 .

26. Ross, *G. Stanley Hall*, 75–77, 138–43; WW to Ellen Louise Axson, November 13, 1884, *PWW*, 3:430. For further evidence of Wilson's study under Hall, see editorial note 1, *PWW* 3:335; and class rosters, *Johns Hopkins University Circulars* 4, no. 34 (November 1884): 7.

27. WW to Ellen Louise Axson, June 3, 1884, *PWW*, 3:205; Granville Stanley Hall to WW, August 29, 1884, *PWW*, 3:311; WW to Ellen Louise Axson, October 28, 1884, *PWW*, 3:382; G. Stanley Hall, *Life and Confessions of a Psychologist* (New York: D. Appleton, 1923), 240.

28. No reading list has been discovered. In the *Circulars* for June 1884 (vol. 3, no. 31) Hall's course is described as a "History of Modern Philosophical and Educational Ideas," sketching the "views of representative modern philosophers" and designed for students seeking conversance in "philosophical and educational opinion and method" as well as those "intending to teach philosophy" (117–18).

29. WW, memoranda for "The Modern Democratic State," ca. December 1–20, 1885, *PWW*, 5:60; WW, "Modern Democratic State," 90–92; WW, "Note on the Democratic State," ca. August 1, 1888, *PWW*, 5:758.

30. WW, "Modern Democratic State," 90–91.

31. WW, "The Study of Administration" (1887), *PWW*, 5:359–80, esp. 371–72, 376, 379. Even the keenest eyes have mistaken Wilson's essay as advocating "separation of politics and administration": Dorothy Ross, *The Origins of American Social Science* (Cambridge: Cambridge UP, 1991), 277.

32. WW, "The Functions of Government," ca. February 17, 1888, quoted in Cooper, *Woodrow Wilson*, 60.

33. WW to Joseph Ruggles Wilson, March 20, 1890, *PWW*, 6:554; WW, confidential journal, December 28, 1889, *PWW*, 463 (emphasis in original).

34. Seminal portrayals of Wilson as economic conservative include William Diamond, *The Economic Thought of Woodrow Wilson* (Baltimore, MD: Johns Hopkins UP, 1943); and Richard Hofstadter, *The American Political Tradition and the Men Who Made It* (New York: Knopf, 1948), chap. 10, esp. 239–41. A vehement argument for the "counterrevolutionary" implications of Wilson's political science is Vincent Ostrom, *The Intellectual Crisis in American Public Administration* (Tuscaloosa: University of Alabama Press, 1974), 133. For a softer but still overstated argument that Wilson's writings on government justified enhancement of state power at the expense of popular participation, see Thorsen, *Political Thought of Woodrow Wilson*, esp. 218, 233.

35. Burke's *Reflections on the Revolution in France* (London: James Dodsley, 1790) scathingly criticized the wholesale overthrow of the ancien régime. For Wilson's thoughts on Burke's view of law as a better tool of change, see WW lecture notes, July 2–10, 1894, and September 22, 1894, to January 20, 1895, *PWW*, 8:597–99 and 9:5–106.

36. WW, "Edmund Burke: The Man and His Times," ca. August 31, 1893, *PWW*, 8:333, 342. Also WW, *The State*, esp. 614–15; Cooper, *Warrior and the Priest*, esp. 53. The term "anti-ideological" is Cooper's; the association to pragmatism is not. Recently, historians of political thought have rediscovered a Burke today's liberals might even embrace: Drew Maciag, *Edmund Burke in America: The Contested Career of the Father of Modern Conservatism* (Ithaca, NY: Cornell UP, 2013); David Bromwich, *The Intellectual Life of Edmund Burke* (Cambridge, MA: Harvard UP, 2014).

37. WW, *Leaders of Men by Woodrow Wilson*, ed. T. H. Vail Motter (Princeton, NJ: Princeton UP, 1952), 23–24, 41–45, esp. 41–42. For the effects of the Homestead, Pullman, and other strikes on prominent intellectuals, see Shelton Stromquist, *Re-inventing the People: The Progressive Movement, the Class Problem, and the Origins of Modern Liberalism* (Urbana: University of Illinois Press, 2006), chap. 1.

38. Marked by WW in Edmund Burke, *The Works of the Right Honorable Edmund Burke*, 7th ed., 12 vols. (Boston: Little, Brown, 1881), 1:525–26, WWLLC.

39. Ibid., 527, 530.

40. Wilson's views on party government are explicated and analyzed in Daniel D. Stid, *The President as Statesman: Woodrow Wilson and the Constitution* (Lawrence: UP of Kansas, 1998), chap. 1.

41. WW, *Leaders of Men*, 45.

42. Ibid., 28–29; WW, "Edmund Burke," *PWW*, 8:340.

43. News release of a speech on Thomas Jefferson, April 13, 1906, *PWW*, 16:362; WW speech of February 12, 1909, *PWW*, 19:41. In Wilson's copy of *Democracy in America* the following is marked: "When the members of a community are forced to attend to public affairs, they are necessarily drawn from the circle of their own interests. . . . As soon as a man begins to treat of public affairs in public, he begins to perceive that he is not so independent of his fellow-men as he had at first imagined, and that, in order to obtain their support, he must often lend them his co-operation." Alexis de Tocqueville, *Democracy in America*, trans. Henry Reeve, 2 vols. (London: Longmans, Green, 1875), 2:94, WWLLC.

44. WW, "Modern Democratic State," 65–66.

45. News release, April 16, 1906, *PWW*, 16:360–61, 362 (emphasis added); WW

address on Thomas Jefferson, April 16, 1906, *PWW*, 366–67. Although Mulder, *Years of Preparation*, 240–44, demonstrates Wilson's commitment to individual responsibility and fear of overregulation in these years, his beliefs in social interdependence and federal supremacy clearly persisted.

46. WW, "Princeton for the Nation's Service," October 25, 1902, *PWW*, 14:170–85; WW to Ellen Axson Wilson, July 19, 1902, 14:27 (on his prime minister role). Bragdon's *Wilson: Academic Years*, 269–384, was long the standard account of Wilson's Princeton presidency, but his characterizations of Wilson as generally intransigent and philosophically antimodernist are overdrawn and bizarre, respectively. More balanced is Cooper, *Woodrow Wilson*, chaps. 4–5.

47. Cooper, *Woodrow Wilson*, chap. 5; James Axtell, "The Bad Dream: Woodrow Wilson on Princeton—After Princeton," *Princeton University Library Chronicle* 69 (Spring 2008): 401–36.

48. A detailed account of these events is Link, *Road to the White House*, 97–106.

49. William O. Inglis, "Helping to Make a President" (1916), in David W. Hirst, *Woodrow Wilson: Reform Governor* (Princeton, NJ: Van Nostrand, 1965), 7–9. For Wilson's corroborating impressions, see WW to David B. Jones and Edward W. Sheldon, June 27 and July 11, 1910, *PWW*, 20:543–45, 572–73.

50. On Wilson's falling out with Harvey and Smith, see Link, *Road to the White House*, 188, 209–12, 218–37, 360–69. In this and other early works Link, too, portrayed Wilson as an opportunistic progressive; Link, *Woodrow Wilson and the Progressive Era, 1910–1917* (New York: Harper, 1954).

51. WW, *Constitutional Government*, 23; WW, preface to 15th edition, *Congressional Government*, xi, xiii; WW, speech of October 5, 1911, *PWW*, 23:398–99.

52. Regarding Wilson and Adler, see WW, "Notes for Three Lectures," ca. July 2–10, 1894, *PWW*, 8:597–608; "Savants at Plymouth," *Boston Daily Globe*, July 17, 1894; WW address book for 1909, WWmss, reel 1; WW address, November 24, 1910, *PWW*, 22:91, 91n5; Juliet Clannon Cushing to WW, December 8, 1910, *PWW*, 2:157, 157n1. Regarding James and Adler, see WJ to Felix Adler, January 11, 1888, *CWJ*, 6:299; Howard B. Radest, *Toward Common Ground: The Story of the Ethical Societies in the United States* (New York: Frederick Ungar, 1969), 69, 99, 100, 159, 166. Although Adler often criticized James's ethical writings, preferring a modified Kantianism, his criticisms of Kant strongly resemble James's, and he republished his major work on the subject in a 1908 Festschrift for James. Felix Adler, undated notes on James, Felix Adler Papers, Butler Library, Columbia University, New York, NY, Boxes/Folders 44/3, 46/1, and 49/5; Felix Adler, "A Critique of Kant's Ethics" (1902), in *Essays Philosophical and Psychological in Honor of William James* (New York: Longmans, Green, 1908), 303–66.

53. Francis L. Patton, "Dr. McCosh," *Princeton College Bulletin* 7 (February 1895): 1–3, at 3.

54. "But dear me, *what shall we do without them?*" Wilson wrote Ellen regarding the Hibbens' sabbatical plans. "That's the worst of having friends whom one really loves,—the pain of the inevitable separations." WW to Ellen Axson Wilson, March 11, 1900, *PWW*, 11:503.

55. E.g., John Grier Hibben, "The Vocation of the Scholar," in *A Defense of Prejudice and Other Essays* (New York: Charles Scribner's Sons, 1911), esp. 146–47.

56. WJ to John Grier Hibben, April 9, 1896, *CWJ*, 8:579; John Grier Hibben, *Inductive Logic* (New York: Charles Scribner's Sons, 1896), 10–11.

57. John Grier Hibben, "The Heart and the Will in Belief—Romanes and Mill," *North American Review* 166 (January 1898): 121–23, at 123.

58. WJ to Alice Howe Gibbens James, January 31, 1904, *CWJ*, 10:368–69, incl. editorial note 3; John Grier Hibben, "The Test of Pragmatism," *Philosophical Review* 17 (July 1908): 365–82; "Philosophy Lecture," *Daily Princetonian* 35 (October 20, 1910): 1.

59. Hibben, "Vocation of the Scholar," 146.

60. James Mark Baldwin, "Psychology Past and Present," *Psychological Review* 1 (July 1894): 363–91, at 386; James Mark Baldwin, *Mental Development in the Child and the Race: Methods and Processes* (New York: Macmillan, 1894), 226; see 76n1, 79n1, 237n1, and 392 for references to James's theories of instinct, emotion, and motor action. In 1902 Baldwin invoked James's alternative metaphor of the "fringe" of consciousness in *Development and Evolution* (New York: Macmillan, 1902), 310.

61. James Mark Baldwin, *Social and Ethical Interpretations in Mental Development* (New York: Macmillan, 1897), 86–87, 167–69, 169n1.

62. James Mark Baldwin to WJ, [January 1899], *CWJ*, 8:478–79.

63. James Mark Baldwin, "James's Principles of Psychology," *Educational Review* 1 (April 1891): 357–71.

64. *Daily Princetonian* 18 (September 28, 1893): 1; Alexander T. Ormond to WW, December 31, 1909, *PWW*, 19:666; WW to Board of Trustees of Princeton University, January 1, 1910, *PWW*, 19:674–95, including 695 editorial note 1; WW, "Report to the Curriculum Committee of the Board of Trustees of Princeton University," ca. May 13, 1910, *PWW*, 20:445–52, esp. 447. As these last three documents show, James's *Psychology: Briefer Course* (New York: Henry Holt, 1892) was the only text in experimental psychology assigned in the preceptorial philosophy seminar. After consulting the philosophy department on February 10, 1910, Wilson reversed an earlier recommendation to the trustees that laboratory work in experimental psychology be excluded from undergraduate instruction, having been convinced that both reading and laboratory work in the field were essential "to any well-rounded scheme of undergraduate studies" in philosophy and crucial preparation for graduate studies in the discipline.

65. *Daily Princetonian* 25 (December 5, 1900): 1; *Daily Princetonian* 27 (April 11, 1902): 1 (quoted). The latter quoted Baldwin, concluding, "Reality is still unfinished and as it is made up of the actions of individuals, each one of us, by taking attitudes may affect the result. . . . [T]here is no religious attitude which does not affect the lives of many. The will to believe often turns the scale . . . and by taking the attitude of faith and religious power, we throw our influence on the side of right and no one can estimate the magnitude of the result upon those about us."

66. *Daily Princetonian* 28 (December 1, 1903): 1 (front-page announcement repeated December 2, 3); *Princeton Seminary Bulletin* 1 (January 1908): 28. Intriguingly, Wilson saved the *Bulletin* issue; it appears on the inventory of his books and periodicals bequeathed to the Library of Congress (WWmss, reel 2).

67. "The Power of Prayer," *Daily Princetonian* 34 (November 5, 1909): 1; "Saint Augustine," *Daily Princetonian* 35 (December 1910): 1.

68. *Daily Princetonian* 33 (November 17, 1908): 1; *Daily Princetonian* 34 (November 23, 1909): 1; *Daily Princetonian* 35 (November 30, 1910): 1. For Wilson's pride in his editorship, see WW diary, March 20, 1877, *PWW*, 1:253.

69. *Princeton University Bulletin* 14 (September 3, 1903): 210; entries for January 1, 2, 17, and 18, 1904, WW diary, January–February 1904, WWmss, reel 1.

70. Frank Thilly, "Freedom of the Will," *Philosophical Review* 3 (July 1894): 385–411, esp. 389 (endorsing a "determinism" not excluding deliberation and choice, thus aligning himself with James against Wilhelm Wundt); Frank Thilly, *Introduction to Ethics* (New York: Charles Scribner's Sons, 1900); Frank Thilly, "Causality," *Philosophical Review* 16 (March 1907): 116–35, esp. 132–33, 135.

71. *Daily Princetonian* 19 (December 19, 1894): 4; *Daily Princetonian* 19 (January 3, 1895): 1. James's address, "The Unity of Consciousness," appeared in Baldwin's *Psychological Review* as "The Knowing of Things Together" (1895), reprinted in *CER*, 371–400.

72. *Daily Princetonian* 21 (October 23, 1896): 4; *Sesquicentennial Committees, 1896*, Sesquicentennial Celebration Records, Princeton University Archives, Princeton, NJ (hereafter SCR), Box 16, Folder: Sesquicentennial—Miscellaneous; Table Chart, dinner of October 23, 1896, SCR Box 16, Folder: Printed ephemera.

73. *Daily Princetonian* 21 (October 23, 1896): 1 (Hall's election); *Alumni Princetonian* 3 (October 22, 1896): 14 (James's election); minutes, American Whig Society, September 25, 1875, *PWW*, 1:75. Wilson is listed as "representing the American Whig Society" in *Sesquicentennial Celebration, Second Day*, pamphlet program in SCR Box 16, Folder: Printed ephemera. At least one correspondent recalled Wilson acquainting himself with James at the sesquicentennial. A fellow honoree, congratulating Wilson on acceding to the presidency of Princeton, wrote: "Today I have another link with Princeton—for the book I have had for hours in my hand—Professor James's Gifford Lectures [*The Varieties of Religious Experience*], reminds me of the conferring of Degrees at the celebration." Edward Dowden to WW, December 16, 1902, *PWW*, 14:295.

74. "Topics of the Times," *Century Magazine* 54 (August 1897): 635; Henry Van Dyke, "Fisherman's Luck" (the issue's "opening meditation"), *Century Magazine* 58 (June 1899): 171–83, at 174; "Topics of the Time," *Century Magazine* 64 (July 1902): 484; C. T. Winchester, "John Wesley," part 1, *Century Magazine* 66 (July 1903): 389–408, at 401. See also "Topics of the Times," *Century Magazine* 54 (August 1897): 950, quoting James's Shaw Oration to the effect that the fighting instinct needs no encouragement; and "Topics of the Times," *Century Magazine* 56 (September 1898): 794, again quoting the Shaw Oration in arguing that war channels the human desire to suffer for a great cause. The discussion directly follows a pair of articles on the Spanish-American War and its potential territorial spoils (781–94), subjects on which Wilson was then writing. The issue also contained a retrospective on Tocqueville's *Democracy in America* by Daniel Coit Gilman, president of Wilson's alma mater Johns Hopkins (703–15).

75. "James's Psychology," *Atlantic Monthly* 67 (April 1891): 552–56; John Winthrop Platner, "Recent Religious Literature," *Atlantic Monthly* 90 (September 1902): 423–27, esp. 423–25. The *Principles* review was the second mention of that work in the journal's pages; see "Comment on New Books," *Atlantic Monthly* 67 (February 1891): 273–74.

76. See the inventory in WWmss, end reel 1.

77. WJ, "Talks to Teachers on Psychology: I," *Atlantic Monthly* 83 (February 1899): 155–62, esp. 158–60, 161.

78. WJ, "Talks to Teachers on Psychology: II," *Atlantic Monthly* 83 (March 1899): 320–29, esp. 325–27 (sociality), 328 (experimentality/practicality); WJ, "Talks to Teachers on Psychology: III," *Atlantic Monthly* 83 (April 1899): 510–17 (effort, interest, meaning, novelty); WJ, "Talks to Teachers on Psychology: IV," *Atlantic Monthly* 83 (May 1899): 617–26, esp. 620–26 (quoted 624).

79. WW, "Mr. Cleveland as President," *Atlantic Monthly* 79 (March 1897): 289–300; WW, "The Making of the Nation," *Atlantic Monthly* 80 (July 1897): 1–14; WW, "On Being Human," *Atlantic Monthly* 80 (September 1897): 320–29; WW, "A Lawyer with a Style," *Atlantic Monthly* 82 (September 1898): 363–74; WW, "A Wit and a Seer," *Atlantic Monthly* 82 (October 1898): 527–40. Soon after *Talks to Teachers* was serialized, Wilson's "Spurious versus Real Patriotism in Education" appeared in *School Review*, which also carried a glowing review of James's book: *School Review* 7 (December 1899): 599–620, 434–435, respectively.

80. *Craftsman* 19 (November 1910): 116–23 (by the editor), 135–39 (by M. Irwin Mac-Donald); *Independent* 69 (November 17, 1910): 1067–1086.

81. WJ, *Talks to Teachers on Psychology, and to Students on Some of Life's Ideals* (1899; repr., New York: Henry Holt, 1910); WJ, *On Some of Life's Ideals* (New York: Henry Holt, 1913); both in WWLLC.

82. WW, "On Being Human," ca. June 2, 1897 (published September), *PWW*, 10:250, 252, 255–56.

83. WW, "The Ideals of America" (1902), *PWW*, 12:211, 212–13. Compare James: "Our nation had been founded in what we may call our American religion, baptized and reared in the faith that a man requires no master to take care of him, and that common people can work out their salvation well enough together if left free to try."

84. WW, "Ideals of America," 223, 224–25. James: "Our great western republic had from its very origin been a singular anomaly. A land of freedom, boastfully so called, with human slavery at the heart of it. . . . What Shaw and his comrades stand for and show us is that . . . Americans of all complexions and conditions can go forth like brothers, and meet death cheerfully if need be, in order that this religion of our native land shall not become a failure on earth."

85. WW, "Ideals of America," 225–26. James: "The nation blest above all nations is she in whom the civic genius of the people does the saving day by day. . . . Such nations have no need of wars to save them."

86. WW, "Princeton in the Nation's Service," October 21, 1896, *PWW*, 10:29.

87. WW, "Princeton for the Nation's Service," 183–84.

88. News report of a religious address in Trenton, NJ, April 17, 1905, *PWW*, 16:63–64. Compare Wilson's notes for a chapel talk delivered January 13, 1895, *PWW*, 9:121, which the *PWW* editors determined are the same Wilson used in 1905 yet contain none of the later talk's Jamesian characteristics.

89. WW, *Constitutional Government*, 4, 57.

90. Ibid., 170, 178.

91. Ibid., 54, 59, 68, 106.

92. Ibid., 106.

93. WW to Edgar Williamson, 23 August 1910, *PWW*, 21:59–61; Link, *Road to the White House*, 155–66.

94. WW acceptance speech, September 15, 1910, *PWW*, 21:91–93; WJ, "Moral Philosopher," 254–55 (see Intro., n. 21); news report, September 15, 1910, *PWW*, 21:119. For the party platform, see *PWW*, 21:94–96.

95. George Lawrence Record to WW, 17 October 1910, and WW to Record, October 24, 1910, *PWW*, 21:338–339, 406–411; news report of a speech at Jersey City, NJ, September 20, 1910, *PWW*, 21:147; WW speeches in Jersey City, Trenton, and Newark, NJ, *PWW*, 21:190–91, 229–30, 565; Hirst, *Reform Governor*, 110 ("methods of right"), 113.

96. Link, *Road to the White House*, 247–67 (quoted at 249); Cooper, *Woodrow Wilson*, 131–36.

97. *Nation* 93 (August 17, 1911): 137. On the initiatives, achievements, and changes spanning Wilson's governorship, see Trygve Throntveit, "New Jersey's Modern Radical: Governor Woodrow Wilson and the American Pragmatist Tradition," in *The American Governor: Power, Constraint, and Leadership in the States*, ed. David P. Redlawsk (New York: Palgrave, 2015), 117–36.

98. On the convention, including Ellen Wilson's and Bryan's roles, see Link, *Road to the White House*, 317–26, 352–57, 433–62.

99. William Howard Taft, "The Judiciary and Progress: Address of Hon. William H. Taft at Toledo, Ohio, Friday Evening, March 8, 1912" (Washington, DC: GPO, 1912), 3; WW speech in Sea Girt, NJ, August 7, 1912, *PWW*, 25:6.

100. *NYT*, July 11, 1912. For Brandeis's relations with Frankfurter, Weyl, and Lippmann, see LDB to FF, November 15, 1911, April 9, 1912, and July 12, 1912, FFmss, reel 15; LDB to WL, May 26 and 27, 1913, copies in Alpheus T. Mason Papers, Box 15, Mudd Manuscript Library, Princeton University, Princeton, NJ; and LDB to Walter Weyl, December 6, 1913 and January 8, 1914, Walter E. Weyl Papers, Box 2, Folder 1, Rutgers University Library, New Brunswick, NJ. On Wilson's campaign prior to August 28, see Link, *Road to the White House*, 309–488; James Chace, *1912: Roosevelt, Wilson, Taft, and Debs—The Election That Changed the Country* (New York: Simon and Schuster, 2004), 128–42, 209–15, 227–29.

101. *NYT*, July 11, 1912; WW speech in Sea Girt, 4–6 (emphasis added).

102. WW speech in Sea Girt, 7. On the tariff's failure to arouse the electorate, see Chace, *1912*, 192.

103. WW quoted in Eleanor Wilson McAdoo, *The Woodrow Wilsons* (New York: Macmillan, 1937), 172 ("principles" versus "personalities"); WW and LDB quoted in *NYT*, August 28, 1912.

104. WW address in Buffalo, NY, September 2, 1912, *PWW*, 25:75. Brandeis's personal influence is clear from his September correspondence, LDBmss, reel 29. He reached wider audiences through two signed *Collier's* articles and two essays printed as editorials in Norman Hapgood's *Collier's* column: LDB, "Trusts, Efficiency and the New Party," *Collier's Weekly* 49 (September 14, 1912): 14–15; LDB, "Trusts, the Export Trade, and the New Party," *Collier's Weekly* 50 (September 21, 1912): 10–11; [LDB], "Concentration" and "Trusts and

the Interstate Commerce Commission," *Collier's Weekly* 50 (October 5, 1912): 8–9. For Brandeis's authorship, see Norman Hapgood to LDB, August 29, 1912, LDBmss, reel 29.

105. LDB, "Suggestions for Letter of Governor Wilson on Trusts," enclosed in LDB to WW, September 30, 1912, *PWW*, 25:289, 290, 291–94.

106. Ibid., 290, 292; LDB, *Scientific Management and Railroads* (1911; repr., New York: Engineering Magazine, 1912), WWLLC. For Wilson's intention to publish the letter and his ultimate decision to let Brandeis make the case in the press instead, see LDB to Norman Hapgood, October 2, 1912, and LDB memorandum, October 2, 1912, copies in Mason Papers, Box 15.

107. WW address in Indianapolis, IN, October 3, 1912, *PWW*, 25:321, 323–24, 329.

108. See WW addresses in Kokomo, Omaha, Denver, and Topeka, October 4–8, 1912, *PWW*, 25:330–32, 339–47, 369–85.

109. WW address in Cleveland, OH, October 11, 1912, *PWW*, 25:411; WW, "A Public Letter," October 19, 1912, *PWW*, 25:434. Wilson won 41.8 percent of the popular vote, compared to Roosevelt's 27.4 percent, Taft's 23.2 percent, and Debs's 6 percent—the record for a Socialist Party candidate. Wilson garnered a huge majority in the electoral college, winning 435 of 531 votes and carrying 40 of 48 states.

110. WW to Alexander Mitchell Palmer, February 5, 1913, *PWW*, 37:100.

111. *Washington Post*, April 9, 1913; WW address to Congress, April 8, 1913, *PWW*, 37:269–70.

112. WW to Furnifold M. Simmons, September 4, 1913, *PWW*, 28:254. On the bill's drafting, the significance of the income tax amendment, and Wilson's role, see Sidney Ratner, *Taxation and Democracy in America* (New York: Wiley, 1967), 321–38.

113. Before Wilson's inauguration, he and Virginia Representative Carter Glass formulated a plan for a centralized private system with a federal "capstone." Treasury Secretary William Gibbs McAdoo and Oklahoma Senator Robert Owen favored incorporating the reserve into the treasury department. The dispute was widely acknowledged as serious: see *Washington Post*, June 16, 1913.

114. LDB to WW, June 14, 1913, *PWW*, 27:520–21; Carter Glass, *An Adventure in Constructive Finance* (Garden City, NY: Doubleday, Page, 1927), 81–84, 112–13; Link, *Wilson and the Progressive Era*, 47–52. On the Fed's development and importance, see Milton Friedman, *A Monetary History of the United States, 1867–1960* (Princeton, NJ: Princeton UP, 1963); Martijn Konings, "The Construction of U.S. Financial Power," *Review of International Studies* 35 (January 2009): 69–94.

115. Throntveit, "New Jersey's Modern Radical," 131–32. The "rule of reason" doctrine, limiting the prohibitions of the Sherman Act to "contracts and combinations which amount to an unreasonable or undue restraint of trade," was codified in *Standard Oil Co.* v. *United States*, 221 US 1 (1911).

116. Arthur S. Link, *Wilson: The New Freedom* (Princeton, NJ: Princeton UP, 1956), 427–33; WW to LDB, April 24, 1913, *PWW*, 27:353–54; LDB to WW, May 19 and 26, 1913, and WW to LDB, May 29, 1913, *PWW*, 27:456, 476–77, 487. For Gompers's pen request, see William B. Wilson to WW, October 7, 1914, *PWW*, 30:131.

117. LDB to Franklin K. Lane, December 12, 1913, in *The Letters of Louis D. Brandeis*, 5 vols., ed. Melvin I. Urofsky and David W. Levy (Albany: SUNY Press, 1971–78), 3:218–20;

LDB, "The Solution of the Trust Problem: A Program," *Harper's Weekly* 58 (November 8, 1913): 18–19.

118. WW address to Congress, January 20, 1914, *PWW*, 29:153. On the Stevens bill, see Link, *New Freedom*, 435–42.

119. John B. Daish, "The Federal Trade Commission," *Yale Law Journal* 24, no. 1 (1914): 43–55; Melvin I. Urofsky, *Louis D. Brandeis: A Life* (New York: Pantheon, 2009), 395–96; [HC], "An Unseen Reversal," *NR* 1 (January 9, 1915): 8; also HC, "Restraint of Trade," *NR* 1 (November 7, 1914): 9–10. For the evolution and legacies of the FTC, see the symposium in *Antitrust Law Journal* 72, no. 3 (2005): 745–1206.

120. WW remarks at a press conference, November 3, 1913, *PWW*, 28:487; William English Walling, *Progressivism—And After* (New York: Macmillan, 1914), 10–11; Robert M. La Follette, "Legalizing the 'Money Power,'" *La Follette's Weekly*, December 27, 1913, 1.

121. HC, "Presidential Complacency," *NR* 1 (November 21, 1914): 7.

CHAPTER THREE

1. WEBD, "An Open Letter to Woodrow Wilson," *Crisis* 5 (March 1913): 236; *La Prensa*, March 4, 1913; Ugarte quoted from an interview in *La Argentina* (Buenos Aires), reprinted in *El Mercurio* (Valparaiso), April 27, 1914; Elizabeth Hines and Eliza Steelwater, *Project HAL: Historical American Lynching Data Collection Project*, http://people.uncw.edu/hinese/HAL/HAL%20Web%20Page.htm, accessed and sorted June 26, 2015. Robert E. Quirk, *An Affair of Honor: Woodrow Wilson and the Occupation of Veracruz* (New York: McGraw-Hill, 1964), is a classic, detailed analysis of the Veracruz invasion, but better on Wilson's decision and its context are Mark T. Gilderhus, *Diplomacy and Revolution: U.S.–Mexican Relations under Wilson and Carranza* (Tucson: University of Arizona Press, 1977), 10–11; Frederick S. Calhoun, *Power and Principle: Armed Intervention in Wilsonian Foreign Policy* (Kent, OH: Kent State UP, 1986), 39–42, 45–53, 72–74; and Linda B. Hall and Don M. Coerver, *Revolution on the Border: The United States and Mexico, 1910–1920* (Albuquerque: University of New Mexico Press, 1988), 50–56.

2. Stephen Skowronek, "The Reassociation of Ideas and Purposes: Racism, Liberalism, and the American Political Tradition," *American Political Science Review* 100 (August 2006): 385–401; Gary Gerstle, "Race and Nation in the Thought and Politics of Woodrow Wilson," in *Reconsidering Woodrow Wilson: Progressivism, Internationalism, War, and Peace*, ed. John Milton Cooper Jr. (Washington, DC: Woodrow Wilson Center Press; Baltimore, MD: Johns Hopkins UP, 2008), 93–123; Lloyd E. Ambrosius, "Democracy, Peace, and World Order," in Cooper, *Reconsidering Woodrow Wilson*, 225–49; Eric S. Yellin, *Racism in the Nation's Service: Government Workers and the Color Line in Woodrow Wilson's America* (Chapel Hill: University of North Carolina Press, 2013).

3. Edith Bolling Galt to WW, 20 May 1915, *PWW*, 33:228; WW statement of late 1913 to Sir William Tyrrell, quoted in Burton J. Hendrick, *The Life and Letters of Walter H. Page*, 3 vols. (Garden City, NY: Doubleday, Page, 1923–26), 1:204.

4. Alongside works cited in note 2, see David Steigerwald, *Wilsonian Idealism in America* (Ithaca, NY: Cornell UP, 1994); Mary A. Renda, *Taking Haiti: Military Occupation and the Culture of U.S. Imperialism, 1915–1940* (Chapel Hill: University of North Carolina Press, 2001), 108–29; Joseph A. Fry, *Dixie Looks Abroad: The South and U.S.*

Foreign Relations, 1789–1973 (Baton Rouge: Louisiana State UP, 2002), 139–74; Adriane Lentz-Smith, *Freedom Struggles: African Americans and World War I* (Cambridge, MA: Harvard UP, 2009).

5. Erez Manela, *The Wilsonian Moment: Self-Determination and the International Origins of Anticolonial Nationalism* (New York: Oxford UP, 2007); Susan Pedersen, *The Guardians: The League of Nations and the Crisis of Empire* (New York: Oxford UP, 2015).

6. John Milton Cooper Jr., *Woodrow Wilson: A Biography* (New York: Knopf, 2009), 23–24.

7. Among historians, see Anthony Gaughan, "Woodrow Wilson and the Legacy of the Civil War," *Civil War History* 43 (September 1997): 225–42; Gerstle, "Race and Nation"; Yellin, *Racism in the Nation's Service*. The function of racism in Wilson's thought and politics has garnered extensive attention from political scientists working in the American political development tradition. See Skowronek, "Reassociation of Ideas and Purposes"; Desmond S. King, "The Racial Bureaucracy: African Americans and the Federal Government in the Era of Segregated Race Relations," *Governance: An International Journal of Policy and Administration* 12 (October 1999): 345–77; Desmond S. King and Rogers M. Smith, "Racial Orders in American Political Development," *American Political Science Review* 99 (February 2005): 75–92.

8. WW to Harriet Augusta Woodrow, May 10, 1881, *PWW*, 2:64; WW to John Hanson Kennard Jr., November 18, 1884, *PWW*, 3:455–56. On the varied attitudes of Wilson's immediate and extended family toward the Civil War, see Cooper, *Woodrow Wilson*, 16–18.

9. WW, "Mr. Gladstone: A Character Sketch" (1880), *PWW*, 2:642.

10. WW to Richard Heath Dabney, October 31, 1889, *PWW*, 6:406; WW to Albert Bushnell Hart, June 3, 1889, *PWW*, 6:243.

11. WW speech at Chapel Hill, NC, January 9, 1909, *PWW*, 18:631.

12. WW, *Division and Reunion, 1829–1889* (New York: Longmans, Green, 1893) (quoted 273); WW, *A History of the American People*, 5 vols. (New York: Harper and Brothers, 1901), vol. 5, chap. 1. *Division and Reunion* was commissioned for the *Epochs in American History* series of semipopular syntheses. Wilson wrote the twelve (later consolidated to five) volumes of *A History of the American People* in under a year between 1900 and 1901, for the princely sum of $12,000—an astonishing $320,000 of 2015 purchasing power. A friend on the Princeton faculty called it a "gilt-edged pot-boiler" (Cooper, *Woodrow Wilson*, 73–76). Still unsurpassed in its dismantling of the Reconstruction consensus and its racist, ahistorical assumptions is WEBD, *Black Reconstruction in America, 1860–1880* (New York: Harcourt, Brace, 1935).

13. WW, *History of the American People* 5:60, 64. Few critics of Wilson's Reconstruction narrative mention his ultimate and crucial condemnation of the Klan or his scathing indictment of corrupt northern whites for bribing black legislators and public officials.

14. WW, *Division and Reunion*, 260–61; WW, "The Politics and Industries of the New South" (1881), *PWW*, 2:53–54; WW, "The Study of Administration" (1887), *PWW*, 5:369–70.

15. WW marginalia in James Bryce, *The American Commonwealth* (1888), December 29, 1888, reproduced in *PWW*, 6:35; WW to Richard Heath Dabney, May 10, 1883, *PWW*, 2:349 ("ignorant"); WW to Albert Bushnell Hart, February 28, 1893, *PWW*, 8:141 (Smith);

Cooper, *Woodrow Wilson*, 68–69. Despite professing love for the state and institution, Wilson immediately used the Virginia offer as leverage for a raise at Princeton.

16. WW quoted in Edith Gittings Reid, *Woodrow Wilson: The Caricature, the Myth, and the Man* (New York: Oxford UP, 1934), 22.

17. WW speech at Hampton, VA, January 31, 1897, *PWW*, 10:130, 132–33; WW to Ellen Axson Wilson, February 1 and 4, 1897, *PWW*, 10:137, 143.

18. WW to Ellen Louise Axson, December 11, 1884, *PWW*, 3:532; WW to John Rogers Williams, September 2, 1904, *PWW*, 15:462; Jesse Wilson Sayre to RSB, April 27, 1925, RSBmss, reel 82; WW address in Princeton, NJ, April 3, 1909, *PWW*, 19:149. On Washington's ideas at this stage in his career, see Louis R. Harlan, *Booker T. Washington: The Making of a Black Leader, 1856–1901* (New York: Oxford UP, 1972); Michael R. West, *The Education of Booker T. Washington: American Democracy and the Idea of Race Relations* (New York: Columbia UP, 2006).

19. Studies placing Wilson under this pejorative umbrella include Yellin, *Racism in Nation's Service*, 2, 209n6; and Desmond S. King and Stephen Tuck, "Decentering the South: America's Nationwide White Supremacist Order after Reconstruction," *Past and Present* 194 (February 2007): 213–53. A variant interpretation presenting Wilson as philosophically committed to *segregation* without labeling him a white supremacist is Gerstle, "Race and Nation," 108–10.

20. WW, *Division and Reunion*, esp. 119, 105–7.

21. WW, *The State: Elements of Historical and Practical Politics*, 15th ed. (1889; repr., Boston: D. C. Heath, 1909), 30; WW, "Liberty Is Not Anarchy," February 22, 1895, *PWW*, 9:217.

22. WW, "The Making of the Nation" (1897), *PWW*, 10:217–36, esp. 230.

23. Yellin, *Racism in Nation's Service*, 2–3. See also Morton Sosna, "The South in the Saddle: Racial Politics during the Wilson Years," *Wisconsin Magazine of History* 54 (Autumn 1970): 30–49; Nicholas Patler, *Jim Crow and the Wilson Administration: Protesting Federal Segregation in the Early Twentieth Century* (Boulder: UP of Colorado, 2004). On segregation under Wilson's Republican predecessors, see August Meier and Elliott Rudwick, "The Rise of Segregation in the Federal Bureaucracy, 1900–1930," *Phylon* 28, no. 2 (1967): 178–84; Vincent P. De Santis, *Republicans Face the Southern Question: The New Departure Years, 1877–1897* (Westport, CT: Greenwood, 1969); Rayford W. Logan, *The Betrayal of the Negro, from Rutherford B. Hayes to Woodrow Wilson* (New York: Collier, 1969); Richard B. Sherman, *The Republican Party and Black America from McKinley to Hoover, 1896–1933* (Charlottesville: UP of Virginia, 1973).

24. Manning Marable, *W. E. B. Du Bois: Black Radical Democrat* (Boston: Twayne, 1986), chapter 3; Meier and Rudwick, "Rise of Segregation in Federal Bureaucracy," 178–81. On the "Tuskegee Machine" and the advantages it secured for black office seekers, businesses, and communities, see Louis R. Harlan, *Booker T. Washington: The Wizard of Tuskegee, 1901–1915* (New York: Oxford UP, 1983).

25. WEBD, "My Impressions of Woodrow Wilson" (1939), printed in *Journal of Negro History* 58 (October 1973): 453–59, esp. 453. For Du Bois's analysis of reconstruction and its historiography in this period, see his "Reconstruction and Its Benefits," *American Historical Review* 15 (1910), 781–99.

26. WW statement of July 16, 1912, quoted in Henry Blumenthal, "Woodrow Wilson and the Race Question," *Journal of Negro History* 48 (January 1963), 1–21, at 20; WW to Alexander Walters, October 21, 1912, *PWW*, 25:449; WEBD, "Politics," *Crisis* 4 (August 1912): 180–181; WEBD, "The Last Word in Politics," *Crisis* 5 (November 1912): 29.

27. African Americans fared little better under Wilson's Republican successors. Meier and Rudwick, "Rise of Segregation in the Federal Bureaucracy"; Sherman, *Republican Party and Black America*; Richard D. Kane, "The Federal Segregation of Blacks during the Presidential Administrations of Warren G. Harding and Calvin Coolidge," *Pan-African Journal* 7 (Summer 1974): 153–71.

28. WEBD, "Open Letter to Woodrow Wilson," 236–37; JA quoted in "Opinion" section, *Crisis* 5 (March 1913): 229.

29. Josephus Daniels diary, April 11, 1913, *PWW*, 27:290–91. On Burleson as Wilson's "political ambassador," see RSB, notes of an interview with Albert Sidney Burleson, ca. March 17–19, 1927, RSBmss, reel 72.

30. Daniels diary, April 11, 1913, 291; Arthur S. Link, *Wilson: The New Freedom* (Princeton, NJ: Princeton UP, 1956), 246–52; Yellin, *Racism in the Nation's Service*, 114–19. Yellin notes that McAdoo, though no racial egalitarian, was responding to pressure both from congressmen and from high-ranking Treasury subordinates (96–98, 99–100, 106–7). For glimpses of Wilson's battle for mastery over Congress and Democratic state and local machines, see EMH diary, April 11, April 18, and May 7, 1913, *PWW*, 27: 292, 333, 407; EMH to WW, May 4, 1913, *PWW*, 27:396–97; James Alexander Reed to WW, June 11, 1913, and WW to Reed, June 13, 1913, *PWW*, 27:508–9, 515.

31. Oswald Garrison Villard to Robert Hayne Leavell, May 15, 1913, *PWW*, 27: 442.

32. Oswald Garrison Villard to WW, July 21, 1913, and WW to Villard, July 23, 1913, *PWW*, 28:60–61, 65; Blumenthal, "Wilson and the Race Question," esp. 6.

33. WEBD, "Impressions of Woodrow Wilson," 456; Oswald Garrison Villard to WW, August 18, 1913, enclosing Booker T. Washington to Villard, August 10, 1913, *PWW*, 28:185–87; Alfred B. Cosey to JPT, August 22, 1913, *PWW*, 28:209–12; William Frank Powell to WW, August 26, 1913, *PWW*, 28:221–23.

34. WEBD, "Another Open Letter to Woodrow Wilson," *Crisis* 6 (September 1913): 232–36, quoted 233, 236.

35. WW to Oswald Garrison Villard, August 19, 1913, *PWW*, 28:64; William Monroe Trotter address to WW, and WW response, November 6, 1913, *PWW*, 28:491–96. For the reports of Wilson's inquiry, see editorial note 1, *PWW*, 28:498–99. For efforts to legislate segregation by act of Congress see, e.g., H.R. 5968 (1913), "To effect certain reforms in the civil service by segregating clerks and employees of the white race from those of African blood or descent" (James P. Aswell, D-Louisiana); and H.R. 13772 (1914), "To segregate Government employees of the white race from those of African blood or descent" (Charles G. Edwards, D-Georgia).

36. William Monroe Trotter address to WW, and WW response, November 12,1914, *PWW*, 31:298–308, esp. 300–304.

37. Ibid., 305–8.

38. For Daniels's recollection see *PWW*, 31:309n2.

39. WW remarks to the University Commission on the Southern Race Question, December 15, 1914, *PWW*, 31:464–65; Charlotte Everett Wise Hopkins to WW, June 21, 1915, *PWW*, 33:430–31, 432nn1, 6; WW proclamation, July 2, 1915, *PWW*, 33:464.

40. Thomas W. Dixon Jr. to JPT, May 1, 1915, quoted in *PWW*, 32:142n1 (editor's note appended to Thomas W. Dixon Jr. to JPT, January 27, 1915).

41. WW to JPT, ca. April 22, 1918, *PWW*, 47:388n3; John Milton Cooper Jr., "American Sphinx: Woodrow Wilson and Race," in *Jefferson, Lincoln, and Wilson: The American Dilemma of Race and Democracy*, ed. Cooper and Thomas J. Knock (Charlottesville: University of Virginia Press, 2010), 145–62, esp. 154–55, 161n18. See also the editors' discussion of the "lightning" misattribution in *PWW*, 32:267n1; and Mark E. Benbow, "Birth of a Quotation: Woodrow Wilson and 'Like Writing History with Lightning,'" *Journal of the Gilded Age and Progressive Era* 9 (October 2010): 509–33, esp. 512–16. Benbow notes that Wilson's program, saved by White House physician and friend Cary Grayson, was crumpled, but interprets this as evidence of emotional investment rather than lack of interest (514). On the misleading use of Wilson's writings in *Birth of a Nation*'s intertitles, see Melvyn Stokes, *D. W. Griffith's "Birth of a Nation": A History of "The Most Controversial Motion Picture of All Time"* (New York: Oxford UP, 2007), 198–200.

42. WEBD, "The Presidential Campaign," *Crisis* 12 (October 1916): 268–69.

43. John Sharp Williams to WW, March 31, 1914, *PWW*, 29:388. For the violent reaction of southerners to Wilson's appointments of African Americans, see Sosna, "South in the Saddle," 36; George C. Osborn, "The Problem of the Negro in Government, 1913," *Historian* 23 (May 1961): 331.

44. WW statement of July 28, 1918, *PWW*, 44:98.

45. WW speech in Waterbury, CT, December 14, 1899, *PWW*, 11:298.

46. WW, "Democracy and Efficiency" (1901), *PWW*, 12:7–8, 16, 19.

47. Andrew Clarke Imbrie, lecture notes on WW, "International Law," Wilson Collection, Box 59, Folder 5, Mudd Manuscript Library, Princeton University (hereafter cited as "Imbrie notes"), lecture 8 (April 3, 1894—original emphasis), lecture 3 (March 13, 1894). Compare Immanuel Kant, *Idea for a Universal History with a Cosmopolitan Purpose* (1784) and *Toward Perpetual Peace* (1795), in *Kant: Political Writings*, ed. H. S. Reiss (Cambridge: Cambridge UP, 1970), 41–53, 93–130.

48. Imbrie notes, lecture 2 (March 6, 1894; original emphasis), and lecture 4, March 19, 1894.

49. Kant, *Perpetual Peace*, 105.

50. WW, "Study of Administration," 380.

51. WW, "The Ideals of America" (1902), *PWW*, 12:222–224.

52. WW, "Religion and Patriotism" (1902), *PWW*, 12:476.

53. WW, "Education and Democracy" (1907), *PWW*, 17:134–36.

54. WW address in Omaha, NE, October 5, 1912, *PWW*, 25:341; Burton I. Kaufman, *Efficiency and Expansion: Foreign Trade Organization in the Wilson Administration, 1913–1921* (Westport, CT: Greenwood, 1974).

55. WW statement of November 2, 1912, *PWW*, 25:502; WW address at Mary Baldwin Seminary, Staunton, VA, December 28, 1912, *PWW*, 25:629.

56. An updated study of Wilson's Asian diplomacy is overdue. In 1952 Tien-yi Li

judged Wilson's policy both democratic and adaptable, if ultimately unsuccessful in stemming foreign (particularly Japanese) incursions into China. Later that decade, Roy Curry deemed Wilson largely successful in meeting the "challenge to a responsible American policy in the Far East." Tien-yi Li, *Woodrow Wilson's China Policy, 1913–1917* (Kansas City, MO: Kansas City UP, 1952); Roy Watson Curry, *Woodrow Wilson and Far Eastern Policy, 1913–1921* (New York: Bookman Associates, 1957), 322.

57. WW statement of March 18, 1913, *PWW*, 27:193–94; Kendrick Clements, *Woodrow Wilson: World Statesman* (1987; repr., Chicago: Ivan R. Dee, 1999), 137; Li, *Wilson's China Policy*, 212.

58. Daniels diary, March 12, 1913, *PWW*, 27:175; *La Follette's Weekly*, March 29, 1913, 9; Paul S. Reinsch to Robert Lansing, December 8, 1916, enclosed in Lansing to JPT, January 23, 1917, *PWW*, 40:563. Favorable commentary appeared in *NYT*, March 19, 1913; *Washington Post*, March 19, 1913; *Wall Street Journal*, March 21, 1913; *Chicago Tribune*, March 20, 1913. For the response of the Chinese political class and press, see Li, *Wilson's China Policy*, 45–46.

59. *NYT*, May 3, 1913; *Outlook* 104 (May 10, 1913): 41; Reinsch to Lansing, December 8, 1916.

60. WW to unknown recipient, August 15, 1911, *PWW*, 23:267 (emphasis added); Lindley Miller Garrison to WW, April 24, 1913, *PWW*, 27:354–356; FF, "Memorandum for the Secretary of War Re: Government and Administration of the Philippine Islands," April 11, 1913, FFmss, reel 120.

61. See William Jennings Bryan to WW, August 16, 1913, *PWW*, 28:175; WW to Lindley Miller Garrison and Garrison to WW, August 19, 1913, *PWW*, 28:192; Manuel Luis Quezon to Bryan, August 16, 1913, enclosed in Bryan to WW, August 19, 1913, *PWW*, 28:192–93.

62. Francis Burton Harrison to Lindley Miller Garrison, October 18, 1913, *PWW*, 28:416. Ford's report is quoted at length in the editorial note under WW to Henry Jones Ford, August 28, 1913, *PWW*, 28:242–45.

63. Many prominent Filipinos, including Quezon, resisted plans for a speedier transition. For the full story of Wilson's Philippine policy, see Curry, *Wilson and Far Eastern Policy*, chap. 3. On US–Philippine relations from the Spanish-American War through Philippine independence, see Paul A. Kramer, *The Blood of Government: Race, Empire, the United States, and the Philippines* (Chapel Hill: University of North Carolina Press, 2006).

64. Ford's report quoted in *PWW*, 28:244; WW to Francis Burton Harrison, September 25, 1913, *PWW*, 28:323–24 (read aloud by Harrison during a speech at Manila on October 6); WW message to Congress, December 7, 1920, *PWW*, 66:490.

65. WW remarks at press conference, April 14, 1913, *PWW*, 27:304–5.

66. Edwin S. Corwin to WW, April 13, 1913, and WW to Corwin, April 19, 1913, *PWW*, 27:299, 336; William Kent to WW, with enclosures, April 9, 1913, *PWW*, 27:280–82; William Jennings Bryan to Hiram Warren Johnson, April 18, 1913, *PWW*, 27:326.

67. WW to Hiram Johnson et al., April 22, 1913, *PWW*, 27:343–44; Daniels diary, April 22, 1913, *PWW*, 27:349–50.

68. Daniels diary, May 13, 1913, appending Bradley A. Fiske to Daniels, May 14, 1913, *PWW*, 27:425–28; Daniels diary, May 15 and 16, 1913, *PWW*, 27:441–45;

Arthur S. Link, *Woodrow Wilson and the Progressive Era, 1910–1917* (New York: Harper, 1954), 87.

69. *Outlook* 104 (May 3, 1913): 16.

70. *El Diario* (Mexico City), November 16, 1912; *El Pais* (Mexico City), November 8, 1912.

71. WW statement on relations with Latin America, March 12, 1913, *PWW*, 27:172.

72. Ibid. (emphasis added).

73. William Jennings Bryan to WW, May 18, 1913, *PWW*, 27:448.

74. For the text of these treaties—all nearly identically worded—see the agreement with Guatemala signed September 20, 1913, in *Treaties, Conventions, International Acts, Protocols, and Agreements between the United States of America and Other Powers, 1776–1923*, 3 vols. (Washington, DC: GPO, 1910–23), 3:2666–2667.

75. Charles A. Douglas draft treaty, enclosed in William Jennings Bryan to WW, June 16, 1913, *PWW*, 27:529. See also Paolo E. Coletta, *William Jennings Bryan*, 3 vols. (Lincoln: University of Nebraska Press, 1964–69), 2:188–89; Lars Schoultz, *Beneath the United States: A History of U.S. Policy toward Latin America* (Cambridge, MA: Harvard UP, 1998), 224–26.

76. Bryan to WW, August 16, 1913; WW to William Jennings Bryan, January 26, 1914, *PWW*, 29:172–73.

77. Coletta, *William Jennings Bryan*, 2:191–93; *NYT*, October 15, 1914; *NYT*, January 3, 1915.

78. Schoultz, *Beneath the United States*, 227–29.

79. WW memorandum, July 27, 1914, *PWW*, 30:307–9.

80. Arthur S. Link, *Wilson: The Struggle for Neutrality, 1914–1915* (Princeton, NJ: Princeton UP, 1960), 514–16.

81. Ibid. 539–48; Schoultz, *Beneath the United States*, 230–31; also Alan L. MacPherson, *The Invaded: How Latin Americans and Their Allies Fought and Ended U.S. Occupations* (New York: Oxford UP, 2014), chaps. 3 and 6.

82. Schoultz, *Beneath the United States*, 516–532; Calhoun, *Power and Principle*, 88–93.

83. McPherson, *Invaded*, 24–25; Link, *Struggle for Neutrality*, 528–35.

84. WEBD to WW, August 3, 1915, WEBDmss, reel 5.

85. WW to Robert Lansing, August 4, 1915, *PWW*, 34:8; Link, *Struggle for Neutrality*, 537–38; Calhoun, *Power and Principle*, 100–102. Renda, *Taking Haiti*, thoroughly reconstructs the Jim Crow thinking and practices common among US occupiers.

86. "Hayti," *Crisis* 10 (October 15, 1915): 291.

87. Erez Manela, "'Peoples of Many Races': The World Beyond Europe in the Wilsonian Imagination," in Cooper and Knock, eds. *Jefferson, Lincoln, and Wilson*, 184–208, esp. 200.

88. The literature on Wilson's Mexican policy is extensive. Especially useful for the period covered in this chapter are Gilderhus, *Diplomacy and Revolution*; and Kendrick A. Clements, "Woodrow Wilson's Mexican Policy, 1913–1915," *Diplomatic History* 4 (Spring 1980): 113–36. Richly detailed but too narrow in its emphasis on Wilson's religious motives is Mark Benbow, *Leading Them to the Promised Land: Woodrow Wilson, Covenant Theology, and the Mexican Revolution, 1913–1915* (Kent, OH: Kent State UP, 2010).

89. Eleanor Wilson McAdoo, *The Woodrow Wilsons* (New York: Macmillan, 1937), 135–36; Francis G. Wickware , ed., *American Yearbook, 1918* (New York: T. Nelson and Sons, 1919), 552.

90. WW quoted in Link, *New Freedom*, 350; WW statement on relations with Latin America, March 12, 1913, 172; John Bassett Moore to WW, May 14, 1913, *PWW*, 27:437–40; Daniels diary, March 11, 1913, *PWW*, 27:170. Long dismissed as paranoia, US suspicions that Britain, especially, sought surreptitiously to control events in Mexico to advance its economic interests there were not unfounded. See Friedrich Katz, *The Secret War in Mexico: Europe, the United States, and the Mexican Revolution* (Chicago: University of Chicago Press, 1981).

91. For complaints from businessmen and landholders, see *Los Angeles Times*, March 20 and May 11, 1913; for pressure from bankers, see EMH to WW, May 6, 1913, *PWW*, 27:404n2.

92. *Nation* 96 (March 13, 1913): 245; *La Follette's Weekly* 5 (March 1, 1913): 3; *La Follette's Weekly* 5 (March 29, 1913): 1; WW remarks at press conference, April 11, 1913, *PWW*, 27:289.

93. WW, draft instructions to Henry Lane Wilson, May 15, 1913, *PWW*, 27:435; WW remarks at press conference, July 28, 1913, *PWW*, 28:89.

94. WW to John Lind, August 4, 1914, *PWW*, 28:110–11; Link, *New Freedom*, 358–60 (Foreign Minister Federico Gamboa quoted 359).

95. WW address to Congress, August 27, 1913, *PWW*, 28:228–31.

96. E.g., *Nation* 97 (September 4, 1913): 201.

97. Link, *Wilson and the Progressive Era*, 115–16; WW to Ellen Axson Wilson, September 28, 1913, *PWW*, 28:334. For the current of opinion, see William Jennings Bryan to WW, September 25, 1913, *PWW*, 28:325; and the previously critical *NYT*, September 26, 1913.

98. WW, draft circular note, October 24, 1913, *PWW*, 27:432; WW address in Mobile, AL, October 27, 1913, *PWW*, 27:450–51.

99. See the press review in *Literary Digest* 47 (November 8, 1913): 855–57.

100. John Barrett to WW, July 26, 1913, *PWW*, 28:139; Mark T. Gilderhus, *Pan American Visions: Woodrow Wilson in the Western Hemisphere, 1913–1921* (Tucson: University of Arizona Press, 1986), 16–17.

101. Link, *New Freedom*, 387–88; Clements, "Wilson's Mexican Policy," 120.

102. EMH diary, October 30, 1913, *PWW*, 28:478; *NYT*, November 20, 1913.

103. Sir Cecil Arthur Spring-Rice to Sir Edward Grey, February 6, 1914, *PWW*, 29:228.

104. Gilderhus, *Diplomacy and Revolution*, 9–10; Link, *New Freedom*, 396.

105. Hall and Coerver, *Revolution on the Border*, 22–23.

106. WW address in Mobile, AL, October 27, 1913, 450; Link, *New Freedom*, 392.

107. Sir Cecil Arthur Spring-Rice to Sir Edward Grey, February 7, 1914, *PWW*, 29:228–30.

108. Quirk, *Affair of Honor*, 53.

109. *El Murcurio* (Valparaiso), April 25, 1914; "American Intervention in Mexico: A Poll of the European Press," *Outlook* 107 (May 2, 1914): 17–18. Exceptions included the London *Times* and *Frankfurter Zeitung*, echoing the more sympathetic response of British and German officials who hoped Wilson would take the logical next steps of ousting Huerta and pacifying Mexico.

110. See *Chicago Tribune*, April 23, 1914, for that paper's position and a digest of press opinion. Also *Nation* 98 (April 23, 1914): 451; *Nation* 98 (April 30, 1914): 487–88; *Independent* 78 (April 27, 1914): 151–52; *La Follette's Weekly* 6 (May 2, 1914): 1. The labor press frequently invoked the simultaneous "war" then raging between striking coal miners and paramilitaries working for John D. Rockefeller at Ludlow, Colorado—a conflict in which Wilson eventually intervened, with federal troops, on the side of the miners and their families. See *Seattle Union Record*, April 15 and May 9, 1914.

111. *NYT*, April 22, 1914; WEBD, "Mexico," *Crisis* 8 (June 1914): 79; *NR* 1 (November 21, 1914): 3.

112. H. J. Forman to RSB, quoted in Link, *New Freedom*, 402.

113. Link, *New Freedom*, 402–7; WW, confidential memorandum for ABC representatives, April 15, 1914, *PWW*, 29:507; WW interview with Samuel G. Blythe, April 27, 1914, *PWW*, 29:516–24.

114. WW interview with John Reed, June 15, 1914, enclosed in John Reed to JPT, 30 June 1914, *PWW*, 30:231–38, esp. 237. Wilson's Pan-American efforts are treated in chapter 4.

115. WW address at Arlington National Cemetery, May 30, 1914, *PWW*, 30:111.

116. WW to George Lawrence Record, June 1, 1914, *PWW*, 30:131; WW to Lindley Miller Garrison, August 8, 1914, *PWW*, 30:362; WW to Edith Bolling Galt, August 18, 1915, *PWW*, 34:242.

117. WW state of the Union address, December 7, 1915, *PWW*, 35:296.

CHAPTER FOUR

1. JA, *Peace and Bread in Time of War* (New York: Macmillan, 1922), 1.

2. Quoted in *Literary Digest* 49 (August 22, 1914): 293–95.

3. Charles Seymour, ed., *The Intimate Papers of Colonel House, Arranged as a Narrative*, 4 vols. (Boston: Houghton Mifflin, 1926–28), 1:298; Theodore Roosevelt, "The Foreign Policy of the United States," *Outlook* 107 (August 22, 1914): 1011–1015; Walter Hines Page to WW, August 9, 1914, *PWW*, 30:371.

4. A. Lawrence Lowell, "A League to Enforce Peace," *Atlantic Monthly* 116 (September 1915): 392–400, quoted at 392; League to Enforce Peace, "Platform," *League to Enforce Peace: American Chapter* (New York: LEP, 1915), 4; William Howard Taft address in Philadelphia, PA, June 17, 1915, in *League to Enforce Peace*, 13.

5. *Current Opinion* 57 (December, 1914): 377–81, esp. 378; *Democratic Textbook for 1916* (Washington, DC: Democratic National Committee, 1916).

6. Robert M. La Follette, "A World Power—For Peace," *La Follette's Weekly* 6 (October 3, 1914): 1.

7. JA, *Peace and Bread*, 4; RB to Alyse Gregory, January 21, 1916, in Randolph Bourne, *The Letters of Randolph Bourne: A Comprehensive Edition*, ed. Eric J. Sandeen (Troy, NY: Whitston, 1981), 363.

8. WEBD, "World War and the Color Line," *Crisis* 9 (November, 1914): 29. WEBD, "The African Roots of War," *Atlantic Monthly* 115 (May 1915), 707–14, explores the war's roots in an inherently racist international competition for extra-European resources. On Du Bois's wartime views generally, see Mark Ellis, " 'Closing Ranks' and 'Seeking

Honors': W. E. B. Du Bois in World War I," *Journal of American History* 79 (June 1992): 94–124; and David Levering Lewis, *W. E. B. Du Bois, 1868–1919: Biography of a Race* (New York: Henry Holt, 1993), chaps. 18–19.

9. HC, *The Promise of American Life* (New York: Macmillan, 1909), 289.

10. HC, "The Structure of Peace," *NR* 9 (January 13, 1917): 290.

11. David W. Levy's biography, *Herbert Croly of "The New Republic": Life and Thought of an American Progressive* (Princeton, NJ: Princeton UP, 1985), is also the best history of the journal's first twenty years.

12. Walter E. Weyl, *The New Democracy: An Essay on Certain Political and Economic Tendencies in the United States* (New York: Macmillan, 1912), 2, 20, 162, 269.

13. *NR* 1 (November 7, 1914): 3, 7–8.

14. *NR* 7 (June 24, 1916): 182; HC to FF, October 10, 1913, FFmss, reel 102; FF, undated memorandum on "The Republic," FFmss, reel 102; JD, "The Problem of Truth" (1911), *MW*, 6:31.

15. *NR* 7 (June 24, 1916), 182.

16. Graham Wallas, *Human Nature in Politics* (London: Archibald Constable, 1908); WL, *A Preface to Politics* (New York: Mitchell Kennerley, 1913). For Wilson's borrowing of both books from the Library of Congress in July and August 1914, see the overdue notice from William Warner Bishop to WW, November 14, 1914, *PWW*, 31:316–17; for his reading of the *New Republic*, see RSB to WL, October 25, 1928, RSBmss, reel 79.

17. WW address to the Senate, August 18, 1914, *PWW*, 30:393–94 (delivered August 19).

18. "The End of American Isolation," *NR* 1 (November 7, 1914): 10; Roland G. Usher, "The War and the Future of Civilization," *NR* 1 (November 7, 1914): 22–23.

19. WW address to Senate, August 18, 1914, 394.

20. RB, "American Use for German Ideals," *NR* 4 (September 4, 1915), 117. The influence of German economic theory and social policy on Gilded Age and Progressive Era American reformers is confirmed in Daniel T. Rodgers, *Atlantic Crossings: Social Politics in a Progressive Age* (Cambridge, MA: Harvard UP, 1998).

21. *Nation* 99 (September 10, 1914): 305.

22. *Nation* 99 (December 17, 1914): 712; *Nation* 99 (December 31, 1914): 771; "Timid Neutrality," *NR* 1 (November 7, 1914): 8.

23. Seymour, *Intimate Papers of Colonel House*, 1:114. The best window into House's views on world politics is his massive diary, preserved in EMHmss; a focused account of his diplomatic initiatives is Joyce Grigsby Williams, *Colonel House and Sir Edward Grey: A Study in Anglo-American Diplomacy* (Lanham, MD: Rowman and Littlefield, 1984). The only full-length biography, and the most detailed examination of his significant but often exaggerated influence on Wilson, is Charles E. Neu, *Colonel House: A Biography of Woodrow Wilson's Silent Partner* (New York: Oxford UP, 2015). A recent account of the House–Wilson relationship that largely credits House's own assessments of his influence is Godfrey Hodgson, *Woodrow Wilson's Right Hand: The Life of Colonel Edward M. House* (New Haven, CT: Yale UP, 2006). More skeptical is John M. Cooper Jr., *Woodrow Wilson: A Biography* (New York: Knopf, 2009).

24. WW quoted in Sir Cecil Arthur Spring-Rice to Sir Edward Grey, September 3, 1914, *PWW*, 30:472.

25. Memorandum, WW interview with Herbert Bruce Brougham, December 14, 1914, *PWW*, 31:458–59.

26. EMH diary, December 16, 1914, *PWW*, 31:469. Texas Democrat James Slayden first proposed a Pan-American Pact to William Jennings Bryan in November 1913, but Wilson thought the idea impractical as long as the Mexican crisis remained unresolved. See William Jennings Bryan to WW, November 6, 1913, and WW to Bryan, November 7, 1913, *PWW*, 28:491, 505.

27. *NR* 1 (December 12, 1914): 3; Mark T. Gilderhus, "Pan-American Initiatives: The Wilson Presidency and 'Regional Integration,' 1914–1917," *Diplomatic History* 4 (Fall 1980): 410n5, 414; EMH diary, November 25 and 30, 1914, EMHmss; WW message to Congress, December 8, 1914, *PWW*, 31:416.

28. EMH diary, December 16, 1914, *PWW*, 31:470.

29. WW, draft Pan-American Treaty, December 16, 1914, *PWW*, 31:471–72. For the draft's transmission to the ABC countries, see *PWW*, 31:473n1.

30. Thomas J. Knock, *To End All Wars: Woodrow Wilson and the Quest for a New World Order* (1992; repr., Princeton, NJ: Princeton UP, 1995), 39.

31. WW address aboard the *Moreno*, March 29, 1915, *PWW*, 32:452.

32. Quoted in *NYT*, August 5, 1914.

33. "Pan-Americanism," *NR* 1 (December 19, 1914): 10.

34. Gilderhus, "Pan-American Initiatives," 416–22. Efforts to strengthen commercial ties met with greater success; see Burton I. Kaufman, "United States Trade and Latin America: The Wilson Years," *Journal of American History* 58 (September 1971): 355–59.

35. Clarence Poe to Josephus Daniels, October 5, 1914, enclosed in Josephus Daniels to WW, October 6, 1914, *PWW*, 31:126–29; WW instructions to the American Ambassador in London, December 24–26, 1914, *PWW*, 31:525.

36. Robert Lansing to WW, with enclosures, October 23, 1914, *PWW*, 31:216–20.

37. WW address to Pittsburgh YMCA, October 24, 1914, *PWW*,. 31:226–27.

38. EMH diary, December 3, 1914, *PWW*, 31:385.

39. *NR* 1 (January 2, 1915): 3; "Security for Neutrals," *NR* 1 (January 2, 1915): 7–9; TV, *Imperial Germany and the Industrial Revolution* (New York: Macmillan, 1915).

40. WW press conference remarks, December 29, 1914, *PWW*, 31:543–44; *NR* 1 (January 9, 1915): 8–9. For evidence of other support, see the reporting in *Chicago Tribune*, December 30, 1914.

41. See correspondence printed in *PWW*, 31:276–78, 293, 336–40.

42. Press release, *PWW*, 30:342; WW to EMH, January 29, 1915, *PWW*, 32:157–58; EMH diary, January 24, 1915, *PWW*, 32:117.

43. N. Gordon Levin, *Woodrow Wilson and World Order: America's Response to War and Revolution* (New York: Oxford UP, 1968); Victoria de Graza, *Irresistible Empire: America's Advance through Twentieth-Century Europe* (Cambridge, MA: Harvard UP, 2005).

44. Quoted in Patrick Devlin, *Too Proud to Fight: Woodrow Wilson's Neutrality* (New York: Oxford UP, 1975), 176. See also Robert Lansing to WW, November 28, 1914, and WW to Lansing, November 30, 1914, *PWW*, 31:359, 369.

45. Seymour, *Intimate Papers of Colonel House* 1:355; Robert Lansing, *War Memoirs of Robert Lansing, Secretary of State* (Indianapolis: Bobbs-Merrill, 1935), 54–55, quotation

at 59. On the embargo debate, see Arthur S. Link, *Wilson the Diplomatist: A Look at His Major Foreign Policies* (Baltimore, MD: Johns Hopkins UP, 1957), 35–46.

46. WW to Charles William Eliot, February 23, 1915, *PWW*, 32:276.

47. On the bill and its fate see Arthur S. Link, *Wilson: The Struggle for Neutrality, 1914–1915* (Princeton, NJ: Princeton UP, 1960), 84–91, 143–49.

48. See enclosure in WW to William Gibbs McAdoo, March 8, 1915, *PWW*, 32:336–37. McAdoo's original draft of this public statement was reviewed and emended by Wilson.

49. WW quoted in Link, *Struggle for Neutrality*, 151–52. For a survey of editorial comment, see *Current Opinion* 58 (February 1915): 71–72.

50. *NR* 2 (February 13, 1915): 29.

51. Link, *Struggle for Neutrality*, 179–83 (Bryan quoted at 180); Devlin, *Too Proud to Fight*, 187.

52. Enclosed in WW to William Jennings Bryan, January 22, 1915, *PWW*, 32:104–5. The note, originally drafted by Lansing, was to be sent to Ambassador Page for relay to Grey. Quoted are Wilson's additions to Lansing's draft.

53. Link, *Struggle for Neutrality*, 157–58.

54. WW to Robert Newton Page, February 23, 1915, *PWW*, 32:275. Page was brother to Walter Hines Page, American ambassador in London.

55. WW draft (March 3) and public (March 5) statements quoted in Link, *Struggle for Neutrality*, 159, 160–61.

56. WW to Thomas W. Hardwick, March 15, 1915, *PWW*, 32:375–76; WJ, "Robert Gould Shaw" (1897), in *Memories and Studies*, ed. Henry James Jr. (New York: Longmans, Green, 1911), 61.

57. Link, *Struggle for Neutrality*, 187.

58. "The Goose and the Gander," *NR* 2 (February 20, 1915): 60.

59. The German declaration was reported in the *Washington Post* of February 5 and confirmed the next day by the American ambassador to Germany, James W. Gerard: *PWW*, 32:193, notes 1, 3.

60. WW, draft note to Germany, February 6, 1915, *PWW*, 32:194–95; William Jennings Bryan to WW, February 18, 1915, *PWW*, 32:249–51, esp. 251n1 on the German reply.

61. EMH to WW, May 11, 1915, in Seymour, *Intimate Papers of Colonel House* 1:434; Roosevelt quoted in John Milton Cooper, Jr., *The Warrior and the Priest: Woodrow Wilson and Theodore Roosevelt* (Cambridge, MA: Harvard UP, 1983), 289.

62. The Bryce group's findings were published as the *Report of the Committee on Alleged German Outrages* (London: HM Stationery Office, 1915). For American reactions, see *Literary Digest* 50 (May 29, 1915): 1257–59.

63. WW address in Philadelphia, PA, May 10, 1915, *PWW*, 33:149.

64. JA, "What War is Destroying" (delivered at the founding of the Woman's Peace Party in Washington, January 10, 1915), *Advocate of Peace* 77 (March 1915): 64; "Lusitania," *Crisis* 10 (June 1915): 81; "Dealing with Germany," *NR* 3 (May 15, 1915): 28.

65. David Lawrence, *The True Story of Woodrow Wilson* (New York: George H. Doran, 1924), 197–98; Lansing, *War Memoirs*, 34.

66. WW note, emended by Lansing, printed as Enclosure II in William Jennings Bryan to WW, June 7, 1915, *PWW*, 33:355–60 (quotation at 358–59).

67. On Bryan's resignation, see Cooper, *Woodrow Wilson*, 291–94. Bryan's role in securing the Volstead Act's passage was critical, though prohibition was by then a century-old movement. Its complexity and consequences are delineated in Lisa McGirr, *The War on Alcohol: Prohibition and the Rise of the American State* (New York: Norton, 2016).

68. *Washington Post*, May 15, 1915.

69. WW to Robert Lansing, with enclosure, July 21, 1915, *PWW*, 33:548; Lansing, *War Memoirs*, 37–38.

70. EMH to WW, August 22, 1915, in Seymour, *Intimate Papers of Colonel House* 2:31; WW to Edith Bolling Galt, August 19, 1915, *PWW*, 34:261.

71. "The Arabic—Germany's Answer," *Outlook* (August 25, 1915): 931–32; "An Act of Deliberate Unfriendliness," *Independent* 83 (August 30, 1915): 279.

72. Link, *Struggle for Neutrality*, 569, 578–79. Actually, Lansing was pretending. He wrote Wilson of his "optimism" that the situation would be "amicably arranged." Robert Lansing to WW, August 26, 1915, *PWW*, 34:340.

73. Lansing, *War Memoirs*, 47–53.

74. Quoted in Knock, *To End All Wars*, 61.

75. *NR* 4 (September 4, 1915): 111.

76. *NR* 4 (September 18, 1915): 166–67.

77. Lansing, *War Memoirs*, 106.

78. For the negotiations and administration reactions, see Robert Lansing to WW, February 16, 1916, *PWW*, 36:182.

79. *NYT*, February 16, 1916; *NR* 6 (February 19, 1916): 53–54. See Arthur S. Link, *Wilson: Confusions and Crises, 1915–1916* (Princeton, NJ: Princeton UP, 1964), 167–94 for the confrontation with pacifist Democrats in Congress following the modus vivendi and declaration on submarine warfare.

80. See the front pages of *NYT*, *New York Tribune*, *Boston Daily Globe*, *Chicago Tribune*, *Los Angeles Times*, *San Francisco Chronicle*, and *Atlanta Constitution* for February 16, 1916.

81. WW to William J. Stone, February 24, 1916, *PWW*, 36:213–14.

82. WL, "Washington Notes," *NR* 6 (March 18, 1916): 181–82.

83. Link, *Confusions and Crises*, 110–13, WW to EMH quoted at 112.

84. Ibid. 131–33; J. Williams, *Colonel House and Sir Edward Grey*, 79–89.

85. For Wilson's reception of the House-Grey Memorandum, see EMH diary, March 6, 1916, *PWW*, 36:262–63; for his addition of *probably* to the text, see EMH to Sir Edward Grey, March 7, 1916, *PWW*, 36:266

86. EMH to WW, February 3, 1916, *PWW*, 36:125; Link, *Confusions and Crises*, 137–38.

87. Michael Parrish, *Felix Frankfurter and His Times: The Reform Years* (New York: Free Press, 1982), FF quoted at 79.

88. "The Sum of All Villainies," *NR* 2 (February 13, 1915): 36–37.

89. *NR* 5 (November 20, 1915): 58; *NR* 6 (March 11, 1916): 144.

90. "The Case of the *Sussex*—the Latest Crisis in Our Relations with Germany," *Current Opinion* 60 (May 1916): 3–5. A detailed account of the *Sussex* crisis is Link, *Confusions and Crises*, 222–55.

91. WW (with EMH) to Sir Edward Grey, April 16, 1916, *PWW*, 36:421; Grey to EMH, April 8, 1916, enclosed in EMH to WW, April 8, 1916, *PWW*, 36:444.

92. Bethmann quoted in Link, *Confusions and Crises*, 242; EMH to WW, April 8,

1916, *PWW*, 36:446; deciphered telegram from Jagow to Bernstorff, April 17, 1916, enclosed in Robert Lansing to WW, April 17, 1916, *PWW*, 36:499.

93. WW address to Congress, April 19, 1916, *PWW*, 36:509–10.

94. For the official German reply to Wilson's ultimatum, see enclosures in Robert Lansing to WW, May 6, 1916, *PWW*, 36:621–27; for Wilson's response, see enclosure in WW to Lansing, May 8, 1916, *PWW*, 650–51.

95. See, e.g., *NR* 7 (July 8, 1916): 237.

96. "A White Peace and its Consequences," *NR* 9 (December 16, 1916): 168; WW to EMH, July 23, 1916, *PWW*, 37:467.

CHAPTER FIVE

1. Max Eastman, *Understanding Germany, the Only Way to End War, and Other Essays* (New York: Mitchell Kennerley, 1916), 70. The preparedness movement is well documented in John Patrick Finnegan, *Against the Specter of a Dragon: The Campaign for American Military Preparedness, 1914–1917* (Westport, CT: Greenwood, 1974); and Michael Pearlman, *To Make Democracy Safe for America: Patricians and Preparedness in the Progressive Era* (Urbana: University of Illinois Press, 1984). For concise analyses of antipreparedness thought, see Ross A. Kennedy, *The Will to Believe: Woodrow Wilson, World War I, and America's Strategy for Peace and Security* (Kent, OH: Kent State UP, 2009), 1–2, 25–27; and Thomas J. Knock, *To End All Wars: Woodrow Wilson and the Quest for a New World Order* (1992; repr., Princeton, NJ: Princeton UP, 1995), 50–55, 62–64.

2. "Hypocritical Neutrality," *NR* 7 (May 13, 1916): 28–29.

3. See, e.g., "A League of Peace," *NR* 2 (March 20, 1915): 167–69.

4. "Mr. Wilson's Great Utterance," *NR* 7 (June 3, 1916): 103.

5. WW to Lindley Miller Garrison and Josephus Daniels, July 21, 1917, *PWW*, 34:4–5; EMH to WW, July 14, 1915, in Charles Seymour, ed., *The Intimate Papers of Colonel House, Arranged as a Narrative*, 4 vols. (Boston: Houghton Mifflin, 1926–28), 2:19.

6. Arthur S. Link, *Wilson: Confusions and Crises* (Princeton, NJ: Princeton UP, 1964), 15–19; William Jennings Bryan, "The People vs. the Special Interests," *Commoner* 15 (October 1915): 1.

7. Wilson had worked to gain the support of leading congressional Democrats by involving them in deliberations with the defense-related departments. See WW to James Hay, August 2, 1915, *PWW*, 34:58, including editorial note 1.

8. WW address to the Manhattan Club, November 4, 1915, *PWW*, 35:168–69.

9. "Evasions by Mr. Wilson," *NR* 5 (November 13, 1915): 29–30; Link, *Confusions and Crises*, 23–37; Lodge to Moreton Frewen, January 13, 1916, quoted in Link, *Confusions and Crises*, 44; Wister quoted in the Springfield (Massachusetts) *Republican*, February 24, 1916.

10. Link, *Confusions and Crises*, 37–39; Lindley Miller Garrison to WW, January 14, 1916, *PWW*, 35:480–81; WW to James Hay, January 18, 1916, *PWW*, 35:499–500.

11. WW address in New York, NY, January 27, 1916, *PWW*, 36:8–12.

12. WW address in Cleveland, OH, January 29, 1916, *PWW*, 36:47–48.

13. WW address in St. Louis, MO, February 3, 1916, *PWW*, 36:118–19, 120–21.

14. *NR* 6 (February 15, 1916): 1–2. For national reaction to Wilson's tour, see *Literary Digest* 52 (February 12, 1916): 359–61; Link, *Confusions and Crises*, 48–50.

15. Link, *Confusions and Crises*, 38–39.

16. WW to Lindley Miller Garrison, February 10, 1916, *PWW*, 36:163.

17. EMH diary, March 29, 1916, EMHmss.

18. WL, "Integrated America," *NR* 6 (February 19, 1916): 62–63.

19. Ibid., 65.

20. *NYT*, February 17 and March 1, 1916 (on NSL rallies); *Literary Digest* 53 (June 3, 1916): 1618 (on Roosevelt's attacks).

21. "Pacifism Versus Passivism," *NR* 1 (December 12, 1914): 7.

22. "'Preparedness' for What?" *NR* 3 (June 26, 1915): 188–89. Contrast Christopher Lasch's argument in *The New Radicalism in America: The Intellectual as a Social Type* (New York: Knopf, 1965), chapter 6, that the *New Republic* editors were committed to a more technocratic, antidemocratic social program—an argument neither their writings nor the policies they supported corroborate.

23. "Preparedness—A Trojan Horse," *NR* 5 (November 6, 1915): 6–7.

24. WL, "Integrated America," 63.

25. Ibid., 62, 64.

26. Ibid., 62–63.

27. Ibid., 65.

28. Ibid., 64–65.

29. Ibid., 66.

30. Ibid., 67. Plans along the lines of Lippmann's—some more ambitious, some less—were central to the reform agendas of many European and American publicists and theorists in the twentieth century's opening decades. See James T. Kloppenberg, *Uncertain Victory: Social Democracy and Progressivism in European and American Thought, 1880–1920* (New York: Oxford UP, 1986), part 2.

31. WL, "Integrated America," 67.

32. JD, "Our Educational Ideal in Wartime," *NR* 6 (April 15, 1916): 283–84; JD, "The Schools and Social Preparedness," *NR* 7 (May 6, 1916): 15–16.

33. WL, "The Issues of 1916," *NR* 7 (June 3, 1916): 109–10.

34. Lippmann related his habit of calling on cabinet officials in WL to Graham Wallas, February 21, 1916, WLmss, reel 32.

35. WL to Graham Wallas, April 21, 1916, WLmss, reel 32. "Our own emphasis," Lippmann continued, "as you will see in The New Republic, is to invent some kind of coercive policy which would have an actual relation to the submarine issue."

36. [WL], "An Appeal to the President," *NR* 6 (April 22, 1916): 303–5. Though the editorial was unsigned, Lippmann laid out its argument in the letter to Wallas (re: cabinet relations) cited in note 34.

37. WL, "Appeal," 303, 304.

38. Ibid., 304.

39. Ibid., copy in WWmss, reel 513.

40. "'Preparedness' for What?" 189.

41. WL, "Appeal," 303.

42. For the pacifist charge and Baker's gentle objection, see *NYT*, March 7, 1916.

43. NDB to WL, May 10 and July 27, 1916, WLmss, reel 2; NDB to WW, September 23, 1916, *PWW*, 38:238. On Baker, see Frederick Palmer, *Newton D. Baker: America at War*, 2 vols. (New York: Dodd, Mead, 1931); Daniel R. Beaver, *Newton D. Baker and the American War Effort, 1917–1919* (Lincoln: University of Nebraska Press, 1966); Douglas Craig, *Progressives at War: William G. McAdoo and Newton D. Baker, 1863–1941* (Baltimore, MD: Johns Hopkins UP, 2013).

44. NDB to WW, April 7, 1916, *PWW*, 37:431.

45. Ibid., 431–34.

46. Link, *Confusions and Crises*, 327–34.

47. WW to NDB, May 5, 1916, *PWW*, 36:612; WW address at Arlington National Cemetery, May 30, 1916, *PWW*, 37:127.

48. NDB to WL, April 22, 1916, WLmss, reel 2; Link, *Confusions and Crises*, 334–39; press release, October 10, 1916, *PWW*, 38:387.

49. Ironically, Theodore Roosevelt, Wilson's cruelest critic, was among the first Americans to suggest "a great world league for the peace of righteousness" in response to the outbreak of war in Europe. Having called for such an organization on accepting the Nobel Peace Prize in 1910, he revived the idea in a series of articles; see *NYT*, September 27; *NYT*, October 4, 11, and 18 (quoted); *NYT*, November 1, 8, 15, 22, and 29, 1914. Later Roosevelt's mushrooming hatred of Germany and Wilson led him to denounce neutrality and anything smacking of it, including Wilson's plans for a nonpunitive peace secured by a League of Nations.

50. Knock, *To End All Wars*, 55–56. The classic work on the LEP is Ruhl J. Bartlett, *The League to Enforce Peace* (Chapel Hill: University of North Carolina Press, 1944); the best recent study is Stephen Wertheim, "The League That Wasn't: American Designs for a Legalist-Sanctionist League of Nations and the Intellectual Origins of International Organization," *Diplomatic History* 35 (November 2011): 797–836. On legalism in American internationalist thought, see Benjamin Allen Coates, *Legalist Empire: International Law and American Foreign Relations in the Early Twentieth Century* (New York: Oxford UP, 2016); for the transatlantic context, see Francis Anthony Boyle, *Foundations of World Order: The Legalist Approach to International Relations, 1898–1922* (Durham, NC: Duke UP, 1999). On internationalist thought generally, see Warren F. Kuehl, *Seeking World Order: The United States and International Organization to 1920* (Nashville, TN: Vanderbilt UP, 1969); Christian Birebent, *Militants de la paix et de la SDN* (Paris: Harmattan, 2007); Jean-Michel Guieu, *Le Rameau et le glaive: les militants français pour la Société des Nations* (Paris: Presses de Sciences Po, 2008); George Egerton, *Great Britain and the Creation of the League of Nations* (Chapel Hill: University of North Carolina Press, 1978); Peter Yearwood, *Guarantee of Peace: The League of Nations in British Policy, 1914–1925* (Oxford: Oxford UP, 2009).

51. JA, "A Toast to John Dewey," *Survey* 63 (November 15, 1929); 204; JA, *Peace and Bread in Time of War* (New York: Macmillan, 1922), 6–7; "Women Foes of War," *Washington Post*, January 11, 1915. For Addams's access to the Wilson administration, see David S. Patterson, *The Search for Negotiated Peace: Women's Activism and Citizen Diplomacy in World War I* (New York: Routledge, 2008), 49, 115–26, 128–30.

52. JA quoted in Patterson, *Search for a Negotiated Peace*, 183; cf. 382n3 for the veracity of her account, misdated in *Peace and Bread*, 59.

53. Knock, *To End All Wars*, 55–56; WW to Lillian Wald, July 3, 1915, *PWW*, 33:472; WW to Robert Lansing, August 19 and 30, 1915, *PWW*, 34:247–48, 399.

54. JA, "Toast to John Dewey," 204; "Security for Neutrals," *NR* 1 (January 2, 1915): 7–9.

55. "A League of Peace," *NR* 2 (March 20, 1915): 168.

56. HC to WL, June 18, 1915, WLmss, reel 7.

57. WL, *The Stakes of Diplomacy* (1915; repr., New York: Macmillan, 1932), 141–42, 212–13, 215, 216–17.

58. WL, "Appeal," 303, 304.

59. Ibid., 304; WJ, "Robert Gould Shaw" (1897), in *Memories and Studies*, ed. Henry James Jr. (New York: Longmans, Green, 1911), 61.

60. WL, "Appeal," 304. Wilson made two dark vertical lines in the margin beside the passage cited, his typical marker of interest and approval. See copy in WWmss, reel 513; cf. RSB, *Woodrow Wilson, Life and Letters*, 8 vols. (Garden City, NY: Doubleday, Page, 1927–39), 6:203n.

61. WL, "Appeal," 304, 305.

62. On these early commitments, see Knock, *To End All Wars*, 34–38.

63. WW address to Pan-American Scientific Congress, January 6, 1916, *PWW*, 35:444–46; EMH to WW, February 9 and 11, 1915, *PWW*, 32:205–6, 220–21.

64. WW to EMH, December 24, 1915, *PWW*, 35:387–88.

65. EMH diary, February 21, 1916, EMHmss.

66. Knock, *To End All Wars*, 76.

67. AUAM memorial to WW, ca. May 8, 1916, *PWW*, 36:632; "A Colloquy with a Group of Antipreparedness Leaders," May 8, 1916, *PWW*, 36:641.

68. "Colloquy with Antipreparedness Leaders," 645–46, 644.

69. Knock implies that a harmony of views emerged between the AUAM and Wilson, which reflects the same cognitive dissonance that Wilson's linking of American readiness for war and influence for peace created for his visitors. While Knock emphasizes Eastman's comment that Wilson "sincerely hates his preparedness policies," it is at least equally accurate to emphasize Eastman's hope "that the President might point the way to all as boldly as he did to our committee." Knock, *To End All Wars*, 66–67.

70. WL to Wallas, April 21, 1916.

71. *NR* 8 (May 13, 1916): 26–27.

72. William Howard Taft to WW, 9 May 1916, and WW to Taft, May 18, 1916, *PWW*, 37:6, 69; see also Taft to WW, April 11, 1916, and WW to Taft, April 14, 1916, *PWW*, 36:458–59, 481. The *New Republic*'s influence on Wilson's decision to endorse international organization was not unique, but it was substantial. Although House urged Wilson on March 30 to make a public statement that would "strike at the system which had caused this world tragedy," he said nothing of a league, preoccupied instead with the prospect of a Wilson-mediated peace conference. According to the record, House never suggested endorsing a league until Taft's invitation arrived on May 9, the day after Wilson's colloquy with the AUAM and more than two weeks after his meeting with Lippmann. EMH diary, entries from March 30 to May 9, 1916, EMHmss.

73. Sir Edward Grey to EMH, April 7, 1916, enclosed in EMH to WW, April 19, 1916,

PWW, 36:511–12; EMH diary, February 22, 1916, EMHmss; WW to EMH, May 16, 1916, *PWW*, 37:57–58.

74. Sir Edward Grey to EMH, May 12, 1916, in Seymour, *Intimate Papers of Colonel House* 2:282–83.

75. WW to EMH, May 16, 1916.

76. WL, "The Reminiscences of Walter Lippmann," Columbia University Oral History Collection, part 2, no. 118, 89–90.

77. WW to EMH, May 16, 1916.

78. Wilson's address is printed under May 27, 1916, *PWW*, 37:113–16.

79. This was not mere rhetoric. Wilson told Ray Stannard Baker on May 12 that his Mexican policy reflected his "shame as an American over the first Mexican war." RSB memorandum, May 12, 1916, *PWW*, 37:30.

80. *NYT*, May 28, 1916; Knock, *To End All Wars*, 77–78; "A Declaration of Interdependence," *Independent* 86 (June 5, 1916): 357 (inset). For the positive American media response, see Arthur S. Link, *Wilson: Campaigns for Progressivism and Peace, 1916–1917* (Princeton, NJ: Princeton UP, 1965), 26–27.

81. Contrast House's May 21 draft, which imagined Britain preventing the war by a public commitment to defend France against German attack—a clear implication of German culpability that Wilson omitted. "Appendix: Comparison of the House Draft and Wilson's Speech of May 27, 1916," in Seymour, *Intimate Papers of Colonel House* 2:337.

82. James Viscount Bryce to EMH, June 8, 1916, *PWW*, 37:289. See also Knock, *To End All Wars*, 76, 78–79; Link, *Campaigns for Progressivism and Peace*, 27.

83. See London *Times*, May 31, 1916, and London *Spectator*, June 3, 1916, accusing Wilson of endorsing Europe's capitulation to tyranny. For additional European comment, see *Literary Digest* 52 (June 10, 1916): 1684–85.

84. Sir Edward Grey to EMH, May 29, 1916, enclosed in EMH to WW, May 31, 1916, *PWW*, 37:131–32. The French ambassador in London, Paul Cambon, opined that Wilson was "surely obeying German instigations when he speaks the word of peace," a sentiment eerily similar to that predicted by Grey when rejecting Wilson's mediation proposal. Quoted in Link, *Campaigns for Progressivism and Peace*, 27.

85. WW Memorial Day address, 126; WL to NDB, 1 June 1916, WLmss, reel 2. For other positive responses, see Oswald Villard's *Nation* 102 (June 1, 1916): 583; Hamilton Holt's *Independent* 86 (June 5, 1916): 357; and Paul U. Kellogg's *Survey* 36 (June 10, 1916): 281–82.

86. "Wilson's Great Utterance," 102–3 (emphasis added).

87. Ibid. "Let that alternative be offered to the German people," the *New Republic* editors continued, "and if radical and social democratic Germany does not make the decent choice, it is because Germany is incapable of learning anything." Then, in words laden with tragic irony: "You can fool and frighten people into aggression once, but when the price is as terrible as the price has been, you cannot do it again if there is a plain alternative in sight."

88. Ibid., 103–4.

89. Ibid., 104.

90. Ibid., 103.

91. The article is in a scrapbook of clippings arranged after Wilson's death by Edith Wilson and filmed in WWmss, reel 503.

92. *NR* 7 (June 17, 1916), 156.

93. Eight of the civilian deaths occurred in Columbus itself, four en route. On the Columbus crisis, see Link, *Confusions and Crises*, chaps. 7 and 10; Mark T. Gilderhus, *Diplomacy and Revolution: U.S.-Mexican Relations under Wilson and Carranza* (Tucson: University of Arizona Press, 1977); Lloyd C. Gardner, "Woodrow Wilson and the Mexican Revolution," in *Woodrow Wilson and a Revolutionary World, 1913–1921*, ed. Arthur S. Link (Chapel Hill: University of North Carolina Press, 1982), 3–48. On Villa's motives, see Friedrich Katz, "Pancho Villa and the Attack on Columbus, New Mexico," *American Historical Review* 83 (February 1978): 101–30.

94. *NYT*, March 10, 1916.

95. *NYT*, March 11, 1916; Link, *Confusions and Crises*, 210–11.

96. *NYT*, March 14, 1916; WW to Robert Lansing, with enclosure, March 13, 1916, *PWW*, 36:298; Link, *Confusions and Crises*, 215.

97. JPT, *Woodrow Wilson as I Know Him* (Garden City, NY: Doubleday, Page, 1921), 159–60. For corroboration, see EMH diary, March 17, 1916, *PWW*, 36:335.

98. NDB to WW, with enclosure, March 16, 1916, *PWW*, 36:322–24. On the Pershing expedition, see Frederick S. Calhoun, *Power and Principle: Armed Intervention in Wilsonian Foreign Policy* (Kent, OH: Kent State UP, 1986), 51–67; James W. Hurst, *Pancho Villa and Black Jack Pershing: The Punitive Expedition in Mexico* (Westport, CT: Praeger, 2008).

99. For the unofficial compromise on withdrawal, see WW to Robert Lansing, March 30, 1916, and editorial note 2, *PWW*, 36:382. For awkward but mostly sincere attempts by actors on both sides to achieve compromise, see the editorial note under David Lawrence to WW, March 14, 1916, *PWW*, 36:309; and relevant documents under March 14–17 and 19–21, 1916, *PWW*, 36:309–50.

100. On the Parral clash, see Link, *Confusions and Crises*, 282–83. For Carranza's note, see *NYT*, April 14, 1916; for Pershing's report that Carranza's forces instigated the fighting, see *NYT*, April 21, 1916.

101. For the Scott–Obregón conference and its results, see Hugh L. Scott and Frederick Funston to NDB, May 3, 1916, *PWW*, 36:592–94; NDB to WW, May 4, 1916, and Robert Lansing to WW, May 4, 1916, *PWW*, 36:603–5; WW draft statement to the press, May 5, 1916, *PWW*, 36:607–8. For the bandit raid (later determined to have no connection with Villa) and its impact on the Scott–Obregón conference, see the series of front-page articles in *NYT*, May 8, 1916.

102. *NYT*, May 21 and 22, 1916. Borah's speech transcribed in *NYT*, May 9, 1916; US and *Carrancista* military maneuvers reported in *NYT*, May 13, 14, 15, and 17, 1916.

103. WW to Robert Lansing, with enclosure, June 18, 1916, *PWW*, 37:249–63, esp. 262 and editorial note 8; WW draft address to Congress, June 26, 1916, *PWW*, 37:298–304, esp. 301–3. For the events described in foregoing text, see *NYT*, May 22, June 16, and June 25, 1916; also Link, *Confusions and Crises*, 300–308.

104. *NYT*, June 29, 1916; Gilderhus, *Diplomacy and Revolution*, 46.

105. *NYT*, June 25 (Taft) and 28 (Roosevelt), 1916; RSB memorandum, May 12, 1916, *PWW*, 37:36; EMH to WW, June 25, 1916, *PWW*, 37:295. For a contrary reading emphasizing an "eruption in public opinion" in favor of peace, see Link, *Confusions and Crises*, 315.

106. WW to EMH, June 22, 1916, *PWW*, 37:281; WW draft address to Congress, June 26, 1916, 303.

107. RSB memorandum, May 12, 1916, 36.

108. Ibid.

109. Knock, *To End All Wars*, 82–83; Robert Lansing memorandum, June 26, 1916, *PWW*, 37:306–7, and editorial note 1; *NYT*, June 27 and 29, 1916; Link, *Confusions and Crises*, 311.

110. WW remarks to the New York Press Club, June 30, 1916, *PWW*, 37:333–34; Robert Lansing to WW, July 3, 1916, *PWW*, 37:348–50; Eliseo Arredondo to Lansing, with enclosure, July 4, 1916, *PWW*, 37:360–61. For the "Peace Pledge" headline, see *NYT*, July 1, 1916.

111. WW address to the National Press Club, May 15, 1916, *PWW*, 37:49.

112. "Sovereign Mexico," *NR* 8 (June 10, 1916): 132–33.

113. WW draft address to Congress, June 26, 1916, 303.

114. Ibid.

115. Calhoun, *Power and Principle*, 102–3; Arthur S. Link, *Wilson: The Struggle for Neutrality, 1914–1915* (Princeton, NJ: Princeton UP, 1960), 534–35, 544–45.

116. Lasch, *New Radicalism*, chap. 6.

117. "Sovereign Mexico," 133–34.

118. "The Larger Anarchy," *NR* 8 (July 8, 1916): 238–39.

CHAPTER SIX

1. JA, *Peace and Bread in Time of War* (New York: Macmillan, 1922), 54; [Max Eastman], "A Plea from Mexico," *Masses* 8 (August 1916): 39; [Max Eastman], "American Internationalists," *Masses* 8 (September 1916): 38; WEBD, "To the Rescue," *Crisis* 12 (May 1916): 31 (quoted); WEBD, "Carrizal," *Crisis* 12 (August 1916): 165. Black soldiers were fighting and, at Carrizal, dying in the chase after Villa.

2. WL, "What Program Shall the United States Stand for in International Relations?" *Annals of the American Academy of Political and Social Science* 66 (July 1916): 60–70, esp. 62.

3. *The American Yearbook, 1914* (New York: D. Appleton, 1915), 47–55.

4. WW to William G. McAdoo, 17 November 1914, *PWW*, 31:325–27.

5. HC, "Presidential Complacency," *NR* 1 (November 21, 1914), 7. On Wilson's opposition to rural credits, see WW to Carter Glass, May 12, 1914, *PWW*, 30:24. For Wilson's position on woman suffrage and eventual endorsement, in 1918, of a constitutional amendment granting the franchise, see Victoria Bissell Brown, "Did Woodrow Wilson's Gender Politics Matter?" in *Reconsidering Woodrow Wilson: Progressivism, Internationalism, War, and Peace*, ed. John Milton Cooper Jr. (Washington, DC: Woodrow Wilson Center Press; Baltimore, MD: Johns Hopkins UP, 2008), 125–62.

6. Robert L. Owen to WW, June 8, 1916, *PWW*, 37:174–75. "Progressive democracy" was Owen's shorthand for the "enlightened measures of social and industrial justice" he hoped to see adopted in the Democratic platform.

7. HC, *Progressive Democracy* (New York: Macmillan, 1914), esp. 178.

8. Ibid., 18–19, 20.

9. Ibid., 16, 18–19, 25, 279.

10. Edith Bolling Galt to WW, May 20, 1915, *PWW*, 33:228; see also Wilson's creased and separating copy of WJ, *On Some of Life's Ideals* (New York: Henry Holt, 1913), WWLLC.

11. WJ, "On a Certain Blindness in Human Beings" (1899), in *Talks to Teachers on Psychology, and to Students on Some of Life's Ideals* (New York: Longman's, Green, 1899), 264.

12. John Milton Cooper Jr., *The Warrior and the Priest: Woodrow Wilson and Theodore Roosevelt* (Cambridge, MA: Harvard UP, 1983), 294; Kristie Miller, *Ellen and Edith: Woodrow Wilson's First Ladies* (Lawrence: UP of Kansas, 2010), chaps. 3–4.

13. WJ, "What Makes a Life Significant?" (1899), in *Talks to Teachers*, 297–99.

14. "The Democratic Platform of 1916," in *National Party Platforms*, ed. Kirk H. Porter (New York, 1924), 373–88. Wilson wrote a comprehensive draft platform that was sent to the party's resolutions committee for review sometime around June 10. Except for a few compactions, the text of Wilson's draft was adopted by the committee, which later worked with Wilson to add statements on the tariff, Mexico, and "Protection of Citizens" (all discussed subsequently). See *PWW*, 37:190, editorial note 1; *PWW*, 37:202, editorial note 3.

15. "Democratic Platform," 375–76. The plank also condemned "subversives" seeking "to injure this government in its foreign relations or cripple or destroy its industries at home," along with any who "by arousing prejudices of a racial, religious, or other nature creates discord and strife among our people so as to obstruct the wholesome process of unification" (376).

16. Ibid., 377, 378, 385–86. The last statement is absent from Wilson's draft.

17. Ibid., 378.

18. Ibid., 379–80; cf. *PWW*, 37:200, editorial note 3.

19. See Wilson's draft at *PWW*, 37:196.

20. One might also hazard that despite the Mexican plank's apologies, Wilson decided the banner of "guaranteed" territorial integrity would serve only as a target for potshot accusations of presidential hypocrisy. Regardless, it is doubtful that Wilson's was a philosophical choice; his awareness of the inherent tension between effective international organization and inviolate territorial integrity was still developing.

21. *NYT*, June 15, 1915 (quoted); Arthur S. Link, *Wilson: Campaigns for Progressivism and Peace, 1916–1917* (Princeton, NJ: Princeton UP, 1965), 42–48.

22. "Democratic Platform," 388.

23. "Woodrow Wilson," *NR* 7 (June 24, 1916): 186. The events surrounding Brandeis's nomination and confirmation receive thorough treatment in Melvin I. Urofsky, *Louis D. Brandeis: A Life* (New York: Pantheon, 2009), chap. 18.

24. *NR* 7 (July 15, 1916): 261.

25. *NYT*, January 24 and March 6, 1916; see also *NYT*, January 27 and June 14, 1916.

26. WW state of the Union address, December 7, 1915, *PWW*, 35:305.

27. W. Elliot Brownlee, "Wilson and Financing the Modern State: The Revenue Act of 1916," *Proceedings of the American Philosophical Society* 129 (June 1985); 176–82, 187, 190–93, 199–201. Although Wilson never directly commented on the AEFIT, his support

for a munitions tax dates to February 1, days after McAdoo received the group's "memorial." See WW address in Des Moines, IA, February 1, 1916, *PWW*, 36:83.

28. "The Democratic Revenue Bill," *NR* 8 (August 26, 1916): 81–82.

29. WW, "A Plan," ca. August 16, 1916, *PWW*, 38:38; Arthur S. Link, *Woodrow Wilson and the Progressive Era, 1910–1917* (New York: Harper, 1954), 235–36.

30. WW address to Congress, August 29, 1916, *PWW*, 38:97, 99; on Wilson's anticipation of the crisis, see 103, editorial note 1.

31. "The Railroad Crisis and After," *NR* 8 (August 26, 1916): 80–81; " 'The Reign of Reason,' " *NR* 8 (September 16, 1916): 152–53. For the journal's earliest endorsement of such a program, see William Z. Ripley, "To Prevent Industrial War," *NR* 7 (May 6, 1916): 13. To the editors' dismay, Wilson's provisions for compulsory suspension of strikes and presidential power over railways in wartime were struck from the bill passed as the Adamson Act. "The Averted Railway Strike," *NR* 8 (September 9, 1916): 130.

32. *NR* 8 (September 2, 1916): 100.

33. RB diary, September 2, 1916, RBmss (support for Wilson); RB to Elizabeth Shepley Sargeant, September 20, 1916, RBmss (*NR* relations); Walter E. Weyl, *American World Policies* (New York: Macmillan, 1917). Charles Forcey argues that "Weyl supported Wilson as the pacific and cautious leader he actually was," in contrast to Croly and Lippmann, who invented a crusader Wilson to worship. Yet in the summer of 1916, Weyl urged arming the United States to levels "adequate" to modern conditions—conditions under which "the age of *laissez-faire*, of non-interference between the nations, is passing," and which demanded experiments in international organization for which "some nation must take the initiative." That "natural leadership," he asserted, "belongs to America." Later, mere weeks before the election, Weyl described as "brilliant" Lippmann's contrast between the pragmatism of Wilson—including his policy of preparedness for war—and the "puzzle" of Hughes. Charles Forcey, *The Crossroads of Liberalism: Croly, Weyl, Lippmann, and the Progressive Era, 1900–1925* (New York: Oxford UP, 1961), 257–59; Walter E. Weyl, "American Policy and European Opinion," *Annals of the American Academy of Political and Social Science* 66 (July 1916): 140–46; Walter Weyl to WL, October 10, 1916, WLmss, reel 167; WL, "The Puzzle of Hughes," *NR* 8 (September 30, 1916): 210–13.

34. WL to Graham Wallas, August 29, 1916, WLmss, reel 32.

35. WL to Graham Wallas, February 21, 1916, WLmss, reel 32; WL diary, March 22, 1916, WLmss, reel 160. From bullet points in the diary entry, it appears Wilson "showed his mind" on "Mexico, liberty, [and the] Virginia Bill of Rights"; his conviction that "Pan-Americanism" was the fulfillment of the "Monroe Doctrine"; the "armed ship question"; German designs on Brazil; naval preparedness; and "his [unreadable], ashamed." Shedding light on the last, Lippmann recalled years later that he and the president had "talked mainly about Mexico." Wilson had often condemned the history of American interference there, and Lippmann remembered him "talking about the Jeffersonian principle of the sacred right of revolution. It's something that no President would say today. He was defending his own policy and his belief that [Victoriano] Huerta was a counter-revolutionist. He believed in the Madero Revolution." WL, "The Reminiscences of Walter Lippmann," Columbia University Oral History Collection, part 2, no. 118, 89.

36. "The talk last week with the President has been a great help to all of us here [at

the *New Republic*]," wrote Lippmann to the president's secretary, Joseph P. Tumulty, on March 27 (WLmss, reel 31).

37. For the apology, and the editors' call for Roosevelt to apologize as well, see "Mr. Roosevelt's Afterthought," *NR* 6 (March 25, 1916): 204. The piece, which Roosevelt saw as a despicable betrayal, permanently ended his friendship with the editors.

38. See Hapgood to WW, August 28, 1916, with enclosure, *PWW*, 38:86–88; WW to Norman Hapgood, August 30, 1916, *PWW*, 38:117. Hapgood, editor of *Harper's*, was vice-chair of the "Woodrow Wilson Independent League" and one of Wilson's most important progressive allies. Lippmann and Croly's break with Roosevelt signaled the beginning of a concerted and successful effort by Hapgood to bring those two voices not only into Wilson's camp but also into his counsels.

39. WL to NDB, August 2, 1916, enclosed in NDB to WW, August 4, 1916, *PWW*, 38:524–25; WW to NDB, August 7, 1916, *PWW*, 38:537; JPT to WL, August 5, 1916, WLmss, reel 31.

40. JPT to WL, August 25, 1916, WLmss, reel 31; WW speech in Sea Girt, NJ, September 2, 1916, *PWW*, 38:126 (editorial note 1), 137.

41. WL to JPT, July 26, 1916, WLmss, reel 31.

42. Probably James Watson Gerard to Robert Lansing, August 8, 1916, enclosed in Lansing to WW, August 22, 1916, *PWW*, 38:71–73. Lippmann's recollection that the cable predicted an election-timed shift in German strategy was either his own embellishment or the president's interpretation.

43. WL, "Reminiscences," 91.

44. WL to Wallas, August 29, 1916.

45. WL, "Reminiscences," 92; WL to Wallas, August 29, 1916.

46. Straight had worried about the editors' attitude toward Roosevelt since publication of their apology to Wilson. Ultimately, he voted for Hughes. But in a letter published in the *New Republic*, he reaffirmed his support of the journal, his admiration of the editors' willingness to disagree with their primary source of funding, and his faith that he and they were "in essential agreement . . . as to the general cause which it should serve." This public openness, not to mention the staff's frequent criticism of Wilson, undermines Christopher Lasch's claim that the journal "deliberately sought to work in closest harmony with the government, even at the expense of its editorial independence." Lasch quotes an entry from House's diary (January 15, 1917) in which the colonel claims he "gave them enough food for thought to keep them on the right road"; yet Lasch neglects House's complaint of March 10, 1917, that he was "finding it difficult to keep [*The New Republic*] in line because of the President's slowness of action." Willard Straight, "A Letter From Mr. Straight," *NR* 8 (October 28, 1916): 313–14; Christopher Lasch, *The New Radicalism in America: The Intellectual as a Social Type* (New York: Knopf, 1965), 220n4; EMH diary, March 10, 1917, EMHmss.

47. For particularly biting remarks, see WL to Henry F. Hollis June 12, 1916, *PWW*, 37:212; WL to NDB, August 2, 1916.

48. WL, "Reminiscences," 92; Norman Hapgood to WW, with enclosure, September 25, 1916, and WW to Hapgood, September 27, 1916, *PWW*, 38:273–75, 281; WW to WL, September 29, 1916, *PWW*, 38:295.

49. JD, "The Hughes Campaign," *NR* 8 (October 28, 1916): 319–21; *NYT*, October 14,

1916 (Eastman); New York *World*, October 20, 1916 (Walling); JA, *Peace and Bread*, 58; RB diary, November 7, 1916, RBmss; Ralph Barton Perry, "On Changing One's Mind," *NR* 8 (November 4, 1916): 9–11.

50. WL, "The Case for Wilson," *NR* 8 (October 14, 1916): 263, 264.

51. Ibid., 263, 264.

52. HC, "The Two Parties in 1916" (I), *NR* 8 (October 21, 1916): 287.

53. Ibid., 287–88.

54. Ibid., 288–89.

55. Ibid., 290–91.

56. Link, *Campaigns for Progressivism and Peace*, 124–25.

57. WL to Mabel Dodge, December 14, 1916, quoted in Ronald Steel, *Lippmann and the American Century* (Boston: Atlantic-Little, Brown, 1980), 108.

58. Link, *Campaigns for Progressivism and Peace*, 209–13; Ernest R. May, *The World War and American Isolation, 1914–1917* (Cambridge, MA: Harvard UP, 1959), 393–402.

59. Johann Heinrich von Bernstorff to EMH, December 12, 1916, EMHmss, Box 12, Folder 402; Chargé Grew to Robert Lansing, December 12, 1916, *FRUS, 1916, Supplement: The World War* (Washington, DC: GPO, 1929), 87.

60. Enclosed in WW to Robert Lansing, December 15, 1916, *PWW*, 40:242–43.

61. *NYT*, December 21, 1916.

62. *NR* 9 (December 16, 1916): 165–166.

63. *NYT*, December 22, 1916; Link, *Campaigns for Progressivism and Peace*, 227–32.

64. *NYT*, December 22, 1916. House also repudiated the president's note—but privately. Sympathetic toward the Allies, he was also convinced that German victory was impossible and that strained relations with Britain must be avoided. EMH diary, December 20, 1916, EMHmss; EMH to WW, December 20, 1916, *PWW*, 40:294.

65. WW to Robert Lansing, December 21, 1916, *PWW*, 40:307; see also editorial note 1, 307–11; and Link, *Campaigns for Progressivism and Peace*, 221, 223–24. In an analysis of both statements published on December 22, the *New York Times* concluded that Wilson had "no sympathy for the German cause" and that it was "ridiculous to suppose that the American Government has any sympathetic interest in German success"—a widespread interpretation boding ill for Wilson's plans to persuade the Allies to accept a negotiated peace.

66. James W. Gerard to Robert Lansing, December 26, 1916, *PWW*, 40:331; *NYT*, January 12, 1917. On Bethmann's predicament, see May, *World War and American Isolation*, 402–4.

67. "Peace Without Victory," *NR* 9 (December 23, 1916): 201.

68. Ibid., 201.

69. Ibid., 201–2. Contrast Steel, who argues that the editors took a "very different" position on "peace without victory" than Wilson would a month later. According to Steel, Lippmann persuaded Croly and colleagues that "the German offer was simply a ploy to consolidate territorial gains" which "would humiliate the democracies and leave Prussian militarists in control of Central Europe," then "laid out his argument in the lead editorial" (Steel, *Lippmann and the American Century*, 109). Lippmann, however, though sympathetic to the Allies, deplored their war aims and had argued for months that victory on their terms would preclude lasting peace. Moreover, his editorial did *not* advise rejecting the German offer but rather warned the Allies to weigh carefully the costs of doing so and

take seriously the notion of a "peace without victory" even were their military fortunes to improve.

70. May, *World War and American Isolation*, 404–15.

71. EMH diary, January 3 and 4, 1917, EMHmss.

72. Lansing memorandum, February 4, 1917, *PWW*, 41:120–21. Wilson knew that the territory dominated by ostensibly democratic white civilization was in turn dominated in less-than-democratic fashion by white people. Nevertheless, he was committed to making the genuinely democratic features of "white civilization" those of a world civilization, and he believed that possibility hinged upon an "intact" United States helping to "rebuild" Europe. He was keenly aware that the greatest nonwhite power was imperial Japan, then bidding to make a colony of China and dominate East Asia, and it was this perception that seems to have fueled his chromatically inflected fears. "With the terrific slaughter taking place in Europe," he asked his cabinet, "if we, also, entered the war, what effect would the depletion of man power have upon the relations of the white and yellow races? Would the yellow races take advantage of it and attempt to subjugate the white races?" (ibid. 120). This question is remarkable from a man who had deprecated fears of a "yellow peril" in 1915 and reveals a confused and frantic Wilson entertaining scenarios and considering judgments from all possible quarters, as his secretaries of state, navy, and labor all recalled (ibid.; Josephus Daniels to WW, 2 February 1917, *PWW*, 41:94; William B. Wilson to RSB, September 17, 1932, RSBmss, reel 85).

73. *NR* 9 (December 30, 1916): 225–26; see also "The Note as Americanism" at 228–30 of the same issue.

74. EMH to WW, January 15, 1917, and WW to EMH, January 17, 1917, *PWW*, 40:477–78, 507; WW to EMH, January 19, 1917, *PWW*, 40:524.

75. WW to HC, January 25, 1917, *PWW*, 41:13. Although some scholars have questioned the degree to which Wilson drew upon the ideas as opposed to the mere language of the *New Republic* in his speech, the evidence of the journal's influence on his thinking is substantial. Since the summer of 1916, the editors had repeatedly urged Wilson to press the belligerents for moderate peace terms, most recently in "Moving toward Peace," *NR* 9 (November 25, 1916): 81–83, published just before Wilson started work on his December 18 appeal for clarified war aims. Wilson clipped and saved the editorial after underlining its main assertions—namely, that the world needed to know "the precise political objects" for which the belligerents fought and also whether particular American commitments would modify those objects. More to the point, House sent Wilson a copy of the "Peace without Victory" editorial sometime before January 5, 1917, to aid him in composing his address. Wilson's previous short outline raised the main questions around which he organized his final speech but left most unanswered, including, "What [America] wants," and "What she is prepared to take part in and willing to do." After receiving the editorial, Wilson produced another outline titled "Americanism for the World," which answered the first draft's questions with the speech's most memorable phrases, including "a community of power" and "peace without victory." These ideas were transferred to a January 11 draft largely reflecting the speech as delivered. See WWmss, reels 513, 85, 479; *PWW*, 40:446, editorial note 1.

The case that Wilson merely lifted a phrase from the journal rests primarily on recollections Lippmann published years later as "Notes for a Biography," *NR* 69 (July 16,

1930): 250–51: "Once the President horrified us by appropriating a phrase ['peace without victory'] and employing it in a sense we had never intended. . . . We did not like the [German proposal] ourselves and did not mean to praise it. . . . However sound the idea, the phrase itself, as I think Colonel House agreed, was inept." Aside from his self-contradictory admission of the idea's soundness, Lippmann's failure of memory here is so great as to suggest a purposeful retreat from ideas he held deeply in 1917 but considered discredited by 1930. Five days after the "Peace without Victory" address, the editors asserted that "America could not share in a settlement which was dictated by the victor" and that however "hurtful" to Allied ears, "peace without victory" was an "idea that had to be expressed." See "America Speaks," *NR* 9 (January 27, 1917): 341; cf. "The Facts Behind the Phrase," *NR* 10 (February 3, 1917): 5–7. Lippmann's later confusion perhaps stemmed from the fact that while endorsing peace without victory generally, he and Croly thought its advent likelier if the Allies first gained at least one decisive battlefield victory to scare the Germans into good-faith negotiations, as explained in "The Will to Believe," *NR* 9 (January 13, 1917): 283–85. The conviction that a negotiated, cooperatively guaranteed peace founded on principles of self-government and national equality was the only sort that could last did not spontaneously germinate in Wilson's mind upon reading one editorial. Rather, it had implanted itself in both Wilson and the *New Republic* editors over the course of a two-year dialogue grown increasingly intimate over its last ten months.

76. EMH to WW, with enclosure, January 20, 1917, *PWW*, 40:526, 528–29.

77. Wilson's address to the Senate is printed under January 22, 1917, *PWW*, 40:533–39.

78. *NYT*, January 23, 1917. On the myths surrounding Wilson and the principle of "self-determination," see chapter 8 in this volume.

79. WW, address to Senate, January 22, 1917.

80. *NYT*, February 1, 1917.

81. WW, second inaugural address, March 5, 1917, *PWW*, 41:332–35, esp. 333.

82. *NYT*, January 23, 1917. Senator Tillman of South Carolina called the message "the noblest utterance that has fallen from human lips since the Declaration of Independence"; Senator Sherman of Illinois thought the president's principles amounted to "a future Hague convention up in a balloon" that would "make Don Quixote wish he had not died so soon." One House Democrat called Wilson's speech "the most remarkable and wonderful in one hundred and fifty years," while a Republican gasped, "It is a most revolutionary proposal and cannot find an echo in Europe."

83. "The Declaration of Interdependence," *Independent* 89 (February 15, 1917): 202. See also John A. Thompson, *Reformers and War: American Progressive Publicists and the First World War* (Cambridge: Cambridge UP, 1987), 143ff.; Knock, *To End All Wars*, 113–14.

84. EMH to WW, 22 January 1917, *PWW*, 40:539; WW quoted in *NYT*, January 23, 1917.

CHAPTER SEVEN

1. "The Will to Believe," *NR* 9 (January 13, 1917): 283–85.

2. Ibid., 284.

3. Quoted in John L. Heaton, ed., *Cobb of "The World"* (New York: E. P. Dutton, 1924), 269. Cobb recalled the meeting occurring April 1, the day before Wilson asked Congress to declare war; it actually took place March 19, the day before Wilson's cabinet endorsed war. See Arthur S. Link, *Wilson: Campaigns for Progressivism and Peace* (Princeton, NJ: Princeton UP, 1965), 393n33. Doubts about Cobb's recollection were largely silenced by Link in 1985; Arthur S. Link, "That Cobb Interview," *Journal of American History* 72 (June 1985): 7–17.

4. WW, draft peace note (unsent), ca. November 25, 1916, *PWW*, 40:70–71; WW, unpublished "Prolegomenon" to a peace note, ca. November 25, 1916, *PWW*, 40:70.

5. WW, "Appeal to the American People," April 15, 1917, *PWW*, 42:75.

6. JPT, *Woodrow Wilson as I Know Him* (New York: Doubleday, Page, 1921), 253. Great War casualty figures are disputed; those given in the text represent averages of estimates from multiple sources. On the specific engagements mentioned, see Robert T. Foley, *German Strategy and the Path to Verdun: Erich von Falkenhayn and the Development of Attrition, 1870–1916* (Cambridge: Cambridge UP, 2005); William Philpott, *Bloody Victory: The Sacrifice on the Somme and the Making of the Twentieth Century* (London: Little, Brown, 2009); Timothy C. Dowling, *The Brusilov Offensive* (Bloomington: Indiana UP, 2008). The best single-volume military history is John Keegan, *The First World War* (1998; repr., New York: Vintage, 2000).

7. JPT, *Wilson as I Know Him*, 255; Robert Lansing to WW, February 1, 1917, *PWW*, 41:99; WW address to Congress, February 3, 1917, *PWW*, 41:108–12; EMH diary, February 1, 1917, *PWW*, 41:87–88.

8. RSB, *Woodrow Wilson: Life and Letters*, 8 vols. (Garden City, NY: Doubleday, Page, 1927–39), 6:465–66; "A Visit to the President," *Friends' Intelligencer* 74 (March 10, 1917): 147.

9. John Milton Cooper Jr., *Woodrow Wilson: A Biography* (New York: Knopf, 2009), 373–79.

10. WW press release, March 4, 1917, *PWW*, 41:318–20; A. Scott Berg, *Wilson* (New York: G. P. Putnam's Sons, 2013), 430–32.

11. JA, *Peace and Bread in Time of War* (New York: Macmillan, 1922), 64.

12. Heaton, *Cobb of "The World,"* 269.

13. Wilson's address is printed under April 2, 1917, *PWW*, 41:519–27. Details of the scene are drawn from Berg, *Wilson*, 434–38.

14. The original of this interpretation is Cooper, *Woodrow Wilson*, 387–88. Luther's point was that knowledge of one's sinfulness should encourage humility rather than apathy, and that it provided the necessary foundation for appreciating both the possibilities faith discloses and the sinner's duty to seek them. A brief war-era interpretation of Luther's famous dictum is John Alfred Faulkner, "Pecca Fortiter," *American Journal of Theology* 18 (October 1914): 600–604.

15. Emphasis added.

16. JPT, *Wilson as I Know Him*, 256.

17. David M. Kennedy, *Over Here: The First World War and American Society* (New York: Oxford UP, 1980), and Christopher Capozzola, *Uncle Sam Wants You: World War I and the Making of the Modern American Citizen* (New York: Oxford UP, 2008), are the two best works on the domestic effects of mobilization and intervention.

18. John Whiteclay Chambers II, *To Raise an Army: The Draft Comes to Modern America* (New York: Free Press, 1987); W. Elliot Brownlee, *Federal Taxation in America: A Short History* (Washington, DC: Woodrow Wilson Center Press; New York: Cambridge UP, 1996), 50–51, 51n4.

19. NDB, *First Annual Report of the Council of National Defense* (Washington, DC: GPO, 1917), 5–6, 8–9; Bernard M. Baruch, *American Industry in the War: A Report of the War Industries Board* (Washington, DC: GPO, 1921), 20–21. David Kennedy (*Over Here*, 114–17) discounts the CND's galvanization of the centralized, functional approach to economic and social mobilization the various War Boards perfected; contrast William J. Breen, *Uncle Sam at Home: Civilian Mobilization, Wartime Federalism, and the Council of National Defense, 1917–1919* (Westport, CT: Greenwood, 1984).

20. Robert D. Cuff, *The War Industries Board: Business-Government Relations during World War I* (Baltimore, MD: Johns Hopkins UP, 1973); Valerie Jean Conner, *The National War Labor Board: Stability, Social Justice, and the Voluntary State in World War I* (Chapel Hill: University of North Carolina Press, 1983); Kennedy, *Over Here*, 116–25 (on Food and Fuel Administrations); Douglas B. Craig, *Progressives at War: William G. McAdoo and Newton D. Baker, 1863–1941* (Baltimore, MD: Johns Hopkins UP, 2013), 197–212 (on Railroad Administration.

21. United States War Industries Board, *An Outline of the Board's Origin, Functions, and Organizations, Compiled as of November 10, 1918* (Washington, DC: GPO, 1918), 11–14.

22. Veblen chastised the government for failing to cooperate with labor radicals to relieve the worker shortage. His memorandum was eventually published with an introduction by Joseph Dorfman: TV, "Using the I. W. W. to Harvest Grain," *Journal of Political Economy* 40 (December 1932): 796–807.

23. Michael E. Parrish, *Felix Frankfurter and His Times: The Reform Years* (New York: Free Press, 1982), 82–85.

24. Ibid., 87–94, esp. 88, 93. Frankfurter did not entirely fail the cause of radicalism during his PMC tenure. Prompted by Frankfurter's investigation of and recommendations regarding the sentencing to death of Tom Mooney, accused of planting a bomb that killed Preparedness Day paradegoers in San Francisco on July 22, 1916, Wilson interceded to get Mooney's death sentence suspended, though he was unable to secure a retrial (California governor Hiram Johnson commuted Mooney's sentence to life in prison, served until his pardon in 1939). Frankfurter meanwhile enraged conservatives by demanding justice for a group of miners roused and abducted from their beds in Bisbee, Arizona, early on the morning of July 12, 1917, by vigilantes who then stranded them in the New Mexican desert. The abductees were rescued from death by federal troops. In his report to the president, Frankfurter recommended that Attorney General Gregory consider bringing federal charges against the vigilantes on grounds that the "deportations" obstructed enforcement of the draft. Joseph P. Lash, "A Brahmin of the Law: A Biographical Essay," in *From the Diaries of Felix Frankfurter*, ed. Joseph P. Lash, 23–24 (New York, 1975); FF, *Felix Frankfurter Reminisces*, ed. Harlan B. Phillips (New York, 1960), 130–39; President's Mediation Commission, *Report on the Bisbee Deportations*, dated November 6, 1917 (Washington, DC: GPO, 1918).

25. President's Mediation Commission, *Report of President's Mediation Commission to the President of the United States* (Washington, DC: GPO, 1918), 21.

26. On Baker's visits, see Melvin I. Urofsky, *Louis D. Brandeis: A Life* (New York: Pantheon, 2009), 498. Brandeis, Frankfurter, and Lippmann frequently dined at the so-called House of Truth, a Washington residence used by Frankfurter, Lippmann, and several friends.

27. Ibid., 500; LDB to EMH, January 9, 1918, copy in FFmss, reel 15; Parrish, *Frankfurter and His Times*, 103–13; Joseph A. McCartin, *Labor's Great War: The Struggle for Industrial Democracy and the Origins of Modern American Labor Relations, 1912–1921* (Chapel Hill: University of North Carolina Press, 1997) 84–91.

28. WL quoted in Ronald Steel, *Walter Lippmann and the American Century* (Boston: Atlantic-Little, Brown, 1980), 116–17; NDB to WL, May 22, 1917, WLmss, reel 2.

29. Steel, *Lippmann and the American Century*, 123.

30. WL to NDB, February 6, 1917, WLmss, reel 2; WL to WW, February 6, 1917, *PWW*, 41:134–35.

31. NDB to WL, February 7, 1917, and WL to NDB, April 3, 1917, WLmss, reel 2; WL to WW, April 3, 1917, *PWW*, 41:538 (proposal quoted).

32. Craig, *Progressives at War*, 157; Kennedy, *Over Here*, 147; Theodore Roosevelt to NDB, March 19, 1917, and NDB to Theodore Roosevelt, March 20, 1917, in Elting E. Morison et al., eds., *The Letters of Theodore Roosevelt*, 8 vols. (Cambridge, MA: Harvard UP, 1951–54), 8:1164; *NYT*, April 6, 1917.

33. NDB to WL, April 4, 1917, WLmss, reel 2; WW to WL, April 7, 1917, *PWW*, 42:4.

34. Craig, *Progressives at War*, 158; Kennedy, *Over Here*, 148 (WW quoted).

35. Capozzola, *Uncle Sam Wants You*, chap. 1, is excellent.

36. See the national press survey in *NYT*, April 3, 1917.

37. JD, "Conscience and Compulsion," *NR* 11 (July 14, 1917): 297–98; JD, "What Are We Fighting For?" *Independent* 94 (June 22, 1918): 474, 480–83; JA, "Patriotism and Pacifists in War Time," *City Club Bulletin* 10 (June 18, 1917): 184–90; Richard Schneirov, "The Odyssey of William English Walling: Revisionism, Social Democracy, and Evolutionary Pragmatism," *Journal of the Gilded Age and Progressive Era* 2, no. 4 (October 2003): 403–30, esp. 413–19; William L. O'Neill, *The Last Romantic: A Life of Max Eastman* (New York: Oxford UP, 1978), 59, 73–74; WEBD, "The World Last Month," *Crisis* 14 (May 1917): 8; WEBD, "Close Ranks," *Crisis* 16 (July 1918): 111. Some contemporaries suspected that Du Bois's conciliatory message was influenced by the offer of an army captaincy; see David Levering Lewis, *W. E. B. Du Bois: Biography of a Race, 1868–1919* (New York, 1993), 552–60. The early advent and consistent reiteration of his support for the war should dispel those suspicions among scholars.

38. Kennedy, *Over Here*, 46–47; Borah quoted in Ralph Stone, *The Irreconcilables: The Fight against the League of Nations* (Lexington: University of Kentucky Press, 1970), 14.

39. RB, "Twilight of Idols" (1917), in *The Radical Will: Selected Writings 1911–1919*, ed. Olaf Hansen (1977; repr., Berkeley: University of California Press, 1992), 339–40; RB, "The War and the Intellectuals" (1917), in *Radical Will*, 312–13. For the war as a "plastic juncture" in history, see JD, "The Future of Pacifism," *NR* 11 (July 28, 1917): 358–60.

40. RB, "Conscience and Intelligence in War," *Dial* 63 (September 13, 1917): 194; RB, "War and Intellectuals," 316; RB, "A War Diary" (1917), in *Radical Will*, 330.

41. RB, "Those Columbia Trustees," *NR* 12 (October 20, 1917): 328–29; RB, "Think-

ing at Seventy-Six," *NR* 12 (August 25, 1917): 111, 113; RB, "Sociologic Fiction," *NR* 12 (October 27, 1917), 359–60; RB, "H. L. Mencken," *NR* 13 (November 24, 1917): 102–3; RB, "Making Over the Body," *NR* 15 (May 4, 1918): 28–29.

42. Charles Forcey, *The Crossroads of Liberalism: Croly, Weyl, Lippmann, and the Progressive Era, 1900–1925* (New York: Oxford UP, 1961), chap. 7, §4: "A Moth-Like Gyration"; RB, "The Collapse of American Strategy" (1917), in *War and the Intellectuals*, ed. Carl Resek (New York: Harper and Row, 1964), 22–35. The best known of Bourne's historical vindications is Christopher Lasch, *The New Radicalism in America: The Intellectual as a Social Type* (New York: Knopf, 1965), chap. 6; more recently, see Moshik Temkin, "Culture vs. *Kultur*, or a Clash of Civilizations: Public Intellectuals in the United States and the Great War, 1917–1918," *Historical Journal* 58, no. 1 (2015): 157–82, esp. 177–78, 182. For Wilson's thoughts on the submarine conundrum, see WW to Matthew Hale, March 31, 1917, WWmss, reel 86; for the *New Republic*'s evolving position, "Postscript: Thursday Morning, February 1, 1917," *NR* 10 (February 3, 1917); "Justification," *NR* 10 (February 10, 1917): 36–38; WL, "The Defense of the Atlantic World," *NR* 10 (February 17, 1917): 59–61.

43. RB, "Twilight of Idols," *Seven Arts* 2 (October 1917): 688–702, esp. 694–96; JD, "In a Time of National Hesitation," *Seven Arts* 2 (May 1917): 3–7.

44. HC to EMH, ca. 28 December 1916, quoted in EMH to WW, 29 December 1916, *PWW*, 40:359–360.

45. For the *New Republic*'s criticism of Wilson's inattention to domestic reconstruction, willingness to curtail civil liberties, and failure to stem the tide of war hysteria, see, e.g., *NR* 11 (July 21, 1917): 316; "War Propaganda," *NR* 12 (October 6, 1917): 255–57; "The Bigelow Incident," *NR* 13 (November 10, 1917): 35–37; "The President's Commission at Bisbee," *NR* 13 (December 8, 1917), 140–41; "Lynching: An American Kultur?" *NR* 14 (April 13, 1918): 311–12; "America Tested by War," *NR* 15 (June 22, 1918): 220–21; "Mob Violence and War Psychology," *NR* 16 (August 3, 1918): 5–7.

46. [HC,] "A War Program for Liberals," *NR* 10 (March 31, 1917): 249–50. See also "The Future of the State," *NR* 12 (September 15, 1917): 179–83; "Counsel of Humility," *NR* 12 (December 15, 1917): 173–76; "After the War—Reaction or Reconstruction," *NR* 13 (January 19, 1918): 331–33; "The Uses of an Armistice," *NR* 17 (November 16, 1918): 59–61.

47. Walter E. Weyl, *The End of the War* (New York: Macmillan, 1918), 71–72, 22.

48. [WL,] "Defense of the Atlantic World," 61.

49. WL to WW, with enclosure, March 11, 1917, *PWW*, 41:388–90.

50. WL to WW, February 6, 1917, *PWW*, 41:135; WL to EMH, April 12, 1917, WLmss, reel 14.

51. Robert Lansing, NDB, and Josephus Daniels to WW, April 13, 1917, *PWW*, 42:55.

52. Kennedy, *Over Here*, 59–60; Stephen Vaughn, *Holding Fast the Inner Lines: Democracy, Nationalism, and the Committee on Public Information* (Chapel Hill: University of North Carolina Press, 1980), 3–22; WW to Robert Goodwyn Rhett, September 4, 1917, *PWW*, 44:148. Vaughn's is the standard account of the CPI. Creel's own account illuminates the ideology behind the CPI and how it became a justification for actions inconsistent with the CPI's mandate, not to mention civil liberties. The title alone suggests Creel's rocky relationship with objectivity: George P. Creel, *How We Advertised*

America: The First Telling of the Amazing Story of the Committee on Public Informa-tion that Carried the Gospel of Americanism to Every Corner of the Globe (New York: Harper, 1920).

53. *Complete Report of the Chairman of the Committee on Public Information, 1917:1918:1919* (Washington, DC: GPO, 1919), esp. 32–40; Wallace Notestein and Elmer E. Stoll, comp., *Conquest and Kultur: Aims of the Germans in Their Own Words* (Wash-ington, DC: CPI, 1918); Dana C. Munro et al., eds., *German Treatment of Conquered Territory* (Washington, DC: CPI, 1918); Earl E. Sperry with Willis M. West, *German Plots and Intrigues in the United States During the Period of Our Neutrality* (Washington, DC: CPI, 1918); Vaughn, *Inner Lines,* esp. chaps. 6–7, 9–10; Kennedy, *Over Here,* 53–69. Creel's was an awkward position; though his propaganda campaign was at times reaction-ary, his defense of the rights of labor and other groups to organize and be heard led Illinois Republican Lawrence Sherman of Illinois to assail him on the Senate floor as "a Socialist of the most pronounced type." *NYT,* April 24, 1918.

54. Kennedy, *Over Here,* 69–73 (Wilson's "contempt" quoted at 72). On the motives behind the Wobbly raids, see William Preston Jr., *Aliens and Dissenters: Federal Repres-sion of Radicals, 1903–1933,* (Cambridge, MA: Harvard UP, 1963), 119–22.

55. For impassioned but balanced reporting on the Illinois riots, see *Chicago Defender,* July 7 and 14, 1917 (East St. Louis) and August 2, 1919 (Chicago). Elliot M. Rudwick, in his *Race Riot at East St. Louis, July 2, 1917* (Carbondale: Southern Illinois UP, 1964), implies (without evidence) that Wilson purposefully stirred up racial hatred in East Saint Louis during the 1916 election to intimidate a traditionally Republican voting bloc and thus bore responsibility for the riot three years later (8). Wilson did erroneously assume that most of the city's blacks had been lured there by Republican politicians promising jobs. These charges, though levied against white politicians, probably did incite animos-ity toward the city's blacks among white laborers. See Emmett J. Scott, *Negro Migration during the War* (New York, 1920), 100.

56. Robert V. Haynes, *A Night of Violence: The Houston Riot of 1917* (Baton Rouge: Louisiana State UP, 1976), esp. 115–92; WEBD, "An Essay toward a History of the Black Man in the Great War," *Crisis* 18 (June 1918): 64–65.

57. Lash, "Brahmin of the Law," 23–24; Liva Baker, *Felix Frankfurter* (New York: Coward-McCann, 1969), 66–69; WW to Thomas W. Gregory, July 7, 1917, *PWW,* 43:116; WW public statement, July 26, 1918, *PWW,* 49:97–98. On the White House conferences following the East Saint Louis riots, see WW to JPT, July 6, 1917; JPT to WW, with en-closure, August 1, 1917; and the series of editorial notes printed under Alfred B. Cosey to WW, August 9, 1917; all in *PWW,* 43:106–7, 342–43, 412–13. David Kennedy's assertion that Wilson "refused even to see the black delegations begging for an appointment" after the riots is inaccurate (*Over Here,* 282). After refusing a small number of individual visi-tors, Wilson received the Committee of the Negro Silent Protest Parade on August 14.

58. William Walling to WW, July 3, 1917, *PWW,* 43:103–4; *NR,* July 7, 1917, 259. Also Lester Aglar Walton to JPT, June 12, 1918, *PWW,* 48:302; Robert Russa Morton to WW, June 15, 1918, *PWW,* 48:323–24; Leonidas C. Dyer to WW, July 23, 1918, *PWW,* 49:61–62; John R. Shillady to WW, July 25, 1918, *PWW,* 49:88–89.

59. JPT to Nick Chiles (editor, *Topeka Plaindealer*), n.d., 1918, enclosed in WW to

JPT, October 1, 1918, *PWW*, 51:170 (emphasis added); WW remarks to the National Race Congress, October 1, 1918, *PWW*, 51:168.

60. WW to JPT, August 1, 1917, *PWW*, 43:343; WW to George Creel, June 18, 1918, *PWW*, 48:346.

61. Josephus Daniels diary, April 6, 1917, *PWW*, 41:556; EMH diary, February 11, 1918, *PWW*, 46:327; WW to Albert Sidney Burleson, September 4, 1917, *PWW*, 44:147.

62. Max Eastman to WW, September 8, 1917, *PWW*, 44:169–72.

63. Eastman et al. to WW, July 12, 1917, enclosed in WW to Albert Sidney Burleson, July 13, 1917, *PWW*, 43:164–165.

64. WW to Max Eastman, September 18, 1917, *PWW*, 44:210–11.

65. WW to George Creel, November 5, 1917, *PWW*, 44:511.

66. WL to EMH, October 17, 1917, enclosed in EMH to WW, October 17, 1917, *PWW*, 44:392–94.

67. HC to WW, October 19, 1917, *PWW*, 44:408–10.

68. Ibid., 410; WW to HC, October 22, 1917, *PWW*, 44:420. In the June 22, 1918, issue of the *New Republic*, Croly published an appeal for funds to help secure a fair trial for 110 prominent Wobblies, bearing the signatures of John Dewey, Walter Weyl, and Thorstein Veblen, among others, prompting an investigation. Eight months earlier, Wilson had complained to Burleson that the case against the allegedly disloyal *Milwaukee Leader* was likewise unconvincing. "I must frankly say that I do not think most of what is quoted [as evidence of sedition] ought to be regarded as unmailable," he wrote, adding, "I think that doubt ought always to be resolved in favor of the utmost freedom of speech." Wilson asked if the paper, as its officers had requested, had been "given another chance?" Burleson replied that they had not and that the courts had sustained the action. And with that the matter was dropped. David W. Levy, *Herbert Croly of "The New Republic": Life and Thought of an American Progressive* (Princeton, NJ: Princeton UP, 1985), 254; WW to Albert Sidney Burleson, October 18, 1917, *PWW*, 44:396–97.

69. JD, "Conscription of Thought," *NR* 12 (September 1, 1917), 129; JD, "In Explanation of Our Lapse," *NR* 13 (November 3, 1917): 17.

70. Creel, *How We Advertised America*, Part II.

71. WW to EMH, September 2, 1917, *PWW*, 44:120. The only comprehensive study of the Inquiry is Lawrence E. Gelfand, *The Inquiry: American Preparations for Peace, 1917–1919* (New Haven, CT: Yale UP, 1963). Its other "chiefs" were Isaiah Bowman of the American Geographical Society, James T. Shotwell of Columbia University, and David Hunter Miller, law partner of House's son-in-law Gordon Auchincloss. The Inquiry's titular head was House's brother-in-law, Sidney Mezes, of whose personal devotion, if not competence, House could be sure.

72. NDB to WL, May 10, 1916, WLmss, reel 2; HC to EMH, September 7 and 28, 1917, EMHmss, Box 31, Folder 0993.

73. EMH diary, April 17 and July 26, 1917, EMHmss; *NR* 11 (July 21, 1917): 316.

74. WL, *The Stakes of Diplomacy* (1915; repr., New York: Henry Holt, 1917), 211; WL to WW, with enclosure, March 11, 1917. Wilson requested *Stakes* via Baker, who had received a copy and discussed its contents with the president. Wilson personally thanked Lippmann for the "great profit" he expected from reading it. NDB to WL, January 29,

1917, and WL to NDB, January 31, 1917, WLmss, reel 2; WW to WL, February 3, 1917, *PWW*, 41:113.

75. The pope's appeal is printed in *FRUS, 1917, Supplement 2: The World War*, 2 vols. (Washington, DC: GPO, 1932), 1:162–64.

76. WW to EMH, August 16, 1917, *PWW*, 43:488.

77. WL, "Memorandum for the Secretary of War," n.d., enclosed in NDB to WW, August 20, 1917, *PWW*, 43:532–534.

78. WW to NDB, August 22, 1917, *PWW*, 44:27; WW addresses of June 14 and June 19, 1917, *PWW*, 42:503, 537.

79. WW, draft reply to the pope, printed under WW to EMH, August 23, 1917, *PWW*, 44:33–36.

80. WW to EMH, August 23 and September 2, 1917, *PWW*, 44:33 (WW quoted), 120–21; EMH to WW, August 31 and September 4, 1917, and Robert Lansing to WW, September 10, 1917 (with enclosure), *PWW*, 44:105, 149–50, 180–81 (European comment); Eastman to WW, September 8, 1917. "The American negotiators," Lippmann wrote in March 1918, "must be in a position to judge whether a claim put forth by a power is supported by the democracy at home, or whether it is merely a traditional diplomatic objective or the design of an imperialistic group. In the fiercely disputed areas they must be prepared freely to offer friendly suggestions either of compromise or of constructive experiment, but if these suggestions are to have much weight they must be supported by a body of reliable fact and must be presented tersely and graphically so as to carry conviction." WL, "Report on the Inquiry: Its Scope and Method," March 20, 1918, Doc. 889, IDNA, reel 43.

81. WL to EMH, September 24, 1917, WLmss, reel 14; WL to NDB, May 16, 1918, in *FRUS: The Paris Peace Conference, 1919*, 13 vols. (Washington, DC: GPO, 1942–47), 1:97–98.

82. See especially WL, "Report on Inquiry." The breadth of topics investigated by the Inquiry is clear from only a passing glance at the record of its work. To take a single example, consider Document No. 553, by L. D. Steefel: "Report on the geography, history, government, economic resources, population, schools, religion, newspapers and periodicals, Danish organization, bibliography and [sic] etc., of North Schleswig." List of Papers, IDNA, reel 1.

83. TV, "Suggestions Touching the Working Program of an Inquiry into the Prospective Terms of Peace," ca. December 31, 1917, copy in Manley O. Hudson Papers, Box 4, Folder 19, Harvard Law School Library, Cambridge, MA; Walter Weyl, "Proposed Organization for Research," n.d., and WL, "Memorandum Regarding the Organization of the Inquiry," November 13, 1917, both quoted in Gelfand, *Inquiry*, 81–82, 346; WL, "Memorandum on the Inquiry," October 26, 1918, WLmss, reel 35. On the Inquiry's working relationship with its British and French counterparts, see Gelfand, *Inquiry*, 119–21, 125–30, 132–33. As Gelfand's book describes, the Inquiry's work was often disorganized, especially as the scope of its mandate expanded in the last half of 1918. There was no precedent for the undertaking, and House provided no detailed scheme for its organization. In many fields, competent specialists were scarce. The tasks assigned were enormous and performed under severe time pressure. Contrary to Gelfand's conclusion, however, Lippmann's work on the League of Nations alone, informed as it was by the technical work of his colleagues,

qualifies the Inquiry as one of the most influential policy planning groups in international history.

84. Steel, *Lippmann and the American Century*, 129. Perhaps the most articulate and widely read exponent of a liberal peace was Lippmann's British friend Norman Angell—incidentally, also given to quoting and citing James's works. Norman Angell, *The Great Illusion: A Study of the Relation of Military Power in Nations to Their Economic and Social Advantage* (1909; repr., London: William Heinemann, 1912), James, on psychology of war, quoted at 170, 287; Norman Angell, *The Foundations of International Polity* (London: William Heinemann, 1914).

85. WL, "The World Conflict in Its Relation to American Democracy," *Annals of the American Academy of Political and Social Science* 72 (July 1917): 1–10.

86. WL, "Report on Inquiry"; WL, "Memorandum: The Context of the Inquiry" n.d. [October/November 1917], Doc. 885, IDNA, reel 43. References to the Reichstag peace resolution of July 1917 and the failure of the Stockholm Conference in September 1917 provide internal evidence of Doc. 885's late autumn date. Its language, subject, and purpose clearly point to Lippmann's authorship.

87. WL, "Context of Inquiry"; WL, "League of Nations," n.d., Doc. 741, IDNA, reel 35; also WL, "Draft of a Reply to the Proposals of the Central Powers," December 31, 1917, Doc. 688, IDNA, reel 34.

88. WL, "Report on Inquiry"; WL, untitled memorandum, n.d., enclosed in WL to Learned Hand, 5 October 1918, Learned Hand Papers, Box 106, Folder 16, Harvard Law School Library, Cambridge, MA.

89. TV, *An Inquiry Into the Nature of Peace and the Terms of Its Perpetuation* (New York: Macmillan, 1917), 217, 238.

90. JD, "What America Will Fight For," *NR* 12 (August 18, 1917): 69; "Tentative Program . . . Presented by the American Section," quoted in Lucia Ames Mead, "The International Committee of Women for Permanent Peace," *World Court* 4 (February 1918): 761–63; Walter E. Weyl, *American World Policies* (New York: Macmillan, 1917), 245; RB, "Arbitration and International Politics," *International Conciliation* 70 (September 1913): 1–14.

91. WL, "Context of Inquiry"; WL to NDB, December 5, 1917, WLmss, reel 2.

CHAPTER EIGHT

1. Norman Angell to George Creel, March 3, 1918, in George Creel to WW, July 15, 1918, *PWW*, 48:619–20.

2. George V quoted in John Milton Cooper Jr., *Pivotal Decades: The United States, 1900–1920* (New York: Norton, 1990), 314; John Keegan, *The First World War* (1998; repr., New York: Vintage, 2000), esp. 373; WW quoted in Sir Cecil Arthur Spring-Rice to Arthur James Balfour, January 4, 1918, *PWW*, 45:456–57.

3. David Lloyd George, speech at Gray's Inn, London, December 14, 1917, in *The Great Crusade: Extracts from Speeches Delivered during the War*, comp. F. L. Stevenson (New York: George H. Doran, 1918); David Stevenson, "French War Aims and the American Challenge, 1914–1918," *Historical Journal* 22 (December 1979): 883–84.

4. Keegan, *First World War*, 357–59; Tasker H. Bliss, "Report of the Representative of the War Department," December 14, 1917, *FRUS, 1917, Supplement 2: The World War*, 2 vols. (Washington, DC: GPO, 1932), 1:386–87. On the Russian collapse, see Norman Stone, *The Eastern Front, 1914–1917* (1975; repr., London: Penguin, 1998), 282–301; on the November revolution and its consequences for Allied strategy, see Arno J. Mayer, *The Political Origins of the New Diplomacy, 1917–1918* (New Haven, CT: Yale UP, 1959), chaps. 5–6. A recent, cogent synthesis is Joshua A. Sanborn, *Imperial Apocalypse: The Great War and the Destruction of the Russian Empire* (New York: Oxford UP, 2014).

5. On the Allies' growing sense of dependence on US land reinforcements, and for the pace of the latter's deployment, see John J. Pershing, *Final Report of Gen. John J. Pershing, Commander-in-Chief, American Expeditionary Forces* (Washington, DC: GPO, 1919), 18–19, 23. On the reversal of momentum at sea following US intervention, see Holger H. Herwig and David F. Trask, "The Failure of Germany's Undersea Offensive against World Shipping, February 1917–October 1918," *Historian* 33 (August 1971): 611–36.

6. "Statement by the Provisional Government Regarding the War," April 9, 1917, in C. K. Cumming and Walter W. Pettit, eds., *Russian-American Relations, March, 1917–March, 1920: Documents and Papers* (New York: Harcourt, Brace and Howe, 1920), 10; Lenin quoted in Derek B. Heater, *National Self-Determination: Woodrow Wilson and His Legacy* (New York: St. Martin's, 1994), 34. For the background of early Soviet foreign policy in relation to the war and Wilsonianism, see Mayer, *Origins of New Diplomacy*, 245–66.

7. "Soviet Government's First Note to Allied Ambassadors," November 22, 1917, in Cumming and Pettit, *Russian-American Relations*, 44; "Note from Trotsky to the Allied Ambassadors," December 6, 1917, in Cumming and Pettit, *Russian-American Relations*, 57; "Note from Trotsky to the Peoples and Governments of Allied Countries Regarding Peace Negotiations," December 29, 1917, in Cumming and Pettit, *Russian-American Relations*, 61–62, 63–64; Erez Manela, *The Wilsonian Moment: Self-Determination and the International Origins of Anticolonial Nationalism* (New York: Oxford UP, 2007), chap. 1.

8. Mayer, *Origins of New Diplomacy*, chap. 7.

9. Thomas J. Knock, *To End All Wars: Woodrow Wilson and the Quest for a New World Order* (1992; repr., Princeton, NJ: Princeton UP, 1995), 140–41; US Department of State, *Proceedings of the Brest-Litovsk Peace Conference: The Peace Negotiations between Russia and the Central Powers, 21 November, 1917–3 March, 1918* (Washington, DC: GPO, 1918), 38, 40 (quoting Austro-Hungarian Foreign Minister Czernin); *NYT*, December 23, 1917 (French Socialists); *NYT*, December 29, 1917 (British Labour).

10. EMH diary, 18 December 1917, *PWW*, 45:324. For Walter Lippmann's recollection of Wilson and House's purposes, see WL, "The Reminiscences of Walter Lippmann," Columbia University Oral History Collection, part 2, no. 118, 107.

11. For Wilson's reading of Lippmann's July article, see WL, "The World Conflict in Its Relation to American Democracy," *Annals of the American Academy of Political and Social Science* 72 (July 1917): 1–10, marked copy in WWmss, reel 90. Baker had forwarded the article: NDB to WW, August 13, 1917, *PWW*, 43:454, and editorial note 1.

12. Sidney Edward Mezes, David Hunter Miller, and WL, "The Present Situation: The War Aims and Peace Terms it Suggests," December 22, 1917, printed at January 4, 1918,

PWW, 45:459–74, and editorial note 1; WL, "Draft of a Reply to the Proposals of the Central Powers," December 31, 1917, Inquiry Doc. 688, copy in WLmss, reel 34 (quoted); WL, "Reminiscences," 108. The expanded memorandum dated January 2, 1918 ("A Suggested Statement of Peace Terms," WWmss, reel 384), demonstrates multiple debts to Lippmann's of December 31, particularly the discussions of the public moral imperative of restoring Belgium et al. For Germany's insistence on the "return of colonial territory, forcibly occupied and captured, during the war," see US Department of State, *Proceedings of the Brest-Litovsk Peace Conference*, 41.

13. Wilson's address laying out the Fourteen Points before a joint session of Congress is printed under January 8, 1918, *PWW* 45:534–539.

14. Careful scholars acknowledge that Wilson never intended to arrange the entire world into ethnic nation-states. Nevertheless, it has long been the habit of historians to present national self-determination as the vital principle animating his peace aims, chalking up its ostensible betrayals to his geopolitical naïveté, ethnic and racial biases, or both. The unqualified version of this interpretation is largely a relic of the mid-twentieth century, when the vogue was to blame Wilson and his counterparts at Paris for the toxic nationalism that ignited World War II. Later treatments exhibit a kind of cognitive dissonance, identifying a civic-nationalist Wilsonianism compatible with international citizenship and an ethnonationalist version that would seem to preclude it. Trygve Throntveit, "The Fable of the Fourteen Points: Woodrow Wilson and National Self-Determination," *Diplomatic History* 35 (June 2011): 445–81, esp. 447–50. Contrast Heater, *National Self-Determination*, asserting that while the "Fourteen Points were anything but a wholehearted exposition of the principle of national self-determination," there nevertheless "can be no doubt that, in his heart, Woodrow Wilson was deeply committed to national self-determination" (43–44).

15. Knock, *To End All Wars*, 138, 145; WW to Robert Lansing, January 1, 1918, *PWW*, 45:417 (quoted), with enclosure, *PWW*, 45:417–19. Influential interpretations of the Fourteen Points as "countermanifesto" include Mayer, *Origins of New Diplomacy*, chap. 9; and N. Gordon Levin Jr., *Woodrow Wilson and World Politics: America's Response to War and Revolution* (New York: Oxford UP, 1968), chap. 3.

16. WW address to Congress, April 2, 1917, *PWW* 41:525; WW, message to the Russian Provisional Government, May 26, 1917, *PWW*, 42:365–67; WL, "Reminiscences," 108; Mezes, Miller, and WL, "Present Situation," 470–71.

17. Spring-Rice to Balfour, January 4, 1918. Michla Pomerance has analyzed Wilson's peace program as "a fusion and confusion of several ideas" about "self-determination," including "freedom from 'alien' rule ('external self-determination'), freedom to select one's own form of government ('internal self-determination'), a form of continuing self-government (democracy), [and] the principle of one nation-one state." While all of these informed Wilson's policies, it is argued subsequently in this chapter that "continuing self-government" was the fundamental principle from which the other permutations derived. Michla Pomerance, "The United States and Self-Determination: Perspectives on the Wilsonian Conception," *American Journal of International Law* 70 (January 1976): 1–27, esp. 20.

18. *PWW*, 45:536.

19. *PWW*, 45:536, 538–39; EMH diary, January 9, 1918, *PWW*, 45:553.

20. The relevant alternative interpretations are Levin, *Wilson and World Politics;* and William Appleman Williams, *The Tragedy of American Diplomacy* (New York: Dell, 1959). By the time he reached Paris in December 1918, Wilson did worry over Europe's susceptibility to Bolshevism's "poison." But by then stories of the Bolsheviks' brutal measures proliferated, and regardless he still sympathized with—and hoped to learn from— the revolutionary mood of peoples whose "Governments have been run for the wrong purposes." William Christian Bullitt diary, December 10, 1918, *PWW*, 53:352.

21. WW quoted in Sir Cecil Arthur Spring-Rice to British Foreign Office, January 9, 1918, *PWW*, 45:549 ("good sense"). For details of Wilson's Russian interventions, see Betty Miller Unterberger, *The United States, Revolutionary Russia, and the Rise of Czechoslovakia* (Chapel Hill: University of North Carolina Press, 1989); George Schild, *Between Ideology and Realpolitik: Woodrow Wilson and the Russian Revolution, 1917–1921* (Westport, CT: Greenwood, 1995); and David S. Foglesong's significantly more critical treatment (stressing Wilson's antipathy toward Bolshevism), *America's Secret War against Bolshevism: U.S. Intervention in the Russian Civil War, 1917–1920* (Chapel Hill: University of North Carolina Press,1995).

22. For the Miller plank and Wilson's rejection of it, see Mezes, Miller, and WL, "Present Situation," 473–74; EMH diary, January 9, 1918.

23. Mezes, Miller, and WL, "Present Situation," 469.

24. Ibid., 463, 471–72. For the administration's decision to recognize nations that had declared independence from Austria-Hungary during the war, including Czechoslovakia (recognized before the empire's disintegration), see WW draft note to the Austro-Hungarian government, ca. October 19, 1918, *PWW*, 51:383; and Unterberger, *United States, Revolutionary Russia, and Rise of Czechoslovakia*, esp. 283–86.

25. Mezes, Miller, and WL, "Present Situation," 470. Cf. Lloyd E. Ambrosius, "Democracy, Peace, and World Order," in *Reconsidering Woodrow Wilson: Progressivism, Internationalism, War, and Peace*, ed. John Milton Cooper Jr. (Washington, DC: Woodrow Wilson Center Press; Baltimore, MD: Johns Hopkins UP, 2008), 225–49, esp. 234–39, identifying both civic-nationalist and ethnic-nationalist strains in Wilson's thought but emphasizing the latter. On Wilson's relative indifference to Irish independence, see John B. Duff, "The Versailles Treaty and the Irish Americans," *Journal of American History* 55 (December 1968): 582–98. Contrasting studies of Wilson and Baltic nationalism agreeing on his lack of sympathy (if not specific attitude) toward Bolshevism are Albert N. Tarulis, *American-Baltic Relations, 1918–1922: The Struggle over Recognition* (Washington, DC: Catholic University of America Press, 1965); and David S. Foglesong, "The United States, Self-Determination, and the Struggle against Bolshevism in the Eastern Baltic Region, 1918–1920," *Journal of Baltic Studies* 26 (Summer 1995): 107–44.

26. Mezes, Miller, and WL, "Present Situation," 470–71; WW quoted in Paul Mantoux, *The Deliberations of the Council of Four (March 24–June 28, 1919): Notes of the Official Interpreter*, trans. and ed. Arthur S. Link and Manfred F. Boemke, 2 vols. (Princeton, NJ: Princeton UP, 1992), 2:131.

27. See Wilson's transcript of his shorthand draft, *PWW*, 45:513–15; and EMH diary, January 9, 1918, 552–53.

28. EMH diary, January 9, 1918, 551.

29. Ibid.

30. WL, "Draft of Reply to Central Powers."

31. The major prophet of "the harmony of interests" that commercial integration would create was Norman Angell, some of whose *New Republic* articles Wilson read; e.g. *PWW*, 34:135–36, 217.

32. American pacifism in the Progressive Era is explored in C. Roland Marchand, *The American Peace Movement and Social Reform, 1898–1918* (Princeton, NJ: Princeton UP, 1972).

33. See WW address to the Senate, January 22, 1917, *PWW* 40:534.

34. EMH diary, January 9, 1918, 552.

35. Spring-Rice to British Foreign Office, January 9, 1918, 549; also RSB diary, March 8, 1919, *PWW*, 55:463. For a similar reading of point 5, see Manela, *Wilsonian Moment*, 40–41.

36. At Paris, Wilson consistently emphasized the evolutionary and impermanent nature of the colonial trusteeships, or mandates system, established by the treaties adopted. All mandated territories were "candidates for full admission to the League," with but "one general condition": "a truly democratic government." Mandates, he explained, would protect "untutored" peoples while accelerating their education in designing and controlling self-governing institutions. Mantoux, *Deliberations of Council of Four*, 2:99.

37. Isaiah Bowman memorandum, December 10, 1918, *PWW*, 53:354; EMH diary, December 10, 1918, *PWW*, 45:552–53.

38. JA to WW, January 14, 1918, *PWW*, 45:586; Stephen Vaughan, *Holding Fast the Inner Lines: Democracy, Nationalism, and the Committee on Public Information* (Chapel Hill: University of North Carolina Press, 1980), 129–30; *NR* 13 (January 12, 1918): 292; WL quoted in Ronald Steel, *Walter Lippmann and the American Century* (Boston: Atlantic-Little, Brown, 1980), 134. Lippmann later recalled that he "did a good deal of the work . . . deciding what were the points at issue and determining what the structure of the thing was to be. . . . I think I wrote the final draft of all the memoranda on the basis of scholarly studies that we had from the various experts." Though his obvious pride in this formative role rankled Bowman, Lippmann credited the Inquiry geographer with important contributions. WL, "Reminiscences," 110.

39. New York *World*, January 9, 1918; Max Eastman, "Wilson and the World's Future," *Liberator* 1 (May 1918): 19, 21.

40. Lloyd George quoted in *NYT*, January 6, 1918.

41. EMH diary, January 9, 1918. Croly hailed Wilson for redressing "the ambiguities and the inadequacies of Lloyd George's" and tried vainly to persuade the nation that neither statesman had endorsed "absolute independence of the subject nationalities" as a universal principle. *NR* 13 (January 12, 1918): 292, 294.

42. "The Genesis of the Fourteen Commandments," *North American Review* 209 (February 1919): 145–52. Harvey presumably authored this unsigned piece. Tellingly, its paraphrase of Wilson's "Twelfth Commandment" regarding "autonomous development" of peoples in the Ottoman Empire read: "the non-Turkish nationalities must be set free" (149).

43. *NYT*, January 11, 1918; *NYT*, January 16, 1918; *Washington Post*, June 10, 1918. The best analysis of the phrase's impact on the colonial world is Manela, *Wilsonian Moment*. Studies of reactions among American ethnic groups include Elizabeth McKillen,

"Ethnicity, Class, and Wilsonian Internationalism Reconsidered: The Mexican-American and Irish-American Immigrant Left and U.S. Foreign Relations, 1914–1922," *Diplomatic History* 25 (Fall 2001): 553–87; and Joseph Cuddy, *Irish America and National Isolationism* (New York: Arno, 1976).

44. WW address to Congress, February 11, 1918, *PWW*, 46:321, 320. Compare Klaus Schwabe, *Woodrow Wilson, Revolutionary Germany, and Peacemaking, 1918–1919: Missionary Diplomacy and the Realities of Power*, trans. Rita and Robert Kimber (Chapel Hill: University of North Carolina Press, 1985), arguing that Wilson sought to cultivate left-leaning Germans by endorsing national self-determination (18, 417n44).

45. WW address to Congress, February 11, 1918, 320–21.

46. WW remarks to the Senate Foreign Relations Committee, quoted in H. W. V. Temperley, ed., *A History of the Peace Conference of Paris*, 6 vols. (London: Frowde, Hodder and Stoughton, 1920–24), 4:429.

47. WW, "The Study of Administration," (1887), *PWW*, 5:369; WW, *Leaders of Men by Woodrow Wilson*, ed. T. H. Vail Motter (1890; repr., Princeton, NJ: Princeton UP, 1952), 41; WW, *Constitutional Government in the United States* (New York: Columbia UP, 1908), 59; WW to A. Mitchell Palmer, February 5, 1913, *PWW* 27:100.

48. "National Self-Determination," *NR* 14 (March 16, 1918): 192–93.

49. RSB to EMH, August 19, 1918, EMHmss, Box 9, Folder 0274; WL to EMH, August 21, 1918, EMHmss, Box 70, Folder 2326.

50. WW address to Congress, February 11, 1918, 318, 322–323. Count Ottokar Czernin's and Georg F. von Hertling's addresses of January 24 are printed in *FRUS, 1918, Supplement 1: The World War*, 2 vols. (Washington, DC: GPO, 1933), 2:38–63.

51. WW address to Congress, February 11, 1918, 321, 323, 319.

52. WW address in Baltimore, MD, April 6, 1918, *PWW*, 47:270; WW address in Mount Vernon, VA, July 4, 1918, *PWW*, 47:514–17. For the military events of spring and summer 1918 and Wilson's response, see Arthur S. Link, *Wilson the Diplomatist: A Look at His Major Foreign Policies* (Baltimore, MD: Johns Hopkins UP, 1957), 105–6.

53. Link, *Wilson the Diplomatist*, 106–7.

54. WL to EMH, August 9, 15, and 21, and September 2, 1918, EMHmss Box 70, Folder 2326.

55. WW address in New York, NY, September 27, 1918, *PWW*, 51:128–31, 132–33.

56. EMH diary, January 10, 1918, EMHmss.

57. WW draft League Covenant, September 7, 1918, *PWW*, 49:467–71; compare EMH draft in EMH to WW, July 16, 1918, *PWW*, 48:630–37. Wilson also excised House's provision for an international court. He had long worried that the type of League favored by conservative internationalists like the LEP's leaders would be *merely* an international court, enforcing preexisting laws and norms that favored the status quo. He hoped instead to invest an international representative body with power to address disputes and adapt to changing circumstances through broad-based collective inquiry. It appears that at this stage Wilson feared dividing League authority between rival branches to the disadvantage of the representative.

58. Knock, *To End All Wars*, 152–53.

59. Ibid., 176–77; John Milton Cooper Jr. *The Warrior and the Priest: Woodrow Wilson and Theodore Roosevelt* (Cambridge, MA: Harvard UP, 1983), 331. See also the penetrat-

ing critique of the League's opponents in "The Defeatists," *NR* 16 (October 19, 1918): 327–29.

60. WW to EMH, March 22, 1918, *PWW*, 47:105; WW quoted in EMH diary, August 16, 1918, *PWW*, 49:266.

61. Knock, *To End All Wars*, 149–50, 160–61; Wolfgang J. Helbich, "American Liberals in the League of Nations Controversy," *Public Opinion Quarterly* 31 (December 1967): 568–96.

62. WW quoted in Rufus Isaacs to David Lloyd George, July 12, 1918, *PWW*, 48:603. For Wilson's resistance to intervention and the reasoning behind his acquiescence, see Frank L. Polk to Roland S. Morris, 5 March 1918, *PWW*, 46:545; WW to EMH, July 8, 1918, *PWW*, 48:550; Sir William Wiseman, memorandum of an interview with WW, October 16, 1918, *PWW*, 51:350. On the negative response of progressive internationalists see Knock, *To End All Wars*, 157–58. George F. Kennan's literary triumph, *Soviet-American Relations, 1917–1920*, vol. 2, *The Decision to Intervene* (Princeton, NJ: Princeton UP, 1958), evades tough questions about Wilson's motives and ends with the arrival of US forces at Vladivostok. For a fuller picture, compare Unterberger, *United States, Revolutionary Russia, and Rise of Czechoslovakia*; and Foglesong, *America's Secret War against Bolshevism*. Unterberger has criticized Foglesong for downplaying Wilson's resistance to anti-Bolshevists in his administration and on the Supreme War Council as well as the nonideological moral and security arguments for supporting the White armies. Betty Miller Unterberger, "Wilson vs. the Bolsheviks," *Diplomatic History* 21 (Winter 1997): 127–31.

63. New York *World*, September 22, 1918; *NR* 16 (September 28, 1918): 240.

64. Seward W. Livermore, *Politics Is Adjourned: Woodrow Wilson and the War Congress, 1916–1918* (Middletown, CT: Wesleyan UP, 1966), 185–205; David M. Kennedy, *Over Here: The First World War and American Society* (New York: Oxford UP, 1980), 233–36.

65. JD, "Internal Social Reorganization after the War," (1918), *MW*, 11:81. Alongside the biweekly *Dial*'s editorials from October 5 forward, see Harold Stearns, "Why Reconstruction?" *Dial* 65 (October 5, 1918): 249–52; TV, "The Modern Point of View and the New Order" (six installments) *Dial* 65 (October 19, November 2, November 16, November 30, December 14, December 28, 1918): 289–93, 349–54, 409–15, 482–89, 543–50, 605–11; and Helen Marot, "Reconstruction at Work," *Dial* 65 (October 19, 1918): 303–6. Whereas most *Dial* articles on reconstruction addressed its domestic and international aspects simultaneously, Dewey's tended to focus on the necessity for international political and economic cooperation to secure peace, free trade, and labor rights. See "An Approach to the League of Nations" (November 2, 1918); "The League of Nations and the New Diplomacy" (November 16, 1918); "The Fourteen Points and the League of Nations" (November 30, 1918); "A League of Nations and Economic Freedom" (December 14, 1918); all in *MW*, vol. 11.

66. TV, "Outline of a Policy for the Control of the 'Economic Penetration' of Backward Countries and of Foreign Investments," *Political Science Quarterly* 47 (June 1932): 189–203. First published January 15, 1918.

67. WL to EMH, December 19, 1917 and May 11, 1918, WLmss, reel 14.

68. "After the War—Reconstruction or Reaction," *NR* 13 (January 19, 1918): 331–33.

69. *NR* 16 (October 19, 1918): 327; FF to EMH, with enclosure, October 15, 1918, EMHmss, Box 45, Folder 1455.

70. WW public statement, October 25, 1918, *PWW*, 53:381. A thorough analysis of the election and results is Livermore, *Politics Is Adjourned*, 206–47.

71. *NR* 17 (November 9, 1918): 26.

72. WW to EMH, October 28, 1918, *PWW*, 51:473. For Wilson's exchanges with Germany and handling of the Allies, Congress, and American public opinion during election season, see Knock, *To End All Wars*, 170–89.

73. Steel, *Lippmann and the American Century*, 141–46, 149–50 (quoting WL, "Reminiscences," 15). Steel misquotes Lippmann's recollection of House's request, though citing the original source, from which the quotation in my text is taken.

74. WL to EMH, August 15, 1918, EMHmss, Box 70, Folder 2326. Also WL to EMH, September 2, 1918 (first of that date), and EMH to WL, September 6, 1918, EMHmss, Box 70, Folder 2326

75. EMH to WW, October 29, 1918 (sixth of that date), *PWW*, 49:504 (re: Cobb); WL and Frank I. Cobb, memorandum on peace terms, October 29, 1918, *PWW*, 49:495–504; on House's recollection, see Charles Seymour, ed., *The Intimate Papers of Colonel House*, 4 vols. (Boston: Houghton Mifflin, 1926–28), 4:153–54. That Lippmann was the memorandum's primary author is clear from the handwritten original in his papers. The only instance of Cobb's hand is the noninterpretation of point 14, though the glosses of points 1–4 and 7 are missing (WLmss, reel 35). Seymour reaches the same conclusion in *Intimate Papers*, 4:153n1. Lippmann recalls writing all but the final gloss; in fact, he anticipated House's request, having prepared a gloss on the Balkans in the days just prior. See WL, "Reminiscences," 15–17; WL to Sidney Edward Mezes, October 26, 1918, WLmss, reel 35.

76. EMH diary, November 4, 1918, EMHmss; Link, *Wilson the Diplomatist*, 107–8; Schwabe, *Woodrow Wilson, Revolutionary Germany, and Peacemaking*, 30–39, 81–94. On historiographical disputes about the overall success or failure of these negotiations, see Bullitt Lowry, *Armistice 1918* (Kent, OH: Kent State UP, 1996), 183–84.

77. "The Pivot of History," *NR* 17 (November 16, 1918): 58; *NR* 17 (November 23, 1918): 82.

78. WL to Learned Hand, October 5, 1918, Learned Hand Papers, Harvard Law School Library, Cambridge, MA, Box 106, Folder 16.

79. League of Free Nations Association, *Statement of Principles* (New York: LFNA, 1918). Helbich, "American Liberals," demonstrates that the LFNA's principles—guaranteed security and equality of economic opportunity of all nations, substitution of cooperative internationalism for competitive nationalism, and for perpetual revision of the international order as circumstances dictated—were invoked by the majority of liberal League of Nations enthusiasts before the ratification debate. Indeed, Helbich argues effectively that the major part of liberal opinion, pacifist and interventionist, supported Wilson's Fourteen Points peace program between the Armistice and the peace conference.

80. JD, "The League of Nations and the New Diplomacy" (1918), *MW*, 11:134; JD, "The Fourteen Points and the League of Nations" (1918), *MW*, 11:135.

81. JD, "The League of Nations and Economic Freedom" (1918), *MW*, 11:139, 142. Robert Westbrook argues that Dewey was attempting to articulate a more "radical" alter-

native to Wilson's (and the LFNA's) vision for the League. This may be true as regards the LFNA (though the equally radical vision of at least one other member, Croly, casts some doubt on it). Dewey's invocation of the "New Diplomacy" (a term identified in the public discourse with Wilson) and praise for the Fourteen Points, however, suggests he did not consider the president to be the "liberal-capitalist" of Robert B. Westbrook's interpretation. Robert B. Westbrook, *John Dewey and American Democracy* (Ithaca, NY: Cornell UP, 1991), 236–37.

82. JD, "Fourteen Points and League of Nations," 138.

83. JD, "League of Nations and Economic Freedom," 139.

84. HC to JA, July 26, 1918, quoted in David W. Levy, *Herbert Croly of "The New Republic": The Life and Thought of an American Progressive* (Princeton, NJ: Princeton UP, 1985), 254; *NR* 17 (November 23, 1918): 82.

85. WL to EMH, 7 November 1918, quoted in Steel, *Lippmann and the American Century*, 150.

CHAPTER NINE

1. John Maynard Keynes, *The Economic Consequences of the Peace* (London: Macmillan, 1919), 43, 54–55. For more balanced accounts, see Thomas J. Knock, *To End All Wars: Woodrow Wilson and the Quest for a New World Order* (1992; repr., Princeton, NJ: Princeton UP, 1995); and (somewhat less sympathetic) Margaret MacMillan, *Paris 1919: Six Months That Changed the World* (New York: Random House, 2001). Two eloquent earlier replies to Keynes are RSB, *Woodrow Wilson and World Settlement*, 3 vols. (Garden City, NY: Doubleday, Page, 1922); and Étienne Mantoux, *The Carthaginian Peace; or, The Economic Consequences of Mr. Keynes* (London: Oxford UP, 1946).

2. William Emmanuel Rappard memorandum, ca. November 20, 1918, *PWW*, 63: 626–27.

3. Balfour and Smuts quoted in T. Harry Williams, Richard N. Current, and Frank Freidel, *A History of the United States*, 2 vols. (1959; New York: Knopf, 1965), 2:403 (caption). Initially the only observer of the Big Four meetings was Professor Paul Mantoux of the Sorbonne, who interpreted Wilson's, Lloyd George's, and Clemenceau's English into French for Orlando's benefit. His was the only record of negotiations until mid-April, when the secretary to the British cabinet, Sir Maurice Hankey, was invited to take minutes for Balfour's information. Paul Mantoux, *Deliberations of the Council of Four, March 24–June 28, 1919: Notes of the Official Interpreter*, trans. and ed. Arthur S. Link and Manfred F. Boemke, 2 vols. (Princeton, NJ: Princeton UP, 1992), 1:xiii–xviii, xxxiii–xl.

4. *NR* 19 (May 24, 1919): 103; WL to EMH, March 18, 1919, EMHmss, Box 70, Folder 2327. For Lippmann's departure from Paris, see Ronald Steel, *Walter Lippmann and the American Century* (Boston: Atlantic-Little, Brown, 1980), 151–53.

5. The best interpretive narratives of Wilson's role in drafting the League Covenant are Knock, *To End All Wars*, chaps. 11–12; and John Milton Cooper Jr., *Breaking the Heart of the World: Woodrow Wilson and the Fight for the League of Nations* (Cambridge: Cambridge UP, 2001). The best critical counterpoint is Lloyd E. Ambrosius, *Woodrow Wilson and the American Diplomatic Tradition: The Treaty Fight in Perspective* (Cambridge: Cambridge UP, 1987).

6. League of Nations Commission (LNC) minutes, February 11, 1919, *PWW*, 55:79–80; "The Cecil Plan," January 14, 1919, and "British Draft Convention," January 20, 1919, both in David Hunter Miller, *The Drafting of the Covenant*, 2 vols. (New York: G. P. Putnam's, 1928), 2:61–64, 106–16. Miller's first volume remains the best of few secondary works addressing French contributions to the Covenant. On British hopes and plans, see George W. Egerton, *Great Britain and the Creation of the League of Nations: Strategy, Politics, and International Organization, 1914–1919* (Chapel Hill: University of North Carolina Press, 1978); Peter Yearwood, *Guarantee of Peace: The League of Nations in British Policy, 1914–1925* (Oxford: Oxford UP, 2009).

7. D. Miller, *Drafting of Covenant* 2:94–97 (Bliss's suggestions), 98–106 (Second Paris Draft).

8. Ibid., 37–59 (Smuts's proposal), 66–67 (First Paris Draft); Robert Cecil memorandum, December 26, 1918, *PWW*, 53:415–17.

9. D. Miller, *Drafting of the Covenant* 2:94–97; for the quotations regarding a noncompliant member's ipso facto status, see 101 (Second Paris Draft), 79 (First Paris Draft).

10. Knock, *To End All Wars*, 202–5; D. Miller, *Drafting of the Covenant* 2:70, 87, 90–91.

11. See EMH, Robert Cecil, and Sir William Wiseman diaries, all February 3, 1919, *PWW*, 54:459–61. For Wilson's handwritten comments on the Hurst-Miller draft, see *PWW*, 54:441–48.

12. Knock, *To End All Wars*, 215–20; Robert Cecil diary, February 6, 1919, *PWW*, 54:514.

13. Carole Fink, "The Paris Peace Conference and the Question of Minority Rights," *Peace and Change* 21 (July 1996): 273–88.

14. D. Miller, *Drafting of the Covenant*, 2:101–2 (Article 7 of WW's second Paris Draft), 727 (final wording, Article 11, para. 2).

15. WW address in Indianapolis, IN, September 4, 1919, *PWW*, 63:27–28. On Wilson's vision of "incipient global governance" as revealed in his original draft of Article 10 and enthusiasm for Article 11, see Erez Manela, "A Man Ahead of His Time? Wilsonian Globalism and the Doctrine of Preemption," *International Journal* 60 (Autumn, 2005): 1115–23. On Wilson's interpretation of Article 11 as a mechanism for peaceful change, as well as the varied but politically significant interpretations of the article by League opponents and supporters, see Robert David Johnson, "Article XI in the Debate on the United States' Rejection of the League of Nations," *International History Review* 15 (August 1993): 502–24.

16. The preceding text draws on F. P. Walters, *A History of the League of Nations* (1952; repr., London: Oxford UP, 1960), 43–53.

17. WW quoted in D. Miller, *Drafting of the Covenant* 2:562–63; WW address in Billings, MT, [early 1919], *PWW*, 63:176.

18. For a survey of opinion, see *Literary Digest* 60 (March 1, 1919): 11–13. Also RSB, memorandum for WW, March 6, 1919, *PWW*, 55:449–50; Ellery Sedgwick to JPT, March 21, 1919, *PWW*, 56:162–63; NDB to WW, March 27, 1919, *PWW*, 56:331.

19. 65 Cong. Rec. S603 (daily ed. December 18, 1918). On Borah as isolationist, see John Milton Cooper, Jr., *The Vanity of Power: American Isolationism and the First World War, 1914–1917* (Westport, CT: Greenwood, 1969), 136–42. Lodge repeatedly expressed himself "anxious to have the nations, the free nations of the world, united in a league,"

but even conservative internationalists had to ask, with Harvard President A. Lawrence Lowell, "If this Covenant were amended as you wish, would you vote for it?" *The Lodge-Lowell Debate on the Proposed League of Nations . . . Held in Symphony Hall, Boston, March 19, 1919* (Boston: Old Colony Trust, 1919), 8, 39.

20. *NYT*, February 27, 1919.

21. 65 *Cong. Rec.* S4974 (daily ed. March 3, 1919). On the Round Robin's origins and effect see Cooper, *Breaking the Heart of the World*, chap. 2.

22. On Wilson's stroke and its effects on his character, see the article by neurologist Edwin A. Weinstein, "Woodrow Wilson's Neurological Illness," *Journal of American History* 57 (September 1970): 324–51.

23. LNC minutes, April 10, 1919, in D. Miller, *Drafting of the Covenant*, 2:370; WW quoted in C. P. Scott diary, December 29, 1918, *PWW*, 53:576n1.

24. See Article 1, paragraph 2 of the League Covenant: "Any fully self-governing State, Dominion, or Colony . . . may become a Member of the League if its admission is agreed to by a two-thirds majority of the Assembly."

25. For the deliberations over the mandate system, see D. Miller, *Drafting of the Covenant* 1:40–41, 101–17. For Wilson's hopes for a different system, see Arthur S. Link, *Wilson the Diplomatist: A Look at His Major Foreign Policies* (Baltimore, MD: Johns Hopkins UP, 1957), 112–13; and the records of Wilson's remarks, en route to France, by William C. Bullitt and Isaiah Bowman, both December 10, 1918, *PWW*, 53:351, 355. That it was Wilson, through his wartime rhetoric and efforts at Paris, who did most to prevent the outright annexation of the territories that became mandates, insisted on the primacy of indigenous over imperial interests, and imposed the requirement, however long the timeline, of eventual self-government, is clear from Knock, *To End All Wars*, 210–16; and MacMillan, *Paris 1919*, chap. 8. The indispensable history of the mandates system is Susan Pedersen, *The Guardians: The League of Nations and the Crisis of Empire* (New York: Oxford UP, 2015). Pedersen shows that the League's Permanent Mandates Commission functioned from the start as a bulwark for the British and French empires against the anti-imperialist tide unleashed by the war. Nevertheless, indigenous and international demands to fulfill their mandated duties forced the mandatories, especially Britain, into compromise arrangements that served to make statehood normative. Moreover, the commission, by publicizing both the policies of mandatories and the resentments and claims of their legal wards, inadvertently undermined the colonial system of political tutelage that several of its members intended it to preserve. Though neither the PMC nor the mandatory powers were interested in "extending the right of self-determination," the mandates system nonetheless became "the tool through which the imperial order would be transformed" (3–4).

26. John Milton Cooper Jr., *Woodrow Wilson: A Biography* (New York: Knopf, 2009); 490, 492; WW quoted in Mantoux, *Deliberations of Council of Four*, 2:131. Wilson, recalled Harold Nicolson, a conference observer, "did in truth maintain his principles intact" when it came to Italy's territorial claims. Harold Nicolson, *Peacemaking, 1919: Being Reminiscences of the Paris Peace Conference* (Boston: Houghton Mifflin, 1933), 183. On Wilson's Italian diplomacy and Italo-American relations, see Daniela Rossini, *Woodrow Wilson and the American Myth in Italy: Culture, Diplomacy, and War Propaganda* (Cambridge, MA: Harvard UP, 2008), richly informative despite indulging in

outdated psychologizing of Wilson. A focused study of the Italian–Yugoslav disputes emphasizing Wilson's flexibility and concern for Italian League membership is Dragan R. Zivojinic, *America, Italy, and the Birth of Yugoslavia (1917–1919)* (New York: East European Monographs, 1972).

27. WW quoted in RSB diary, April 25 and May 1, 1919, *PWW*, 58:327. On Wilson and Japan, see Noriko Kawamura, "Wilsonian Idealism and Japanese Claims at the Paris Peace Conference," *Pacific Historical Review* 66 (November 1997): 503–26; Knock, *To End All Wars*, 249–50. For Wilson's support of the Chinese and anguished decision to recognize Japan's Shandong claim, see Russell H. Fifield, *Woodrow Wilson and the Far East: The Diplomacy of the Shantung Question* (New York: Crowell, 1952); Wunz King, *Woodrow Wilson, Wellington Koo, and the China Question at the Paris Peace Conference* (Leyden: A. W. Sythoff, 1959); and Cooper, *Woodrow Wilson*, 491–94.

28. The account offered here draws on MacMillan, *Paris 1919*, 157–206. See also Arno J. Mayer, *Politics and Diplomacy of Peacemaking: Containment and Counterrevolution at Versailles 1918–1919* (New York: Knopf, 1967), excellent on the connection between domestic and foreign policy and on Wilson, though eliding the disparity between his mild worries about Bolshevism's spread and the deep concerns of his counterparts. The richest, most multifaceted picture of the negotiations and their consequences can be gleaned from Manfred F. Boemke, Gerald D. Feldman, and Elisabeth Glaser, eds., *The Treaty of Versailles: A Reassessment after 75 Years* (New York: Cambridge UP, 1998).

29. RSB, *Wilson and World Settlement*, 2:353–408; Link, *Wilson the Diplomatist*, 109–12; Inga Floto, *Colonel House in Paris: A Study of American Policy at the Paris Peace Conference 1919* (Princeton, NJ: Princeton UP, 1980), 152–55, 164–208. An alternative account emphasizing House's realism in accommodating the Allies is Godfrey Hodgson, *Woodrow Wilson's Right Hand: The Life of Colonel Edward M. House* (New Haven, CT: Yale UP, 2007), chap. 16. House's most learned biographer joins Knock and Cooper in downplaying his role in Wilson's capitulation on reparations; see Charles E. Neu, *Colonel House: A Biography of Woodrow Wilson's Silent Partner* (New York: Oxford UP, 2015), 410–11; Knock, *To End All Wars*, 250; Cooper, *Woodrow Wilson*, 488.

30. MacMillan, *Paris 1919*, 459–71; Cooper, *Woodrow Wilson*, 486–89. On divergent French and British security and economic priorities, see Ruth Henig, *The League of Nations* (London: Haus, 2012); Marc Trachtenberg, *Reparation in World Politics: France and European Economic Diplomacy, 1916–1923* (New York: Columbia UP, 1980); Robert E. Bunselmeyer, *The Cost of the War, 1914–1919: British Economic War Aims and the Origins of Reparation* (Hamden, CT: Archon, 1975).

31. MacMillan, *Paris 1919*, 63–82, 109–42, 207–56; Cooper, *Woodrow Wilson*, 497; WW interview with Frank Worthington, December 28, 1918, enclosed in Edward Price Bell to Lawrence Lanier Winslow, December 31, 1918, *PWW*, 53:573–75.

32. RSB diary, 27 June 1919, *PWW*, 61:254.

33. *NR* 19 (May 24, 1919): cover, 100–106; "Defeat Article X," *NR* 18 (March 29, 1919): 263–65. For similar attitudes from other pragmatist-progressives, see TV, "Peace," *Dial* 66 (May 17, 1919): 485–87; and JA (with Florence Kelley and Lillian Wald) in *NYT*, May 15, 1919, 5.

34. Quoted in Charles Forcey, *The Crossroads of Liberalism: Croly, Weyl, Lippmann, and the Progressive Era, 1900–1925* (New York: Oxford UP, 1961), 288.

35. Croly's anguish on learning the treaty terms is poignantly conveyed in David W. Levy, *Herbert Croly of "The New Republic": The Life and Thought of an American Progressive* (Princeton, NJ: Princeton UP, 1985), 263–66. On Croly's increasing preoccupation with humanity's "spiritual distempers," see Forcey, *Crossroads of Liberalism*, 281–83.

36. WL to FF, July 28, 1917, WLmss, reel 9; WL to RSB, May 19, 1919, WLmss, reel 2.

37. *NR* 18 (February 22, 1919): 100–102; *NR* 19 (June 7, 1919): 170. For the editors' thinking at a transitional stage, see "Agitation for a League of Nations without Criticism," *NR* 18 (March 15, 1919): 200–202, in which Article 10 is described as "dangerous" because "ambiguous."

38. WL to NDB, June 9, 1919, WLmss, reel 2. On Lippmann's correspondence with Wilson's Senate opponents, see Steel, *Lippmann and the American Century*, 160, 163.

39. Forcey, *Crossroads of Liberalism*, 292; Levy, *Herbert Croly*, 271–72. Forcey's figure of ten thousand lost subscribers is exaggerated, but Levy's accounting still reveals a decline well exceeding 20 percent, and overall readership may have declined further. Among the dailies that were consistent in denouncing both treaty and Covenant were all the Hearst papers, as well as the New York *Sun*, New York *Herald*, Philadelphia *North American*, Providence *Journal*, St. Paul *Pioneer Press*, Minneapolis *Journal*, Kansas City *Star*, *Detroit Free Press*, Detroit *Journal*, *Chicago Tribune*, and *San Francisco Chronicle*. A survey of editorial pages from May through July 1919 reveals far more dailies supporting ratification, including the *New York Times*, New York *World*, New York *Globe*, New York *Evening Post*, Springfield (Massachusetts) *Republican*, Philadelphia *Press*, Philadelphia *Public Ledger*, Baltimore *American*, Baltimore *Sun*, Louisville *Courier-Journal*, St. Louis *Republic*, *St. Louis Post-Dispatch*, Omaha *World-Herald*, Des Moines *Register*, Indianapolis *News*, Detroit *News*, Detroit *Times*, Chicago *Evening Post*, Minneapolis *Tribune*, Milwaukee *Journal*, Raleigh *News and Observer*, Richmond *Times-Dispatch*, Atlanta *Constitution*, and New Orleans *Times-Picayune*. Most independent papers supported ratification while affiliated papers broke along partisan lines, but there were important exceptions to this last rule, mostly on the Republican side. However, the positions of these pro-League Republican organs tended to evolve over time: the New York *Tribune*, *Los Angeles Times*, and *Ohio State Journal*, for instance, were generally supportive of Wilson's cause in the early summer of 1919 and gradually turned against it in favor of one or another reservationist alternative.

40. WW press conference remarks, July 10, 1919, *PWW*, 61:424; WW address to Senate, July 10, 1919, *PWW*, 61:426–36. Attempts to diagnose Wilson posthumously as psychologically deformed by a messiah complex and paranoia of betrayal include Sigmund Freud and William C. Bullitt, *Thomas Woodrow Wilson, Twenty-eighth President of the United States: A Psychological Study* (Boston: Houghton Mifflin, 1967), written over three decades before publication, when Wilson's papers were unavailable to scholars; and Alexander L. George and Juliette L. George, *Woodrow Wilson and Colonel House: A Personality Study* (New York: J. Day, 1956). Arthur Link savaged Freud and Bullitt's work in *The Higher Realism of Woodrow Wilson, and Other Essays* (Nashville: Vanderbilt UP, 1971), chap. 11; Edwin A. Weinstein demolished the Georges' thesis in *Woodrow Wilson: A Medical and Psychological Biography* (Princeton, NJ: Princeton UP, 1981). For cogent analysis and historiographical summary, see Cooper, *Breaking the Heart of the World*, 416–22.

41. Cooper, *Woodrow Wilson*, 509–12.

42. A story told thoroughly and well in Cooper, *Breaking the Heart of the World*, chaps. 5–8.

43. WW address in Cheyenne, WY, September 24, 1919, *PWW*, 63:479–80.

44. The quotation is from Thomas A. Bailey, *Woodrow Wilson and the Great Betrayal* (New York: Macmillan, 1945), 277.

45. Thomas W. Brahamy diary, 2 April 1917, *PWW*, 41:532.

46. Link, *Wilson the Diplomatist*, 129.

47. Charles Seymour to his family, December 10, 1918, *PWW*, 53:356.

48. Bullitt diary, December 10, 1918, 351; William Christian Bullitt to WW, May 17, 1919, *PWW*, 59:233.

49. "Censorship and the Peace Conference," *NR* 17 (November 16, 1918): 63.

50. Cooper, *Breaking the Heart of the World*, 414–23, quoted at 422, 423.

51. Quoted in Cooper, *Woodrow Wilson*, 560.

52. *Literary Digest* 60 (March 1, 1919): 11–13; *Current Opinion* 69 (September 1920): 1–7.

53. *NYT*, June 30, 1919 (on financing, referenda); William R. Boyd, Jr. to Executive and National Committees and Vice Presidents of the League, with enclosures, ca. December 1918, and schedule of regional congresses, February 5–28, 1919, both in William Howard Taft Papers, Library of Congress, Washington, DC (microfilm), reel 639 (on the national petition drive);William Howard Taft, "League of Nations Wins Public Favor," *Detroit Free Press*, March 1, 1919 (on rally attendance); William Howard Taft, "President and Senate Must Ratify Treaty," *Philadelphia Public Ledger*, November 21, 1919.

54. See, e.g., *Federal Council Bulletin* 2 (January 1919): 12–14; *Federal Council Bulletin* 2 (March 1919): 42; *Federal Council Bulletin* 2 (June 1919): 94. Frederick Allen Lynch asserted that the Federal Council represented thirty-three million congregants in a letter to Wilson printed under January 25, 1919, *PWW*, 54:277. Antistatist resistance to the League was more common in the burgeoning fundamentalist movement, but pro-League sentiment among Protestant clergy, theologians, and laity completely overwhelmed these dissenting voices. See Markku Ruotsila, *The Origins of Christian Anti-Internationalism: Conservative Evangelicals and the League of Nations* (Washington, DC: Georgetown UP, 2008); James L. Lancaster, "The Protestant Churches and the Fight for Ratification of the Versailles Treaty," *Public Opinion Quarterly* 31 (Winter 1967–68): 597–619.

55. *Federal Council Bulletin* 2 (June 1919): 94; Frederick Allen Lynch to the editors, *NYT*, July 20, 1919; *New Era Magazine* 25 (July 1919): 371–72; Samuel Zane Batten, "The Churches and Social Reconstruction," *Biblical World* 53 (November 1919): 594–617, esp. 609; "Address of the Bishops" (May 2, 1920), *Journal of the Twenty-Eighth Delegated Conference of the Methodist Episcopal Church, 1920* (New York: Eaton and Mains, 1920), 145–98, esp. 193–97.

56. *Annual Report of the Federal Council of Churches of Christ in America, 1919* (New York: FCCCA, 1919), 116–21.

57. *Federal Council Bulletin* 2 (December 1919): 186; *NYT*, December 12, 1919; *Boston Daily Globe*, June 8, 1920. Eventually well over 17,000 clergy signed the October petition; and though this represents less than a quarter of the 80,000 clergy contacted, only 816 actually responded in the negative.

58. *Handbook of the National Catholic War Council* (Washington, DC: NCWC, 1918), 1. On NCWC activities during the League fight, see the autobiography of its leader, John A. Ryan, *Social Doctrine in Action* (New York: Harper, 1941), 141–45.

59. *Biblical World* 54 (January 1920): 79, 82.

60. *CCAR Yearbook* 29 (Cincinnati, OH: CCAR, 1919), 100; Samuel Schulman, "The Jew and the New Age," *Proceedings of the Union of American Hebrew Congregations* 9, 1916–20 (n.p., 1920), 8468–8477, esp. 8473, copy in Union for Reform Judaism Records, American Jewish Archives, Cincinnati, OH.

61. Proceedings of the Eleventh General Convention of the Constitution Grand Lodge, Independent Order of B'nai B'rith (n.p., n.d.), 21–100, esp. 85, copy in Records of B'nai B'rith, District # 2, Box B-33, American Jewish Archives, Cincinnati, OH; Fifth and Sixth Annual Reports and Proceedings of the Third Biennial Meeting of the National Federation of Temple Sisterhoods, Boston, 1919 (n.p., 1919), 31, copy in Women for Reform Judaism Records, Box 1, American Jewish Archives, Cincinnati, OH.

62. *General Federation Magazine* 18 (December 1919): 1; New York *Tribune*, January 14, 1920; *Handbook of the National American Woman Suffrage Association and Proceedings of the Jubilee Convention* (New York: NAWSA, 1919), 249.

63. *Red Cross Bulletin* 3 (January 13, 1919): 5; *Red Cross Bulletin* 3 (March 3, 1919): 8; *Red Cross Bulletin* 3 (June 2, 1919): 1–2. ARC membership numbers are from official reports in the March 3 and October 20, 1919, issues of the *Bulletin*. A fine study of the ARC's activities, growth, and impact during and after the war is Julia F. Irwin, *Making the World Safe: The American Red Cross and a Nation's Humanitarian Awakening* (New York: Oxford UP, 2013).

64. C. Howard Hopkins, *John R. Mott, 1865–1955: A Biography* (Grand Rapids, MI: Eerdmans, 1979), 476–597. For the YMCA's army camp activities, see James H. Beach to Frank L. Weil, April 14 and 22, 1919, Frank L. Weil Papers, Box 2, Folder 1, American Jewish Archives, Cincinnati, OH.

65. Hartford (Kentucky) *Herald*, November 26, 1919; New York *Tribune*, January 14, 1920.

66. *Philadelphia Tribune*, January 18, 1919 (quoting NAACP resolution); *Washington Post*, August 29, 1919. William Monroe Trotter's Equal Rights League did not explicitly endorse the League of Nations, instead petitioning the Senate to submit a racial-equality amendment to the Covenant (ibid.).

67. New York *Tribune*, June 29, 1919; December 14, 1919; and June 20, 1920.

68. *Atlanta Constitution*, February 13, 1919; *NYT*, March 4, 1919.

69. *NYT*, May 6 and June 16, 1919.

70. Minutes of the Board of Directors, January 20, 1920, Chamber of Commerce of the United States Records, Series 1, Box 2, Hagley Museum and Library, Wilmington, DE; New York *Tribune*, October 22, 1919. For Filene's advocacy and the US Chamber's promotional efforts, see *Chicago Daily Tribune*, February 5, 1919; *San Francisco Chronicle*, February 20, 1919; *NYT*, June 30, 1919.

71. 66 Cong. Rec. S558–561, 674–695 (daily eds. June 3 and 5, 1919); *NYT*, April 28, 1920 (on banker support/excursion). Among the financial community, even most critics of the settlement's economic features were dismayed at the Versailles treaty's rejection:

Joan Hoff Wilson, *American Business and Foreign Policy, 1920–1933* (Lexington: UP of Kentucky, 1971), 21–30.

72. Ralph M. Easley to Theodore Marburg, June 16, 1919, and Easley to Haley Fiske, June 20, 1919 (quoted), National Civic Federation Records, New York Public Library, New York (microfilm), reel 329; ; Frank Moore Colby, ed. *The New International Yearbook, 1919* (New York: Dodd, Mead, 1920), 375, 453. For pro-League resolutions by local Rotaries, see *Rotarian* 14 (April–June 1919):165–66, 251–252, 294; *Rotarian* 15 (September 1919):162; *Rotarian* 16 (September 1920):129.

73. New York *Tribune*, September 14, 1919, and January 14, 1920.

74. Quoted in New York *Tribune*, September 26, 1920. For state Legion endorsements, see New York *Tribune*, October 12, 1919; *NYT*, January 11, 1920; and *Atlanta Constitution*, October 26, 1919.

75. *NYT*, April 28, 1919. Petitions on both sides of the issue are preserved in Record Group 46, Records of the US Senate, Petitions and Memorials (RG 46), and Record Group 233, Records of the US House of Representatives, Petitions and Memorials, both in National Archives, Washington, DC. A highly conservative estimate would be that proratification petitions outnumbered antiratification petitions by five to one.

76. The resolutions passed March 28 and April 8, 1919. For Massachusetts constituent opinion, see RG 46, Box 80, Folder 1, 2; Box 101, Folders 1–12; Box 103, Folders 4, 5, 8, and esp. 10; Box 104, Folder 2; Box 105, Folder 5. The majority of anti-League expression was organized by the Massachusetts League for the Preservation of American Independence; see postcards in Box 106, Folders 1, 5, and 9, amounting to perhaps five hundred total signatures.

77. Hiram Johnson to Jack Johnson, May 31, 1919, in Robert E. Burke, ed. *The Diary Letters of Hiram Johnson, 1917–1945*, 7 vols. (New York: Garland, 1983), vol. 3, unpaginated. Evidence and analysis of pro-League sentiment in California appears in several collections at the Huntington Library, San Marino, CA, including the Clara Burdette Collection, Henry Mauris Robinson Papers, Philip Ackerley Stanton Papers, and Marshal Stimson Papers, and from perusal of the Los Angeles City Club *Bulletin*, California Federation of Women's Clubs *Clubwoman*, and *Transactions of the Commonwealth Club of California*, ca. April 1919 through the early 1920s.

78. JA, *Peace and Bread in Time of War* (New York: Macmillan, 1922), 189.

79. WEBD, "The League of Nations," *Crisis* 18 (May 1919): 10–11.

80. WL, "Notes for a Biography," *NR* 63 (July 16, 1930): 252; WL, "The Reminiscences of Walter Lippmann," Columbia University Oral History Collection, part 2, no. 118, 121.

81. WL, "Reminiscences," 121; Steel, *Lippmann and the American Century*, chap. 13.

82. JD to his children, May 13, 1919, in JD and Alice Chipman Dewey, *Letters from China and Japan* (New York: E. P. Dutton, 1920), 166–69.

83. JD, "Our National Dilemma" (1920), *MW*, 12:7.

84. *Searchlight* 4 (March 1920): 8; *Searchlight* 4 (April 1920): 14. On Lodge's wavering, see H. N. Rickey (LEP Washington Bureau chief) to William H. Short, October 13, 1919, League to Enforce Peace—Additional Records, Series 1A, Folder 37, Houghton Library, Harvard University, Cambridge, MA.

85. Quoted in *NYT*, September 18, 1920.

86. *NYT*, March 5, 1921.

87. See *Bulletin of the National Council for Limitation of Armaments* 1 (December 3, 1921): 1, urging that the Washington conference take steps "towards the constitutions of world machinery for the maintenance of peace." Among many other bodies (several previously mentioned), the NCLA's constituents included the American Association of University Women, American Union Against Militarism, Foreign Policy Association, National Congress of Mothers and Parent–Teachers' Associations, National Federation of Business and Professional Women's Clubs, National Women's Trade Union League, Veterans of Foreign Wars, Women's Christian Temperance Union, Women's International League for Peace and Freedom, and World Friendship Information Bureau. On the persistence of American internationalism after World War I, see Warren F. Kuehl and Lynne K. Dunn, *Keeping the Covenant: American Internationalists and the League of Nations, 1920–1939* (Kent, OH: Kent State UP, 1997); Akira Iriye, *Cultural Internationalism and World Order* (Baltimore, MD: Johns Hopkins UP, 1997).

88. E.g., resolutions of the National League of Women Voters, 1922 annual convention, copy in Louise Leonard Wright Papers, Box 1, Folder 19, Schlesinger Library, Harvard University, Cambridge, MA.

89. Frank Costigliola, *Awkward Dominion: American Political, Economic, and Cultural Relations with Europe, 1919–1933* (Ithaca, NY: Cornell UP, 1984); Warren I. Cohen, *Empire without Tears: America's Foreign Relations, 1921–1933* (New York: Knopf, 1987). For a résumé of early League accomplishments, see Hamilton Holt, "The League of Nations Effective," *Annals of the American Academy of Political and Social Science* 96 (July 1921): 1–10. A concise overview of American philanthropic, administrative, and technical support for the League is Manley O. Hudson, "Many Americans Active in the League," *NYT*, April 6, 1924. An indictment of their inadequacy and lament for the domestic distractions impeding formal ties between the League, World Court, and United States—from the dean of Republican foreign-policy thought—is Elihu Root, *America's International Responsibilities* (New York: FCCCA, 1926).

CONCLUSION

1. WJ to James Mark Baldwin, October 24, 1901, *CWJ*, 9:552; WJ to L. T. Hobhouse, August 12, 1904, *CWJ*, 10:449.

2. WL, *The Phantom Public* (New York: Harcourt, Brace, 1925), 38–39, 126.

3. JD, *The Public and Its Problems* (1927), in Jo Ann Boydston et al., eds., *The Later Works of John Dewey*, 17 vols. (Carbondale: Southern Illinois UP, 1981–90), 2:319, 327, 332.

4. WL, "H. G. Wells and an Altered World," *Vanity Fair* 15 (December, 1920): 39–40, esp. 40.

5. Detailed and luminous in this regard is Quincy Wright, *Research in International Law since the War: A Report to the International Relations Committee of the Social Science Research Council* (Washington, DC: Carnegie Endowment for International Peace, 1930). Harvard President A. Lawrence Lowell collected opinion and analysis in a Wilsonian vein from across the academy; see Abbott Lawrence Lowell Peace Papers, Houghton Library, Harvard University, Cambridge, MA.

6. Frederick Bausman, *Let France Explain* (London: George Allen and Unwin, 1922); John Kenneth Turner, *Shall It Be Again?* (New York: B. W. Huebsch, 1922); Harry Elmer Barnes, "Assessing the Blame for the World War: A Revised Judgment Based on All the Available Documents," *Current History* 20 (May 1924): 171–95.

7. Charles Beard, *The Idea of National Interest* (New York: Macmillan, 1934), is representative.

8. Even shrewd critics of realism have failed to grasp the significance of this fact. See Frank Ninkovich, *The Global Republic: America's Inadvertent Rise to World Power* (Chicago: University of Chicago Press, 2014), arguing that American participation could not have improved the "institutional elaboration of a bad idea," but also, confusingly, reading history backwards from the 1920s and 1930s to argue that even granting participation, American popular indifference to collective security would have hampered the League—as, indeed, formal abstention did (101–3).

9. The venerable pedigree of this analytical gambit includes E. H. Carr, *The Twenty Years' Crisis, 1919–1939: An Introduction to the Study of International Relations* (London: Macmillan, 1940); WL, *U.S. Foreign Policy: Shield of the Republic* (Boston: Little, Brown, 1943); George F. Kennan, *American Diplomacy, 1900–1950* (Chicago: University of Chicago Press, 1951); Hans J. Morgenthau, *In Defense of the National Interest: A Critical Examination of American Foreign Policy* (New York: Knopf, 1951); Henry Kissinger, *Diplomacy* (New York: Touchstone, 1994); John J. Mearsheimer, *The Tragedy of Great Power Politics* (New York: Norton, 2001); Norman A. Graebner and Edward M. Bennet, *The Versailles Treaty and Its Legacy: The Failure of the Wilsonian Vision* (Cambridge: Cambridge UP, 2011).

10. The triangular failure of Anglo-Franco-American diplomacy deserves a dedicated, updated monograph, but see Melvin P. Leffler, *The Elusive Quest: America's Pursuit of European Stability and French Security, 1919–1933* (Chapel Hill: University of North Carolina Press, 1979); Patrick Cohrs, *The Unfinished Peace after World War I: America, Britain and the Stabilisation of Europe, 1919–1932* (Cambridge: Cambridge UP, 2006); Zara Steiner, *The Lights That Failed: European International History, 1919–1933* (Oxford: Oxford UP, 2005); Zara Steiner, *The Triumph of the Dark: European International History, 1933–1939* (Oxford: Oxford UP, 2011); Ruth Henig, *The League of Nations* (London: Haus, 2012); Anthony D'Agostino, *The Rise of Global Powers: International Politics in the Era of the World Wars* (New York: Cambridge UP, 2012).

11. Robert Divine, *Second Chance: The Triumph of Internationalism in America during World War II* (New York: Atheneum, 1967); Christopher D. O'Sullivan, *Sumner Welles, Postwar Planning, and the Quest for a New World Order, 1937–1943* (New York: Columbia UP, 2008).

12. The plans are reprinted in Ruth B. Russell, *A History of the United Nations Charter: The Role of the United States, 1940–1945* (Washington, DC: Brookings Institution, 1958), 472–85, 526–34.

13. Divine, *Second Chance*, esp. chaps. 9–11; Robert F. Dallek, *Franklin D. Roosevelt and American Foreign Policy* (New York: Oxford UP, 1979), part 4; Townsend Hoopes and Douglas Brinkley, *FDR and the Creation of the U.N.* (New Haven, CT: Yale UP, 1997).

14. Daniel Yergin, *Shattered Peace: The Origins of the Cold War and the National Security State* (New York: Houghton Mifflin, 1977); Lloyd C. Gardner, *Spheres of Influence:*

The Great Powers Partition Europe, from Munich to Yalta (Chicago: Ivan R. Dee, 1993); Frank Costigliola, *Roosevelt's Lost Alliances: How Personal Politics Helped Start the Cold War* (Princeton, NJ: Princeton UP, 2012).

15. Clark M. Eichelberger, *The UN: The First Twenty-Five Years* (New York: Harper and Row, 1970); Carole Fink, "The United Nations after Fifty Years," *Global Justice* 2 (Winter 1996): 6–8.

16. E.g., Frank Ninkovich, *The Wilsonian Century: U.S. Foreign Policy since 1900* (Chicago: University of Chicago Press, 1999); David M. Kennedy, "What 'W' owes to 'WW,'" *Atlantic Monthly* (March 2005): 36–40; Joan Hoff, *A Faustian Foreign Policy from Woodrow Wilson to George W. Bush: Dreams of Perfectibility* (New York: Cambridge UP, 2008). By no means do these works represent an exhaustive or interpretatively coherent list.

17. For example, William Appleman Williams, *The Tragedy of American Diplomacy* (New York: World, 1959); Carl P. Parrini, *Heir to Empire: United States Economic Diplomacy, 1916–1923* (Pittsburgh, PA: University of Pittsburgh Press, 1969).

18. Seminal on the topic is Erez Manela, *The Wilsonian Moment: Self-Determination and the International Origins of Anticolonial Nationalism* (New York: Oxford UP, 2007).

19. Alonzo L. Hamby, "Progressivism: A Century of Change and Rebirth," in Sidney M. Milkis and Jerome M. Mileur, eds., *Progressivism and the New Democracy* (Amherst: University of Massachusetts Press, 1999), 40–80, esp. 53; James T. Kloppenberg, "Pragmatism: An Old Name for Some New Ways of Thinking?" *Journal of American History* 83 (June 1996): 100–138.

20. Hamby, "Progressivism," 58–59; Daniel T. Rodgers, *Atlantic Crossings: Social Politics in a Progressive Age* (Cambridge, MA: Harvard UP, 1998), chap. 10.

21. Sidney M. Mileur, "The Legacy of Reform: Progressive Government, Regressive Politics," in Milkis and Mileur, *Progressivism and the New Democracy*, 276–78.

22. The burgeoning civic studies field of interdisciplinary scholarship and transdisciplinary public practice offers hope. See Peter Levine, *We Are the Ones We Have Been Waiting For: The Promise of Civic Renewal in America* (New York: Oxford UP, 2013); Peter Levine and Karol Edward Soltan, eds., *Civic Studies: Approaches to the Emerging Field* (Washington, DC: Bringing Theory to Practice, 2014); Harry C. Boyte, "Deliberative Democracy, Public Work, and Civic Agency," *Journal of Public Deliberation* 10, no.1 (2014): article 15, accessed September 28, 2016, http://www.publicdeliberation.net /jpd/vol10/iss1/art15. The complexity of the civic task confronting would-be pragmatist progressives is illustrated by the contrasting styles and implicit definitions of *progressivism* embraced by President Barack Obama and 2016 Democratic presidential candidate Bernie Sanders, as well as by the charges of accomodationism and ideological absolutism leveled at each respectively and by the vexed efforts of Sanders's primary-campaign rival, Hillary Clinton, to triangulate between them. The campaign and election of Donald J. Trump further suggests the ease with which passions can be mobilized as compared to the deliberative, reflective work through which citizens get themselves organized.

23. Elizabeth Borgwardt, *A New Deal for the World: America's Vision for Human Rights* (Cambridge, MA: Harvard UP, 2005), 250.

24. WW address in Pueblo, CO, September 25, 1919, *PWW*, 63:511.